# BENJAMIN FRANKLIN, PENNSYLVANIA, AND THE FIRST NATIONS

# Benjamin Franklin, Pennsylvania, & the First Nations

## *The Treaties of 1736–62*

EDITED BY

SUSAN KALTER

UNIVERSITY OF ILLINOIS PRESS

URBANA AND CHICAGO

c 5 4 3 2 1
Manufactured in the United States of America
∞ This book is printed on acid-free paper.

Library of Congress Cataloging-in-Publication Data
Benjamin Franklin, Pennsylvania, and the first nations:
the treaties of 1736–62 / edited by Susan Kalter.
p. cm.
Includes bibliographical references and index.
ISBN-13: 978-0-252-03035-2 (cloth : alk. paper)
ISBN-10: 0-252-03035-4 (cloth : alk. paper)
1. Indians of North America—Pennsylvania—Treaties.
2. Indians of North America—Legal status, laws, etc.—
Pennsylvania—Sources. 3. Franklin, Benjamin, 1706–1790.
I. Kalter, Susan.
KF8202 2006
342.7308'720261—dc22 2005028933

# CONTENTS

LIST OF ILLUSTRATIONS vii
PREFACE ix
INTRODUCTION 1
EDITOR'S NOTE 45

## TREATIES

September and October 1736 49
July 1742 63
June and July 1744 86
October 1745 123
November 1747 142
July 1748 149
October 1753 160
July and November 1756 181
March, April, and May 1757 226
July and August 1757 255
October 1758 290
August 1761 334
August 1762 358
GLOSSARY OF PERSONS AND GROUPS MENTIONED IN THE TREATIES 407
INDEX 425

# ILLUSTRATIONS

Map 1. Key locations in eastern North America *9*

Map 2. Key locations in Pennsylvania and Iroquoia, and on Lenape lands *18*

Map 3. The British colonies circa 1763 *22*

A page from an original treaty, dated July 19, 1748, printed by Benjamin Franklin *46*

# PREFACE

This interdisciplinary edition of the Pennsylvania treaties that Benjamin Franklin printed is the first since Julian Boyd's limited-issue printing of five hundred library-bound copies in 1938. A new edition to update his work could not realistically have been accomplished any sooner. Since the late thirties, a sea change in the approach to tribal-colonial relations and the interpretation of written records of Native American speech has begun to occur. Significant theoretical and applied advances in established fields like colonial American history and the history of linguistics, and newly emerged fields such as Native American Studies and literary theory, make possible a complete reconsideration of the place of the treaties in both general and intellectual history.

Some of this sea change arises directly from the intervention of twentieth-century Native intellectuals and activists in reclaiming their intellectual heritage and its treatment in our social institutions. Without the emergence of a Native American Studies field increasingly influenced and directed by Native Americans, it would be difficult to imagine an American Studies field that in the past decade has destabilized the idea of natural borders for the United States. Native American Studies has restored to our imaginary about the North American continent the realization that its early colonial-age international borders were constituted mainly by tribal Indian nations and that many of these nations still form the geopolitical terrain of the continent's historical development. Historical actors like Franklin lived within this terrain, not beyond it. The conceptual perspectives of Native Americans and the work of Native American Studies in recovering Native American intellectual history are also beginning to have an impact on other arenas like natural resource management, the U.S. federal court system, and segments of the film industry such as historical documentary.

This revolution in thought has allowed us to see that these treaties are not merely concrete artifacts bearing witness to historical events. It has allowed us to recognize that they are not uncomplicated vehicles for the rhetorical eloquence of

Native American leaders. It has allowed us to understand Franklin's role in their printing as interconnected with his other roles as a legislative leader in Pennsylvania's young government. The treaties are complex, intercultural instruments that demand recognition of how both colonial politics and Native American politics shaped them. In addition, as readers approaching the treaties from historical, literary, biographical, or legal angles, we begin to recognize how our own contexts shape our interpretations of them. Understanding the treaties is an exercise not only in historical self-awareness but also in looking from a number of different contemporary angles. A reader feels compelled now to step across national, social, and vocational boundaries to ask persons in different positions to describe what they see.

A short history of interpretation from just one angle—that of my own field, literary studies—helps us understand the changing event that the reading of a treaty through history has been. When Benjamin Franklin first printed the treaties, he considered them one of the first native American literary forms.[1] He justified his printing of them in part on the basis of their uniqueness in comparison to European literary forms. He promoted their sale with a kind of self-evident acceptance of their status and reception as literature. By 1928, when a literature professor named Lawrence C. Wroth rediscovered the treaties, he faced the neglect of this literary type "as literature" among the sea of genres like narrative prose, nonfiction prose, poetry, and drama, which seemed to his contemporaries more obviously literary.[2]

Subsequent renditions tended to collapse these distinctions. The spate of interest in Indian oratory and Indian eloquence, especially from around 1930 until about 1979, was characterized by the extraction of particular speeches and passages from larger records such as complete treaties. Through this movement, the utterances of Native American leaders were wrested from their original contexts and political particularities, with a resulting abstraction of their protests and of their societal critiques. The focus on mere oratorical eloquence not only tore fragments of utterances out of the social space of the treaty, assigning them to the realm of nonfiction prose as essay, sermon, and the like, but it also cast those fragments in a melancholic or tragic mode which, Ojibwa scholar Gerald Vizenor has observed, relegated both U.S. injustice toward Native Americans and their resistance against that injustice to the irrecoverable past.[3]

Treatments of this specific series of treaties by anthropologists and historians, while more attentive to contexts, have also produced some troubled designations. Anthropologist William N. Fenton emphasized how the treaties might be seen as dramas, in which the members of the League of the Haudenosaunee, or Iroquois Confederacy, were the playwrights and stage directors while Franklin and other commissioners from the colonies might be seen as actors reciting their lines.[4] However, the reality is neither so sanguine nor so total. As others have pointed out, the oral utterances of Native American subjects are nearly always mediated in their handling and packaging for select and mass distribution by non-Natives who have political, social, and/or ideological stakes in their rhetorical effects.[5] The comparison of the treaties to dramas applied mainly to the originally indigenous genre—the Condolence Ritual—that frames many of the treaty negotiations also recorded in the treaty minutes. The negotiations themselves were both much less predictable than a scripted drama and at times much more scripted by British participants than Fenton's optimistic and apolitical metaphor implies. Though the Iroquois certainly were no pawns in the British Empire's chess game, neither did they dictate their own terms.

If the sense of the treaties as dramas produces a false impression of the serious ramifications of a treaty council as compared to the elusive social influence of any dramatic performance, no matter how much it may intervene in the course of history, their last reprinting in 1938 may swing too far in another direction. Julian P. Boyd and Carl Van Doren were not inclined to consider the literary dimensions of these treaties, which they edited and introduced, speaking mainly to their historical significance. Yet, if we do not lift the words off the historical page, so to speak, we fall into the trap of excessive credulity relating to how much one might read the "truth" of historical events from a single, isolated record. It would be a grave mistake to dismiss these texts as pure fictions or instruments of imperial power so tainted by white colonial control as to be rendered useless as historical evidence. However, one of the finest implements of a healthy historical skepticism is a talent for recognizing and bringing to the surface the play of words, the indeterminacy and ambiguity, that renders the urge for definite historical knowledge insatiable.

With this edition, I hope to allow the reader to take into consideration the most important elements of the language contexts surrounding the treaties. The treaties can no longer be looked at in isolation: they interacted with other texts, whether oral or written or cartographic, on a number of different levels in both the colonial society and Native American societies. Conversations among cross-cultural in-laws are as important to comprehending the treaties as knowledge of Iroquois ceremonies, revelations about deceptive maps, and attention to the governmental, public, and private writings that structured colonial Pennsylvania, including the prolific issue of Franklin's pen. We must also enter history with some notion of the changing connotations of words, because historical interpretations often hinge on assumptions about tone and mutual intelligibility across time. Translation itself leaves much room for interpretive ambiguity, so we should be particularly careful about drawing certain conclusions from words first spoken in Mohawk or Lenape.

Moreover, because nations that dominate in international affairs often have a silencing effect on the speech of less powerful nations and their members, we must remain cognizant of the many ways this silence takes shape. Political dominance may literally silence an individual's utterance; it may keep one's comments out of the historical record; it may cause one's words to be inscribed in a way that softens or sharpens a criticism of the listeners; or it may render itself invisible in such a way that present-day readers fail to understand the words that they read (silencing them, in a sense). We may not see how our continuing self-interested allegiance to the politically dominant nation interferes with our understanding. Indeed, past attention to the figurative features of Native American speech has illustrated this last kind of silencing. In comparing Iroquois oratory to Roman oratory, past generations dislocated eighteenth-century figures to a more ancient era in a way that neutralized their relevance to the modern world. They also forgot to account for the independent development of Native American genres of speech and their historical significances that would have arisen and evolved upon a fundamentally distinct and changing economic base during the tens of thousands of years prior to modern contact with Europeans.[6] Readers who basked in the picturesque use of metaphoric language by Iroquois speakers romanticized Native Americans of the past. In the mid-twentieth century, when U.S. policy called for termination of tribal governments, the idea of the long-gone romantic Indian severed the more evident connections between the arguments of contemporary tribal leaders against termination and the figurative verbal techniques of their eighteenth-century forebears.[7]

It is my hope that this edition will help connect eighteenth-century centers of Native American thought and intellectual exchange to those more contemporary exercises of political and intellectual sovereignty—especially their legacies in Iroquois and Lenape communities—as well as to the cross-cultural conversations that preceded European presence on the continent.[8] Cherokee scholar Jace Weaver's concept of communitism therefore seems an important perspective to bring to these texts.[9] Representatives of the various Indian nations participating in these treaty councils often worked at cross purposes to one another, but most had a commitment to Native community on a familial, national, or pan-tribal level. It would be too easy to place the events of these years into a divide-and-conquer rubric that separates Iroquois from Lenape. Once we surface the complex political and social character of Native American identities and affiliations, Weaver's concept helps us to further refigure this colonizing perspective. We can no longer operate on the false assumption that Native Americans ought to have had a natural solidarity through membership in a common race. Race and the idea of racial homogeneity were socially imposed and enforced on the huge array of diverse people in the Western Hemisphere.

This way of thinking produced the chimera of a mythic pan-tribal unity and the retrospective nostalgic regret that, if only Native Americans had joined together to resist colonial encroachment, they might have succeeded. Instead of imagining a racial solidarity that never existed because it was a figment of the colonist's imagination, Weaver asks us to look at the solidarities and allegiances that Native Americans have recognized and have upheld in the process of defending their communities against a systematic and ruthless colonization. Faced with a British government that promised to police its own borders but did not, and European settlers whose public morality honored property and frowned on trespassers but whose private actions contradicted these values, Iroquois and Lenape leaders and individuals formed alliances with one another when it served their strategic interests. But they also recognized that all their relations with other nations, whether Native or European, were international relations. Such alliances required both care and caution: care to maintain and caution to see that the partnership remained balanced and continued to serve their communities.

If we can read with a sense of the communitism that these treaties display, we might also be able to imagine "the power of the oral tradition to destabilize commonsense categories, to promote nonconfrontational ways of reevaluating hegemonic concepts, to encourage dialogue rather than monologue."[10] These treaties offer fragmentary glimpses into the oral tradition even while the text seems always to be closing the window upon it. Perhaps the effect will be a delayed but sincere reevaluation of the hegemonic concepts regarding land, purchase, conquest, savagism, and rights that continue to determine our perceptions of the world and of our nation. Certainly within the texts, various voices are in energetic interplay in ways that subvert their controlling authority, as the concept of dialogue might predict. Although Benjamin Franklin and others attempted to channel the "Indian language" of the treaties to serve their own purposes, this language exceeds the control that any particular British subject or U.S. citizen can exert upon it. Maybe then, a good case can be made that such treaties not only loosened proprietary hold upon the British colonies as Franklin wished, but wrested them away from their allegiance to the crown as he could not have wished or anticipated.

Research by and about Native Americans, and about relationships among Indian nations and European/Euramerican nations, is an ongoing process. No person involved in this process has the definitive last word. I hope that this volume will facilitate further research into the continuing history of diplomacy in which the Iroquois, Lenapes, and others are engaged. There remain questions about these treaties and the events surrounding them that oral traditions and other Native-based sources of knowledge may clear up. My expertise does not extend past a beginner's understanding of the languages in which these traditions have been kept, and I am not a member of the Indian nations about which I write. It is the province of those knowledgeable in these languages and traditions, as established members of these nations, to identify those areas in which the academic sources are still deficient and to improve upon or correct what we think we know.[11] I hope that this more accessible edition of these treaties will assist in these endeavors.

I would like to thank the National Endowment for the Humanities for granting me the summer stipend for 2002 that helped make this edition possible. The Research Proposal Review Committee of the College of Arts and Sciences at Illinois State University also funded a portion of this project. I would also like to thank Illinois State's Research and Sponsored Programs Office; the Research Office for the College of Arts and Sciences; the staff of the Laboratory for Integrated Learning and Technology; and the faculty and staff at ISU's Milner Library and the University of Illinois, in particular Milner's interlibrary loan division, Karen Hogenboom in government documents at the University of Illinois, Joan Winters, and the map librarian at ISU. In addition, I am grateful for the support and encouragement of my mentors, colleagues, and students, many of whom have read portions of the original prospectus or the present work and whose feedback has been indispensable: Rodger Tarr, Richard Dammers, Ron Fortune, Lucinda Beier, Ross Frank, Nicole Tonkovich, Susan Burt, Joe Blaney, Eileen Fowles, Jill Jones, Susan Westbury, Hilary Justice, Christopher Breu, Jeffrey Ludwig, and Chris De Santis; and to the respondents to my queries on the H-Net List for American Indian Studies and the SAIL listserv during the final preparation of the manuscript, especially Jim Rementer and Devon Mihesuah. This volume is dedicated to Linda Poolaw and Barbara Mann for giving of their time and expertise to me, Linda in 1989–90 in teaching myself and others in the Horace Poolaw Photography Project about the Kiowas of Oklahoma, and Barbara in 1998–2000 in helping me to better understand Haudenosaunee history through oral tradition and the written record.

1. William N. Fenton, "Structure, Continuity, and Change in the Process of Iroquois Treaty Making," in *The History and Culture of Iroquois Diplomacy: An Interdisciplinary Guide to the Treaties of the Six Nations and Their League,* ed. Francis Jennings (Syracuse, N.Y.: Syracuse University Press, 1985), 5.

2. Lawrence C. Wroth, "The Indian Treaty as Literature," *Yale Review* 17 (1928): 749–50.

3. Gerald Vizenor, "A Postmodern Introduction," in *Narrative Chance* (Albuquerque: University of New Mexico Press, 1993), 3–6, 9–14; Gerald Vizenor, "Socioacupuncture: Mythic Reversals and the Striptease in Four Scenes," in *The American Indian and the Problem of History* (New York: Oxford University Press, 1987), 183.

4. Fenton, "Structure, Continuity, and Change."

5. See, for example, William Clements, *Native American Verbal Art: Texts and Contexts* (Tucson: University of Arizona Press, 1996). This edition is not an exception to this phenomenon of mediation.

6. See V. N. Voloshinov, *Marxism and the Philosophy of Language,* trans. Ladislav Matejka and I. R. Titunik (Cambridge: Harvard University Press, 1996) for the concept of the speech genre and its relationship to the economic base of a society.

7. Stephen L. Pevar, *The Rights of Indians and Tribes* (Carbondale: Southern Illinois University Press, 1992), 5–7.

8. Literary scholar Robert Warrior has called for Native American intellectuals to exert their leadership in recovering Native American intellectual traditions. He has emphasized the idea that looking at Native American writing and orality as components of an intellectual history is an important and needed perspective in both U.S. and Native American Studies. *Tribal Secrets: Recovering American Indian Intellectual Traditions* (Minneapolis: University of Minnesota Press, 1994), xiii–xxiii.

9. Jace Weaver, *That the People Might Live* (New York: Oxford University Press, 1997), ix.

10. Julie Cruikshank, "Negotiating with Narrative: Establishing Cultural Identity at the Yukon International Storytelling Festival," *American Anthropologist* 99.1 (March 1997): 63.

11. See also the work of Raymond DeMallie, a non-Lakota scholar, for an example of how Lakota language sources may be used to clarify the historical record. "The Lakota Ghost Dance: An Ethnohistorical Account," *Pacific Historical Review* 51 (1982): 385–405; "'These Have No Ears': Narrative and the Ethnohistorical Method," *Ethnohistory* 40.4 (Fall 1993): 515–38.

# BENJAMIN FRANKLIN, PENNSYLVANIA, AND THE FIRST NATIONS

# INTRODUCTION

By the time Benjamin Franklin began to pay attention to the treaties that Pennsylvania colony was making with the Indian nations around its borders, the League of the Haudenosaunee was losing power. Western history has not successfully discovered how much prestige, influence, or dominance this original Iroquois Confederacy might have had with other nations prior to the arrival of European fishermen near the mouth of the St. Lawrence River in the late fifteenth century. However, as far as postcontact power, the Iroquois reached their peak in the middle of the seventeenth century. At the beginning of this century, the intrusion of a European market into the established trading patterns of the St. Lawrence River Valley set off a series of trade wars. From 1649, when fighters from the Mohawk and Seneca nations destroyed the French-allied Huron confederation, until the 1660s, the Iroquois experienced the height of their regional hegemony. For quite a while longer, until France was defeated in the Seven Years' War, they and their allies would continue to be the main buffer between England and France in North America.[1]

The strength and longevity of the League, along with its attentive diplomacy with the English and the French and their trading connections with other Indian nations, were what allowed the Iroquois to continue to exercise significant influence in the region after 1700, despite their declining power. Although most Western experts believe that the League could not have been formed much earlier than 1450, Seneca-Wyandot scholar Barbara Mann argues convincingly that its origins were in the middle of the twelfth century. In correlating archaeological evidence with oral tradition, she demonstrates that the introduction of corn into the region later known as Iroquoia converges with the beginning of palisade building around 1000 C.E. and with evidence of cannibalism and warfare occurring around the same time. Because the traditions about the founding of the League say that it came into being to end internecine warfare that was characterized in part by cannibalism, the archaeological characteristics of this era should draw our attention as being a little bit more than coincidental.[2]

## The Ancient Origins of the Iroquois

The story of the founding of the League gives historical observers insight into the political and social values of the Iroquois nations. Unlike many of the traditions of other Indian nations along the eastern seaboard, Western attention to it and the lengthy political cultivation of the Anglo-Iroquois relationship has made it more available to outsiders. Although this availability has not always meant that readers of English would comprehend clearly its meanings and implications, we seem to be approaching lucidity in the centuries-long translation effort that has surrounded the story cycle of the League's founding.

To understand the resonance of the story for the Iroquois, Mann suggests, we must first grasp the connection between the League Cycle and the earlier Sky Cycle. The Sky Cycle stories are shared by several eastern Native American groups despite differences in language family, political history, and cultural practices, but it is not known how or when this came about. This cycle relates the arrival of the Iroquois's most ancient female ancestor on Earth. Because it commemorates a history several millennia old, Algonquin and Iroquoian origins might converge at some early date. Alternatively, contiguous groups might have acquired the story later, through intermarriages, individual adoptees, membership in common political organizations, or in some other manner.[3]

In the Iroquois versions of the Sky Cycle, Otsitsa the Sky Woman fell through a hole in the Sky World and landed upon the Earth. She literally landed upon earth because the earth animals joined together to create Turtle Island, or North America, for her after being alerted to her descent toward a formless ocean. The already pregnant Sky Woman then gave birth to Lynx, whose place in the Sky Cycle is often obscured or erased in its earliest recorded versions. While Lynx could conceivably be a recent addition to the story, Mann convincingly explains her early omission by the fact that missionaries were the first to record these stories. The elimination of an intermediate daughter between Sky Woman and the male Twins of tradition conforms the story more closely to Eve, Cain, and Abel while lending credence to the Western demonization of Sky Woman that apparently is not part of the original story. (Though it is a story of a fall, it is not The Story of the Fall.) Once Lynx had grown, North Wind courted her, assuming the shape of many different earth animals to woo her. The shape of the human male was finally successful, and soon Lynx became pregnant. Unfortunately, however, Sky Woman's daughter died in childbirth.[4]

The most recent Iroquois interpretations of this event seem to rectify an accumulation of foreign and Christian ideas about Sky Woman and her two grandsons that have prevented our understanding the link between the Sky Cycle and the League Cycle. They reveal that concepts such as good and evil are cultural specific. In both story cycles, profound grief is a prominent force. Following Lynx's death, Sky Woman became wild with grief at the loss of her dearest companion, the only other unadulterated link to the Sky World that she had on Earth. She blamed Flint, the second twin to emerge from Lynx's womb, for Lynx's death. Because Flint was ugly to her, or Earth-like, while Sapling his twin was handsome and Sky-like, Flint was unloved by Grandmother. The loss of the mother-daughter relationship, a central component of traditional Iroquois culture, was not compensated by Flint's birth. This imbalance initiated a rivalry among the siblings, and much of the continuing work of creating the world begun by Grandmother and her beloved daughter resulted from this competition.[5]

In many texts, Flint is known as the Evil Mind and Grandmother is portrayed simply as evil, but Mann tells us that these cultural substitutions do not allow us to grasp the more poignant phenomena that the story relates. Mentally off balance because his grandmother rejects him in her lingering grief, Flint should be thought of instead as the Wrinkled Mind. Also, because Christian interpreters were used to seeing women in roles in which they distanced all humankind from God, one of Grandmother's many names—Bad Medicine Woman—seemed to reflect a similar view of women by the Iroquois. However, Bad Medicine Woman may be translated also as Hard Luck Woman. Because her grandson Sapling is ultimately forced to bury Flint beneath a mountain to protect humanity from him, Sky Woman may certainly be understood as a figure constantly down on her luck. Unable to make up for the way the lingering irrationality of her mourning has set off an unfortunate chain of events, she must witness her grandson's passionate spirit hardening into insanity while the Twins are cut off from one another by the generations-long emotional gap created by Lynx's loss.[6]

## The Formation of the League of the People of the Completed Longhouse

Thousands of years later, as the Epoch of the League begins, the sacred story begun during the Sky Epoch resumes. To understand how such a thing is possible, we must understand North American concepts of reincarnation, which survived into the postcontact era. "Although widely recorded . . . the reincarnation aspect of Haudenosaunee spirituality has been studiously ignored" or confused with Eastern, karma-based ideas, and then dismissed as a corrupting insertion of matter foreign to Native American cultures. Early in the eighteenth century, "Lafitau recorded the Haudenosaunee 'idea of metempsychosis, the palingenesis or rebirth, and successive transmigration of souls into other bodies after a long revolution of centuries.' . . . Haudenosaunee concepts of reincarnation are emphatically not Asian, karma-based philosophies; there is no sense of return as punishment." Thus as the League Cycle recounts the story of how Deganawida brings peace to the warring nations of Iroquoia, listeners intimate with the Sky Cycle will recognize Deganawida's cosmic identity as Sapling, the Smooth Mind.[7]

When Deganawida left the north shore of Lake Ontario, where he was born, his grandmother and mother saw him set off in a white stone canoe. The canoe is the first link of Deganawida to Sapling, who in the Sky Cycle traveled in an ice floe (white stone) shaped like a canoe to find land after the glaciers or white stone mountains of an ice age had receded. Deganawida arrived in Iroquoia at a time of great violence among the nations. With the introduction of corn to the Finger Lakes area, which probably came with the intrusive movement north of Iroquoian peoples from the western Susquehanna region of what is now central Pennsylvania, came a shift in the social power of men and women. Maize agriculture was becoming the basis of subsistence in an area where hunting and fishing had formerly filled this role. Because women were responsible for cultivation and men responsible for the predatory methods of food acquisition, men's social importance decreased. Mann hypothesizes that this demotion of hunting activities led to their exaggeration in a cannibal cult resistance to the novel social arrangements that had emerged with the growing dependence upon agriculture. As a symbolic variant of hunting, cannibalism was the logic of the earlier predatory system driven to the extreme. As a result, the warring that Deganawida encountered as he entered Iroquoia was a conflict between advocates (of both genders) dependent upon the older supremacy of hunting and advocates (of both genders) dependent upon the newer supremacy of planting.[8]

Deganawida therefore visited first a woman who lived along a war road that ran from east to west. According to some, she was a member of the Neutral nation and lived in the region of Niagara Falls. She had a solemn obligation to feed the warriors who passed by, so Deganawida's negotiations with Jigonsaseh were aimed not at discontinuing this practice but at asking her to urge them, while they ate, to follow the path of peace. Jigonsaseh's condition for agreeing to this arrangement was that women in the League about to be formed should have the power to nominate leaders of the Confederacy and all its local and national governments. In this encounter between Deganawida and Jigonsaseh we are meant to see the reunion of Sapling with his reincarnate mother Lynx, who has reappeared to help resolve the problems caused by her death in the Sky Cycle. "The primary problem of the first Epoch was the premature removal of the Lynx, whose untimely death so embittered Grandmother that she rejected Flint, turning a minor sibling rivalry into a serious Sky dysfunction. Note that the thrust of the plot in the League Epoch is to repair the central problem of the first Epoch: the Lynx is restored. Jigonsaseh becomes a pivot of the plot, the great Peace Woman. She is not partisan, as Grandmother was, but works to reconcile Flint [Atotarho] and Sapling [Deganawida]."[9]

At the time, a man named Atotarho was both a chief of the Onondagas (Onontakes) and a leader of the faction that was using cannibalism to terrorize the Cultivators. Deganawida journeyed next to Onondaga territory, but rather than confronting Atotarho immediately, he visited the home of the man whose name would become Hiawatha: He Who Combs. Hiawatha too had adopted cannibalism as a defense in these dark times, and Deganawida watched him as he carried home a human carcass to boil in his kettle. From the roof, he looked through the smoke hole into the kettle. Hiawatha below saw Deganawida's face reflected in the water but thought that he was seeing himself. Stunned by the wisdom and nobility of the visage, he resolved to abandon his cannibal activities. Deganawida then descended from the roof to eat with Hiawatha, a meal of deer signifying that the hunters would be included in the Great Peace in a reciprocal balance with the cultivators of corn. The two agreed that for the peace to take hold they must convert Atotarho, so they split up. Hiawatha took on the task of combing the snakes (madness) out of Atotarho's hair (mind), smoothing his Wrinkled Mind, while Deganawida journeyed to Mohawk country.[10]

As Deganawida is undergoing a trial among the Mohawk (Kanienke) to prove to them the truth of his message, Hiawatha meets with tragedy. Here, the theme of grief so central to the Sky Cycle reemerges. Its outgrowths would eventually form the terrain upon which European diplomats would encounter and begin to comprehend Iroquois priorities in international relations. Having convinced the Onondaga people to accept the message of peace, Hiawatha could not persuade Atotarho. In one version of the story, as Hiawatha pursues negotiations with Atotarho, all three of his daughters and his wife die at the mercy of forces only implicitly, and yet quite evidently, linked to the mad, power-hoarding Onondaga chief. Bowed low by grief, Hiawatha finally retreated south. Finding shells at the bottom of a lake, he threaded them on strings to make the first wampum and, as he journeyed east, talked to himself about how with these strings he would console a person in grief such as his own. Upon reaching the edge of a Mohawk village, he was approached by Deganawida, who took up the word strings of condolence that would shape Iroquois diplomacy for centuries to come.[11]

As ethnologist J. N. B. Hewitt once observed, the Ritual of Condolence that developed from this reunion of friends is remarkable for the psychological insight (and spiritual necessity) of its many stages. Perhaps the most striking words are those of the first, second, and third "articles" of the requickening part of the ceremony. In the first, the condoler, who reenacts Deganawida's role with Hiawatha, wipes away the mourner's grief in recognition that an excess of tears can blind the mourner to the world and his responsibility to live in it. In the second, the condoler clears the passages of the ears that have become obstructed from so much crying and caused the mourner to lose his hearing. "It comes to pass where a great calamity has befallen one's person that the passages of the ears become obstructed and the hearing is lost. One then hears not the sounds made by mankind, nothing of what is taking place on the earth." To lose one's hearing is again both literal and figurative: cutting one off from being able to listen to the words of sympathy from those around one and threatening to interfere with the mourner's ability to listen to reason, with respect to seeking retribution for the death, and restitution, as it may be offered by those who caused the death. In the third article, the condoler clears the obstruction from the throat of the mourner who is so choked up with sadness that he is unable to speak.[12]

Literary scholar John Bierhorst recognizes that this symbolic clearing of obstructions might have yet a more heightened meaning in a society battling an unforeseen outbreak of cannibalism. "Now the enemy of society is not merely death itself, but the *cult* of death. The death of a kinsman [sic] may lead one into a state of depression, or 'insanity,' symptomized perhaps by an excessive veneration of the corpse (and cannibalism?) conducive to thoughts of suicide or, alternatively, murder. . . . If murder, then the morbid cycle may be reinduced . . . producing the vendetta, or blood feud, that inevitably rends the fabric of society." Apparently, Deganawida's efforts to prevent Hiawatha's grief and morbidity from casting him into a recidivist cannibalism succeeded. After performing this first wampum-based ceremony, he and Hiawatha traveled to the Oneida (Onenniote), Cayuga (Kayukwa), and Seneca (Sonontowane) and convinced them to take hold of the wampum belt of peace. Finally, with all five nations at their backs, the two approached Atotarho. They convinced this sole remaining holdout after much struggle—and by offering him the leadership of the Confederacy—to accept the Great Peace.[13]

As the Iroquois moved out of this era, the Ritual of Condolence was increasingly adapted to diplomatic needs. Treaty councils would often begin with a performance of the Ritual of Condolence, and frequently its performance was linked to the death of a hereditary chief and the need to install a new one. However, as ethnologist Michael Foster has observed, the concepts surrounding the clearing of the senses after mourning may be closely associated with concepts surrounding the adjustment of one's mind to listen to one's partner in cross-cultural negotiation. The speaker who welcomed a delegation that has traveled a long distance would welcome them at the edge of the woods bordering upon the seat of the treaty. He would "'wipe the eyes' of the weary travelers ([because] their eyes are full of things they have seen on their journey, things which might have distracted them from their mission). . . . Next he 'clears their ears' of all the things they have heard on their journey, things which might cause them to alter the message. . . . Then he 'clears the obstructions from their throats' so that once more they will be able to breathe and speak normally. . . . It is manifestly obvious that the first three 'words'—eyes, ears, and throat—are the physiological organs of speech perception and production. They are the primary channels of communication." Thus, the performance of rites associated with the Condolence Ceremony may sometimes have occurred whether or not the death of a chief had preceded that particular treaty conference.[14]

## Beyond the League: The Lenapes and Shawnees

The institution of a league formed on the concept of peace appears to have had far-reaching and complex effects in the postcontact era and possibly in the period from the twelfth through the fifteenth centuries. Historian Matthew Dennis characterizes the seventeenth-century Iroquois as a confederacy and a culture that sought to extend their particular philosophy of peace to neighboring societies. Like all efforts at expansion historically, the Iroquois's seems to have involved a mixture of genuinely outgoing motives and motives that were at the same time provoked by self-interest: both the need to defend themselves against external hostilities and the desire to position themselves at the center of lucrative networks of trade.[15]

In fact, one recorded version of the League Cycle captures this complicated relationship to the will to peace and the readiness for war that has consistently troubled human societies. Deganawida describes the Great Peace that will become the law or normal state of existence as consisting of three parts, Gáiwoh (Righteousness), Skénon (Health), and Gashasdénshaa (Power): "Righteousness means justice practised [sic] between men and between nations; it means also a desire to see justice prevail. Health means soundness of mind and body; *it also means peace, for that is what comes when minds are sane and bodies cared for.* Power means authority, the authority of law and custom, *backed by such force as is necessary to make justice prevail;* it means also religion, for justice enforced is the will of the Holder of the Heavens and has his sanction." The contradiction that lies at the heart of every effort to institute international peace meant that the Iroquois's neighbors would not always look upon their defenses or their overtures—friendly or hostile—with favor. The institution of the League meant the banning of domestic violence. Yet to expand their peaceful domestic world and to mitigate the dangers posed by outsiders by transforming them symbolically and physically into kinspeople could mean a kind of assimilation and ritual adoption that these outsiders ironically identified as cannibalistic.[16]

The two other principal groups participating in Pennsylvania's eighteenth-century Indian treaties therefore had decisions to make about their preferred relationship to the Iroquois's version of peace. Even within these two large groupings—the Lenapes and Shawnees—there were diverse experiences with the Iroquois prior to the eighteenth century. Most Lenape (a.k.a. Delaware) groups, who had lived to the south and southeast, in either direction out from the Delaware River, until the beginning of land negotiations with Europeans in the seventeenth century, appear at first neither to have disturbed nor to have been disturbed by their Iroquois neighbors. Instead, the southern Lenapes of the 1630s faced threats from the Susquehannocks (Andastes), an Iroquoian group not yet politically affiliated with the Iroquois. These threats surfaced when these Lenapes attempted to maintain control over the new European trade on the Delaware River. The outcome was a mutually advantageous alliance between the two. By the end of the century, however, these relationships would all change.[17]

During the trade wars of this same era, the Iroquois had forced Shawnee (Shawunogi) groups residing to their southwest down the Ohio River toward its southern branches. Information about the fifteenth- and sixteenth-century locations of Shawnee villages either does not exist or has not been reliably sorted out. There seem to be three credible possibilities. Shawnee villages may have extended far and thin during this general time not only from south of the eastern tip of Lake Erie along the Ohio River to the Wabash and along the Cumberland River, but all the way through the area we now know as northern Pennsylvania. In this case, and perhaps in the others, they may have been interspersed among the Eries and the Susquehannocks in a different pattern of political territoriality than we tend to witness in Europe. Alternatively, they may have been located mostly in northern Pennsylvania from the

Susquehanna River to Lake Erie and later retreated west into the Ohio and Cumberland locations. Finally, they may have lived mostly south of Lake Erie and along the Ohio River. In 1692, some Shawnees settled with the Munsee group of Lenapes in the northern regions of the Delaware River. The first and second possibilities would help explain why such a relocation from areas along the Illinois River, instigated by envoys from the Mahicans and the Munsees, would have seemed attractive.[18]

Though many oral traditions of the Lenapes have been recorded since the seventeenth century, no cogent interpretations of the link between these traditions and ancient Lenape political history exist. Much controversy still swirls over the authenticity of the Walum Olum, a translation of a reputedly pictographic record of the last grand migration of the Lenapes' ancestors. As Bierhorst says, "confidence in the document has lately faded." Certainly confidence in the Asian migration interpretations of the document is much fainter, but many, including this editor, find credible evidence that writing devices such as pictographs, hieroglyphs, wampum, and indigenous syllabaries were used extensively across eastern North America prior to European arrival. Rather than engaging in conjecture about the Lenapes' history before the seventeenth century, the editor refers the reader to the Lenape bibliography for the sometimes conflicting sources of information and interpretation.[19]

At least two things can be said with relative certainty about the Lenapes of the seventeenth century. First, unlike the Iroquois, they were not bound together in a formal confederacy that provided for the common defense, and their principal political affiliations were with their town, with the towns along their waterway, and with their clan. Each town and each waterway community operated with relative independence from the others even though all the towns along the Delaware River were united by just two closely related languages and a sense of common kinship. The Unami dialects were spoken in the south while the Munsee dialects were spoken north of a line roughly running from present-day Stroudsburg, Pennsylvania, to immediately southeast of Staten Island. There may have been as many as forty communities who formed the contact-era Lenapes.[20]

Second, like the Iroquois, the oral traditions and ceremonies of the Lenapes marked both the reciprocity between men and women and their different responsibilities for the hunt and the cultivation of crops, respectively. Ethnohistorian Jay Miller describes the Lenape concepts of responsibility and revelation as being linked to expressions of community identity and cosmic harmony. "Responsibility had to do with public good and community welfare under the leadership of the chiefly family of a clan (or clan segment) associated with a specific waterway having a regional or capital town at its mouth. . . . Revelation . . . established the link between a human and a spirit that alone enabled the success of any undertaking. . . . The encounter between the person and the spirit occurred at a specific locale, often a remote elevation, and conferred access to supernatural power." The Gamwing or Big House ceremony, which took place in a special building symbolic of the universe, helped Lenape families renew their spiritual ties with all of creation. The Green Corn

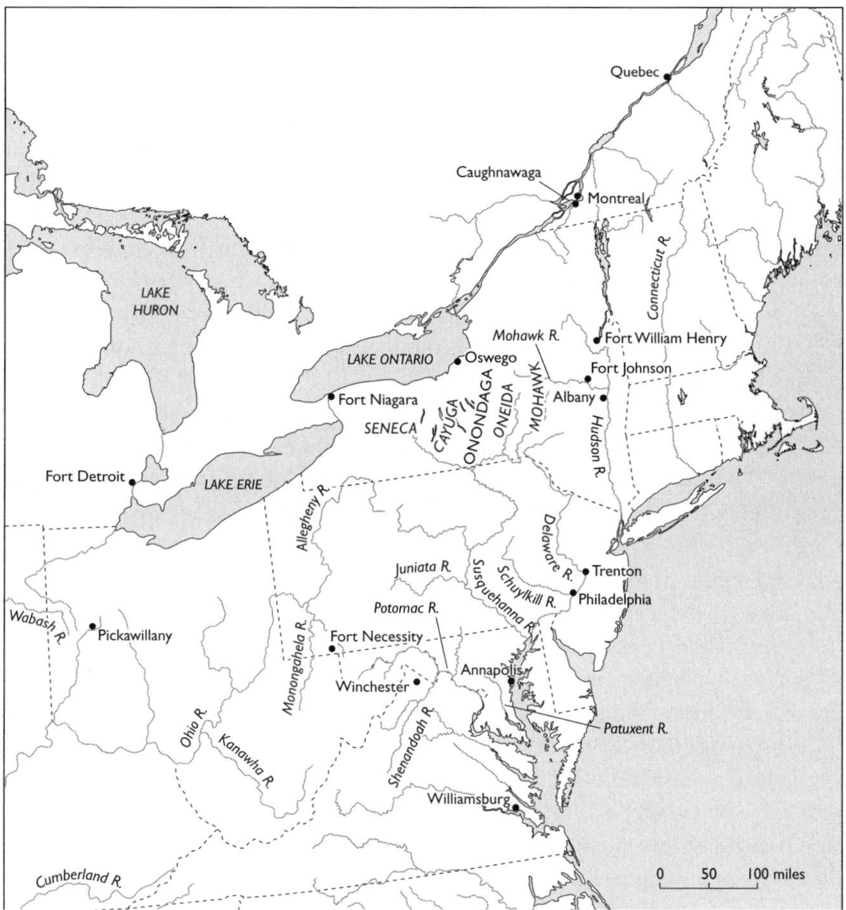


Map 1. Key locations in eastern North America.

ceremony specifically celebrated the maturing harvest. Only plant crops would be served during this time, to honor Mother Corn.[21]

## The Silver Covenant Chain

To understand who the "Delaware" of Pennsylvania's treaties are, we must first understand two elements of the early colonial landscape: how diverse Lenape identities began to consolidate around local land cessions (and eventually around westward migrations and continuing eastern residency rights), as well as reductions in population owing to disease; and how shifts in the trading and military alliances made by the Swedish, Dutch, French, and by each separate, rival English colony created instability in this landscape. The first alliance pertinent to our discussion was created in 1609 when the French, under the leadership of Samuel de Champlain, joined the Huron confederation north of Lake Ontario and some Canadian Algonquins in their attacks on the Iroquois. Who initiated hostilities remains unclear, but motives on all sides once Champlain enters the picture are quite clear. The Huron were the middlemen of an extensive and lucrative trade network reaching the tribal nations to the west on the Great Lakes and in the area east of Hudson Bay to the north. The Iroquois were interested in gaining a share of this trade, if not in supplanting the Huron as middlemen to the French. The French saw that Iroquois alliances with the Huron would destroy their monopoly with the northern and western tribes, allowing trade goods and price competition into the region from other European nations trading in from the seacoast.[22]

Also in 1609, Henry Hudson had discovered the mouth of the Hudson River. By 1613, the Dutch venturing up that river were beginning to ally themselves to the Mohawks. This alliance threatened the French alliance and therefore stabilized the balance of power around the St. Lawrence River. The Dutch also began trading with northern Lenapes (probably the Munsees on Manhattan Island) around this time, as did the English, though no records of formal alliances have been preserved. However, the southern Lenapes put an end to Dutch attempts to settle on Delaware Bay near present-day Lewes, Delaware, in 1631 when the Dutch inadvertently provoked the killing of a Lenape chief because of their authoritarian manner of communicating with the locals. By 1638, the Swedish had begun to settle in Lenape territory on the western side of Delaware Bay and the lower part of the Delaware River. The Swedish alliance with the southern Lenapes would have slightly balanced out the alliance, probably formed around 1610, between English Virginia and the Susquehannocks who lived to the west of the Lenapes along the Susquehanna River. As already noted, these two rival alliances became linked when the Susquehannocks and the Lenapes came to terms over trade, which probably gave the Lenapes access to Virginia English goods and the Susquehannocks access to the Swedish and Dutch goods that the Lenapes could acquire.[23]

The Swedish settlements along the west side of the Delaware River at first extended from present-day Wilmington to the Schuylkill River in what is now Philadelphia. While the Europeans usually believed that they were purchasing the lands outright, the Lenapes saw the result of their negotiations as an agreement to share the lands. They expected to be able to continue to fish, hunt, and plant in the areas "purchased." Eventually, the Swedish "bought" land along the river from Cape Henlopen in southern Delaware to the area that is now Trenton, New Jersey. The Dutch then began to use irregularities and the ambiguities in the use of the word "sale" to obtain land rights from the Lenapes, who were becoming only too happy to welcome a rival to the Swedish governor, who disdained them. Eventually, these maneuvers resulted in the 1655 ouster of Swedish authorities from the region by the Dutch. This expulsion was probably not what the Lenapes had had in mind, given that they held advantage by playing multiple rivals off against one another. Furthermore, the Susquehannock allies of the Lenapes were suddenly placed in a tight spot that would soon become a vise. Having threatened the Dutch-allied Mohawks with an ultimatum to join an Indian trade cartel (which would have ruined them) or to face a fight, the Susquehannocks found a principal cartel ally, the Lenapes, strangely now in the Dutch sphere of influence.[24]

As the Susquehannocks newly allied to Maryland faced the Dutch-allied Iroquois, a point of stability was maintained because the Susquehannocks refused to attack their friends the Lenapes. The events of 1664 began to spell decline for the Susquehannocks. Dutch New Netherlands became English New York. Yet despite the elimination of all other European rivals in the region south of Lake Ontario, the English colonies still found enough to fight about among themselves. So English Maryland continued to encourage Susquehannock assaults on the Iroquois allies of English New York. Then, just as Maryland began militarily to wrest Delaware Bay from New York's control in 1672, the Dutch took over New York again. At this point, Maryland became fearful that the Dutch would incite the Iroquois against them directly and decided in June 1674 to conclude a peace with them. In doing so, they began to turn against the Susquehannocks.[25]

By February 1675, three months after England gained back New York, one hundred Susquehannock families were asking Maryland for refuge in an abandoned Piscatawa village near present-day Washington, D.C. Though great disagreement exists among historians about what happened, it appears probable that Maryland armed the Iroquois for a decisive attack on the Susquehannocks, or at least withdrew their military support from the latter. Fearing a Dutch-Iroquois alliance, Maryland could have set such events in motion prior to the reversion of New York to English hands. Other possibilities exist. For instance, once New York was back in English hands, Maryland may simply have been trying to prevent the Susquehannocks from falling into New York's sphere of influence. In fact, though no record of it exists, either the Dutch or the French could have armed the Iroquois to defeat the Susquehannocks who would have come to Maryland for refuge.[26]

Conflicting interpretations of the event as an English conquest versus an Iroquois conquest profoundly affect our interpretation of the first three treaties reproduced in this collection. However, the attempted massacre in 1675 of one hundred refugee Susquehannock families by the militias of Maryland and Virginia during Bacon's Rebellion does not demonstrate that these colonies "conquered" the Susquehannocks, in the normal sense or in fact at all. These families appear to have capitulated before they were targeted as convenient scapegoats, much like the Moravian Lenapes Benjamin Franklin tried to protect from the Paxton Boys almost a century later. Fortunately for them, the Susquehannocks were clever enough to escape this siege under the cover of night.[27]

They ran not only toward refuge among their allies, the Lenapes, but toward a historic juncture. New York's Edmund Andros was at this very moment finding it an advantageous strategy in the struggle for supremacy among the British colonies to increase his own friendly Indian population by protecting embattled tribes against those other colonies. As King Philip's War came to an end in New England, Andros had invited the Mahicans to take refuge within his jurisdiction, after having armed his Mohawk allies to defeat these, their persistent antagonists. Similarly, when Andros learned early in 1676 that the Susquehannocks had taken refuge with the Lenapes, he welcomed them and pledged his protection to them, certainly aware of the advantage he had won from Maryland's foolish betrayal of its former allies. As Maryland persisted in trying to gain Delaware Bay by planning to set its other Indian allies in pursuit of the Susquehannocks toward that region, Andros attempted to persuade them to move back to their homes along the Susquehanna River. Doing so, as all but twenty-six families did, meant accepting the peace and protection of their former enemies, the Iroquois.[28]

A series of treaties in 1677 formalized these arrangements and also gave rise to the Silver Covenant Chain that helped keep peace among New York, its Indian allies, and the other English colonies until 1755. Though the Susquehannocks had begun moving home in June 1676, a treaty in February and March 1677 at Shackamaxon (a Lenape town where Philadelphia now stands) between the Iroquois, the Lenapes, and the Susquehannocks sealed the arrangements. At this treaty, the Iroquois and the Lenapes may have divided Susquehannock territory between themselves (and their new Susquehannock tribal members) at the falls of the Susquehanna River, for the Susquehannocks ceased to exist for a time as an independent people until some were reborn as the Conestoga Indians. In April 1677, Andros engineered a formal peace and alliance among New York, Massachusetts, Connecticut, the Iroquois, and the Mahicans. By August of that year, he had gotten Maryland and Virginia to join the Chain, though Maryland did not drop their pursuit of the Susquehannocks or their designs on Delaware Bay. (Recall that Pennsylvania colony does not yet exist.) Eventually, continued raids by the Susquehannocks of Iroquoia and their Iroquois friends forced the Piscatawa and Conoy into the Covenant Chain under Iroquois leadership.[29]

## Pennsylvania's Chain of Friendship

Meanwhile, in the decade beginning around 1673, the diverse Lenape communities sometimes referred to collectively as the Unalachtigo, or the people near the ocean, had begun to move. By this time, many Lenape communities may have endured a reduction in their populations to as little as a tenth of their precontact numbers. This grievous death toll was caused largely by disease, reduction of their food supply, and conflicts over trade or trespass with Europeans and other Indian nations. Many downriver communities decided at this time to sell their land rights permanently to the English. They tended then to move north, and they became absorbed into the Unami Lenape communities who lived farther up the Delaware. (Unami means "the people who live down the river," a relative term given the length of the Delaware.) Some may have gone south down the Chesapeake peninsula as well. The Unalachtigo communities relinquished their independent identities while the areas now known as Delaware and southern New Jersey began to fill up with English and other settlers from Europe.[30]

In 1681, the colony of Pennsylvania was carved out of an area that New York had claimed as its jurisdiction. William Penn, the first proprietor of this grant, continued to buy land from the Lenapes (and others). Philadelphia and the counties surrounding it emerged as a result of these sales, which became renowned for the fairness of the compensation that the Indian nations received, the clarity of the terms to which all parties had agreed, and Penn's observance of Lenape protocols of consent in land cessions. These protocols consisted of the chief gaining the consent of all his constituents having claim to the land in question as well as the consent of neighbors who had no direct claim to the land except that they would be neighbors to the newcomers. Penn bought lands from Lenapes who would be referred to as the Brandywine Lenapes, who reserved for themselves a town to the southwest of Philadelphia. He also bought lands as far north as the falls of the Delaware River, across from Trenton, in an area of present-day Bucks County. Those Lenapes in the Philadelphia vicinity who did not stay at Brandywine tended to relocate to their hunting grounds on the upper part of the Schuylkill River, where they became known as the Tulpehocken Lenapes, after the valley and creek of that name. The Tulpehocken Lenapes included a group known as the Okehocking, who had decided to abandon a reservation in Chester County that Penn had promised them.[31]

In addition to the Brandywine Lenapes and the Tulpehocken Lenapes who had been involved in land sales, a third emerging branch of Lenapes known as the Forks Lenapes still lived in the area where the Lehigh and Delaware Rivers converge. By 1718, when William Penn died, they had not sold their lands to him or any other European. Many of the Jersey Lenapes had, by the early eighteenth century, moved across the river into this region in what would become part of Pennsylvania. Generally, these people from the area that became New Jersey already identified with the Forks Lenapes, given that the Delaware River was not the boundary that Europeans tended to turn rivers into, but the waterway that unified their communities as described earlier. The Forks Lenape territory extended along the river from just north of Trenton, around Washington Crossing or New Hope to just south of Stroudsburg at the Delaware Water Gap where the Kittatinny Mountains formed a relative boundary. The watershed of the Lehigh River from these mountains south roughly marked a western boundary that dropped straight south near the southern bend in that river toward Tohiccon Creek, and then continued roughly to the southeast. The Forks Lenapes lived just south of the fourth branch, the Munsee group of Lenapes, who are often referred to as though they were always a separate and coherent nation rather than "the people who live in the stony country," as the Forks were "the people who live up the river," or Unalimi.[32]

When William Penn returned for his second and final visit to Pennsylvania, he bought the Susquehanna Valley. This 1701 treaty was the second in a series that came to be known as Pennsylvania's Chain of Friendship with the Lenapes, the Conestoga Susquehannocks, the Shawnees, and the Conoys. New York and the Iroquois, especially the Mohawks, would see it at first as a rival to the power they held through the Covenant Chain. Yet it was the upper part of the Susquehanna waterway—the part controlled by the Iroquois—where the Brandywine, Tulpehocken, and Forks Lenapes would all end up by the 1740s. Between 1702 and 1729, the Brandywine Lenapes sold off their reservation lands because they were unable to keep white settlers from encroaching upon them or to enlist the help of the less than honest proxies into whose hands Penn had entrusted the government of Pennsylvania. Likewise, the Tulpehocken Lenapes saw Palatine Germans invasively take over their lands at the invitation of Pennsylvania Governor William Keith. The family of Conrad Weiser, perhaps the most prominent interpreter between the Iroquois and the English, was among the squatters. Even before this time, from 1709 or earlier until the final sale in 1732, the Tulpehocken Lenapes had been selling and relocating to the Susquehanna. Pennsylvania had found a compliant chief in Olumapies and pretended that he was their head chief. Both the Brandywine and the Tulpehocken ended up around Paxtang or Harrisburg. The Forks Lenapes would not arrive at Shamokin (now Sunbury), Wyoming, or Nutimy's Town (near Berwick) in great numbers until 1742.[33]

## Pennsylvania Joins the Covenant Chain

The events that brought them there and the effect that these and subsequent events had on Lenape-Iroquois and Lenape-Pennsylvania relations form one of the central dramas of these treaties. In general, we may think of Franklin's printings as covering three indistinctly drawn periods in an era of intense international rivalry. The events that draw the Forks Lenapes to Wyoming and the Susquehanna River belong to the first period. The first three treaties of 1736, 1742, and 1744 occur toward the end of the Iroquois's attempt to secure a regional political hegemony vis-à-vis its nearest southern Indian neighbors through an alliance with Pennsylvania rather than sheer military might. Their first clandestine contact with Pennsylvania, seeking only trade, was in 1704 during Queen Anne's War (1702–1713) between England and France. Prior to 1704, English New York had jealously guarded its alliance with the League against rival English colonies, though they could never prevent the Iroquois from treating with the French. In fact, New York's tight relationship with the Mohawks, New France's ongoing relationship with the Senecas, and the divided allegiances of the Onondagas toward New France and Pennsylvania aided the Confederacy's ability to maintain diplomatic independence even while they eventually led to severe splinters in the unity of the League.[34]

The second three treaties of 1745, 1747, and 1748 all occurred in the midst of King George's War (1744–1748). Unlike the Lancaster Treaty of 1744, however, these three treaties exhibit direct overtures, either from the English to the League or from Ohio Iroquois to the English, to enter the war as an ally against the French. This period is also important because it witnessed the first significant, though indirect, confrontation between England and France over the upper Ohio Valley region that both nations claimed, but that belonged to the Iroquois (through their victories in the trade wars of the previous century), their offshoots, and their allies (such as the Twightwee or Miami Indians). Although Francis Jennings and Richard Aquila point out the extensive weakening of Iroquois power after their defeat by the French in 1687, this decline does not appear to have weakened their hold on territory south of Lake Erie so much as to the north of it. Thus, these treaties record the distress of the third major power claiming the region—the loosely allied Indian nations—at the arrogant encroachments of the other two onto their territory. In this period, we are first introduced to the Ohio Iroquois and the Ohio Lenapes.[35]

The final eight treaties (of which July 1756 and November 1756 formed a single printing) all took place within the sphere of the Seven Years' War, often inaccurately described as the French and Indian War. Here the happenings of the previous two periods, as recorded both within and outside of the treaties Franklin printed, unhappily converged. A series of incidents beginning in 1737 that deprived the Lenapes of their last lands, their shelter among the Iroquois, and their ability to rely upon the friendship, good neighborliness, and defense by Pennsylvania against French invasion culminated in their decision to initiate war against Pennsylvania's illegitimate squatters. Most of these final treaty councils were spent in efforts to reestablish a peace between the British and their longtime allies and to investigate the causes of their war. The peculiar timing of Franklin's selection of treaties for printing (1736–1762), his unusual interventions in 1753 and November 1756, and his subsequent use of their contents for propaganda purposes against William Penn's sons, the proprietors of Pennsylvania under royal charter, suggest that he early had his finger on the pulse of the Penns' dishonesty.[36]

From 1682 until 1701, when William Penn gave control of Indian affairs to James Logan, Pennsylvania enjoyed an unprecedented rapport with their Indian neighbors as compared to the other English colonies. These good relations eroded very slowly as Logan began courting the Iroquois while engaging in profiteering in his trade relationships with all Indians and cheating the Brandywine and Tulpehocken Lenapes out of their lands by undermining their hold upon them. For the Senecas, Cayugas, Onondagas, and Oneidas, the prospect was sweet of opening an alternative trading partnership with Philadelphia to compete with the monopoly that the Mohawk-Albany axis held over the English trade. By this time, the Susquehannocks, the Shawnees, and the Conoys had each been accepted into New York's Covenant Chain through Iroquois mediation, and the League had welcomed them as refugee nations who settled in far southern Iroquoia. They helped protect their southern flank and drew the League nearer to Pennsylvania.[37]

Until about 1721, their relationship with Pennsylvania remained somewhat hidden from New York. During this period, they began to consolidate their power through wars south and far south of Iroquoia. (In 1706, the Conestoga Susquehannocks, the Shawnees, and the Nanticokes expressed fear of them; in 1707, they were at war with the Catawbas in the Carolina backcountry; in 1720, the Conestogas, Shawnees, Conoys, and Lenapes told Pennsylvania that they were afraid of stopping raids by the Iroquois on more southerly Indian nations.) After 1721, as the English colonies began trying to broker peace agreements between the Cherokees and Catawbas and the Iroquois, Pennsylvania's relationship with the latter began to solidify and become more overt. In 1722, Pennsylvania joined the Silver Covenant Chain with New York and the Iroquois. The move suddenly raised the latter to premier status among "Pennsylvania's Indians."[38]

As Pennsylvania-Iroquois relations got stronger, Pennsylvania's relations with the Lenapes were becoming progressively weaker. After William Penn's death in 1718, his three sons, Thomas, Richard, and John, inherited proprietorship of Pennsylvania. Not given to the Quaker ethics of their father and in the kind of debt to which many high-living gentry were prone, they looked opportunistically to land deals from Pennsylvania's Lenapes for their salvation. Repeatedly, they sold tracts to English merchants and manufacturers without first extinguishing Lenape title to the land, as their father had always done. When they and Logan did get around to treating with the Lenapes for title, they were known to offer as little as two pounds per thousand acres for land they were selling at 155 pounds per thousand acres. Finally, in 1737, Thomas and John Penn pulled off their most infamous swindle.[39]

## The Walking Purchase

In 1686, an agent for William Penn appears to have negotiated with a chief named Mechkilikishi for a tract he owned south of Tohiccon Creek and north of Neshaminy Creek. The area is just below where the Delaware River forks into the Lehigh River. However, when the agent (or perhaps William Penn himself) began the leisurely day-and-a-half walk along the course of the Delaware to mark off the extent of the purchase, the deal fell apart. Mechkilikishi and his neighbor Nutimus told the proprietor and his people that they could not cross Tohiccon Creek, because Nutimus was the owner of that land and had not agreed to sell. Because the Lenapes had already made the walk themselves, they knew roughly how much land they were agreeing to and where. Penn agreed to defer the sale until later, but died before he could settle the matter. By the time Thomas and John Penn entered the picture, Mechkilikishi had also died.[40]

In 1734, the brothers started pressuring Nutimus and others living north of Tohiccon Creek to sell their lands at a rock-bottom rate; but they refused. So in 1735, the brothers dug up the 1686 document that was "a preliminary draft of a deed" for Mechkilikishi's land, which Pennsylvania had since bought. They then bullied and threatened Nutimus and the other Lenape chiefs into agreeing to a new walk. Soon after this forced concession, but long before the infamous Walk ever took place, the

Penns began to survey and sell the land that they wanted north of Tohiccon Creek. Benjamin Franklin himself advertised in his *Pennsylvania Gazette* the land lottery by which the Penns attempted to raise some quick cash before Lenape title had actually been extinguished. Though the lottery was stymied by moral objections from the Quakers and their legal restrictions on lotteries, they were able to sell many acres secretly to friends. Franklin knew both Nicholas Scull, the surveyor who assisted the Penns, and William Allen, who was one of his early patrons and who purchased some of this land from the Penns in secret. Given that Franklin soon began to publish the treaties Pennsylvania was making with the Iroquois, it is quite possible that he already had some idea of the shenanigans in which the Penns were engaged.[41]

At this point, Pennsylvania's growing relationship with the Iroquois began to come in handy to the brothers. In 1722, they had made a formal alliance with Pennsylvania, but they still had not resolved an issue they had raised in 1721: Pennsylvania's encroachments upon the Susquehanna River Valley that Logan's trade schemes and land deceptions were encouraging. In 1683, the Iroquois had, with much encouragement from New York merchants, asked its governor to protect the upper Susquehanna from William Penn, who wished to purchase it. This prospective purchase severely threatened the Albany-Mohawk trading monopoly. New York's lieutenant governor Thomas Dongan promptly "sold" to William Penn this land that New York did not own, plus the lower Susquehanna, which the Iroquois had not entrusted to him and did not claim. Penn proceeded to extinguish Conestoga title to the lower Susquehanna in 1701, apparently with the Five Nations' approval on record. The Shawnees and Conoys appear to have benefited from this purchase as well, though it is unclear whether they were witnesses or interested landholders.[42]

By 1720, Logan began to hear complaints from the Cayugas through the Conestoga leader Civility about people settling on Cayuga lands on the Susquehanna, probably north of the falls at Conewaga, between Paxtang (Harrisburg) and Conestoga. However, the Iroquois had not gotten very far when they presented their claims to Pennsylvania in 1721, 1722, and 1727. By 1732, however, the League's potential usefulness to the Penns was becoming more apparent. Thomas Penn removed the duplicitous James Logan from power while continuing to use him to further his ends. Logan had not only blocked Iroquois claims to the Susquehanna but is notorious for having altered treaty minutes, suppressed information in official records, and embezzled from William Penn. Thomas Penn needed the Iroquois to help enforce his land grab from Nutimus and the other Forks Lenapes, so he encouraged the stronger alliance with them that even Logan himself was starting to set in motion. (Logan's own motive was a sudden need to secure his hold on Olumapies's lands in the Tulpehocken Valley west of the Schuylkill River, provoked by the Penns' suspicion of him.)[43]

When the Confederacy came to Philadelphia in 1736 to confirm the terms of the 1732 renewal and the strengthening of their earlier alliance, Penn convinced them after the treaty to "release" their claim to lands in the Delaware Valley. The Iroquois had never claimed these lands; they had always acknowledged the Lenapes' ownership of them. So the paper they signed, which made it seem as though

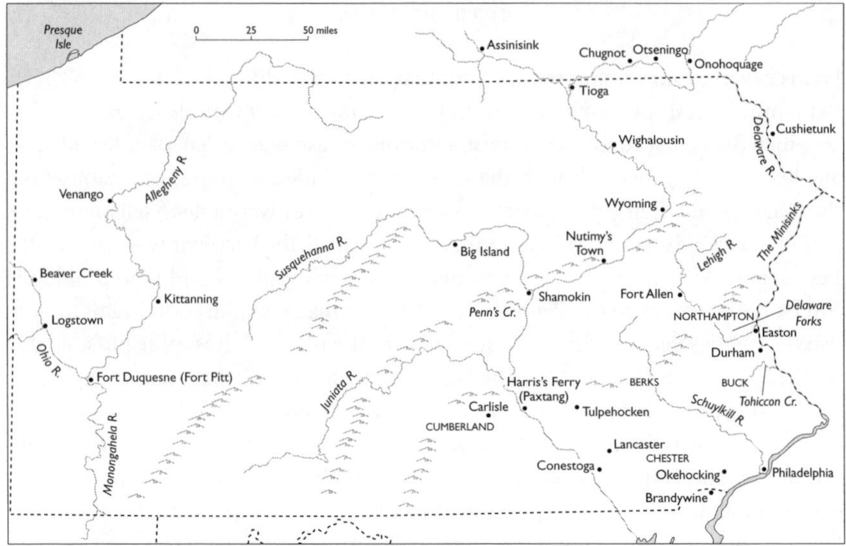


Map 2. Key locations in Pennsylvania and Iroquoia, and on Lenape lands.

they had transferred the lands to Pennsylvania, from their perspective merely reiterated the Lenapes' ownership. In return for their signatures, Penn's agent Conrad Weiser pledged that Penn would intervene for them in their land disputes with Maryland and Virginia, a request denied at the official treaty.[44]

Ironically, in a barely recorded six-day session at the treaty council itself, the League had also agreed to "release" their claims to the Susquehanna River country below the "Kekachtaninius" Hills (or Endless Mountains). It is unclear that they had ever claimed these lands at all, this area being the former territory of those Susquehannocks who had decided in the 1670s to live among the Lenapes rather than the Iroquois. Several persons in the delegation may have been bribed with presents and placed under the influence of alcohol to sign this release, given that the same methods were used several days later to secure the "release" of the Delaware lands. It is possible that the Iroquois signed this release in an unsuccessful attempt to secure the withdrawal of Logan's traders from the upper reaches of the Susquehanna, from the Allegheny, and from the Ohio. They might also have expected the help with Virginia and Maryland that they only got after later agreeing to the Delaware release. In any event, the Susquehanna release helped Pennsylvania and the British build a false image of the League as an empire subordinate to the British empire rather than as an independent and growing confederacy at the center of a network of alliances and expanding national membership.[45]

It seems worthy to note here that this 1736 treaty was the first that Benjamin Franklin printed, though he would have had a chance in 1732 to secure Pennsylvania's treaty printing business. Either Franklin or Pennsylvania or both recognized in the 1736 treaty the beginning of a new era during which public scrutiny of Indian affairs might be important. That ten of the fourteen treaties he chose to print record events related to the Walking Purchase, and that all of the remaining four record events of great significance to England's imperial integrity against the perceived assaults of France, suggest that Franklin foresaw how their publication might serve the empire, and his own political interests, down the road.[46]

The release of the Delaware lands put the Penns in a position to move forward with the walk of the Tohiccon lands. In fact, they had already made a dress rehearsal during which they had discovered that with "due attention to topography and even more attention to semantics, the [boundary] line [for the land they intended to grab] could be made long enough to encompass not only the lands of troublesome old Nutimus but also the entire "Forks of Delaware' region of the Lehigh Valley, between the South and Blue mountains and a large area of Minisink [Munsee Lenape] territory beyond the Blue." Then, in 1737, after they had gotten the League "release," they went back to the Lenapes and obtained signatures from them that released their claim on land represented to them in a map of the area. However, the Penns doctored the map so that the waterway that the Lenapes would have "read" visually as Tohiccon Creek was labeled as the west branch of the Delaware River, much farther north. Because the Penns did not translate the alphabetic labels to them, the Lenapes did not know what they appeared to be agreeing to with their signatures. Jennings believes that they thought they were simply reconfirming the sale of Mechkilikishi's tract.[47]

The Penns' henchmen then performed an actual walk. As described above, the original walk of 1686/1701 had been a leisurely day-and-a-half excursion, complete with rest stops, pauses for meals, loadings and unloadings of horses, and a relaxed smoke of one's pipe. The 1737 Walking Purchase was nothing less than a marathon. Three men raced ahead as far as they could, ignoring the borders they crossed between the Lenape chiefs who held different lands. The boundary line drawn from the endpoint of the fastest, best enduring runner began sixty-four miles from the origin. It took in all the land between the Lehigh and Delaware Rivers south of the Kittatinny Mountains, and then some. When the Lenapes cried foul, the Penns simply invited the League down to the 1742 treaty at Philadelphia.[48]

Here they and their speaker Canasatego either were duped by the same fraudulent maps and "deeds" into confirming the honesty of the purchase or conspired with Pennsylvania to form a threatening alliance against the Lenapes, or both. A conspiracy would have saved face. By figuring their previous "release" of lands as a legitimate exercise of power over the lands of a people who could now be made to appear as a tributary nation, it positioned the Iroquois as indispensable to the borderlands peace of Pennsylvania. In fact, the Lenapes would later reveal that they only removed from the Forks region onto Iroquois lands at Wyoming, Shamokin, and Nutimy's Town to preserve the peace. From 1737 until 1742, they had alternately threatened to defend themselves and complained of the hostilities they faced from the squatters who believed they had legally purchased the Forks lands from the Penns. Clearly, the Lenapes backed away from self-defense when faced with the prospect of an Iroquois-Pennsylvania military alliance, or at minimum the withdrawal of the League's backing.[49]

What remains unclear is the extent to which Canasatego acted on the authority of the Onondaga Council, the extent to which he acted on his own, perhaps influenced by the ubiquitous bribes of Conrad Weiser and the like, and the extent to which the minutes recording his actual words were altered. Though many secondary sources name Canasatego as "chief of the Onondagas" (sometimes as the Atotarho, or head of the entire Iroquois League), none of them substantiate this title, rarely offering their evidence to reveal the source of their certainty on this point. In fact, in the treaties themselves, Canasatego is most often listed as the speaker for the League, and it is generally asserted that speakers were usually different from those chiefs who had been elected by the clan mothers into the hereditary offices of the Confederacy. Speakers were chosen for their oratorical skills and ability to recall lengthy and numerous speeches; chiefs did not always (or perhaps often) possess such outstanding language skills. That the treaties list Canasatego as a chief of the Onondagas does not necessarily mean anything more than that the British wanted to endow him with an authority he might not have had. Moreover, we seldom in the other treaties see evidence that the Atotarho of the League came to Pennsylvania in person to treat; in fact, speakers often told Pennsylvania that they could not confirm an agreement until they got the approval of the Council at Onondaga. Yet the question remains open.[50]

## Lancaster 1744

This 1742 treaty, during which Canasatego appears to have commanded the Lenapes to abandon their rights to the Forks, opened the door for the negotiations that the Iroquois had desired with Maryland and Virginia since 1736. Canasatego took the opportunity offered by Pennsylvania's spotlight to launch a rhetorically clever warning toward the two intransigent colonies. Having ignored Iroquois complaints about settlements along the Potomac and the Shenandoah for seven or eight years, Maryland and Virginia finally came to the bargaining table in 1744 once Canasatego threatened that the Iroquois would do themselves justice. The exchange between the colonies and the League at this treaty gives us insight into the diplomatic history of indigenous North America. Not only does the practice of clever verbal ambiguity to frustrate the designs of other nations appear to be a precontact norm echoed in other sources like John Heckewelder's writings, but the Iroquois appear to be instructing the British in the diplomatic language of the continent. They seem amused that the British react with such alarm to a measure so clearly designed to call their bluff. They had evidently been taken more seriously than even they had expected.[51]

Unfortunately, while the League gained significant concessions at the 1744 treaty, they also inadvertently gave the British the keys to the continent. In addition, their apparent decision to engage the European rhetoric of conquest on their own terms has resulted in profound dismissal and misunderstanding. Attempting to debunk the British rhetoric of Iroquois Empire that enabled British claims to the interior of the continent, scholars have also tried to adjust misperceptions of Native American political phenomena. These attempts to disentangle Native American events from European categories of the politically possible sometimes end ironically in a cynical rejection of the recorded word of Native Americans. As I have described above, no unqualified trust should be placed in the Pennsylvanians who claim to have recorded these treaties faithfully; yet, more often than not, they recorded and published exchanges that operate greatly to their disadvantage rhetorically if not practically. One might therefore proceed with caution when trying to reconstruct or deconstruct relations among Indian nations. It is easy to undermine British propaganda at the expense of understanding Native American history.

The 1744 Treaty at Lancaster is one of the most interesting of Franklin's collection because of the rhetorical strategies employed on both sides. When the treaty council opens on a Friday in late June, Pennsylvania's governor bids the Iroquois to rest from their long journey. When talks begin the following Monday, he tries to hurry them up. But the Iroquois delegation would have no part of this strongly urged "expedition." A careful reader will notice that, in the course of more than twenty years, they almost never return answers to the English colonies on the same day, much less at the same sitting. A deep-seated philosophy of the value of deliberation and consensus precluded them from doing so. They recognized that hasty replies made for ill-conceived decisions; moreover, their political structures would not allow for a single speaker to take upon himself at a moment's notice the authority of the League. The several nations of the League had to consider one another's perspectives, perhaps consult with the clan mothers, and agree to speak with one voice to the outside world. None had the executive prerogative of an English governor.[52]

Even more important perhaps, spontaneous replies would have disrupted the Iroquois's techniques of oral recall that allowed them to preserve their history accurately and reproduce others' speeches with near verbatim accuracy. During the delivery of a speech by the English, different members of the delegation were apparently responsible for memorizing different portions of the speech. Their private deliberations allowed them to reconstruct the whole and allowed the chosen speaker to assemble the whole in his mind. To ensure that both parties were understanding one another, the speaker would always repeat the main points of the speech that had been delivered to the delegation before pronouncing the reply that had been assembled in private council and read into the wampum.[53]

After refusing to abandon their ancient diplomatic practices on the petulant demand of an immature continental power, the Iroquois discover that they are dealing with two very different animals in Maryland and Virginia. Almost immediately, Maryland agrees to compensate them for the lands that settlers have already invaded. Rhetorically, though, the colony rejects all Iroquois claims to the lands, trying to figure their purchase as though it is merely a gift to appease a pretender. The League will have none of it. With no intention to reject the offer on the table, they nevertheless take the opportunity to ridicule Maryland's grandiose claims of a century of possession by comparing them to their own ancient emergence as a people from the land in question. (It is actually a fascinating fit with Dean Snow's later

Map 3. The British colonies circa 1763.

analysis of Iroquois origins!) Toying with Maryland some more over the quality of the goods they offer in their settlement, the League nevertheless wraps up the deal within the week. We might compare the exchange to any of the numerous corporate settlements of today where a company admits no wrong though everyone knows they would have lost their case in court.

On the other hand, Virginia insists that the League prove its claim before it will agree to any deal. Having parsed Maryland's claim that they had already bought the lands in question from the Susquehannocks by clarifying the area claimed and the time sequence Maryland was relying upon, the League discovers that Virginia has no interest in legalities. The colony claims possession of all of its enormous, chartered territory from 1584 on. On June 28, Virginia's commissioners state: "It is true that the Great King holds *Virginia* by Right of Conquest, and the Bounds of that Conquest to the Westward is the Great Sea." They draw, therefore, on the famous right of conquest discussed by Helen Hunt Jackson in *A Century of Dishonor* by which the European powers agreed to divide the Western Hemisphere among them. Anticipating this tactic, the speaker Tachanoontia penetrates into the heart of British hypocrisy. The right of conquest that Virginia would claim is empty and semantic; the right of conquest claimed by the Iroquois was bought with blood. It is real.

It is not pretense. It is not a dream of a future conquest but a memory of a recent one. To back it up, Tachanoontia names four nations, one of which is recognizably the Conoys who appear in later treaties and in recorded history as an adopted nation of the League.[54]

Therefore, the recent debunking of the Six Nations' 1744 claim of conquest as grandiose and exaggerated deserves a second look. If it is widely acknowledged that the Iroquois engaged in southern wars beginning around 1706, if the Conestogas, Shawnees, Nanticokes, Conoys, and Lenapes are all on record as being afraid of them, if they incorporated the Tuscaroras into their union as a result of their involvement in the Carolinas, then it is plausible that they had indeed "conquered" several of the little-known peoples and territories along the Shenandoah River in the Blue Ridge chain of the Appalachian Mountains. That the results of such conquests were not empirical control, but adoption and incorporation, does not mean that Tachanoontia's definition of conquest was semantic or that his use of the word was hypocritical. In fact, a close examination of this treaty suggests that the only exaggerated claim of conquest per se (gain by force of arms) that the League ever made was the one *apparently* made by Canasatego in 1742 about how the Lenapes became "women," peacemaking members of the electorate who could not sell land. The Cayuga speaker Gachradodow reveals that it was indeed Maryland who had backed the Iroquois in their defeat of the Susquehannocks (or Conestogas) in 1675![55]

Like Maryland, Virginia compensates the Iroquois for the lands they claimed without ever admitting their rights to those lands. They then boondoggle the Iroquois with the same trick the Penns had used on the Lenapes in 1737. Believing that the deed they were signing covered only the lands they had explicitly claimed, the League delegates signed away their rights to all lands claimed by Virginia, as it was then or as it would be in the future! Because Virginia's charter covered most of the northern half of the United States and part of western Canada as well as Alaska, the deed was clearly illegal. Even the section that the Six Nations could claim a right in was much bigger than what they thought they were ceding. They were even careful to stipulate that the king of England give them further compensation as westward settlement proceeded. Unfortunately, compensation would become the least of the Iroquois's worries. With this grand key to the continent, Virginia would launch an invasion of the Ohio Valley that ultimately brought down the French empire in North America and compromised the security of the Six Nations, all their adopted nations, and all their allies.[56]

## The Constitutional Controversy

One other national inheritance to arise from the 1744 Treaty at Lancaster is the debate over Iroquois contributions to the political structure of the United States, its Constitution and precedents, and its political philosophies. At the end of the long and tedious wrangle with Maryland and Virginia over their squatters, the Iroquois receive presents from them and Pennsylvania. It was their practice to give a gift in return, but as Canasatego pointedly reiterates, they are poor as a result of English encroachment on and domestication of their hunting grounds. So he presents three bundles of deerskins and some advice: "We heartily recommend Union and a good Agreement between you our Brethren. Never disagree, but preserve a strict Friendship for one another, and thereby you, as well as we, will become the stronger. Our wise Forefathers established Union and Amity between the *Five Nations;* this has made us formidable; this has given us great Weight and Authority with our neighbouring Nations. We are a powerful Confederacy; and, by your observing the same Methods our wise Forefathers have taken, you will acquire fresh Strength and Power; therefore whatever befals you, never fall out one with another." These words remain at the center of the interconnected controversies over the intellectual heritage of the United States, methods of historical research, and the efforts of the last few decades to replace a Eurocentric with a multicultural curriculum.

In the early 1990s, the well-known historian Arthur Schlesinger Jr. was one of the many people to attack the State of New York for instituting a secondary-school curriculum that acknowledged Iroquois thought as one of the precursors to the Constitution of the United States, along with the Magna Charta, John Locke, and other European-based events in political philosophy and practice. Because New York has an Iroquois population still living within its boundaries, Schlesinger and others saw it as folding to an "Iroquois lobby" by including the League in its Constitutional curriculum. The Iroquois and other advocates of multicultural learning were said to be using trumped-up histories of racialized groups to bolster the self-esteem of students who were not "making the grade." An examination of the 1744 Treaty is a necessary part of reaching a decision over the merits of the arguments on all sides; but looking at it alone is not sufficient. One must also examine the scholarly arguments as well, sifting through the rhetorical strategies used to present them; one must assess carefully which scholars possess the most credible knowledge and understanding of Iroquois history and of British-colonial relations with the Iroquois on both official and unofficial levels. One must also decide whether it is possible to access the historical past in a manner that is definitive on this question.[57]

This last point is perhaps the most important to keep in mind. The New Historical principle—that history descends to us in traces that are partly random and partly "consequent upon complex and subtle social processes of preservation and effacement"—bears repeating. To examine Pennsylvania diplomacy with neighboring Indian nations is also to see that that discursive interaction cannot be conceived through frontier models of contact or by concentrating only on the political elite. Cultural historiography has an important role to play here. Most of the colonial lands outside of the larger cities were borderlands where the common British subject could encounter a person of Native American descent or nationality on any given day. Moreover, that subject often lived on tribal lands whose title had not yet been transferred to the colony. Though these encounters produced mutual suspicion and distrust as often as they produced friendship, neighborliness, and respect, the latter were a reality and the former would not necessarily preclude an understanding of native political values. It might, in some cases, require it. In addition, Indian diplomacy required a basic understanding of the values and procedures by which various Indian nations and individuals conducted their affairs, so it is possible that certain facts about these nations would infiltrate into the collective consciousness. Whether the historical traces confirm that they did, and whether the absence of such traces confirms that they did not, form the heart of the debate. Also at issue are which types of traces constitute valid historical evidence.[58]

A number of scholars in the specific arena of Iroquois and British-Iroquois history have weighed in on the question. The foremost proponents of the thesis of Iroquois influence are Bruce Johansen, Donald Grinde, and later Robert Venables. Major opponents of the thesis have been Francis Jennings, Elisabeth Tooker, William Starna, George Hamell, and Robert Berner. (Schlesinger himself is not an authority on the Iroquois or on Iroquois-British relations, but on twentieth-century and nineteenth-century U.S. history and foreign policy.) Because Johansen and Grinde initiated the debate and continue to be key scholars within it, a careful examination of their writings and sources is strictly necessary if one wishes to come to a reasonable understanding of the argument for Iroquois influence on the shape of the emerging nation of 1776.[59]

Proponents argue that most of the fundamental values that shaped the United States derived in part or in large part from contact and interaction with the Iroquois. Other Indian nations are sometimes acknowledged, but the debate has centered on the role of the League. The fundamental values that filtered into European settlements included the concept and practice of popular sovereignty, the exercise of political freedom, and the idea that individuals had basic rights. The idea that a leader is a servant of the people rather than the reverse is said to arise from Native North American origins, along with the ability to rise to positions of leadership from humble beginnings. Though many Indian nations in the east practiced hereditary or electoral-hereditary forms of leadership during peace, war chiefs and others could emerge on their talents alone. Johansen and Grinde aver that the British witnessed some of these ideas in practice only among Native Americans, even if they had also read about European models of them that had since died away. They likewise frame other elements of political life as originally unique to the continent: extreme courtesy in debate rather than constant interruption as the British Parliament practiced; government by reason and consent rather than coercion; relative equality of property; freedom of speech; freedom of religion or absence of strict religious doctrine; and equal rights before the law.[60]

The debate raises an important methodological question. Is it necessary to demonstrate the adoption of very specific particulars to sustain the more general thesis that U.S. conceptions of freedom and U.S. structures of democracy could not have been forged in the absence of Native America's example? Must a direct correspondence between the U.S. separation of powers mechanism, for example, and the Iroquois's own be proved? Does the adherence of a founder of the U.S. system to an argument in favor of a bicameral or a unicameral legislature demonstrate that that position is based in Iroquois thought or a thorough knowledge and careful consideration of League structure? Historians who look to Iroquois precedents for all significant U.S. democratic structures may eventually concede that the textual traces do not always exist, either because they never did or because they were lost. By the same token, those who deny all Native American precedents to U.S. political thought may eventually concede that to privilege text and artifact over formal orality, casual conversation, and the ephemeral is impossible. Ojibwa intellectual Gerald Vizenor calls this type of restriction of academic evidence to Western-dominated discourses "a euphemism for linguistic colonization of oral tradition and popular memories." The question of whether the textual traces exist is secondary to the question of why they may not exist and whether their absence sustains the argument against influence.[61]

## The Question of Iroquois Contributions to the Political Formation of the United States

The political philosophies at issue in the debate were not all the unique reserve of the Iroquois League; many pervaded eastern North America at the time of contact. Nor are all the unique contributions that the Iroquois League might claim illustrated in the 1744 Treaty of Lancaster. It is important, therefore, that we focus on what this particular document and the history of British-Iroquois relations as illustrated in this collection might reveal.[62]

As Francis Jennings has pointed out, most efforts to connect the failed 1754 Albany Plan of Union to the Articles of Confederation to the U.S. Constitution are nationalistic fantasies. To push the origins of the national imaginary back so far is to deny that the major shifts in loyalty from British empire to colonial independence and from colonial affiliation to national occurred only in the immediate aftermath of the Seven Years' War. No straight, uncomplicated line from the League of the Iroquois to the Plan of Union to the Articles to the Constitution would exist even were this not the case. Clearly, the Constitution was a major revision, even a rejection, of the Articles; and while the committee of the Continental Congress that drew up the Articles used Franklin's ideas as a model, it did not simply adopt the draft of the Articles that he submitted, which was partly modeled on his earlier Plan of Union, without major alterations.[63]

However, a potentially significant set of commonalities pervades all three U.S. documents: their emphasis on union; their embrace of the principle of confederation; their structural adoption of a federalist mode in which the central authority exercises only a limited set of powers; and, up until 1860, their strong operational emphasis upon states' rights and a significant amount of decentralized power. These emphases can also be discerned in Canasatego's July 4, 1744, words. In addition,

Canasatego recommended the unprecedented practice of treating with Indian nations using one voice, a practice the new nation adopted. There is no direct evidence that these words influenced Benjamin Franklin's sketch of a plan of union in 1754. However, indirect evidence exists to suggest that he and other revolutionary leaders may have conceived these organizational concepts through observation of and interaction with the Iroquois League.[64]

Many of the arguments for, or against, League influence on these U.S. documents center upon Franklin's role. Certainly Franklin had a central role in the dissemination of the Pennsylvania-Iroquois treaties and used them with the other treaties he printed as propaganda against the Penns. Whether he is ultimately central to the arguments regarding Iroquois influence remains an open question. His printing of the 1744 treaty and other documents demonstrates that hundreds, perhaps thousands, of readers and persons involved in government had access to knowledge of the *external* political organization of the League. This information was also accessible in Cadwallader Colden's *History of the Five Indian Nations,* which Franklin not only read but also offered to sell in 1747. We also know that there were many other individuals in a position to participate in the Continental Congress or influence thinking about the shape of a new government who also had access to knowledge of the League's confederate structure. Frederick Muhlenberg was the grandson of the person with the most intimate knowledge of the Iroquois: Conrad Weiser. Muhlenberg was not only a delegate to the Continental Congress but the first Speaker of the House of Representatives. William Johnson, Charles Thomson, George Croghan, Israel Pemberton, Cadwallader Colden, and Samuel Kirkland all had significant understanding of Iroquois affairs and all were in contact with persons who came to lead the revolution and the new nation. Why many other colonial and revolutionary leaders wrote as though they did not know or would not acknowledge that Native Americans even had governments and national affiliations remains unknown. The League was the only confederacy bordering the British colonies that was unquestionably known at the time to be a stable and enduring confederacy at the time. So the cautions of Vizenor and Montrose against putting too much faith in the ability of textual traces to paint a whole picture cannot be emphasized enough.[65]

An argument in favor of Franklin's centrality can also be established. He had opportunity to consider the external structure if not also the internal workings of the Iroquois League. He may have done both. He himself printed the 1744 Treaty with Canasatego's advice. He knew and conversed or corresponded with Conrad Weiser, Cadwallader Colden, and dozens of others in the Pennsylvania government who dealt in Iroquois affairs. And he treated with the Ohio Iroquois as a commissioner twice, once prior to 1754.[66]

In 1751, Franklin read in manuscript Archibald Kennedy's pamphlet entitled *The Importance of Gaining and Preserving the Friendship of the Indians to the British Interest.* His commentary on the pamphlet was printed with it and included the following lines:

> A voluntary Union entered into by the Colonies themselves, I think, would be preferable to one impos'd by Parliament; for it would be perhaps not much more difficult to procure, and more easy to alter and improve, as Circumstances should require, and Experience direct. It would be a very strange Thing, if six Nations of ignorant Savages should be capable of forming a Scheme for such an Union, and be able to execute it in such a Manner, as that it has subsisted Ages, and appears indissoluble; and yet that a like Union should be impracticable for ten or a Dozen English Colonies, to whom it is more necessary, and must be more advantageous; and who cannot be supposed to want an equal Understanding of their Interests.[67]

Francis Jennings and others deny that Franklin could have taken the Iroquois Confederacy as a working model for a confederated union of colonies. Jennings's three main arguments are that Franklin thought of humans in terms of race and thought Indians' natural attribute was a state of savagery; that his use of the words *ignorant* and *savage* pejoratively precludes having esteem for their intellect and political abilities; and that he was in this response to Kennedy's pamphlet advocating colonial union against the Iroquois. Jennings's source of information on Franklin's racial views is an essay he wrote in 1751 entitled "Observations concerning the Increase of Mankind, Peopling of Countries, &c.," opposing the British Iron Act as detrimental to colonial growth.

Here Franklin embraces his own "White and Red" race as *preferable* to all others, including "Spaniards, Italians, French, Russians . . . Swedes," and all Germans but the Saxon. However, Franklin, like other eighteenth-century thinkers, does not connect race to state of civilization or savagery. When he refers to "natural" attributes, he implies that conditions like slavery by *their* very nature produce certain tendencies in individuals, not that they are incapable of other tendencies under other conditions. Franklin's May 9, 1753, comments in a letter to Peter Collinson about why Native Americans would continue to live in a state of savagery when given the opportunity of civilization point to informed choices about leisure and abundance, not natural limitations of certain races. Jennings's conclusions about Franklin's racial thinking may therefore be anachronistic. The eighteenth-century desire to populate the continent with Anglo-Saxons is certainly racialist. However, the belief that race determines one's intellectual capabilities and state of civilization did not begin to gain hegemony until the second decade of the nineteenth century. It coincided with the dissemination of Wilhelm von Humboldt's philosophies of language.[68]

It is likewise difficult to determine that Franklin's use of the words *ignorant* and *savage* was contemptuous. *Ignorant* in Franklin's day meant that one had not been educated through formal schooling (which Franklin himself had not had much of). It indicated that one had not been exposed to the thinking of what were the great minds of civilization in Franklin's estimation. It could be used pejoratively, but it had not yet acquired the unquestionable connotation of derision that it now has.

The same was true of *savage.* Though it might in some contexts mean ferocious or cruel, it originates as a description of someone who has not been tamed or cultivated and who acts in complete liberty: precisely the picture of freedom from civilized constraint that Johansen and Grinde emphasize. Realistically, one cannot conclude from Franklin's use of this phrase that he was being dismissive; in the context of the commentary on Kennedy's pamphlet as a whole, he may have been complimenting the Iroquois on their independent discovery of an ingenious and enduring scheme of self-government. Also, Franklin was not advocating colonial union against the League at that time. He was reiterating the colonies' need to maintain the friendship of the League. (He only ever acted otherwise when he feared that they might have turned against the British and saw a need for immediate self-defense.) His activities through the last treaty printing in 1763 demonstrate that he was far from antagonistic toward Pennsylvania's Indian neighbors. In any event, enmity has never prevented enemies from learning from one another.[69]

## King George's War and Beyond

The British colonies' first practical test of Canasatego's advice to maintain good agreement with one another failed. Whether Massachusetts had learned of his words or not, they advocated in 1745 the practice of jointly treating with the Iroquois as showing the colonies' union and thus having greater weight with the League. Unfortunately, the urge was opportunistic and Pennsylvania refused to cooperate. Massachusetts had been most vulnerable to the attacks of the French and their Native American allies at the start of King George's War and wanted New York and Pennsylvania to help engage the Six Nations in their cause. Because Pennsylvania's Assembly had not approved such a hasty invitation to war, its commissioners refused to join in Massachusetts's speeches to the League in Albany. They would draw the war closer, put Indian neutrality at risk, do nothing to lessen attacks by French-allied Indians, and would ultimately be a betrayal of the Iroquois unless colonists were willing to join the fight. The Quakers who dominated the Assembly at the time were also morally opposed to war; but their main objection was to bearing the entire financial burden of arming the Iroquois and defending the colonies while the Penns sat back and raked in money from the Pennsylvanians who had to pay annual quitrents on their lands. Moreover, they foresaw that paying for arms and armies would never place control of them in the hands of the people; it would only give the proprietors control of a coercive force by which they could gain a further stranglehold on the population.[70]

Pennsylvania instead coaxed out information about French overtures to the Six Nations to go to war, and Canasatego reiterated his request that the English colonies should be united in their councils so as to speak with one voice. Two years later, the first real warning of trouble arrived on Pennsylvania's doorstep. A delegation of warriors from the Ohio Valley arrived in Philadelphia in November 1747. These Ohio

Iroquois had begun to populate the void that the seventeenth-century trade wars had made of the region. Along with many Lenapes, who had been pushed out of Tulpehocken, Brandywine, and the Delaware Forks, and Shawnees, who had been shunted around the Iroquois hinterlands as protection, they lived in the region under ambiguous political and economic status. Though the League at various times claimed ownership of the lands these groups occupied, some evidence suggests that this claim may have been part of the British scheme of enlarging the Iroquois "empire" in their own self-interest. The Ohio Iroquois would claim ownership themselves, based on the principle that warriors owned what they had won, rather than the chiefs of the League. And though the Ohio Iroquois in these treaties sometimes defer to the League for political direction, they and their allies the Lenapes and Shawnees often acted as independent political entities. Moving away from the Pennsylvania-Iroquois vise gave the Lenapes and Shawnees much greater freedom.[71]

In 1747, the Ohio Iroquois approached Pennsylvania because the French had attempted to recruit all the Ohio Valley nations into joining the war against the English. A faction of one nation—apparently a Shawnee nation—took up the invitation, so the rest had declared war on the French in the name of England. It is unlikely that the declaration reflected anything like intense loyalty to their English allies: they simply needed a way to prevent French encroachment upon their lands and independence. That they kindled a council fire and invited the nations to attend illustrates their political autonomy. However, they came to Philadelphia to receive monetary backing—arms—to enforce their right against France. English traders had already been backing them and inciting them against the French, promising them Pennsylvania's aid as well. According to Michael McConnell, they turned to the colony for help when the League refused to assist them.[72]

Pennsylvania saw their opportunity and took it. Shifting their attention away from the League, they decided to cultivate the relationship with the Ohio nations. They gave them the presents they requested in 1747 and brought the Miami Indians, or Twightwees, into the Chain of Friendship through them in 1748, though League representatives attended the treaty and were nominally in charge. They then sent more presents with a delegation, consisting not only of Conrad Weiser but also of William Franklin, Benjamin's son, to the Ohio Iroquois's council fire at Logstown (or Kittanning) on the Allegheny River. (Franklin had in the meanwhile been organizing a voluntary military association to defend Pennsylvania against potential attacks by French-allied Indian nations and had handed over all but editorial control of his printing press to David Hall.) Weiser ushered into the Chain the Wyandots (Owendaets), a reconstituted group of the old Huron Confederacy defeated by the League in the seventeenth century. Upon his return to Philadelphia, he got Pennsylvania to change its ten-year policy of using the League as the Lenapes' spokesperson. By 1752, they had recognized a Lenape hereditary chief formerly from Tulpehocken named Shingas as the Ohio Lenapes' leader. The Shawnees consequently shifted their attention to the Ohio Lenapes as mediators for them with the British.[73]

The result of these policy shifts was to drive the League itself closer into the arms of the French. It is ironic that in 1745 at Albany, the British colonies had feared League talks with the French, only to begin to abandon them in 1747. Their nervousness over Iroquois neutrality had defied reason in any case. Over the past century, the League's "French" connections had given several northern and northwestern nations, such as the Ottawas, access to English trade under the nose of the French. These arrangements resulted sometimes from Iroquois weakness, sometimes from their strength.

The temporary shift in attention of the Onondagas especially toward the French apparently resulted in the assassination of Canasatego in 1750; but it is likely that two other events contributed to his death.[74] In August 1749, during a treaty that Franklin mysteriously did not print, Canasatego complained to Pennsylvania of settlers on the Juniata lands of the Susquehanna River. Similar complaints had been made in 1742, to no avail. Though Richard Peters's word is not to be trusted, he reported that Canasatego's delegation of 290 persons had arrived in the city after the governor had already treated with a Seneca delegation. Pennsylvania had sent that delegation to the Onondaga Council to get approval for a purchase of the Juniata lands. Apparently they told them to tell the rest of the delegation under Canasatego not to come to town because they were too late to treat. Canasatego had apparently met them and brought them back down to Philadelphia with him anyway. Peters's account accuses him of trying to sell land already sold because he fears they will get no present, having "nothing" to treat over. However, Peters also decided that Pennsylvania could not get the Juniata lands unless they agreed to buy land east of the Susquehanna. The outcome of the talks with Canasatego is another swindle. Thinking he was selling a particular tract apparently between the Susquehanna and the Schuylkill, he signed a deed that took in land much to the north of the agreed-upon northern boundary and extended to the Delaware. It was a partial sale of the Wyoming lands to which many Forks Lenapes had relocated after 1742. Pennsylvania attached a truncated map to the deed and retained for themselves the full map of the land actually "bought."[75]

Also in 1749, Virginia's Ohio Company began its expansion into the Ohio Valley acquired in 1744, by obtaining a crown grant through Virginia of 500,000 acres and proposing to build a fort in the region. The moves put France on the alert. While Canasatego was in Philadelphia, they sent an unsuccessful expedition to the region, trying to enforce their claim. (Though they had concluded a peace with Great Britain in 1748, they never really got to enjoy it.) Unfortunately for them, the Ohio nations responded by doing the same, but with their residency rather than an expedition. By September 1750, Canasatego was dead. Conrad Weiser blamed French factions within the Onondaga nation; if that information was correct, it is possible that they used Canasatego's failing diplomacy with Pennsylvania and Virginia (and possibly his willingness to receive bribes from them) as one justification.[76]

Also by 1750, Pennsylvania and Virginia were competing in their designs to settle the Ohio, and Virginia was winning. The Pennsylvania Assembly rejected a proposal put forth by Thomas Penn to build a fort there. (A year later, Benjamin Franklin was elected as a member of that Assembly; he would continue to win that seat annually until 1764.) The Ohio Company of Virginia's representative, Christopher Gist, began making arrangements for a treaty that would be held in Logstown in June 1752. Virginia's goal was to secure confirmation from the Ohio Iroquois of the Ohio lands signed away in 1744. It was once again a matter of convincing susceptible Iroquois leaders to sell out from under them lands on which mainly Lenapes lived. Tanaghrisson, the Onondaga Council's representative at Ohio, and Andrew Montour, a cross-blood French-Iroquois translator, received the bribes, which were subsequently distributed to their followers to enhance their prestige in the noncapitalist economy to which they belonged. They secretly gave consent to settlements south and east of the Ohio (the Monongahela region) and deferred actual approval of the deed to the Onondaga Council; meanwhile, Virginia failed to inform Pennsylvania that it had purchased land within the other colony's chartered boundaries.[77]

## Preludes to the Seven Years' War

While meeting at Logstown, the parties learned that the French had attacked a Miami town and reasserted their claim to the Ohio Valley. Six months later, France began to build a line of forts from Presque Isle (Erie, Pennsylvania) to Venango to Monongahela to Logstown to Beaver Creek. They also started driving British traders out of the region. Though the clan mothers of the League tried to intervene, they were overwhelmed by the size of the French force and relieved enough that they did not intend war with the League to let them pass. Though Tanaghrisson three times warned the force not to go any farther, some of the Ohio nations actually welcomed the French. They might possibly have solidified emerging claims of ownership over the Ohio lands that defied the 1744 and 1752 "sales."[78]

Another representative of the Ohio Iroquois, Scarouady, went to Winchester, Virginia, and Carlisle, Pennsylvania, in 1753 to ask those colonies' backing against the French through arms, and that they prevent settlement in the region to keep the peace. His delegation included Shawnee, Wyandot, Miami, and Lenape chiefs, including Shingas and his brothers Beaver or Tamaqua, Pisquetomen, and Delaware George, or Nenatchehan. At Winchester, he sold them out by privately encouraging Virginia to build a fort at Monongahela that they publicly refused. He also appeared in public, as at Carlisle, to be working for the release of Shawnee prisoners in South Carolina while actually asking that colony to keep them locked up. Mention appears in the Carlisle treaty that the goods the Pennsylvania commissioners, including Franklin, intended to give to the delegation were being held back. The purported risk of distributing them was fabricated by traders working for the man put in charge of them, George Croghan, the premier but debt-ridden Ohio trader who in 1749 had pocketed Pennsylvania's gift to the Ohio nations to buy a piece of land from them himself. Croghan would later become a deputy for New York colony's Indian agent William Johnson, when the crown in 1755 named Johnson sole superintendent of Indian affairs for the British colonies.[79]

The 1753 Treaty at Carlisle was the first of three attended by Franklin. He was also appointed a commissioner in 1754 for the treaty council held at Albany, which ran concurrent with the Albany Congress and its aborted Plan of Union, and in November 1756 at Easton. It is very intriguing that the two of these three treaties that he was able to print both show unprecedented addendums by the commissioners that appear in no other treaty printings of his. Both of these addendums speak not only to Franklin's active interventions into Indian affairs but also to his respect for his Iroquois and Lenape interlocutors. A single paragraph at the end of the 1753 treaty, signed also by Richard Peters and Isaac Norris, reiterates the complaints of the various Ohio nations that abuses by traders in the region must be stopped or the Ohio nations would be alienated from their friendship with the British. Though there is no doubt that Franklin's first priority was the "national interest" (or in this case the "imperial interest"), he recognized in the delegations of 1753 and 1756 a reasonableness and common sense that was convincing to him. In both cases, Franklin subordinates his own voice to the voices of the Indian delegates. He adopts their point of view even after hostilities had broken out between the parties.[80]

Hostilities would indeed break out in October 1755 when Ohio Lenapes and Shawnees with French officers began to attack Pennsylvania's backcountry settlements. As the treaties indicate, the immediate reason why these nations broke their chain of friendship with the British was British neglect and abuse in the region. This included a failure to provide them with sufficient arms. As an expedition by George Washington to the region late in 1753 would show, the British were simply unable or unwilling to support their own claims with the necessary promise of force. Soon after, Virginia would attempt to erect their fort where the Monongahela and the Allegheny join to become the Ohio. They were immediately kicked out. The fort became Fort Duquesne, where present-day Pittsburgh stands. A few months later, while the Albany Congress and Treaty were going on, Washington surrendered Fort Necessity and the British were essentially in retreat.[81]

Less immediate provocations for the war were being concocted at Albany as Washington withdrew. They were the final straw in the series of betrayals felt most shockingly by the Lenapes. They sealed permanently both their sense of dispossession and its reality. At the treaty, Pennsylvania and Connecticut each got a number of chiefs of the League to cede lands where Lenape stakes were high. Pennsylvania bought land on the western side of the Susquehanna River. However, the League immediately balked when Conrad Weiser attempted to survey the Juniata lands; once again, Weiser's version of the purchase was larger than the League's. Not only did his version of this 1754 tract overlap with the 1744 deed Virginia had made with the League, it also encroached on land "granted" by the League to the Ohio nations, probably Lenapes, and not yet settled by whites. Meanwhile Connecticut engaged in a purchase from a handful of chiefs that the League immediately proclaimed illegal. Pennsylvania also assailed the purchase as encroaching on their chartered boundaries. Unfortunately, the abdication of the sale by both these parties did not prevent Connecticut settlers from invading the Wyoming Valley, harassing the Lenape residents, and ultimately pushing many of these eastern Lenapes to the Ohio and into the arms of the French.[82]

Although Pennsylvania gave back a large portion of its purchase, the damage had already been done. The 1737 Walking Purchase and the 1749 sale that encroached on Wyoming lands had already confirmed to the Lenapes that Pennsylvania under William Penn's sons was neither their friend nor their defender. In the entire course of their hostilities, which coincided with the start of the Seven Years' War, the Lenapes never attacked Pennsylvanians on lands they considered legally acquired. Only squatters on land illegitimately acquired ever suffered at their hands. Images of the savage brutality of Indian attacks are replete in U.S. literature. Squatted lands are often retrospectively figured as frontiers, as though always already part of the invading nation. Yet the Lenapes were starved and bullied out of house and home, and saw their small children die before them as a result. Though the invaders felt themselves to be honest and righteous in their claims, their actions had results at least as savagely brutal as those they condemned.[83]

Following the first attacks in 1755, the remainder of the treaties Franklin printed dealt with trying to reinstitute the peace. Here, Franklin's role became crucial. Though ultimately he proved powerless against the interests of the proprietors and the crown, he took the lead of Pennsylvania's Quakers and helped to uncover at least partially the fraud and deception that had led unnecessarily to a costly war. By no means a pacifist himself, that he was humble enough to recognize and pursue the truth of the pacifist Quakers' claims that the Lenapes would never have initiated a war without just grievances serves as an enduring example of effective conflict resolution methods. The efforts of the Quakers and the Assembly to sound the Nations on the causes of the attacks brought a much swifter end to them than military action alone would have done.

Six months after the attacks begin, Pennsylvania meets with Scarouady and sends messengers to the Lenapes and Shawnees with messages of peace on the condition that prisoners be returned. They discover that the Wyoming Lenapes (formerly Forks Lenapes who had chosen to remain in the east rather than moving to the Ohio) had relocated to Tioga. These eastern Lenapes had raised a man named Teedyuscung to chiefdom; he responds welcomingly to Pennsylvania's invitation, but reminds them that he did not speak for the western Lenapes. He tells them that the Onondaga Council authorized him to treat on their behalf and the eastern Lenapes' own. Teedyuscung reveals that the League asked the eastern Lenapes to help them defend their lands against the French and the English in exchange for a greater voice within and outside the Confederacy. He also intriguingly hints that Pennsylvania had treated with pretenders in the past, which had helped cause the present trouble. Pennsylvania makes Teedyuscung their agent and counselor and sends him and others out to spread the news of the peace proposal.[84]

When Teedyuscung returns in November 1756, a new lieutenant governor is in place and Benjamin Franklin is one of the treaty commissioners. William Denny then asks the questions that the Penns' placemen, Weiser and Peters, do not want him to ask: "how that League of Friendship came to be broken? Have we, the Governor or People of *Pennsylvania,* done you any Kind of Injury? If you think we have, you should be honest, and tell us your Hearts: You should have made Complaints before you struck us, for so it was agreed in our antient League." Denny's questions were the commissioners' idea, and the draft of the speech is written in Franklin's hand. Teedyuscung's answer gives Franklin, the Quakers, and other forces in the Assembly who had been chafing under the Penns' feudal authoritarianism a priceless piece of propaganda to use against them. He first mentions the 1737 Walking Purchase and the proprietor's practice of speculative profiteering; he also mentions complaints about a claim in New Jersey that was ignored.[85]

Ironically, Franklin and his fellow Assemblymen were prepared to put the question to rest when Weiser unwisely intervened. At first ready to accept the commissioners' offer to make satisfaction on the spot and get reimbursement from the Penns later, Teedyuscung defers prompt settlement after Weiser had a suspiciously solitary meeting with him. Weiser claims that Teedyscung had told him he could not accept goods himself but must bring down the interested parties. The incident is one of those Franklin calls attention to in the commissioners' two-paragraph addendum to this treaty. It is here that the commissioners withdraw their generous offer to the Penns. Weiser sends the Lenapes off on a wild goose chase for their money and the truth while the Assembly sends Benjamin Franklin off to England to get justice for the Lenapes, among other things. His own purpose became to convince the crown to revoke the Penns' charter and make Pennsylvania into a crown colony. Both the Lenapes and the Pennsylvania citizenry had suffered at the Penns' hands.[86]

Subsequent treaties trace this wild goose chase and discover the other main causes of the attacks. Franklin is in England for most of this time but follows events closely through his correspondence. In the spring of 1757, the League comes down to listen to Lenape complaints about the Walking Purchase, but Teedyuscung never shows up. Either he suspected that a farce of justice was about to occur or Croghan, Weiser, and Peters manufactured the delay to make him look like a fool in front of the Six Nations. At this conference during which the Iroquois are kept waiting for an unbelievable eight weeks, Pennsylvania learns that a Lenape man's death in New Jersey, a Shawnee chief's death while in custody during the Carolina incident of 1753, and encroachment resulting from the 1754 sales are also significant causes of the attacks. When Teedyuscung finally arrives two months later, the lieutenant governor gives him the run-around. Asking only for a secure place at Wyoming for his people to reside permanently, he is told he must apply to the League for that. It is clearly in Pennsylvania's power. He is then told that the king of England appointed William

Johnson to judge the Walking Purchase dispute, but is prevented from having it judged there and then, even though Johnson's deputy Croghan is supervising the treaty in Johnson's name! Teedyuscung's distrust of Johnson will eventually be validated. Only the peace that Pennsylvania confirms with the Shawnees and Mahicans at the end of this conference is not one of their elaborate word games.[87]

In 1758, Pennsylvania tries to undermine Teedyuscung's authority and power even further. At a treaty council during which the complaints about New Jersey are resolved, George Croghan's father-in-law Nichas, a League Mohawk, leads the League there in accusing Teedyuscung of usurping their power, of being put into Lenape leadership by Pennsylvania, and of improperly negotiating for Tohiccon lands in their stead. The move is one of the last efforts of Confederacy speakers to reassert the bloodless 1742 conquest over the eastern Lenapes. However, the delegation does agree to let the Lenapes live at Wyoming until the Onondaga Council can approve the arrangement permanently. At one point, they also accuse Pennsylvania of speaking insincerely. This implies that Croghan did not have influence with the entire delegation. Pennsylvania here learns still more about the causes of the attacks: an incident between the Senecas and Virginia in which a Seneca boy was captured; British failure to defend the Ohio and help the League against the French; and a 1755 incident in which nine Esopus Indians were killed.[88]

Meanwhile, in London, Benjamin Franklin gets a similar run-around to the one Teedyuscung experienced. After finally getting the King's Privy Council to hear the Walking Purchase complaint, they decide redundantly in May 1759 that William Johnson should judge the case, rather than the king, as Teedyuscung wished. The Penns promptly offer Johnson a bribe; though he did not exactly bite, the results may be witnessed in the final 1762 treaty that Franklin's press printed. As at Lancaster in 1744, the Penns admit no wrong and the Lenapes are paid off anyway. Beaver, the head of the western Lenapes, has come to confirm the peace for the first time. Though he apparently denies any claim among his people for the Forks, he still receives compensation. Yet Franklin's trip had not all been in vain. He had the satisfaction of calling Thomas Penn a "low jockey" as good as to his face; he got Charles Thomson's scathing report of the Walking Purchase fiasco, *An Enquiry into the Causes of the Alienation of the Delaware and Shawanese Indians from the British Interest,* into print; and he returned to the colonies beginning to know that the crown was no better than the proprietors when it came to dealing honestly and seeing justice done.[89]

## Aftermath

Franklin wrote directly or indirectly about Native Americans over much of his life. We may blame our own negligence in gathering together the strands of his ideas about them on the willingness of some to dismiss the possibility that Franklin's mind was large enough to accommodate imperial designs and appreciation for Native American ideas at the same time. Unlike many, more ruthless colonizers, this contradiction in him sometimes gave way to right action when push came to shove. In the most famous instance, Franklin was instrumental in preventing a planned genocide. Confused and often simply wrong in his comprehension of the 1763 renewal of Ohio Nations hostilities that occurred after the French loss of Canada (a continuation of the Forty Years' War with the colony-states that lasted from 1755 until 1795), he was able at least to distinguish belligerents from those not at war. In November 1763, 127 Moravian Indians from a Bethlehem mission took shelter from less discerning Pennsylvanians on an island near Philadelphia. After a group known as the Paxton Boys massacred twenty Conestogas at the Penns' manor near Lancaster, the governor (Thomas Penn's nephew John), his Council, and the Assembly in which Franklin sat decided to send the Moravian Indians to safety in New York under William Johnson's protection. In early January 1764, they sent letters to Franklin's son, then governor of New Jersey, and to Franklin's friend, Cadwallader Colden, then lieutenant governor of New York, asking their permission for the Indians to pass under armed escort. William Franklin complied; Colden refused. The New Yorkers regarded the eastern Susquehanna Indians as "Rogues," "Thieves," and "Runaways," "most obnoxious" and "not to be trusted."[90]

Writing for a committee of the Assembly, Franklin described the Conestogas as having been "barbarously butchered by a Sett of Ruffians, whose audacious Cruelty is checked by no Sentiment of Humanity, and by no Regard to the Laws of their Country." He then printed his now famous "A Narrative of the Late Massacres," an equally impassioned plea for justice and reason. The Indians having been brought back to Philadelphia, news arrived that the Paxton Boys intended to attack the city and murder them with a force of anywhere from fifteen hundred to five thousand men. Rumors flew that they also intended to kill the Quakers, despised as Indian-lovers and hated for their religious tenets. The governor, Council, Assembly, and city magistrates gathered three thousand Philadelphians together and enlisted their aid in the protection of the city and the Indians. Many of the pacifist Quakers took up arms. The following night at midnight, the governor made Franklin's house his headquarters as the alarm bells rang with the approach of a mob numbering about 250 and growing. Clergymen were sent out to warn the Paxton Boys that the city was armed, Quakers and all. The following day, Franklin and six others faced them down. The men dispersed, leaving their complaints in writing. The danger of the moment was past. I can find no record that Franklin ever wrote to his perennial correspondent and intellectual partner, Cadwallader Colden, again.[91]

Savagist ideology told many British subjects and U.S. citizens that they could only assimilate Indians to their own ways or bring about their total extinction. The Iroquois League, the Lenapes, the Shawnees, the Miamis, the Kickapoos, and many others continue to bear the brunt of this ideology. Yet their political persistence and cultural vitality have repeatedly given the lie to a savagism that would freeze them in time; they have given its ultimatums the slip. The League nations retain a greatly reduced portion of their lands in Iroquoia: near Syracuse and Buffalo, and in eastern, far northern, and southwestern New York. They also have one large reserve and several smaller ones in Canada, as well as reservations in Wisconsin and Oklahoma. All are results of the same kinds of land pressures that we witness in these treaties, pressures that deteriorating attitudes and policies, and unlawful maneuvers, accelerated after the Revolutionary War. Many Lenapes moved first to Indiana, then to Missouri, then to Kansas, and then to Oklahoma between 1800 and the 1870s. Gerald Vizenor and others repudiate the notion that Native American history must be seen through the tragic lens of these times, however. Native America today is experiencing renaissance and rebirth.[92]

These treaties do sustain a tragic narrative: America's failure to restrain its land greed and curb the unholy alliance formed between the powerful, like the Penns, and the power-starved, like those who squatted and traded on Indian nations lands beyond their colony's borders. Yet, despite the corruption, the bribery, and the scandals witnessed by these treaties, they also sustain a more powerful principle. Careful deliberation and negotiations made in good faith create long-lasting peace. They create peace even among parties with cultures that appear at first glance to be radically different. Tragedies are still emerging in Native America, still propelled by the neglect of the powerful and by fundamental misconceptions of the relationships between nations and the obligations among them. But they do not have to continue to dominate. We produce them. We proliferate them. We weave them into the fabric of our imagination. We signal our addictive dependence upon them through our literary proclivities. We adhere to them. But there are many, more powerful narratives from which to choose. Understanding (through volumes like this one and those that will improve upon it) the historical reasons why Native Americans are in the situations they are currently in is one step toward creating these new narratives.[93]

1. Francis Jennings, *The Ambiguous Iroquois Empire* (New York: W. W. Norton and Co., 1984), 111–12; Richard Aquila, *The Iroquois Restoration: Iroquois Diplomacy on the Colonial Frontier, 1701–1754* (Detroit: Wayne State University Press, 1983), 70–81; Barbara A. Mann and Jerry L. Fields, "A Sign in the Sky: Dating the League of the Haudenosaunee," *American Indian Culture and Research Journal* 21.2 (1997): 108; Jennings, *Ambiguous Iroquois Empire,* 41–43, 74–112, 99, 112, 210–12. Cf. Wilma Dunaway, "Incorporation as an Interactive Process: Cherokee Resistance to Expansion of the Capitalist World System, 1560–1763," *Sociological Inquiry* 66.4 (Fall 1996): 455–70,on reconfiguration of trade.

2. Aquila, *Iroquois Restoration,* 68–69, 80–81; Mann and Fields, "A Sign in the Sky," 118–29; Dean R. Snow, *The Iroquois* (Cambridge: Blackwell, 1994), 1–20. See also David Henige, "Can a Myth Be Astronomically Dated?" *American Indian Culture and Research Journal* 23.4 (1999): 1–27. I do not rely here on Mann and Fields's astronomical argument.

3. Barbara A. Mann, "The Lynx in Time: Haudenosaunee Women's Traditions and History," *American Indian Quarterly* 21.3 (Summer 1997): 433–37; Mann and Fields, "A Sign in the Sky," 129–32, 150; John Bierhorst, *Mythology of the Lenape: Guide and Texts* (Tucson: University of Arizona Press, 1995), 83; Mann, "The Lynx in Time," 430–31.

4. Mann, "The Lynx in Time," 430–31, 426–27; cf. Snow, *The Iroquois,* 2–4; cf. Matthew Dennis, *Cultivating a Landscape of Peace: Iroquois-European Encounters in Seventeenth Cen-*

*tury America* (Ithaca: Cornell University Press, 1993), 13, 21–23. See J. N. B. Hewitt, "Iroquoian Cosmology," in the *Twenty-first Annual Report of the Bureau of American Ethnology, 1899–1900,* for the importance of Sky Woman, her activities, and place in the Sky World, prior to her descent to earth. Links of the aspects of her mother and father to Hiawatha and Atotarho, as well as other links of both the League Cycle and the later parts of the Sky Cycle with the early part of the Sky Cycle, can be seen.

5. Mann, "The Lynx in Time," 425–28, 430–31; Paul A. W. Wallace, *The White Roots of Peace* (Philadelphia: University of Pennsylvania Press, 1946), 23–25.

6. Mann, "The Lynx in Time," 427, 431.

7. Mann, "The Lynx in Time," 435–36; Mann and Fields, "A Sign in the Sky," 129–30. See also Snow, *The Iroquois,* 8–10, on language changes in Proto-Iroquoian. Several scholars of Iroquois history have observed that these changes may affect classifications of oral traditions and make older traditions less accessible to interpretation. William Fenton points out that the Iroquois called narratives that Westerners commonly label as myths "things which truly happened." To label an oral tradition as "myth" versus "history" can lead to misinterpretation. Father Joseph François Lafitau, *Customs of the American Indians Compared with the Customs of Primitive Times* (Toronto: The Champlain Society, 1974), 66n1.

8. Wallace, *White Roots of Peace,* 14; Mann, "The Lynx in Time," 435–36; Snow, *The Iroquois,* 9, 19–20; cf. Mann and Fields, "A Sign in the Sky," 119; Mann and Fields, "A Sign in the Sky," 122.

9. Mann and Fields, "A Sign in the Sky," 133; Rochester Museum & Science Center Web site (http://www.rmsc.org/museum/exhibits/online/lhm/IAPmain.htm); Wallace, *White Roots of Peace,* 15–16; Mann, "The Lynx in Time," 436, 435.

10. Mann and Fields, "A Sign in the Sky," 126, 127; Wallace, *White Roots of Peace,* 17–21.

11. Wallace, *White Roots of Peace,* 21–25; William N. Fenton, "Structure, Continuity, and Change in the Process of Iroquois Treaty Making," in *The History and Culture of Iroquois Diplomacy: An Interdisciplinary Guide to the Treaties of the Six Nations and Their League,* ed. Francis Jennings (Syracuse, N.Y.: Syracuse University Press, 1985), 3–36. See also Henry Rowe Schoolcraft, *Notes on the Iroquois* (Albany, N.Y.: E. H. Pease and Co., 1847), and Joshua V. H. Clark, *Onondaga, or Reminiscences of Earlier and Later Times* (Syracuse, N.Y.: Stoddard and Babcock, 1849) for variations on the deaths in Hiawatha's family.

12. John Bierhorst, "The Ritual of Condolence," *Four Masterworks of American Indian Literature* (New York: Farrar, Straus and Giroux, 1974), 117, 129–35.

13. Bierhorst, "The Ritual of Condolence," 110; Wallace, *White Roots of Peace,* 27–29.

14. Fenton, "Structure, Continuity, and Change," 5; Bierhorst, "The Ritual of Condolence," 109; Michael K. Foster, "Another Look at the Function of Wampum in Iroquois-White Councils," in Jennings, ed., *The History and Culture of Iroquois Diplomacy,* 106.

15. Dennis, *Cultivating a Landscape of Peace,* 5–9; Jennings, *Ambiguous Iroquois Empire,* 41–46, 84–112.

16. Dennis, *Cultivating a Landscape of Peace,* 5–9, 85–90; Wallace, *White Roots of Peace,* 15–16. In Hewitt's recording of the Onondaga version of the Sky Cycle, a chief named He-holds-the-earth (Hao3'hw ñdjiaw '' g ' ) is Sky Woman's husband in the Sky World, to whom she is guided by her deceased father. The Holder of the Heavens may be a different figure, but the similarity of their names is worth noting. All the major figures in the Sky Cycle have *orenda,* or spiritual power, that implies not "will," "sanction," or enforcement, but foreknowledge. Hewitt, "Iroquoian Cosmology," 150.

17. C. A. Weslager, *The Delaware Indians: A History* (New Brunswick, N.J.: Rutgers University Press, 1972), 114, 100, 119–20; Jennings, *Ambiguous Iroquois Empire,* 116–19.

18. Jerry E. Clark, *The Shawnee* (Lexington: University Press of Kentucky, 1993), 10–11, 1–9, 12–20; James H. Howard, *Shawnee! The Ceremonialism of a Native Indian Tribe and Its Cultural Background* (Athens: Ohio University Press, 1981), 7–10, 1–6; Jennings, "Descriptive Treaty Calendar," in *History and Culture of Iroquois Diplomacy*, 162–63; Jennings, *Ambiguous Iroquois Empire*, 197.

19. Bierhorst, *Mythology of the Lenapes*, 13; Linda Comac, *The Red Record: The Wallum Olum, The Oldest Native North American History* (Garden City Park, N.Y.: Avery Publishing Group, 1993); Jay Miller, Review of *The Red Record, American Indian Culture and Research Journal* 18.1 (1994); James Mooney, *The Ghost-Dance Religion and the Sioux Outbreak of 1890* (Chicago: University of Chicago Press, 1965), 155, 170–71, 176; Garrick Mallery, *Picture-Writing of the American Indians* (New York: Dover Publications, 1972); Eugene Vetromile, *The Abnakis and their History* (New York: J. B. Kirker, 1866); Traveller Bird, *Tell Them They Lie: The Sequoyah Myth* (Los Angeles: Westernlore Publishers, 1971); Susan Kalter, "America's Histories Revisited: The Case of *Tell Them They Lie*," *American Indian Quarterly* 25.3 (Summer 2001); See also Rev. John Heckewelder, *History, Manners, and Customs of the Indian Nations who Inhabited Pennsylvania and the Neighbouring States* (1819) (Philadelphia: Historical Society of Pennsylvania [Lippincott's Press], 1876); Rev. John Heckewelder, *A Narrative of the Mission of the United Brethren among the Delaware and Mohegan Indians* (Philadelphia: McCarty and Davis, 1820); Indiana Historical Society, *Walum Olum or Red Score: The Migration Legend of the Lenni Lenape or Delaware Indians* (Chicago: Lakeside Press, 1954); Francis Jennings, *The Founders of America* (New York: W. W. Norton and Co., 1993), 70–72; and works by David Zeisberger and George Henry Loskiel.

20. Weslager, *Delaware Indians*, 31–47; Jay Miller, "Old Religion among the Delawares: The Gamwing (Big House Rite)," *Ethnohistory* 44.1 (Winter 1997): 114.

21. Jay Miller, "Old Religion among the Delawares," 114–23, 114.

22. Jennings, *Ambiguous Iroquois Empire*, 41–44, 60–72.

23. Jennings, *Ambiguous Iroquois Empire*, 54; Weslager, *Delaware Indians*, 31–32, 99–100, 104–5, 113–15; Francis Jennings, "'Pennsylvania Indians' and the Iroquois," in *Beyond the Covenant Chain*, ed. Daniel K. Richter and James H. Merrell (Syracuse, N.Y.: Syracuse University Press), 76.

24. Weslager, *Delaware Indians*, 116–28; Jennings, "'Pennsylvania Indians,'" 77; Jennings, *Ambiguous Iroquois Empire*, 98.

25. Jennings, "'Pennsylvania Indians,'" 77–78; Jennings, *Ambiguous Iroquois Empire*, 130, 132–33, 136–39.

26. Elisabeth Tooker, "The Demise of the Susquehannocks: A 17th Century Mystery," *Pennsylvania Archaeologist* 54 (1984): 8; Jennings, *Ambiguous Iroquois Empire*, 139; Jennings, "'Pennsylvania Indians,'" 184n14.

27. Jennings, "'Pennsylvania Indians,'" 78; Jennings, *Ambiguous Iroquois Empire*, 145–47.

28. Jennings, *Ambiguous Iroquois Empire*, 148–57.

29. Jennings, *Ambiguous Iroquois Empire*, 154–67; Jennings, "Descriptive Treaty Calendar," 160.

30. Weslager, *Delaware Indians*, 147–50, 45–47, 139–44.

31. Jennings, *Ambiguous Iroquois Empire*, 223, Weslager, *Delaware Indians*, 155–65, 173–76.

32. Weslager, *Delaware Indians*, 178–79, 187, 45–47; Jennings, *Ambiguous Iroquois Empire*, 310.

33. Jennings, *Ambiguous Iroquois Empire*, 236–37, 247–48; Jennings, "'Pennsylvania Indians,'" 83, 86–87; Francis Jennings, *Empire of Fortune: Crowns, Colonies, and Tribes in the Seven Years War in America* (New York: W. W. Norton and Co., 1988), 21; Paul A. W. Wallace,

*Conrad Weiser: Friend of Colonist and Mohawk* (Philadelphia: University of Pennsylvania Press, 1945), 31–35; Weslager, *Delaware Indians,* 184, 192–93, 185, 176–77.

34. Aquila, *Iroquois Restoration,* 80–81, 156; Jennings, *Ambiguous Iroquois Empire,* 239, 105–6, 166, 183–84, 316; Jennings, *Empire of Fortune,* 80–81, 325; Snow, *The Iroquois,* 145–54.

35. Michael N. McConnell, "Peoples 'In Between': The Iroquois and the Ohio Indians, 1720–1768," in Richter and Merrell, eds., *Beyond the Covenant Chain,* 93–96; Jennings, *Ambiguous Iroquois Empire,* 175, 190–96, 205–13; Aquila, *Iroquois Restoration,* 41–69.

36. Jennings, *Ambiguous Iroquois Empire,* xv–xvi.

37. Weslager, *Delaware Indians,* 156–57, 165; Jennings, *Ambiguous Iroquois Empire,* 244–48, 271–73, 155, 162, 196, 170.

38. Aquila, *Iroquois Restoration,* 205–32; Jennings, "Descriptive Treaty Calendar," 166–67, 172–73; Jennings, *Ambiguous Iroquois Empire,* 278–82, 289–94.

39. Jennings, *Ambiguous Iroquois Empire,* 276–77, 309, 316–18, 321; cf. William Apess, "Eulogy on King Philip, as Pronounced at the Odeon, in Federal Street, Boston," in *On Our Own Ground: The Complete Writings of William Apess, a Pequot,* edited and with an introduction by Barry O'Connell (Amherst: University of Massachusetts Press, 1992), 285, 290, on extortionate land speculation in early America.

40. Jennings, *Ambiguous Iroquois Empire,* 330–31, 340, 317, 310.

41. Jennings, *Ambiguous Iroquois Empire,* 320–21, 332, 337, 334–35; Francis Jennings, *Benjamin Franklin, Politician* (New York: W. W. Norton and Co., 1996), 53–54; C. William Miller, *Benjamin Franklin's Philadelphia Printing: A Descriptive Bibliography* (Philadelphia: American Philosophical Society, 1974), 55.

42. Jennings, *Ambiguous Iroquois Empire,* 315, 320–21, 226–29, 236–37.

43. Jennings, *Ambiguous Iroquois Empire,* 280, 160, 229, 225–26n6, 252–53, 281, 292–93, 303, 313, 263–264, 291, 312–21.

44. Jennings, *Ambiguous Iroquois Empire,* 321–24.

45. Jennings, *Ambiguous Iroquois Empire,* xvii; Jennings, *Empire of Fortune,* 25.

46. Miller, *Franklin's Philadelphia Printing,* xxiv–xxv, 67; Leonard W. Labaree, ed., *The Papers of Benjamin Franklin* (New Haven, Conn.: Yale University Press, 1959), 1:277. Jennings, *Benjamin Franklin,* 36.

47. Jennings, *Ambiguous Iroquois Empire,* 333–34, 336–40.

48. Jennings, *Ambiguous Iroquois Empire,* 337, 330, 310, 341–46; Anthony F. C. Wallace, *King of the Delawares: Teedyuscung, 1700–1763* (Freeport, N.Y.: Books for Libraries Press, 1949), 18–30; Wallace, *Conrad Weiser,* 95–101.

49. Jennings, *Ambiguous Iroquois Empire,* 341–46.

50. Cf. Bruce Elliott Johansen and Barbara Alice Mann, eds., *Encyclopedia of the Haudenosaunee (Iroquois Confederacy)* (Westport, Conn.: Greenwood Press, 2000), 43; Jennings, *Ambiguous Iroquois Empire,* 21, 167, 344, 356; Weslager, *Delaware Indians,* 182; Fenton, "Structure, Continuity, and Change," 27; Foster, "Function of Wampum," 104–5; Barbara Alice Mann, "'Are You Delusional?' Kandiaronk on Christianity," in *Native American Speakers of the Eastern Woodlands: Selected Speeches and Critical Analyses,* ed. Barbara Alice Mann (Westport, Conn.: Greenwood Press, 2001), 59.

51. Heckewelder, *History, Manners, and Customs,* 150–53.

52. Carol L. Bagley and Jo Ann Ruckman, "Iroquois Contributions to Modern Democracy and Communism," *American Indian Culture and Research Journal* 7.2 (1983): 56, 64; Elisabeth Tooker, "The United States Constitution and the Iroquois League," *Ethnohistory* 35.4 (Fall 1988): 315; Mann and Fields, "A Sign in the Sky," 137, 162n179.

53. Fenton, "Structure, Continuity, and Change," 14, 34n28, 16–18.

54. Helen Hunt Jackson, *A Century of Dishonor* (Norman: University of Oklahoma Press, 1995), 9–13.

55. Douglas W. Boyce, "'As the Wind Scatters the Smoke': The Tuscaroras in the Eighteenth Century," in Richter and Merrell, eds., *Beyond the Covenant Chain,* 152–57; Johansen and Mann, *Encyclopedia,* 3–6; Dennis, *Cultivating a Landscape,* 6–8; Jennings, *Ambiguous Iroquois Empire,* 45–46. Mann's discussion regarding the Wyandot leader Kandiaronk in "Are You Delusional?" throws into question whether this "women" insult may be attributed to Canasatego or is a self-interested confusion of his words by the official record keepers in the British colonies.

56. Jennings, *Ambiguous Iroquois Empire,* 360–62.

57. Arthur M. Schlesinger Jr., *The Disuniting of America* (New York: Norton, 1992), 96–99; Donald A. Grinde Jr. and Bruce E. Johansen, *Exemplar of Liberty: Native America and the Evolution of Democracy* (Los Angeles: American Indian Studies Center at UCLA, 1991), xxii, xxv. As with many historical debates, it is also necessary to examine carefully the logic, coherence, and relevance of the arguments presented on all sides, whether authors cite evidence to support each claim or denial that they make, whether the evidence cited supports the claim or denial being made, whether an attack on a narrow claim or denial invalidates a more complex body of evidence or argument, whether opponents actually engage with one another's argument, and whether arguments are free of racial bias or other assumptions that tend to discredit otherwise reasonable scholarship. For example, the secrecy of the Constitutional Convention does not equate to an absence of discussion of Native American political structures in that forum. It is also important to rule out casual participants in the debate who have not thoroughly investigated the question or who rely on hearsay. In the case of this particular debate, the publication of materials in relatively inaccessible archives may need to occur before judgments on particular points can be legitimately rendered.

58. Louis Montrose, "Professing the Renaissance: The Poetics and Politics of Culture," in *Literary Theory: An Anthology,* ed. Julie Rivkin and Michael Ryan (Malden, Mass.: Blackwell Publishers, 1998), 781; cf. Jennings, *Ambiguous Iroquois Empire,* 58–60; Jennings, *Founders,* 49–52.

59. Bruce E. Johansen, *Forgotten Founders: Benjamin Franklin, the Iroquois, and the Rationale for the American Revolution* (Ipswitch, Mass.: Gambit, 1982); Donald A. Grinde Jr., *The Iroquois and the Founding of the American Nation* (San Francisco: The Indian Historian Press, 1977); Grinde and Johansen, *Exemplar of Liberty;* Robert W. Venables, "American Indian Influences on the America of the Founding Fathers," *Exiled in the Land of the Free: Democracy, Indian Nations, and the U.S. Constitution,* ed. Oren Lyons, John Mohawk et al. (Santa Fe, N.Mex.: Clear Light Publishers, 1992); Jennings, *Empire of Fortune,* 258–59; Tooker, "The United States Constitution and the Iroquois League," 305–36; William A. Starna and George R. Hamell, "History and the Burden of Proof: The Case of Iroquois Influence on the U.S. Constitution," *New York History* 77.4 (October 1996): 427–52; Robert L. Berner, "Iroquois Influence: A Response to Bruce E. Johansen's "Notes from the 'Culture Wars,'" *American Indian Culture and Research Journal* 24.2 (2000): 111–16; Bruce Johansen, "Data or Dogma? A Reply to Robert L. Berner," *American Indian Culture and Research Journal* 24.2 (2000): 118.

60. Venables, "American Indian Influences," 75–77, 102–4, 111, 115–16; Grinde and Johansen, *Exemplar,* xx, 3, 11–17, 24, 33; Bagley and Ruckman, "Iroquois Contributions," 57, 65–66; Raymond Demallie, "The Lakota Ghost Dance: An Ethnohistorical Account," *Pacific Historical Review* 51 (1982): 385–405; Heckewelder, *History, Manners, and Customs,* 185–86 and passim.

61. Grinde and Johansen, *Exemplar,* 197, 200, 202, 253n14; Bagley and Ruckman, "Iroquois

Contributions," 62; Gerald Vizenor, "Socioacupuncture: Mythic Reversals and the Striptease in Four Scenes," in *The American Indian and the Problem of History,* ed. Calvin Martin (New York: Oxford University Press, 1987), 183.

62. Heckewelder, *History, Manners, and Customs,* 107–54 and passim; Wilma Dunaway, "Incorporation as an Interactive Process: Cherokee Resistance to Expansion of the Capitalist World-System, 1560–1763." *Sociological Inquiry* 66:4 (Fall 1996): 466.

63. Jennings, *Empire of Fortune,* xvii; Jennings, *Founders,* 292; Worthington Ford, ed., *Journals of the Continental Congress, 1774–1789* (Washington, D.C.: U.S. GPO, 1904–1937), 2:195–99; Paul H. Smith, ed., *Letters of Delegates to Congress, 1774–1789* (Washington, D.C.: U.S. GPO 1976–1998), 4:251–52; Labaree, *Papers of Benjamin Franklin,* 22:120–25; cf. Grinde and Johansen, *Exemplar,* 145, 276n16 (which misquotes *Letters of Delegates*).

64. Labaree, *Papers of Benjamin Franklin,* 5:335–41, 344–55, 357–417; Merrill Jensen, *The Articles of Confederation: An Interpretation of the Social-Constitutional History of the American Revolution, 1774–1781* (Madison: University of Wisconsin Press, 1962), 254–70. Grinde and Johansen assert that Hendrick, a Mohawk chief, "was asked to provide insights into the structure of the League . . . for the assembled colonial delegates" at the 1754 Albany Congress, that "during the framing and ratification process of the United States Constitution, the Iroquois lectured to colonial and revolutionary leaders on the virtues of unity and served as an example of democracy," and that editorial opinion during the Convention urged the use of parts of the Iroquois Constitution (*Exemplar,* 104, xxiv, xxiii, 163). They do not provide citations that prove supportive of these three particular claims, perhaps owing to a printing oversight. The 1775 Treaty that they cite resides in the National Archives in Washington, D.C., awaiting re-publication for a more general audience.

65. Labaree, *Papers of Benjamin Franklin,* 3:175, 272; Wallace, *Conrad Weiser,* 212; Richard Barry, *Mr. Rutledge of South Carolina* (New York: Duell, Sloan and Pearce, 1942), 107–10, 339; Nicholas B. Wainwright, *George Croghan, Wilderness Diplomat* (Chapel Hill: University of North Carolina Press, 1959); Theodore Thayer, *Israel Pemberton: King of the Quakers* (Philadelphia: Historical Society of Pennsylvania, 1943); Walter Pilkington, ed., *The Journals of Samuel Kirkland* (Clinton, N.Y.: Hamilton College, 1980), 93–120; Grinde and Johansen, *Exemplar of Liberty,* 113, 278n39.

66. Wallace, *Conrad Weiser,* vii, 40, 105, 171, 199, 250, 418; Labaree, *Papers of Benjamin Franklin,* 2:385–88 and passim through several volumes; Jennings, *Benjamin Franklin,* 85; Franklin also corresponded with naturalist John Bartram, William Bartram's father.

67. Labaree, *Papers of Benjamin Franklin,* 4:117, 119.

68. Jennings, *Empire of Fortune,* 258–59; Labaree, *Papers of Benjamin Franklin,* 4:225–27, 234, 229, 479–86; Susan Kalter, "Keep these words until the stones melt: language, ecology, war, and the written land in nineteenth century U.S.-Indian relations" (Ph.D. diss., University of California, San Diego, 1999).

69. H. W. Brands, *The First American: The Life and Times of Benjamin Franklin* (New York: Doubleday, 2000), 16; "savage" and "ignorant," *Oxford English Dictionary*, online version, 2002; Labaree, *Papers of Benjamin Franklin,* 4:44–46, 49–50, 67–68, 117–21.

70. Jennings, *Benjamin Franklin,* 64, 81–84, 91–92, 94–121.

71. McConnell, "Peoples "In Between,'" 93–112; Jennings, "'Pennsylvania Indians,'" 75–91; Jennings, *Empire of Fortune,* 55.

72. McConnell, "Peoples "In Between,'" 98; Jennings, *Empire of Fortune,* 27–28.

73. McConnell, "Peoples "In Between,'" 99–101; Jennings, *Empire of Fortune,* 28–33, 40–41; Labaree, *Papers of Benjamin Franklin,* 4:320; Jennings, *Benjamin Franklin,* 65–67.

74. Jennings, *Empire of Fortune,* 34; Jennings, "Descriptive Treaty Calendar," 159–82; Aquila, *Iroquois Restoration,* 129–55.

75. Wallace, *Conrad Weiser,* 278–84.

76. Jennings, "Descriptive Treaty Calendar," 184; cf. Jennings, *Empire of Fortune,* 10–13, 16–17; Jennings, *Ambiguous Iroquois Empire,* 363; cf. Bagley and Ruckman, "Iroquois Contributions," 65, on treason by chiefs. Note that an Onondaga faction would not have to be a faction in the French interest to blame Canasatego for the "sale" of the Ohio Valley to Virginia, which threatened the entire region.

77. Jennings, *Empire of Fortune,* 10–20, 37–44; Brands, *The First American,* 208, 356–58.

78. Jennings, *Empire of Fortune,* 49–54.

79. Jennings, *Empire of Fortune,* 54–59, 44–45, 75–79, 148.

80. Jennings, *Empire of Fortune,* 92–95.

81. Jennings, *Benjamin Franklin,* 122–25; Jennings, *Empire of Fortune,* 189–92, 60–68, 125–29.

82. Jennings, *Empire of Fortune,* 90–108; Wallace, *Conrad Weiser,* 359.

83. Jennings, "Descriptive Treaty Calendar," 188; Jennings, *Empire of Fortune,* 72, 261–62, cf. 441–46.

84. Jennings, *Empire of Fortune,* 263.

85. Jennings, *Empire of Fortune,* 278–81; Labaree, *Papers of Benjamin Franklin,* 7:16.

86. Labaree, *Papers of Benjamin Franklin,* 7:137–42; Jennings, *Benjamin Franklin,* 144, 149, 158, 192; cf. Jennings, *Empire of Fortune,* 15, 96, 103–5, 274–81, 345; cf. Wallace, *Conrad Weiser,* 461–65.

87. Labaree, *Papers of Benjamin Franklin,* 7:175, 178–79, 198–99, 264–70, 281–84, 373–77, 385–89, 8:xxiv–xxv, 22–27, 54–79, 81–85, 99–105, 113–14, 149–52, 157–59, 174–77, 199–213, 226–30, 264–76, 291–300, 309–16, 340–56, 360–89, 396–404, 432–33; Jennings, *Empire of Fortune,* 326–37, 342–48.

88. Labaree, *Papers of Benjamin Franklin,* 8:206; Charles Thomson also believed that Weiser and Croghan conspired to "keep Teedyuscung in liquor" at the 1757 Easton conference. It is likely that such tactics continued in 1758. Wallace, *Conrad Weiser,* 481.

89. Jennings, *Benjamin Franklin,* 144–50, 159–60; Labaree, *Papers of Benjamin Franklin,* 8:379–89, 7:362, 362n6.

90. Labaree, *Papers of Benjamin Franklin,* 1:277, 2:32, 156, 160, 188, 239, 318, 391, 415–16, 3:81, 99, 194, 238, 272, 320, 340, 389, 445, 4:67–68, 88, 121, 183–84, 221, 480–82, etc.; also Labaree, *Papers of Benjamin Franklin,* 9:273, 10:286, 293–97, 303–4, 342, 11:22–29; cf. Brands, *The First American,* 524–25.

91. Labaree, *Papers of Benjamin Franklin,* 11:30, 42–75; see Labaree, *Papers of Benjamin Franklin,* volumes 2–23 for record of Colden correspondence and cessation thereof after 26 February 1763.

92. C. A. Weslager, *The Delaware Indian Westward Migration* (Wallingford, Pa.: Middle Atlantic Press, 1978), 231; Gerald Vizenor, "A Postmodern Introduction," in *Narrative Chance* (Albuquerque: University of New Mexico Press, 1993); Vizenor, "Socioacupuncture."

93. See also Devon Mihesuah, "Should American Indian History Remain a Field of Study?" in Mihesuah and Wilson, *Indigenizing the Academy* (Lincoln: University of Nebraska Press, 2004).

# EDITOR'S NOTE

In making editorial changes to the original eighteenth-century treaties, I attempted to make the texts as accessible as possible to a contemporary reader while retaining the most important features of the original. In this endeavor, I faced the sometimes competing imperatives of readability and length.

To modernize and standardize the texts, several typographical and spatial edits were made. To bind as a single bound volume, it was necessary to use a uniform paper size and standardize the margin size. (The originals were printed on both "letter" sized and "legal" sized paper.) The page numbers and page breaks from the original printing were superseded in this process. The typography was modernized: for example, by converting lowercase s's that look like f's to modern-style s's. The type size was regularized and title sizes diminished, and the font was both changed and regularized. Borders that surrounded text, as on the title page of the 1744 treaty, were removed. When quotation marks were placed next to every line in a quoted paragraph, they were removed except before the first and after the last word of that paragraph. Those words on the bottoms of each page that anticipate the word that starts the following page were also removed, as were stray printers' marks. Where I was unable to duplicate Franklin's footnote marker symbols, I converted those symbols. Spaces between letters in the same word (as in T H E E N D) were removed. Running sidebar notations of the year of the treaty that begin to appear in the 1753 treaty were also removed, as were symbols such as } that covered double and triple lines, as in the announcement that several people attending a treaty were esquires (esqrs). Throughout the text, italics, uppercase lettering, punctuation marks, and spelling irregularities were retained wherever they occurred. However, words that opened paragraphs or other passages and lists of names in capital and small capital letters were changed to capital and lowercase letters. In some cases, particularly when the convention was used for emphasis, small caps were converted to all capital letters.

Some effort was made to standardize the page layout and pagination in order to accommodate spatial constraints. Title pages and blank pages were removed and the

[ 1 ]

A

# TREATY, &c.

*At the* Court-House *in* Lancaster, Tuesday, July 19. 1748.

P R E S E N T,

*Benjamin Shoemaker*, *Joseph Turner*, } Esqrs.
*Thomas Hopkinson*, *William Logan*,

*The Magistrates and Inhabitants of* Lancaster *County*, *Fifty-five* Indians *of several Nations*, viz. *of the* Six Nations, Delawares, Shawonese, Nanticokes, *and* Twightwees; Conrad Weiser, *Esq*; *Interpreter for the* Six Nation Indians; *Mr.* Andrew Montour, *Interpreter for the* Shawonese *and* Twightwees.

A PROCLAMATION was made for Silence, and then a Commission, in His Majesty's Name, under the Great Seal of the Province, was read, constituting the honourable *Benjamin Shoemaker*, *Joseph Turner*, *Thomas Hopkinson*, and *William Logan*, Esquires, Commissioners to treat with these *Indians*; and the Interpreter was order'd to tell them the Purport thereof, and to bid them heartily welcome among their Brethren.

The Commissioners having been informed that *Scarrowyady*, a Chief of the *Oneido* Nation, living at *Ohio*, was appointed Speaker for the *Indians*, but was so much hurt by a Fall, that he was unable to attend; order'd the Interpreter to tell them, that they condoled with them on this unfortunate Accident, but hoped, as what they came to transact was of a publick Nature, and well known to them all, this would occasion no Delay. As the Government had shewn them great Indulgence, in granting them a Council at *Lancaster*, so far from the usual Place of Business, and in so hot a Season, it was expected they would not detain the Commissioners, but deliver what they had to say To-morrow Morning at Ten o' Clock; and further, to desire they would use no Manner of Reserve, but open their Hearts freely and fully, the Commissioners promising to treat them with the same Freedom and Plainness.

D *At*

A page from an original treaty, dated July 19, 1748, printed by Benjamin Franklin. This item is reproduced by permission of the Huntington Library, San Marino California.

title spacing was condensed from several lines into one to three lines. In some cases, line breaks in the lists of persons present at treaty councils were removed and these lists were condensed spatially. In cases where long lists of persons present at treaty councils were given in the original, these tables were converted to text in order to condense them. Printers' illustrations and seals of the colony were also removed.

In some cases, nonuniform emendations were made. Where it would not interfere with comprehension, spaces between lines/paragraphs were removed but spaces were retained to indicate a change of speakers. Extra lines announcing that a speaker continued to speak were generally removed, unless they were needed to avoid confusion on the part of the reader. These edits were necessary to provide the reader with a condensed and economical version of the treaties. To improve readability as a result of these spacing edits, indentations of the first line of a paragraph were sometimes added or removed. Where reverse indentation was unnecessary for readability, the indentation of the second through the last line of a paragraph was removed. Also, to improve readability as a result of these spacing edits, some lists that were left-justified or indented-left in the original were centered, while some lines that were centered in the original were left-justified or indented-left. Borders separating one day from the next were converted to modern-style borders, usually straight lines or double lines from left to right. Where it was appropriate or necessary, borders were added, as when the original omitted a border because of a page break or where a change of day or venue had occurred. So that the modern reader might best follow the actions accompanying speeches at the treaty councils, most actions indicating the giving of wampum were right-justified, whether they appeared that way in the original or not.

The most substantive change that was made was the placement of address words such as "Brethren" or "Brother Onas" in the same line as the paragraph that followed them. In the original, these words usually occupied an entire line to themselves. This change will inevitably have an effect on the reader's perception of the pace and ceremony of the speeches made, so it was a regrettable but necessary step toward producing an economical and accessible volume.

The University of Illinois Press asked me to substitute more widely recognized names such as Iroquois (in place of Haudenosaunee) and Susquehannock (in place of Andaste) in the preface, introduction, notes, and glossary for greater readability to a wider audience. Because these names are not the preferred designations chosen by members of these groups, I have indicated self-selected names whenever possible when I first speak of the group.

The treaties in this volume are based on the facsimiles printed in the 1938 collection, which remain in the public domain. Those facsimiles were made from copies found in the Historical Society of Pennsylvania (all but the July 1742, October 1745, November 1747, and July 1748 treaties), in the American Philosophical Society (October 1745, November 1747, and July 1748), and in the Library Company of Philadelphia (July 1742). In some cases, facsimiles of single pages in this earlier collection were made from copies in the Curtis Collection at the University of Pennsylvania or from copies at the Library Company of Philadelphia.

✠

# A TREATY

# OF FRIENDSHIP

HELD WITH

THE CHIEFS OF THE SIX NATIONS,

AT PHILADELPHIA,

IN *SEPTEMBER* and *OCTOBER,* 1736.

---

*PHILADELPHIA:*
Printed and Sold by B. FRANKLIN, at the New Printing-Office
near the Market. MDCCXXXVII

---

## A TREATY of FRIENDSHIP, &c. *September,* 1736.

The Chiefs of the *Six Nations* having been expected at *Philadelphia* these four Years past, to confirm the Treaty made with some of them, who came down in the Year 1732,[1] *Conrad Wyser* our Interpreter, about the Beginning of this Month, advised from *Tulpyhokin,* that he had certain Intelligence from some Indians sent before him, that there was a large Number of those People with their Chiefs, arrived at *Shamokin* on *Sasquehannah;* upon which he was directed to repair thither to attend them, and supply them with Necessaries in their Journey hither.

On the *Twenty-seventh* of this Month, about a Hundred or more of them came with *Conrad* to the President's House, at *Stenton,* being near the Road, where suitable Entertainment was provided for them; and the next Day the Honourable the Proprietor, and some of the Council, with other Gentlemen coming thither from *Philadelphia;* after Dinner

A Council was held at *Stenton, September* 28, 1736.
PRESENT, The Honourable *THOMAS PENN,* Esq; Proprietary.
*JAMES LOGAN,* Esq; President. *Samuel Preston, Ralph Assheton,*
*Clement Plumsted, Thomas Griffitts,* Esqrs;

And the following *Indian* Chiefs, to wit.

Of the TSANANDOWANS or SINEKAS
*Kanickhungo*, Speaker.
*Togachshaholoo,*
*Sagoyatundachquai,*
*Askotax,*
*Hetaquantegechty*, Speaker.

ONANDAGOES
*Kahiskerowane* (Brother *to their former great Chief Conossoorah* at *Albany*)
*Tagunhuntee,*
*Kaxhaayn,*
*Kuchdachary,*
*Saweegatee-o.*

CAYOOGES
*Saguchsauyunt,*
*Sunaretchy,*
*Kanawatoe*
*Teeouchtseegherochgoo.*

ONEIDAS
*Saristagoa,*
*Takashwangarorasor,*
*Shekallamy.*

TUSKARORES
*Sawnutaga,*
*Tyeroi.*

*Of the* CANYINGOES *or* MOHOCKS *none came.*[2]

By the Interpreter's Advice, they were first spoke to in their own Way, with three small Strings of *Wampum* in Hand,[3] one of which was delivered on each of the following Articles.

*Our Friends and Brethren,*

I. *You are come a great way, and have doubtless suffered many Hardships in so long a Journey; but now you are with your Brethren and true Friends, who have long been in Friendship and Alliance with your Nations; you must therefore put away all Grief and Uneasiness, and brighten your Eyes, that we may see and be chearful with each other.*[4]

II. *We desire that as we are now met as Brethren and Friends, you will open your Hearts, as we shall open our Hearts, that we may speak with Freedom and Openness to each other.*

III. *You are come to us as your true Friends, we receive you with Gladness, you shall shelter yourselves under our Covering, and be entertained by us as ourselves, for you are our Brethren.*

The Indians hereupon expressed their Satisfaction with Sounds peculiar to themselves on such Occasions; and then their Speaker with three like Strings in his Hand, repeated all those three several Articles more at large, returning their Thanks for each, delivering a String as each Article was spoke to, and giving Assurances of their Freedom and Openness, and desiring that we would use the same; but on the 3d they said, *They could not receive and treat us as we did them, they are now with us, they give themselves to us, and depend on our Protection.*

Then with five more very short Strings in his Hand, the Speaker proceeded to say on the first, *That they had received on the Road a Message from us delivered by* Conrad Wyser, *welcoming them into the Country.* On the 2d, *That they had at the same time received from us an Account of our late Governor's Death, but that this would not occasion any Alteration, because* W. PENN'S *own Son is here, and also* James Logan, *with the Council.* On the 3d They returned their Thanks, and with the other two confirm'd the whole.

They said, *They were now come, after a full Consultation with all their Chiefs at their great Fire or Place of Counsel, to return an Answer to the Treaty, that some of them had held with us four Years since, at* Philadelphia: *That they intended to stay with their Friend* James Logan *two Nights to rest themselves, and then proceed to the Fire kept for them at* Philadelphia; *where after two Nights more, they would at that Fire give their full Answer.*

They were told, *We were willing to keep them here in the Country the longer, because many People in* Philadelphia *had been sickly, and now the* Small Pox *are there, a Disease that has often proved fatal to the Indians; that it would be a great Trouble to us to see any of them taken with that Distemper, after they had travelled so far to visit us; for we are very desirous they should all return safe, and as healthy as they came to us: That it is proper they should give their Answer at* Philadelphia, *in the same publick Manner we had last treated with them; but it is adviseable they should spend no more of their time in the Town, than will be absolutely necessary, for many Inconveniences may attend it.*[5]

They appeared concerned at this, thanked us, and said they would go together by themselves to advise on it.

*September 29.*

The Gentlemen of the Council having gone home last night to *Philadelphia,* and only the Proprietor staying, Mr *Preston* with some others came again to day; and the *Indian* Chiefs after they had consulted this Morning amongst themselves, meeting the Proprietor, &c. in Council, said,

*That they were much obliged to us for the Care we took of them; we shewed by it our true Friendship for them. That as they are now with us, they put themselves wholly under our Direction, and tho'* Philadelphia *is the Place where their Fire is kept for them, yet it may upon Occasion be brought out hither; and they are free either to proceed to* Philadelphia *to treat at the Fire there, or to stay here, as we shall think fit to order it.*

They were told, *As the last Treaty with them was held in Publick at* Philadelphia, *it would be necessary they should there give their Answer; That we were not wholly against their going to Town, but thought ourselves obliged to acquaint them with the Danger; yet that this is not at present so great that it should wholly prevent their going. The Distemper is as yet but young and just begun in the Place; that it is only in the Heart or near the Middle of the Town; that they will be accommodated at the Edge or Out-Skirts of the Town, where if they take Care, they may for a few Days be in but very little or no Danger.*

They then resolved to set out for *Philadelphia* the next Day; and accordingly having been entertained at *Stenton* three Nights, they went to Town on the last of *September;* and having rested the first of *October,* on the second Day they met as follows.

At a Council held in the *Great Meeting-House* at *Philadelphia,*
the *2nd* Day of *October* 1736.
PRESENT, The Honourable *THOMAS PENN,* Esq; Proprietary,
*JAMES LOGAN,* Esq; President. *Samuel Preston, Ralph Assheton, Anthony Palmer, Thomas Griffitts, Clement Plumsted, Charles Read, Thomas Lawrence,* Esqrs.
Present also The *MAYOR* and *Recorder* of the City,
With divers Gentlemen, and a very large Audience that filled the House and its Galleries.

The *Indian* Chiefs being come and seated,

The President, before proceeding to hear them, thought proper to inform the Audience, that in *August* 1732, a great Treaty having been held in this Place with several Chiefs of the Six Nations, they had made report thereof on their Return to their Great Council, where the several Propositions that had been made to them on the Part of this Government, had been fully considered; and that these Chiefs now present, of whom there never at any time before had been so great a Number met in this Province, were now come to return their Answer.

The *Indians* being made acquainted with what the President had said, were told, that we were ready to hear them.

Whereupon *Kanickhungo* their Speaker, addressing himself to their Brother *ONAS* (which signifies *PENN*) to their Brother *JAMES LOGAN,* and the Gentlemen of the Council, spoke as follows by *Conrad Wyser* the Interpreter;

"*BRETHREN,* WE are now come down from the Towns of our several Nations to give our Answer to the great Treaty, which we and you held together, at this Place, about four Years since: This Answer has been agreed and concluded upon by our great Council, who have carefully considered all that passed between you and us, and expressed their great Satisfaction in the friendly and good Dispositions of you our Brethren, towards all the *Indians* of the *Six Nations;* and as you received us kindly, and at that Treaty undertook to provide and keep for us a Fire in this great City, we are now come to warm ourselves thereat, and we desire and hope it will ever continue bright and burning to the End of the World."

*Hereupon he laid down a large Belt of white* Wampum *of eleven Rows, with four black St.* George's *Crosses in it; and proceeding, said*

"*BRETHREN,* SOON after our Brother *ONAS,* who is now here, came into this Country, he and we treated together; he opened and cleared the Road between this Place and our Nations, which was very much to our good Liking, and it gave us great Pleasure. We now desire that this Road, for the mutual Accommodation and Conveniency of you and us who Travel therein to see each other, may be kept clear and open, free from all Stops or Incumbrances; and if, since the time that we last cleared it with you, any Tree has fallen across it, or if it is any way stopt up, of which however we know nothing, we are now willing to open and clear the same from every Interruption; and it is our hearty Desire that it may so continue, while the Earth endureth."[6]

*Hereupon he presented a Bundle of Skins in the Hair, and went on;*

"*BRETHREN,* ONE of the chief Articles of our late Treaty together, was the brightning of the Chain of Friendship between us, and the preserving it free from all Rust and Spots; and that this Chain was not only between this Government and us, but between all the *English* Governments and all the *Indians.* We now assure you our Brethren, that it is our earnest Desire this Chain should continue, and be strengthned between all the *English* and all our Nations, and likewise the *Delawares, Canays,* and the *Indians* living on *Sasquehannah,* and all the other *Indians* who now are in League and Friendship with the *Six Nations;* in Behalf of all whom, and as a lasting Confirmation of this great Article, to endure until this Earth passeth away and is no more seen, we now deliver you this Beaver Coat."

*Here he laid down a large Beaver Coat.*

*The Proprietor gave them Thanks in Behalf of this Government for what they had spoke touching these three important Articles of the Fire, Road and Chain of Friendship, and told them their Discourse thereon was very satisfactory.*

*The Speaker proceeded and said;*

"*BRETHREN,* TO conclude all that we have now said, it is our Desire that we and you should be as of one Heart, one Mind, and one Body, thus becoming one People, entertaining a mutual Love and Regard for each other, to be preserved firm and entire, not only between you and us, but between your Children, and our Children, to all succeeding Generations.[7]

"We who are now here, are old Men, who have the Direction of Affairs in our own Nations; and as we are old, it may be thought that the Memory of these things may be lost with us, who have not, like you, the Art of preserving it by committing all Transactions to Writing: We nevertheless have Methods of transmitting from Father to Son, an Account of all these Things, whereby you will find the Remembrance of them is faithfully preserved, and our succeeding Generations are made acquainted with what has passed, that it may not be forgot as long as the Earth remains."

They were told, *That it was very agreeable to us to know that they took such effectual Care in this Point.*

*Then proceeding he said;* "*BRETHREN,* WE desire that this brightning of the Chain, and establishing a strong and firm League of Friendship, may be understood by you, as we understand it to be, not only between the Chiefs of our Nations, and the Chiefs or Principal Men of this Government, but likewise between all our People, and all your People, and between you and all our *Warriours* who go abroad and sometimes pass near this Government, to all of whom we have given the strictest

Charge to behave themselves agreeable to the Friendship which is established between you and us, that so we all may continue to be one People for ever.

"At the last Treaty you advised us to strengthen ourselves by entring into firm Leagues of Friendship and Alliance with several other Nations of *Indians* around us; this Advice was truly good, and we thank our Brethren for it; we have accordingly treated with these Six following Nations, *to wit,* the *Onichkaryagoes, Sissaghees, Tioumitihagas, Attawantenis, Twechtwese,* and *Oachtamughs,*[8] and have engaged them so heartily in our Interest, that they acknowledge us for their Elder Brethren, and have promised to join with us as one People, and to act altogether in Concert with us.

"You likewise then advised us to call home all those of our Nations who are at *Canada,* or live amongst the *French,* lest if any Occasion of Difference should arise, they might then be prevented from returning. We esteem this likewise as sound good Advice, and we thank our Brethren for it; the *French* were formerly our cruel Enemies, and we are taking such Measures as we hope will be effectual to bring back our People, if any new Breach should happen."[9]

*The Speaker said,* "To confirm all that we have now said, we would be glad if we had a large Present of Skins to deliver, in Return to the considerable one in Goods which we had of you; but we must own to you that we are at present but very ill provided and poor, and have only a very small Quantity of Skins, which nevertheless we hope our Brethren will accept."

*Here he laid down two small Bundles of Skins.*

"We have now nothing more to say in Publick; but having other Matters to treat on with the Proprietor, we will enter upon them at another time."

They were told, *That the Proprietor, President and Council thank'd them very kindly in Behalf of this Government, for all they had now said; that they had returned full and distinct Answers to all the Chief Articles or Propositions made at the last great Treaty in 1732, they had spoke to each of them like honest Men and true Brethren; and as they had consulted together before they delivered their Answer, so now the Council would meet and consider together of all that had passed at present.*

Which being interpreted to them, they expressed their Satisfaction by a Sound peculiar to them, in which they all joined, and then withdrew.

At a Council held at *Philadelphia, October* 4, 1736.
PRESENT, The Honourable *JAMES LOGAN;* Esq; President.
*Anthony Palmer, Ralph Assheton, Clement Plumsted, Thomas Griffitts, Thomas Lawrence, Charles Read,* Esqrs;

The President representing to the Board the Necessity of dispatching the *Indians* of the *Six* Nations, who being very numerous remain here at a great Charge, proposed that the Consideration of the Value of the Present to be given them, should be now proceeded upon; and accordingly the Board entering upon the same, and observing that for these many Years there has not been so great an Appearance here of Chiefs of these Nations as at this time, and that they have returned very full and distinct Answers to every Article of the Treaty with them in 1732, are of Opinion, that proper Goods for them to the Value of about *Two Hundred Pounds* should be provided and given them; and that to *Conrad Weyser,* the Interpreter, who is extremly useful on all such Occasions, and on the present one has been very serviceable, there be given *Twenty Pounds.*

At a Council held at *Philadelphia, October* 12. 1736.
PRESENT, The Honourable *JAMES LOGAN,* Esq; President.
*Samuel Preston, Samuel Hasell, Clement Plumsted, Thomas Griffitts, Thomas Lawrence, Charles Read.* Esqrs;

The President informed the Board, that agreeable to the Minute of the 4th, Care had been taken to provide Goods for the Indians: But next Day, after Council, consulting with *Conrad Weyser,* the Interpreter, he had advised that the Delivery of the Present should be delayed till the *Indians* had finished with the Proprietary, with whom they were then to treat about the Purchase of Lands; that most of last Week being spent therein, the *Indians* had Yesterday ended with the Proprietary, having signed Releases to him for all the Lands lying between the Mouth of *Sasquehannah,* and *Kekachtaninius* Hills, and that it now remained to conclude on the Quantity and Quality of the several Goods to be given them, and on the Substance of what should be proper to be spoke to them; The Board are of Opinion, that considering the large Quantity of Goods which they have had from the Proprietor on the Purchase, it may not at this time be necessary to give them, in Behalf of this Government, so great a Present as the Value ordered by the aforesaid Minute; but that it may very well be considerably reduced; and accordingly, it is *Ordered,* that it be reduced to between *Sixty* and *Seventy Pounds.*

The President likewise acquainting the Board, that the *Indians,* at a Meeting with the Proprietor and him, had taken Notice that *Conrad Weyser,* and *Shekallamy,* were by the Treaty of 1732, appointed as fit and proper Persons to go between the *Six Nations,* and this Government, and to be employed in all Transactions with one another, whose Bodies the *Indians* said were to be equally divided between them and us, we to have one half, and they the other; that they had found *Conrad* faithful and honest, that he is a true good Man, and had spoke their Words, and our Words, and not his own; and the *Indians* having presented him with a drest Skin to make him Shoes, and two Deer Skins, to keep him warm, they said, as they had thus taken Care of our Friend, they must recommend their's (*Shekallamy*) to our Notice; and the Board judging it necessary that a particular Notice should be taken of him, accordingly, it is, *Ordered,* That *Six Pounds* be laid out for him in such things as he may most want.

It was then recommended to the President, and he undertook, to prepare a Draught of what might be proper to be said to these *Indians* at giving the Present from this Government, and to lay the same before the Board to morrow Morning, at Ten a Clock, to which time the Council adjourned.

At a Council held at *Philadelphia, October* 13th, 1736.
PRESENT, The Honourable *THOMAS PENN,* Esq; Proprietary,
*JAMES LOGAN,* Esq; President. *Samuel Preston, Ralph Assheton,*
*Clement Plumsted, Samuel Hasell, Thomas Lawrence,*
*Thomas Griffitts.* Esqrs;

The President laid before the Board a draught of a concluding Speech to the Indians, which being read and approved, they were sent for, who being come and seated, the said Speech was delivered to them by the Interpreter as follows.

"*OUR BRETHREN,* FOUR Years since at a great Treaty held here with your Chiefs, we confirmed all our former Treaties with you, we brightned the Chain, kindled our Fire to be kept always burning here for you, opened and cleared the Path between your Country and Ours, and made ourselves and you one Body and one People.

"The Chiefs of all your Nations, being met at your great Fire or Council in the Country of the *Onondagoes,* having heard of and considered that Treaty, were so well pleased with it, that it was agreed, as you have told us, that you, who are the principal of all your Chiefs, should come down and visit us, and more fully and absolutely confirm that Treaty, which you accordingly did a few Days since at our great House in Town, in the presence and hearing of some Thousands of our People, and it was done not only in Behalf of us ourselves and yourselves, but for our Children and Children's Children, to all Generations, as long as the Sun, Moon, and Earth, endure.

"Thus this Treaty, by which we are to become as one People, and one Body, is in the strongest Terms confirmed, never to be changed, but to be kept in everlasting Remembrance.

"But, besides what we have already concluded, we shall now for the further brightning the same Chain, and that no Spot or Blemish may be fixt on it, speak to some Particulars for your more full Satisfaction.

"It has been agreed between us, that we should suffer no Injury to be done to one of your People more than to our own, nor without punishing the Offender in the same manner as if it had been done to one of our People; and you also engaged on your parts that you would give us the like Satisfaction for every Injury done by your People to any of ours, and whatever should happen of this kind, it should make no other Difference, than as if the Injury were done by one *English* or White Man to another, and so in the Case of an *Indian.* Now since you came hither, we have heard that a White Man one of our People, and one of yours, being both in Liquor, quarrelled at *Allegheny,* that the *Indian* struck at the White Man with a Knife, and the white Man gave the *Indian* some Blows on the Head, of which he died in four or five Days after; that the White Man got out of the way, and hid, and when he heard the Man was dead, he ran away to the *Southward* of *Virginia:* Who was first in the Fault in this matter we know not, but we have now issued a Proclamation for apprehending the White Man, and proposed a Reward of *Ten Pounds,* to any one who will seize and deliver him to some Magistrate or Officer, that he may be put in Prison and tried for his Life; if then it appears that he willfully kill'd the Man, he will be hanged by our Law; if it was in Defence of his own Life, he is not to die for it, but after he is tried we shall acquaint you how the matter appeared. The first Account we had of it was in a Letter, which the Interpreter shall read and acquaint you with it; but that Story being told only on one side, we do not depend on it for the Truth; and thus we shall act in all such Cases, as Brethren always ought whenever they unfortunately happen.

"We are very sensible Rum is the principal occasion of these Disorders, and we heartily wish any means could be possibly found to prevent the Abuse of it: You have desired us in your Discourse with the Proprietor to recall all our Traders from *Ohio* or *Allegheny* and the Branches of *Sasquehannah;* We desired at our Treaty four Years ago that all our *Indians,* the *Delawares, Shawanese,* and others, should be recalled from *Ohio,* for we knew not then but there might be War with the *French,* and you know the Strength of a People consists in their being drawn close together as into one Body, and not to be scattered; but we know not what you mean by recalling our Traders; for you are sensible the *Indians* cannot live without being supplied with our Goods: They must have Powder and Lead to hunt, and Cloaths to keep them warm; and if our People do not carry them, others will, from *Maryland, Virginia, Jerseys,* or other Places; and we are sure you do not desire that *Indians* should trade with those People rather than with ours. The Traders of all Nations find the *Indians* are so universally fond of Rum, that they will not deal without it: We have made many Laws against carrying it; we have ordered the *Indians* to stave the Caggs of all that is brought amongst them; but the Woods have not Streets like *Philadelphia,* the Paths in them are endless, and they cannot be stopt, so that it will be carried either from one Country or another; and on the other hand the *Indians* are so very fond of the Liquor, even the best of them, that instead of taking it from those who bring it, and staving it, they take and drink it, which is both unjust in it self, and does more Mischief; for the Traders, if they kept it, would hand it out by stealth in small Quantities, but the *Indians* when they take it, drink it off by great Quantities; so that no Method we can find will prevent the *Indians* having it, till they are so wise as to refrain it of themselves; and, Why are they not so wise? they shew very good strong Sense in other things, and why cannot they act like us? All of us here, and all you see of any Credit in the Place, can every Day have as much Rum of their own to drink as they please, and yet scarce one of us will take a Dram, at least not one Man will on any Account be drunk, no not if he were hired to it with great Sums of Money.[10]

"And now to bind and confirm all these our Words, we have provided for you the following Goods, which will be delivered to you to morrow at the President's Lodgings, *to wit.*"

*One Hundred Pounds of Powder,*
*One Hundred & Fifty Pounds of Lead,*
*Twenty five Hatchets,*
*One Hundred Knives,*

*Twelve Strowd Matchcoats,*
*Twelve Kettles,*
*Twelve Blankets,*
*Twelve Duffels,*
*Thirty one Yards and ¼ of half Thicks,*
*Two Hundred Flints,*
*One dozen Looking-Glasses,*
*Three dozen Scissars.*
*With some Tobacco, Pipes, Rum, and Sugar.*

The Council rising, and the President with the Proprietor staying, the *Indians* entered into further Discourse, and said, *They had received a Message with some* Wampum *from the Governor of* Maryland, *informing them, he had received a Letter from the King of* England, *ordering him to see that they should not be wronged of their Lands; that he had understood this Government had wronged them, and if they would send some of their People to him, he would take care they should be righted, he would write to the great King, who would give such Orders as that they should have Justice done them. Being asked how they received that Message, they said, the Man who brought it was here now with them, they had the* Wampum *and would shew it to us; and they earnestly pressed that we would write to the Governors of* Maryland *and* Virginia *to make them Satisfaction for the Lands belonging to them (the Indians) which the People of those Governments were possessed of, that had never been purchased of them; that all the Lands on* Sasquehannah *and at* Chanandowa *were theirs, and they must be satisfied for them; that they had agreed with us for the Lands they now released to us, but they had never received any thing from the other Governments to the Southward, for theirs.*

They were told, That on their receiving the Present to morrow, they should be answered on these Heads; and after being entertained by the Proprietor, they withdrew.

*October* 14.

The Honourable the Proprietor, the President, with some of the Council met this Forenoon, and the *Indian* Chiefs being come and seated.

Their Speaker, having some Parcels of Skins laid before him, rose; and by the Interpreter said;

*That they were now to speak to the Proprietor and our People for the last time this Visit; that we had spoke to them last night, and recapitulated the Heads of all that had been agreed between them and us, as the Fire, the Path, the Chain; that we are now become one People; with every other Article that had been mentioned between us: This they will remember on their Parts through all Generations, and they desire that we may remember the same as long as the Earth endures.*

*That having now brightened the Chain, and confirmed all the Articles necessary for establishing perfect Friendship between them and us, and being thus become one People, they must desire that we would be more reasonable in the Sale of our Goods, which are much dearer (they say) from our Traders than from those of* New-York; *that the Powder sold by Traders of* New-York, *is generally found to be mixed with black Dust, so that the Bullet falls often short of the Mark thro' the Badness of the Powder;*

*that if we would sell cheap, we might thereby draw great Trade to this Province, far beyond that of any others, which would be to our Advantage.*

And hereupon he laid down a Bundle of Skins, and said,

*That amongst them there is never any Victuals sold, the Indians give to each other freely what they can spare; but if they come amongst our People, they can have none without paying; they admire we should take Money on this Score.*[11]

*That having now finished, and preparing to return home, as several of them are old Men, they request that we would help them on their Journey, by assisting them with Horses and some Carriages for their Goods; that as we have many Horses and Carriages, they desire we would spare them some for their Use, who are our Brethren.*

And hereupon he laid down two Bundles of Skins;

Then proceeding, he said, *That they must desire us to write to the Governors of* Virginia *and* Maryland, *who are possessed of their Lands, without ever considering the Indians for them, and request that we would take the Answers of those Governors, which next Spring some of their Nations will come to receive at the Fire kept for them in this Place; That they intend to apply to the great King on the other Side of the Water, and let him know what they expect on this Head from his People.*

*That if* Civility *at* Conestogoe, *should attempt to make a Sale of any Lands to us or any of our Neighbours, they must let us know, that he hath no Power to do so; and if he does any thing of the kind, they the Indians will utterly disown him.*

*That last night we told them the Woods were very dark, and that it was impossible to prevent Rum being carried to* Allegheny; *that if the Case be thus, we had better hinder any Persons from going thither at all, and confine our Traders to the River* Sasquehannah *and its Branches; for as several Indian* Warriours *pass by* Allegheny, *where so much Rum is constantly to be had, they cannot but be very apprehensive that some Mischief may happen; this Consideration often troubles them.*[12]

In Answer to all which, the *Indians* were thus told by the Interpreter. "THAT as to all that had passed relating to the Chain, Road and Fire, we have now firmly and fully established and confirmed all these Articles, to be kept in perpetual Remembrance by them and us, and by our Children and their Children to all Generations.

"That as to the Dearness of Goods carried amongst them, the Government here has no Concern in the Trade, it is entirely carried on by private People; those that go amongst the *Indians* purchase the Goods they carry with them at the easiest Rate, and we are told, that considering the Length of Way they carry them, they are sold so cheap, that these Traders can be but small Gainers; but the Prices of Goods are not under any Regulation, they get for them what they can.

"That all the white People, tho' they live together as Brethren, have each nevertheless distinct Properties and Interests, and none of us can demand from another Victuals or any thing of the Kind without Payment. One Man raises Corn and sells it, another raises Horses and he sells them, and thus every Man lives by his own

Labour and Industry, and no one has a Right to take away from another what he thus earns for himself; and all Victuals cost Money.

"That proper Care will be taken, as has formerly been done, to supply them with Horses and Carriages to make their Journey home as easy as possible.

"That we would be glad to do them any Service with the Neighbouring Governments, but we do not clearly understand this Matter: As to what is said of a Letter from the King of *England*, we do not believe there is any Truth in that Report; we have indeed heard of a Letter sent up to *Sasquehannah* from the Governor of *Maryland;* if he mentions any thing in it of Orders from the King of *England*, they should send some Persons to that Government to enquire into the Matter. As to the Claim they make on the Lands of *Maryland* and *Virginia*, we know not how this is supported; the Lands on *Sasquehannah*, we believe, belong to the *Six Nations*, by the Conquest of the *Indians* of that River; but how their Pretentions are made good to the Lands to the Southward, we know not; and we ought to be better informed before we can write on this Head.

"That we cannot prevent our Traders from going where they may best dispose of their Goods; we shall take the most proper Measures in our Power to hinder their carrying Rum in such Quantities, and we hope the *Indians* will give strict Charge to the Warriours to be cautious and prudent, that all Kind of Mischief may be prevented."

The *Indians* appearing satisfied with what had been spoke to them, said they had nothing further to offer. The Present was then delivered to them, which they received with great Thankfulness, those of each Nation alternately by themselves, and then all of them together, joining in their usual solemn Sound, when they express their Satisfaction. Having afterwards drank a friendly Glass, and taking Leave of the Proprietor, President and Council, they departed; and thus the Treaty ended.[13]

ROBERT CHARLES, *Secr.*

1. In response to New York and French military encroachments on their territory, the Six Nations had tried in 1726 to instigate the Shawnees, Lenapes, and other nations to attack the English while asking their western and northern allies to attack the French. These nations' refusal to join in these attacks prompted them in 1727 to reorient their defenses in an east-west direction. They accordingly tried to sell some part of the lower Susquehanna lands to Pennsylvania, but the colony claimed previous purchase. However, by 1731, James Logan needed their help in legitimating his illegal possession of Tulpehocken Valley lands that he had sold to the Palatine Germans, including Weiser's family, under the Penns' and the Lenapes' noses. The 1732 treaty promised the Iroquois an alliance with Pennsylvania that would strengthen the former's control over its near southern Indian neighbors in exchange for action in retrieving the Shawnees from the French sphere of influence. Many Lenapes and Shawnees had relocated to the Ohio country as a result of the 1727 reorientation. The 1732 treaty was a partial retraction of that new policy, with Pennsylvania being used as a counterweight against both France and New York (Jennings, *Ambiguous Iroquois Empire*, 297–316).

2. The Mohawks' rivalry with the other nations of the Confederacy for control of trade

with the English, as well as their wish to prevent suspicion in Albany about their dealings with Pennsylvania, may explain their absence from this treaty (cf. Jennings, *Ambiguous Iroquois Empire,* 316, 335).

3. Recent research about the use and meaning of wampum has dispelled the erroneous impression that the Iroquois and Lenapes used it as a form of money. As Gordon Brotherston's *Book of the Fourth World* makes clear, people in the precontact Americas used many different forms of writing that differed from the phonetically based forms upon which Europe and its descendents came to rely. The wampum exchanged during these treaties was a record and ratification of the words, promises, and transfers of deeds that occurred during them, but it was much more than a mere record. The Iroquois regarded wampum as a medium for clearing the channel of communication between two parties, for organizing the proceedings at the treaty council, for establishing a psychological connection between the speakers and listeners, for eliciting responses to proposals, and for regulating the flow of business in an orderly fashion. The participants perform a preliminary act of reading a message into the wampum, and the designated speaker of that message to the other party is asked to repeat the message, which is seen to increase the sacred power of the wampum. Whereas nonnative accounts of wampum have emphasized its retrospective function, wampum is seen by natives to function more importantly in a prospective manner. It shapes present and future events, including the needed periodical renewals of treaty agreements without which the parties are bound to forget their promises and obligations. A string of wampum is used for a communication of importance but not of enormous consequence, while a belt is used for a communication or agreement of premier importance and consequence (Foster, "Function of Wampum," 99–114). Wampum affirms a message, stresses its truth, and conveys its particular nature (Fenton, "Structure, Continuity, and Change," 17).

4. Note in these words allusions or enactments of the Condolence Ritual.

5. Jennings interprets this smallpox scare as Logan's method of keeping the Iroquois at his house so that he can ply them with his liquor and bribery tricks into doing his will (*Ambiguous Iroquois Empire,* 321n37).

6. The figure of a road encumbered or stopped up with trees will recur throughout these treaties. Non-Iroquois researchers have characterized this metaphor as part of a "forest diplomacy" in which nations were envisioned as traveling toward one another through the woods to treat and needing a clear path to ensure the success of the diplomatic mission (Jennings, "Glossary of Figures of Speech in Iroquois Political Rhetoric," *The History and Culture of Iroquois Diplomacy,* 121). Mann further notes that because there is an "important spiritual connection between men and (trees)/palisades," it becomes clearer that the idea of a tree falling across one's path refers to a peace messenger being waylaid in his diplomatic journey by a warrior of some sort. Because the Iroquois believed that "the souls of dead warriors travel into trees," even the more innocent image of a path made more difficult to travel because of logs and brush might take on a spiritual significance, wherein hindrances to communication could arise from our continuing connection to a world beyond the material one ("Sign in the Sky," 120–21).

7. The Iroquois frequently characterize their relationships with their allies as being of one heart, one mind, and one body, and as becoming one people. Matthew Dennis attributes this characterization to their "expansive vision of peace" (*Cultivating a Landscape,* 5). He notes that peace "for the Iroquois was not an abstract concept; rather it was concrete, integral, something grounded firmly in the social, economic, and political organization of their everyday lives. Fundamentally, they conceived of peace and lived it in terms of a domestic

harmony—which they institutionalized within households, lineages, clans, and villages. Peace was possibly only within a group cemented by consanguinity and a common sense of moral order" (7). Because consanguinity and a common moral order were not truly possible with the British, the Iroquois "transformed them symbolically . . . into kinspeople" and cultivated them as kinspeople through trade (8–9). Despite these expressions of oneness, the Iroquois knew that the British acted in their own interest first.

8. The six named were newly allied nations to the west of the Iroquois, apparently including the Miamis or Twightwees. These nations likely considered the League their elder brethren only insofar as being a necessary intermediary between themselves and the English.

9. Despite these assurances, Iroquois efforts to bring the Shawnees and Lenapes back toward Pennsylvania largely failed.

10. Because James Logan's traders were major participants in a coercive trading relationship with Native Americans that involved abuses with alcohol, it was very much in his interest for Pennsylvania's speech to blame these abuses on lack of self-control among them, detracting attention from the traders' unethical behavior as well as their illegal presence on Iroquois and other native lands. Franklin and his fellow commissioners in 1753 and 1756 would have a far different view on whether Pennsylvania's laws and powers could be made capable of addressing the problem.

11. The meeting of a noncapitalist economy with a capitalist economy is here revealed in the dialogic struggle between the Iroquois, whose discourse characterizes the English as lacking generosity and hospitality, and the English, whose subsequent discourse arranges the same material situation as a right to just compensation for private expenditures. The economic basis of our society forms the outer limits of our speech and the genres in which they are performed. This struggle for control of the ideological significance of the material conditions that the Iroquois confront shows a rare moment in which neither party is able to make its ideological interpretation dominant or "impart a supraclass, eternal character" to it. While this "social multiaccentuality" is evident in hindsight, it is also evident from subsequent history that on the British side a singular view of the situation continued to reign (Voloshinov, *Marxism and the Philosophy of Language,* 23). But as Johansen and Grinde point out, the Iroquois view may have helped to erode faith in the hierarchical schema upheld by the capitalist ideology of private exchange.

12. Mann has interpreted other such statements of this type as subtle threats (Personal Communications to Susan Kalter. American Literature Association conferences. San Diego, 30 May 1998 and Baltimore, 27–28 May 1999).

13. Pennsylvania always reports the Indians as leaving "satisfied," making it easier for them to blame future conflicts on treachery or ingratitude (Jennings, *Empire of Fortune,* 58). Given the stonewalling over the issues of trade here, the Iroquois more likely decided to leave these issues unresolved for the sake of the more important agreements that they had or might secure.

# THE TREATY

## HELD WITH THE *INDIANS*

## OF THE SIX NATIONS,

## AT *PHILADELPHIA*, IN *JULY*, 1742.

---

*PHILADELPHIA:*
Printed and Sold by B. FRANKLIN, at the New-Printing-Office,
near the Market. MDCCXLIII.

---

### THE TREATY, *&c.*

THE Deputies of the Six Nations having, at their last Visit, agreed to release their Claim to all the Land on both Sides of the River *Sasquehanah,* as far South as this Province extends, and to the Northward to those called the *Endless Mountains* or *Kittochtinny Hills;* in Consideration whereof, they then received a large Quantity of valuable Indian Goods for the Lands situate on the Eastern Side of the said River, but declined at that Time to receive any for those on the Western Side of the said River, chusing to defer the same till another Visit; A large Number arrived from these Nations at *Philadelphia,* on *Wednesday* the *30th* of *June,* with Deputies duly impowered to receive the said Goods; and acquainted the Governor, that being weary from the Fatigue of their long Journey, they should crave three or four Days to rest themselves before they proceeded to their Business: In the mean time they would wait on the Governor to discourse, according to their usual Method, about News and other Occurrences; which the Governor readily agreed to, and ask'd them when they would chuse to pay their first Visit; which they desiring might be on *Friday* the *2d* of *July* in the Afternoon, the Council was accordingly summon'd, and met at Mr. *Logan's* House, where were

PRESENT, The Honourable *GEORGE THOMAS,* Esq; Lieut. Governor.
*James Logan, Samuel Preston, Clement Plumsted, Thomas Lawrence,*
*Samuel Hasell, Ralph Asheton, Abraham Taylor, Robert Strettell,* Esqrs;
The Chiefs of the *Six Nations,* with the Chiefs of the *Shawanese.*
*CANASSATEEGO,* the *Onondago* Chief, Speaker.
*CONRAD WEISER,* Interpreter.

The Governor opened the Conference as follows.

"*BRETHREN,* The Proprietor having purchased certain Lands from your Nations about Six Years ago, a Moiety of what was agreed to be given in Consideration of that Purchase was at that Time delivered to them, and the other being at their own Desire left in the Proprietor's Hands, He pressed you by *Shikalamy* to send last Year for it, and would have been glad to have seen you and taken you by the Hand before his Departure. But as the Design of this Meeting is to hear your News and converse together in a free and friendly Manner, I shall say no more about the Goods than that they lye ready at the Proprietor's House, and will be delivered when you shall have sufficiently rested from the Fatigue of your Journey."

The Chief of the *Onondagoes* spoke

"*BRETHREN,* We propose to rest four Days, and then come to the main Business. At present we are at a private Conference about News, and have something of this Sort to mention to our Brother *Onas.*" And on the Governor's signifying they would be glad to know what it was, the Chief proceeded.

"*BRETHREN,* It is our Way when we come to our Brethren, or any other Persons, whom we live in strict Friendship with, to remove all Obstructions to a good Understanding; with this View we are to inform you of a Piece of disagreeable News that happen'd in our Journey.—Some White People living at a Place called *Conegocheegoe,* whose Names we cannot tell, nor whether they belong to this or the neighbouring Government, but one of them, as we heard, had his House burnt over his Head some Years ago, and he was brought down a Prisoner and committed to the Goal of this City: These People lighting of our young Warriours, as they were hunting, made some Proposals about the Purchasing of Land from them, and our young Men being indiscreet, and unacquainted with Publick Business, were foolish enough to hearken to them, and to receive five Duffil Strowds for two Plantations on the River *Cohongoronto.* A *Conestogo* Indian, and a *French* Indian, and some others that were in Company had three Duffil Strowds, and went away with them; and our young Men carried off the other two. As soon as this came to our Knowledge, we sent for our Warriours, and after examining and rebuking them severely, we took away their two Strowds, and publickly censured them for exposing us to our Brethren of *Pennsylvania* in doing a Thing so inconsistent with our Engagements to them; "You are, said we aloud, that all our People might hear and take Notice, to know and remember, that the Six Nations have obliged themselves to sell none of the Land that falls within the Province of *Pennsylvania* to any other but our Brother *Onas,* and that to sell Lands to any other is an high Breach of the League of Friendship.' Brethren, this rash Proceeding of our young Men makes us ashamed. We always mean well, and shall perform faithfully what we have promised: And we assure you, this Affair was transacted in the Manner we have related, without our Privity or Consent. And that you may be fully convinced of this, and of the Sincerity of our Intentions, we have brought you these Two Strowds [*here he presented two Red Strowds to the Governor*] they are the very

Strowds our foolish young Men received; we took them from them, and we give them to you to return to those white People who made the Bargain, and desire when the Strowds are returned to them, they may be told what we now say, and that we shall not confirm such Bargains nor any other that may interfere with our Engagements to our Brother *Onas.*"[1]

The Governor then spoke:

"*BRETHREN,* I thank you for this Piece of News; you have taken this Matter perfectly right. All Bargaining for Land within this Province, is, to be sure, a manifest Breach of your Contract with the Proprietors, and what we know you will not countenance. We have hitherto found the *Six Nations* faithful to their Engagements, and this is a fresh Instance of their Punctuality. You could not help these Mistakes of your young Men; they were not done in your Presence: But as several Inconveniences may arise from these kind of clandestine Sales, or from any such loose Sales of Land by your People, we desire you will, on your Return home, give publick Notice to all your Warriours not to bargain for any Land; or if they do, that you will not confirm such Bargains; and that this very Affair, together with what you have done therein, may be particularly reported to all your Nation assembled in Council."

The *Onondago* Chief promised to give such publick Notice; and desiring Liberty to mend his former Speech, he proceeded:

"*BRETHREN,* I forgot one Circumstance: Our People who pretended to sell the Land, demanded a Belt of Wampum of the Buyers to carry to their Chiefs; and on their declaring they had no Wampum, our Warriours said, they would not answer that their Chiefs would confirm this Bargain, since they never did any thing of this Nature without Wampum."

The Governor, after a short Pause, spoke:

"*BRETHREN of the Six Nations,* I shall take this Opportunity to relate to you a Piece of disagreeable News I received some Days ago in a Letter from *Le Tort* the Indian Trader, at *Allegheny,* who says, "That in *May* last some Indians of the *Taway* Nation, supposed by us to be the *Twightwees,* in their Return from War, called and stayed some Time with the *Shawanese;* who being asked, and denying they had brought either Scalps or Prisoners, the *Shawanese* suspecting them, had the Curiosity to search their Bags, and finding two Scalps in them that by the Softness of the Hair did not feel like Indian Scalps, they wash'd them clean and found them to be the Scalps of some Christians. On this Discovery, the *Twightees* were so much ashamed, that they stole away from their Town in the Night-time; and coming, as they afterwards understood, to a little Village belonging to the *Shawanese,* they told our People that their Hearts were full of Grief; for, as they came along the Road, they found it all bloody; and having good Cause to believe it was made bloody with the Blood of some of the White Brethren, they had very sorrowfully swept the Road; and desired them to inform the Governor of *Pensilvania* of their (the *Twightwees*) Grief;

and how they had swept the Road clean.' *Le Tort* adds, on Behalf of the *Shawanese*, "That they were much troubled and grieved at this unfortunate Accident; and prayed, as they had no Concern in it, more than by being Instruments to discover it, their Brethren would not blame them, nor suffer a Misunderstanding to arise between them on this Account: They would sweep the Road clean, and wipe all the Blood away; and desired their Brethren would be satisfied with this, and not weep too much for a Misfortune that might not happen again as long as the Sun and Moon shone.'

"The Person who delivered me *Le Tort*'s Letter, brought this Bundle of Skins as a Present to me; but I told the Messenger, I would not meddle with it; he might leave it if he pleased: The Affair appear'd to me in a bad Light, and I would represent it to the *Six Nations*, who were expected in Town every Day. This is the Fact as I have it from *Le Tort:* I desire to be inform'd if you know any thing of this Matter; and if you do not, that you will make diligent Enquiry who committed the Murder, and who are the unhappy Sufferers, and assist us to obtain Satisfaction, if it shall appear to be any of our Fellow-Subjects that have been treated in this Manner."

*To inforce this Request, I present you with this String of Wampum.*

The *Onondago* Chief, in Reply, said:

"*BRETHREN,* We take this Information kindly at your Hands; we will take this String of Wampum Home with us to our Lodgings, and there consult about the most regular and proper Steps to be taken by us to answer your Expectations; and when we have duly considered the Matter, we will return you an Answer."

Upon this the Governor put an End to the Conference; and calling for Wine and other Liquors, according to the *Indian* Custom, after a decent and chearful Entertainment, the *Indians* withdrew.

At a COUNCIL held at the Proprietor's House, *July* 5. 1742.
PRESENT The Honourable *GEORGE THOMAS,* Esq; Lieut. Governor.
*James Logan, Clement Plumsted,* Esqrs.
With several Gentlemen of the Town.
*The Chiefs of the Six Nations.*

It being judg'd proper, at this critical Time, when we are in daily Expectation of a *French* War, to sound the *Indians,* and discover what Dependance we might have on them, in case their Aid should be wanted; an handsome Dinner was provided for their Chiefs; and after they had made an hearty Meal, and drank his Majesty's Health, the Proprietors, and the Health of the *Six Nations,* the Chiefs gave the solemn Cry, in Testimony of their Thanks, for the Honour done them. And soon after the Governor began, in a free Way, to enquire for what Reason the *Senecas* were not come down, since they had an equal Right to a Share of the Goods with the other Nations.——*Canassateego,* their Speaker, said, "The *Senecas* were in great Distress, on Account of a Famine that raged in their Country, which had reduced them to such Want, that a

Father had been obliged to kill two of his Children to preserve his own and the rest of his Family's Lives; and they could not now come down, but had given Directions about their Share of the Goods."——The Governor express'd his Concern for the unhappy Circumstances of their Brethren of the *Seneca* Nation; and, after a short Respite, enquired if any of their Deputies were then at *Canada,* and whether the *French* Governor was making any warlike Preparations. And on their answering, *Yes;* the Governor said, with a smiling, pleasant Countenance, "I suppose if the *French* should go to War with us, you will join them." The *Indians* conferr'd together for some Time, and then *Canassateego,* in a cheerful lively Manner, made Answer.—"We assure you, the Governor of *Canada* pays our Nations great Court at this Time, well knowing of what Consequence we are to the *French* Interest: He has already told us, he was uncovering the Hatchet and sharpening it, and hoped, if he should be obliged to lift it up against the *English,* their Nations would remain neuter and assist neither Side.——But we will now speak plainly to our Brethren: Why should we, who are one Flesh with you, refuse to help you, whenever you want our Assistance?—We have continued a long Time in the strictest League of Amity and Friendship with you, and we shall always be faithful and true to you our old and good Allies.—The Governor of *Canada* talks a great deal, but ten of his Words do not go so far as one of yours.—We do not look towards them; We look towards you; and you may depend on our Assistance." Whilst the *Onondago* Chief made this open and hearty Declaration, all the other *Indians* made frequently that particular Kind of Noise which is known to be a Mark of Approbation.—The Governor bid the Interpreter tell *Canassateego,* "He did not set on foot this Enquiry from any Suspicion he had of the *Six Nations* wanting a due Regard for the *English.*—Our Experience of their Honour and Faith would not permit us to think any other of them than that they would esteem our Friends their Friends, and our Enemies their Enemies, agreeable to the strict Union which had ever subsisted between us.—As to the Governor of *Canada,* they need not mind what he said.—The *English,* on equal Terms, had beat the *French,* and could beat them again: And were they but to consider the Advantages which the *English* have, by possessing so many large and populous Countries and so many good Ports on the Continent of *America,* they would soon see who had most Reason to fear a War, the *French* or the *English.*[2]

Here the Conversation drop'd; and, after another Glass of Wine, the *Indians* resumed the Discourse, by asking whether their Brethren had not been for some time engaged in a War with the King of *Spain,* and what Successes they had met with.

The Governor told them, the King of *Great Britain* lived in an Island, and being surrounded with the Sea, his chief Strength lay in his Ships; in which he was so much superior to his Enemies, that they were seldom to be met with on the broad Ocean, but sculk'd and hid themselves, only venturing out now and then; and whenever they did they were almost sure to be taken; and that the King of *Great Britain* had, with his Ships, beat down or taken several of the *Spaniards* Great Forts in *Ameri-*

*ca.*—The *Indians* said they were pleased to hear their Brethren were an Over-match for their Enemies, and wish'd them good Success.

The Governor then inquired into the State and Condition of the Nations to the Westward of the Great Lakes, and whether they had any Warriours then in those Countries? Whether they had concluded Peace with the Southern *Indians?* And whether they had heard what their Deputies had done at *Albany?*

They made Answer: That they had always Abundance of their Men out amongst the Nations situate to the West of their Lakes.—That they had kindled a Fire with a vast many Nations, some whereof were Tributaries,[3] and they had a good Understanding with all.—They set out from their own Country in Company with two Sets of Deputies, one going to hold a Treaty with the Southern *Indians,* and they believed a Peace would be concluded: The other going to meet the Governor of *New-York,* at *Albany;* but they could not tell what had been done at either Place.—On their Return, they were to hold a General Council, and would inform their Brethren of these Particulars.

Then the Governor put an End to the Conference, by telling the *Indians* the Goods would be delivered to them at a Council to be held to morrow Afternoon at the Meeting-House.

At a COUNCIL held in the Meeting-House, *Philadelphia, July* 6. 1742.
PRESENT, The Honourable *GEORGE THOMAS,* Esq; Lieut. Governor.
*James Logan, Samuel Preston, Clement Plumsted, Ralph Asheton,*
*Abraham Taylor, Robert Strettell,* Esqrs;
*CANASSATEEGO,* Chief of the *Onondagoes,* Speaker.
SHICALAMY; and a great Number of Indians,
whose Names are as follows, *viz.*

ONONTOGOES. *Sawegaty, Caxhayion,* Counsellors. *Saguyassatha, Kayadoghratie* alias *Slanaghquasy, Rotier-uwughton, Tokaughaah, Tiorughwaghthe, Tokanoungoh, Aronty-oony, Tohanohawighton, Tioghwatoony, Auughrahysey.*

CAIYOUQUOS. *Sahugh-sowa, Tohatgaghthus,* Chiefs. *Tokany-esus, Runho-hihio, Kanadoghary, Zior-aghquaty, Sagu-iughwatha,* alias *Cadcaradasey. Sca-yenties, Tats-heghteh, Alligh-waheis, Tayo-quario, Hogh degh runtu, Rotehn Haghtyackon,* Captain. *Sawoalieselhohaa, Sagughsa-eck, Uwantakeraa, Horuhot, Osoghquaa, Tuyanoegon.*

ANOYIUTS *or* ONEIDAS. *Saristaquoh, Ungquaterughiathe* alias *Shikelimo,* Chiefs. *Tottowakerha, Taraghkoerus, Onughkallydawwy,* a noted young Chief. *Onughnaxqua,* Chief. *Tawyiakaarat, Tohathuyongochtha, Sughnakaarat, Taghneghdoerus, Tokanyiadaroeyon, Sagogughyatha, Rahehius, Tokanusoegon.*

JENONTOWANOS *or* SENECAS. *Karugh iagh Raghquy,* Captain. *Tahn heentus, Onontyiack.*

TUSCARROROS. *Sawontka, Ti-ieroes, Cloghsytowax,* Chiefs. *Tokaryhoegon,* Captain. *Oghioghseh, Tieleghweghson, Tougrotha, Yorughianego, Ot-quehig, Squagh-*

*ky, Sayadyio, Onughsowûghton, Cherigh wâstho, Aghsûnteries, Tion ogh scôghtha, Saligh wanaghson, Ohn-wâasey, Tocar-eher* [died since at Tulpehokin.] *Tohan-atâkqua, Kanyhâag.*

SHAWANOES. *Wehwehlaky,* Chief. *Aset teywa, Asoghqua, Maya minickysy, Wawy-ia Beeseny.*

Canestogo *Indians that speak the* Onayiut's *Language. Tior Haasery,* Chief. *Ta-nigh wackerau, Karha Cawyiat, Kayen quily quo.*

CANOYIAS *or* NANTIKOKES *of* Canestogo. *Des-seheg, Ichqua que heck, Quesa-maag, Ayiok-ius.*

DELAWARES *of* Shamokin. *Olumapies, Lingehanoah,* Chiefs. *Kelly macquan, Quitie-yquont, Pishquiton, Nena chy haut.*

DELAWARES *from the* Forks. *Onutpe, Lawye quohwon al. Nutimus,* Chiefs. *Towe-ghkappy. Cornelius Spring,* and others.

CONRAD WEISER, CORNELIUS SPRING, *Interpreters.*

And a great Number of the Inhabitants of *Philadelphia.*

The Governor, having commanded Silence, spoke as follows:

"*Friends and Brethren of the Six Nations,* Six Years ago a Number of your Chiefs obliged us with a Visit, when they agreed, on Behalf of your Nations, to the Release of certain Lands on both Sides the River *Sasquehannah,* to the Southward of the *Endless-Mountains,* and within the Limits and Bounds of the King's Grant of this Province. In Consideration of which, a certain Quantity of Goods was agreed on and delivered as a full Satisfaction for the said Lands lying on the Eastern Side of the said River: And for the Lands on the Western Side of the said River, you desired the Payment should be deferr'd till another Opportunity. These Goods, which are exactly the same in Quantity as those you received the last Time the Chiefs of your Nations were here, have been ready a considerable Time, and kept in Expectation of your Coming for them: And now you are come down fully impowered by your respective Councils to receive them, we are well pleased to deliver them: Leaving it to you to make a fair and equal Division of them amongst yourselves. We are sorry for the Absence of our Brethren the *Senecas,* and much more so that it should be owing to their Distress at Home by a Famine that rages in their Country:—A Famine so great that you tell us a Father has been obliged to sacrifice one Part of his Family, even his own Children, for the Support and Preservation of himself, and the other Part.—We heartily commiserate their Condition, and do not doubt but you will do them fair and ample Justice in the Disposal of their Part of the Goods in such Manner as they have instructed you. You shall now hear the List of the Goods read to you."

Here, by the Governor's Order, the List of the Goods was read over, *viz.*

500 *Pounds of Powder.*
600 *Pounds of Lead.*
45 *Guns.*
60 *Kettles.*
100 *Tobacco-Tongs.*
100 *Scissars.*

| | | | |
|---|---|---|---|
| 60 | *Strowd-Matchcoats.* | 500 | *Awl-Blades.* |
| 100 | *Blankets.* | 120 | *Combs.* |
| 100 | *Duffel Matchcoats.* | 2000 | *Needles.* |
| 200 | *Yards Half-thick.* | 1000 | *Flints.* |
| 100 | *Shirts.* | 24 | *Looking-Glasses.* |
| 40 | *Hats.* | 2 | *Pounds of Vermilion.* |
| 40 | *Pair Shoes & Buckles.* | 100 | *Tin-Pots.* |
| 40 | *Pair Stockings.* | 1000 | *Tobacco-Pipes.* |
| 100 | *Hatchets.* | 200 | *Pounds of Tobacco.* |
| 500 | *Knives.* | 24 | *Dozen* of *Gartering,* and |
| 100 | *Hoes.* | 25 | *Gallons of Rum.* |

Then the Governor told them that the Goods, of which the Particulars had been just read to them, were in the Meeting-House, and would be sent to whatever Place they would direct.

The Governor then proceeded:

"*BRETHREN,* You have often heard of the Care that your great and good Friend and Brother *William Penn* took at all Times to cultivate a perfect good Harmony with all the *Indians:* Of this your Nations have ever been fully sensible; but more especially a Number of your Chiefs, about ten Years ago, when, on the Arrival of a Son of your said great Friend *William Penn,* large and valuable Presents were exchanged by us with you; a new Road was made and clear'd; a new Fire kindled; and the Chain of Friendship made stronger so as to last while the Sun and Moon endure.

"And now we cannot but congratulate ourselves that your Coming should happen at a Time when we are in daily Expectation of a War being declared between the King of *England,* and the *French* King, well knowing that should such a War happen, it must very sensibly affect you, considering your Situation in the Neighbourhood of *Canada.* Your Coming at this Juncture is particularly fortunate, since it gives us an Opportunity of mentioning several Things that may be necessary to be settled between People so strictly and closely united as we are.—An Union not to be express'd by any thing less than the affectionate Regards which Children of the same Parents bear for each other, as conceiving ourselves to be one Flesh and one People.[4]

"The utmost Care therefore ought mutually to be taken by us on both Sides, that the Road between us be kept perfectly clear and open, and no Lets nor the least Obstruction be suffered to lie in the Way; or if any should by Accident be found, that may hinder our free Intercourse and Correspondence, it must forthwith be removed."

*To inforce this, We lay down a String of Wampum.*

"In next Place, We, on our Part, shall inlarge our Fire that burns between us. We shall provide more Fewel to increase it and make it burn brighter and clearer, and give a stronger and more lasting Light and Warmth."

*In Evidence of our sincere Intentions, We lay down this Belt of Wampum.*

"In the last Place, considering the Obligations we are mutually under by our several Treaties, "That we should hear with our Ears for you, and you hear with your Ears for us.' We shall at all Times very willingly give you the earliest and best Intelligence of any Designs that may be form'd to your Disadvantage.—And if you discover any Preparations that can hurt us, we desire you will immediately dispatch some suitable Person in whom we can place a Confidence, to give us a proper Information."

*To inforce this Request, as well as to brighten the Chain, we lay down this other Belt of Wampum.*

On the Governor's concluding the Speech, the solemn Cry by way of Approbation was repeated by the *Indians* as many Times as there were Nations present; and then *Canassateego* rose up and spoke.

"*BRETHREN,* We thank you for your kind Speech: What you have said is very agreeable to us; and to-morrow when we have deliberated on the several Matters recommended to us, we will give you our Answer. We desire, as our Time will be wholly taken up in Council, you will order the Goods, to be carried back to the Proprietaries to prevent their being lost, and that they may continue there till we call for them."

At a COUNCIL held in the Meeting-House, *July* 7. 1742.
PRESENT, The Honourable *GEORGE THOMAS,* Esq; Lieut. Governor.
*James Logan, Samuel Preston, Thomas Lawrence, Samuel Hasell, Abraham Taylor, Robert Strettell,* Esqrs;

*CANASSATEEGO*'s Speech on Behalf of the *Six Nations.*

"*BRETHREN, the Governor and Council, and all present,*

According to our Promise we now propose to return you an Answer to the several Things mentioned to us Yesterday, and shall beg Leave to speak to Publick Affairs first, tho' they were what you spoke to last. On this Head you Yesterday put us in Mind, first, "Of *William Penn's* early and constant Care to cultivate Friendship with all the *Indians;* of the Treaty we held with one of his Sons, about ten Years ago; and of the Necessity there is at this Time of keeping the Roads between us clear and free from all Obstructions.' We are all very sensible of the kind Regard that good Man *William Penn* had for all the *Indians,* and cannot but be pleased to find that his Children have the same. We well remember the Treaty you mention held with his Son on his Arrival here, by which we confirmed our League of Friendship that is to last as long as the Sun and Moon endure: In Consequence of this, We, on our Part, shall preserve the Road free from all Incumbrances; in Confirmation whereof we lay down this String of Wampum.

"You in the next Place said you would inlarge the Fire and make it burn brighter, which we are pleased to hear you mention; and assure you, we shall do the same, by adding to it more Fewel, that it may still flame out more strongly than ever: In the last Place, you were pleased to say that we are bound, by the strictest Leagues, to watch for each others Preservation; that we should hear with our Ears for you, and you hear with your Ears for us: This is equally agreeable to us; and we shall not fail to give you early Intelligence whenever any thing of Consequence comes to our Knowledge: And to encourage you to do the same, and to nourish in your Hearts what you have spoke to us with your Tongues, about the Renewal of our Amity and the Brightening of the Chain of Friendship; we confirm what we have said with another Belt of Wampum.

"*BRETHREN,* We received from the Proprietors, yesterday, some Goods in Consideration of our Release of the Lands on the West-Side of *Sasquehannah.* It is true we have the full Quantity according to Agreement; but if the Proprietor had been here himself, we think, in Regard of our Numbers and Poverty, he would have made an Addition to them.—If the Goods were only to be divided amongst the *Indians* present, a single Person would have but a small Portion; but if you consider what Numbers are left behind, equally entitled with us to a Share, there will be extremely little. We therefore desire, if you have the Keys of the Proprietor's Chest, you will open it, and take out a little more for us.

"We know our Lands are now become more valuable. The white People think we do not know their Value; but we are sensible that the Land is everlasting, and the few Goods we receive for it are soon worn out and gone. For the Future we will sell no Lands but when Brother *Onas* is in the Country; and we will know beforehand the Quantity of the Goods we are to receive. Besides, we are not well used with respect to the Lands still unsold by us. Your People daily settle on these Lands, and spoil our Hunting.—We must insist on your Removing them, as you know they have no Right to settle to the Northward of *Kittochtinny-Hills.*—In particular, we renew our Complaints against some People who are settled at *Juniata,* a Branch of *Sasquahannah,* and all along the Banks of that River, as far as *Mahaniay;* and desire they may be forthwith made to go off the Land; for they do great Damage to our Cousins the *Delawares.*

"We have further to observe, with respect to the Lands lying on the West Side of *Sasquahannah* that tho' Brother *Onas* (meaning the Proprietor) has paid us for what his People possess, yet some Parts of that Country have been taken up by Persons whose Place of Residence is to the South of this Province, from whom we have never received any Consideration. This Affair was recommended to you by our Chiefs at our last Treaty; and you then, at our earnest Desire, promised to write a Letter to that Person who has the Authority over those People, and to procure us his Answer: As we have never heard from you on this Head, we want to know what you have done in it. If you have not done any thing, we now renew our Request, and desire you will inform the Person whose People are seated on our Lands, that that Country belongs to us, in Right of Conquest; we having bought it with our Blood, and taken it from our Enemies in fair War; and we expect, as Owners of that Land, to receive such a Consideration for it as the Land is worth. We desire you will press him to send us a positive Answer: Let him say *Yes* or *No:* If he says Yes, we will treat with him; if No, we are able to do ourselves Justice; and we will do it, by going to take Payment ourselves.

"It is customary with us to make a Present of Skins whenever we renew our Treaties. We are ashamed to offer our Brethren so few; but your Horses and Cows have eat the Grass our Deer used to feed on.[5] This has made them scarce, and will, we hope, plead in Excuse for our not bringing a larger Quantity: If we could have spared more we would have given more; but we are really poor; and desire you'll not consider the Quantity, but, few as they are, accept them in Testimony of our Regard."

*Here they gave the Governor a Bundle of Skins.*

The Governor immediately replied:

"*BRETHREN,* We thank you for the many Declarations of Respect you have given us in this solemn Renewal of our Treaties: We receive, and shall keep your String and Belts of Wampum, as Pledges of your Sincerity, and desire those we gave you may be carefully preserved, as Testimonies of ours.

"In Answer to what you say about the Proprietaries,—They are all absent, and have taken the Keys of their Chest with them; so that we cannot, on their Behalf, enlarge the Quantity of Goods: Were they here, they might, perhaps, be more generous; but we cannot be liberal for them.—The Government will, however, take your Request into Consideration, and, in Regard to your Poverty, may perhaps make you a Present. I but just mention this now, intending to refer this Part of your Speech to be answered at our next Meeting.

"The Number of Guns, as well as every thing else, answers exactly with the Particulars specified in your Deed of Conveyance, which is more than was agreed to be given you. It was your own Sentiments, that the Lands on the West Side of *Sasquahannah* were not so valuable as those on the East; and an Abatement was to be made, proportionable to the Difference in Value: But the Proprietor overlooked this, and ordered the full Quantity to be delivered, which you will look on as a Favour.

"It is very true, that Lands are of late become more valuable: but what raises their Value? Is it not entirely owing to the Industry and Labour used by the white People in their Cultivation and Improvement? Had not they come amongst you, these Lands would have been of no Use to you, any further than to maintain you. And is there not, now you have sold so much, enough left for all the Purposes of Living?——What you say of the Goods, that they are soon worn out, is applicable to every thing; but you know very well, that they cost a great deal Money, and the Value of Land is no more than it is worth in Money.[6]

"On your former Complaints against People's Setling the Lands on *Juniata,* and from thence all along on the River *Sasquahannah* as far as *Mahaniahy,* some Magistrates were sent expressly to remove them; and we thought no Persons would presume to stay after that."

Here they interrupted the Governor, and said:—"These Persons who were sent did not do their Duty: So far from removing the People, they made Surveys for themselves, and they are in League with the Trespassers. We desire more effectual Methods may be used, and honester Persons imploy'd."

Which the Governor promised, and then proceeded:
"*BRETHREN,* According to the Promise made at our last Treaty with you, Mr. *Logan,* who was at that Time President, did write to the Governor of *Maryland,* that he might make you Satisfaction for such of your Lands as his People had taken up; but did not receive one Word from him upon that Head. I will write to him again, and endeavour to procure you a satisfactory Answer. We do not doubt but he will do you Justice: But we exhort you to be careful not to exercise any Acts of Violence towards his People, as they likewise are our Brethren, and Subjects of the same Great King; and therefore Violence towards them must be productive of very evil Consequences.

"I shall conclude what I have to say at this Time with Acknowledgments for your Present; which is very agreeable to us, from the Expressions of Regard used by you in presenting it: Gifts of this Nature receiving their Value from the Affection of the Giver, and not from the Quantity or Price of the Thing given."

At a COUNCIL held at *Philadelphia, July* 8. *1742.*
PRESENT, The Honourable *GEORGE THOMAS,* Esq; Lieut. Governor.
*James Logan, Samuel Preston, Clement Plumsted, Thomas Lawrence,*
*Samuel Hasell, Ralph Asheton, Abraham Taylor, Robert* Strettell, Esqrs.

The Board taking into Consideration, whether it be proper or not at this Time to make a Present to the *Indians* of the Six Nations now in Town, in Return for their Present to this Government at Yesterday's Treaty:

*Resolved,*

That it is highly fit and proper that a Present be made to the said *Indians* at this Time.

And it is the Opinion of this Board, that the said Present should be of the Value of £.500, or at least £.300.

And it is recommended to Mr. *Logan,* Mr. *Preston,* and Mr. *Lawrence* to acquaint Mr. *Kinsey;* the Speaker of the Assembly, with the Opinion of this Board; and that they request him to confer with such other Members of Assembly as are in Town, and report their Sentiments thereupon.

The Board taking into Consideration the Threats express'd by the *Indians* at the Treaty yesterday, against the Inhabitants of *Maryland,* settled on certain Lands on the West Side of *Sasquahannah,* which the *Indians* claim, and for which they require Satisfaction; and considering, that should those Threats, in any sort, be put in Execution, not only the Inhabitants of *Maryland,* but of this Government, and all His Majesty's Subjects on the Northern Continent of *America,* may thereby be involved in much Trouble: It is the Opinion of this Board, that the Governor write to the Governor of *Maryland* without Delay, to inform him of the *Indians* Complaints and Threats, and to request a satisfactory Answer; and that his Letter be sent by a special Messenger, at the Publick Expence.

At a COUNCIL held *July* 9. 1742.
PRESENT, The Honourable *GEORGE THOMAS*, Esq; Lieut. Governor,
*James Logan, Samuel Preston, Clement Plumsted, Ralph Asheton,*
*Samuel Hasell, Thomas Lawrence, Robert Strettell,* Esqrs.
And Mr. *Peters.*

The Governor informed the Board, that the *Indian* Chiefs dining with him Yesterday, after Dinner delivered their Answer to two Affairs of Consequence:

The first related to the violent Battery committed on *William Webb,* in the Forks of *Delaware,* whereby his Jaw-Bone was broke, and his Life greatly endangered, by an unknown *Indian.*[7] *Canassatego* repeating the Message delivered to the *Six Nations* by *Shickcalamy,* in the Year 1740, with a String of Wampum, said in Answer: "The *Six Nations* had made diligent Enquiry into the Affair, and had found out the *Indian* who had committed the Fact; he lived near *Asopus,* and had been examined and severely reprov'd: And they hoped, as *William Webb* was recovered, the Governor would not expect any further Punishment; and therefore they returned the String of Wampum received from their Brethren, by the Hand of *Shickcalamy,* in Token that they had fully comply'd with their Request."

I thank'd them for their Care; but reminded them, that tho' the Man did not die, yet he lay a long Time in extreme Misery, and would never recover the free Use of his Speech, and was rendered less able to get his Livelihood, and in such Cases the *English* Laws obliged the Assailant to make good all Damages, besides paying for the Pain endured.—But as the *Indian* was, in all Probability, poor and unable to make Satisfaction, I told them, that for their Sake I would forgive him; adding, had *Webb* died I make no Doubt but you would have put the *Indian* to Death, just as we did two of our People who had killed an *Indian;* we caused them to be hung on a Gallows, in the Presence of many Hundreds of our People, to deter all others from doing the like.[8] *Canassatego* made me this Reply: "The *Indians* know no Punishment but Death; they have no such Thing as pecuniary Mulcts; if a Man be guilty of a Crime, he is either put to Death, or the Fault is overlook'd. We have often heard of your Hanging-up those two Persons; but as none of our *Indians* saw the Men die, many believe they were not hanged, but transported to some other Colony: And it would be satisfactory to the *Indians,* if, for the Future, some of them be sent for, to be Witnesses of such Executions." I assured them, that whoever gave them that Information, abused them; for the Persons certainly suffered Death, and in the Presence of all the People.

*Canassatego* then proceeded to give an Answer to what was said to them the 2d Instant relating to *Le Tort's* Letter: "That they had, in Council, considered in what

Manner the Matter recommended to them ought to be conducted; and they were of Opinion, that as the *Shawanese,* not the *Twightwys* (for they knew so much of it that the People were of the *Twightwy* Nation in whose Bags the Scalps were found) had sent me a Present of Skins, I should, in return, send them a Blanket or a Kettle, and with it a very sharp Message, that tho' they had done well in sweeping the Road from Blood, yet that was but a small Part of their Duty; they ought not to have suffered the *Twightwys,* after their Lie and the Discovery of the Scalps, to have left them, "til they had given a full and true Account how they came by them, whose Scalps they were, and in what Place, and for what Reason the Men were kill'd; and when they had been fully satisfied of all these Particulars, then it was their Duty to have given Information to the Government where the white People lived, that the Murderers might be complained against, and punished by the Nation they belong'd to: And as the *Shawanese* had omitted to perform the Part of Brethren, that I should reprove them for it, and charge them to make Amends for their Neglect, by using all possible Expedition to come at the Knowledge of these Things, and to aid their Brethren the white People in obtaining Justice.

The Minutes of the preceding Council being read, Mr. *Logan,* in Pursuance of the Board's Direction of Yesterday, reported, on Behalf of himself and the other Gentlemen to whom it was recommended, that they had confer'd with Mr. *Kinsey,* and requested him to consult the other Members of the Assembly concerning the making a Present to the *Indians;* and that Mr. *Kinsey* having collected the Sentiments of several Members of the Assembly in Town whom he had confer'd with on that Subject, found them generally of Opinion, that a Present should at this Time be made; but that they had declined nominating any Sum: However, that Mr. *Kinsey* had given it as his own Opinion, that the Governor and Council might go as far as *Three Hundred Pounds.*

And accordingly it is refer'd to Mr. *Logan,* Mr. *Preston* and Mr. *Lawrence,* to consider of and prepare a proper List of the Goods whereof the Present should be composed, to the Value of *Three Hundred Pounds* as aforesaid; advising with the Interpreter as to the Quantity and Quality.

At a COUNCIL held at the Proprietor's the 9th of *July,* P. M, 1742.
PRESENT, The Honourable *GEORGE THOMAS,* Esq; Lieut. Governor,
*James Logan, Robert Strettell, Samuel Preston,*
*Abraham Taylor,* Esqrs;
The CHIEFS of the *Six Nations.* *SASSOONAN,* and *Delawares.*
NUTIMUS, and the *Fork-Indians.* *CONRAD WEISER,* Interpreter.

The Governor spoke to the Chiefs of the *Six Nations* as follows:

"*BRETHREN,* The last Time the Chiefs of the *Six Nations* were here, they were informed, that your Cousins, a Branch of the *Delawares,* gave this Province some Disturbance about the Lands the Proprietor purchased from them, and for which their Ancestors had received a valuable Consideration above *Fifty-five* Years ago, as appears by a Deed now lying on the Table.—Sometime after this, *Conrad Weiser* delivered to your Brother *Thomas Penn* your Letter, wherein you request of him and *James Logan* that they would not buy Land, &c.—This has been shewn to them and interpreted; notwithstanding which they have continued their former Disturbances, and have had the Insolence to write Letters to some of the Magistrates of this Government, wherein they have abused your good Brethren our worthy Proprietaries, and treated them with the utmost Rudeness and Ill-Manners. Being loth, from our Regard to you, to punish them as they deserve, I sent two Messengers to inform them that you were expected here, and should be acquainted with their Behaviour.—As you, on all Occasions, apply to us to remove all white People that are settled on Lands before they are purchased from you, and we do our Endeavours to turn such People off; we now expect from you, that you will cause these *Indians* to remove from the Lands in the Forks of *Delaware,* and not give any further Disturbance to the Persons who are now in Possession.

*To inforce This we lay down a String of Wampum.*

Then were read the several Conveyances, the Paragraph of the Letter wrote by the Chiefs of the *Six Nations* relating to the *Delawares;* the Letters of the *Fork-Indians* to the Governor and Mr. *Langhorne,* and a Draught of the Land; and then delivered to *Conrad Weiser,* who was desired to interpret them to the Chiefs when they should take this Affair into their Consideration.

At a COUNCIL held *July* 10. 1742.

PRESENT, The Honourable *GEORGE THOMAS,* Esq; Lieut. Governor.

*James Logan, Samuel Preston, Clement Plumsted, Samuel Hasell, Thomas Lawrence, Robert Strettell, Abraham Taylor,* Esqrs.

The Governor laid before the Board an Extract from the Treaty held here the 7th Instant with the *Indians* of the *Six Nations,* so far as it related to the Inhabitants of *Maryland;* as also a Letter he had prepared for the Governor of *Maryland* upon that Subject; both of which being approved were ordered to be transcribed fair, in order to be dispatch'd to morrow Morning: The Letter is as follows:

*SIR,* *Philadelphia, July 10. 1742.*

*THE inclosed Extract of the Speech made by the Chiefs of the* Six Nations, *before a very numerous Audience, in this Place, with my Answer to it, is of so great Importance to all his Majesty's Colonies in this Part of his Dominions, and to your Government in particular, that I have imploy'd a special Messenger to deliver it you. I hope you will enable me to send them a satisfactory Answer. It would be impertinent in me to say more to one so well informed as you are of these Nations, and of their absolute Authority over all the* Indians *bordering upon us, or of the Advantages of maintaining a strict Friendship with them at all Times, but most especially at this critical Juncture.*

I am, Yours, *&c.*

An Account exhibited by *Conrad Weiser* of his Expences upon the *Indians* and *Indian* Affairs, from *February* last to *July* 1. 1742, amounting to £. 36 18 *s.* 3 *d.* was laid before the Board, and examined, and allow'd to be a just and very moderate Account.

And the Board taking into Consideration the many signal Services performed by the said *Conrad Weiser* to this Government, his Diligence and Labour in the Service thereof, and his Skill in the *Indian* Languages and Methods of Business, are of Opinion that the said *Conrad* should be allowed as a Reward from the Province at this Time the Sum of *Thirty Pounds,* at least, besides Payment of his said Account.

At a COUNCIL held at the Great Meeting-House. *July* 10. *P. M.* 1742.
PRESENT The Honourable *GEORGE THOMAS,* Esq; Lieut. Governor.
*James Logan, Samuel Preston, Thomas Lawrence, Samuel Hasell,*
*Abraham Taylor, Robert Strettell,* Esqrs.
*CANASSATEGO, SHICKCALAMY,* And other *Indian* Chiefs.
*CONRAD WEISER,* Interpreter.
And a great Number of the Inhabitants of *Philadelphia.*

The Governor spoke to the *Indians* as follows:

"*BRETHREN,* This Meeting will be short: It is in order to make you a Present from the Governor, the Council, the Assembly, and all our People. *William Penn* was known to you to be a good and faithful Friend to all the *Indians:* He made a League of Friendship with you, by which we became one People. This League has often since been renew'd by friendly Treaties; and as you have declared that the Friendship shall always last on your Parts, so we would have you believe that it shall remain inviolable on ours while Sun and Moon endure.

"I gave you some Expectation of a Present, and we have it now ready to deliver to you. This Present is made you by the Governor, Council, Assembly, and all our People, in Consideration of the great Miseries and Distresses which you our good Friends have lately suffered. This will be some Relief to you for the present, and it's to be hoped your own Industry will soon retrieve your Circumstances.

"It has sometimes happened, and may happen again, that idle and untrue Stories are carried to you concerning us your Brethren; but our Desire is, and we expect it from you, that you will give no Credit to them; for we are, and always will be, your steady and sincere Friends.

"It is a Custom when we renew our Treaties with our good Friends the *Indians,* to clear the Road and make our Fire burn bright: We have done so upon this Occasion; and, in Token of our Sincerity, we deliver you, as a Present from the Governor, the Council, the Assembly, and all the People of *Pennsylvania,* the following Goods, *viz.*

24 *Guns.*
600 *Pounds of Lead.*
50 *Hoes*
50 *Hatchets.*

| | | | |
|---|---|---|---|
| 600 | *Pounds of Powder.* | 5 | *Pounds of Vermilion.* |
| 25 | *Strowdes* } *Matchcoats.* | 10 | *Dozen of Knives.* |
| 90 | *Duffel* } *Matchcoats.* | 8 | *Dozen of Gimblets.* |
| 30 | *Blankets.* | 2 | *Dozen of Tobacco-Tongs.* |
| 62 | *Yards of Half-Thicks.* | 25 | *Pair of Shoes.* |
| 60 | *Ruffled Shirts.* | 25 | *Pair of Stockings,* |
| 25 | *Hats,* | 25 | *Pair of Buckles,* |
| 1000 | *Flints.* | | |

Whereupon the Chiefs, and all the *Indians,* returned their solemn Thanks; and *Canassatego* said, "They had no more to say as to Publick Business at present; but they had somewhat under Deliberation, which when they had duly considered they would communicate."

At a COUNCIL held at the Proprietor's, *July* 12.1742.
PRESENT The Honourable *GEORGE THOMAS,* Esq; Lieut. Governor.
*James Logan, Clement Plumsted, Thomas Lawrence, Abraham Taylor, Robert Strettell,* Esqrs. Mr. *Richard Peters.*
*CANASSATEGO, SHICKCALAMY,* And sundry Chiefs of the *Six Nations.*
*SASSOONAN* and *Delawares. NUTTIMUS,* and *Fork-Indians.*
*CONRAD WEISER,* Interpreter.
*Pisquetoman, Cornelius Spring, Nicholas Scull,* Interpreters to the *Fork Indians.*

*CANASSATEGO* said:

"*BRETHREN the Governor and Council,*

The other Day you informed us of the Misbehaviour of our Cousins the *Delawares,* with respect to their continuing to claim, and refusing to remove from some Land on the River *Delaware,* notwithstanding their Ancestors had sold it by a Deed under their Hands and Seals to the Proprietaries for a valuable Consideration, upwards of *Fifty* Years ago; and, notwithstanding that they themselves had about [blank] Years ago, after a long and full Examination, ratified that Deed of their Ancestors, and given a fresh one under their Hands and Seals; and then you requested us to remove them, inforcing your Request with a String of Wampum.—Afterwards you laid on the Table our own Letters by *Conrad Weiser,* some of our Cousins Letters, and the several Writings, to prove the Charge against our Cousins, with a Draught of the Land in Dispute.—We now tell you, we have perused all these several Papers: We see with our own Eyes, that they have been a very unruly People, and are altogether in the Wrong in their Dealings with you.—We have concluded to remove them, and oblige them to go over the River *Delaware,* and quit all Claim to any Lands on this Side for the Future, since they have received Pay for them, and it is gone thro' their Guts long ago.—To confirm to you that we will see your Request executed, we lay down this String of Wampum in return for yours."

Then turning to the *Delawares,* holding a Belt of Wampum in his Hand, he spoke to them as follows:

"*COUSINS,* Let this Belt of Wampum serve to chastise you. You ought to be taken by the Hair of the Head and shaked severely, till you recover your Senses and become sober. You don't know what Ground you stand on, nor what you are doing. Our Brother *Onas's* Cause is very just and plain, and his Intentions to preserve Friendship. On the other Hand, Your Cause is bad; your Heart far from being upright; and you are maliciously bent to break the Chain of Friendship with our Brother *Onas* and his People. We have seen with our Eyes a Deed sign'd by nine of your Ancestors above *Fifty* Years ago for this very Land, and a Release sign'd, not many Years since, by some of yourselves and Chiefs now living, to the Number of fifteen or upwards.—But how came you to take upon you to sell Land at all: We conquered you; we made Women of you; you know you are Women, and can no more sell Land than Women; nor is it fit you should have the Power of selling Lands, since you would abuse it.[9] This Land that you claim is gone through your Guts; you have been furnish'd with Cloaths, Meat and Drink, by the Goods paid you for it, and now you want it again, like Children as you are.—But what makes you sell Land in the Dark. Did you ever tell us that you had sold this Land. Did we ever receive any Part, even the Value of a Pipe-Shank, from you for it. You have told us a blind Story, that you sent a Messenger to us to inform us of the Sale, but he never came amongst us, nor we never heard any thing about it.—This is acting in the Dark, and very different from the Conduct our *Six* Nations observe in their Sales of Land; on such Occasions they give publick Notice, and invite all the *Indians* of their united Nations, and give them all a Share of the Present they receive for their Lands.—This is the Behaviour of the wise united Nations.—But we find you are none of our Blood: You act a dishonest Part, not only in this but in other Matters: Your Ears are ever open to slanderous Reports about our Brethren; you receive them with as much Greediness as lewd Women receive the Embraces of bad Men. And for all these Reasons we charge you to remove instantly; we don't give you the Liberty to think about it. You are Women. Take the Advice of a wise Man, and remove immediately. You may return to the other Side of *Delaware* where you came from: But we do not know whether, considering how you have demean'd yourselves, you will be permitted to live there; or whether you have not swallowed that Land down your Throats as well as the Land on this Side. We therefore assign you two Places to go, either to *Wyomen* or *Shamokin.* You may go to either of these Places, and then we shall have you more under our Eye, and shall see how you behave. Don't deliberate; but remove away, and take this Belt of Wampum."

This being interpreted by *Conrad Weiser* into *English,* and by *Cornelius Spring* into the *Delaware* Language, *Canassatego* taking a String of Wampum, added further.

"After our just Reproof, and absolute Order to depart from the Land, you are now to take Notice of what we have further to say to you. This String of Wampum serves to forbid you, your Children and Grand-Children, to the latest Posterity forever, medling in Land-Affairs; neither you nor any who shall descend from you, are ever hereafter to presume to sell any Land: For which Purpose, you are to preserve this String, in Memory of what your Uncles have this Day given you in Charge.— —We have some other Business to transact with our Brethren, and therefore depart the Council, and consider what has been said to you."

*Canassatego* then spoke to the Governor and Council:
"*BRETHREN,* We called at our old Friend *James Logan's,* in our Way to this City, and to our Grief we found him hid in the Bushes, and retired, thro' Infirmities, from Publick Business. We press'd him to leave his Retirement, and prevailed with him to assist once more on our Account at your Councils. We hope, notwithstanding his Age, and the Effects of a Fit of Sickness, which we understand has hurt his Constitution, that he may yet continue a long Time to assist this Province with his Counsels. He is a wise Man, and a fast Friend to the *Indians.* And we desire, when his Soul goes to GOD, you may chuse in his Room just such another Person, of the same Prudence and Ability in Counselling, and of the same tender Disposition and Affection for the *Indians.* In Testimony of our Gratitude for all his Services, and because he was so good as to leave his Country-House, and follow us to Town, and be at the Trouble, in this his advanced Age, to attend the Council; we present him with this Bundle of Skins.

"*BRETHREN,* It is always our Way, at the Conclusion of a Treaty, to desire you will use your Endeavours with the Traders, that they may sell their Goods cheaper and give us a better Price for our Deer-Skins. Whenever any particular Sort of *Indian* Goods is scarce, they constantly make us pay the dearer on that Account. We must now use the same Argument with them: Our Deer are killed in such Quantities, and our Hunting-Countries grown less every Day by the Settlement of white People, that Game is now difficult to find, and we must go a great Way in Quest of it; they therefore ought to give us a better Price for our Skins; and we desire you would speak to them to do so. We have been stinted in the Article of Rum in Town. We desire you will open the Rum-Bottle, and give it to us in greater Abundance on the Road."

*To inforce our Request, about the* Indian *Traders,*
*we present you with this Bundle of Skins.*

"*BRETHREN,* When we first came to your Houses, we found them clean and in Order: But we have staid so long as to dirty them; which is to be imputed to our different Way of Living from the white People: And therefore, as we cannot but have been disagreeable to you on this Account, we present you with some Skins to make your Houses clean, and put them into the same Condition they were in when we came amongst you.

"*BRETHREN,* The Business the *Five* Nations transact with you is of great Consequence, and requires a skilful and honest Person to go between us; one in whom both you and we can place a Confidence.—We esteem our present Interpreter to be such a Person, equally faithful in the Interpretation of whatever is said to him by either of us, equally allied to both; he is of our Nation, and a Member of our

Council as well as of yours. When we adopted him, we divided him into Two equal Parts: One we kept for our selves, and one we left for you. He has had a great deal of Trouble with us, wore out his Shoes in our Messages, and dirty'd his Cloaths by being amongst us, so that he is become as nasty as an *Indian.*[10]

"In Return for these Services, we recommend him to your Generosity; and on our own Behalf, we give him *Five Skins* to buy him Clothes and Shoes with.

"*BRETHREN,* We have still one more Favour to ask. Our Treaty, and all we have to say about Publick Business, is now over, and to morrow we design to leave you. We hope, as you have given us plenty of good Provision whilst in Town, that you will continue your Goodness so far as to supply us with a little more to serve us on the Road. And we likewise desire you will provide us with Waggons, to carry our Goods to the Place where they are to be conveyed by Water."

To these several Points the Governor made the following Reply.

"*BRETHREN of the Six Nations,* The Judgment you have just now pass'd on your Cousins the *Delawares,* confirms the high Opinion we have ever entertained of the Justice of the *Six Nations.* This Part of your Character, for which you are deservedly famed, made us waive doing our selves Justice, in order to give you another Opportunity of convincing the World of your inviolable Attachment to your Engagements. These unhappy People might have always liv'd easy, having never receiv'd the least Injury from us; but we believe some of our own People were bad enough to impose on their Credulity, and engage them in these wrong Measures, which we wish, for their Sakes, they had avoided.

"We hoped, from what we have constantly given in Charge to the Indian Traders, that they would have administred no just Cause of Complaint: If they do you Wrong, it is against our Inclinations, and contrary to our express Directions. As you have exhibited no particular Charge against them, we shall use our best Endeavours to persuade them to give you as much for your Skins as they can possibly afford; and to take Care that their Goods which they give in Exchange for Skins, be of the best Sort. We will likewise order you some Rum to serve you on your Journey home, since you desire it.

"We wish there had been more Room and better Houses provided for your Entertainment; but not expecting so many of you, we did the best we could. 'Tis true there are a great many Houses in Town, but as they are the Property of other People, who have their own Families to take Care of, it is difficult to procure Lodgings for a large Number of People, especially if they come unexpectedly.

"We entertain the same Sentiments of the Abilities and Probity of the Interpreter as you have express'd. We were induc'd at first to make use of him in this important Trust, from his being known to be agreeable to you, and one who had lived amongst you for some Years, in good Credit and Esteem with all your Nations; and have ever found him equally faithful to both. We are pleas'd with the Notice you have taken of him, and think he richly deserves it at your Hands. We shall not be wanting to make him a suitable Gratification, for the many good and faithful Services he hath done this Government.

"We have already given Orders for Waggons to carry your Goods, and for a Supply of Provisions to serve you on the Road in your Return home, where we heartily wish you may arrive in good Health."

After the Governor had concluded, Mr. *Logan* return'd an Answer to that Part of *Canassateego*'s Speech which related to him, and said, "That not only upon the Account of his Lameness, of which the Indians themselves were Witnesses; but on Account of another Indisposition which about three Years since had laid him under an Incapacity of expressing himself with his former usual Freedom, he had been obliged to live retired in the Country. But that our first Proprietor, the Honourable *William Penn,* who had ever been a Father and true Friend to all the Indians, having above Forty Years since recommended them to his particular Care, he had always, from his own Inclination as well as from that strict Charge, endeavoured to convince all the Indians, that He was their true Friend; and was now well pleased, that after a Tract of so many Years, they were not insensible of it. He thanked them kindly for their Present, and heartily joined with them in their Desires, that this Government may always be furnished with Persons of equally good Inclinations, and not only with such, but also with better Abilities to serve them."

And then *Canassatego* said, he had forgot to mention, that *Shickcalamy* and *Caxhayn* had been employ'd on several Messages to this Government, and desir'd they might be consider'd on that Account.

At a COUNCIL held the 12th *of July,* P. M. 1742.
PRESENT, The Honourable *GEORGE THOMAS,* Esq; Lieut. Governor,
*James Logan, Samuel Preston, Clement Plumsted, Thomas Lawrence,*
*Samuel Hasell, Abraham Taylor, Robert Strettell,* Esqrs.
Mr. *Richard Peters.*

The Board taking into Consideration the Regulation of the necessary Expences of the *Indians* Travelling down hither, and Returning; and upon an Estimate made by *Conrad Weiser,* amounting to about *One Hundred Pounds,* it appearing that the said Sum of £. 100. will be necessary to be advanced to *Conrad Weiser* to defray those Expences, Mr. *Logan* on the Proprietaries Behalf, proposes to advance 40 *l.* and the Treasurer declaring he had no Publick Money in his Hands, and that if he had, he would not advance Money without the Assembly's Order; it is recommended to Mr. *Preston* and Mr. *Lawrence,* to confer with Mr. *Kinsey,* and know whether he, as Speaker of the Assembly, and Trustee of the Loan-Office, will advance the other 60 *l.*

And the *Indians* having requested that they might have a small Quantity of Rum, to be added to their Provisions, to comfort them on the Road: The Board is of Opinion that there be added to the said Estimate for Twenty Gallons of Rum for the aforesaid Use. And in Return for their Present of Skins, at Requesting that the Indian Traders be enjoyn'd to sell their Goods cheaper, the Board directs that two

Strouds be presented. And that *Five Pounds* be given to *Caxhayn* on the Account of the Province, for his Services; and to *Shickalamy* the like Sum.

*A just Copy, compared by PATRICK BAIRD*, Secry.

1. The agreement between the League and Pennsylvania that land exchanges would only be made on the level of the two governments reinforces our understanding of British-Indian relations as international relations. While the agreement clearly gave Pennsylvania a monopoly over the purchase of lands, it also clearly acknowledged the Iroquois Confederacy and others as "foreign" (sovereign) and independent nations rather than the domestic and dependent nations that the U.S. Supreme Court would later label them. There is a certain amount of delight and humor to be derived from the young warriors' sale of the land. They were apparently acquainted with public business enough to know that their sale had no value without the sanction of the Onondaga Council. So, for once, they turned the tables on the English and swindled them as they were used to being swindled.

2. In this paragraph, Canasatego demonstrates the renowned skill of the League in balancing their English and French interests, maintaining their neutrality while offering flattering words that played into the English imaginary that the League had somehow subjected themselves to English rule. Possibly, the absence of the Senecas in this delegation was because of this balancing act in addition to the famine reported.

3. The meaning of "tributaries" here remains ambiguous. It was in the British interest to figure these western nations as subordinate to the League, but it is possible that they mean only to describe a relationship of protection from other nations or a situation in which the League would act as intermediary in the trade with the British (cf. Jennings, *Ambiguous Iroquois Empire*, 94).

4. This characterization of the Anglo-Iroquois relationship is another attempt to figure the latter as subjects of the King of England: a seemingly equal sibling relationship that obfuscated the real favoritism shown the "true sons."

5. This complaint and others like it reveal that the squatting and gradual encroachments by British (and later, U.S.) subjects that were to drive Native Americans off their lands were far from lacking in real violence, although this violence was silent. They were starved by systematic land greed and disrespect for international borders.

6. The reasoning here is specious. The lands were either sold before improvements had been made or were "improved" without consent of the owners—squatted upon. The Penns commonly made profits that were seventy to eighty times their costs in acquiring the land. The Iroquois had already shown that the value of the land was indeed more than its worth in money because its worth included its future, as well as its present, value. Demand *for* the land raised its market value, not improvements upon it.

7. Webb had been assaulted as a result of the Walking Purchase (Wallace, *Conrad Weiser*, 125).

8. The British will raise this example several more times in an unsuccessful effort to show the impartiality of their justice.

9. There continues to be much confusion and controversy over the Lenapes' relationship to the League and this 1742 characterization of them as women. The well-documented Iroquois respect for women precludes this characterization as one of societal contempt. Given the League's political structure, it makes some sense that women would be unable to sell land without consulting their male kin and the hereditary chiefs they elect. But even if the

Lenapes are being called women in *this* politically specific way, they would later report that the Iroquois had fabricated the conquest that Canasatego here claims to recall. Wallace puts it this way: "Neither in 1736 nor at any other time during Weiser's career (except for an outburst of rhetoric by Canasatego in 1742—an outburst that unfortunately has been quoted as though this . . . windjammer were the Iroquois Blackstone) did the Six Nations deny the right in principle of the Delawares to own land" (*Conrad Weiser,* 73).

Apparently, the Iroquois had been at war with the Lenapes in 1661, around the same time that they were warring with the Susquehannocks. (The Lenapes and Susquehannocks were allies at the time.) It appears from records of nations paying tribute that the Munsee group of Lenapes had become an adopted nation of the League by 1682 (Weslager, *Delaware Indians,* 179–80). Later records indicate that the Munsees and perhaps other Lenapes may have been tricked into dependent status when the Iroquois falsely reported that they were about to be attacked by another nation (Wallace, *Conrad Weiser,* 464). However, this alliance would not have included the laying down of arms that one might associate with "woman" status. In 1677, the Lenapes had apparently taken on the role of women, or peacemakers and mediators between the Iroquois and other tribes, possibly the Susquehannocks, but reported as Algonquin nations (Jennings, *Ambiguous Iroquois Empire,* 23; Jennings, "Pennsylvania Indians," 80). Yet the role had not been the result of a military defeat by the League.

It seems that the real conquest occurred precisely here at the 1742 treaty itself, as the League and Pennsylvania allied themselves against the Forks Lenapes, just as Jennings has observed. This passage may then be interpreted as an artistic verbal fabrication: an "intentional effort of one or more individuals to manage activity so that a party of one or more others [we as readers] will be induced to have a false belief about what it is that is going on" (Goffman in Greg Sarris, *Keeping Slug Woman Alive,* 24; Jennings, *Ambiguous Iroquois Empire,* 343–46).

Various reports of Lenape status conceivably depend upon both deliberate and accidental confusion of the different bands of Lenapes by both British and Iroquois informants and by subsequent historians. They also rely on wars, cold wars, and differing European and Native American connotations of "woman." The Lenapes who together could have clarified the entire story were not asked in time and most of their versions are apparently lost.

10. Conrad Weiser, the interpreter of whom Canasatego speaks, became less worthy of League trust as the years went on. Records show that the Penns gave him a great deal of land in return for his services to them.

✠

# A TREATY,

Held at the TOWN of *Lancaster*,

in PENNSYLVANIA,

By the HONOURABLE the Lieutenant-Governor

of the PROVINCE,

And the HONOURABLE the Commissioners

for the PROVINCES OF VIRGINIA

*and* MARYLAND,

WITH THE *INDIANS* OF THE SIX NATIONS,

In *JUNE*, 1744.

---

*PHILADELPHIA:*

Printed and Sold by B. FRANKLIN, at the New-Printing-Office, near the Market. MDCCXLIV.[1]

---

## A TREATY WITH THE *INDIANS* OF THE SIX NATIONS.

In the COURT-HOUSE in the Town of *Lancaster*, on *Friday*, the Twenty Second of *June*, 1744,

PRESENT, The Honourable *GEORGE THOMAS*, Esq; Lieut. Governor of the Province of *Pennsylvania*, and Counties of *Newcastle*, *Kent* and *Sussex*, on *Delaware*.

The Honourable *Thomas Lee*, Esq; Colonel *William Beverly*, Commissioners of *Virginia*.

The Honble *Edmund Jennings*, Esq; *Philip Thomas*, Esq; Colonel *Robert King*, Colonel *Thomas Colville*, Commissioners of *Maryland*.

The Deputies of the *Onandagoes, Senecas, Cayogoes,*
*Oneidas* and *Tuscaroraes.*
*Conrad Weiser,* Interpreter.

The Governor and the Commissioners took some of the *Indian* Chiefs by the Hand, and, after they had seated themselves, the Governor bid them welcome into the Government; and there being Wine and Punch prepared for them, the Governor and the several Commissioners drank Health to the *Six Nations;* and *Canassatego, Tachanoontia,* and some other Chiefs, returned the Compliments, drinking the Healths of *Onas,** *Assaragoa,*† and the Governor of *Maryland.*

After they were all served with Wine, Punch, Pipes and Tobacco, the Governor told the *Indians,* that as it was customary, and indeed necessary, they should have some Time to rest after so long a Journey, and as he thought three Days would be no more than sufficient for that Purpose, he proposed to speak to them on *Monday* next; after which, the honourable Commissioners would take their own Time to deliver what they had to say.

*CANASSATEGO* answered the Governor: We thank you for giving us Time to rest; we are come to you, and shall leave it intirely to you to appoint the Time when we shall meet you again. We likewise leave it to the Governor of *Maryland,* by whose Invitation we came here, to appoint a Time when he will please to mention the Reason of his inviting us. As to our Brother *Assaragoa,* we have at this present Time nothing to say to him; not but we have a great deal to say to *Assaragoa,* which must be said at one Time or another; but not being satisfied whether he or we should begin first, we shall leave it wholly to our Brother *Onas* to adjust this between us, and to say which shall begin first.

In the COURT-HOUSE at *Lancaster, June* 25, 1744. *A. M.*
PRESENT, The Honourable *GEORGE THOMAS,* Esq; Governor, *&c.*
The Honourable the Commissioners of *Virginia.*
The Honourable the Commissioners of *Maryland.*
The Deputies of the *Six Nations.*
*Conrad Weiser,* Interpreter.

The GOVERNOR spoke as follows:

*Honourable Gentlemen, Commissioners for the Governments of* Virginia *and* Maryland, *and Brethren, Sachims, or Chiefs of the* Indians *of the* Six Nations:

At a Treaty, held by me two Years ago, in Behalf of the Government of *Pennsylvania,* with a Number of the Chiefs of the *Indians* of the *Six Nations,* I was desired by them to write to the Governor of *Maryland* concerning some Lands in the back Parts

* *Onas,* the Governor of *Pennsylvania*
† *Assaragoa,* the Governor of *Virginia*

of that Province, which they claim a Right to from their Conquests over the ancient Possessors, and which have been settled by some of the Inhabitants of that Government, without their Consent, or any Purchase made from them. It was at that time understood that the Claim was upon *Maryland* only; but it has since appeared, by some Letters formerly wrote by Mr. President *Logan* to the late Governor of *Maryland,* that it related likewise to some Lands in the back Parts of *Virginia.* The Governors of those Colonies soon manifested a truly equitable Disposition to come to any reasonable Terms with the *Six Nations* on account of those Lands, and desired, that for that End a Time and Place might be fixed for a Treaty with them; but before this could be effected, an unfortunate Skirmish happened in the back Parts of *Virginia,* between some of the Militia there, and a Party of the *Indian* Warriors of the *Six Nations,* with some Loss on both Sides. Who were the Aggressors is not at this time to be discussed, both Parties having agreed to bury that Affair in Oblivion, and the Government of *Virginia* having, in Token of the Continuance of their Friendship, presented the *Six Nations,* through my Hands, with Goods to the Value of One Hundred Pounds Sterling. To prevent further Hostilities, and to heal this Breach, I had, before the Present was given, made a Tender of my good Offices; which both Parties accepted, and consented, on my Instances, to lay down their Arms: Since which the Faith pledged to me has been mutually preserved, and a Time and Place has been agreed upon, through my Intervention, for accommodating all Differences, and for settling a firm Peace, Union and Friendship, as well between the Government of *Virginia* as that of *Maryland,* and the *Indians* of the *Six Nations.** The honourable the Commissioners for these two Governments, and the Deputies of the *Six Nations,* are now met at the Place appointed for the Treaty. It only remains therefore for me to say, That if my further good Offices shall be thought useful for the Accomplishment of this Work, you may rely most assuredly upon them.

But I hope, honourable Gentlemen Commissioners, it will not be taken amiss if I go a little further, and briefly represent to you, how especially necessary it is at this Juncture, for his Majesty's Service, and the Good of all his Colonies in this Part of his Dominions, that Peace and Friendship be established between your Governments and the *Indians* of the *Six Nations.*

These *Indians,* by their Situation, are a Frontier to some of them; and, from thence, if Friends, are capable of defending their Settlements; if Enemies, of making cruel Ravages upon them; if Neuters, they may deny the *French* a Passage through their Country, and give us timely Notice of their Designs. These are but some of the Motives for cultivating a good Understanding with them; but from hence the Disadvantages of a Rupture are abundantly evident. Every Advantage you gain over them in War will be a weakening of the Barrier of those Colonies, and consequently be, in effect, Victories over yourselves and your Fellow Subjects. Some Allowances for their Prejudices

* This was allowed, at a Conference had by the Governor with the Commissioners, to be a just State of the Transactions preceding the Treaty.

and Passions, and a Present now and then for the Relief of their Necessities, which have, in some Measure, been brought upon them by their Intercourse with us, and by our yearly extending our Settlements, will probably tie them more closely to the *British* Interest. This has been the Method of *New-York* and *Pennsylvania,* and will not put you to so much Expence in twenty Years, as the carrying on a War against them will do in one. The *French* very well know the Importance of these Nations to us, and will not fail by Presents, and their other usual Arts, to take Advantage of any Misunderstandings we may have with them.* But I will detain you, Gentlemen, no longer. Your own superior Knowledge will suggest to you more than I can say on this Subject.

*Friends and Brethren, Sachims, or Chiefs of the* Indians *of the* Six Nations: These, your Brethren of *Virginia* and *Maryland,* are come to enlarge the Fire, which was almost gone out, and to make it burn clearer; to brighten the Chain which had contracted some Rust, and to renew their Friendship with you; which it is their Desire may last so long as the Sun, the Moon and the Stars, shall give Light.[2] Their Powers are derived from the *Great King of* ENGLAND, your Father; and whatever Conclusions they shall come to with you, will be as firm and binding as if the Governors of these Provinces were themselves here. I am your Brother, and, which is more, I am your true Friend. As you know, from Experience, that I am so, I will now give you a few Words of Advice. Receive these your Brethren with open Arms; unite yourselves to them in the Covenant Chain, and be you with them as one Body, and one Soul. I make no doubt but the Governor of *Canada* has been taking Pains to widen the Breach between these your Brethren of *Virginia* and you; but as you cannot have forgot the Hatred the *French* have always borne to your Nations, and how kindly, on the contrary, you have been treated, and how faithfully you have been protected by the *Great King of* ENGLAND and his Subjects, you will not be at a Loss to see into the Designs of that Governor. He wants to divide you from us, in order the more easily to destroy you, which he will most certainly do, if you suffer yourselves to be deluded by him.

As to what relates to the Friendship established between the Government of *Pennsylvania* and your Nations, I will take another Day to speak to you upon it.

*To enforce what had been said, the* GOVERNOR *laid down a Belt of Wampum; upon which the* Indians *gave the*† Yo-hah.

After a short Pause, the Governor ordered the Interpreter to tell the *Indians,* that as they had greatly exceeded their appointed Time for meeting the Commis-

* The two preceding Paragraphs were allowed by the Commissioners of *Virginia,* whilst they were at *Philadelphia* to be very proper to be spoken by the Governor of *Pennsylvania* at the Opening of the Treaty; but taking up an Opinion, from what passed at the first friendly Interview with the *Indians,* that they would not make any Claim upon Lands within the Government of *Virginia,* the Governor consented to decline speaking them in the Presence of the *Indians.*

† The *Yo-hah* denotes Approbation, being a loud Shout or Cry, consisting of a few Notes pronounced by all the *Indians* in a very musical Manner, in the Nature of our Huzza's.

sioners, he recommended to them to use all the Expedition possible in giving their Answer to what had been said, that they might forthwith proceed to Treat with the respective Commissioners on the Business they came about.[3]

Then *Canassatego* repeated to the Interpreter the Substance of what the Governor had spoke, in order to know if he had understood him right (a Method generally made use of by the *Indians*) and when the Interpreter told him he had taken the true Sense,[4] *Canassatego* proceeded to return the Thanks of the *Six Nations* for the Governor's kind Advice, promising to follow it as far as lay in their Power; but as it was their Custom when a Belt was given to return another, they would take Time till the Afternoon to provide one, and would then give their Answer.

In the COURT-HOUSE at *Lancaster, June 25*, 1744. *P. M.*
PRESENT, The Honourable *GEORGE THOMAS*, Esq;. Governor, &c.
The Honourable the Commissioners of *Virginia.*
The Honourable the Commissioners of *Maryland.*
The Deputies of the *Six Nations.*
*Conrad Weiser*, Interpreter.

Canassatego's *Answer to the Governor's Speech delivered in the Morning.*

*Brother* Onas, You spoke in the Presence of *Assaragoa* and the Governor of *Maryland* to us, advising us to receive them as our Brethren, and to unite with them in the Covenant Chain as one Body, and one Soul. We have always considered them as our Brethren, and, as such, shall be willing to brighten the Chain of Friendship with them; but since there are some Disputes between us respecting the Lands possessed by them, which formerly belonged to us, we, according to our Custom, propose to have those Differences first adjusted, and then we shall proceed to confirm the Friendship subsisting between us, which will meet with no Obstruction after these Matters are settled.

*Here they presented the* GOVERNOR *with a Belt of Wampum, in return for the Belt given them in the Morning by the* GOVERNOR; *and the Interpreter was ordered to return the* Yo-hah.

*Then the* GOVERNOR, *in Reply, spoke as follows:*

I receive your Belt with great Kindness and Affection; and as to what relates to the Governments of *Virginia* and *Maryland*, the honourable Commissioners, now present, are ready to treat with you. I shall only add, that the Goods for the Hundred Pounds Sterling, put into my Hands by the Governor of *Virginia*, as a Token of his good Dispositions to preserve Friendship with you, are now in Town, and ready to be delivered, in consequence of what was told you by *Conrad Weiser* when he was last at *Onandago.*

Then the Governor, turning to the Commissioners of *Virginia* and *Maryland*, said, Gentlemen, I have now finished what was incumbent upon me to say by way of Introduction to the *Indians;* and as you have a full Authority from your respective Governments to treat with them, I shall leave the rest intirely to you, and either stay or withdraw, as you shall think most for your Service.

The Commissioners said, They were all of Opinion, it would be for their Advantage that the Governor should stay with them; and therefore they unanimously desired he would favour them with the Continuance of his Presence whilst they should be in Treaty with the *Indians:* Which his Honour said he would at their Instance very readily do, believing it might expedite their Business, and prevent any Jealousy the *Indians* might conceive at his withdrawing.

*The Commissioners of* Maryland *ordered the Interpreter to acquaint the* Indians *that the Governor of* Maryland *was going to speak to them, and then spoke, as follows:*

*Friends and Brethren of the united* Six Nations,

We, who are deputed from the Government of *Maryland* by a Commission under the Great Seal of that Province, now in our Hands (and which will be interpreted to you) bid you welcome; and in Token that we are very glad to see you here as Brethren, we give you this String of Wampum.

*Upon which the* Indians *gave the* Yo-hah.[5]

When the Governor of *Maryland* received the first Notice, about seven Years ago, of your Claim to some Lands in that Province, he thought our good Friends and Brethren of the *Six Nations* had little Reason to complain of any Injury from *Maryland,* and that they would be so well convinced thereof, on farther Deliberation, as he should hear no more of it; but you spoke of that Matter again to the Governor of *Pennsylvania,* about two Years since, as if you designed to terrify us.

It was very inconsiderately said by you, that you would do yourselves Justice, by going to take Payment yourselves: Such an Attempt would have intirely dissolved the Chain of Friendship subsisting, not only between us, but perhaps the other *English* and you.

We assure you, our People, who are numerous, courageous, and have Arms ready in their Hands, will not suffer themselves to be hurt in their Lives and Estates.

But, however, the old and wise People of *Maryland* immediately met in Council, and upon considering very coolly your rash Expressions, agreed to invite their Brethren, the *Six Nations,* to this Place, that they might learn of them what Right they have to the Land in *Maryland,* and, if they had any, to make them some reasonable Compensation for it; therefore the Governor of *Maryland* has sent us to meet and treat with you about this Affair, and the brightening and strengthening the Chain which hath long subsisted between us. And as an Earnest of our Sincerity and Good-will towards you, we present you with this Belt of Wampum.

*On which the* Indians *gave the* Yo-hah.

Our *Great King of* ENGLAND, and his Subjects, have always possessed the Province of *Maryland* free and undisturbed from any Claim of the *Six Nations* for above one hundred Years past, and your not saying any thing to us before, convinces us you thought you had no Pretence to any Lands in *Maryland;* nor can we yet find out to what Lands, or under what Title, you make your Claim: For the *Sasquahannah Indians,* by a Treaty above ninety Years since (which is on the Table, and will be interpreted to you) give, and yield to the *English* Nation, their Heirs and Assigns for ever, the greatest Part (if not all) of the Lands we possess, from *Patuxent* River, on the Western, as well as from *Choptank* River, on the Eastern Side of the Great Bay of *Chessapeak.* And, near Sixty Years ago, you acknowledged to the Governor of *New-York* at *Albany,* "That you had given your Lands, and submitted yourselves to the King of *England.*"

We are that Great King's Subjects, and we possess and enjoy the Province of *Maryland* by virtue of his Right and Sovereignty thereto; why, then, will you stir up any Quarrel between you and ourselves, who are as one Man, under the Protection of that Great King?

We need not put you in mind of the Treaty (which we suppose you have had from your Fathers) made with the Province of *Maryland* near Seventy Years ago, and renewed and confirmed twice since that time.

By these Treaties we became Brethren; we have always lived as such, and hope always to continue so.

We have this further to say, that altho' we are not satisfied of the Justice of your Claim to any Lands in *Maryland,* yet we are desirous of shewing our Brotherly Kindness and Affection, and to prevent (by any reasonable Way) every Misunderstanding between the Province of *Maryland* and you our Brethren of the *Six Nations.*

For this Purpose we have brought hither a Quantity of Goods for our Brethren the *Six Nations,* and which will be delivered you as soon as we shall have received your Answer, and made so bright and large a Fire as may burn pure and clear whilst the Sun and Moon shall shine.

We have now freely and openly laid our Bosoms bare to you; and that you may be the better confirmed of the Truth of our Hearts, we give you this Belt of Wampum.

*Which was received with the* Yo-hah.

*After a little Time* Canassatego *spoke as follows:*

*Brother, the Governor of* Maryland, We have heard what you have said to us; and, as you have gone back old Times, we cannot give you an Answer now, but shall take what you have said into Consideration, and return you our Answer some Time to Morrow. He then sat down, and after some Time he spoke again.

*Brother, the Governor of* Maryland, If you have made any Enquiry into *Indian* Affairs, you will know, that we have always had our Guns, Hatchets and Kettles, mended when we came to see our Brethren. Brother *Onas,* and the Governor of *York* always do this for us; and we give you this early Notice, that we may not thereby be delayed, being desirous, as well as you, to give all possible Dispatch to the Business to be transacted between us.

The Commissioners of *Virginia* and *Maryland* said, since it was customary, they would give Orders to have every Thing belonging to them mended that should want it.

In the COURT-HOUSE at *Lancaster, June* 26, 1744, *P. M.*
PRESENT, The Honourable *GEORGE THOMAS,* Esq; Governor, &c.
The Honourable the Commissioners of *Virginia.*
The Honourable the Commissioners of *Maryland.*
The Deputies of the *Six Nations.*
*Conrad Weiser,* Interpreter.

*CANASSATEGO spoke as follows:*
*Brother, the Governor of* Maryland, When you invited us to kindle a Council Fire with you, *Conedogwainet* was the Place agreed upon; but afterwards you, by Brother *Onas,* upon second Thoughts, considering that it would be difficult to get Provisions and other Accommodations where there were but few Houses or Inhabitants, desired we would meet our Brethren at *Lancaster,* and at his Instances we very readily agreed to meet you here, and are glad of the Change; for we have found Plenty of every thing; and as Yesterday you bid us welcome, and told us you were glad to see us, we likewise assure you we are as glad to see you; and, in Token of our Satisfaction, we present you with this String of Wampum.

*Which was received with the usual Ceremony.*

*Brother, the Governor of* Maryland, You tell us, that when about Seven years ago you heard, by our Brother *Onas,* of our Claim to some Lands in your Province, you took no Notice of it, believing, as you say, that when we should come to reconsider that Matter, we should find that we had no Right to make any Complaint of the Governor of *Maryland,* and would drop our Demand. And that when about two Years ago we mentioned it again to our Brother *Onas,* you say we did it in such Terms as looked like a Design to terrify you; and you tell us further, that we must be beside ourselves, in using such a rash Expression as to tell you, We know how to do ourselves Justice if you still refuse. It is true we did say so, but without any ill Design; for we must inform you, that when we first desired our Brother *Onas* to use his Influence with you to procure us Satisfaction for our Lands, we, at the same time, desired him, in case you should disregard our Demand, to write to the Great King beyond the Seas, who would own us for his Children as well as you, to compel you to do us Justice: And, two Years ago, when we found that you had paid no Regard to our just Demand, nor that Brother *Onas* had convey'd our Complaint to the Great King over the Seas, we were resolved to use such Expressions as would make the greatest Impressions on your Minds, and we find it had its Effect; for you tell us,

"That your wise Men held a Council together, and agreed to invite us, and to enquire of our Right to any of your Lands, and if it should be found that we had a Right, we were to have a Compensation made for them: And likewise you tell us, that our Brother, the Governor of *Maryland,* by the Advice of these wise Men, has sent you to brighten the Chain, and to assure us of his Willingness to remove whatever impedes a good Understanding between us." This shews that your wise Men understood our Expressions in their true Sense. We had no Design to terrify you, but to put you on doing us the Justice you had so long delayed. Your wise Men have done well; and as there is no Obstacle to a good Understanding between us, except this Affair of our Land, we, on our Parts, do give you the strongest Assurances of our good Dispositions towards you, and that we are as desirous as you to brighten the Chain, and to put away all Hindrances to a perfect good Understanding; and, in Token of our Sincerity, we give you this Belt of Wampum.

*Which was received, and the Interpreter ordered to give the* Yo-hah.

*Brother, the Governor of* Maryland, When you mentioned the Affair of the Land Yesterday, you went back to old Times, and told us, you had been in Possession of the Province of *Maryland* above One Hundred Years; but what is One Hundred Years in Comparison of the Length of Time since our Claim began? since we came out of this Ground? For we must tell you, that long before One Hundred Years our Ancestors came out of this very Ground, and their Children have remained here ever since. You came out of the Ground in a Country that lies beyond the Seas, there you may have a just Claim, but here you must allow us to be your elder Brethren, and the Lands to belong to us long before you knew any thing of them. It is true, that above One Hundred Years ago the *Dutch* came here in a Ship, and brought with them several Goods; such as Awls, Knives, Hatchets, Guns, and many other Particulars, which they gave us; and when they had taught us how to use their Things, and we saw what sort of People they were, we were so well pleased with them, that we tied their Ship to the Bushes on the Shore; and afterwards, liking them still better the longer they staid with us, and thinking the Bushes too slender, we removed the Rope, and tied it to the Trees; and as the Trees were liable to be blown down by high Winds, or to decay of themselves, we, from the Affection we bore them, again removed the Rope, and tied it to a strong and big Rock [*here the Interpreter said, They mean the* Oneido *Country*] and not content with this, for its further Security we removed the Rope to the big Mountain [*here the Interpreter says they mean the* Onandago *Country*] and there we tied it very fast, and rowll'd Wampum about it; and, to make it still more secure, we stood upon the Wampum, and sat down upon it, to defend it, and to prevent any Hurt coming to it, and did our best Endeavours that it might remain uninjured for ever. During all this Time the New-comers, the *Dutch,* acknowledged our Right to the Lands, and sollicited us, from Time to Time, to grant them Parts of our Country, and to enter into League and Covenant with us, and to become one People with us.

After this the *English* came into the Country, and, as we were told, became one

People with the *Dutch.* About two Years after the Arrival of the *English,* an *English* Governor came to *Albany,* and finding what great Friendship subsisted between us and the *Dutch,* he approved it mightily, and desired to make as strong a League, and to be upon as good Terms with us as the *Dutch* were, with whom he was united, and to become one People with us: And by his further Care in looking into what had passed between us, he found that the Rope which tied the Ship to the great Mountain was only fastened with Wampum, which was liable to break and rot, and to perish in a Course of Years; he therefore told us, he would give us a Silver Chain, which would be much stronger, and would last for ever. This we accepted, and fastened the Ship with it, and it has lasted ever since. Indeed we have had some small Differences with the *English,* and, during these Misunderstanding, some of their young Men would, by way of Reproach, be every now and then telling us, that we should have perished if they had not come into the Country and furnished us with Strowds and Hatchets, and Guns, and other Things necessary for the Support of Life; but we always gave them to understand that they were mistaken, that we lived before they came amongst us, and as well, or better, if we may believe what our Forefathers have told us. We had then Room enough, and Plenty of Deer, which was easily caught; and tho' we had not Knives, Hatchets, or Guns, such as we have now, yet we had Knives of Stone, and Hatchets of Stone, and Bows and Arrows, and those served our Uses as well then as the *English* ones do now. We are now straitened, and sometimes in want of Deer, and liable to many other Inconveniencies since the *English* came among us, and particularly from that Pen-and-Ink Work that is going on at the Table (*pointing to the Secretary*)[6] and we will give you an Instance of this. Our Brother *Onas,* a great while ago, came to *Albany* to buy the *Sasquahannah* Lands of us, but our Brother, the Governor of *New-York,* who, as we suppose, had not a good Understanding with our Brother *Onas,* advised us not to sell him any Land, for he would make an ill Use of it; and, pretending to be our good Friend, he advised us, in order to prevent *Onas*'s, or any other Person's imposing upon us, and that we might always have our Land when we should want it, to put it into his Hands; and told us, he would keep it for our Use, and never open his Hands, but keep them close shut, and not part with any of it, but at our Request. Accordingly we trusted him, and put our Land into his Hands, and charged him to keep it safe for our Use; but, some Time after, he went to *England,* and carried our Land with him, and there sold it to our Brother *Onas* for a large Sum of Money; and when, at the Instance of our Brother *Onas,* we were minded to sell him some Lands, he told us, we had sold the *Sasquahannah* Lands already to the Governor of *New-York,* and that he had bought them from him in *England;* tho' when he came to understand how the Governor of *New-York* had deceived us, he very generously paid us for our Lands over again.

Tho' we mention this Instance of an Imposition put upon us by the Governor of *New-York,* yet we must do the *English* the Justice to say, we have had their hearty Assistances in our Wars with the *French,* who were no sooner arrived amongst us than they began to render us uneasy, and to provoke us to War, and we have had several Wars with them; during all which we constantly received Assistance from the *English,* and, by their Means, we have always been able to keep up our Heads against their Attacks.

We now come nearer home. We have had your Deeds interpreted to us, and we acknowledge them to be good and valid, and that the *Conestogoe* or *Sasquahannah Indians* had a Right to sell those Lands to you, for they were then theirs; but since that Time we have conquered them, and their Country now belongs to us, and the Lands we demanded Satisfaction for are no Part of the Lands comprized in those Deeds; they are the **Cohongorontas* Lands; those, we are sure, you have not possessed One Hundred Years, no, nor above Ten Years, and we made our Demands so soon as we knew your People were settled in those Parts. These have never been sold, but remain still to be disposed of; and we are well pleased to hear you are provided with Goods, and do assure you of our Willingness to treat with you for those unpurchased Lands; in Confirmation whereof, we present you with this Belt of Wampum.

*Which was received with the usual Ceremonies.*

*CANASSATEGO* added, that as the three Governors of *Virginia, Maryland,* and *Pennsylvania,* had divided the Lands among them, they could not, for this Reason, tell how much each had got, nor were they concerned about it, so that they were paid by all the Governors for the several Parts each possessed, and this they left to their Honour and Justice.[7]

In the COURT-HOUSE at *Lancaster, June* 27, 1744, A.M.
PRESENT, The Honourable *GEORGE THOMAS,* Esq; Governor, *&c.*
The Honourable the Commissioners of *Virginia.*
The Honourable the Commissioners of *Maryland.*
The Deputies of the *Six Nations.*
*Conrad Weiser,* Interpreter.

*The Commissioners of* Virginia *ordered the Interpreter to let the* Indians *know the Governor of* Virginia *was going to speak to them, and then they spoke as follows:*

*Sachims and Warriors of the* Six United Nations, *our Friends and Brethren,* At our Desire the Governor of *Pennsylvania* invited you to this Council Fire; we have waited a long Time for you, but now you are come, you are heartily welcome; we are very glad to see you; we give you this String of Wampum.

*Which was received with their usual Approbation.*

*Brethren,* In the Year 1736, four of your Sachims wrote a Letter to *James Logan,* Esq; then President of *Pennsylvania,* to let the Governor of *Virginia* know that you expected some Consideration for Lands in the Occupation of some of the People of *Virginia.* Upon seeing a Copy of this Letter, the Governor, with the Council of

* *Cohongorontas,* i.e. *Potomack.*

*Virginia,* took some Time to consider of it. They found, on looking into the old Treaties, that you had given up your Lands to the Great King, who has had Possession of *Virginia* above One Hundred and Sixty Years, and under that Great King the Inhabitants of *Virginia* hold their Land, so they thought there might be some Mistake.

Wherefore they desired the Governor of *New-York* to enquire of you about it. He sent his Interpreter to you in *May,* 1743, who laid this before you at a Council held at *Onandago,* to which you answer, "That if you had any Demand or Pretensions on the Governor of *Virginia* any way, you would have made it known to the Governor of *New-York.*" This corresponds with what you have said to Governor *Thomas,* in the Treaty made with him at *Philadelphia* in *July,* 1742; for then you only make your Claim to Lands in the Government of *Maryland.*

We are so well pleased with this good Faith of you our Brethren of the *Six Nations,* and your Regard to the Treaties made with *Virginia,* that we are ready to hear you on the Subject of your Message eight Years since.

Tell us what Nations of *Indians* you conquered any Lands from in *Virginia,* how long it is since, and what Possession you have had; and if it does appear, that there is any Land on the Borders of *Virginia* that the *Six Nations* have a Right to, we are willing to make you Satisfaction.

*Then laid down a String of Wampum, which was accepted with the usual Ceremony, and then added,*

We have a Chest of new Goods, and the Key is in our Pockets. You are our Brethren; the Great King is our common Father, and we will live with you, as Children ought to do, in Peace and Love.

We will brighten the Chain, and strengthen the Union between us; so that we shall never be divided, but remain Friends and Brethren as long as the Sun gives Light; in Confirmation whereof, we give you this Belt of Wampum.

*Which was received with the usual Ceremony.*

*TACHANOONTIA* replied:

*Brother Assaragoa,* You have made a good Speech to us, which is very agreeable, and for which we return you our Thanks. We shall be able to give you an Answer to every Part of it some Time this Afternoon, and we will let you know when we are ready.

In the COURT-HOUSE at *Lancaster, June* 27, 1744, *P. M.*
PRESENT, The Honourable *GEORGE THOMAS,* Esq; Governor, &c.
The Honourable the Commissioners of *Virginia.*
The Honourable the Commissioners of *Maryland.*
The Deputies of the *Six Nations.*
*Conrad Weiser, Interpreter.*

*TACHANOONTIA spoke as follows:*

*Brother* Assaragoa, Since you have joined with the Governor of *Maryland* and brother *Onas* in kindling this Fire, we gladly acknowledge the Pleasure we have in seeing you here, and observing your good Dispositions as well to confirm the Treaties of Friendship, as to enter into further Contracts about Land with us; and, in Token of our Satisfaction, we present you with this String of Wampum.

*Which was received with the usual Ceremonies.*

*Brother* Assaragoa, In your Speech this Morning you were pleased to say we had wrote a Letter to *James Logan,* about seven Years ago, to demand a Consideration for our Lands in the Possession of some of the *Virginians;* that you held them under the Great King for upwards of One Hundred and Sixty Years, and that we had already given up our Right; and that therefore you had desired the Governor of *New-York* to send his Interpreter to us last Year to *Onandago,* which he did; and, as you say, we in Council at *Onandago* did declare, that we had no Demand upon you for Lands, and that if we had any Pretensions, we should have made them known to the Governor of *New-York;* and likewise you desire to know if we have any Right to the *Virginia* Lands, and that we will make such Right appear, and tell you what Nations of *Indians* we conquered those Lands from.

Now we answer, We have the Right of Conquest, a Right too dearly purchased, and which cost us too much Blood, to give up without any Reason at all, as you say we have done at *Albany;* but we should be obliged to you, if you would let us see the Letter, and inform us who was the Interpreter, and whose Names are put to that Letter; for as the whole Transaction cannot be above a Year's standing, it must be fresh in every Body's Memory, and some of our Council would easily remember it; but we assure you, and are well able to prove, that neither we, nor any Part of us, have ever relinquished our Right, or ever gave such an Answer as you say is mentioned in your Letter.[8] Could we, so few Years ago, make a formal Demand, by *James Logan,* and not be sensible of our Right? And hath any thing happened since that Time to make us less sensible? No; and as this Matter can be easily cleared up, we are anxious it should be done; for we are positive no such thing was ever mentioned to us at *Onandago* nor any where else. All the World knows we conquered the several Nations living on *Sasquahannah, Cohongoronta,* and on the Back of the Great Mountains in *Virginia;* the *Conoy-uch-such-roona, Coch-now-was-roonan, Tohoa-irough-roonan,* and *Connutskin-ough-roonaw,* feel the Effects of our Conquests, being now a Part of our Nations, and their Lands at our Disposal. We know very well, it hath often been said by the *Virginians,* that the *Great King of* ENGLAND, and the People of that Colony, conquered the *Indians* who lived there, but it is not true. We will allow they have conquered the *Sachdagughroonaw,* and drove back the *Tuscarroraws,* and that they have, on that Account, a Right to some Part of *Virginia;* but as to what lies beyond the Mountains, we conquered the Nations residing there, and that Land, if the *Virginians* ever get a good Right to it, it must be by us; and in Testimony of the Truth of our Answer to this Part of your Speech, we give you this String of Wampum.

*Which was received with the usual Ceremony.*

*Brother* Assaragoa, We have given you a full Answer to the first Part of your Speech, which we hope will be satisfactory. We are glad to hear you have brought with you a big Chest of new Goods, and that you have the Key in your Pockets. We do not doubt but we shall have a good Understanding in all Points, and come to an Agreement with you.

We shall open all our Hearts to you, that you may know every thing in them; we will hide nothing from you; and we hope, if there be any thing still remaining in your Breast that may occasion any Dispute between us, you will take the Opportunity to unbosom your Hearts, and lay them open to us, that henceforth there may be no Dirt, nor any other Obstacle in the Road between us; and in Token of our hearty Wishes to bring about so good an Harmony, we present you with this Belt of Wampum.

*Which was received with the usual Ceremony.*

*Brother* Assaragoa, We must now tell you what Mountains we mean that we say are the Boundaries between you and us. You may remember, that about twenty Years ago you had a Treaty with us at *Albany,* when you took a Belt of Wampum, and made a Fence with it on the Middle of the Hill, and told us, that if any of the Warriors of the *Six Nations* came on your Side of the Middle of the Hill, you would hang them; and you gave us Liberty to do the same with any of your People who should be found on our Side of the Middle of the Hill. This is the Hill we mean, and we desire that Treaty may be now confirmed. After we left *Albany,* we brought our Road a great deal more to the West, that we might comply with your Proposal; but, tho' it was of your own making, your People never observed it, but came and lived on our Side of the Hill, which we don't blame you for, as you live at a great Distance, near the Seas, and cannot be thought to know what your People do in the Back-parts: And on their settling, contrary to your own Proposal, on our new Road, it fell out that our Warriors did some Hurt to your People's Cattle, of which a Complaint was made, and transmitted to us by our Brother *Onas;* and we, at his Request, altered the Road again, and brought it to the Foot of the Great Mountain, where it now is; and it is impossible for us to remove it any further to the West, those Parts of the Country being absolutely impassable by either Man or Beast.

We had not been long in the Use of this new Road before your People came, like Flocks of Birds, and sat down on both Sides of it, and yet we never made a Complaint to you, tho' you must be sensible those Things must have been done by your People in manifest Breach of your own Proposal made at *Albany;* and therefore, as we are now opening our Hearts to you, we cannot avoid complaining, and desire all these Affairs may be settled, and that you may be stronger induced to do us Justice for what is past, and to come to a thorough Settlement for the future, we, in the Presence of the Governor of *Maryland,* and Brother *Onas,* present you with this Belt of Wampum.

*Which was received with the usual Ceremony.*

*Then* Tachanoontia *added:*

He forgot to say, that the Affair of the Road must be looked upon as a Preliminary to be settled before the Grant of Lands; and that either the *Virginia* People must be obliged to remove more Easterly, or, if they are permitted to stay, that our Warriors, marching that Way to the Southward, shall go Sharers with them in what they plant.

In the COURT-HOUSE at *Lancaster, June* 28, 1744, *A. M.*
PRESENT, The Honourable *GEORGE THOMAS,* Esq; Governor, &c.
The Honourable the Commissioners of *Virginia.*
The Honourable the Commissioners of *Maryland.*
The Deputies of the *Six Nations.*
*Conrad Weiser,* Interpreter.

*The* GOVERNOR *spoke as follows:*

*Friends and Brethren of the* Six Nations,

I Am always sorry when any thing happens that may create the least Uneasiness between us; but as we are mutually engaged to keep the Road between us clear and open, and to remove every Obstruction that may lie in the Way, I must inform you, that three of the *Delaware Indians* lately murdered *John Armstrong,* an *Indian* Trader, and his two Men, in a most barbarous Manner, as he was travelling to *Allegheny,* and stole his Goods of a considerable Value. *Shick Calamy,* and the *Indians* settled at *Shamokin,* did well; they seized two of the Murderers, and sent them down to our Settlements; but the *Indians,* who had the Charge of them, afterwards suffered one of them to escape, on a Pretence that he was not concerned in the bloody Deed; the other is now in *Philadelphia* Goal. By our Law all the Accessaries to a Murder are to be tried, and put to Death, as well as the Person who gave the deadly Wound. If they consented to it, encouraged it, or any ways assisted in it, they are to be put to Death, and it is just it should be so. If, upon Trial, the Persons present at the Murder are found not to have done any of these Things, they are set at Liberty. Two of our People were, not many Years ago, publickly put to Death for killing two *Indians;* we therefore expect you will take the most effectual Measures to seize and deliver up to us the other two *Indians* present at these Murders, to be tried with the Principal now in Custody.[9] If it shall appear, upon their Trial, that they were not advising, or any way assisting in this horrid Fact, they will be acquitted, and sent home to their Towns. And that you may be satisfied no Injustice will be done to them, I do now invite you to depute three or four *Indians* to be present at their Trials. I do likewise expect that you will order strict Search to be made for the Remainder of the stolen Goods, that they may be restored to the Wife and Children of the Deceased. That what I have said may have its due Weight with you, I give you this String of Wampum.

*Which was accepted with the* Yo-hah.

The Governor afterwards ordered the Interpreter to tell them, he expected a very full Answer from them, and that they might take their own Time to give it; for he did not desire to interfere with the Business of *Virginia* and *Maryland.*

They said they would take it into Consideration, and give a full Answer.

Then the Commissioners of *Virginia* let them know, by the Interpreter, that they would speak to them in the Afternoon.

In the COURT-HOUSE Chamber at *Lancaster, June* 28, 1744, *P. M.*
PRESENT, The Honourable the Commissioners of *Maryland.*
The Deputies of the *Six Nations.*
*Conrad Weiser,* Interpreter.

*The Commissioners desired the Interpreter to tell the* Indians *they were going to speak to them. Mr.* Weiser *acquainted them herewith. After which the said Commissioners spoke as follows:*

*Our good Friends and Brethren, the* Six *united* Nations,

We have considered what you said concerning your Title to some Lands now in our Province, and also of the Place where they lie. Altho' we cannot admit your Right, yet we are so resolved to live in Brotherly Love and Affection with the *Six Nations,* that upon your giving us a Release in Writing of all your Claim to any Lands in *Maryland,* we shall make you a Compensation to the Value of Three Hundred Pounds Currency, for the Payment of Part whereof we have brought some Goods, and shall make up the rest in what Manner you think fit.

As we intend to say something to you about our Chain of Friendship after this Affair of the Land is settled, we desire you will now examine the Goods, and make an End of this Matter.

We will not omit acquainting our good Friends the *Six Nations,* that notwithstanding we are likely to come to an Agreement about your Claim of Lands, yet your Brethren of *Maryland* look on you to be as one Soul and one Body with themselves; and as a broad Road will be made between us, we shall always be desirous of keeping it clear that we may, from Time to Time, take care that the Links of our Friendship be not rusted. In Testimony that our Words and our Hearts agree, we give you this Belt of Wampum.

*On presenting of which the* Indians *gave the usual Cry of Approbation.*

Mr. *Weiser* acquainted the *Indians,* they might now look over the several Goods placed on a Table in the Chamber for that Purpose; and the honourable Commissioners bid him tell them, if they disliked any of the Goods, or, if they were damaged, the Commissioners would put a less Price on such as were either disliked or damnified.

The *Indians* having viewed and examined the Goods, and seeming dissatisfied at the Price and Worth of them, required Time to go down into the Court-House, in order for a Consultation to be had by the Chiefs of them concerning the said Goods, and likewise that the Interpreter might retire with them, which he did. Accordingly they went down into the Court-House, and soon after returned again into the Chamber.

Mr. *Weiser* sat down among the *Indians,* and discoursed them about the Goods, and in some short Time after they chose the following from among the others, and the Price agreed to be given for them by the *Six Nations* was, *viz.*

| | *L.* | *s.* | *d.* |
|---|---|---|---|
| Four Pieces of Strowds, at 7 *L.* | 28 | 00 | 00 |
| Two Pieces Ditto, 5 *L.* | 10 | 00 | 00 |
| Two Hundred Shirts, | 63 | 12 | 00 |
| Three Pieces Half-Thicks, | 11 | 00 | 00 |
| Three Pieces Duffle Blankets, at 7 *L.* | 21 | 00 | 00 |
| One Piece Ditto, | 6 | 10 | 00 |
| Forty Seven Guns, at 1 *L.* 6 *s.* | 61 | 2 | 00 |
| One Pound Vermillion, | 00 | 18 | 00 |
| One Thousand Flints, | 00 | 18 | 00 |
| Four Dozen Jews Harps, | 00 | 14 | 00 |
| One Dozen Boxes, | 00 | 1 | 00 |
| One Hundred Two Quarters Bar-Lead, | 3 | 00 | 00 |
| Two Quarters Shot, | 1 | 00 | 00 |
| Two Half-Barrels of Gun-Powder, | 13 | 00 | 00 |
| | *L.* 220 | 15 | 00 |
| | *Pennsylvania Currency* | | |

When the *Indians* had agreed to take these Goods at the Rates above specified, they informed the Interpreter, that they would give an Answer to the Speech made to them this Morning by the honourable the Commissioners of *Maryland,* but did not express the Time when such Answer should be made. At 12 o'Clock the Commissioners departed the Chamber.

In the COURT-HOUSE at *Lancaster, June* 28, 1744, *P. M.*
The Honourable *GEORGE THOMAS,* Esq; Governor, &c.
The Honourable the Commissioners of *Virginia.*
The Honourable the Commissioners of *Maryland.*
The Deputies of the *Six Nations.*
*Conrad Weiser,* Interpreter.

*The Commissioners of* Virginia *desired the Interpreter to let the* Indians *know, that their Brother* Assaragoa *was now going to give his Reply to their Answer to his first Speech, delivered them the Day before in the Forenoon.*

*Sachims and Warriors of the united* Six Nations,

We are now come to answer what you said to us Yesterday, since what we said to you before on the Part of the Great King, our Father, has not been satisfactory. You have gone into old Times, and so must we. It is true that the Great King holds *Virginia* by Right of Conquest, and the Bounds of that Conquest to the Westward is the Great Sea.

If the *Six Nations* have made any Conquest over *Indians* that may at any Time have lived on the West-side of the Great Mountains of *Virginia*, yet they never possessed any Lands there that we have ever heard of. That Part was altogether deserted, and free for any People to enter upon, as the People of *Virginia* have done, by Order of the Great King, very justly, as well by an ancient Right, as by its being freed from the Possession of any other, and from any Claim even of you the *Six Nations*, our Brethren, until within these eight Years. The first Treaty between the Great King, in Behalf of his Subjects of *Virginia*, and you, that we can find, was made at *Albany*, by Colonel *Henry Coursey*, Seventy Years since; this was a Treaty of Friendship, when the first Covenant Chain was made, when we and you became Brethren.

The next Treaty was also at *Albany*, above Fifty-eight Years ago, by the Lord *Howard*, Governor of *Virginia;* then you declare yourselves Subjects to the Great King, our Father, and gave up to him all your Lands for his Protection. This you own in a Treaty made by the Governor of *New-York* with you at the same Place in the Year 1687, and you express yourselves in these Words, "Brethren, you tell us the King of *England* is a very great King, and why should not you join with us in a very just Cause, when the *French* join with our Enemies in an unjust Cause? O Brethren, we see the Reason of this; for the *French* would fain kill us all, and when that is done, they would carry all the Beaver Trade to *Canada*, and the *Great King of* England would lose the Land likewise; and therefore, O Great Sachim, beyond the Great Lakes, awake, and suffer not those poor *Indians*, that have given themselves and their Lands under your Protection, to be destroyed by the *French* without a Cause."

The last Treaty we shall speak to you about is that made at *Albany* by Governor *Spotswood*, which you have not recited as it is: For the white People, your Brethren of *Virginia*, are, in no Article of that Treaty, prohibited to pass, and settle to the Westward of the Great Mountains. It is the *Indians*, tributary to *Virginia*, that are restrained, as you and your tributary *Indians* are from passing to the Eastward of the same Mountains, or to the Southward of *Cohongorooton*, and you agree to this Article in these Words; "That the Great River of *Potowmack*, and the high Ridge of Mountains, which extend all along the Frontiers of *Virginia* to the Westward of the present Settlements of that Colony, shall be for ever the established Boundaries between the *Indians* subject to the Dominion of *Virginia*, and the *Indians* belonging and depending on the *Five Nations;* so that neither our *Indians* shall not, on any

Pretence whatsoever, pass to Northward or Westward of the said Boundaries, without having to produce a Passport under the Hand and Seal of the Governor or Commander in Chief of *Virginia;* nor your *Indians* to pass to the Southward or Eastward of the said Boundaries, without a Passport in like Manner from the Governor or Commander in Chief of *New-York.*"[10]

And what Right can you have to Lands that you have no Right to walk upon, but upon certain Conditions? It is true, you have not observed this Part of the Treaty, and your Brethren of *Virginia* have not insisted upon it with a due Strictness, which has occasioned some Mischief.

This Treaty has been sent to the Governor of *Virginia* by Order of the Great King, and is what we must rely on, and, being in Writing, is more certain than your Memory. That is the Way the white People have of preserving Transactions of every Kind, and transmitting them down to their Childrens Children for ever, and all Disputes among them are settled by this faithful kind of Evidence, and must be the Rule between the Great King and you. This Treaty your Sachims and Warriors signed some Years after the same Governor *Spotswood,* in the Right of the Great King, had been, with some People of *Virginia,* in Possession of these very Lands, which you have set up your late Claim to.

The Commissioners for *Indian* Affairs at *Albany* gave the Account we mentioned to you Yesterday to the Governor of *New-York,* and he sent it to the Governor of *Virginia;* their Names will be given you by the Interpreter.

*Brethren,* This Dispute is not between *Virginia* and you; it is setting up your Right against the Great King, under whose Grants the People you complain of are settled. Nothing but a Command from the Great King can remove them; they are too powerful to be removed by any Force of you, our Brethren; and the Great King, as our common Father, will do equal Justice to all his Children; wherefore we do believe they will be confirmed in their Possessions.

As to the Road you mention, we intended to prevent any Occasion for it, by making a Peace between you and the Southern *Indians,* a few Years since, at a considerable Expence to our Great King, which you confirmed at *Albany.* It seems, by your being at War with the *Catawbas,* that it has not been long kept between you.[11]

However, if you desire a Road, we will agree to one on the Terms of the Treaty you made with Colonel *Spotswood,* and your People, behaving themselves orderly like Friends and Brethren, shall be used in their Passage through *Virginia* with the same Kindness as they are when they pass through the Lands of your Brother *Onas.* This, we hope, will be agreed to by you our Brethren, and we will abide by the Promise made to you Yesterday.

We may proceed to settle what we are to give you for any Right you may have, or have had to all the Lands to the Southward and Westward of the Lands of your Brother the Governor of *Maryland,* and of your Brother *Onas;* tho' we are informed that the Southern *Indians* claim these very Lands that you do.

We are desirous to live with you, our Brethren, according to the old Chain of

Friendship, to settle all these Matters fairly and honestly; and, as a Pledge of our Sincerity, we give you this Belt of Wampum.

*Which was received with the usual Ceremony.*

In the COURT-HOUSE Chamber at *Lancaster, June* 29, 1744, *A. M.*
PRESENT, The Honourable the Commissioners of *Maryland.*
The Deputies of the *Six Nations.*
*Conrad Weiser,* Interpreter.

*Mr.* Weiser *informed the honourable Commissioners, the* Indians *were ready to give their Answer to the Speech made to them here Yesterday Morning by the Commissioners; whereupon* Canassatego *spoke as follows, looking on a Deal-board, where were some black Lines, describing the courses of* Potowmack *and* Sasquahanna:

*Brethren,* Yesterday you spoke to us concerning the Lands on this Side *Potowmack* River, and as we have deliberately considered what you said to us on that Matter, we are now very ready to settle the Bounds of such Lands, and release our Right and Claim thereto.

We are willing to renounce all Right to Lord *Baltimore* of all those Lands lying two Miles above the uppermost Fork of *Potowmack* or *Cohongoruton* River, near which *Thomas Cressap* has a hunting or trading Cabin, by a North-line, to the Bounds of *Pennsylvania.* But in case such Limits shall not include every Settlement or Inhabitant of *Maryland,* then such other Lines and Courses, from the said two Miles above the Forks, to the outermost Inhabitants or Settlements, as shall include every Settlement and Inhabitant in *Maryland,* and from thence, by a North-line, to the Bounds of *Pennsylvania,* shall be the Limits. And further, If any People already have, or shall settle beyond the Lands now described and bounded, they shall enjoy the same free from any Disturbance whatever, and we do, and shall accept these People for our Brethren, and as such always treat them.

We earnestly desire to live with you as Brethren, and hope you will shew us all Brotherly Kindness; in Token whereof, we present you with a Belt of Wampum.

*Which was received with the usual Ceremony.*

Soon after the Commissioners and *Indians* departed from the Court-House Chamber.

In the COURT-HOUSE Chamber at *Lancaster, June* 30, 1744, *A. M.*
PRESENT, The Honourable the Commissioners of *Virginia.*
The Deputies of the *Six Nations.*
*Conrad Weiser, Interpreter.*

Gachradodow, *Speaker for the* Indians, *in Answer to the Commissioners Speech at the last Meeting, with a strong Voice, and proper Action, spoke as follows:*

*Brother* Assaragoa, The World at the first was made on the other Side of the Great Water different from what it is on this Side, as may be known from the different Colours of our Skin, and of our Flesh, and that which you call Justice may not be so amongst us; you have your Laws and Customs, and so have we. The Great King might send you over to conquer the *Indians,* but it looks to us that God did not approve of it; if he had, he would not have placed the Sea where it is, as the Limits between us and you.

*Brother* Assaragoa, Tho' great Things are well remembered among us, yet we don't remember that we were ever conquered by the Great King, or that we have been employed by that Great King to conquer others; if it was so, it is beyond our Memory. We do remember we were employed by *Maryland* to conquer the *Conestogoes,* and that the second time we were at War with them, we carried them all off.

*Brother* Assaragoa, You charge us with not acting agreeable to our Peace with the *Catawbas,* we will repeat to you truly what was done. The Governor of *New-York* at Albany, in Behalf of *Assaragoa,* gave us several Belts of Wampum from the *Cherikees* and *Catawbas,* and we agreed to a Peace, if those Nations would send some of their great Men to us to confirm it Face to Face, and that they would trade with us; and desired that they would appoint a Time to meet at *Albany* for that Purpose, but they never came.

*Brother* Assaragoa, We then desired a Letter might be sent to the *Catawbas* and *Cherikees,* to desire them to come and confirm the Peace. It was long before an Answer came; but we met the *Cherikees,* and confirmed the Peace, and sent some of our People to take care of them, until they returned to their own Country.

The *Catawbas* refused to come, and sent us word, That we were but Women, that they were Men, and double Men, for they had two P——s; that they could make Women of us, and would be always at War with us. They are a deceitful People. Our Brother *Assaragoa* is deceived by them; we don't blame him for it, but are sorry he is so deceived.

*Brother* Assaragoa, We have confirmed the Peace with the *Cherikees,* but not with the *Catawbas.* They have been treacherous, and know it; so that the War must continue till one of us is destroyed. This we think proper to tell you, that you may not be troubled at what we do to the *Catawbas.*

*Brother* Assaragoa, We will now speak to the Point between us. You say you will agree with us as to the Road; we desire that may be the Road which was last made (the Waggon-Road.) It is always a Custom among Brethren or Strangers to use each other kindly; you have some very ill-natured People living there; so that we desire the Persons in Power may know that we are to have reasonable Victuals when we are in want.

You know very well, when the white People came first here they were poor; but now they have got our Lands, and are by them become rich, and we are now poor; what little we have had for the Land goes soon away, but the Land lasts for ever. You told us you had brought with you a Chest of Goods, and that you have the Key in your Pockets; but we have never seen the Chest, nor the Goods that are said to be in it; it may be small, and the Goods few; we want to see them, and are desirous to come to some Conclusion. We have been sleeping here these ten Days past, and have not done any thing to the Purpose.

The Commissioners told them they should see the Goods on *Monday.*

In the COURT-HOUSE at *Lancaster, June* 30, 1744, *P. M.*
PRESENT. The Honourable *GEORGE THOMAS,* Esq; Governor, &c.
The Honourable the Commissioners of *Virginia.*
The Honourable the Commissioners of *Maryland.*
The Deputies of the *Six Nations.*
*Conrad Weiser,* Interpreter.

The three Governments entertained the *Indians,* and all the Gentlemen in Town, with a handsome Dinner. The *Six Nations,* in their Order, having returned Thanks with the usual Solemnity of *Yo-ha-han,* the Interpreter informed the Governor and the Commissioners, that as the Lord Proprietor and Governor of *Maryland* was not known to the *Indians* by any particular Name, they had agreed, in Council, to take the first Opportunity of a large Company to present him with one; and as this with them is deemed a Matter of great Consequence, and attended with Abundance of Form, the several Nations had drawn Lots for the Performance of the Ceremony, and the Lot falling on the *Cayogo* Nation, they had chosen *Gachradodow,* one of their Chiefs, to be their Speaker, and he desired Leave to begin; which being given, he, on an elevated Part of the Court-House, with all the Dignity of a Warrior, the Gesture of an Orator, and in a very graceful Posture, spoke as follows:

"As the Governor of *Maryland* had invited them here to treat about their Lands, and brighten the Chain of Friendship, the united Nations thought themselves so much obliged to them, that they had come to a Resolution in Council to give to the great Man, who is Proprietor of *Maryland,* a particular Name, by which they might hereafter correspond with him; and as it had fallen to the *Cayogoes* Lot in Council to consider of a proper Name for that chief Man, they had agreed to give him the Name of *Tocarry-hogan,* denoting Precedency, Excellency, or living in the middle or honourable Place betwixt *Assaragoa* and their Brother *Onas,* by whom their Treaties might be better carried on." And then, addressing himself to his Honour the Governor of *Pennsylvania,* the honourable the Commissioners of *Virginia* and *Maryland,* and to the Gentlemen then present, he proceeded:

"As there is a Company of great Men now assembled, we take this Time and Opportunity to publish this Matter, that it may be known *Tocarry-hogan* is our Friend, and that we are ready to honour him, and that by such Name he may be always called and known among us. And we hope he will ever act towards us according to the Excellency of the Name we have now given him, and enjoy a long and happy Life."

The honourable the Governor and Commissioners, and all the Company present, returned the Compliment with three Huzza's, and, after drinking Healths to our gracious King and the *Six Nations,* the Commissioners of *Maryland* proceeded to Business in the Court-House Chamber with the *Indians,* where *Conrad Weiser,* the Interpreter, was present.

The honourable the Commissioners ordered Mr. *Weiser* to tell the *Indians,* that a Deed, releasing all their Claim and Title to certain Lands lying in the Province of *Maryland,* which by them was agreed to be given and executed for the Use of the Lord Baron of *Baltimore,* Lord Proprietary of that Province, was now on the Table, and Seals ready fixed thereto. The Interpreter acquainted them therewith as desired, and then gave the Deed to *Canassatego,* the Speaker, who made his Mark, and put his Seal, and delivered it; after which, thirteen other Chiefs or Sachims of the *Six Nations* executed it in the same Manner, in the Presence of the honourable the Commissioners of *Virginia,* and divers other Gentlemen of that Colony, and of the Provinces of *Pennsylvania* and *Maryland.*

At the House of Mr. *George Sanderson* in *Lancaster, July* 2, 1744, *A. M.*
PRESENT, The Honourable the Commissioners of *Maryland.*
The Deputies of the *Six Nations.*
*Conrad Weiser,* Interpreter.

The several Chiefs of the *Indians* of the *Six Nations,* who had not signed the Deed of Release of their Claim to some Lands in *Maryland,* tendered to them on *Saturday* last, in the Chamber of the Court-House in this Town, did now readily execute the same, and caused Mr. *Weiser* likewise to sign it, as well with his *Indian,* as with his.own proper Name of *Weiser,* as a Witness and Interpreter.

In the COURT-HOUSE at *Lancaster, July* 2, 1744, *A.M.*
PRESENT, The Honourable *GEORGE THOMAS,* Esq; Governor, *&c.*
The Honourable the Commissioners of *Virginia.*
The Honourable the Commissioners of *Maryland.*
The Deputies of the *Six Nations.*
*Conrad Weiser,* Interpreter.

*CANASSATEGO spoke as follows:*
*Brother* Onas, The other Day you was pleased to tell us, you were always concerned whenever any thing happened that might give you or us Uneasiness, and that we were mutually engaged to preserve the Road open and clear between us; and you informed us of the Murder of *John Armstrong,* and his two Men, by some of the *Delaware Indians,* and of their stealing his Goods to a considerable Value. The *Delaware Indians,* as you suppose, are under our Power. We join with you in your Concern for such a vile Proceeding; and, to testify that we have the same Inclinations with you to keep the Road clear, free and open, we give you this String of Wampum.

*Which was received with the usual Ceremony.*

*Brother* Onas, These Things happen frequently, and we desire you will consider them well, and not be too much concerned. Three *Indians* have been killed at different Times at *Ohio,* and we never mentioned any of them to you, imagining it might have been occasioned by some unfortunate Quarrels, and being unwilling to create a Disturbance. We therefore desire you will consider these Things well, and, to take the Grief from your Heart, we give you this String of Wampum.

*Which was received with the usual Ceremonies.*

*Brother* Onas, We had heard of the Murder of *John Armstrong,* and, in our Journey here, we had Conference with our Cousins the *Delawares* about it, and reproved them severely for it, and charged them to go down to our Brother *Onas,* and make him Satisfaction, both for the Men that were killed, and for the Goods. We understood, by them, that the principal Actor in these Murders is in your Prison, and that he had done all the Mischief himself; but that, besides him, you had required and demanded two others who were in his Company when the Murders were committed. We promise faithfully, in our Return, to renew our Reproofs, and to charge the *Delawares* to send down some of their Chiefs with these two young Men (but not as Prisoners) to be examined by you; and as we think, upon Examination, you will not find them guilty, we rely on your Justice not to do them any Harm, but to permit them to return home in Safety.

We likewise understand, that Search has been made for the Goods belonging to the Deceased, and that some have been already returned to your People, but that some are still missing. You may depend upon our giving the strictest Charge to the *Delawares* to search again with more Diligence for the Goods, and to return them, or the Value of them, in Skins. And, to confirm what we have said, we give you this String of Wampum.

*Which was received with the usual Ceremonies.*

*Brother* Onas, The *Conoy Indians* have informed us, that they sent you a Message, some Time ago, to advise you, that they were ill used by the white People in the Place where they had lived, and that they had come to a Resolution of removing to *Shamokin,* and requested some small Satisfaction for their Land; and as they never have received any Answer from you, they have desired us to speak for them; we heartily recommend their Case to your Generosity. And, to give Weight to our Recommendation, we present you with this String of Wampum.

*Which was received with the usual Ceremony.*

*The Governor having conferred a little Time with the honourable Commissioners of* Virginia *and* Maryland, *made the following Reply:*

*Brethren,* I am glad to find that you agree with me in the Necessity of keeping the Road between us clear and open, and the Concern you have expressed on account of the barbarous Murders mentioned to you, is a Proof of your Brotherly Affection for us. If Crimes of this Nature be not strictly enquired into, and the Criminals severely punished, there will be an End of all Commerce between us and the *Indians*, and then you will be altogether in the Power of the *French*. They will set what Price they please on their own Goods, and give you what they think fit for your Skins; so it is for your own Interest that our Traders should be safe in their Persons and Goods when they travel to your Towns.

*Brethren*, I considered this Matter well before I came from *Philadelphia*, and I advised with the Council there upon it, as I have done here with the honourable the Commissioners of *Virginia* and *Maryland*. I never heard before of the Murder of the three *Indians* at *Ohio;* had Complaint been made to me of it, and it had appeared to have been committed by any of the People under my Government, they should have been put to Death, as two of them were, some Years ago, for killing two *Indians*. You are not to take your own Satisfaction, but to apply to me, and I will see that Justice be done you; and should any of the *Indians* rob or murder any of our People, I do expect that you will deliver them up to be tried and punished in the same Manner as white People are. This is the Way to preserve Friendship between us, and will be for your Benefit as well as ours. I am well pleased with the Steps you have already taken, and the Reproofs you have given to your Cousins the *Delawares*, and do expect you will lay your Commands upon some of their Chiefs to bring down the two young Men that were present at the Murders; if they are not brought down, I shall look upon it as a Proof of their Guilt.

If, upon Examination, they shall be found not to have been concerned in the bloody Action, they shall be well used, and sent home in Safety: I will take it upon myself to see that they have no Injustice done them. An Inventory is taken of the Goods already restored, and I expect Satisfaction will be made for such as cannot be found, in Skins, according to their Promise.

I well remember the coming down of one of the *Conoy Indians* with a Paper, setting forth, That the *Conoys* had come to a Resolution to leave the Land reserved for them by the Proprietors, but he made no Complaint to me of ill Usage from the white People. The Reason he gave for their Removal was, That the settling of the white People all round them had made Deer scarce, and that therefore they chose to remove to *Juniata* for the Benefit of Hunting. I ordered what they said to be entered in the Council-Book. The old Man's Expences were born, and a Blanket given him at his Return home. I have not yet heard from the Proprietors on this Head; but you may be assured, from the Favour and Justice they have always shewn to the *Indians*, that they will do every thing that can be reasonably expected of them in this Case.

In the COURT-HOUSE at *Lancaster, July* 2, 1744, *P. M.*
PRESENT, The Honourable the Commissioners of *Virginia*.
The Deputies of the *Six Nations*.
*Conrad Weiser*, Interpreter.

*The* Indians *being told, by the Interpreter, that their Brother* Assaragoa *was going to speak to them, the Commissioners spoke as follows:*

"*Sachims and Warriors, our Friends and Brethren,*

As we have already said enough to you on the Subject of the Title to the Lands you claim from *Virginia,* we have no Occasion to say any thing more to you on that Head, but come directly to the Point.

"We have opened the Chest, and the Goods are now here before you; they cost Two Hundred Pounds *Pennsylvania* Money, and were bought by a Person recommended to us by the Governor of *Pennsylvania* with ready Cash. We ordered them to be good in their Kinds, and we believe they are so. These Goods, and Two Hundred Pounds in Gold, which lie on the Table, we will give you, our Brethren of the *Six Nations,* upon Condition that you immediately make a Deed recognizing the King's Right to all the Lands that are, or shall be, by his Majesty's Appointment in the Colony of *Virginia.*

"As to the Road, [we] agree you shall have one, and the Regulation is in Paper, which the Interpreter now has in his Custody to shew you. The People of *Virginia* shall perform their Part, if you and your *Indians* perform theirs; we are your Brethren, and will do no Hardships to you, but, on the contrary, all the Kindness we can."

The *Indians* agreed to what was said, and *Canassatego* desired they would represent their Case to the King, in order to have a further Consideration when the Settlement increased much further back. To which the Commissioners agreed, and promised they would make such a Representation faithfully and honestly; and, for their further Security that they would do so, they would give them a Writing, under their Hands and Seals, to that Purpose.

They desired that some Rum might be given them to drink on their Way home, which the Commissioners agreed to, and paid them in Gold for that Purpose, and the Carriage of their Goods from *Philadelphia,* Nine Pounds, Thirteen Shillings, and Three-pence, *Pennsylvania* Money.

*Canassatego* further said, That as their Brother *Tocarry-hogan* sent them Provision on the Road here, which kept them from starving, he hoped their Brother *Assaragoa* would do the same for them back, and have the Goods he gave them carried to the usual Place; which the Commissioners agreed to, and ordered Provisions and Carriages to be provided accordingly.

After this Conference the Deed was produced, and the Interpreter explained it to them; and they, according to their Rank and Quality, put their Marks and Seals to it in the Presence of several Gentlemen of *Maryland, Pennsylvania* and *Virginia;* and when they delivered the Deed, *Canassatego* delivered it for the Use of their Father, the Great King, and hoped he would consider them; on which the Gentlemen and *Indians* then present gave three Shouts.

In the COURT-HOUSE at *Lancaster, Tuesday, July* 3, 1744, *A.M.*
PRESENT, The Honourable *GEORGE THOMAS,* Esq; Governor, *&c.*

The Honourable the Commissioners of *Virginia.*
The Honourable the Commissioners of *Maryland.*
The Deputies of the *Six Nations.*
*Conrad Weiser,* Interpreter.

*The* GOVERNOR *spoke as follows:*
*Friends and Brethren of the* Six Nations,

At a Treaty held with many of the Chiefs of your Nations Two Years ago, the Road between us was made clearer and wider; our Fire was enlarged, and our Friendship confirmed by an Exchange of Presents, and many other mutual good Offices.

We think ourselves happy in having been instrumental to your meeting with our Brethren of *Virginia* and *Maryland;* and we persuade ourselves, that you, on your Parts, will always remember it as an Instance of our Goodwill and Affection for you. This has given us an Opportunity of seeing you sooner than perhaps we should otherwise have done; and, as we are under mutual Obligations by Treaties, we to hear with our Ears for you, and you to hear with your Ears for us, we take this Opportunity to inform you of what very nearly concerns us both.

The *Great King of* ENGLAND and the *French* King have declared War against each other. Two Battles have been fought, one by Land, and the other by Sea. The *Great King of* ENGLAND commanded the Land Army in Person, and gained a compleat Victory. Numbers of the *French* were killed and taken Prisoners, and the rest were forced to pass a River with Precipitation to save their Lives. The Great God covered the King's Head in that Battle, so that he did not receive the least Hurt; for which you, as well as we, have Reason to be very thankful.

The Engagement at Sea was likewise to the Advantage of the *English.* The *French* and *Spaniards* joined their Ships together, and came out to fight us. The brave *English* Admiral burnt one of their largest Ships, and many others were so shattered, that they were glad to take the Opportunity of a very high Wind, and a dark Night, to run away, and to hide themselves again in their own Harbours. Had the Weather proved fair, he would, in all Probability, have taken or destroyed them all.

I need not put you in mind how much *William Penn* and his Sons have been your Friends, and the Friends of all the *Indians.* You have long and often experienced their Friendship for you; nor need I repeat to you how kindly you were treated, and what valuable Presents were made to you Two Years ago by the Governor, the Council, and the Assembly, of *Pennsylvania.* The Sons of *William Penn* are all now in *England,* and have left me in their Place, well knowing how much I regard you and all the *Indians.* As a fresh Proof of this, I have left my House, and am come thus far to see you, to renew our Treaties, to brighten the Covenant Chain, and to confirm our Friendship with you. In Testimony whereof, I present you with this Belt of Wampum.

*Which was received with the* Yo-hah.

As your Nations have engaged themselves by Treaty to assist us, your Brethren of *Pennsylvania,* in case of a War with the *French,* we do not doubt but you will punctually perform an Engagement so solemnly entred into. A War is now declared, and we expect that you will not suffer the *French,* or any of the *Indians* in Alliance with them, to march through your Country to disturb any of our Settlements; and that you will give us the earliest and best Intelligence of any Designs that may be formed by them to our Disadvantage, as we promise to do of any that may be to yours. To enforce what I have now said to you in the strongest Manner, I present you with this Belt of Wampum.

*Which was received with the* Yo-hah.

*After a little Pause his Honour, the* GOVERNOR, *spoke again:*
*Friends and Brethren of the* Six Nations,

What I have now said to you is in Conformity to Treaties subsisting between the Province of which I am Governor and your Nations. I now proceed, with the Consent of the honourable Commissioners for *Virginia* and *Maryland,* to tell you, that all Differences having been adjusted, and the Roads between us and you made quite clear and open, we are ready to confirm our Treaties with your Nations, and establish a Friendship that is not to end, but with the World itself. And, in Behalf of the Province of *Pennsylvania* I do, by this fine Belt of Wampum, and a Present of Goods, to the Value of Three Hundred Pounds, confirm and establish the said Treaties of Peace, Union and Friendship, you on your Parts doing the same.

*Which was received with a loud* Yo-hah.

The Governor further added, The Goods bought with the One Hundred Pounds Sterling, put into my Hands by the Governor of *Virginia,* are ready to be delivered when you please. The Goods bought and sent up by the People of the Province of *Pennsylvania,* according to the List which the Interpreter will explain, are laid by themselves, and are likewise ready to be delivered to you at your own time.

*After a little Pause the Commissioners of* Virginia *spoke as follows:*
*Sachems and Warriors of the* Six Nations,

The Way between us being made smooth by what passed Yesterday, we desire now to confirm all former Treaties made between *Virginia* and you, our Brethren of the *Six Nations,* and to make our Chain of Union and Friendship as bright as the Sun, that it may not contract any more Rust for ever; that our Childrens Children may rejoice at, and confirm what we have done; and that you and your Children may not forget it, we give you One Hundred Pounds in Gold, and this Belt of Wampum.

*Which was received with the usual Ceremony.*

*Friends and Brethren,* Altho' we have been disappointed in our Endeavours to bring about a Peace between you and the *Catawbas,* yet we desire to speak to you something more about them. We believe they have been unfaithful to you, and spoke of you with a foolish Contempt; but this may be only the Rashness of some of their young Men. In this Time of War with our common Enemies the *French* and *Spaniards,* it will be the wisest Way to be at Peace among ourselves. They, the *Catawbas,* are also Children of the Great King, and therefore we desire you will agree, that we may endeavour to make a Peace between you and them, that we may be all united by one common Chain of Friendship. We give you this String of Wampum.

*Which was received with the usual Ceremony.*

*Brethren,* Our Friend, *Conrad Weiser,* when he is old, will go into the other World, as our Fathers have done; our Children will then want such a Friend to go between them and your Children, to reconcile any Differences that may happen to arise between them, that, like him, may have the Ears and Tongues of our Children and yours.

The Way to have such a Friend, is for you to send three or four of your Boys to *Virginia,* where we have a fine House for them to live in, and a Man on purpose to teach the Children of you, our Friends, the Religion, Language and Customs of the white People. To this Place we kindly invite you to send some of your Children, and we promise you they shall have the same Care taken of them, and be instructed in the same Manner as our own Children, and be returned to you again when you please; and, to confirm this, we give you this String of Wampum.

*Which was received with the usual Ceremony.*

*Then the Commissioners of* Maryland *spoke as follows:*

*Friends and Brethren, the Chiefs or Sachims of the* Six *united* Nations,

The Governor of *Maryland* invited you hither; we have treated you as Friends, and agreed with you as Brethren.

As the Treaty now made concerning the Lands in *Maryland* will, we hope, prevent effectually every future Misunderstanding between us on that Account, we will now bind faster the Links of our Chain of Friendship by a Renewal of all our former Treaties; and that they may still be the better secured, we shall present you with One Hundred Pounds in Gold.

What we have further to say to you is, Let not our Chain contract any Rust; whenever you perceive the least Speck, tell us of it, and we will make it clean. This we also expect of you, that it may always continue so bright as our Generations may see their Faces in it; and, in Pledge of the Truth of what we have now spoken, and our Affection to you, we give you this Belt of Wampum.

*Which was received with the usual Ceremony.*

*CANASSATEGO, in return, spoke as follows:*

*Brother* Onas, Assaragoa, *and* Tocarry-hogan, We return you Thanks for your several Speeches, which are very agreeable to us. They contain Matters of such great

Moment, that we propose to give them a very serious Consideration, and to answer them suitably to their Worth and Excellence; and this will take till To-morrow Morning, and when we are ready we will give you due Notice.

You tell us you beat the *French;* if so, you must have taken a great deal of Rum from them, and can the better spare us some of that Liquor to make us rejoice with you in the Victory.

The Governor and Commissioners ordered a Dram of Rum to be given to each in a small Glass, calling it, *A French Glass.*

In the COURT-HOUSE at *Lancaster, July* 4, 1744, *A.M.*
PRESENT, The Honourable *GEORGE THOMAS,* Esq; Governor, *&c.*
The Honourable the Commissioners of *Virginia.*
The Honourable the Commissioners of *Maryland.*
The Deputies of the *Six Nations.*
*Conrad Weiser,* Interpreter.

*CANASSATEGO Speaker.*

*Brother* Onas, Yesterday you expressed your Satisfaction in having been instrumental to our meeting with our Brethren of *Virginia* and *Maryland.* We, in return, assure you, that we have great Pleasure in this Meeting, and thank you for the Part you have had in bringing us together, in order to create a good Understanding, and to clear the Road; and, in Token of our Gratitude, we present you with this String of Wampum.

*Which was received with the usual Ceremony.*

*Brother* Onas, You was pleased Yesterday to inform us, "That War had been declared between *the Great King of* ENGLAND and the *French* King; that two great Battles had been fought, one by Land, and the other at Sea; with many other Particulars." We are glad to hear the Arms of the King of *England* were successful, and take part with you in your Joy on this Occasion. You then came nearer Home, and told us, "You had left your House, and were come thus far on Behalf of the whole People of *Pennsylvania* to see us; to renew your Treaties; to brighten the Covenant Chain, and to confirm your Friendship with us." We approve this Proposition; we thank you for it. We own, with Pleasure, that the Covenant Chain between us and *Pennsylvania* is of old Standing, and has never contracted any Rust; we wish it may always continue as bright as it has done hitherto; and, in Token of the Sincerity of our Wishes; we present you with this Belt of Wampum.

*Which was received with the* Yo-hah.

*Brother* Onas, You was pleased Yesterday to remind us of our mutual Obligation to assist each other in case of a War with the *French,* and to repeat the Substance of what we ought to do by our Treaties with you; and that as a War had been already entered into with the *French,* you called upon us to assist you, and not to suffer the *French* to march through our Country to disturb any of your Settlements.

In answer, We assure you we have all these Particulars in our Hearts, they are fresh in our Memory. We shall never forget that you and we have but one Heart, one Head, one Eye, one Ear, and one Hand. We shall have all your Country under our Eye, and take all the Care we can to prevent any Enemy from coming into it; and, in Proof of our Care, we must inform you, that before we came here, we told **Onantio,* our Father, as he is called, that neither he, nor any of his People, should come through our Country, to hurt our Brethren the *English,* or any of the Settlements belonging to them; there was Room enough at Sea to fight, there he might do what he pleased, but he should not come upon our Land to do any Damage to our Brethren.[12] And you may depend upon our using our utmost Care to see this effectually done; and, in Token of our Sincerity, we present you with this Belt of Wampum.

*Which was received with the usual Ceremony.*

*After some little Time the Interpreter said,* Canassatego *had forgot something material, and desired to mend his Speech, and to do so as often as he should omit any thing of Moment, and thereupon he added:*

The *Six Nations* have a great Authority and Influence over sundry Tribes of *Indians* in Alliance with the *French,* and particularly over the praying *Indians,* formerly a Part with ourselves, who stand in the very Gates of the *French;* and, to shew our further Care, we have engaged these very *Indians;* and other *Indian* Allies of the *French* for you. They will not join the *French* against you. They have agreed with us before we set out. We have put the Spirit of Antipathy against the *French* in those People. Our Interest is very considerable with them, and many other Nations, and as far as ever it extends, we shall use it for your Service.

The Governor said, *Canassatego* did well to mend his Speech; he might always do it whenever his Memory should fail him in any Point of Consequence, and he thanked him for the very agreeable Addition.[13]

*Brother* Assaragoa, You told us Yesterday, that all Disputes with you being now at an End, you desired to confirm all former Treaties between *Virginia* and us, and to make our Chain of Union as bright as the Sun.

We agree very heartily with you in these Propositions; we thank you for your good Inclinations; we desire you will pay no Regard to any idle stories that may be told to our Prejudice. And, as the Dispute about the Land is now intirely over, and we perfectly reconciled, we hope, for the future, we shall not act towards each other but as becomes Brethren and hearty Friends.

We are very willing to renew the Friendship with you, and to make it as firm as possible, for us and our Children with you and your Children to the latest Generation, and we desire you will imprint these Engagements on your Hearts in the stron-

* *Onantio,* the Governor of *Canada.*

gest Manner; and, in Confirmation that we shall do the same, we give you this Belt of Wampum.

*Which was received with the* Yo-hah *from the Interpreter and all the Nations.*

*Brother* Assaragoa, You did let us know Yesterday, that tho' you had been disappointed in your Endeavours to bring about a Peace between us and the *Catawbas,* you would still do the best to bring such a Thing about. We are well pleased with your Design, and the more so, as we hear you know what sort of People the *Catawbas* are, that they are spiteful and offensive, and have treated us contemptuously. We are glad you know these Things of the *Catawbas;* we believe what you say to be true, that there are, notwithstanding, some amongst them who are wiser and better; and, as you say, they are your Brethren, and belong to the Great King over the Water, we shall not be against a Peace on reasonable Terms, provided they will come to the Northward to treat about it. In Confirmation of what we say, and to encourage you in your Undertaking, we give you this String of Wampum.

*Which was received with the usual Ceremonies.*

*Brother* Assaragoa, You told us likewise, you had a great House provided for the Education of Youth, and that there were several white People and *Indians* Children there to learn Languages, and to write and read, and invited us to send some of our Children amongst you, *&c.*

We must let you know we love our Children too well to send them so great a Way, and the *Indians* are not inclined to give their Children Learning. We allow it to be good, and we thank you for your Invitation; but our Customs differing from yours, you will be so good as to excuse us.[14]

We hope * *Tarachawagon* will be preserved by the good Spirit to a good old Age; when he is gone under Ground, it will be then time enough to look out for another; and no doubt but amongst so many Thousands as there are in the World, one such Man may be found, who will serve both Parties with the same Fidelity as *Tarachawagon* does; while he lives there is no Room to complain. In Token of our Thankfulness for your Invitation, we give you this String of Wampum.

*Which was received with the usual Ceremony.*

*Brother* Tocarry-hogan, You told us Yesterday, that since there was now nothing in Controversy between us, and the Affair of the Land was settled to your Satisfaction, you would now brighten the Chain of Friendship which hath subsisted between you and us ever since we became Brethren; we are well pleased with the Proposition, and we thank you for it; we also are inclined to renew all Treaties, and keep a good Correspondence with you. You told us further, if ever we should perceive the Chain had contracted any Rust, to let you know, and you would take care to take the Rust out,

---

* *Tarachawagon, Conrad Weiser*

and preserve it bright. We agree with you in this, and shall, on our Parts, do every thing to preserve a good Understanding, and to live in the same Friendship with you as with our Brother *Onas* and *Assarogoa;* in Confirmation whereof, we give you this Belt of Wampum.

*On which the usual Cry of* Yo-hah *was given.*

*Brethren,* We have now finished our Answer to what you said to us Yesterday, and shall now proceed to *Indian* Affairs, that are not of so general a Concern.

*Brother* Assaragoa, There lives a Nation of *Indians* on the other Side of your Country, the *Tuscaroraes,* who are our Friends, and with whom we hold Correspondence; but the Road between us and them has been stopped for some Time, on account of the Misbehaviour of some of our Warriors. We have opened a new Road for our Warriors, and they shall keep to that; but as that would be inconvenient for Messengers going to the *Tuscaroraes,* we desire they may go the old Road. We frequently send Messengers to one another, and shall have more Occasion to do so now that we have concluded a Peace with the *Cherikees.* To enforce our Request, we give you this String of Wampum.

*Which was received with the usual Cry of Approbation.*

*Brother* Assaragoa, Among these *Tuscaroraes* there live a few Families of the *Conoy Indians,* who are desirous to leave them, and to remove to the rest of their Nation among us, and the straight Road from them to us lies through the Middle of your Country. We desire you will give them free Passage through *Virginia,* and furnish them with Passes; and, to enforce our Request, we give you this String of Wampum.

*Which was received with the usual Cry of Approbation.*

*Brother* Onas, Assaragoa, *and* Tocarry-hogan, At the Close of your respective Speeches Yesterday, you made us very handsome Presents, and we should return you something suitable to your Generosity; but, alas, we are poor, and shall ever remain so, as long as there are so many *Indian* Traders among us. Theirs and the white Peoples Cattle have eat up all the Grass, and made Deer scarce. However, we have provided a small Present for you, and tho' some of you gave us more than others, yet, as you are all equally our Brethren, we shall leave it to you to divide it as you please.—And then presented three Bundles of Skins, which were received with the usual Ceremony from the three Governments.

We have one Thing further to say, and that is, We heartily recommend Union and a good Agreement between you our Brethren. Never disagree, but preserve a strict Friendship for one another, and thereby you, as well as we, will become the stronger.

Our wise Forefathers established Union and Amity between the *Five Nations;* this has made us formidable; this has given us great Weight and Authority with our neighbouring Nations.

We are a powerful Confederacy; and, by your observing the same Methods our wise Forefathers have taken, you will acquire fresh Strength and Power; therefore whatever befals you, never fall out one with another.

The Governor replied:
The honourable Commissioners of *Virginia* and *Maryland* have desired me to speak for them; therefore I, in Behalf of those Governments, as well as of the Province of *Pennsylvania,* return you Thanks for the many Proofs you have given in your Speeches of your Zeal for the Service of your Brethren the *English,* and in particular for your having so early engaged in a Neutrality the several Tribes of *Indians* in the *French* Alliance. We do not doubt but you will faithfully discharge your Promises. As to your Presents, we never estimate these Things by their real Worth, but by the Disposition of the Giver. In this Light we accept them with great Pleasure, and put a high Value upon them. We are obliged to you for recommending Peace and good Agreement amongst ourselves. We are all Subjects, as well as you, of the Great King beyond the Water; and, in Duty to his Majesty, and from the good Affection we bear to each other, as well as from a Regard to our own Interest, we shall always be inclined to live in Friendship.

Then the Commissioners of *Virginia* presented the Hundred Pounds in Gold, together with a Paper, containing a Promise to recommend the *Six Nations* for further Favour to the King; which they received with *Yo-hah,* and the Paper was given by them to *Conrad Weiser* to keep for them. The Commissioners likewise promised that their publick Messengers should not be molested in their Passage through *Virginia,* and that they would prepare Passes for such of the *Conoy Indians* as were willing to remove to the Northward.

Then the Commissioners of *Maryland* presented their Hundred Pounds in Gold, which was likewise received with the *Yo-hah.*

*Canassatego* said, We mentioned to you Yesterday the Booty you had taken from the *French,* and asked you for some of the Rum which we supposed to be Part of it, and you gave us some; but it turned out unfortunately that you gave us it in *French* Glasses, we now desire you will give us some in *English* Glasses.

The Governor made answer, We are glad to hear you have such a Dislike for what is *French.* They cheat you in your Glasses, as well as in every thing else. You must consider we are at a Distance from *Williamsburg, Annapolis,* and *Philadelphia,* where our Rum Stores are, and that altho' we brought up a good Quantity with us, you have almost drunk it out; but, notwithstanding this, we have enough left to fill our *English* Glasses, and will shew the Difference between the Narrowness of the *French,* and the Generosity of your Brethren the *English* towards you.

The *Indians* gave, in their Order, five *Yo-hahs;* and the honourable Governor and Commissioners calling for some Rum, and some middle sized Wine Glasses, drank Health to the *Great King of* ENGLAND, and the *Six Nations,* and put an End to the Treaty by three loud Huzza's, in which all the Company joined.

In the Evening the Governor went to take his Leave of the *Indians*, and, presenting them with a String of Wampum, he told them, that was in return for one he had received of them, with a Message to desire the Governor of *Virginia* to suffer their Warriors to go through *Virginia* unmolested, which was rendered unnecessary by the present Treaty.

Then, presenting them with another String of Wampum, he told them, that was in return for theirs, praying him, that as they had taken away one Part of *Conrad Weiser's* Beard, which frightened their Children, he would please to take away the other, which he had ordered to be done.

*The* Indians *received these two Strings of Wampum with the usual* Yo-hah.

The Governor then asked them, what was the Reason that more of the *Shawanaes,* from their Town on *Hohio,* were not at the Treaty? But seeing that it would require a Council in Form, and perhaps another Day to give an Answer, he desired they would give an Answer to *Conrad Weiser* upon the Road on their Return home, for he was to set out for *Philadelphia* the next Morning.

*CANASSATEGO in Conclusion spoke as follows:*

We have been hindered, by a great deal of Business, from waiting on you, to have some private Conversation with you, chiefly to enquire after the Healths of *Onas* beyond the Water; We desire you will tell them, we have a grateful Sense of all their Kindnesses for the *Indians.* Brother *Onas* told us, when he went away, he would not stay long from us; we think it is a great While, and want to know when we may expect him, and desire, when you write, you will recommend us heartily to him; which the Governor promised to do, and then took his Leave of them.

The Commissioners of *Virginia* gave *Canassatego* a Scarlet Camblet Coat, and took their Leave of them in Form, and at the same time delivered the Passes to them, according to their Request.

The Commissioners of *Maryland* presented *Gachradodow* with a broad Gold-laced Hat, and took their Leave of them in the same Manner.

*A true Copy, compared by RICHARD PETERS,* Secry.

*THE END.*

1. Franklin competed against other printers in the colonies to sell the 1744 treaty, historically one of the most significant of the era. He sent two hundred extra copies to England to be sold there. Between 1766 and 1776, forty-five treaties were printed altogether in at least fifty different publications (Wroth, "The Indian Treaty as Literature," 749–50).

2. Franklin was particularly interested in the metaphors of Iroquois origin used by the two parties. Phrases like "enlarge the Fire," "brighten the Chain," and "so long as the Sun, the Moon and the Stars, shall give light" show that Native Americans exercised much control over the discourse of the treaty councils, bending the British to their language. When drafting speeches for Governor Denny in 1756 and elsewhere, Franklin too used Iroquois metaphors. His linguistic absorption of Native American thought and phrasing represents a larger phenomenon

among British subjects in the Americas. It shows that the British were not impervious to Iroquois intellect (Labaree, *Papers of Benjamin Franklin,* 6:22–23). The addition of the Chain, however, was British.

Franklin and Colden are credited with the "discovery of the Indian treaty as a native American literary form" and with recognizing their literary appeal (Fenton, "Structure, Continuity, and Change," 5; Wroth, "The Indian Treaty as Literature," 750–51). Yet readers have often admired the eloquence and drama of the treaties without understanding what is going on. Literary interpretations cannot thrive or maintain legitimacy in the absence of contextual historical support (Jennings, Introduction, *The History and Culture of Iroquois Diplomacy,* xiv).

3. Note that the mood shifts abruptly from one of relaxation and mutual accommodation to one of haste. The Pennsylvania government fails in its attempt to rush Iroquois deliberations, as can be seen by Canasatego's reply. The Iroquois consistently operated under a principle of deliberation, understanding that immediate responses to political propositions were both unwise and dangerous because they did not allow for a cooling of emotion or a just consideration of the perspectives of each of the five nations in the confederacy. In any case, the orator was not authorized to respond without consulting the elected leaders of the confederacy.

4. Notice here and elsewhere that the Iroquois always demonstrate an ability to repeat previous utterances by the British with near verbatim accuracy. Their methods of preserving speech orally are not fully understood, but may have included, in the long term, annual or semiannual readings of the wampum, which recorded significant events in their political history. Certain participants with excellent skills in oral recall may have been expected to remember the speeches as they were being spoken, just as other participants were assigned the role of orators. (cf. Fenton, "Structure, Continuity, and Change," 17).

5. Despite the note on the meaning of the yo-hah above, there is some doubt over what it meant. According to Colden, the practice entailed a call and response where a chief called out "Do you hear?" and the rest answered "We attend and remember, or understand" (Wroth, "The Indian Treaty as Literature," 755–56). Pennsylvanians likely converted this confirmation that the company had remembered the speeches into approval of all their words and actions (Wallace, *Conrad Weiser,* 68).

6. It sometimes surprises today's students that the Iroquois so consistently defend the reliability of their oral methods of historiography. Yet their distrust of the reliability of "Pen-and-Ink work" is well corroborated by recent investigations. The surviving written record is often quite unreliable; the oral tradition is frequently much more reliable.

7. This day's speech, and those spoken on June 30 and July 4, were probably responsible for Richard Peters's remark: "I make no doubt that the Indian treaty will give everyone pleasure that reads it and as the Indians really appear superior to the Commissioners in point of sense and argument, it will raise people's opinions of the wisdom of the Six Nations and give the government at home higher notions of their consequence than they could have before," Julian Boyd, "Indian Affairs in Pennsylvania, 1736–1762," in *Indian Treaties Printed by Benjamin Franklin, 1736–1762* (Philadelphia: Historical Society of Pennsylvania, 1938), xl).

8. Thomas Lee, President of Virginia's Council, stole a letter from Governor William Gooch that promised the League satisfaction for these lands (Boyd, "Indian Affairs," xxxviii); Lee later served as acting governor of the colony and corresponded with Weiser to satisfy his intense curiosity about the government of the Six Nations (Wallace, *Conrad Weiser,* 198–99).

9. By previous treaty agreements, the Iroquois had the right to administer justice in their own territories. Pennsylvania's insistence that the crime on the Juniata be tried in Pennsylvania is in disregard of those covenants.

10. Virginia's claim that the lands in question were "deserted and free for any people to

enter upon" might have its origin in any number of conditions, such as the characterization of native uses of and claims over open space as "emptiness," or a devastation resulting from disease, starvation, or war. The myth that hunters needed more land for subsistence than farmers disregarded the cash-crop character that the hunting economy had acquired since European arrival. Many more animals were killed than were needed for local subsistence (Jennings, *Ambiguous Iroquois Empire,* 274).

The difference between the League's interpretation of the 1722 boundary and Virginia's likely reflects a situation in which the League had agreed to one version while the British recorded a version more favorable to themselves. The wampum record may say otherwise (Jennings, *Ambiguous Iroquois Empire,* 294–96).

11. The British were constantly involved in efforts to create peace among their native allies so as to reduce the costs of trade and maintain the illusion of a coherent empire over people it had never subjected to its rule. James Merrell believes that Iroquois incursions into Catawba territories began around the 1660s. He offers several explanations for the cause of the war, but does not really consider trade, mourning (attempts to adopt new members into the nation to replace lost members), or instigation by newly adopted members who had been victims of Catawba raids ("'Their Very Bones Shall Fight': The Catawba-Iroquois Wars," in Richter and Merrell, eds., *Beyond the Covenant Chain,* 115–33). Theda Perdue offers these as possible explanations for the simultaneous conflicts with the Cherokees ("Cherokee Relations with the Iroquois in the Eighteenth Century," in Richter and Merrell, eds., *Beyond the Covenant Chain,* 135–49). This passage shows that the Iroquois had been able to negotiate against the routine British peace efforts and that these efforts may not have been so consistent as they appear.

12. Fathers in Iroquois culture did not have the power to order their children around as they did in European and Euramerican families. A man's mother and her female relatives determined his political opportunities. When the New York governor once attempted to call the Mohawks children, they balked. France, however, refused to treat with the League unless they accepted the terms. So while the terms used here may have a great deal of significance, they may not always have the significance we assume and may not always have been taken as seriously as they seem to have been. (Jennings, *Ambiguous Iroquois Empire,* 44–45, 193). They may have been taken seriously, but in Iroquois rather than British ways.

13. It appears that a process of review and recall was built into the delivery of a speech so that the speaker would have a space prior to the close of a session to add anything that he might have left out. Cues from fellow delegates may have recalled to Canasatego his omission.

14. This refusal of Virginia's invitation to provide education for some of the League's young people demonstrates its savvy regarding the latent motivations behind the offer: an attempt to control the mind and heart of the budding translator. Because European-style educations had been available to some natives since almost the beginning of colonization, League members may have heard of abuses that these children met with. (Wolfgang Hochbruck and Beatrix Dudensing-Reichel, "'Honoratissimi Benefactores': Native American Students and Two Seventeenth Century Texts in the University Tradition," in *Early Native American Writing: New Critical Essays,* ed. Helen Jaskoski [New York: Cambridge University Press, 1996], 1–14). Abuses in the education of young natives became widespread during the boarding school era of the late nineteenth century and by then included virtual kidnappings, punishment for speaking one's own language, and harsh corporal punishment.

✠

# AN ACCOUNT OF THE TREATY

Held at the CITY of *Albany,* in the Province of *NEW-YORK,* By His EXCELLENCY the Governor of that PROVINCE,

And the HONOURABLE the COMMISSIONERS for the Provinces OF *MASSACHUSETTS, CONNECTICUT,* AND *PENNSYLVANIA,*

WITH THE INDIANS OF THE SIX NATIONS,

In *OCTOBER,* 1745.

---

*PHILADELPHIA:*
Printed by B. FRANKLIN, at the NEW-PRINTING-OFFICE, near the Market, MDCCXLVI.

---

## AN ACCOUNT OF THE TREATY, *&c.*

TO THE HONOURABLE *GEORGE THOMAS,* Esq; With the King's Royal Approbation, Lieutenant Governor of the Province of *Pennsylvania,* and Counties of *Newcastle, Kent,* and *Sussex,* on *Delaware,* under the Honourable JOHN PENN, THOMAS PENN, and RICHARD PENN, Esqs; true and absolute Proprietors of the said Province and Counties.

*May it please the* GOVERNOR,

Having been honoured with a Commission, authorizing us, the Subscribers, in Conjunction with the Governors of the Neighbouring Colonies, or their Delegates, or separately, to treat with the *Indians* of the Six United Nations at *Albany,* in *October* last; we think it our Duty to tender an Account of our Conduct therein; which be pleased to receive as follows.

The next Day after the Receipt of the Commission, that is, on the *Twenty-seventh* Day of *September* last, we set out for *Albany,* where we arrived on the *Third* of *October* following. On the *Fourth* of *October,* the Day appointed to treat with the *Indians,* pursuant to the Instructions given us, we waited on the Governor of *New-York,* acquainted him with our Appointment, and shewed him the Commission by which we were impowered to treat.

The Governor desired his Secretary might take a Copy of it; to which we consented. The *Indians* of Five of the Six United Nations, in Number about Four Hundred and Sixty, arrived the same Day, none of them *Senecas;* it being, as we were inform'd, a Time of great Sickness and Mortality among them, which prevented their Coming.

But the Commissioners from the *Massachusetts* not being come, the Treaty was deferred until their Arrival. Two Days after, being the *Sixth* of *October* in the Evening, we received a Message from the Governor of *New-York,* by his Secretary, desiring to know of us at what Time we would confer with a Committee of his Council, either alone, or with the Commissioners of the other Colonies, all then arrived, *viz.*

For the *Massachusetts,*
*Jacob Wendal,* Esq; a Member of the Council,
*John Stoddart, Samuel Wells, Thomas Hutchinson,* Esqs;
Members of Assembly
For *Connecticut* Colony,
——*Wolcot,* Esq; Lieutenant Governor, And Col.——*Stanley.*

We agreed to return our Answer to his Message in the Morning.

Accordingly in the Morning we returned our Answer by *James Read,* that we would meet the Committee of Council at a Quarter after Ten that Day, and chose to have our first Conference with them only. About the Time appointed we went; but the Commissioners from the other Colonies coming into the Room soon after, deprived us of the separate Conference proposed. Being all thus met, the Gentlemen of the Council, *to wit, Daniel Horsmanden,* and *Joseph Murray,* Esqs; let us know, they were appointed by the Governor of *New-York,* a Committee to confer with us concerning the Treaty which was to ensue; that their Governor desired to be inform'd of our Sentiments, whether we were inclinable to speak to the *Indians* of the United Nations separately, or whether we thought a joint Speech to be delivered on Behalf of all the Colonies, might be best, either being indifferent to him.

The Commissioners from *New-England* declared their Opinions for a joint Speech, as what would show our Union, and consequently, have the greater Weight with the *Indians.* On the Part of *Pennsylvania* it was objected, that we had divers Matters in Charge which related to our own Government only, which would be improper in such a joint Speech; and perhaps it might be the Case of other of the

Colonies: That such a joint Speech would require much Time in forming; and with Difficulty, if at all likely to be agreed on.

But it was replied, this would be best judged of when the Heads of such joint Speech were read; and the Committee of Council producing what they had prepared to this Purpose, it was agreed to be read. On Reading of which we observed, that it mentioned a Complaint against the Eastern *Indians* for killing some white People; and therefore, among other Things, proposed the *Indians* of the Six United Nations should be put on declaring War against the Eastern *Indians;* and to assure them that the several Colonies would support them in it. To this Article it was objected, on the Part of *Pennsylvania,* That it was necessary the Legislature of each Government should be consulted before the *Indians* were put on Declaring of War: That it would be very mischievous to all the Colonies, as it would be a Means of drawing the War nearer on their Borders: That the *Indians* did not seem disposed to enter into a War with each other, but rather to remain Neutral: That in this Disposition, little better could be expected from them than what was remarked to be the Case in the last War, when the *Indians* of opposite Parties passed each other without fighting, and only scalp'd the white People: That as to the People who had been killed, the *Indians* might be put on demanding Satisfaction, and might possibly obtain it, and prevent the Cause of War; or if they were put on Declaring of War, at least Care should be first taken to provide them with the Requisites necessary for defending themselves, and carrying on such War; without which, it would in Effect, be a Betraying them. What Provision was made by the Government of *New-York,* the Gentlemen of the Council best knew. In *Pennsylvania* we knew no Provision was made for them. That therefore if this Article was inserted in the Speech proposed, we must insist on Treating separately. To the Proposal for putting the *Indians* of the Six United Nations on demanding Satisfaction, one of the Commissioners of the *Massachusetts* answered, That Proposal ought to come on the Part of the *Indians;* for that if no more was proposed to them on the Behalf of the Governments, than that they should demand Satisfaction for the Injury done, they would offer something yet less. At length it was agreed all the other Governments, *Pennsylvania* excepted, should treat jointly; and we were desired to be assistant in their joint Treaty so far as we judged fit.

A Committee was then named to prepare the joint Speech to be delivered by the Governor of *New-York.* When it was prepared we were to meet again to consider the same.

It was two Days after this before the Speech was ready; and in the mean Time the Governor and Council of *New-York* made Enquiry concerning the Alarm which happened the last Winter amongst the *Mohawks,* occasioned by a Report spread amongst them that the *English* were coming to cut them off. To this Purpose the Governor of *New-York* sent for the *Mohawks,* and let them know that the String of Wampum which had been sent him by them not to make any further Enquiry concerning that Affair, he could not accept of; that it was necessary the Authors of this false Rumour should be known and punished; and therefore he insisted they would discover all they knew concerning the Authors; and if they had any other Cause of

Uneasiness, to communicate it to him: And thereupon he delivered back the String of Wampum sent him. The *Mohawks* agreed to return their Answer the next Day. Some of the *Mohawks* accordingly attended the Governor of *New-York* the next Day, and named to him a Person who they said was the Author of this false Alarm. The Person being sent for, owned his having heard and mentioned the Report; but deny'd his being the Author of it.

After the strictest Enquiry and Examination, the Governor and Council seemed to believe him innocent, and that the Rumour had been raised and spread by Means of some one or more of the *Mohawks* themselves.

On the Tenth of *October,* the Speech proposed to be delivered to the *Indians* by the Governor of *New-York,* being prepared, we were desired to meet the other Commissioners, and hear the same read. Accordingly, about Ten of the Clock in the Forenoon, we met them; the Speech was read; after which it was objected on the Part of *Pennsylvania* that it contain'd a Narrative of many Facts to which we were altogether Strangers; and therefore were not proper to be made Parties in the Relation: That it pressed the *Indians* on making of War; which we thought ought be attended with mischievous Consequences to all the Colonies: That as we are to treat separately, and they had already heard our Reasons against a War, they must judge for themselves how far it would be prudent in them to press it. The Result was, the Commissioners of the other Colonies agreed to the Speech, as it had been prepared; and in the Afternoon of the same Day, the Deputies of the *United Nations* were desired to attend the Governor of *New-York:* They came accordingly; and the Governor in Behalf of his Government, and those of the *Massachusetts* and *Connecticut,* and in the Presence of the Commissioners from thence, read the Speech agreed on; which was interpreted to the Indians: A Copy whereof was delivered to us, and follows in these Words, *viz.*

BRETHREN, Here are present upon the Occasion of this Interview, Commissioners from the Governments of the *Massachusetts-Bay* and *Connecticut,* conven'd with me on the same righteous Intention of Renewing, Bright'ning, and Strengthening the Covenant Chain which has tied you and His *Britannick* Majesty's several Colonies on this Continent, in the firmest Engagements to each other, for Supporting and Maintaining our Common Cause.[1]

We are glad to see, so many of our Brethren, and we bid you Welcome here; at the same Time, that we heartily condole the Absence of our Brethren the *Senecas,* and the Calamities which have occasioned it; may the Almighty comfort them under their grievous Afflictions, and soon wipe off all Tears from their Eyes.

We do with you our Brethren, and with you as their Representatives, ratify, confirm, and establish all former Engagements entred into by us and our Brethren of the Six United Nations; and assure you, that we shall ever hold them inviolable, and we doubt not of the same from you.

*A BELT.*

Brethren, The Rumour which last Winter gave an Alarm to our Brethren the

*Maquas,* and was from thence spread to the other Nations, now appears to have been without Foundation; and I cannot help observing on this Occasion, that you ought not for the future to suffer any such idle Tales to be raised or propagated among you, as they not only tend to separate your and our Affections each from the other; but also to make us jealous of our own People, without sufficient Grounds for it.

*A String of Wampum.*

Brethren, It must be further observed to you, that we hear several of the Chiefs and others of our Brethren of the *Six Nations,* have contrary to our Inclinations, and against our express Advice, had an Interview with the Governor of *Canada* this Summer at *Montreal.*

And that your Pretence for holding this Correspondence with our declared Enemies, was for the publick Good and the Preservation of the House at *Oswego.*[2]

To tell the Governor of *Canada* that they must not make any Attack or Attempt upon that Place, for that our Brethren are resolved to defend it, and that it should remain a Place of Peace and Trade.

You declared your Intent was Good, and that the Governor of *Canada* should never prevail upon you in any Thing hurtful to your Brethren the *English,* who you knew did not like your going thither; that yet upon your Return from thence, your Brother the Governor of *New-York* should know all that passed between them and the Governor of *Canada.*

We will tell our Brethren what we hear was done, whilst they were with the Governor of *Canada,* and we expect the whole Truth from them according to their Promise, and whether what we hear is true or not.

We hear that whilst our Brethren were with the Governor of *Canada,* the *French Indians* took up the Hatchet against the *English;* which we believe to be true, for Reasons you shall hear by and by; and thereby the Treaty of Neutrality concluded between you and them, is become vain.

We hear likewise, that our Brethren of the *Six Nations* there present, were so far prevailed upon by our Enemies the *French,* as to accept of the Hatchet, upon Condition to carry it home to their Council to deliberate upon, and then to return the Governor of *Canada* their Answer; which we cannot believe to be true, till we have it from our Brethrens own Mouths.

We expect a plain and full Answer from our Brethren concerning these Matters, that the Way may be cleared, for wiping off all Stains from the Covenant Chain; and that we may preserve it bright, firm, and inviolable, as long as the Sun shall shine.

*A BELT.*

*Brethren,* We must now acquaint you of some Things relating to the War; the Success of his Majesty's Arms against the *French* in this Part of the World; and the Rise and Occasion of our Attacks upon the Enemy in this Quarter.

When you were here last Summer, you were told that War was declar'd between the Crowns of *Great-Britain* and *France:* The Events that have since happened are too numerous to relate particularly.

His Majesty's Subjects in this Country lay still the last Summer without attempting any Thing against the *French* Settlements: But the *French* first attack'd and destroyed a small Place belonging to us call'd *Canso,* about twenty five Leagues from *Cape Breton.*

Afterwards they laid Siege to *Annapolis-Royal;* but therein they proved unsuccessful.

They then agreed to make another Trial for that Place next Spring; and in the mean Time they sent to *France,* hoping to obtain some of the King's Ships to facilitate the Reduction of it.

They having proceeded thus far, Mr. *Shirley,* the Governor of the *Massachusetts-Bay,* thought it high Time to do something to curb the Insolence of that haughty People; and did therefore raise a small Army, which was joined by a Number of Men from the Governments of *Connecticut* and *New-Hampshire,* and sent them early last Spring against *Louisburgh.*

They were likewise joined by a Number of His Majesty's Ships of War; and after about seven Weeks Siege, that important and strong fortified Place was, through the Goodness of Divine Providence, delivered up to our Forces.

Whereupon the rest of the Inhabitants of the Island of *Cape Breton,* together with those that were settled in Parts adjacent, surrendred themselves Prisoners to the *English.*

And during the Siege, and since, many *French* Ships were taken, and divers of them of great Value; and the Design of the *French* against *Annapolis-Royal* was frustrated.

We have in this Part of the Country lain still, both the last Summer and this, hoping that our Neighbours in *Canada* would either be quiet, or carry on the War in a manly and christian-like Manner.

And to induce them thereto, a Message was sent from this Place to the Government of *Canada* the last Summer, by which he was assured, that if he should renew their former vile Practice of treating His Majesty's Subjects inhumanly, the several Governors, together with the *Six Nations,* would join and make Reprisals on them.

And at the same Time you publickly declared, That if any of His Majesty's Subjects, in any of His Governments, should be killed by any *Indian,* you would immediately join in the War against them and the *French.*

You likewise sent your Delegates last Summer to the Eastern *Indians* to warn them not to engage in the War against the *English,* threatning them in Case they should do so.

Notwithstanding these Things, divers Hostilities have been committed.

Some Months ago the Eastern *Indians,* who had formerly acknowledged their Subjection to the Crown of *Great Britain,* entred into solemn Engagements with the King's Subjects, and had been since treated by them with great Kindness.

But at the Instigation of the *French,* they have lately killed one *Englishman,* and also great Numbers of Horses and Cattle; burnt a Saw-Mill, and many Dwelling-houses, and attack'd an *English* Garrison.

Notwithstanding such outrageous Insults, the Governor of *Massachusetts-Bay* was so tender of them, that he resented it no further than to send a Message to them, demanding the Delivery of the Murderers, as they would avoid the Consequence of their Neglect.

This Proposal was rejected by them, and since that Time they have killed two or three others; whereupon the Governor of the *Massachusetts* declared War against them.

And we are informed the *English* have killed two of them, and taken another Prisoner.

About three Months since some of the *Canada-Indians* killed two *Englishmen* near *Connecticut* River; the Body of one of them was treated in a most barbarous Manner, by which they left a Hatchet of War, thereby daring us to take it up and return it.

There has likewise been several other Parties that have attempted to destroy his Majesty's Subjects of *New-England,* but have hitherto been prevented.

These Facts plainly shew that the *French* are still acted by the same Spirit that they were formerly governed by; and they seem never pleased but when they are at War, either with the *English,* or some of the Tribes of *Indians;* and if they had it in their Power, they would doubtless destroy all about them.

It is likewise evident, that the most solemn and sacred Engagements are broken through by those *Indians* that have committed the late Murders.

That Belts of Wampum will not bind them to the Performance of their Promises.

That we are slighted, and you contemned, as though they thought you not worthy to be regarded.

But now the *French* and their *Indians,* by the little Regard they have shewn to your Threatnings, or to the Covenants they have made with you, do declare that they think you do not intend to perform what you have threatned, or that they do not fear your Displeasure; both which do reflect equal Dishonour on you.

It is high Time for us and you to exert our selves and vindicate our Honour; and although it is well known that we delight not in the Destruction of our Fellow-creatures, but have chosen rather to suffer our selves to be abused; yet we cannot think our selves obliged any longer to bear their Insults and evil Treatment.

Therefore since neither our peaceable Dispositions, nor Examples, nor any Methods we have been able to use, have been sufficient to prevail upon them to forbear their barbarous Treatment of us, but they will force our Resentments; in the Name of GOD, we are resolved, not only to defend our selves, but by all proper Ways and Methods to endeavour to put it out of their Power to misuse and evil intreat us as they have hitherto done.

And we doubt not of your ready and chearful Concurrence with us, agreeable to your solemn Promise made in this Place last Summer, in joining with us against our Enemies the *French*, and such *Indians* as are or shall be instigated by them; for we esteem them Enemies to God, as well as to all their Fellow-Creatures who dwell round about them.

*A large Belt, with the Figure of a Hatchet hung to it.*

The publick Affairs of my Government have prevented my Meeting you sooner.

I was apprehensive I should not have been able to meet you this Fall, and it was determined upon on a sudden, so that there could not be timely Notice sent to the rest of His Majesty's Governments, or, I doubt not, they would likewise have sent Commissioners to be present at this Interview.

We are all subject to the same Prince, united in the same Bonds of Duty and Allegiance to the Great King, our common Father, and in Friendship and Affection to each other; and in this Union consists that Strength that makes us formidable to our Enemies, and them fearful of our Resentments.

We are all united with you in the same Covenant-chain, which as long as we preserve it free from Rust, must remain impregnable: And you on your Parts, have declared that you will preserve it so strong and bright, that it shall not be in the Power of the Devil himself, with all his Wiles and Art, to break or dirty it.[3]

You are also united with all the far Nations of *Indians* in League with our Great King, with whom we recommend to you to preserve strict Friendship, and hold frequent Correspondence.

That your selves, who many of you live scattered and dispersed, should dwell in Bodies closer together, as you have heretofore promised to do.

And we advise you to keep your young Men at home, and within Call, excepting such as may be sent from Time to Time a Hunting, or against our Enemies; and you may depend upon the most ready and effectual Assistance from us in all Times of Danger.

*A BELT.*

The *Indians* of the United Nations promised to call a Council the next Morning; and, if they could, to return their Answer to this Speech the same Day.

The next Day we waited on the Governor of *New-York*, and delivered to him, according to our Agreement, the Speech we propos'd to make to the *Indians* of the United Nations, in order for his Perusal, and then to be returned us; which he promised to do by the next Morning.

*OCTOBER* the Twelfth, in the Morning, we received a Message from the Governor of *New-York*, with the Speech he proposed to make to the *Mohiggans*, or River *Indians*; which we perused, and returned to the Secretary, without making any Objections against what was proposed to be said to them. Some Time after we received a second Message, desiring us to be present when the Governor delivered this Speech, and at the Receiving the Answer of the *Six Nations* to the Speech made to them.

We attended accordingly. The Commissioners for the *Massachusetts* and *Connecticut* also attended: And the Speech prepared for the River *Indians* was read by Paragraphs, and translated to them; a Copy of which was delivered us, and is as follows:

CHILDREN, I am glad to see you here, and bid you welcome. I sent for you to meet me at this Place, that I might have an Opportunity to renew and confirm the Covenants and Engagements made from Time to Time between us. And I do now publickly promise, that nothing shall be wanting on my Part; but that the Covenant Chain shall remain bright and strong for ever.

*Children,* I must put you in mind of what you promised me last Year. You engaged that you would keep your People at Home, which, I am informed, you have not done; but many of your People have lately left *Schahkook,* and are gone to *Canajoherie,* and some to *Attowawie.* I want to know for what Reason they have left their Habitations, and charge you to send for them back as soon as you can; and that you would live together at *Schahkook.*

*A String of Wampum.*

*Children,* Last Year I acquainted you that War was declared between the Great King, your Father, and the *French* King; and told you what I expected of you. You answered me, that in all Things relating to the War you would take the *Six Nations* for an Example, which I expect you will do.

*A BELT.*

To this Speech the River *Indians* the same Day returned their Answer; of which, with what further past between them and the Governor of *New-York* we obtained a Copy, which follows in these Words:

FATHER, We are glad to see you here in Health. Your Children here present bid you all welcome.

*Father,* You have renewed the Covenant, and have assured us that you will keep it inviolable. We do now likewise assure you, that nothing shall be wanting on our Parts, but that we will keep the Covenant Chain clear and free from Rust.

*Father,* When we were here last, you told us that you was glad to see so great a Number of us together; and now you ask us what is the Reason so many of us have left *Schahkook* and are gone to *Canajoherie* and *Attowawie;* and that you are sorry so many of us have left our Habitations.

*Father,* You have told us that War is proclaimed between the *English* and *French,* and that you designed to go and fight the *French.* You told us that we should do as our Uncles the *Six Nations* did with respect to the War.

*Father,* You told us that you would keep the Covenant; and we are resolved to do the same; as a Token whereof we give this

*BELT.*

Father, You must not be surprized that so many of our People have left *Schah-*

*kook.* They are not gone to a strange Country, but are only among our Uncles the *Six Nations,* with whom we are united in Covenant.[4]

*A String of Wampum.*

Father, Respecting the War with the *French,* we will do as the *Six Nations,* and our Father; and will take them for Examples in all Things relating thereto.

*A BELT.*

Father, We are glad the *Six Nations* design to send some of their People to *Canada,* to treat with the *Indians* there. We have been two or three Times to the Carrying-place to treat with some of those *Indians,* in order to keep Peace; and design to send some of our People to *Canada,* to speak with some of the *Indians* there, upon the same Business.

*Give some Skins.*

His Excellency recommended to them, that they should use their Edeavours to prevail upon the *Aschicanhcook Indians,* and all the rest of the *Indians* who have left their old dwelling Place, to return to *Schahkook.*

They answered, they would.

The *Indians* of the United Nations then delivered their Answer to the Speech made to them, *Canassatego* being Speaker: A Copy of which, with what ensued, as we received it, follows in these Words.

BRETHREN, Two Days ago you spoke to us, and we are now come to give you our Answer. You must not expect that we can answer particularly to the several Heads you mentioned to us, but only to the principal Articles. You have renewed to us the Covenant Chain, and we do now renew the same on our Parts; and it is impossible that it can ever Rust, for we daily wipe off the Rust and Dirt, and keep it clean; which we will ever continue to do.

*A BELT.*

*Brethren,* You thought fit to mention to us, that there had been an Uproar among us last Winter, and told us, We ought not to entertain any such Notions of you our Brethren, especially as we had no Grounds to believe any such Thing. It is true, Brethren, there was such a Rumour among us; but it was immediately buried and forgot; and we did not expect that our Brethren would have mentioned any Thing concerning that Affair to us, at this Interview; and we desire you to think no more of it. We are always mindful of the Covenants between us and our Brethren; and here is a Certificate,* whereby it appears, that we are in Covenant with our Brethren of *Boston.*[5]

*A String of Wampum.*

* They here produc'd a Certificate under the Seal of the *Massachusetts.*

*Brethren,* You spoke to us concerning our going to *Canada,* and told us, that the Commissioners of *Indian* Affairs had last Winter told us not to go there; but some of us went. As to what you tell us, that we had taken up the Hatchet against you our Brethren, and promised him to consider of it at home, it is not so. The *Mohawks* and *Tuskaroroes* at their Return, gave the Commissioners of *Indian* Affairs, an Account of all that passed there; and we are convinced that that Account is true.

*A BELT.*

*Brethren,* You have thought fit to relate to us several Particulars concerning the War between you and the *French,* and what Reason you had for taking up the Hatchet against the *French* and their *Indians.* We thank you for giving us a particular Account of the Provocations and Inducements you had for declaring War against them. You have also mentioned to us, that we are one Body and one Flesh, and that if one of us is touched or hurt, the other is likewise; and you have informed us; that you were molested and attacked by the Enemy, and had therefore taken up the Hatchet against them, and desired, as we are one Flesh with you, that we would also take up the Hatchet against the *French,* and those under their Influence, in Conjunction with you. We *Six Nations* accept of the Hatchet, and will keep it in our Bosom. We are in Alliance with a great Number of far *Indians,* and if we should so suddenly lift up the Hatchet without acquainting our Allies, it would perhaps disoblige them; we will therefore, before we make Use of the Hatchet against the *French,* or their *Indians,* send four of our People who are now ready, to *Canada,* to demand Satisfaction for the Wrongs they have done our Brethren; and if they refuse to make Satisfaction, then we will be ready to use the Hatchet against them, whenever our Brother the Governor of *New-York,* orders us to do it.

*A BELT.*

His Excellency ask'd them what Time they thought necessary to see whether the *French Indians* would make such Satisfaction?

They answered, Two Months.

His Excellency asked them, That if in Case the Enemy should commit any further Hostilities in the mean time, Whether they would then, upon his Commands, immediately make Use of the Hatchet?

They answered, Yes.

*Brethren,* You desired us to gather together our People who are scattered, and to settle in a Body; especially as it is very uncertain how soon we may have occasion for them: Your Request is very reasonable, and we will use our Endeavours to that End.

*A BELT.*

*Brethren,* We have now finished our Answer; and have nothing further to say, but only one Request to make to you all; which is, That you our Brethren should be all united in your Councils, and let this Belt of Wampum serve to bind you all together; and if any Thing of Importance is to be communicated to us, by any of you, this is the Place where it should be done.[6]

*A BELT.*

The Answer thus delivered by the United Nations, was received with the Approbation of the Governor of *New-York;* the Commissioners from the *Massachusetts* only expressed their Dissatisfaction; for that, as they alledged, the *Indians* the last Year had engaged, that if Hostilities were committed against the *English,* they would in such Case, declare War: That Hostilities had been since committed; and therefore that by those Engagements, the *Six Nations* ought now to declare War with the *French* and *Indians.*

This Day we proposed to have delivered our Speech to the *Indians;* but the Time being too far spent, and this the last Day of the Week, we were obliged to postpone it, until the Beginning of the next.

The Fourteenth of *October,* being the Time we appointed for speaking with the *Indians,* we gave Directions to *Conrad Weiser* to give them Notice to attend. But before they came to the Place appointed, we received a Message from the Governor of *New-York,* that he was then met in Council, and desired to speak with us. We went accordingly. When we came to the Governor's, besides himself and his Council, there were present the Commissioners from the *Massachusetts;* who then presented to the Governor Letters that they had received by an Express, giving an Account that a Party of *French* and *Indians,* had a few Days before made an Attack on the Great Meadow Fort, about Fifty Miles, as we are informed, from *Albany.* That they had taken Prisoner a Person whom they found at some Distance from it. That two others coming down a Creek near that Fort, were shot at, one killed, the other made his Escape. The Number of *French* and *Indians* was not mentioned. On reading of these Letters, the Commissioners for the *Massachusetts* were requested to be explicit in what they desired on this Occasion. They thereupon represented, That their Government thought it unreasonable the whole Burden of the War should remain on one Province, whilst the rest remained Neutral: That they desired the *Indians* of the *Six Nations* might be engaged to assist them: That tho' they thought it was reasonable other Provinces should bear a Part of the Expence; yet rather than want the Assistance of the *Indians* on the present Occasion, they would be at the whole Expence themselves. The Governor of *New-York* complained, the *Massachusetts* Government had been too precipitate in their Declaration of War: That the other Governments were not obliged to follow the Example: Said that he had done all in his Power towards being better provided for a War: That in the Condition the Inhabitants of that Province were in on the Borders, it would be imprudent in him to engage the *Indians* of the *Six Nations* in a War: That proper Provision should first be made, which could not be done without his Assembly, who were to sit in a little Time, and before whom he would lay this Affair. After this, and more of like Import said, we parted. The Governor of *New-York* having delivered the Presents from that Government to the *Indians* of the United Nations, embarked for the City of *New-York* and we proceeded to meet the *Indians* according to our Appointment. When we came to the Place agreed on for this Purpose, we found the Deputies of the United Nations attending, and the Speech we had before agreed on was now read, and interpreted to them by *Conrad Weiser;* the Interpreters of *New-York* and the *Massachusetts* being also present, and assisting: Which Speech follows in these Words:

*Brethren of the* Six Nations, Altho' it is not long since a Treaty was held with you in *Pennsylvania,* yet our Governor, and the Assembly of the Province, being informed of your coming hither, have, at the Invitation of the Governor of *New-York,* sent us here, to be present at the Treaty now held with you. We attend accordingly, and are glad to see you. In Token whereof, we present you with this

*String of Wampum.*

*Brethren,* Before your last going to *Canada,* you promised our Governor, That on your return you would open your Hearts, and give a full Account of all that passed between you and the *French* Governor; and we have it in Charge to desire you now to perform this Promise.

*Brethren,* We are also to put you in Mind, that, by the Treaty made last Year with our Governor, at *Lancaster,* you promised him, that neither the Governor of *Canada,* nor any of his People, should come through your Country to hurt your Brethren the *English,* nor any of the Settlements belonging to them: Notwithstanding which, some of the *Shawnese* Indians, in Conjunction with some *Frenchmen* from *Canada,* committed a Robbery on our Traders, and took from them a great Quantity of Goods. This, our Governor sometime since gave you Notice of by *Conrad Weiser,* and you undertook to demand Satisfaction for the Injury, of the Governor of *Canada* and the *Shawnese Indians.* We therefore now desire to be informed whether you have made this Demand, and what Satisfaction you have obtained. The *Frenchmen* who did this Injury came through the Lands you claim, and the Robbery was committed on our Traders on those Lands. It was therefore a manifest Breach of the Neutrality the Governor of *Canada* pretended to observe towards you, and shews the Perfidy of the *French,* and that they regard the Treaties they make, no longer than whilst they think it their Interest so to do.

We hope their Example will not influence you, but that you will fulfil all the Treaties you have entered into with your Brethren the *English.* To impress this on your Minds, and to enforce our Request, we present you with this

*Belt of Wampum.*

*Brethren,* Besides what we have already said, we are also to remind you, that our Governor, at the Request of the Government of *Virginia,* became a Mediator between you and the Southern *Indians* called *Catabaws:* And you promised him next

Spring to send Deputies to *Philadelphia,* to meet some of that Nation, in order to conclude a Peace with them: And that in the mean Time all Hostilities shall be suspended. But our Governor is since informed that a Party of the *Oneides* Warriors are gone to attack the *Catabaws.* Whether this be true or not, or whether any of your young Men went without your Knowledge, we do not know; and therefore desire you now to inform us of all the Particulars; and if any of your Warriors are gone against the *Catabaws,* that you will forthwith recal them, and take Care that no more go against them during the Time agreed on.

*Brethren,* You may remember, that at a Treaty held with our Government at *Philadelphia,* in the Year One Thousand Seven Hundred and Thirty Two, you were advised, "To call home all those of your Nations who were at *Canada,* or live amongst the *French;* lest if any Occasion or Difference should arise, they might be prevented from returning." This, in your Answer made to our Governor in the Year One Thousand Seven Hundred Thirty Six, you call "Sound Advice, say the *French* were formerly your cruel Enemies, and that you were taking such Measures as you hoped would be effectual to bring back your People if any new Breach should happen."

*Brethren,* The French are a subtle People. A Breach hath now happened, occasioned by an unjust Declaration of War made by the *French* King against the King of *Great Britain* and His Subjects; and, no doubt, if any of your People live amongst the *French,* they will endeavour to engage them in their Service; and, therefore, we think you would act very prudently, as soon as is possible, to persuade them to return and settle amongst you. To enforce this Request, we present you with this

*Belt of Wampum.*

*Brethren,* We have more to say to you from our Governor; but this we must defer until we hear your Answer to what we have already said.

This Speech being interpreted to them, and the *Indians,* by *Cannassetego* their Chief, signifying their Intention of an immediate Consultation, and in a little Time to return us an Answer, we withdrew.

Some Time after being informed the *Indians* were come to a Result, we again met them, and received their Answer; the Substance of which, as the same was translated to us, is as follows, the aforesaid *Canassatego* being Speaker.

BRETHREN, You that come from *Pennsylvania* to represent our Brother *Onas,* you tell us that you come hither at the Invitation of the Governor of *New-York,* to the Council Fire at *Albany,* to hear what passes between us and our Brother the Governor of *New-York.* You were pleased to signify to us, that you were glad to see us, for which we return you our hearty Thanks. We are likewise glad to see you, in Token wherefore we return you this

*String of Wampum.*

*Brethren,* The first Thing you required of us this Morning was, that we would give you an Account of all that passed between us and the Governor of *Canada* at our last Visit to him, according to the Promise we made the last Summer to *Conrad Weiser,* your Interpreter, at *Oswego.* And since you desire to hear with your own Ears, we are now ready to do it, tho' it will take up Time, and, therefore, another Opportunity might have suited better. Our Going to *Montreal* was at the Invitation of the Governor of *Canada.* At our coming there, several great Men, as well of the *French,* as *Indians,* being dead since our last Journey there, we, according to our Custom, spent some Days in bewailing their Death. During this Time, divers of the *French* Council took an Opportunity of sounding us, to learn from us how the War went on with the *English,* and how far we were engaged therein. On which Occasion we told them, That formerly we had inconsiderately engaged in Wars, but that we looked upon this War, as a War between the *English* and *French* only, and did not intend to engage on either Side; for that the *French* and *English* made War, and made Peace, at Pleasure; but when the *Indians* once engaged in Wars, they knew not when it would end. We also told the *French,* that they knew, and all the World knew, the Countries on which we were settled, and particularly the Lakes, were ours; and, therefore, if they would fight our Brethren, the *English,* they ought to fight on the salt Water, and that they must not come over our Land to disturb them, or to obstruct the Trade at *Oswego.* That they, the *French,* had two trading Houses on those Lakes, with which they ought to be contented. The Governor of *Canada* promised us he would not do it unless the King his Master should command him, and then he must obey. While these Things pass'd, News arrived at *Montreal,* of the taking of *Cape Breton* by the *English,* at which the *French* were much alarmed; and the Governor thereupon sent for all the *Indians* then at *Montreal, to wit,* the *French Indians,* and us, the Deputies of the *Six Nations,* who met together in a large House, where the Governor of *Canada* taking in his Hand a large Belt of Wampum, in which the Figure of a Hatchet was wrought, speaking to us of the *Six Nations,* said as follows:

*Children,* Your Brethren the *English* have already taken one of my Towns (meaning *Cape Breton*) and their Fleet I suppose is now coming up to *Quebec;* and therefore I must take up the Hatchet to defend my self against them. As for you, my Children (speaking to the *French Indians*) I have no Occasion to say much to you, for you must live and die with me, and cannot deny me your Assistance. And as for you, my Children of the *Six Nations* (speaking to us) he further said, I know you love your Brethren the *English,* and therefore I shall not say much to you; perhaps you would not be pleased with it: But Children, said he, should know their Duty to their Father. Then speaking to us all, he desired such who loved him to go with him and assist him in defending *Quebec;* and that those who went with him need not to take any thing with them save their Tobacco Pouches; that he would provide Guns, Pistols, Swords, Ammunition, Provisions, and every Thing, even Paint to paint them; and thereupon delivered the Belt to the Interpreter, who threw it at the Feet of the *Indians* present, some of whom inconsiderately, and without any Consultation first had, took it up, and danced the War Dance; and afterwards divers of the *Indians* present, chiefly of the Praying *Indians,* went with the *French* Governor to *Quebec,* where they staid eight or ten Days, but no Notice was taken of them, nor any Arms or Necessaries, so much as a Knife, provided for them, nor were they admitted to speak to the Governor; which so exasperated the Praying *Indians,* that they left *Quebec,* and are since gone against their common Enemies to the Southward. *Canassatego* added,

*Brethren,* You also put us in mind this Morning of the Treaties of Friendship subsisting between you and us. The Last we made with the Governor of *Pennsylvania,* was at *Lancaster,* the last Year. By this Treaty we were to be Neutral (and we with the *English* of all the Provinces would agree that we should remain so) unless the *French* should come through our Settlements to hurt our Brethren the *English,* which we would not permit. This, and all other our Treaties, with our Brethren the *English,* we are determined to observe; and in Token thereof, we return you this

*Belt of Wampum.*

*Brethren,* You also put us in mind of our Brother *Onas* his Mediation between us and the *Catabaws;* and that you heard some of our Warriors were, notwithstanding, gone against them. It is not in our Power to restrain our Warriors as the *English* can do, until a Peace be finally concluded. This the *Catabaws* know. We have used our Endeavours to restrain them from going, and shall continue so to do; during the Time agreed on, altho' we doubt whether the *Catabaws* are so desirous of Peace as they would have our Brother *Onas* believe; otherwise they would have done as the *Cherokees* did, who, tho' they were at War with us, came to desire Peace; but the *Catabaws* have neither come to us, nor have they come to our Brother *Onas:* But the Account he has received, is only from the Government of *Virginia.* When *Conrad Weiser* brought us an Account of this Matter, we were going to *Canada;* and at our Return we had kindled a Council Fire; but receiving a Message from the Governor of *New-York,* we were obliged to rake it up until we return. *Canassatego* further said, We have spoke to the Governor of *Canada* concerning *Peter Chartier,* and the Robbing of your *Indian* Traders; the Governor of *Canada* said, He knew nothing of the Matter. At our Council before-mentioned, we were to have considered what we should do further in this Affair; but were called away before we had come to any Resolution. He added, Your Traders go very far back into the Country, which we desire may not be done, because it is in the Road of the *French.* At our Return, we will hold a Council; and in the Spring, when our Deputies come to meet those of the *Catabaws* at *Philadelphia,* we shall send our Brother *Onas* our Result. *Canassatego* further said,

*Brethren,* You put us in Mind of a Promise we made our Brother *Onas* at his coming over to *Pennsylvania,* That we would recal our People from *Canada,* who were settled there. We have invited them back to us, and have done all we can to effect it; but cannot prevail: The Governor of *Canada* has taken them into his Lap, suckles them as his Children, and they are so well pleased with him, it is impossible for us to prevail with them to come and settle with us. We return you this Belt instead of that we received from you.

After we had received this Answer of the *Indians,* we acquainted them by our Interpreter, that what we had farther to say to them, would be early the next Morning. In the mean Time we ordered them a Pair of Oxen and some Beer for their Subsistence, and then parted.

The next Morning, being the Fifteenth of *October,* the *Indians* met us pursuant to our Appointment; when we spoke to them to the Effect following.

BRETHREN, We now put you in Mind, there are two Things remaining under your Consideration, concerning which, you have received Belts from our Governor, and have, as yet, return'd no full Answer: The First relates to the *Catabaws,* the Second to our *Indian* Traders. As you have signified to us your Inability of doing it at this time, we expect when you return home, a Council will be called, and that you will give our Governor a full Answer in the Spring.

*Brethren,* When our Governor and Assembly sent us hither, they did not think it fitting we should come empty handed; but have directed us to provide you a Present. We considered Winter was approaching, that our Brethren would want Cloathing to preserve them from the Cold, and Powder and Lead to acquire their Livelihood by Hunting; we have therefore provided the Goods which now lie before you, *to wit,*

Six Pieces of Strouds.
Four Pieces of *Indian* Blankets.
Two Pieces of striped Blankets.
Four Pieces of half Thicks.
One Piece of *Shrewsbury* Cotton.
Eight Dozen of Knives.
Four Hundred and Twenty-five Bars of Lead.
Four half Barrels of Pistol Powder.

These we present to you on Behalf of our Government, and have no more to say, but to wish you a good Journey Home.

This Speech being interpreted to the *Indians,* after a short Consultation between themselves, they brought six Bundles of Skins; and by *Canassatego,* spoke as follows:

BRETHREN, We thank you for the Goods you present to us. We are Poor, and have little to return; however, out of what we have, we present you with the six Bundles of Skins which you see. These we desire may be accepted of, as a Token of our Affection.

To this we replied. We accepted them in the Manner they desired, wished them well, and then took Leave of them.

The Sloop which brought us, waiting our Return, we embarked, arrived at *New-York* on the Nineteenth of *October.* The same Day took Boat, and got to *Elizabeth* Town Point. Then mounted our Horses; and on the Twenty-second of *October,* reached Home.

Permit us to add, That in the foregoing Relation, we do not pretend to have delivered the several Conversations which past, *verbatim;* but only the Substance, so far as we judge them material; and where we have made any Omissions, they are of such Things as we think of too little Consequence to be inserted. If the Governor's Health, and other Affairs of Importance, had permitted his Attendance at this Treaty, we make no Question it would have been managed with greater Skill and Delicacy. Thus much, however, we may say, That so far as we were able, we have, pursuant to the Instructions we received, faithfully endeavoured to acquit ourselves of the Trust, to the Honour and Interest of the Province: But whether we are so happy as in any Degree to have succeeded herein, is humbly submitted to the Governor,

*By*
THO. LAWRENCE,
JOHN KINSEY.

1. Signaling both its previous entry into New York's Covenant Chain and a reassertion by New York of primary influence over League affairs, Pennsylvania treats in the capital of its rival New York (Boyd, "Indian Affairs," xlv).

2. New York had established a trading house at Oswego in 1722. The French destroyed it in 1756. Because it intercepted trade from Iroquoia to France that would have crossed Lake Ontario and trade from northern and northwestern Indians who would otherwise have had to use the League nations as middlemen, it had vexed both Iroquois and French (Jennings, *Empire of Fortune,* 74, 290).

3. As the behind-the-scenes bickering shows, these outward protestations of union were far from the reality.

4. On a literal level, the uncle-nephew relationship in matrilineal societies would be a relation between men with elected authority and experience, often on a more national than local level, and men with newfound authority, less experience, and local reputation. The Mahicans (here spelled Mohiggans and easily confused with the Mohegans of New England except for their designation as [Hudson] River Indians) had been adopted into the League in 1677 as a result of their defeat in King Philip's War (Jennings, *Ambiguous Iroquois Empire,* 148). Thus the nation as a whole was characterized in League terms as still learning the political ropes.

5. League speakers frequently expressed impatience with the British when they raised issues at treaty councils that should have been forgotten, considered trivial, or dealt with in less formal ways. The British were violating North American diplomatic protocols that had preceded their arrival on the continent, though of course many protocols had arisen from the previous century of intercontinental diplomacy.

6. Canasatego here intriguingly reiterates his 1744 urge to the British colonies to be united in their councils. At both treaties, their inability to speak with one voice had both frustrated the Iroquois and created problems for them. At Lancaster, the treaty had been unnecessarily prolonged and the League must have found it difficult to keep track of all the multiple lines of

diplomatic concern at once. This may have contributed to their unwittingly signing away the Ohio Valley. At Albany, it must have been clear from the starkly different tones of the speeches from the various colonies that the British did not know what they wanted or how to get it. The two speeches by Canasatego support the idea that the reassignment of the power to negotiate with Indian nations from the state to the federal level, beginning in the 1750s, was spurred on by League complaints.

✠

# A TREATY

## BETWEEN THE PRESIDENT *and* COUNCIL

## OF THE Province of PENNSYLVANIA,

## AND THE *INDIANS* of *OHIO*,

## Held at *PHILADELPHIA, Nov.* 13. 1747.

---

*PHILADELPHIA:*
Printed and Sold by B. FRANKLIN, at the New Printing-Office,
near the Market. MDCCXLVIII.

---

### A TREATY, *&c.*

*At a Council held at* Philadelphia, *the* 13*th of* November, 1747.
PRESENT, *The Honourable* ANTHONY PALMER, *Esq; President.*
*Thomas Lawrence, Samuel Hassell, William Till, Abraham Taylor, Robert Strettell, Benjamin Shoemaker, Joseph Turner, William Logan,* Esqrs.

THE *Indian* Warriors from *Ohio,* having arriv'd in Town on *Wednesday,* the President sent them a Message Yesterday, by Mr. *Weiser,* the Interpreter, to bid them welcome: And understanding that they were desirous to be heard To-day, he summon'd the Council for this Purpose. Mr. *Weiser* attending, he was sent to tell the *Indians* the Council was sitting, and ready to receive them. They immediately came. The President inform' d them, the Council were glad to see their Brethren, took their Visit very kindly, and desired to know what they had to communicate.

After a Pause, the principal Warrior rose up, and spoke as follows:

*Brethren, the* English, *the Governor of* York, *the Commissioners at* Albany,[1] *the Governor and Councellors of* Pennsylvania,

WE who speak to you are Warriors, living at *Ohio,* and address you on Behalf of ourselves, and the rest of the Warriors of the *Six Nations.*

You will, perhaps, be surprized at this unexpected Visit; but we cou'd not avoid coming to see you, the Times are become so critical and dangerous. We are of the

*Six Nations,* who are your ancient Friends, having made many Treaties of Friendship with the *English,* and always preserv'd the Chain bright. You know when our Father, the Governor of *Canada,* declar'd War against our Brethren, the *English,* you the Governor of *New-York,* the Commissioners of *Indian* Affairs at *Albany,* the Commissioners for this Province, sent to inform the Council at *Onondago* of it, and to desire that they wou'd not meddle with the War; that they wou'd only look on, and see what wou'd be done; that we, the *Indians,* wou'd let you fight it out by yourselves, and not pity either Side; and that we would send to all the Nations in Alliance with us, to do the same: And accordingly the *Indians* did send to all their Friends and Allies, and particularly to the *Indians* about the Lakes, and in the Places where we live, requesting they wou'd not engage on either Side; and they all stood Neuters, except the *French* Praying *Indians,* who, tho' they promis'd, yet were not as good as their Words. This is the first Thing we have to say to our Brethren, and we hope they will receive this in good Part, and be willing to hear what we have further to say.

*Brethren,* When the *Indians* received the first Message from the *English,* they thought the *English* and *French* would fight with one another at Sea, and not suffer War to be made on the Land: But some Time after this, Messengers were sent by all the *English* to *Onondago,* to tell us that the French had begun the War on the Land in the *Indian* Countries, and had done a great deal of Mischief to the *English,* and they now desired their Brethren, the *Indians,* would take up the Hatchet against the *French,* and likewise prevail with their Allies to do the same. The old Men at *Onondago* however refus'd to do this, and would adhere to the Neutrality; and on their declaring this, the *English* sent other Messengers again and again, who pressed earnestly that the *Indians* would take up their Hatchet, but they were still denied by the old Men at the Fire at *Onondago,* who, unwilling to come into the War, sent Message after Message to *Canada* and *Albany,* to desire both Parties would fight it out at Sea. At last the young *Indians,* the Warriors, and Captains, consulted together, and resolved to take up the *English* Hatchet against the Will of their old People, and to lay their old People aside, as of no Use but in Time of Peace.[2] This the young Warriors have done, provoked to it by the repeated Applications of our Brethren the *English;* and we now come to tell you, that the *French* have hard Heads, and that we have nothing strong enough to break them. We have only little Sticks, and Hickeries, and such Things, that will do little or no Service against the hard Heads of the *French:* We therefore present this Belt, to desire that we may be furnished with better Weapons, such as will knock the *French* down; and in Token that we are hearty for you, and will do our best if you put better Arms into our Hands, we give you this Belt.

*Here they gave a Belt of seven Rows.*

*Brethren,* When once we, the young Warriors, engaged, we put a great deal of Fire under our Kettle, and the Kettle boil'd high, and so it does still *(meaning they carried the War on briskly)* that the *Frenchmens* Heads might soon be boil'd. But when we look'd about us, to see how it was with the *English* Kettle, we saw the Fire was almost out, and that it hardly boil'd at all; and that no *Frenchmens* Heads were like to be in it. This truly surprizes us, and we are come down on Purpose to know the Reason of it. How comes it to pass, that the *English,* who brought us into the War, will not fight themselves? This has not a good Appearance, and therefore we give you this String of Wampum to hearten and encourage you, to desire you wou'd put more Fire under your Kettle.[3]

*Here they presented the String of Wampum of seven Strings.*

*Brethren,* We have now done with general Matters; but old *Scaiohady* desires to inform the Council, that he was here in *James Logan*'s Time, a long Time ago, when he had but one Child, and he a little one: That he was then employed in the Affairs of the Government: That *James Logan* gave him this String, to assure him, if ever he should come to want, and apply to this Government, they wou'd do something for him. *Scaiohady* is now grown old and infirm, and recommends himself to *James Logan*'s and the Council's Charity.

*Here he laid down a String of Wampum.*

The *Indians* withdrew, and the Council adjourn'd to To-morrow Morning, Eleven a Clock.

*In the Council-Chamber, 14th November* 1747.
PRESENT, *Thomas Lawrence, Robert Strettell, Benjamin Shoemaker, William Logan,* Esqrs.

THE President being indispos'd, and the other Members not attending, there could be no Council; the Members present, judg'd that before the Heads of an Answer to the Speech of the *Indians* could be considered, it was necessary previously to learn from Mr. *Weiser,* the particular History of these *Indians,* their real Disposition towards us, and their future Designs; and accordingly sent for him. He said the *Indians,* had in Part told him their Mind, and he thought they might be brought to tell him more; and when they did, he would inform the Council. The Members likewise judg'd, that it might be of Service to know Mr. *Logan*'s Sentiments about what might be proper to be said to the *Indians,* and requested Mr. *Weiser* and the Secretary to wait on him for that Purpose.

*At a Council held at* Philadelphia, *16th November* 1747.
PRESENT, The Honourable the PRESIDENT, *Thomas Lawrence, Samuel Hassell, William Till, Abr. Taylor, Robert Strettell, Benj. Shoemaker, Thomas Hopkinson, William Logan,* Esqrs.

MR. *Weiser* attending was called in, and inform'd the Council, that he had learn'd the following Particulars from the *Indians,* viz. That last Summer the Governor of *Canada* had sent the Hatchet to the *Indians* about the Lakes, and on the Branches of *Ohio;* that one Nation took it up; and that these *Indians,* and the *Indians* in those Quarters, consisting principally of Warriors, being afraid others would do the like, to prevent this took up the *English* Hatchet, and proclaim'd War against the *French;* which had a good Effect, no more daring after this to meddle with the *French* Hatchet: That these *Indians* on *Ohio,* had concluded to kindle a Fire in their Town, and had invited all the *Indians* at a considerable Distance round about them to come to their Fire in the Spring; and that they had consented to it. Mr. *Weiser* added, that the *Indians* in the Parts these People came from, were numerous, not less than Five Hundred Men, and had many Allies more numerous than themselves: That it was always the Custom in War Time, to put the Management into the Hands of the young People; and that it would be of the most pernicious Consequence not to give them Encouragement at this Time; and particularly he thought the Council should at least tell them, they approv'd of their taking up the Hatchet; and aknowledge the Service done to the *English* by their seasonable Declaration in their Favour: He thought Providence had furnished this Province with a fine Opportunity of making all the *Indians* about the Lakes their Friends, and warm Friends too.——Mr. *Weiser* being asked what Sort of a Present should be given them at this Time, He said Goods were now so dear, that the Value of 100 Pounds would appear but small, that they should have so much given them at least, and Half as much to the *Canayiahaga Indians.* Not that this was by any Means sufficient, but would be a good Salutation-Present, and preparatory to a larger to be sent in the Summer. This he judged necessary to be done, and that they should now be told of this future Present: And, tho' he had never been in those Parts, yet he judged the attaching these *Indians* and their Friends to the *English* Cause to be so necessary, that he would, if the Council pleased, and his Health should permit, go with the Present himself, and see with his own Eyes what Number of *Indians* was there, and in what Disposition. He said further, that he accompanied the Secretary to Mr. *Logan*'s Yesterday, and that the Secretary had informed Mr. *Logan* of all these Particulars, and taken his Sentiments in Writing, and on them form'd the Plan of an Answer. The Board ordered the Secretary to read what he had wrote; and on considering this, and Mr. *Weiser*'s Information, an Answer was agreed to, and the Presents settled. The Council adjourned to Four o'Clock in the Afternoon, and directed that the *Indians* should be told to be there, in order to receive the Answer of the Council to their Speech.

*At a Council held at* Philadelphia, *the* 16*th of* November, 1747. *P. M.*
PRESENT, The Honourable ANTHONY PALMER, Esq; President;
And the same Members as in the Forenoon.

The *Indians* having taken their Seats, the President spoke as follows:

*Brethren Warriors of the* Six Nations,

WE the President and Council of the Province of *Pennsylvania,* have taken what you said to us into Consideration, and are now going to give you an Answer.

We are always glad to see our Brethren, and are particularly pleased at this critical Time, with your present Visit. You are sensible of the constant Friendship this Government has always shewn to the *Indians* of the *Six Nations;* and that, from their first Settlement in the Country, their Interest has been put on the same Foot with our own. And as long as you shall act up to your Engagements, you will never want the most substantial Proofs that we can give of our Regard for your Nations.

You tell us, that at the Beginning of the War, you receiv'd a Message from all the *English,* to stand neuter, and to prevail with your Allies to do the same; that in Compliance therewith, you did stand neuter, and all your Allies, except the Praying *Indians,* who promis'd, but broke their Word: That the *French* commencing Hostilities, you received repeated Messages from the *English* to continue neuter no longer, but to take up their Hatchet against the *French;* and that you and your Allies have accordingly done this. *Brethren,* You did well to hearken to the Messages sent by the *English.* Your Allies so readily concurring with you, shews you keep up a good Understanding with them; for which you are to be commended. You live in small Tribes at a Distance from one another: Separate, you will be easily overcome; united, it will be difficult, if not impossible, to hurt you: Like the Strings on which you put your Wampum, a single Thread is soon snapp'd, a few require more Strength; but if you weave them into a Belt, and fasten them tight together, it must be a strong Hand that can break it.[4]

We are pleased to hear, that at the pressing Instances of the Governors of *New-York* and *New-England,* you have taken up the Hatchet against the *French;* who you know, notwithstanding their fair Speeches, have been from the Beginning your inveterate Enemies: And in Confirmation that we approve of what you have done, we give you this *Belt.*

By your String of Wampum you tell us, that you observe the *English* Kettle does not boil high, and you give the String to all the *English,* to encourage them to put more Fire under their Kettle.

As you address this to all the *English,* we shall send your String to the other Governors: But to lessen your Concern on this Account, we are to apprize you, that the *French* were sending large Forces in big Ships, well arm'd with great Cannon, over the Seas to *Canada;* that the *English* pursued them, attack'd them, took their Men of War, killed a Number of their Men, and carried the rest Prisoners to *England.* This Victory put a Stop for the Present to the Expedition intended against *Canada:* You are therefore not to judge by the Appearance Things make now, that the *English* Fire is going out; but that this is only accidental, and it will soon blaze again.

As this is the first Visit paid us by our Brethren the Warriors living on the Branches of *Ohio,* to shew that we take it kindly of them, and are desirous to cultivate and improve the Friendship subsisting between the *Six Nations* and us, we have provided a Present of Goods; a List whereof will be read to you at the Close of our Answer. They are at *John Harris*'s, and the Interpreter will go along with you, and deliver them to you there. In the Spring we propose to send Mr. *Weiser* to you, and he will be furnished with a proper Present to be distributed to all the *Indians* at *Ohio,* at *Canayiahaga,* and about the Lake *Erie.* In Confirmation of what we say, we give you this *String of Wampum.*

Having receiv'd by the Traders a kind Message from the *Canayiahaga Indians*, to let them see we are pleased with it, we have sent them a small Present of Powder and Lead, by Mr. *Croghan*, which you will inform them of, and likewise of our further Intentions in their Favour, with this *String of Wampum*, which is given you for that Purpose.

The President and Council at your Recommendation will take Care to give *Scaiohady* a Present for his own private Use, and his old Friend Mr. *Logan* will do the same.

*A String of Wampum.*

The *Indian* Speaker having consulted with *Scaiohady*, took up the Belt and Strings of Wampum in the Order they were presented, and repeating the Substance of every Paragraph, express'd high Satisfaction at what the Council had said, and promis'd to send the String of Wampum to the *Canayiahaga Indians*, who being their own Flesh and Blood, they were pleased with the Regards shewn to them. And in Testimony of their intire Satisfaction and Devotion to the *English* Interest, they gave the *Indian* Marks of Approbation, and danc'd the Warrior Dance.

*A true Copy.*

*Nov.* 25. 1747. RICHARD PETERS, *Secretary*.

1. These addresses are puzzling, as no governor of New York nor commissioners from Albany appear to be present. A few possibilities present themselves. Conceivably, Pennsylvania added these names to the speech to avoid trouble with New York's government or with the League Iroquois who may have been jealous of the meeting between a rival colony and Ohio "upstarts." On the other hand, the speaker and warriors may have been confused about who they were meeting with or asked the messages to be conveyed to New York.

2. The phrasing may appear disrespectful on first glance. However, the speaker seems merely to be explaining an ordinary provision of the Iroquois political structure: the shift from peacetime leadership to wartime leadership, which would not destabilize the continuing operation and legitimacy of the peacetime council at Onondaga. In many North American nations, there were separate leaders for war and for peace. Each nation in the confederacy could choose independently of the others whether to wage war; within a nation, no persons had the power to restrain individuals who wished to go to war. Because it seems that the younger men were leaders on a more local level, the phrasing might make sense in this respect as well. However, it also appears that this pronouncement is a first step in the "declaration of independence" of the Ohio Iroquois, albeit very minute.

3. The expressions regarding the kettle, the fire, and the boiling of heads are metaphoric. There is one unconfirmed report of cannibalism by Iroquois occurring in the early decades of the century, but there appears to be no evidence from this war to suggest that it was practiced against the French. Later publications, such as David Cusick's 1823 historical sketch, would portray the Six Nations as having repudiated the practice prior to contact, but there is evidence from the seventeenth century to suggest that it was being practiced at that time.

At this time, the Pennsylvania Assembly was involved in a power struggle with Thomas

Penn over the support of military action against the French and their Indian allies. One main motivation was conscientious objection, but it appears they were also concerned during this earlier war over the same issue that rankled in the later war: who would control a militia once formed. Franklin created a voluntary military association for the defense of Pennsylvania. Rather than applauding his ingenuity, Penn regarded the move as contemptuous toward government and little short of treason. It appears that his main objection was not that the association might undercut the Assembly, because opposition members in that body and in the Council supported Franklin, but that it undercut Penn's ability to control Pennsylvanians (Jennings, *Benjamin Franklin,* 63–66). The Ohio Indians saw only the result: a hypocritical unwillingness on the part of British colonials in Pennsylvania to back their own government's war against France personally while encouraging Iroquois involvement in a war that they had not made.

4. Johansen and Grinde identify this metaphor as an Iroquois metaphor that was picked up by British colonials and that goes toward proving the influence of Iroquois ideas on the West. The metaphor could show that the British colonials knew the principle behind the League or behind the Covenant Chain. Colonials who knew about the Chain did not necessarily have knowledge of the League or its inner workings. It is hard to verify the actual provenience of the concept.

✠

# A TREATY

HELD BY COMMISSIONERS,

MEMBERS of the COUNCIL of the

PROVINCE of *PENNSYLVANIA*, At the TOWN

of *LANCASTER*, With some CHIEFS of the

*SIX NATIONS* at *OHIO*, and others, for the

Admission of the TWIGHTWEE NATION

into the Alliance of his MAJESTY, *&c.*

in the Month of *July*, 1748.

---

*PHILADELPHIA:*
Printed and Sold by B. FRANKLIN, at the New Printing-Office,
near the Market. MDCCXLVIII.

---

To the HONOURABLE the PRESIDENT *and* COUNCIL OF THE Province of PENNSYLVANIA.

WE, the Subscribers, having been honoured with a Commission, authorizing us to hold a Treaty with some of the *Six Nations, Twigtwees,* and others, at *Lancaster,* do make the following Report of our Proceedings therein.

WE hope what we have done will be of Service to the Province, and to your Satisfaction. We are,

HONOURABLE GENTLEMEN,

*Your most Obedient, Humble Servants,*
Benjamin Shoemaker,
Joseph Turner.
Thomas Hopkinson.
William Logan.

*Philadelphia, July* 25. 1748.

## A TREATY, *&c.*

*At the* Court-House *in* Lancaster, Tuesday, July 19. 1748.
PRESENT, *Benjamin Shoemaker, Joseph Turner, Thomas Hopkinson, William Logan,* Esqrs.

*The Magistrates and Inhabitants of* Lancaster *County, Fifty-five* Indians *of several Nations,* viz. *of the* Six Nations, Delawares, Shawonese, Nanticokes, *and* Twightwees; Conrad Weiser, *Esq; Interpreter for the* Six Nation Indians; *Mr.* Andrew Montour, *Interpreter for the* Shawonese *and* Twightwees.

A PROCLAMATION was made for Silence, and then a Commission, in His Majesty's Name, under the Great Seal of the Province, was read, constituting the honourable *Benjamin Shoemaker, Joseph Turner, Thomas Hopkinson,* and *William Logan.* Esquires, Commissioners to treat with these *Indians;* and the Interpreter was order'd to tell them the Purport thereof, and to bid them heartily welcome among their Brethren.

The Commissioners having been informed that *Scarrowyady,* a Chief of the *Oneido* Nation, living at *Ohio,* was appointed Speaker for the *Indians,* but was so much hurt by a Fall, that he was unable to attend; order'd the Interpreter to tell them, that they condoled with them on this unfortunate Accident, but hoped, as what they came to transact was of a publick Nature, and well known to them all, this would occasion no Delay. As the Government had shewn them great Indulgence, in granting them a Council at *Lancaster,* so far from the usual Place of Business, and in so hot a Season, it was expected they would not detain the Commissioners, but deliver what they had to say To-morrow Morning at Ten o' Clock; and further, to desire they would use no Manner of Reserve, but open their Hearts freely and fully, the Commissioners promising to treat them with the same Freedom and Plainness.

*At the* Court-House *in* Lancaster, Wednesday, July 20. 1748.
PRESENT, *Benjamin Shoemaker, Joseph Turner, Thomas Hopkinson, William Logan,* Esqrs.
*The Magistrates, and many of the Inhabitants of* Lancaster *County,*
*The same* Indians *as Yesterday.*

THE Interpreter inform'd the Commissioners, that *Scarrowyady* still continuing ill, and unable to attend, had deputed *Andrew Montour* to deliver his Speech, which the *Indians* desir'd might be receiv'd on their Behalf, the Substance thereof having been deliberated upon, and settled by them in Council

The Commissioners saying they had no Objection to this, *Andrew Montour* said he was now going to speak for the *Indians* of the *Six Nations,* living at *Ohio.*

*Brethren, the Governor of* Pennsylvania, *and all the Governors of the great King of* England, *over the Seas;*

You have often sent pressing Messages to the Council Fire at *Onondago,* to engage in your Interest as many of their Allies as they could influence: These Messages they have transmitted to us, desiring we would take all Opportunities of complying with your Request; in Consequence whereof we have now the Pleasure to present to you some of the Chiefs of the *Twightwee* Nation, a large and powerful Tribe, living on *Ouabache,* a great River running into *Ohio,* who come as Deputies sent by the whole Nation, with a Request that you would be pleased to admit them into your Amity. We join with them in the Petition; take their Hands, and let them, together with ours, be lock'd close in yours, and there held fast: We have opened unto you the Occasion of our Visit; and to make it acceptable, we lay down this String of Wampum.

*Brethren,* Onas, *and all the King of* England*'s Governors,* It will be necessary to lay before you what has passed between the *Twightwees* and us, previous to our coming here, that you may be sensible of our Zeal for your Service, and of the ardent Desire of that Nation to enter into your Alliance.

Last Fall they sent a Message addressed to all the Tribes of *Indians* at *Ohio* and elsewhere, in Amity with the *English,* which was delivered to the *Shawonese,* as living the nearest to them, and by them communicated to us to this Effect.

"*Brethren,* We, the *Twightwees,* are desirous to enter into the Chain of Friendship with the *English;* and as you are the next to us of the *Indians* in their Alliance, we entreat you to signify this our Desire to the other *Indians,* and that you and they will open us a Council Road to the *English* Governments: Make it so open and clear for us, that neither we, nor our Wives or Children, may hurt their Feet against any Log or Stump; and when once you have cleared a Road for us, we assure you we will keep it so, and it shall not be in the Power of *Onontio* to block up or obstruct the Passage. We further desire of you that when you have cleared a Council Road for us to the *English,* you, and the other *Indians,* will join your Interest to recommend us in the most effectual Manner to them to be admitted into their Chain." Upon receipt of this Message from the *Twightwee* the following Answer was sent them.

"*Brethren, the* Twightwees, We received your String of Wampum expressing your Desire to enter into Friendship with our Brethren the *English,* and praying our Assistance to obtain this for you. We are glad you are in this Disposition, and wou'd by all Means encourage you in it; but we are afraid lest you should have taken this Resolution too hastily. Are you Proof against the Solicitations that the Governor of *Canada* and his People will certainly use to engage your Adherence to him? Can you withstand his Resentment? Consider this well, lest when we shall have recommended you to our Brethren the *English,* you shou'd prove unsteady, and so we shou'd lose their Esteem. Take, therefore, we urge you, Time to consider, and let us know your Mind, and we will give you all the Assistance in our Power."

The *Twightwees* having received this Answer, sent in the Spring a second Message, addressed to all the *Indians* on *Ohio* in Alliance with the *English,* to this purport:

"*Brethren,* Our Message in the Fall was not sent rashly or unadvisedly. We thought many Nights and Days of this Affair. We weighed every Thing well relating thereto before we took the Resolution of seeking the Friendship of the *English,* and we now repeat to you our Assurances, that this Request does not come from the Mouth only; no, it comes from the Heart, and is what we ardently wish to accomplish; and that we may not fail of Success, we desire your Assistance, and that of all the *Indians* in the *English* Chain, to help us to obtain this Favour; and particularly we desire some of you will go along with us, and present us to *Onas.*"

*Brethren,* We have now faithfuly related what passed between the *Twightwees* and us. We deliver over to you the Strings of Wampum which we received with their Messages. Their Nation has sent thirty Beaver Skins, which we desire you would accept; and now be pleased to hear what their Deputies have to say.

*Here were laid down two Strings of Wampum, and 30 Beaver Skins.*

Then *Andrew Montour* acquainted the Commissioners, that he was now going to be the Mouth of the *Twightwee* Deputies.

*Brethren,* We present to you the Calumet Pipe, and pray we may be admitted to become a Link in your Chain of Friendship, and give you the strongest Assurances, if this Favour be granted to us, that we will keep it bright as long as the Rivers run.

*Here the Deputies laid down a Calumet Pipe, with a long Stem, curiously wrought, and wrapp'd round with Wampum of several Colours, and fill'd with Tobacco, which was smoked by the Commissioners and the* Indians *according to Custom.*[1]

*Brethren,* We the Deputies of the *Twightwees* have it in Charge further to tell you, that our Nation received a Calumet Pipe from some of the Allies, consisting of twelve Towns or Nations, with a Message to this Effect: That they had a Report among them that we intended to solicit the *English* to be received into their Friendship and Alliance: That if such Report was true, they desired us to acquaint them with our Success, that they might apply for the same Favour, which they earnestly desire, and said they would wait a Day and a Night for an Answer.* Then the Deputies offered another Pipe to the Commissioners, not to keep, but that they might speak to it, and return it, with their Answer.

*Andrew Montour* said he was now going to resume the Speech of the *Six Nation Indians* at *Ohio.*

*Brethren,* You have now heard the *Twightwees* speak for themselves. We heart-

* *N.B.* A Day and a Night in the *Indian* Language signifies a whole Year.

ily join with them in their Petition. They are numerous, and, tho' poor, yet they are worthy of your Friendship, and, as such we most heartily recommend them to you by this Bundle of Skins.

*Here they laid down a Bundle of Deer Skins.*

*Brethren,* We beg Leave before we conclude to become Intercessors for the *Shawonese,* who have given you just Cause of Complaint. They have told us, that the Governor of *Pennsylvania* sent them a Letter some Years ago, requiring them to come down; but being conscious they had acted wrong, they had delay'd hitherto to do it; and have taken this Opportunity of our coming, to make use of us; desiring us to ask that for them which they dare not ask for themselves; that is, That they may be receiv'd again into Favour, they having owned their Fault, and given us the strongest Assurances of their better Behaviour for the future. Forgive us, therefore, if we entreat you wou'd be pleas'd to drop your Resentment; and however they have behav'd hitherto, we hope a Sense of your Goodness will prevail with them to become good and faithful Allies for the future.

*Gave a String of Wampum.*

*Andrew Montour* informing the Commissioners he had delivered all that was given him in Charge to say at present, the *Indians* withdrew.

*At a Meeting of the Commissioners held at* Lancaster, *the 21st* July, 1748.
PRESENT, *Benjamin Shoemaker, Joseph Turner, Thomas Hopkinson, William Logan,* Esqrs.

THE Secretary having settled the Minutes of Yesterday, the same were taken into Consideration, and that Part thereof which relates to the *Shawonese* not giving the Commissioners Satisfaction, Mr. *Weiser* was sent to *Scarrowyady* to consult with him thereupon; who return'd, and inform'd the Board, that according to Order he had consulted with *Scarrowyady,* and he, in the Presence of *Andrew Montour,* deliver'd himself as follows:

"*Neucheconno, Kekewatcheky, Sonatziowanah,* and *Sequeheton,* Chiefs of the *Shawonese,* now left at *Allegheny,* met in Council, and address'd themselves to the *Delawares,* and to the *Six Nations* on *Ohio,* in the following Manner:

"*Grand Fathers* and *Brethren,*

We the *Shawonese* have been misled, and have carried on a private Correspondence with the *French,* without letting you, or our Brethren, the *English,* know of it. We travell'd secretly thro' the Bushes to *Canada,* and the *French* promised us great Things, but we find ourselves deceiv'd. We are sorry that we had any Thing to do with them: We now find that we cou'd not see, altho' the Sun did shine; We earnestly desire you wou'd intercede with our Brethren, the *English, for us who are left at* Ohio, that we may be permitted to be restor'd to the Chain of Friendship, and be looked upon as heretofore the same Flesh with them. Thus far the *Shawonese**.*"

Whereupon the *Indians* of the *Six Nations*, and the *Delawares*, having received these Assurances of their Concern for their past Behaviour, undertook to become their Intercessors, and have brought along with them three of the principal *Shawonese*, to make their Submissions in Person.

*At the Court House at* Lancaster, *Friday the 22d* July, 1748.
PRESENT, *Benjamin Shoemaker, Joseph Turner, Thomas Hopkinson, William Logan*, Esqrs.
*The Magistrates and many of the Inhabitants of* Lancaster *County, The same* Indians *as on Wednesday.*

*The Commissioners order'd the Interpreter to let the* Indians *know they were going to give them an Answer.*

*Brethren, you who live at* Ohio, *of the* Six Nations, *and others,* WE are concern'd that *Scarrowyady* continues so ill as not to be able to attend, but are pleas'd to hear he is in a fair Way of Recovery, and that he cou'd give the necessary Instructions to Mr. *Andrew Montour* about the Business which brought you here; We take it for granted, that your Sentiments are fully and truly express'd in the Speeches delivered, and shall therefore answer the several Matters contain'd therein in the Order they were spoke.

*Brethren of the* Six Nations, *and others, living at* Ohio, It gives us no small Satisfaction to observe the Regard you have shewn to the Messages sent you by the Governors of his Majesty's Provinces, in endeavouring to gain over to His Majesty's Interest as many of your Allies as you cou'd influence: This is agreable to your Duty, and was recommended to you in a particular Manner by the Governor of this Province at the Commencement of the *French* War. As the *Twightwee* shew'd so great an Inclination to enter into our Friendship, and desir'd you to conduct them hither, the Part you have acted on this Occasion was kind and prudent, and we think ourselves oblig'd to you for encouraging them, and shewing them the Way.

*Our Approbation of your Conduct is testified by this String of Wampum.*

*Brethren,* As there is Reason to think from the Manner in which the *Twightwees* have made their Application for a Council Road to the *English* Provinces, that it is not a sudden, or a hasty Step, but well consider'd by them, and may take its Rise from the different Treatment which *Indians* of all Nations meet with at the Hands of the

* Some of the *Shawonese* were seduc'd by *Peter Chartier*, a noted *Indian* Trader and Inhabitant of *Pennsylvania* at the Beginning of the *French* War, and remov'd from their Towns to be nearer to the *French* Settlements on the *Mississippi*. Some Time after, several of these Deserters return'd; of which *Neucheconno* and his Party were some; these, it seems, together with *Kakewatcheky*, the old *Shawonese* King, and his Friends, who had withstood the Sollicitations of *Chartier*, join'd together, and apply'd in this submissive Manner to *Scarrowyady*.

*English,* from what they experience while in the *French* Interest, we are inclinable to think them sincere, and that when admitted into our Chain, they will not lightly break it.

A Council Road to this Province is a Measure which nearly concerns you, as it is to be laid out thro' your Towns, and no doubt you have thought well of this, and conceive you may depend on the Sincerity of their Professions, and that it may be for our mutual Benefit, or you wou'd not join with them in making this Request. At your Instance therefore, and from the Opinion we have of your Prudence and Integrity, we consent that such Road may be opened; and it may be depended on, that on our Parts it will always be kept clean, not the least Obstruction shall be suffer'd to remain in it. In Confirmation whereof

*We give this String of Wampum.*

*Brethren of the* Twightwee *Nation,* At the Intercession of our good Friends and Allies the *Six Nations,* we have granted you a Council Road, whereby you have free Access to any of His Majesty's Provinces; we admit you into our Friendship and Alliance, and therefore now call you BRETHREN, an Appellation which we hold sacred, and in which is included every Thing that is dear. It obliges us to give you Assistance on all Occasions, to exercise unfeign'd Affection towards you, to take you into our Bosoms, to use our Eyes, and Ears, and Hands, as well for you, as for ourselves. Nothing is put in Competition by an *Englishman* with the Faith and Honour due to those whom our gracious King pleases to take into his Protection, admit into his Chain of Friendship, and make them our Fellow Subjects: From that Moment they become our own Flesh and Blood, and what hurts them will equally hurt us. Do you, on your Parts, look upon this important Name of Brethren in the same Light; You must no more think of *Onontio,* and his *Children;* all that sort of Relationship now ceases; His Majesty's Friends are your Friends, and His Majesty's Enemies are Your Enemies. On these Conditions we accept your Calumet Pipe, and shall lay it up very carefully, that it may be always ready for Use when you and we come together. In Token of our Readiness to receive you into our Chain of Friendship, we present you

*With this double Belt of Wampum, as an Emblem of our Union.*

*Brethren of the* Twigthwee *Nation,* We understand that by an antient Custom observ'd by your Ancestors, the Delivery and Acceptance of the Calumet Pipe are the Ceremonies which render valid, and bind fast your Alliances: We must now tell you what our Usages are on these Occasions. The *English* when they consent to take any Nation into their Alliance, draw up a Compact in Writing, which is faithfully interpreted to the contracting Parties, and when maturely consider'd, and clearly and fully understood by each Side, their Assent is declar'd in the most publick Manner, and the Stipulation render'd authentick by sealing the Instrument with Seals, whereon are engraven their Families Arms, writing their Names, and publishing it as their Act and Deed, done without Force or Constraint, freely and voluntarily. This is the *English,*

Method of ratifying Treaties; this is the grand Security each gives of his Faith; and our Brethren of the *Six Nations,* the *Delawares, Shawonese,* and all other *Indian* Nations, when they first enter'd into the Chain of Friendship with us, executed Instruments of this Nature; and as you are now one People with us, in the same Manner with all other of our *Indian* Allies, it will be expected by this, and His Majesty's other Governments, that you will do the same. For your Satisfaction we now shew you some of the Deeds that the *Indians* executed when they first enter'd into our Alliance.

*Brethren, Deputies of the* Twigtwees, You say some of your Allies having heard of your Intentions to apply for Admittance into the Friendship and Alliance with the *English,* desired you to acquaint them with the Success of such Application, to the End that they might have an Opportunity of asking the same Favour. As we don't know the Names of those of your Allies, their Number or Situation, we cannot be more particular at present on this Head, than to tell you, that we are always ready to receive favourably the Applications of all those whom our Brethren of the *Six Nations* shall recommend as worthy of our Friendship and Regard.

*In Testimony whereof we have wrapped a String of Wampum round the Calumet Pipe sent by your Allies.*

*Brethren of the* Six Nations, *&c,* at Ohio, You perceive that at your Request we have received the *Twightwees* into our Friendship: We take kindly your conducting them to us for that End; and as a Proof of our being well pleased with your Conduct on this Occasion, we have ordered our Interpreter to deliver to you at Mr. *Croghan*'s some *English* Goods, that are lodged there for the use of the *Indians.*

*Brethren,* Your Intercession for the *Shawonese* puts us under Difficulties. It is at least two Years since the Governor of *Pennsylvania* wrote to *Cackewatcheka* a Letter, wherein he condescended, out of regard to him, and a few other *Shawonese,* who preserved their Fidelity, to offer those who broke the Chain a Pardon on their Submission, on their Return to the Towns they had deserted, and on their coming down to *Philadelphia* to evidence in Person the Sincerity of their Repentance. This they should have immediately complied with, and they would have readily been admitted into Favour; but as they did not do it, what can be said for them? You who live amongst them best know their Dispositions, and wou'd not, it may be hoped, become Mediators for them, were you not persuaded they wou'd return to their Duty. Some of them, it may be allowed, are weak People, and were preverted from their Duty by the Perswasions of others; but this cannot be thought to be the Case of *Neucheconno,* and a few more. As therefore you have taken upon you the Office of Intercessors, take this String of Wampum, and therewith chastise *Neucheconno* and his Party in such Terms as shall carry a proper Severity with them, tho' the Expressions are left to your Discretion; and then tell the delinquent *Shawonese,* that we will forget what is pass'd, and expect a more punctual Regard to their Engagements hereafter.

*Here was deliver'd a String of Wampum.*

'Tis but Justice to distinguish the Good from the Bad; *Cackewatcheky* and his Friends, who had Virtue enough to resist the many fine Promises made by the Emissaries of the *French*, will ever be remember'd with Gratitude, and challenge our best Services. To testify our Regard for these, we present them with this

*Belt of Wampum.*

And have order'd our Interpreter, who is going to *Ohio*, to give them a Present of Goods.

The Commissioners gave a handsome Entertainment to the Deputies of the *Twightwees*, and the *Indians* who conducted them from *Ohio*, and after Dinner enter'd into a free Conversation with them about the Numbers and Situation of their Towns, and those of their Allies; and by their Informations it appears that the River *Ouabache* takes its Rise from a Lake at a small Distance from the West-End of Lake *Erie*, from which it runs South Westerly four or 500 Miles, and falls into the *Ohio*, about three hundred Miles from the *Mississippi;* that on this River, and another River call'd the *Hatchet*, the *Twightwees* and their Allies have twenty Towns, and that they count One Thousand fighting Men; that it is a plain Country, and of a rich Soil, abounding with Game. The principal Deputy of the *Twightwees* laid down with Chalk the Courses of the *Mississippi*, of *Ouabache* and of *Ohio*, marking the Situation of their own Towns, of Lake *Erie*, and of two Forts that the *French* have on the *Mississippi;* whereby it is manifest, that if these *Indians* and their Allies prove faithful to the *English*, the *French* will be depriv'd of the most convenient and nearest Communication with their Forts on the *Mississippi*, the ready Road lying thro' their Nations, and that there will be nothing to interrupt an Intercourse between this Province and that great River.[2]

*At the* Court-House *at* Lancaster, Friday, July 22. 1748. P. M.
PRESENT, *The same as in the Morning.*

Taminy Buck, *one of the Chiefs of the* Shawonese, *stood up, and spoke as follows:*

*Brethren*, WE, the *Shawonese*, sensible of our ungrateful Returns for the many Favours we have been all along receiving from our Brethren the *English*, ever since we first made the Chain of Friendship, came along the Road with our Eyes looking down to the Earth, and have not taken them from thence till this Morning, when you were pleased to chastise us, and then pardon us. We have been a foolish People, and acted wrong, tho' the Sun shone bright, and shew'd us very clearly what was our Duty. We are sorry for what we have done, and promise better Behaviour for the future. We produce to you a Certificate of the Renewal of our Friendship in the Year 1739 by the Proprietor and Governor. Be pleased to sign it afresh, that it may appear to the World we are now admitted into your Friendship, and all former Crimes are buried, and intirely forgot.

The Commissioners receiv'd the Deed, but refused to sign it, letting them know they were forgiven on Condition of better Behaviour for the future; and when they shall have performed that Condition, it will be time enough to apply for such Testimonials.[3] Orders were given for mending their Guns and Hatchets, and then the *Twightwees* were told that the Secretary was preparing an Instrument for rendering authentick our Treaty of Friendship with them, which wou'd be ready at Nine o' Clock in the Morning, to which Time the Commissioners adjourn'd.

*At the* Court-house *at* Lancaster, Saturday *the* 23d July 1748.
PRESENT, *Benjamin Shoemaker, Joseph Turner, Thomas Hopkinson, William Logan,* Esqrs.
*The Magistrates, and many of the Inhabitants of* Lancaster *County, The same* Indians *as Yesterday.*

THE Instrument and Counterpart having been prepar'd and approv'd by the Commissioners, the Contents thereof were read, and carefully Interpreted to, and approv'd by the *Indians,* and then they were executed by the Commissioners, and the three Deputies of the *Twightwees,* the other *Indians* mention'd therein signing as Witnesses, together with the Magistrates and Inhabitants present.

The Commissioners then enquired if the *Indians* had any particular News to communicate, and, after some Time spent in Conference, *Suchraquery* spoke as follows:

The *Indians* of the several Nations, living at *Ohio* return you Thanks for your Acceptance of their good Offices in conducting the *Twightwees,* and admitting them into your Alliance; likewise for your Goodness in accepting their Mediation on Behalf of the *Shawonese,* and thereupon forgiving their late Breach of Faith. Our new Brethren the *Twightwees* tell us, that they have brought a few Skins to begin a Trade, and they desire you will be pleased to order the Traders to put less Stones into their Scales, that their Skins may weigh more, and that they may allow a good Price for them, which will encourage them and their Nation to trade more largely with you. This the Commissioners promised to do.

The Commissioners informed the *Indians,* that there was likely to be a Peace between the King of *England* and the *French* King; that the News was but just arriv'd, and imperfectly told; but that there was actually a Cessation of Arms. The *Indians* making no Reply, the Commissioners, after ordering a Present to the *Twightwee* Deputies, rose, and put an End to the Treaty.

*FINIS*

1. This first appearance of this calumet pipe ceremony at a Pennsylvania-Ohio Iroquois treaty is as exciting and significant as the presence of the Miamis (Twightwees) themselves. The calumet pipe indicates that we are witnessing the meeting of two cultural modes in an ancient borderlands of Native North America. Little information has been published about the meanings the Miamis associated with the calumet and its use in diplomacy. However, the use of pipes was widespread throughout the area of the Great Lakes, the Mississippi, and the

extensive cultural area known as the Mississippian, which between 800 and 1500 C.E. extended into the southeast and along the many valleys of the rivers that feed the Mississippi, such as the Ohio. The use of pipes transcends tribal boundaries, language families, and historical periods of enmity among different groups, but it is not clear whether the various origins of these traditions would converge if one could trace the history of the calumet back through time.

The Iroquois Ritual of Condolence includes smoking and the use of pipes, but it appears that this particular ceremony may be Miami given the change of speakers.

Among the Lakotas, the pipe is believed to carry the thoughts and prayers of its holders to the sky and to Wah'kon-tah when filled with tobacco and smoked (Joseph Epes Brown, recorder and ed., *The Sacred Pipe: Black Elk's Account of the Seven Rites of the Oglala Sioux* [Baltimore: Penguin, 1953], xiv, xix–xx, 3–9).

That Pennsylvania's commissioners are being asked to participate in a smoking of the pipe shows another diplomatic method and belief system by which they are being asked to deliberate in sober consultation with the higher spiritual powers before taking any action.

It is remarkable that the Iroquois are acting as intermediaries for the Shawnees and their sponsors, the Miamis, given that less than a hundred years earlier, the League had attacked and severely threatened Miami towns in the region below Lake Michigan. One story tells of their cannibalizing the Miami's small children and staking an entrance to the Miami town with the skull of one of their victims. The Miamis in return mutilated two of the attackers by cutting off their hands, noses, and lips and sent the warriors back to their villages with heads of two of their companions around their necks (Stewart Rafert, *The Miami Indians of Indiana: A Persistent People, 1654–1994* [Indianapolis: Indiana Historical Society, 1996], 9–11, 4–5, 19).

2. We see here the Pennsylvania government taking advantage of their new friendship with the Miamis. They begin mapping out future encroachments and strategizing against the French over a region to which neither was entitled.

3. Here is one instance of the coercive style of diplomacy often practiced by the British. Whereas the Shawnees approach them in good faith to renew an abrogated agreement, the British insist upon proof after proof of their sincerity, which amounted to proof of their submission.

✠

# A TREATY

## HELD WITH THE *OHIO* INDIANS,

## AT *CARLISLE,* In OCTOBER, 1753.

---

*PHILADELPHIA:*
Printed and Sold by B. FRANKLIN and D. HALL,
at the New-Printing Office, near the Market. MDCCLIII.

---

### A TREATY, *&c.*

*To the Honourable* JAMES HAMILTON, *Esq; Lieutenant-Governor, and Commander in Chief, of the Province of* Pennsylvania, *and Counties of* New-Castle, Kent *and* Sussex, *upon* Delaware,

The REPORT of Richard Peters, Isaac Norris, *and* Benjamin Franklin, *Esquires, Commissioners appointed to treat with some Chiefs of the* Ohio Indians, *at* Carisle, *in the County of* Cumberland, *by a Commission, bearing Date the 22d Day of* September, 1753.[1]

*May it please the* Governor,

Not knowing but the *Indians* might be waiting at *Carlisle,* we made all the Dispatch possible, as soon as we had received our Commission, and arrived there on the Twenty-Sixth, but were agreeably surprized to find that they came there only that Day.

Immediately on our Arrival we conferred with *Andrew Montour,* and *George Croghan,* in order to know from them what had occasioned the present coming of the *Indians,* that we might, by their Intelligence, regulate our first Intercourse with them; and were informed, that tho' their principal Design, when they left *Ohio,* was to hold a Treaty with the Government of *Virginia,* at *Winchester,* where they had accordingly been; yet they intended a Visit to this Province, to which they had been frequently encouraged by *Andrew Montour,* who told them, he had the Governor's repeated Orders to invite them to come and see him, and assured them of an hearty Welcome; and that they had moreover some important Matters to propose and transact with this Government.

The Commissioners finding this to be the Case, and that these *Indians* were some of the most considerable Persons of the *Six Nations, Delawares, Shawonese,* with Deputies from the *Twightwees,* and *Owendaets,*[2] met them in Council, in which the Commissioners declared the Contents of their Commission, acknowledged the Governor's Invitation, and bid them heartily welcome among their Brethren of *Pennsylvania,* to whom their Visit was extremely agreeable.—*Conrad Weiser* and *Andrew Montour* interpreting between the Commissioners and *Indians,* and several Magistrates, and others, of the principal Inhabitants of the County, favouring them with their Presence.

The *Twightwees* and *Delawares* having had several of their great Men cut off by the *French* and their *Indians,* and all the Chiefs of the *Owendaets* being lately dead, it became necessary to condole their Loss; and no Business could be begun, agreeable to the *Indian* Customs, till the Condolances were passed; and as these could not be made, with the usual Ceremonies, for want of the Goods, which were not arrived, and it was uncertain when they would, the Commissioners were put to some Difficulties, and ordered the Interpreters to apply to *Scarrooyady,* an *Oneido* Chief, who had the Conduct of the Treaty in *Virginia,* and was a Person of great Weight in their Councils, and to ask his Opinion, whether the Condolances would be accepted by Belts and Strings, and Lists of the particular Goods intended to be given, with Assurances of their Delivery as soon as they should come. *Scarrooyady* was pleased with the Application; but frankly declared, that the *Indians* could not proceed to Business while the Blood remained on their Garments, and that the Condolances could not be accepted unless the Goods, intended to cover the Graves, were actually spread on the Ground before them.[3] A Messenger was therefore forthwith sent to meet and hasten the Waggoners, since every Thing must stop till the Goods came.

It was then agreed to confer with *Scarrooyady,* and some other of the Chiefs of the *Shawonese* and *Delawares,* on the State of Affairs at *Ohio,* and from them the Commissioners learned, in sundry Conferences, the following Particulars, *viz.*

"That when the Governor of *Pennsylvania's* Express arrived at *Ohio,* with the Account of the March of a large *French* Army to the Heads of *Ohio,* with Intent to take Possession of that Country, it alarmed the *Indians* so much, that the *Delawares,* at *Weningo,* an *Indian* Town, situate high up on *Ohio* River, went, agreeable to a Custom established among the *Indians,* and forbad, by a formal Notice, the Commander of that Armament, then advanced to the *Straits,* between Lake *Ontario* and Lake *Erie,* to continue his March, at least not to presume to come farther than Niagara. This had not however any Effect, but, notwithstanding this Notice, the *French* continued their March; which, being afterwards taken into Consideration by the Council, at *Logs-town,* they ordered some of their principal *Indians* to give the *French* a second Notice to leave their Country, and return Home; who meeting them on a River running into Lake *Erie,* a little above *Weningo,* addressed the Commander in these Words:

*The second Notice delivered to the Commander of the* French *Army, then near* Weningo.

*Father* Onontio, Your Children on *Ohio,* are alarmed to hear of your coming so far this Way. We at first heard you came to destroy us; our Women left off planting, and our Warriors prepared for War. We have since heard you came to visit us as Friends, without Design to hurt us; but then we wondered you came with so strong a Body. If you have had any Cause of Complaint, you might have spoke to *Onas,* or *Corlaer* (meaning the Governors of *Pennsylvania,* and *New-York)* and not come to disturb us here. We have a Fire at *Logs-town,* where are the *Delawares,* and *Shawonese,* and Brother *Onas;* you might have sent Deputies there, and said openly what you came about, if you had thought amiss of the *English* being there; and we invite you to do it now; before you proceed any further.

*The* French *Officer's Answer.*

*Children,* I find you come to give me an Invitation to your Council Fire, with a Design, as I suppose, to call me to Account for coming here. I must let you know that my Heart is good to you; I mean no Hurt to you; I am come by the great King's Command, to do you, my Children, Good. You seem to think I carry my Hatchet under my Coat; I always carry it openly, not to strike you, but those that shall oppose me. I cannot come to your Council Fire, nor can I return, or stay here; I am so heavy a Body that the Stream will carry me down, and down I shall go, unless you pull off my Arm:[4] But this I will tell you, I am commanded to build four strong Houses, *viz.* at *Weningo, Mohongialo Forks, Logs-Town,* and *Beaver Creek,* and this I will do. As to what concerns *Onas,* and *Assaragoa* (meaning the Governors of *Pennsylvania* and *Virginia)* I have spoke to them, and let them know they must go off the Land, and I shall speak to them again; if they will not hear me, it is their Fault, I will take them by the Arm, and throw them over the Hills. All the Land and Waters on this Side *Allegheny* Hills are mine, on the other Side theirs; this is agreed on between the two Crowns over the great Waters. I do not like your selling your Lands to the *English;* they shall draw you into no more foolish Bargains. I will take Care of your Lands for you, and of you. The *English* give you no Goods but for Land, we give you our Goods for nothing."

We were further told by *Scarrooyady,* that when the Answer to this Message was brought to *Logs-Town,* another Council was held, consisting of the *Six Nations, Delawares,* and *Shawonese,* who unanimously agreed to divide themselves into two Parties, one to go to *Virginia,* and *Pennsylvania,* with *Scarrooyady,* and the other to go with the *Half King* to the *French* Commander, who had it in Charge to make the following Declaration, as their third and last Notice.

*The third Notice, delivered by the* Half King *to the Commander of the* French *Forces.*

*Father,* You say you cannot come to our Council Fire at *Logs-Town,* we therefore now come to you, to know what is in your Heart. You remember when you were tired with the War (meaning Queen *Anne*'s War) you of your own Accord sent for us, desiring to make Peace with us; when we came, you said to us, Children, we make a Council Fire for you; we want to talk with you, but we must first eat all with one Spoon out of the Silver Bowl, and all drink out of this Silver Cup; let us exchange Hatchets; let us bury our Hatchets in this bottomless Hole; and now we will make a plain Road to all your Countries, so clear, that *Onontio* may sit here and see you all eat and drink out of the Bowl and Cup, which he has provided for you. Upon this Application of yours we consented to make Peace; and when the Peace was concluded on both Sides, you made a solemn Declaration, saying, Whoever shall hereafter transgress this Peace, let the Transgressor be chastised with a Rod, even tho' it be I, your Father.

Now, Father, notwithstanding this solemn Declaration or yours, you have whipped several or your Children; you know best why. Of late you have chastised the *Twightwees* very severely, without telling us the Reason;[5] and now you are come with a strong Band on our Land, and have, contrary to your Engagement, taken up the Hatchet without any previous Parley. These Things are a Breach of the Peace; they are contrary to your own Declarations: Therefore, now I come to forbid you. I will strike over all this Land with my Rod, let it hurt who it will. I tell you, in plain Words, you must go off this Land. You say you have a strong Body, a strong Neck, and a strong Voice, that when you speak all the *Indians,* must hear you. It is true, you are a strong Body, and ours is but weak, yet we are not afraid of you. We forbid you to come any further; turn back to the Place from whence you came.

Scarrooyady, who was the Speaker in these Conferences, when he had finished this Relation, gave his Reason for setting forth these three Messages to the *French* in so distinct a Manner; because, said he, the Great Being who lives above, has ordered us to send three Messages of Peace before we make War:—And as the *Half King* has, before this Time, delivered the third and last Message, we have nothing now to do but to strike the *French.*

The Commissioners were likewise informed, by Mr. *Croghan,* that the *Ohio Indians* had received from the *Virginia* Government a large Number of Arms in the Spring, and that at their pressing Instances a suitable Quantity of Ammunition was ordered in the Treaty at *Winchester* to be lodged for them, in a Place of Security, on this Side the *Ohio* which was committed to the Care of three Persons, *viz.* [blank] *Guest. William Trent* and *Andrew Montour,* who were impowered to distribute them to the *Indians* as their Occasions and Behaviour should require. That all the Tribes settled at or near *Allegheny* would take their Measures from the Encouragement which these *Indians* should find in the Province of *Virginia;* and that the kind Intentions of this Government in the Appropriation of a large Sum of Money for the Use of these *Indians,* in case they should be distressed by their Enemies, and their Hunting and Planting prevented, were well known to them by the repeated Informations of *Andrew Montour* and the Traders.

*CONRAD WEISER,* to whom it was earnestly recommended by the Commissioners, to procure all the Information possible from the *Indians* of his Acquaintance, touching their Condition and Disposition, and the real Designs of the *French,* did likewise acquaint us, that all Persons at *Ohio* would have their Eyes on the Reception of those *Indians,* now at *Carlisle,* and judge of the Affection of this Province by their Treatment of them; and that as the intended Present was no Secret to those *Indians,* it was his Opinion, that the Whole should, at this Time, be distributed; for if any Thing can, such a generous Donation must needs attach the *Indians* entirely to the *English.*[6]

These several Matters being taken into Consideration by the Commissioners, and the Governor having given them express Directions to accommodate themselves to the Circumstances of the *Indians,* as they should appear in examining them at the Place of Treaty, we were unanimously of Opinion, that an Addition should be made to the Goods bought at *Philadelphia,* in which a Regard should be had to such Articles as were omitted or supplied in less Quantities than was suitable to the present Wants of the *Indians.* On this Resolution the Lists of Goods were examined, and an additional Quantity bought of *John Carson,* at the *Philadelphia* Price, and usual Rate of Carriage.

During these Consultations, it was rumoured that the *Half King* was returned to *Logs-Town,* and had received an unsatisfactory Answer, which was confirmed, but not in such Manner as could be positively relied on, by a Brother of *Andrew Montour,* and another Person who came directly from *Allegheny.* This alarmed the Commissioners, and made them willing to postpone Business till they should know the Certainty thereof, judging, that if the *Half King* was returned, he would certainly send a Messenger Express to *Carlisle,* with an Account of what was done by him; and from this the Commissioners might take their Measures in the Distribution of the Present.

A Letter, wrote by *Taaf,* and *Callender,* two *Indian* Traders, dated the Twenty-eighth Day of *September,* from a Place situate a little on this Side *Allegheny* River, directed to *William Buchanan,* was given him the Morning of the first Day of *October,* and he immediately laid it before the Commissioners for their Perusal. In this Letter an Account is given, that the *Half King* was returned, and had been received in a very contemptuous Manner by the *French* Commander, who was then preparing with his Forces to come down the River; and that the *Half King,* on his Return, shed Tears, and had actually warned the *English* Traders not to pass the *Ohio,* nor to venture either their Persons or their Goods, for the *French* would certainly hurt them.[7] On this News the Conferences with *Scarrooyady,* and the Chiefs of the *Six Nations, Delawares,* and *Shawonese,* were renewed, and the Letter read to them, at which they appeared greatly alarmed; but, after a short Pause, *Scarrooyady,* addressing himself to the *Delawares* and *Shawonese,* spoke in these Words:

*Brethren and Cousins,* I look on this Letter as if it had been a Message from the

*Half King* himself: We may expect no other Account of the Result of his Journey. However, I advise you to be still, and neither say nor do any Thing till we get Home, and I see my Friend and Brother the *Half King,* and then we shall know what is to be done.

The Forms of the Condolences, which depend entirely on *Indian* Customs, were settled in Conferences with *Scarrooyady,* and *Cayanguileguoa,* a sensible *Indian,* of the *Mohock* Nation, and a Person intimate with and much consulted by *Scarrooyady,* in which it was agreed to take the *Six Nations* along with us in these Codolances; and accordingly the proper Belts and Strings were made ready, and *Scarrooyady* prepared himself to express the Sentiments of both in the *Indian* Manner. And as the Goods arrived this Morning before Break of Day, the several Sorts used on these Occasions were laid out; and the *Indians* were told that the Commissioners would speak to them at Eleven a Clock.

*At a Meeting of the Commissioners, and* Indians, *at* Carlisle,
*the first Day of* October, 1753.
PRESENT, Richard Peters, Isaac Norris, Benjamin Franklin, Esquires,
Commissioners.
The Deputies of the *Six Nations, Delawares, Shawonese, Twightwees,*
and *Owendaets.*
Conrad Weiser, Andrew Montour, Interpreters.
James Wright, John Armstrong, Esquires, Members of Assembly.
The Magistrates, and several other Gentlemen and Freeholders of
the County of *Cumberland.*
*The* SPEECH *of the Commissioners.*

Brethren, *Six Nations, Delawares, Shawonese, Twightwees,* and *Owendaets,* THOUGH the City of *Philadelphia* be the Place where all *Indians* should go, who have Business to transact with this Government, yet at your Request, signified to Colonel *Fairfax,* at *Winchester,* and by him communicated to our Governor, by an Express to *Philadelphia,* he has been pleased on this particular Occasion to dispense with your coming there, and has done us the Honour to depute us to receive and treat with you at this Town, in his Place and Stead; this is set forth in his Commission, which we now produce to you, under the Great Seal of this Province, the authentick Sign and Testimony of all Acts of Government.

*Brethren,* By this String we acquaint you, that the *Six Nations* do, at our Request, join with us in condoling the Losses you have of late sustained by the Deaths of several of your Chiefs and principal Men; and that *Scarrooyady* is to deliver for both what has been agreed to be said on this melancholy Occasion.

*Here the Commissioners gave a String of Wampum.*

*Then* Scarrooyady *spoke as follows:*

Brethren, the Twightwees *and* Shawonese, It has pleased Him who is above, that we shall meet here To-day, and see one another; I and my Brother *Onas* join together to speak to you. As we know that your Seats at Home are bloody, we wipe away the Blood, and set your Seats in Order at your Council Fire, that you may sit and consult again in Peace and Comfort as formerly; that you may hold the antient Union, and strengthen it, and continue your old friendly Correspondence.

*Here a String was given.*

*Brethren,* Twightwees, *and* Shawonese, We suppose that the Blood is now washed off. We jointly, with our Brother *Onas,* dig a Grave for your Warriors, killed in your Country; and we bury their Bones decently; wrapping them up in these Blankets; and with these we cover their Graves.

*Here the Goods were given to the* Twightwees, *and* Shawonese.

*Brethren,* Twightwees, *and* Shawonese, I, and my Brother *Onas,* jointly condole with the Chiefs of your Towns, your Women and Children, for the Loss you have sustained. We partake of your Grief, and mix our Tears with yours. We wipe your Tears from your Eyes, that you may see the Sun, and that every Thing may become clear and pleasant to your Sight; and we desire you would mourn no more.

*Here a Belt was given.*

The same was said to the *Delawares, mutatis mutandis.*

And then he spoke to the *Owendaets,* in these Words:

*Our Children, and Brethren, the* Owendaets, You have heard what I and my Brother *Onas* have jointly said to the *Twightwees, Shawonese,* and *Delawares:* We now come to speak to you. We are informed that your good old wise Men are all dead, and you have no more left.

We must let you know, that there was a Friendship established by our and your Grandfathers; and a mutual Council Fire was kindled. In this Friendship all those then under the Ground, who had not yet obtained Eyes or Faces (that is, those unborn) were included; and it was then mutually promised to tell the same to their Children, and Childrens Children: But so many great Men of your Nation have died in so short a Time, that none but Youths are left; and this makes us afraid, lest that Treaty, so solemnly established by your Ancestors, should be forgotten by you: We therefore now come to remind you of it, and renew it; we rekindle the old Fire, and put on fresh Fuel.

*Here a String was given.*

The other Speeches, of burying the Dead, &c. were the same as those to the *Twightwees, &c.*

After each had been spoken to, *Scarrooyady* proceeded thus:

*Brethren,* Delawares, Shawonese, Twightwees, *and* Owendaets, We, the *English,* and *Six Nations,* do now exhort every one of you to do your utmost to preserve this Union and Friendship, which has so long and happily continued among us: Let us keep the Chain from rusting, and prevent every Thing that may hurt or break it, from what Quarter soever it may come.

Then the Goods allotted for each Nation, as a Pesent of Condolance, were taken away by each, and the Council adjourn'd to the next Day.

*At a Meeting of the Commissioners, and* Indians, *at* Carlisle,
*the 2d of* October, 1753.
PRESENT, The Commissioners, The same *Indians* as Yesterday,
The Magistrates, and several Gentlemen of the County.
*The* Speech *of the Commissioners.*

*Brethren,* Six Nations, Delawares, Shawonese, Twightwees, *and* Owendaets, NOW that your Hearts are eased of their Grief, and we behold one another with chearful Countenances, we let you know that the Governor, and good People of *Pennsylvania,* did not send us to receive empty-handed; but put something into our Pockets, to be given to such as should favour us with this friendly Visit: These Goods we therefore request you would accept of, and divide amongst all that are of your Company, in such Proportions as shall be agreeable to you. You know how to do this better than we. What we principally desire, is, that you will consider this Present as a Token of our cordial Esteem for you; and use it with a Frugality becoming your Circumstance, which call at this Time for more than ordinary Care.

*Brethren,* With Pleasure we behold here the Deputies of five different Nations, *viz.* the *United Six Nations,* the *Delawares,* the *Shawonese,* the *Twightwees,* and the *Owendaets.* Be pleased to cast your Eyes towards this Belt, whereon six Figures are delineated, holding one another by the Hands. This is a just Resemblance of our present Union: The five first Figures representing the five Nations, to which you belong, as the sixth does the Government of *Pennsylvania;* with whom you are linked in a close and firm Union. In whatever Part the Belt is broke, all the Wampum runs off, and renders the Whole of no Strength or Consistency. In like Manner, should you break Faith with one another, or with this Government, the Union is dissolved. We would therefore hereby place before you the Necessity of preserving your Faith entire to one another, as well as to this Government. Do not separate: Do not part on any Score. Let no Differences nor Jealousies subsist a Moment between Nation and Nation; but join all together as one Man, sincerely and heartily. We on our Part shall always perform our Engagements to every one of you. In Testimony whereof, we present you with this Belt.

*Here the Belt was given.*

*Brethren,* We have only this one Thing further to say at this Time: Whatever

Answers you may have to give, or Business to transact with us, we desire you would use Dispatch; as it may be dangerous to you, and incommodious to us, to be kept long from our Homes, at this Season of the Year.

*At a Meeting of the Commissioners, and* Indians, *the* 3d *of* October, 1753
PRESENT, The Commissioners, The same *Indians* as before.
Several Gentlemen of the County.

*Scarrooyady,* Speaker.

*Brother* Onas, WHAT we have now to say, I am going to speak, in Behalf of the *Twightwees, Shawonese, Delawares,* and *Owendaets.*

You have, like a true and affectionate Brother, comforted us in our Affliction. You have wiped away the Blood from our Seats, and set them again in order. You have wrapped up the Bones of our Warriors, and covered the Graves of our wise Men; and wiped the Tears from our Eyes, and the Eyes of our Women and Children: So that we now see the Sun, and all Things are become pleasant to our Sight. We shall not fail to acquaint our several Nations with your Kindness. We shall take Care that it be always remembered by us; and believe it will be attended with suitable Returns of Love and Affection.

*Then one of the* Twightwees *stood up, and spoke as follows:* (Scarrooyady *Interpreter.)*

*Brother* Onas, The *Outawas, Cheepaways,* and the *French,* have struck us.—The Stroke was heavy, and hard to be borne, for thereby we lost our King, and several of our Warriors; but the Loss our Brethren, the *English* suffered, we grieve for most. The Love we have had for the *English,* from our first Knowledge of them, still continues in our Breasts; and we shall ever retain the same ardent Affection for them.—We cover the Graves of the *English* with this Beaver Blanket. We mourn for them more than for our own People.

*Here he spread on the Floor some Beaver Skins, sewed together in the Form of a large Blanket.*

*Then* Scarrooyady *spoke as follows:*

*Brother* Onas, I speak now on Behalf of all the *Indians* present, in Answer to what you said when you gave us the Goods and Belt. What you have said to us Yesterday is very kind, and pleases us exceedingly. The Speech which accompanied the Belt, is particularly of great Moment. We will take the Belt home to *Ohio,* where there is a greater and wiser Council than us, and consider it, and return you a full Answer.[8] We return you Thanks for the Present.

*Gave a String.*

*Brother* Onas, Last Spring, when you heard of the March of the *French* Army, you were so good as to send us Word, that we might be on our Guard: We thank you for this friendly Notice.

*Brother* Onas, Your People not only trade with us in our Towns, but disperse themselves over a large and wide extended Country, in which reside many Nations: At one End live the *Twightwees,* and at the other End the *Caghnawagas,* and *Adirondacks;* these you must comprehend in your Chain of Friendship, they are, and will be, your Brethren, let *Onontio* say what he will.

*Gave a String.*

*Brother* Onas, I desire you would hear and take Notice of what I am about to say now. The Governor of *Virginia* desired Leave to build a strong House on *Ohio,* which came to the Ears of the Governor of *Canada;* and we suppose this caused him to invade our Country. We do not know his Intent; because he speaks with two Tongues. So soon as we know his Heart, we shall be able to know what to do; and shall speak accordingly to him. We desire that *Pennsylvania* and *Virginia* would at present forbear settling on our Lands, over the *Allegheny* Hills. We advise you rather to call your People back on this Side the Hills, lest Damage should be done, and you think ill of us. But to keep up our Correspondence with our Brother *Onas,* we will appoint some Place on the Hills, or near them; and we do appoint *George Croghan,* on our Part, and desire you to appoint another on your Part, by a formal Writing, under the Governor's Hand. Let none of your People settle beyond where they are now; nor on the *Juniata* Lands, till the Affair is settled between us and the *French.* At present, *George Croghan*'s House, at *Juniata,* may be the Place where any Thing may be sent to us. We desire a Commission may be given to the Person intrusted by the Government of *Pennsylvania;* and that he may be directed to warn People from settling the *Indians* Lands, and impowered to remove them.

*Gave a Belt and String.*

*Brother* Onas, All we who are here desire you will hear what we are going to say, and regard it as a Matter of Moment: The *French* look on the great Number of your Traders at *Ohio* with Envy; they fear they shall lose their Trade. You have more Traders than are necessary; and they spread themselves over our wide Country, at such great Distances, that we cannot see them, or protect them. We desire you will call back the great Number of your Traders, and let only three Setts of Traders remain; and order these to stay in three Places, which we have appointed for their Residence, *viz. Logs-Town,* the Mouth of *Canawa,* and the Mouth of *Mohongely;* the *Indians* will then come to them, and buy their Goods in these Places, and no where else. We shall likewise look on them under our Care, and shall be accountable for them. We have settled this Point with *Virginia* in the same Manner.

*Gave a String.*

*Brother* Onas, The *English* Goods are sold at too dear a Rate to us. If only honest and sober Men were to deal with us, we think they might afford the Goods cheaper: We desire therefore, that you will take effectual Care hereafter, that none but such be suffered to come out to trade with us.

*Gave a String.*

*Brother* Onas, Your Traders now bring scarce any Thing but Rum and Flour: They bring little Powder and Lead, or other valuable Goods.[9] The Rum ruins us. We beg you would prevent its coming in such Quantities, by regulating the Traders. We never understood the Trade was to be for Whiskey and Flour. We desire it may be forbidden, and none sold in the *Indian* Country; but that if the *Indians* will have any, they may go among the Inhabitants, and deal with them for it. When these Whiskey Traders come, they bring thirty or forty Cags, and put them down before us, and make us drink; and get all the Skins that should go to pay the Debts we have contracted for Goods bought of the Fair Traders; and by this Means, we not only ruin ourselves, but them too. These wicked Whiskey Sellers, when they have once got the *Indians* in Liquor, make them sell their very Clothes from their Backs.—In short, if this Practice be continued, we must be inevitably ruined: We most earnestly therefore beseech you to remedy it.

*A treble String.*

*Brother* Onas, I have now done with generals; but have something to say for particular Nations.

The *Shawonese* heard some News since they came here, which troubled their Minds; on which they addressed themselves to their Grandfathers, the *Delawares;* and said, Grandfathers, we will live and die with you, and the *Six Nations:* We, our Wives and Children; and Children yet unborn.

N. B. *This was occasioned by* Conrad Weiser'*s having told them in private Conversation, that while he was in the* Mohock *Country, he was informed, that the* French *intended to drive away the* Shawonese (*as well as the* English) *from* Ohio.

Scarrooyady then proceeded, and said, I have something farther to say on Behalf of the *Shawonese.*

*Brother* Onas, At the Beginning of the Summer, when the News was brought to us, of the Approach of the *French,* the *Shawonese* made this Speech to their Uncles, the *Delawares,* saying, "Uncles, you have often told us, that we were a sensible and discreet People; but we lost all our Sense and Wits, when we slipp'd out of your Arms; however, we are now in one another's Arms again, and hope we shall slip out no more. We remember, and are returned to our former Friendship, and hope it will always continue. In Testimony whereof, we give you, our Uncles, a String of ten Rows."

The *Shawonese* likewise, at the same time, sent a Speech to the *Six Nations,* saying, "Our Brethren, the *English,* have treated us as People that had Wit: The *French* deceived us: But we now turn our Heads about, and are looking perpetually to the Country of the *Six Nations,* and our Brethren, the *English,* and desire you to make an Apology for us; and they gave eight Strings of Wampum." The *Delawares* and *Six Nations* do therefore give up these Strings to *Onas,* and recommend the *Shawonese* to him as a People who have seen their Error, and are their and our very good Friends.

*Gave eight Strings.*

*Brother* Onas, Before I finish, I must tell you, we all earnestly request you will please to lay all our present Transactions before the Council of *Onondago,* that they may know we do nothing in the Dark. They may perhaps think of us, as if we did not know what we were doing; or wanted to conceal from them what we do with our Brethren; but it is otherwise; and therefore make them acquainted with all our Proceedings: This is what we have likewise desired of the *Virginians* when we treated with them at *Winchester.*

*Brother* Onas, I forgot something which I must now say to you; it is to desire you would assist us with some Horses to carry our Goods; because you have given us more than we can carry ourselves. Our Women and young People present you with this Bundle of Skins, desiring some Spirits to make them chearful in their own Country; not to drink here.

*Presented a Bundle of Skins.*

*Then he added:*

The *Twightwees* intended to say something to you; but they have mislaid some Strings, which has put their Speeches into Disorder; these they will rectify, and speak to you in the Afternoon.[10]

*Then the* Indians *withdrew.*

*At a Meeting of the Commissioners and* Indians,
*the 3d of* October, 1753. P. M.
PRESENT, The Commissioners, The same *Indians* as before.
The Magistrates, and several Gentlemen of the County.

*The* Twightwees *speak by* Andrew Montour.

*Brother* Onas, HEARKEN what I have to say to the *Six Nations, Delawares, Shawonese,* and *English.*

The *French* have struck us; but tho' we have been hurt, it is but on one Side; the other Side is safe. Our Arm on that Side is entire; and with it we laid hold on our Pipe, and have brought it along with us, to shew you it is as good as ever: And we shall leave it with you, that it may be always ready for us and our Brethren to smoak in when we meet together.

*Here he delivered over the Calumet, decorated with fine Feathers.*

*Brother* Onas, We have a single Heart. We have but One Heart. Our Heart is green, and good, and sound: This Shell, painted green on its hollow Side, is a Resemblance of it.

The Country beyond us, towards the Setting of the Sun, where the *French* live, is all in Darkness; we can see no Light there: But towards Sun-rising, where the *English* live, we see Light; and that is the Way we turn our Faces. Consider us as your fast Friends, and good Brethren.

*Here he delivered a large Shell, painted green on the Concave-side, with a String of Wampum tied to it.*

*Brother* Onas, This Belt of Wampum was formerly given to the King of the *Piankashas,* one of our Tribes, by the *Six Nations;* that if at any Time any of our People should be killed, or any Attack made on them by their Enemies, this Belt should be sent with the News, and the *Six Nations* would believe it.

The *Twightwees,* when they brought this Belt to the Lower *Shawonese* Town, addressed themselves to the *Shawonese, Six Nations, Delawares,* and then to the *English,* and said;

*Brethren,* We are an unhappy People: We have had some of our Brethren, the *English,* killed and taken Prisoners in our Towns. Perhaps our Brethren, the *English,* may think, or be told, that we were the Cause of their Death: We therefore apply to you the *Shawonese,* &c. to assure the *English* we were not. The Attack was so sudden, that it was not in our Power to save them. And we hope, when you deliver this Speech to the *English,* they will not be prejudiced against us, but look on us as their *Brethren:* Our Hearts are good towards them.

*A large Belt of fourteen Rows.*

*Brethren,* One of our Kings, on his Death-bed, delivered to his Son, the young Boy who sits next to me, these eight Strings of Wampum, and told him, Child, "I am in Friendship with the *Shawonese, Delawares, Six Nations,* and *English;* and I desire you, if by any Misfortune I should happen to die, or be killed by my Enemies, you would send this String to them, and they will receive you in Friendship in my Stead.

*Delivers the Strings.*

The following is a Speech of the Wife of the *Piankasha* King, after her Husband's Death, addressed to the *Shawonese, Six Nations, Delawares,* and *English:* "Remember, Brethren, that my Husband took a fast Hold of the Chain of Friendship subsisting between your Nations: Therefore I now deliver up his Child into your Care and Protection, and desire you would take Care of him; and remember the Alllance his Father was in with you, and not forget his Friendship, but continue kind to his Child."

*Gave four Strings black and white.*

*Brethren,* Shawonese, Delawares, Six Nations, *and* English. We acquaint all our Brethren, that we have prepared this Beaver Blanket as a Seat for all our Brethren to sit on in Council. In the Middle of it we have painted a green Circle, which is the Colour and Resemblance of our Hearts; which we desire our Brethren may believe are sincere towards our Alliance with them.

*Delivered a Beaver Blanket.*

*Then* Scarrooyady *stood up and said:*
*Brother* Onas, The *Shawonese* and *Delawares* delivered this Speech to the *Six Nations,* and desired they would deliver it to the *English;* and now I deliver it on their Behalf.

*Brethren,* We acquaint you, that as the Wife of the *Piankasha* King delivered his Child to all the Nations, to be taken Care of, they desire that those Nations may be interceeded with, to take Care that the said Child may be placed in his Father's Seat, when he comes to be a Man, to rule their People. And the *Six Nations* now, in Behalf of the Whole, request, that this Petition may not be forgot by the *English,* but that they would see the Request fulfilled.

*Gave four Strings.*

Then *Scarrooyady* desired the *Six Nations* Council might be made acquainted with all these Speeches: And added, that they had no more to say; but what they have said is from their Hearts.

*At a Meeting of the Commissioners, and* Indians, *the* 4*th of* October, 1753.
PRESENT, The Commissioners, The same *Indians* as before. The Gentlemen of the County.

*The Commissioners, unwilling to lose any Time, prepared their Answers early this Morning, and sent for the* Indians; *who having seated themselves, the following Speech was made them:*

*Brethren,* Six Nations, Delawares, Shawonese, Twightwees, *and* Owendaets, THE several Matters delivered by you Yesterday have been well considered; and we are now going to return you our Answers.

The Concern expressed by the *Twightwees* for the Death and Imprisonment of the *English,* with their Professions of Love and Esteem, denotes a sincere and friendly Disposition, which entitles them to our Thanks, and the Continuance of our Friendship; this they may certainly depend on.

*Brethren,* You have recommended to us the several Nations, who, you say, live in that great Extent of Country, over which our Traders travel to dispose of their Goods, and especially the *Twightwees, Adirondacks,* and *Caghnawagas,* who you say live at different Extremities, and have good Inclinations towards the *English.*—We believe you would not give them this Character unless they deserved it. Your Recommendations always will have a Weight with us, and will dispose us in Favour of them, agreeable to your Request.

*Brethren,* The several Articles which contain your Observations on the *Indian* Traders, and the loose straggling Manner in which that Trade is carried on, thro' Countries lying at great Distances from your Towns—Your Proposals to remedy this, by having named three Places for the Traders to reside in, under your Care and Protection, with a Request, that the Province would appoint the particular Persons to be concerned in this Trade, for whom they will be answerable—What you say about the vast Quantities of Rum, and its ill Effects, and that no more may be brought amongst you; all these have made a very strong Impression upon our Minds; and was it now in our Power to rectify these Disorders, and to put Matters on the Footing you propose, we would do it with great Pleasure: But these are Affairs which more immediately concern the Government; in these therefore, we shall imitate your Example, by laying them before the Governor, assuring you, that our heartiest Representations of the Necessity of these Regulations shall not be wanting, being convinced, that unless something effectual be speedily done in these Matters, the good People of this Province can no longer expect Safety or Profit in their Commerce, nor the Continuance of your Affection.

*Brethren,* We will send an Account to *Onondago* of all that has been transacted between us.

We will assist you with Horses for the Carriage of the Goods given you.

We grant your Women and young Men their Request for Rum, on Condition it be not delivered to them until you shall have passed the Mountains.

Scarrooyady some Days ago desired us to give Orders for the Mending of your Guns, *&c.* and we did so; being obliged to send for a Gunsmith out of the Country, as no One of that Trade lived in the Town; who promised to come: But having broke his Word, it has not been in our Power to comply with this Request.

*Here the String given with the Request was returned.*

Having delivered our general Answer, we shall now proceed to give one to what was said by particular Nations, as well by the *Shawonese* in the Forenoon, as by the *Twightwees* in the Afternoon.

*Brethren,* Delawares, *and* Shawonese, We are glad to see you in such good Dispositions to each other. We entreat you to do every Thing you can to preserve the Continuance of this agreeable Harmony. The *Shawonese* may be assured we retain no Manner of Remembrance of their former Miscarriages: We are perfectly reconciled, and our Esteem for their Nation is the same as ever.

*Gave a large String.*

*Brethren,* Twightwees, We shall take your several Presents, Shells, Strings, Beaver Blanket, and Calumet Pipe, with us, and deliver them to the Governor; that these, and the several Things said at the Delivery of them, may remain in the Council Chamber, at *Philadelphia,* for our mutual Use and Remembrance, whenever it shall please the Great Being, who sits above, to bring us together in Council again.

*Gave a long String.*

*Brethren,* We desire you will send these two Strouds to the young King, as an Acknowledgment of our affectionate Remembrance of his Father's Love to us, and of our Good-will to him.

Be pleased to present to the Widow of the *Piankasha* King, our late hearty Friend, these Handkerchiefs, to wipe the Tears from her Eyes; and likewise give her Son these two Strouds to clothe him.

*Here two Handkerchiefs and two Strouds were given.*

*Brethren* Twightwees, We assure you we entertain no hard Thoughts of you; nor in any wise impute to you the Misfortune that befel the *English* in your Town; it was the Chance of War: We were struck together; we fell together; and we lament your Loss equally with our own.

*Brethren,* Six Nations, Delawares, Shawonese, Twightwees, *and* Owendaets, We have now finished our Answers; and we hope they will be agreeable to you: Whatever we have said, has been with a hearty Good-will towards you; our Hearts have accompanied our Professions, and you will always find our Actions agreeable to them. Then the Commissoners were silent; and, after a Space of Time, renewed their Speeches to them.

*Brethren,* Six Nations, Delawares, Shawonese, Twightwees, *and* Owendaets, We have something to say to you, to which we entreat you will give your closest Attention, since it concerns both us and you very much.

*Brethren,* We have held a Council on the present Situation of your Affairs. We have Reason to think, from the Advices of *Taaf* and *Callender,* that it would be too great a Risque, considering the present Disorder Things are in at *Ohio,* to encrease the Quantity of Goods already given you: We therefore acquaint you, that, though the Governor has furnished us with a larger Present of Goods, to put into your publick Store-house, as a general Stock, for your Support and Service, and we did intend to have sent them along with you; we have, on this late disagreeable Piece of News, altered our Minds, and determined, that the Goods shall not be delivered till the Governor be made acquainted with your present Circumstances, and shall give his own Orders for the Disposal of them. And that they may lie ready for your Use, to be applied for, whenever the Delivery may be safe, seasonable, and likely to do you the most Service; we have committed them to the Care of your good Friend *George Croghan,* who is to transmit to the Governor, by Express, a true and faithful Account how your Matters are likely to turn out; and on the Governor's Order, and not otherwise, to put you into the Possession of them.[11]

This we hope you will think a prudent Caution, and a Testimony of our Care for your real Good and Welfare.

*Brethren,* We have a Favour of a particular Nature to request from your Speaker, *Scarrooyady,* in which we expect your Concurrence, and joint Interest; and therefore make it to him in your Presence. Here the Commissioners applying to *Scarrooyady,* spoke as follows:

*Respected Chief and Brother* Scarrooyady, We have been informed by *Andrew Montour,* and *George Croghan,* that you did at *Winchester,* in pubick Council, undertake to go to *Carolina,* to sollicit the Release of some Warriors of the *Shawonese* Nation, who are said to be detained in the publick Prison of *Charles-Town,* on Account of some Mischief committed by them, or their Companions, in the inhabited Part of that Province; and these two Persons, who are your very good Friends, have given it as their Opinion, if, after you know what has passed at *Ohio,* you shall now leave this Company of *Indians,* and not return with them to their Families, and assist in the Consultations with the *Half King,* and their other Chiefs, what Measures to take in this unhappy Situation of your Affairs, all may be irrecoverably lost at *Allegheny,* and the Loss with Justice be laid at your Door. You may, perhaps, be afraid to disoblige the *Shawonese,* as it was at their Instance you undertook this Journey; but we intend to speak to them, and have no Doubt of obtaining their Consent; convinc'd as we are, that the Release of these Prisoners will be sooner and more effectually procur'd by the joint Interposition of the Governors of *Pennsylvania* and *Virginia,* than by your personal Sollicitation; in as much as our Governor, to whom we shall very heartily recommend this Affair, can send, with greater Dispatch, his Letters to *Carolina,* than you can perform the Journey; for at this Season, Opportunities present every Day of sending by Sea to *Charles-Town;* and an Express by Land may be dispatched to Governor *Dunwiddie,* as soon as we return to *Philadelphia.*

*Gave a String.*

The *Shawonese* Chiefs expressing Dissatisfaction at this Endeavour of the Commissioners to stop *Scarrooyady,* it gave us some Trouble to satisfy them, and obtain their Consent; but at last it was effected; and when this was signified to *Scarrooyady,* he made this Answer.

*Brother* Onas, I will take your Advice, and not go to *Virginia* at this Time,—— but go Home, and do every Thing in my Power for the common Good. And since we are here now together, with a great deal of Pleasure I must acquaint you, that we have set a Horn on *Andrew Montour*'s Head,[12] and that you may believe what he says to be true, between the *Six Nations* and you, they have made him one of their Counsellors, and a great Man among them, and love him dearly.

Scarrooyady *gave a large Belt to* Andrew Montour, *and the Commissioners agreed to it.*

After this Difficulty was got over, nothing else remained to be done; and as the Absence of these *Indians* was dangerous, the Commissioners put an End to the Treaty, and took their Leave of them, making private Presents at parting, to such of the Chiefs, and others, as were recommended by the Interpreters to their particular Notice.

Thus, may it please the Governor, we have given a full and just Account of all our Proceedings, and we hope our Conduct will meet with his Approbation. But, in Justice to these *Indians,* and the Promises we made them, we cannot close our Report, without taking Notice, That the Quantities of strong Liquors sold to these *Indians* in the Places of their Residence, and during their Hunting Seasons, from all Parts of the Counties over *Sasquehannah,* have encreased of late to an inconceivable Degree, so as to keep these poor *Indians* continually under the Force of Liquor, that they are hereby become dissolute, enfeebled and indolent when sober, and untractable and mischievous in their Liquor, always quarrelling, and often murdering one another: That the Traders are under no Bonds, nor give any Security for their Observance of the Laws, and their good Behaviour; and by their own Intemperance, unfair Dealings, and Irregularities, will, it is to be feared, entirely estrange the Affections of the *Indians* from the *English;* deprive them of their natural Strength and Activity, and oblige them either to abandon their Country, or submit to any Terms, be they ever so unreasonable, from the *French.* These Truths, may it please the Governor, are of so interesting a Nature, that we shall stand excused in recommending in the most earnest Manner, the deplorable State of these *Indians,* and the heavy Discouragements under which our Commerce with them at present labours, to the Governor's most serious Consideration, that some good and speedy Remedies may be provided, before it be too late.[13]

*RICHARD PETERS,*
*November* 1, 1753. *ISAAC NORRIS,*
*BENJ. FRANKLIN.*

1. Between July 1748 and September 1753, several important events had occurred. The problematic 1749 land sale was accompanied by two proclamations issued by the Pennsylvania government, both of which Franklin's press printed. One forbad settlers from occupying Iroquois lands west of the Blue Hills; the other forbad the sale of liquor to Indians within the borders of Pennsylvania (Miller, *Philadelphia Printing,* 262–63). Governor Hamilton was afraid that the squatters on the Juniata might form an alliance with the Iroquois against Pennsylvania (Boyd, "Indian Affairs," lvii). That possibility may strike today's reader as unthinkable. Yet it was very real in an eighteenth-century borderlands where the colony was run by moneyed interests along the coasts, where race unified less than region, and where Irish heritage may have been as damning, in terms of perceived "savagery," as Native American. Weiser and Richard Peters both received two thousand acres of prime land from Thomas Penn for their participation in this sale. Unfortunately, the land they tried to survey for themselves was already squatted upon by "wild" Irish settlers (Wallace, *Conrad Weiser,* 377–78).

The land sale itself may have been one contributing factor to Canasatego's assassination in September 1750 a few days before Weiser was to treat with him (Wallace, *Conrad Weiser,* 309). Jennings interprets his death as a rejection of the policy associated with him of the League acting as policeman for Pennsylvania with respect to other Indian nations (Jennings, *Ambiguous Iroquois Empire,* 363–64).

During this treaty, though not recorded in these minutes, Andrew Montour would deny to

Weiser that the League had ever sold the Ohio Valley to Virginia in 1744 (Wallace, *Conrad Weiser,* 348). Franklin knew as early as August 1751 that Croghan had misrepresented the Ohio Indians as encouraging Virginia and/or Pennsylvania in constructing forts there, which had led to the French march through the territory that is at the center of discussion here. He made this discovery while investigating the costs that his colony had incurred in Indian affairs. One of his first charges as a newly elected member of the Pennsylvania Assembly, this investigation would show Franklin and his colleagues that these costs had skyrocketed since 1733 when Thomas Penn had become actively involved in treaty conferences and land sales (Labaree, *Papers of Benjamin Franklin,* 4:181–83). Yet while the Penns had reaped much of the reward for these "Indian expenses," the Assembly (and the people) had footed the entire bill. Pennsylvania's "citizens were paying for the acquisition and preservation of the Penn's enormous estate, of which the same citizens then had to purchase individual tracts and pay perpetual quitrent upon them" (Jennings, *Benjamin Franklin,* 83–84).

2. Wyandots.

3. Note that Franklin is witness not only to the condolence ceremonies that open this treaty but also to this negotiation with Scarouady. Though many have characterized the arrival of the commissioners ahead of their own presents as a blunder, it gave them a unique opportunity to comprehend native priorities in diplomatic procedure. For the Ohio Indians at Carlisle, a treaty council was no mere matter of getting down to and over with business. No matter that the delay might inconvenience the participants or keep them away from the defense of their land in time of danger, the parties had first to adjust their minds both to one another and with clarity to the realities surrounding the negotiations. Only then could any lasting agreement possibly emerge as a result of the conferences.

4. Note that the French had also adopted the figurative language of the League and other native diplomats.

5. The "Half King" who would have been speaking these words is Tanaghrisson. Here he refers to the French assault on the Miami town of Pickawillany that had occurred on June 21, 1752, while the Ohio Indians were meeting with Virginia at Logstown. An Indian agent, Charles Langlade, led the assault in which the chief, Memeskia, was killed, and reportedly cannibalized, and British traders were killed or captured. The assault was meant to "discipline" the Miamis, and most returned to the French alliance after their brief, four-year membership in the Covenant Chain (Jennings, *Empire of Fortune,* 42, 49).

6. Weiser seems to overestimate the power that such a present would have when land was at stake. Though they were unlikely to betray any weapons and provisions suppliers they might find allied with them, the natives were not terribly "attached" to the English when the English later tried to take over these same lands.

7. It is unclear whether the tears shed by Tanaghrisson were literal or figurative, diplomatic or personal. This event and others similar are referred to in a few places. They resonated in the British colonial imaginary in a way that must at that time have called the subject's masculinity and maturity into question (cf. Wallace, *Conrad Weiser,* 333 and Boyd, *Indian Treaties,* lxvii). Such is the gulf among societies regarding displays of emotion. Though some native interpretations may have been similar, several other possibilities present themselves. On the personal and literal level, Tanaghrisson might have been crying for what he and others would surely have understood to be the immanent violence over the territorial incursion that he had been unable to prevent and the potential loss of both life in and sovereignty over that territory. Quite possibly, the act was public and formal, however, rather than private and informal: an expected, almost conventional, rejoinder to the unreasonable responses of the

French. The image of a native leader crying for his land was revived in pro-environmental discourse during the 1970s. Such images have been adopted and co-opted by British and U.S. entities under changing social circumstances.

8. Because a similar procedure was used by the Iroquois proper in deferring certain questions to the Onondaga Council, this sentence makes it clear that the Ohio Indians had established a semi-independent government for the region. Their subsequent request that Onondaga be informed of the proceedings demonstrates their unwillingness to have this act read as an act of defiance or aggression.

9. This failure by the British traders to supply arms to the Ohio region became a major problem for the British, and may indeed have led to unnecessary casualties in the Seven Years' War. Had the Ohio Indians been able to present a more formidable opposition to French forces, they likely would not have turned against the British in 1755. Wallace describes the situation as urgent: "On the 15th [of August 1755] the conference [in Philadelphia] was held. The hearty thanks of the government were extended to the Wyandots for their visit and to the Six Nations warriors for the valor they had displayed at the battle of the Monongahela. But Scaroyady, Silver Heels, the Belt, and the other warriors who received these compliments, wanted more than words of praise. They had made a dangerous journey from the Ohio to get men and munitions. Scaroyady told Weiser privately that all was at stake on the decisions now made. If the Wyandots were sent back to their people without positive assurance of support in the war, they would be forced to go over to the French. And not only the Wyandots, but also the Delawares, Shawnees, and Ohio Mingoes (Six Nations Indians)" (*Conrad Weiser,* 389).

Prior to this battle, General Edward Braddock had alienated many of these Ohio Indian nations from favor toward the British by revealing that that empire intended to take their land from them once they drove the French off. Braddock thus stymied his own attempt to initiate such a French retreat and recover from Washington's 1754 failure. Because the Ohio Indians refused to fight for land that would be stolen from them upon victory and because Braddock had contemptuously sent away Croghan's reinforcements, (bragging that he did not need Indians to win during an era when native participation in wars was generally the decisive factor), he led his troops into a virtual ambush. Because he had neither the advice from these warriors about how to fight a wilderness war, nor would he have heeded it, his orders resulted in the deaths and casualties of more than two-thirds of his men (Jennings, *Empire of Fortune,* 152–58).

This August 1755 treaty was one of several that Franklin did not print. Did he or the Quaker-dominated Assembly decide that it did not fit into the narrative of the Walking Purchase and Pennsylvania-League alliance that was forming through many of the other treaties that had already been printed?

10. It is unclear whether the wampum strings were literally mislaid or whether something figurative is meant here.

11. This decision, made on the basis of false reports by Croghan's traders, may have been a "fatal" mistake. See footnote 9 above. It is reasonable to suggest that British traders on the Ohio were actively trying to incite a war so that their own empire would gain legitimate access to the region. Their trickery alienated the longstanding native allies of Pennsylvania and the British.

12. New peacetime chiefs are installed in the League government by the placing of antlers on the head. The synethnic son of a French Canadian woman, Montour became a member of the Onondaga Council in this ceremony (Jennings, *Empire of Fortune,* 38, 516).

13. This coda is the first of two extraordinary additions that appear only at the ends of the

two treaties in which Franklin participated. The second appears at the end of the November 1756 treaty council minutes from Easton. They strongly suggest Franklin's personal intervention. He and the other commissioners clearly find convincing the reasoning presented to them by their Ohio Indian interlocutors and see in it an opportunity to gain or maintain advantage for the British Empire in its long-term bid for the Ohio Valley.

✠

# MINUTES OF CONFERENCES,

## HELD WITH THE *INDIANS*, at *EASTON*,

### In the Months of *July* and *November*, 1756;

TOGETHER WITH TWO MESSAGES sent by the GOVERNMENT to the *Indians* residing on *Sasquehannah;* and the REPORT of the COMMITTEE appointed by the ASSEMBLY to attend the GOVERNOR at the last of the said Conferences.

---

*PHILADELPHIA:*
Printed and Sold by B. FRANKLIN, and D. HALL,
at the *New-Printing-Office*, near the Market. MDCCLVII.

---

## MINUTES OF CONFERENCES, *&c.*

*PHILADELPHIA.*

*After the Ending of the Conferences between* Scarroyady *and some of the People called* Quakers, *the three* Indians, Newcastle, Jagrea, *and* William Locquies, *being prepared to set out for* Wioming, *the Governor (who, during these Conferences, received Messages from the Governor of* New-York) *delivered them the following Message to the* Delaware *and* Shawanese Indians, *living on* Sasquehannah, *viz.*

*BRETHREN, April* 26, 1756.

I HAVE received an Account from Sir *William Johnson,* sent me by Sir *Charles Hardy,* Governor of *New-York,* that, immediately after the Council held at *Fort Johnson,* Deputies were dispatched by the *Six Nations* to *Atsaningo,* and that they convened the *Delawares, Shawanese,* and other *Indians,* from the several Towns on the *Sasquehannah,* to the Number of Three Hundred, to whom they delivered Messages from that Council, blaming them for taking up the Hatchet against their Brethren the *English,* and commanding them to lay it down immediately; and that they had hearkened to this Message, and agreed to strike no more.——What I tell you is in this Letter. [*Here the Governor gave Mr.* Weiser *Sir* Charles Hardy*'s Letter of the* 16*th of* April, *to interpret to them. And when he had made them understand what Sir* Charles Hardy *had wrote, the Governor took a Belt in his Hand, and proceeded.*]

*Brethren,* I think it necessary that the *Indians* at *Wioming,* as well Enemies as Friends, should know, that Sir *Charles Hardy* has sent this Account to me from Sir *William Johnson;* and as two of you are of the *Six Nations,* and one a *Delaware,* I think it proper that you should undertake to notify this to them; and at the same Time to let them know, as from yourselves, that if they are sincerely disposed to Peace, and will deliver up the *English* Prisoners to the *Six Nations,* and hearken to their Advice in laying down the Hatchet, and abide by such Terms as shall be agreed on, you can venture to assure them; that tho' much Blood has been spilt, and that the *English,* in Resentment of this, are well prepared to avenge themselves, yet they have so great Regard for the *Six Nations,* that it will be in their Power to perswade the *English* not to prosecute the War, but to accept fair, just and honourable Terms; and I provide you with this Belt, to deliver it to them with such a Speech.[1]

*Brethren,* I speak my own sincere Inclinations, when I say I am for Peace; and not only my own, but the Sentiments of others, and particularly the earnest Desire of a Number of People, who are the Descendants of those that came over with the first Proprietor; all those are extremely desirous to interpose with the Government, to receive the Submission of the *Delawares,* and to overlook what is past, and establish for the future a firm and lasting Agreement, Peace and Affection between us, and have repeatedly applied to me for this Purpose.

*Brethren,* As many Stories have been told to the *Indians* to our Prejudice, I desire you will undeceive them; and particularly I do charge *William Locquies* to acquaint the *Delawares,* that those of their Tribe who live among us, have not had any Mischief done them, but are treated with our usual Kindness, and are at Liberty, and live in Peace and Plenty among us.——I charge you *William Locquies,* to declare the Truth to the *Indians,* and to assure them that they have been imposed on; and relate the Care that has been taken, as well by the Government of *New Jersey,* as this, of all the *Indians* who have staid with us, and that they enjoy our Protection, and live as happily as ever.

*A String.*

*Brethren, Paxinosa,* and some other *Shawanese,* and other *Indians,* have not broke Faith with us, but endeavoured to dissuade the *Delawares* from striking us.——When they could not succeed, they separated from them, and now live together in some Place near *Wioming;* I would have you go to them, and let them likewise know this Account from Sir *William Johnson,* and assure them from me, that if they are inclined to come within the Inhabitants, you have my Orders to conduct them; or if they do not incline to come now, but at any other Time, they will, on sending me a Message, be provided with a safe Conduct, and meet with an hearty Welcome.——Let them know that *Scarroyady* related to me what had passed between him and them; and that *Aroas* and *David* have likewise made me acquainted with what was said by them when they were last at *Wioming.*

*Then the Governor gave them a String to give to* Paxinosa.

Newcastle, Jagrea, *and* William Locquies, *returned the Governor an Answer;* viz.

That the Messages were very good, and what they approved mightily, and would undertake the Journey, and deliver them faithfully; but then they must desire the Governor would make their Apology to Colonel *Clapham,* and tell him, that nothing but the Governor's Commands would have induced them to delay their coming to him.

The Governor promised he would; and then told them, that Mr. *Spangenberg* was desired to be present, having some *Delaware Indians* under his Care, that he might hear what was delivered to them.——He desired they would go by Way of *Bethlehem,* and take with them one or more of the *Indians* there, and that Mr. *Spangenberg* would prepare those *Indians* for their Visit, and perswade some of them to accompany them to *Wioming.*

The Messengers returned, and on the 31st of *May,* 1756, made the following Report, *viz. That on their Arrival at* Wioming, *they found the* Indians *had left the Town, and gone up the River; they therefore proceeded to* Teaogon, *where they met with a great Number of* Indians, *and informed them they had brought a Message from the Governor of* Pennsylvania, *and desired a Meeting of all their People in that Town and near it; which being obtained in two Days, they then delivered their Message.——After which,* Paxinosa, *as Speaker of their Council, returned the following Answer,* viz.

*Brethren, The Governor, and People of* Pennsylvania, THE dark Clouds overspread our Country so suddenly, that we have been all at once separated, and that dark Cloud got in between us; and as it has pleased the most High to dispel it a little, so that we can just see one another again, our Eyes are now running with Tears, because of the melancholy Sight of seeing our Country covered with our own Blood (we mean yours and ours.) Give me Leave to wipe off the Tears from your Eyes, though at the same Time my own Eyes run with Tears in Abundance for what has passed.

*Gave a String.*

*Brethren,* As you came a great Way, and through dangerous Places, where evil Spirits reign, who might have put several Things in your Way to obstruct your Business, this String serves to clear your Mind, and the Passage from your Heart to your Mouths that you may speak freely to us.

*Gave a String.*

Teedyuscung, *a* Delaware *Chief, spoke next.*

*Brother* Onas, *and the People of* Pennsylvania, We rejoice to hear from you, and that you are willing to renew the old good Understanding, and that you call to Mind the first Treaties of Friendship made by *Onas,* our great Friend, deceased, with our Fore-Fathers, when himself and his People first came over here. We take hold of these Treaties with both our Hands, and desire you will do the same, that a good Understanding and true Friendship may be re-established. Let us both take hold of these Treaties with all our Strength, we beseech you; we on our Side will certainly do it.

*Gave a Belt.*

*Brother* Onas, What you said to us we took to Heart, and it entered into our Heart; and we speak to you from our Heart; and we will deal honestly with you in every Respect.

*Gave a String.*

*Brother Onas,* We desire you will look upon us with Eyes of Mercy. We are a very poor People; our Wives and Children are almost naked. We are void of Understanding, and destitute of the Necessaries of Life. Pity us.

*Gave a String.*

*The* Delawares, Memskies, *and* Mohickons, *to* Onas, *and the People of* Pennsylvania.

*Brethren,* There is a great Number of our People among you, and in a Manner confined; we desire you will set them at Liberty, or rather give them a safe Conduct to *Wioming,* where we intend to settle as on your Fire Side; there we will jointly with you kindle a Council-Fire, which shall always burn, and we will be one People with you.

*Gave two Belts.*

*Brother* Onas, *and all the People of* Pennsylvania, We had the Misfortune that a great and dark Cloud overspread our Country; but by our Prudence, and that of our Uncles, the *Six Nations,* it is now almost dispelled, and we see the clear Heavens again. We the *Delawares,* the *Shawanese,* the *Mohickons,* and *Memskies,* give you this String of Wampum, and desire you, that the Bitterness which might have gathered in this dark and unhappy Time may be removed, and that you may by this Means spit it out; take or accept this as a certain Cure for that Purpose, and pass by all that is past, and think on your poor foolish Brethren with Mercy, and forget all the Evil done to you by them.

*Gave several Strings of Wampum.*

*Brother* Onas, What our Uncles the *Six Nations* required of us, in your and their Behalf, by their Delegates, at *Otsaningo,* we that live on the River *Sasquehannah* have agreed to. We have laid aside our Hatchet, and will never make use of it any more against you or your Brethren, the *English:* All our young Men have been consulted about this, and all earnestly agree to it; and we now speak in their Presence.

We must give you this Caution, not to charge them with any Thing that may be done by the *Ohio Indians,* who are under the Influence of the *French* against you. We assure you, our young Men will do no more Mischief to your People.

*Gave a String.*

*At a* COUNCIL *held at* Philadelphia, *on* Tuesday, *the* 8*th of* June, 1756.
PRESENT, The Honourable *ROBERT HUNTER MORRIS,* Esq; Lieutenant-Governor.
Benjamin Shoemaker, Joseph Turner, Richard Peters, John Mifflin, Esquires.
Captain Newcastle, Jagrea, or Satagarowyes, *Indians* of the *Six Nations.*
Conrad Weiser, Esq; Interpreter.

*The Governor and the People of* Pennsylvania, *to the* Indians *on* Sasquehannah, *gathered at* Teaogon.

*Brethren,* I RETURN you the Thanks of this Government for the kind Reception you gave to my Messengers: This I look upon as an Act of Friendship, and a Token of your good Intentions.

*A String of four Rows*

*Brethren,* I am glad to find a good Spirit at last prevailing amongst you, and that you hearkened to my Message, and laid it to Heart; you will ever find us, your Brethren, sincerely disposed to consult and act for your truest Interest, and in the several Matters which were or shall now be particularly promised on our Part, you may rest assured we mean punctually to perform them, and expect the same Disposition in you.

*A String of four Rows.*

*Brethren, the* Shawanese, Delawares, Memskies, *and* Mohickons, As you on your Parts have confirmed the Treaties and Leagues of Amity subsisting between you and this Government, and given a Belt in Confirmation thereof, and desire the same be done on our Part; I do now, by this Belt, ratify and confirm all former Treaties and Engagements, and assure, that they shall be most inviolably observed as long as the Sun shines.

*Here a large Belt was given.*

*Brethren,* As Your Confirmation of former Treaties was accompanied with Professions of Sincerity, so I make you the strongest Assurances of Truth in the Confirmation this Government has now made.

*A String of four Rows.*

*Brethren,* That you and I may have an Opportunity of making these mutual

Declarations at a publick Convention, I now kindle a Council-Fire at the House of *Conrad Weiser,* who is one of the Council of the *Six Nations,* and the publick Interpreter of the Province.

*A large Belt of fourteen Rows.*

N. B. *Mr.* Weiser *said it was necessary to name a particular Place; but the* Indians *were, notwithstanding this, always at Liberty to name another; and he believed, from something Captain* Newcastle *had dropped, the* Indians *would chuse the* Forks-of-Delaware.

*Brethren,* Having appointed a Place for us to meet in Council, I now clear the Roads to this Place, and remove the Logs and other Obstructions out of it, so that it may be perfectly safe for every one desirous to use it to travel to their Brethren when met in Council.

*A Belt of eight Rows, and eight Strings tied to it.*

*Brethren,* It is offensive to see Blood spilt upon the Road used by People who have lived in Friendship together; I therefore remove all Blood out of the Road that leads to the Council Fire.

*A Belt of nine Rows.*

*Brethren,* Your *Indians* who live among us go where they please; they live as we do; and enjoy their Liberty. We only hinder them from going to the Frontiers, where they might be mistaken for Enemies, and hurt or killed; and that the *Indians* may know the Truth of this, we send some of them along with our Messengers *to Teaogon,* who will declare what Treatment they have had from us. What few we have in Confinement shall be set at Liberty when the Council meets, and be brought there.

*A String.*

*Brethren,* This last is a very important Article, and what we absolutely depend upon, That all Prisoners taken on both Sides shall be delivered up, as there can be no Sincerity on either Side where this is not done, and that in the most faithful and ample Manner, without keeping back a single Prisoner; this Belt assures you that it shall be punctually performed by us, and we expect the same punctually on your Side.[2]

*Two Belts, the one of seven, the other of eight Rows.*

*Brethren,* You have mentioned to us the Distresses you have been, and are, in, for Want of Necessaries; these are owing to your having given Way to the Influences of an evil Spirit, and struck us your Brethren without any Cause; and as you have brought it on yourselves, you have the less Reason to complain: But now that a good Spirit begins to shew itself in you, and you desire to meet us in Council, I shall bring with me a Sufficiency of Clothes and Provisions to relieve those Distresses.

*A String.*

*Brethren,* As you have laid down the Hatchet, and desire the same may be done by us, our Messenger carries with him our Proclamation for Suspension of Hostilities within the Limits therein specified, of which we have informed the *Six Nations.*

*Brethren,* Agreeable to the repeated Advice and Request of *Scarroyady,* and other *Indians* of the *Six Nations,* then residing in this Province, I engaged to build a Fort at *Shamokin,* for the Protection of our Friendly *Indians,* their Wives and Children; and I now acquaint you with the March of the Forces, in order to effect this useful Work, that it may give no Umbrage; the Commander having my Orders not to act offensively.

*Brethren,* You are to take Notice, that nothing proposed by me is to interfere with any Invitation you may have received from Sir *William Johnson,* or your Uncles, the *Six Nations;* they have acquainted me, that a great Council is to be held in the Country of the *Six Nations;* and those *Indians* at *Teaogon* are invited to it: I would have them by all Means give their Attendance there. You may go to either Place as you incline, for we are both in the Service of one King, and act by his Direction.

*Brother* Newcastle, I have now finished what I would have you say in the Name of this Province to the *Indians* gathered at Teaogon. You will adapt the several Articles to *Indian* Customs, retaining the Spirit and Substance of them.

*At a* CONFERENCE *held at* Easton, *on* Wednesday *the 28th of* July, 1756.
PRESENT, *The Honourable* ROBERT HUNTER MORRIS, *Esq; Lieutenant-Governor.*
William Logan, Richard Peters, Benjamin Chew, John Mifflin, *Esquires, of the Council.*
Joseph Fox, John Hughes, William Edmonds, *Commissioners.*
Teedyuscung, *the* Delaware *Chief, and* 14 *other Chiefs,*
Conrad Weiser, *Esq; Interpreter for the* Six Nations.
John Pumpshire, Joseph Peepy, Ben, *Interpreters for the* Delawares.

*A large Company, consisting of Officers of the* Royal American *Regiment, and of the Provincial Forces; Magistrates and Freeholders, of this and the neighbouring Province; and about forty Citizens of the City of* Philadelphia, *chiefly of the People called* Quakers.

*The Governor acquainted the* Indians *he was going to speak, and desired them to be attentive.*

*Brethren,* BY a Belt which I sent by *Newcastle,* and the other *Indian* Messengers, to *Diahogo,* I informed the *Indians* there, that I had kindled a Council Fire; by another String I invited them to it; and by a String of Wampum I cleared the Road, that they might come in Safety to us. I assured you of an hearty Welcome as soon as I came here, and of my Protection; and I now, in the Name of this Government, again bid you welcome. As Captain *Newcastle* brought me no Answer to some Part of the Messages I sent last by him, I expect to receive them by you. I hope you come prepared to speak to us freely, sincerely, and openly, and desire you may do so.

*A String.*

To which *Teedyuscung* immediately answered.

Last Spring you sent me a String; and as soon as I heard the good Words you sent, I was glad; and as you told us, we believe it came from your Hearts, so we felt it in our Hearts, and received what you said with Joy.

*Brethren,* The first Messages you sent me, came in the Spring; they touched my Heart; they gave me Abundance of Joy. I returned an Answer to them, and waited for your second Messages, which came after some Time, and were likewise very agreeable. By the last you acquainted me that you had kindled a Council Fire, and invited me and my People to it. We accepted the Invitation; and I came accordingly, and have staid several Days, smoaking my Pipe with Patience, expecting to meet you here. We are ready to hear what you have to say, and not only we, but five other Nations, in all ten Nations, are now turning their Eyes this Way, and wait what will be said and done at this Meeting.

*Brother,* I solemnly, and with the utmost Sincerity, declare, that tho' you may think I am alone here, yet it will not be long before you will be convinced that I am here by the Appointment of ten Nations, among which are my Uncles the *Six Nations,* authorizing me to treat with you, and what I do they will all confirm. The Truth of this you will soon have made evident to you.

*Brother,* Hearken to what I am going to say: I declare, in the most solemn Manner, that what I now relate is the Truth. Abundance of Confusion, Disorder and Distraction has arisen among the *Indians,* from People taking upon them to be Kings, and Persons of Authority.[3] In every Tribe of *Indians* there have been such Pretenders, who have held Treaties, sometimes publick, and sometimes in the Bushes; sometimes what these People did came to be known, but frequently it remained in Darkness, or at least no more was imparted to the Publick than they were pleased to publish. To some they held up their Belts, but others never saw them; this bred among the *Indians* great Heart-burnings and Quarrels, and I can assure you, that the present Clouds do, in a great Measure, owe their Rise to this wild and irregular Way of doing Business.—The *Indians,* sensible of this Mistake of our Ancestors, are now determined to put an End to this Multitude of Kings, and to this dark Way of proceeding; they have agreed to put the Management of their Affairs into the Hands of a very few, and these shall no longer have it in their Power to huddle up and give partial Representations of what is done. I assure you, that there are only two Kings appointed to transact publick Business, of which I am one. For the future, Matters will go better on both Sides; you as well as we will know who we are to deal with. We must beseech the most High to scatter the Clouds which have arisen between us, that we may settle Peace as heretofore,

*A String.*

*Brethren, the* English, *and particularly the Governor of* Pennsylvania, You know you have invited me here; I came therefore; my Uncles, the *Six Nations,* will confirm what I say. In your Messages to the *Indians* at *Diahogo* you signified to us, that you heard we were in Want and Distress, which to be sure we are, and pitied us and our poor Wives and Children. We took it kindly, and as a Word that came from your Heart. Now is the Time for you to look about, and act the Part of a charitable and wise Man.—Be therefore strong—be assured that, though I am poor, I will do my Share. Whatever Kindness you do to me, or my People, shall be published to ten *Indian* Nations. We will not hide any Presents you shall give us; every Body shall know that we have heard your good Words. We will not do as others, and some of our Uncles, the *Six Nations,* have done, sneak away, and hide your Words and Presents in the Bushes, but shall publish far and near, that all may join with us. Exert yourselves now in the best Maner you can, and you will obtain your End.[4]

*Brother,* The Conclusion of my Words is no more than this; the Matter in Hand is of too great Moment for one Man. I am but a Messenger from the *United Nations,* though I act as a Chief Man for the *Delawares.* I must now hear what you have to say to my People at this Council-Fire. If it be good, I shall lay hold of it, and carry it to the *United Nations,* who will smile and be pleased to hear good News. If what you will say be disagreeable, I will, notwithstanding, keep it close *(here he closed his Fist)* and deliver it faithfully to the *United Nations,* and let them, as they are my Superiors, do as they see Cause.

Being asked if he had done, he said he had for the present; the main Thing, he added, is yet in my Breast, laying his Hand to his Heart, but this will depend on what Words the Governor will speak to us. Then he repeated the *Delaware* Word, *Whish-shicksy,* the same in *Mohock* Language as *Jago,* with great Earnestness, and in a very pathetick Tone. Mr. *Weiser,* who knew the Word to have a very extensive and forcible Sense, desired the Interpreter to ask him what he meant by *Whish-shicksy* on this particular Occasion, and explained himself in the following Manner. Suppose you want to remove a large Log of Wood, that requires many Hands, you must take Pains to get as many together as will do the Business; if you fall short but one, though never so weak an one, all the rest are to no Purpose. Though this be in itself nothing, yet, if you cannot move the Log without it, you must spare no Pains to get it. *Whish-shicksy;* be strong; look round you; enable us to engage every *Indian* Nation we can; put the Means into our Hands; be sure perform every Promise you have made to us; in particular do not pinch Matters neither with us or other *Indians;* we will help you; but we are poor, and you are rich; make us strong, and we will use our Strength for you; and, besides this, what you do, do quickly; the Times are dangerous; they will not admit of Delay.—*Whish-shicksy;* do it effectually, and do it with all possible Dispatch.[5]

*The Governor then spoke.*

*Brother,* I have heard with Attention all you have said. I thank you for the Openness with which you have declared your Sentiments; the Matters mentioned are of Importance; I have laid them to Heart; I will consider them with my Council; when I am prepared to speak, I will let you know; I will use Dispatch, the Times being, as you justly observe, very dangerous.

*At a* CONFERENCE *held at* Easton, *on* Thursday *the* 29*th of* July, 1756.
PRESENT, The Honourable the GOVERNOR.
The Gentlemen of the Council. The same *Indians.*
The Commissioners. The same Interpreters. The same Audience.

*Brethren,* I AM going to speak to you on the Affair we are met about; my Speech will contain Matters of great Moment: By this String of Wampum therefore I open your Ears, that you may give a proper Attention.

*A String.*

*Brethren,* The Inhabitants of this Province have ever been a peaceable People, and remarkable for their Love and constant Friendship to the *Six Nations,* and other *Indians* in Alliance with them.

When our Back Inhabitants were attacked last Fall, we at first were at a Loss to know from whence the Blow came; and were much surprized when we were informed that it was given by our old Friends and Neighbours the Cousins of our Brethren the *Six Nations;* we wondered at it; and the more so, as we had not, to our Knowledge, given them any just Cause of Offence.—As soon as we knew this, we sent to the *Six Nations,* and informed them of it, and desired to know, whether this Blow had been struck by their Direction, or with their Privity or Consent: And on receiving Assurances from them, that it was not done with their Consent, and that they greatly disapproved such Conduct, we made ready to revenge the Injury we had received, and we wanted neither Men or Arms, Ammunition, nor Strength to do it, and to take Vengeance for the Injury done us; yet, when we had the Hatchet in our Hands, and were prepared not only to defend ourselves, but to carry the War into the Country of those who had struck us, we sent again to the *Six Nations,* agreeable to the Treaties subsisting between us, to acquaint them of our Intentions. They let us know they had held a Grand Council, at *Fort Johnson,* on this Matter, and that Deputies from thence were sent to summon a Meeting of *Delawares* and *Shawanese* at *Otsaningo,* who were returned with an Account, That their Nephews had, at their Interposition, laid down the Hatchet, and would strike the *English* no more. The *Six Nations* having received these Assurances from the *Delawares* and *Shawanese,* requested us not to execute our hostile Purposes, but to suspend Hostilities; declaring, that they would fully accommodate this Breach, and bring about a Peace. At this Request of the *Six Nations*, we kept our Warriors at Home, for guarding and protecting our Frontiers. I then sent *Newcastle*, and other *Indian* Messengers to you, to notify the Advices of the *Six Nations*, with respect to what had been determined at *Otsaningo*, instructing him, in case he found you sincerely disposed for Peace, and inclined to return to your Alliance with us, to assure you, on the Behalf of this Government, that we were willing to it, on just and honourable Terms. *Newcastle*, and the other Messengers, returned with your Answers; in which you acknowledged, you had been under the Influence of an Evil Spirit, but were well disposed to return to your old Amity and Friendship; at the same Time letting us know, that you was sorry for what had passed; that you was in Distress, and desired we would pity your Distresses. To shew our Readiness to enter into a Treaty, and our Sincerity in what was said by *Newcastle*, I sent him back again to you, to let you know, on the Behalf of this Government, that I had kindled a Council-Fire, invited all your People to it, cleared the Road, washed off the Blood, and promised, if your People would come to Council, and renew former Leagues, and do what is further necessary on the Occasion, I would bring something with me to relieve your Distresses.—I thought it right to go through this Account in this particular Manner, that you might know from myself what was the Subject of the Messages sent by *Newcastle*, and what was the Substance of the Answers I received by him. And now, I suppose (as I do not see the Body of your *Indians* here) your People, in general, did not believe *Newcastle*, but sent you to know if he had my Authority for the several Matters he delivered to you, and to hear them from my own Mouth. I do not blame you for this Caution, it bespeaks your Care. The Matters he was charged with being of the last Concern, for the Satisfaction of all your People, how wide soever they are dispersed, I do in this publick Assembly, in the Name of the Government, and People of this Province, assure you, that Captain *Newcastle* acted by my Authority; and in Confirmation of what I have said, and that what he delivered, was by Authority from me, I give you this Belt.

*A Belt.*

*Brethren*, Being now convinced out of my Mouth, of the Sincerity of my Professions made to you by Captain *Newcastle*, and of the Dispositions of the People of this Province, to renew the antient Friendship that subsisted between *William Penn* and the *Indians*, I desire you will report this to the *Indians* at *Diahogo*, and to the *Six Nations*, and to all the *Indians* far and near, as my Words, spoken to them in the Name, and on the Behalf of the Government of *Pennsylvania*. I invite them all to this Council-Fire; the greater the Number that shall come, the more acceptable it will be to me. I invite, and desire you will bring with you, your whole People; but then you must bring here with you also all the Prisoners you have taken during these Disturbances; I must insist on this, as an Evidence of your Sincerity to make a lasting Peace, for, without it, though Peace may be made from the Teeth outwards, yet while you retain our Flesh and Blood in Slavery, it cannot be expected we can be Friends with you, or that a Peace can come from our Hearts. I repeat this Article of the Prisoners as a necessary Condition of Peace, and desire you will consider it as such: If in this you deal with us sincerely, we shall esteem you sincere in every Thing else, and proceed to renew our former Leagues and Covenants, and become again one Flesh as before. And I must remind you (as we are acting in Consort with the *Six Nations)* to bring some of your Uncles along with you, that they may see all that passes, and be Witnesses of the good Effects of their and our Messages to you.

*A Belt.*

*Brethren,* In Testimony of the Satisfaction you have given all our People by your coming to this Council-Fire, they have put into my Hands a small Present for you and your young Men, which will be given you at any Time you shall think proper. I have likewise given Orders to the Captains of the Forts, on the Frontiers, to furnish you with as much Provisions as you can carry, for the Use of the People you have left behind you.

*Brethren,* Only a few of you are now come down; this Present of Goods therefore is but small; when the Body of your Nation comes here, which I expect they will, and the Prisoners are delivered up, and a firm Peace made, larger Presents will be given, and your Distresses relieved in a more ample Manner.

*Brother,* Great Works require strong Hands and many; this is a good and a great one, the Work of Peace; it requires strong Heads, and sound Hearts; we desire many such may be joined together: I therefore desire your Assistance for *Pennsylvania* in this Matter; having great Influence with many who live far distant from us, you are esteemed, and will be heard; we therefore chuse you as Agent and Counsellor for this Province; engage in it heartily. You ought to do it; you owe it to the Country in which you was born; you owe it to your Brethren the *English;* you owe it to your Uncles the *Six Nations;* you owe it to your own People over which you preside: We desire you will heartily undertake it, and use your utmost Endeavours to bring about this great and good Work we have now begun.

*A large Belt.*

*Teedyuscung* answered, that he had received the Governor's Words kindly, and would, in a few Words, answer him. Then taking a large Belt in his Hand, he proceeded.

*Brother,* At the very Time *Newcastle* came with your last Messages, I was in Treaty with the *Six Nations,* and then received this Authority from them. *[Lifting up the Belt.]* This Belt denotes, that the *Six Nations,* by their Chiefs, have lately renewed their Covenant Chains with us; formerly we were accounted Women, and employed only in Womens Business; but now they have made Men of us, and as such we are now come to this Treaty. Having this Authority as a Man to make Peace, I have it in my Hand, but have not opened it; but will soon declare it to the other Nations. This Belt holds together ten Nations; we are in the Middle, between the *French* and *English;* look at it. There are but two Chiefs of the ten Nations; they are now looking on, and their Attention is fixed, to see who are disposed really for Peace.—This Belt further denotes, that whoever will not comply with the Terms of Peace, the ten Nations will join against him and strike him; see the dangerous Circumstances I am in; strong Men on both Sides; Hatchets on both Sides; whoever does incline to Peace, him will I join.

*Brother,* This is a good Day; whoever will make Peace, let him lay hold of this Belt, and the Nations around shall see and know it. I desire to conduct myself according to your Words, which I will perform to the utmost of my Power. I wish the same good Spirit that possessed the good old Man *William Penn,* who was a Friend to the *Indians,* may inspire the People of this Province at this Time.

*Then delivered the Belt.*

The Governor received it, and said, I take hold of the Belt, and am pleased with what has been said; it is all very good.

*Teedyuscung* then explained the Belt, saying, it was sent him by the *Six Nations,* and he accepted of it: You see, says he, a Square in the Middle, meaning the Lands of the *Indians,* and at one End the Figure of a Man, indicating the *English;* and at the other End another, meaning the *French;* our Uncles told us, that both these coveted our Lands; but let us join together to defend our Lands against both, you shall be Partakers with us of our Lands.

*Teedyuscung* and his Son came and dined with the Governor; and after Dinner, some more of the *Indians* coming in, the Governor acquainted *Teedyuscung* that he had something of Importance to communicate to him. The Governor then informed him, That as he was going to Council this Morning, he received a Letter from the Northern Frontiers, with very bad News, that gave him a great deal of Concern. By this Letter he received Advice, that some *Indians* had killed four of our White People at the *Minisinks;* this occasioned our Forces to be upon their Guard, and a Party of them fell in with three *Indians,* and judging them to be Enemy *Indians,* one of them was killed in endeavouring to make his Escape; and then the Governor entered into the Particulars related in *Van Etten's* Letter. The Governor said, he did not know what *Indians* had done this Mischief. If the *Indian* who was killed was our Friend, he was sorry for it; but if our Enemy, he was glad of it.

*Teedyuscung* said, that when he came here to Council, all the *Indians* thereabouts knew of it; and therefore he believed it must be the *French Indians* that killed our People; but that if his People were so foolish as to come on our Borders at this Time, and were killed any how, they must take the Reward of their Folly. None of these private Deaths ought to affect a publick Measure; nor would this make any Alterations in his Councils.

*At a* CONFERENCE *held at* Easton, *on* Friday, *the* 30*th of* July, 1756.
PRESENT, The Honourable the GOVERNOR,
The Gentlemen of the Council. The same *Indians.*
The Commissioners. The same Interpreters. The same Audience.

*The Goods were brought, and placed on the Council Table, and were delivered to the* Indians, *the Governor speaking as follows.*

*Brethren,* I ACQUAINTED you Yesterday, that the People of *Pennsylvania* had put into my Hands a small Present to relieve you, and your Wives and Children, from their present Distresses. I think it further necessary to inform you, That a Part of this Present was given by the People called *Quakers* (who are the Descendants of those who first came over to this Country with your old Friend *William Penn)* as a particular Testimony of their Regard and Affection for the *Indians,* and their earnest Desire to promote the good Work of Peace in which we are now engaged.

*Brethren,* This is not only their Sentiments but my own, and those of the People of this Province; who will all rejoice to see this good Work of Peace perfected; and therefore, as you have now received from us this substantial Proof of our Disposition to relieve your Distresses, you will be the better enabled to encourage others to return to their former Friendship with us. I say, Brother, by this we give you a clear Testimony of our Readiness and good Dispositions for Peace. Shew you the same Readiness, and comply with the Terms I have proposed to you.

*A String.*

*Teedyuscung* returned Thanks; and repeated his Assurances of doing all in his Power to perfect a general Peace with the *Indians.*—From the Council, the Governor proceeded to an Entertainment that was provided for the *Indians,* the Officers, and all the Company then in Town, accompanying him.

*Teedyuscung,* whilst at Dinner, was so well pleased with his kind Reception and generous Entertainment, that he declared, in the warmest Manner, no Endeavours of his should be wanting to bring over to the Peace, all the *Indians* far and near, that he could speak or send to; and repeatedly desired the Governor would publish what was done, through his and the neighbouring Provinces, and he would do the same at Home.——The *Philadelphia Quakers* going after Dinner to take their Leave of him, he parted with them in a very affectionate Manner; but the other Part of the Company staying, he entered into a free Conversation with the Governor; wherein he related many entertaining Particulars respecting his Journey to *Niagara,* and afterwards made a Council Speech with a String of Wampum, saying:

*Brother,* You are so good, and received us so kindly, I will also give you some of that good Tobacco that the *Six Nations* have put into my Pipe; you shall smoak of it yourselves; you will find it is good, and I will give of the same Tobacco wherever I go (meaning the Message from the *Six Nations* to them, to be at Peace with the

*English.)* The same Thing that I have offered to you I will offer to all the *Indians,* and at the same time tell them, that you have smoaked of this Tobacco; but to do this requires me to be rich, and yet I am poor.—It will take up a long Time, as there are many Nations to send the Pipe to; but in two Months I hope to go my Rounds, and be here again with a large Number, of different Nations; I say it may be in two Months, but it may be longer, as the People live at a great Distance from one another. I assure you I will execute every Thing you have desired of me, and let the *Six Nations* know all that has passed between us; and that I am your Agent and Counsellor in the *Delaware* Nation.

*A String.*

*Brethren,* I would not have you mistake me, as if I meant that I could prevail on the *Ohio Indians:* I cannot tell that they will leave off doing Mischief.—I hope you will strengthen yourselves against them; pray make yourselves as strong as possible on that Side. I must warn you likewise of another Thing; perhaps on the East Side of *Sasquehannah* there may be Mischief done by *Indians* in my Absence; but be assured it will not be by any of my People; it will be by the *French Indians* from *Ohio,* who can easily pass over *Sasquehannah,* and do what Mischief they please: Against these, you must be sure to arm yourselves in the best Manner you can; remember I give you this Warning.

*A String.*

*At a* COUNCIL *held at* Easton, *on* Friday, *the* 30*th of* July, 1756, P. M.
PRESENT, The Honourable the GOVERNOR.
William Logan, Benjamin Chew, Richard Peters, John Mifflin, Esquires.
Conrad Weiser, Esquire.

MR. *WEISER* was ask'd, Whether it was intended the Governor should keep the Belt *Teedyuscung* gave, or return it? Mr. *Weiser* answered, That having some Doubts about it, he put the same Question to *Newcastle,* who said the Belt was sent by the *Six Nations* to the *Delawares,* and as it was given by them to the Governor, it ought to be preserved among the Council Wampum, being a Belt of great Consequence; and it would be well to return another of a Fathom long, and at the Delivery of it, which must be in Council To-morrow, to make a proper Address to *Teedyuscung,* that he would be diligent, and carry it to all the Nations within his Influence. *Newcastle* said further, That *Teedyuscung* would want Abundance of Wampum, and if he had it not, the Cause would suffer exceedingly. He hoped the Council Bag was full, and desired it might be emptied into the Lap of *Teedyuscung.* Mr. *Weiser* concurring in Opinion, and saying, that the *French* gave great Quantities of Wampum to their *Indians,* and on Matters of Consequence their Belts were several Fathom long, and very wide, the Secretary was ordered to bring what Wampum he had into Council, *viz.* Fifteen Strings, and seven Belts, a Parcel of new black Wampum, amounting to seven Thousand; and having no new white Wampum, nor any proper Belts to give in return for *Teedyuscung*'s Peace Belt, a Messenger was sent to *Bethlehem*, and he returned with five Thousand; upon which the *Indian* Women were employed to make a Belt of a Fathom long, and sixteen Beads wide; in the Center of which was to be the Figure of a Man, meaning the Governor of *Pennsylvania*, and on each Side five other Figures, meaning the ten Nations mentioned by *Teedyuscung*.

The King, who was very irregular in his Visits, as well as in his Discourses, bolted all of a sudden into the Room, and with a high Tone of Voice spoke as follows, *viz.*

*Brother*, I desire all that I have said, and you have said to one another, may be taken down aright; some speak in the Dark; do not let us do so; let all be clear and known. What is the Reason the Governor holds Councils so close in his Hands, and by Candle Light? The *Five Nations* used to make him sit out of Doors like a Woman.—If the *Five Nations* still make him a Woman, they must; but what is the Reason the Governor makes him a Woman, meaning, Why does he confer with *Indians* without sending for him, to be present and hear what was said?

The Governor answered, That he holds Councils on a Hill; has no Secrets; never sits in Swamps, but speaks his Mind openly to the World; what happens here he has a Right to hear: The Women were sent for to make a Belt, not to Council. The *Six Nations* may be wrong, they are not under his Direction; and therefore he is not answerable for their Conduct, if they have not treated the *Delawares* as Men.

The Chief thanked the Governor, seemed well pleased, and said, To-morrow he would speak more, and what he had to say was from the *Six Nations:*—He that won't make Peace must die.

*A String.*

It was agreed in the Morning the Governor should deliver the new Belt, then in making, to *Teedyuscung*, with a proper Speech; that by two Belts tied together, *Newcastle* and *Teedyuscung* should be made joint Agents for this Government, and they be desired to consult together, to love one another, and to act for the best; that the new black Wampum, and all the Belts and Strings, should be given to *Teedyuscung*, and a private Present made to him and his Interpreter, *Ben*.

*At a* COUNCIL *held at* Easton, *on* Saturday, *the* 31st *of* July, 1756
PRESENT, The Honourable the Governor.
The same Members as before. TEEDYUSCUNG.
CONRAD WEISER. Esq; NEWCASTLE.

*The Names of the* Indians *present at the Treaty were taken down by Mr.* Edmonds, *and ordered to be entered.*

*Mr.* Weiser *having enquired of* Newcastle *what Messages had been received by the* Delawares, *at* Diahogo, *from the* Six Nations, *received the following Information, which he took down in Words that are the literal Interpretation of what* Newcastle *said,* viz. *"The large Belt, given by* Teedyuscung, *was sent to the* Delawares *by the Council of the* Six United Nations, *with a Message to the following Purport.*

*Cousins, the* Delaware Indians, YOU will remember that you are our Women; our Fore-Fathers made you so, and put a Petticoat on you, and charged you to be true to us, and lie with no other Man; but of late you have suffered the String that tied your Petticoat to be cut loose by the *French,* and you lay with them, and so became a common Bawd, in which you acted very wrong, and deserve Chastisement; but notwithstanding this, we have still an Esteem for you, and as you have thrown off the Cover of your Modesty, and become stark naked, which is a Shame for a Woman, you must be made a Man; and we now give you a little Power, but it will be some Time till you shall be a complete Man; we advise you not to act as a Man yet, but be first instructed by us, and do as we bid you, and you will become a noted Man.

*Cousins,* The *English* and *French* fight for our Lands; let us be strong, and lay our Hands to it, and defend it; in the mean time turn your Eyes and Ears to us, and the *English,* our Brethren, and you will live as well as we do.

Then the Governor sent to *Newcastle* and *Teedyuscung* the new Belt; not being finished, he explained the proposed Figure to them, and desired the Women might finish it on rainy Days, or resting on their Journey, which was promised.

*Then the Governor spoke as follows:*

*Brother* Newcastle, *and* Teedyuscung, I set an high Value upon this Belt; it is the Peace Belt which *Teedyuscung* delivered in Council; I very chearfully lay hold of it; I will lay it up with the Council Belts, and declare to you, I am most heartily disposed to effect the Meaning of this Belt, a speedy and honourable Peace, and a Return of the Offices of Love and Friendship between the *Indians* and their Brethren the *English.*—In Return, I give you the Belt now making, which you will consider as finished; and when done, shew it every where, and make our Dispositions and the Treatment you have met with known to your own People, the *Six Nations,* and all your Allies.—*[Here the Governor gave the new Belt, so far as it was made, and all the Wampum prepared for it, desiring, if it was not enough to complete it, that they would add more.*] Then taking up the two Belts, joined together, in his Hands, and addressing *Newcastle* and *Teedyuscung,* he declared them Agents for the Province, and gave them Authority to do the publick Business together. He recommended to them a mutual Confidence, Esteem and Intimacy, and wished them Success in their Negotiations.

To which they answered, That they would be mutual good Friends, and lay their Heads together, and do every Thing in their Power to promote the weighty Matters entrusted to them.

*Teedyuscung* added, If his Memory should not serve him in every Thing committed to his Charge, or Things should be crooked, he would return to us, and make them straight. What he says comes from his Heart, and not from his Lips; his Heart and ours should be one, and be true to one another; for if different Liquors are put in a Cask, and shaked, they will mix, and come out one.

The Governor said, that he had written down what *Teedyuscung* said on the Belt delivered by him, and will keep it in his Heart. It is very agreeable to him and the People of *Pennsylvania.* He will lay up the Belt in the Council-chamber as a Mark of his Friendship. As he is appointed Agent for *Pennsylvania,* with Captain *Newcastle,* he puts into his Hands all the Belts and Wampum he has here, to be made use of by him in the Course of his Negotiations, as he may judge most proper, and most for the Interest of the People of this Province.

*Teedyuscung* answered, That he might meet with Difficulties in transacting the important Business committed to his Charge; but as he is now one of the Council of the Province of *Pennsylvania,* he assures his Brethren, that he will exert himself faithfully, and to the utmost of his Abilities, in the Service; and if he meets with crooked Paths, he will endeavour to make them straight.

The Governor thanked *Teedyuscung* and *Newcastle* for their undertaking to be Agents for *Pennsylvania* on this Occasion, desired that they might unite and co-operate one with another, and consult together on the proper Measures to be entered into by them, and delivered them two Belts tied together, as a Sign or Symbol of that Harmony and Unanimity that ought to subsist between them.

*Teedyuscung* said, That he was pleased with being joined with *Newcastle* in the publick Business; that he hoped Matters would be brought to a happy Issue; that he wished there might be a firm Friendship and lasting Union between the *Six Nations,* the other *Five Nations,* and the People of *Pennsylvania,* and that they might be as one Man. He further said, that he had a large Family, and having a great Way to go, he had no Means of carrying any more Provisions than would serve him on the Road; he therefore desired that he might be furnished with a Horse, that he might be enabled to carry Necessaries for his Family.—Whereupon the Governor promised to let him have a Horse, and he promised to return him again the next Time he came down.

The Governor then taking into his Hands all the Belts, Strings, and Bundles of new black Wampum, gave them to *Teedyuscung,* and desired he would use them to the best Advantage among the Nations he should apply to.

The private Presents were then given, and the Governor and Council took their Leave, the Council returning to *Philadelphia,* and the Governor going to *New-York,* on an Express received from General *Shirley.*

*A List of the* Indians *present at a* Treaty *held at* Easton,
*on the* 26*th of* July, 1756.

Captain *Newcastle,* one of the Counsellors of the *Six Nations,*

*Wecmochwee,*

*Mongeest,*

| | |
|---|---|
| *Teedyuscung*, alias *Gideon*, King of the *Delawares*, | *Hachchaon*, |
| *Tapascawen*, Counsellor, | *Ben*, that speaks *English*, |
| *Amos*, *Kesmitas*, *John Jacobs*, } *Teedyuscung*'s three Sons, | *John Pumpshire*, |
| *Matchmetawchunk*, his Son-in-Law, | *Joseph Michty*, |
| *John Smalling*, his Grand-Son, | *Thomas Storer*, |
| *Christian*, | *Joseph Peepy*, |
| *William*, | *Nicodemus*, |
| *Josiah*, | *Zacharias*, |
| *Baronet Rewman*, an *Onondago Indian*, | *Christian*, |
| | *Machawehelly*, |
| | And sundry Women and Children. |

I have carefully perused the foregoing Minutes, and do find them to give a true Account of what passed between the Governor and the *Indians*, in my Presence, at *Easton*.

*Philadelphia, September* 11, 1756. *CONRAD WEISER.*

*At a* CONFERENCE *with the* Indians, *held at* Easton, *on* Monday, *the* 8*th of* November, 1756.

PRESENT, *The Honourable* WILLIAM DENNY, *Esq; Lieutenant-Governor.*

William Logan, Richard Peters, Esquires.

Benjamin Franklin, Joseph Fox, William Masters, John Hughes, *Commissioners.*

Teedyuscung, *the* Delaware *King, Speaker of the* Six Nations, Delaware Indians, Shawanese, Mohiccons,

Pumpshire, *a* Jersey Delaware Indian, *Interpreter.*

*Colonel* Weiser, *Major* Parsons, *Capt.* Weatherholt, *Capt.* Van Etten, *Capt.* Reynolds, *Officers of the Provincial Forces.*

*Lieutenant* McAlpin, *and Ensign* Jeffrys, *Recruiting Officers, of the* Royal Americans.

*A Number of Gentlemen and Freeholders, from the several Counties, and from the City of* Philadelphia.

ON *Saturday* Morning the Governor, whilst at *Samuel Dean*'s, received Intelligence from Mr. *Horsfield,* that a Party of *Indians,* who came with *Teedyuscung* from *Diahogo,* staid behind at a little Distance from Fort *Allen,* and had some bad Designs in doing so; whereupon the *Moravian* Brother who brought the Intelligence, was immediately dispatched to *Easton,* and the next Morning the Governor received a Letter from Colonel *Weiser,* informing him, that the Matter communicated to him by Mr.

*Horsfield,* had been examined into along with *Teedyuscung,* and was without Foundation; on which the Governor proceeded on his Journey, and came to Town in the Afternoon; and as soon as he alighted, the *Delaware* King, and two of the Six Nation Indians, came to wait on him, by whom he was told, that Colonel *Weiser,* and two other of the *Six Nations,* were gone to meet him, but had taken a different Road.

Mr. *Weiser,* and the two *Indians* came afterwards, and expressed their Concern at missing the Governor.

This Morning the Governor sent Mr. *Weiser* with his Compliments to the *Indian* Chief, and desired to know whether he intended to speak first, and when; and the King saying it was his Duty to speak first, wished it might be this Forenoon; on which the Governor appointed Eleven a Clock; at which Time the Governor marched from his Lodging to the Place of Conference, guarded by a Party of the *Royal Americans* in the Front, and on the Flanks, and a Detachment of Colonel *Weiser's* Provincials, in Sub-divisions, in the Rear, with Colours flying, Drums beating, and Musick playing; which Order was always observed in going to the Place of Conference.[6]

Teedyuscung opened the Conferences with the following Speech.

Brother the Governor, May it please your Excellency to hear a few Words; I will put the Governor and Gentlemen in mind, that Conferences were held here in the Summer, and what passed there is well known.

I have taken all the Pains possible to execute what I then undertook, and have brought with me several of different Tribes, as well *Delawares* as *Six Nation Indians.*

I held up the Encouragements I received from the *English,* and spread them far and near to all the Tribes I promised to go to, as well among the *Delawares* as *Six Nations;* and I assure you, I have been true and faithful to my Promises, and used all the Diligence in my power; in Testimony whereof I give these

*Four Strings.*

In Confirmation that I have faithfully published what was committed to my Care, several *Indians* of different Places, as well *Six Nations Indians* as *Delawares,* are come along with me, and being now present, will put their Hands and Seals to the Truth of what I say; they have acted upon what I delivered in Behalf of this Government, and their Minds are intent on the good Work that is going on; some of them were here before.

In Conformity to an antient and good Custom established among our Ancestors, I now proceed to open your Eyes and Ears, and remove all Obstructions out of your Throats, that nothing may impede the Attention necessary to be used in a Matter of such Importance as is now going on.

Some bad Reports have lately been spread, which deserve to be no more minded than the Whistling of Birds; these I would remove by this Belt, and take away all bad Impressions that may have been made by them.

*Gave a Belt of eight Rows.*

*Brother,* I have done for the present, and another Time, if God spares Life, I will begin the main Matter I came to do.

*The Governor replied.*

*Brother,* I return you Thanks for your kind Speech, and likewise for the Regard you shewed me in sending two of the *Six Nations Indians* along with Mr. *Weiser* to meet me. I unfortunately took a different Road, and so we missed of one another; but it gave me great Satisfaction to hear by Mr. *Weiser,* that he and those *Indians* were desirous to meet me, and conduct me to Town.

*Brother,* Many idle Reports are spread by foolish and busy People; I agree with you, that on both Sides they ought to be no more regarded than the Chirping of Birds in the Woods.

*A String.*

*Brother,* By this Belt I open your Eyes and Ears, and particularly the Passage from your Heart to your Mouth, that in what you have to say to this Government they may both concur, nor the Mouth utter any Thing but what is first conceived in the Heart: And I promise you Openness and Sincerity in every Thing I shall speak.

*A Belt.*

The Governor said, he would be ready to hear what *Teedyuscung* had further to say at Eleven o'Clock To-morrow Morning.

*At a* CONFERENCE *with the* Indians, *on* Tuesday,
*the 9th Day of* November, 1756.
PRESENT, The Honourable *WILLIAM DENNY,* Esq;
Lieutenant-Governor.
William Logan, Richard Peters, Esquires. The Commissioners,
Mr. Weiser,
Gentlemen, Officers. *Indians* as before.

*The Governor ordered the Interpreter to acquaint* Teedyuscung *that he was ready to hear him and he delivered himself as follows.*

*Brother,* THIS is to notify to you, that at the Treaty held here in the Summer, I promised to publish what was then delivered to me to all the Nations I could have any Influence on; and that I have performed all I promised, and done my Duty faithfully, with Respect to all these Nations, I can evidence by some of them who are come with me, and are now here, at your Pleasure, ready to hear what you have to say to us, and disposed to do every Thing in their Power, in Confirmation of what has been, or will be, transacted.

*A String.*

*Brethren,* This Belt signifies that I took Notice of, and paid a due Regard to, every Thing sent by the Messengers you sent to me at *Diahogo,* whom I received kindly. You may in particular remember, that you took hold of my Hand, and thereupon I came to this Place, where the Council-Fire was appointed to be kindled: When I came here, I found every Thing said by your Messengers true; which, on my Return, I made known, as well as every Thing else that was then delivered to me, to ten different Nations, *Delawares* and *Six Nations;* and as many of them as I have prevailed upon to come with me, can evidence the Truth of this.

We are all put in mind of the ancient Leagues and Covenants made by our Fore-Fathers, and of the former Union and mutual kind Actions of our and their Ancestors; what was proposed here renewed the Remembrance of these former happy Times.

Though we are but Children in Comparison of them, and of little Ability, as you well know, yet we have picked up a few Chips, and will add them to the Fire, and hope it will grow a great Fire, and blaze high, and be seen by all the different *Indian Nations,* Spectators of what we are now doing.

*A Belt of ten Rows.*

*Brethren,* I remember what has passed in Discourse and Conversation among our old antient People, especially about Governor *Penn;* what he said to the *Indians* is fresh in our Minds and Memory, and I believe it is in yours. The *Indians* and Governor *Penn* agreed well together; this we all remember, and it was not a small Matter that would then have separated us: And now, as you fill the same Station he did in this Province, it is in your Power to act the same Part.

I am now before you just what you see me; I represent myself only to be a Boy; I am really no more. Now as Misfortunes have happened by the bad Spirit, by our Enemy, and by some of our foolish young People, I declare unto you the Truth, that I have ever been sorry to see it thus, and, as far as I know myself, if it costs me my Life, I would make it otherwise.—As I have already proceeded a great Way, and prevailed on those who have stept out of the Way, and on many of whom I had little or no Expectation, to enter into peaceable Measures, I now call upon you to use your Ability, which is much greater than ours, to assist this good Work, to encourage it, and to confirm it to good Advantage.

*A Belt of seven Rows.*

Taking the Belt up again, he added, What you have said I have truly imparted to all, and what you shall now say I shall likewise hold up; I shall not put it into my Bosom, but declare it, and distribute it to all, that it may have a good Effect.

*At a* COUNCIL *held at* Easton, *on* Wednesday,
*the* 10th *Day of* November, 1756
PRESENT, The Honourable *WILLIAM DENNY,* Esq;
Lieutenant-Governor.
William Logan, Richard Peters, Esquires.

*CONRAD WEISER,* from *Teedyuscung,* acquainted the Governor, That last Night an *Indian,* named *Zaccheus,* brought an Account from *Fort Allen,* that about Forty *Indian* Warriors were come to *Nishamekatchton,* a Creek about three Miles beyond that Fort, from *Diahogo,* where they were informed by some *Indians,* who first set out with *Teedyuscung* to accompany him to the Treaty at *Easton,* that he and all his Company were cut off, and they were come to revenge his Death, in case they should have found it true; but hearing *Teedyuscung* was safe, and kindly received by the *English,* they were glad, and would remain there. *Teedyuscung* being asked by Mr. *Weiser,* if it would not be proper to send an Invitation to them to come to the Treaty, he said it would, and desired the Governor might join with him in it; which being approved by the Governor, *Moses Tattamy,* and Lieutenant *Holler,* were dispatched with the Message.

The Minutes of Yesterday's Conference were read, and the Answer considered and agreed to, but referred till the Return of the Messengers from the *Indians* beyond *Fort Allen.*

*Conrad Weiser* was ordered to inform the *Indians* by *Moses Tattamy,* that Parties of the Enemy *Indians* had lately committed Murders on the Borders of this County, even since *Teedyuscung*'s coming amongst us, but were retreated, and that the Inhabitants were determined to pursue the Murderers, and to desire the *Indians* not to straggle, but keep together, lest they should be mistaken for Enemy *Indians.*

At a Meeting of the Governor and Commissioners, it was mentioned, that the *Indians* had surmized as if Injustice had been done them in Land Affairs, the Governor therefore added to his Answer a Paragraph, putting the Question in plain Terms.[7]

*At a* COUNCIL *held at* Easton, *on* Friday, *the* 12*th of* November, 1756.
PRESENT, The Honourable *WILLIAM DENNY,* Esq; Lieutenant-Governor.
William Logan, Richard Peters, Esquires.

THE Messenger, *Moses Tattamy,* returned this Morning from the *Indians,* and reported, That in his Journey, near *Hayes*'s, about Half-way to *Fort-Allen,* he met two *Indians* and a Soldier coming down to see their Friends, and know what they were doing, and how received; but as he told the *Indians* he was going up with a Message from the Governor and *Teedyuscung,* they were satisfied, and returned to hear it: That he came to the *Indians* at Nine o'Clock Yesterday Forenoon, and delivered his Message; after which they were in Council till Three in the Afternoon, and then gave him an Answer to the following Effect.—"That they thanked the Governor for the kind Notice he had taken of them, and for his Invitation to come to the Treaty, but as it was agreed between *Teedyuscung* and them that they should come no farther than the Place where they were, and that the Goods, in case of Success, were to be brought and divided at *Fort-Allen,* they intended to stay whilst the Treaty continued; they were glad to hear the *Indians* were treated as Friends, and that a

Peace was likely to be made, and if it should be so, they should all heartily rejoice, and would agree to, and confirm, every Thing *Teedyuscung* should do."—*Tattamy* told the Governor, that he had likewise informed them of the Murders lately committed, desiring them to be cautious of straggling, or going at a great Distance; for which Notice they were thankful, and promised to keep their *Indians* together; and if they saw any Tracts of *Indians* going towards this Province, to give immediate Notice of it to the Governor,

The Messenger being asked if those *Indians* had impowered *Teedyuscung* to transact Business for them at the Treaty, he answered, that they said, in express Terms, they had given him their Authority, and if any Good should be done (meaning if a firm Peace should be concluded) not only they, but all the *Indians* at *Diahogo,* and many more different Tribes, or Towns, would be exceedingly pleased with it, and would confirm it.

The Draught of the Governor's Answer to the *Indians* as settled at the last Council, was read, and some Alterations made; then the *Indians* had Notice that the Governor would speak to them this Afternoon.

*At a* CONFERENCE *with the* Indians, *on* Friday,
*the* 12*th of* November, 1756, P. M.
PRESENT, The Honourable *WILLIAM DENNY,* Esq;
Lieutenant-Governor.
William Logan, Richard Peters, Esquires.
The same Commissioners, Officers, Gentlemen, *Indians,* as before.

*The Governor spoke as follows.*

*Brother,* I AM going to give you an Answer to what was said by you at our last Meeting, and would have done it sooner, if I had not expected to have seen more of our *Indian* Brethren here; I shall use the utmost Sincerity on my Part, and desire you will hearken attentively.

*A String.*

*Brother,* I observe what you have said, in regard to your faithful Performance of all the Matters given you in Charge by this Government when you were last here, and do heartily thank you for the diligent Care you have taken to make known to all the *Indian* Nations our good Dispositions for Peace, and for inviting them to come to this Council-Fire, and for the further Assurances you make in Behalf of those present, and of many more who are absent, even some of whom you had little Expectations of, that all will be done in their and your Power to bring the same to a happy Issue.

*A Belt.*

*Brother,* You have done well to consider the antient Leagues, subsisting between you and this Government from its very first Beginning. I am pleased to hear you express yourself so affectionately in Favour of the first Proprietor; he very well deserves it at the Hands of all the *Indians;* he was always just and kind to them, and he gave it in Charge to his Governors, and to his Children, the present Proprietaries, to treat them, as he did, with the utmost Affection, and to do them all Manner of good Offices, which has always been done by them, as far as is come to my Knowledge.

As to myself, after the present Proprietaries had appointed me to this Government, they recommended the Care of the *Indians* to me in a very particular Manner; and I assure you, I shall be ready on all Occasions to do the *Indians* every Service in my Power, and most heartily assist in bringing about a lasting and durable Peace.—I throw a large Log into the Council-Fire, that it may blaze up to the Heavens, and spread the Blessings of Peace far and wide; this Belt confirms my Words.

*A Belt.*

*Brother* Teedyuscung, What I am now going to say to you should have been mentioned some Time ago: I now desire your strict Attention to it.

You was pleased to tell me the other Day, that the League of Friendship made by your Fore-fathers was as yet fresh in your Memory; you said that it was made so strong that a small Thing would not easily break it. As we are now met together, at a Council-Fire, kindled by us both, and have promised on both Sides to be free and open to one another, I must ask you, how that League of Friendship came to be broken? Have we, the Governor or People of *Pennsylvania,* done you any Kind of Injury? If you think we have, you should be honest, and tell us your Hearts: You should have made Complaints before you struck us, for so it was agreed in our antient League: However, now the great Spirit has thus happily brought us once more together, speak your Mind plainly on this Head, and tell us if you have any just Cause of Complaint, what it is; that I may obtain a full Answer to this Point, I give this Belt.

*A Belt.*

*Teedyuscung* thanked the Governor, and desired Time to consider till To-morrow, and he would give an Answer at such Time as the Governor would be pleased to appoint.

The Governor desired he would take full Time to consider it, as it was a Matter of Consequence, and let him know when he was ready; and desired at the same Time he would offer what he had further to say on any other Matter.

*At a* CONFERENCE *held on* Saturday, November, 13, 1756.
PRESENT, *The Honourable* WILLIAM DENNY, *Esq;*
*Lieutenant-Governor.*
William Logan, Richard Peters, Esquires.
The same Commissioners, Gentlemen, Officers, *Indians,* as before.

Teedyuscung *spoke as follows, laying before him the several Strings and Belts given him Yesterday by the Governor.*

*Brother,* I REMEMBER Yesterday by these Strings that you would have had a Conference sooner, had you not expected that the *Indians* who were invited would have come to this Council.—I thank you for the kind Things you have spoke, and for reminding me of what passed in former Times; I will endeavour to tell you the Truth from the Bottom of my Heart, and hope you will have Patience to hear me; all I shall deliver shall be according to the Authority I have received, as those who are now with me will witness.

*Gave three Strings of black and white Wampum.*

*Brother,* The Times are not now as they were in the Days of our Grandfathers; then it was Peace, but now War and Distress; I am sorry for what has happened, and I now take and wipe the Tears from your Eyes, as there is great Reason for Mourning. This I not only do on my own Part, but on the Part of the *Six Nations,* who will put their Seal to it.—I take away the Blood from your Bodies, with which they are sprinkled: I clear the Ground, and the Leaves, that you may sit down with Quietness: I clear your Eyes, that when you see the Day-light you may enjoy it.—I declare this not only for the *Indians* I represent, but for the *Six Nations,* who, with them, make up Ten in all, which have with us put their Hands to these Words.

*Gave a Belt of nine Rows.*

*Brother,* Now I have done wiping your Eyes and Bodies, and cleaning the Ground where you sit; I will also heal your Wounds, not only at the Top, but at the Bottom; I will apply to them the good Plaister which the Great Creator has made for these Purposes. I say I will heal the Wound, so as it may never break out more, but be compleatly cured; in this the *Six Nations* also join with me.

*Gave a Belt of eight of Rows.*

*Brother,* Now as I have healed the Wound, our Case is like that of two Brothers; when one has been sick, and has recovered his Health, it is usual for the other to be glad; just so it is with me now: Your Wound is cured;—I am glad to see you Face to Face, as it has pleased the good Spirit to bring us together. I also remember every thing you have said; and as to what I have said, or still have to say, the other Nations will confirm.[8]

*Gave a Belt of eleven Rows.*

*Brother,* I am now going to tell you something in a few Words, in Answer to your Request last Night, that I should give you a true Account how I came to strike you.

In the Beginning of the Confusion and War that happened the Fall before this, I lived in the Middle of the Road leading from the *Six Nations* to *Philadelphia,* where I was ordered by my Uncles to sit down; and there I sat in profound Peace, under no Apprehension of Danger; and when I looked towards *Philadelphia,* I saw my Brother the Governor, and nothing but Peace and Friendship; and when I looked the other Way towards my Uncles the *Six Nations,* every thing was also Peace there; so it was with me, until all at once a Man, whose Name is called *Charles Broadhead,* an Inhabitant of this Province, came to me at *Wioming,* and told me, as if he had such a Message from the Governor, that I had struck my Brethren the *English,* which I denied over and over; and when I could not prevail with him to believe me, I took two Handfuls of Wampum, and desired him to go down with them to the Governor, and assure him that it was not I who struck the *English.*[9] I also desired the Governor to let me know what further Measures I should take, to satisfy him and my Brethren the *English,* of the Truth of this.—I also desired, by the same Messenger, that the Governor would take all the prudent Methods he could to relate this to Colonel *Johnson,* and to my Uncles the *Six Nations,* as I was under a good deal of Concern that this Charge was laid against me.——There were two Kings present besides me, who joined with me in the Message; and I likewise desired the Governor to send me Word what to do, for which I waited till I was out of Patience, and obliged to flee, and leave my Inheritance, on that Account.

*Gave a String.*

*Brother,* According to your other Question or Request last Night, to know of me why I struck you, without first giving you a Reason for it; I will tell you the Truth why I have unfortunately struck you.[10] I say, Brother, I will tell you the very Truth, in Answer to your Question. I never knew any of our ancient Kings ever to have this in their Minds, I now tell you that it came from a great King, at least I think so: The King of *England,* and of *France,* have settled or wrought this Land, so as to coop us up as if in a Pen. Our foolish and ignorant young Men, when they saw the Proceeding of this Enemy, and the Things that were told them, believed them, and were perswaded by this false-hearted King to strike our Brethren the English.—According to your Desire I will now tell you the Truth with an honest Heart, as far as is in my Power: After this unfortunate Management once prevailed, it is easy for all you *English,* if you look into your Hearts, to find the Cause why this Blow came harder upon you than it would have otherwise done;—but this is not the principal Cause; some Things that have passed in former Times, both in this and other Governments, were not well pleasing to the *Indians;* indeed, they thought them wrong; but as I said before, they were not the Principal Cause. Being asked in what other Governments, he answered, in the Province of *New-Jersey.* Now, Brother, I have told you the Truth, as you desired me, and also the Uneasiness of my Mind, because I verily believe it was our Duty to go to the very Bottom, be it as bad as it will, and that it is necessary we should both open our whole Minds to one another, that we may agree to heal the Wound.

*Gave a Belt of twelve Rows.*

*Brother,* When I was here at the last Treaty, I did according to what I promised. I took the Belt I received from this Government, and held it up to all the Nations I undertook to go to, and I took them all by the Hand (meaning I invited them all to come to the Council-Fire.) One of the *Delaware* Nations, meaning the *Minisink Indians,* now about *Fort Allen,* gave me this Belt, saying, he was glad to hear what I said, and laid hold of the same Hand, meaning, he accepted the Invitation; but said he would only go Part of the Way, no further than to a certain Place, and there he would stay, but that I might proceed, for he would agree to whatever I did, being led by the same Hand, and giving me Authority to act for him at this Council.

*Then delivered the Belt, of ten Rows, given him by those* Indians, *who he said were* Minisinks.

*Brother,* By this String I also let you know, that I would not have you think I have finished every Thing at this Meeting, though what I have now done is of great Moment; if we are spared till another Day, that is, until next Spring, I will let you know something further in another Meeting, for you must be sensible we cannot at one Time finish a Thing of so great Moment. In the mean time, I will use my faithful Endeavours to accomplish every Thing for the Good of both of us.

*Gave a String.*

Then, pausing a while, he said he had forgot something, and taking up the String again, he proceeded.

I will let you know fully and freely my Mind, and what is my Determination to do.—When I return into my Country, I will look about me, I will see and hear for you.—If I hear of any Enemy going towards you, I will send a suitable Messenger to give you Notice, though it should be at Midnight. I will also take every prudent Measure to prevent any Danger that may befal you; perhaps, if the Enemy be but few, I may not come to know of it, but if the Number be great, I shall be the liklier to know it: However, be they more or less, I will let you know it.

*Then laid down the String again.*

Then, the Governor desired of *Teedyuscung,* as he had mentioned Grievances received by the *Indians* from this and other Governments, to let him know what they were; and to speak his Mind freely and fully without any reserve; upon which *Teedyuscung* spoke as follows.

*Brother,* You have not so much Knowledge of Things done in this Country as others who have lived longer in it, being but lately come among us.—I have not far to go for an Instance: This very Ground that is under me (striking it with his Foot) was my Land and Inheritance, and is taken from me by Fraud; when I say this Ground, I mean all the Land lying between *Tohiccon Creek* and *Wioming,* on the River *Sasquehannah.* I have not only been served so in this Government, but the same Thing has been done to me as to several Tracts in *New-Jersey,* over the River. When I have sold Lands fairly, I look upon them to be really sold.—A Bargain is a Bargain.—Though I have sometimes had nothing for the Lands I have sold but broken Pipes, or such

Trifles, yet when I have sold them, though for such Trifles, I look upon the Bargain to be good: Yet I think I should not be ill used on this Account by those very People who have had such an Advantage in their Purchases, nor be called a Fool for it. *Indians* are not such Fools as to bear this in their Minds.—The Proprietaries, who have purchased their Lands from us cheap, have sold them too dear to poor People, and the *Indians* have suffered for it. It would have been more prudent, in the Proprietaries to have sold the Lands cheaper, and have given it in Charge to those who bought from them, to use the *Indians* with Kindness on that Account.[11]

Now, Brother, hear me; supposing you had a Pipe in your Mouth, smoaking, of little Value; I come and take it from you; by and by, when you see me again, you remember it, and take a Revenge: I had forgot, and wonder at the Cause, and ask you, Brother, Why you have done so? This makes me remember the Injury I did you, and more careful for the future. Now, although you have purchased our Lands from our Fore-fathers on so reasonable Terms, yet now at length you will not allow us to cut a little Wood to make a Fire; nay, hinder us from Hunting, the only Means left us of getting our Livelihood.

Now, Brother, I am pleased you asked me this Question, having thereby given me an Opportunity of speaking my Mind freely, as to any Uneasiness I was under.—You are wise enough to see these Things, and to provide a Remedy for them

Then *Teedyuscung* produced a Receipt from *William Parsons,* for a Bundle of Deer-skins he had sent from *Fort Allen* as a Present to Governor *Morris,* and desired Mr. *Peters* to let him know if he had received them for the Governor; which he said he had.

He then asked Mr. *Peters* what was done with the Memorandum he gave to Governor *Morris,* when he was in *Philadelphia* in *April,* 1755, containing a Claim to a small Pine Tract in *New-Jersey;* to which Mr. *Peters* said, that Governor *Morris* had promised to enquire into the Matter, and the Memorandum would be returned to him at any Time, with Governor *Morris*'s Report on it.

The Governor then asked him, what he meant by Fraud; having said his Lands were taken from him by Fraud, what it meant?

To which *Teedyuscung* replied.—When one Man had formerly Liberty to purchase Lands, and he took the Deed from the *Indians* for it, and then dies; after his Death the Children forge a Deed like the true One, with the same *Indian* Names to it, and thereby take Lands from the *Indians* which they never sold—this is Fraud. Also, when one King has Land beyond the River, and another King has Land on this Side, both bounded by Rivers, Mountains and Springs, which cannot be moved, and the Proprietaries, greedy to purchase Lands, buy of one King what belongs to the other—this likewise is Fraud.[12]

The Governor then asked *Teedyuscung,* Whether he had ever been used in that Manner?

He answered, Yes;—I have been served so in this Province: All the Land extending from *Tohiccon,* over the *Great-Mountain,* to *Wioming,* has been taken from me by Fraud; for when I had agreed to sell the Land to the old Proprietary by the Course of the River, the young Proprietaries came and got it run by a straight Course by the Compass, and by that Means took in double the Quantity intended to be sold.

*Brother,* As you have desired me to be very particular, I have told you the Truth, and have opened my Mind fully. I did not intend to speak thus, but I have done it at this Time, at your Request; not that I desire you should now purchase these Lands, but that you should look into your own Hearts, and consider what is right, and that do.

The Governor thanked him for the Freedom and Openness he had used with him, and told him, when he was ready to speak to him, he would let him know it.

*At a* COUNCIL *held at* Easton, November 14, 1756.
PRESENT, The Honourable *WILLIAM DENNY,* Esq; Lieutenant-Governor.
William Logan, Richard Peters, Esquires.[13]

MR. *WEISER,* by the Governor's Order, attended the Council. The Minutes of Yesterday's Conference were read over, and then each Paragraph by itself. Mr. *Weiser* said, he apprehended *Teedyuscung's* Relation, of what passed between him and *Charles Broadhead,* in a Light something different from what was set down in the Minutes, *viz.* That *Charles Broadhead* had, in the Name of the Governor, charged on *Teedyuscung* the Murders committed on the Inhabitants of this Province, and demanded Satisfaction for them; that the King denied the Charge, and sent a Message by him, with a Bundle of Wampum, to the Governor of *Pennsylvania,* to assure him of his not having committed Hostilities. And further, desired he might receive Orders from the Governor what to do, promising to execute them faithfully; and if it should be judged necessary, he would even go to Colonel *Johnson,* and the *Six Nation* Country, with any Message the Governor would please to send there by him, but desired it might be sent in a certain Number of Days, after which, if it did not come, he would take it for granted the Governor believed the Stories told of him.

The Governor enquired of Mr. *Weiser* into the Foundation of the Complaint made by the *Indians,* as to the Frauds said to be committed in Purchases of Land made of them by the Proprietaries; and he told the Governor, That few or none of the *Delawares* present, as he could recollect, originally owned any of these Lands, or any Land in this Province; that, if any Injury was done, it was done to others, who were either dead or gone, some to the *Ohio,* and some to other Places.—That as to the Lands particularly instanced by *Teedyuscung,* he heard that they were sold to, and the Consideration Money paid by, the first Proprietary, *William Penn.*—That when Mr. *John Penn* and Mr. *Thomas Penn* were here, a Meeting was then had with the principal *Indians* living on these Lands, and the former Agreement renewed, and the Limits again settled between the Proprietaries and those Chiefs of the *Delawares;* and accordingly a Line was soon after run by *Indians* and Surveyors. That the *Delawares* complaining afterwards, their Complaint was heard in a great Council of the *Six Nations,* held at *Philadelphia,* in the Year 1743, in which several Deeds, executed by the *Delawares* to the Proprietaries, were read, and interpreted, and the Signers Names and Marks examined; and, after a long Hearing, the *Six Nations* declared the Complaints of their Cousins, the *Delawares,* to be unreasonable, and were very angry with them for complaining without Cause.

Mr. *Peters,* being asked by the Governor, said, he had likewise heard Things to the same Effect, and was present at the Council when the *Delawares* Complaints were heard and settled by the *Six Nations;* that it was a very large Council, consisting of the principal Chiefs of the *Delawares.*—And added, he believed when the Matter should come to be well examined into, the Proprietaries would not be found to have done Injustice to the *Delawares,* or to hold any of their Lands, for which those *Indians* had not given Deeds, truly interpreted to them, and received a Consideration.

But as neither Mr. *Weiser,* nor he, was concerned in this Transaction, and the Papers to prove it were at *Philadelphia,* this Matter might, on the Governor's Return, be thorougly enquired into, and if it should appear that Injustice had been done the *Delawares* in this, or any other of their Sales, they ought to receive Satisfaction.—After which the Governor proposed to let the *Indians* know, that as to the particular Grievances they had mentioned, they should be thoroughly examined into, well considered, and, if justly founded, amply redressed as quickly as the Nature of the Business would admit.

But upon conferring with the Commissioners, he was told by them, that such Promises had been frequently made the *Indians* by Governors of other Provinces, and not performed, and these People might consider them as now made with a Design to evade giving them Redress.

The Commissioners said further, as more Goods were brought than were proper at this Time to be given to the small Number of *Indians* come down, it would be better, whether the Claim was just or unjust, to offer them Immediate Satisfaction, which they, on the Part of the Publick, with the Governor's Approbation, were willing to do, judging this would effectually remove all their Uneasiness. The Governor concurring with them in Sentiments, an Answer to their Complaints was framed accordingly.

*At a* CONFERENCE *held on* Monday, November 15, 1756.
PRESENT, The Honourable *WILLIAM DENNY,* Esq;
Lieutenant-Governor.
William Logan, Richard Peters, Esquires.
The Commissioners, Officers, Gentlemen, *Indians,* as before.

*The Governor spoke as follows.*

*Brother,* YOU expressed your Concern for what had happened, wiped the Tears from our Eyes, and the Blood from our Bodies, and having made clean the Council Seat, I heartily thank you for it. I do likewise wipe the Tears from your Eyes; I wash away the Blood from your Bodies, and from the Council Seat, that there may not remain the lest Defilement,

*A Belt.*

*Brother,* I make you my Acknowledgments for your having searched our Wounds to the Bottom, and the good Remedies you have applied for their Cure, and I pray the Great Creator may bless our mutual Endeavours, that they may be so effectually healed as not to leave behind them the least Scar, or ever break out again, whilst the Rivers run, or the Sun and Moon give Light to the Earth.

*A Belt.*

*Brother,* As to what you say of the Message delivered to you at *Wioming,* by *Charles Broadhead,* the Governor did send him, and I could have wished you had sent some of your own People to me on so weighty an Occasion; and for the future, I must caution you not to hearken to any Messages as from this Government, unless the Persons charged with them are known to be publick Officers, usually employed for such Purposes, and the Papers they produce are sealed with the Seal of the Government.

*A String.*

*Brother,* I thank you for the Openness with which you have expressed yourselves as to the Causes why you struck us. The *French* practice every Artifice they are Masters of to deceive the *Indians,* and I am sorry your young Men should have been so foolish as to have hearkened to them. I hope they have sufficiently seen their Errors, and will not hereafter suffer themselves to be so deluded by that deceitful People.

*A String.*

*The Governor taking the Belt given by the* Minisink Indians, *repeated what* Teedyuscung *said on it, and then answered it.*

*Brother,* As I conceive this Belt to be your Authority for acting at this Council-Fire, in Behalf of the *Minisink Indians,* who only came Part of the Way, I will keep it, and put it into the Council Bag, being glad to hear they have put their Hand to the Belt I sent, though I should have been better pleased to have seen them here.

*Brother,* You give me Hopes of another Visit. Assure yourself it will always give me Pleasure to receive you, and any other of our *Indian* Friends with you. Your kind Offer of giving me timely Notice of the Approach of an Enemy, is an incontestable Proof of the Warmth of your Heart for me; and as you have so freely offered it, I shall ever have an entire Dependance upon you; and whatever Persons are sent with Intelligence of this Sort, shall be handsomely rewarded. I expect and desire you will give the same Intelligence to any other Governor whose Country you apprehend to be in Danger, as all the *English* are of the same Flesh and Blood, and Subjects of the same King.

*Gave a large String.*

*Brother,* I am very glad you have been as good as your Word in coming down to the Council-Fire, which was kindled on this particular Occasion. I believe you have used your best Endeavours, with great faithfulness, to effect every Thing you undertook. I heartily agree to the Peace as you have proposed it, provided all the *English* Colonies be included in it. But we cannot agree to make Peace for this Government alone, and leave you at Liberty to continue the War with our Brethren of the neighbouring Colonies; for we, the *English,* are all Subjects of one great King, and must, for the future, be all at Peace, or all at War, with other Nations at the same Time.

*A Belt.*

*Brother,* You may remember it was stipulated in the Conferences held last Summer, that all the Prisoners you had taken should be brought to this Council-Fire, and there delivered up; and as you have only delivered up five Prisoners, and I am sure many more have been taken, I desire to know why they have not been brought; they are our own Flesh and Blood, and we cannot be easy whilst they are kept in Captivity.

*A String.*

*Brother,* You have opened your Heart, and shewn us the Reasons you thought you had for differing with us: You have done well in speaking so plainly on that Head; but you should have made your Complaint to us before you lifted your Hand to strike, and that might have prevented the Mischief. When the Great Creator made Man, he gave him a Tongue to complain of Wrongs, two Ears to hear a Brother's Complaints, and two Hands to do him Justice, by removing the Cause.—All these were made before the Hatchet, and should be first used. Had the Man, in your Comparison, whose Pipe was taken from him, said, Brother, you took my Pipe from me at such a Time, and I must have Satisfaction; his Brother might have answered, I did not think you valued a Pipe so much, do not let us differ about a small Matter, here, Brother, take two of mine. That this Method, agreeable to our antient Treaties, may be remembered, and Complaints always made by you to us, or by us to you, in a publick Manner, and Justice demanded before we strike, I give you this

*String.*

*Brother,* I am but lately come among you; the Grievances you mention are of old Date. If former *Indian* Kings have, as you say, sometimes sold more Land than they had a Right to sell, in so doing they injured us, and we, as well as you, have Cause to complain of them.—But sometimes, though they sold no more than their own, they sold it fairly, and it was honestly paid for by the *English;* yet when the *Indian* Children grow up, they may forget that their Fathers sold the Lands, and divided the Goods; and some evil Spirit, or bad Man, that loves to make Mischief, may tell them, the Land is still yours; your Fathers never sold it; the Writings are false. Morever, many People, both *English* and *Indians,* concerned in the former Purchases of Lands, are now dead; and as you do not understand Writings and Records, it may be hard for me to satisfy you of the Truth, though my Predecessors dealt ever so uprightly; therefore, to shew our sincere Desire to heal the present Differences, and live in eternal Peace with you our Brethren, tell me what will satisfy you for the Injustice you suppose has been done you in the Purchase of Lands in this Province; and if it be in my Power, you shall have immediate Satisfaction, whether it be justly due to you or not. The good People of this Province are ready and willing to open their Hands, and help me, by contributing freely to this good Work.—Or if you are not impowered to receive such Satisfaction at this Time, or have not Convenience to carry away the Goods that may be given you on that Account, then I will lodge the Goods in such Hands as you shall appoint, till you bring to our next Meeting your old Men of the several Nations, who may have a Right to a Share in the Division of those Goods, where they shall be ready to be delivered to them and you. This may be done at a Council-Fire, to be rekindled at *Philadelphia* for you and us, or here, as you shall chuse, when we expect, and insist, that you bring down all the Captives that still remain in your Country.

And as you mention Grievances from the Neighbouring Governments, I make no Doubt, but on proper Application, you will have the utmost Justice done you; and if I can be of any Service to you in making the Application, it will give me great Pleasure; in Testimony whereof, I give you this

*Belt.*

*Brother,* You told us last Summer, that formerly there were many *Indian* Chiefs who made Treaties, some in one Place, and some in another, from whence Misunderstandings had often arose.—It was so formerly with the *English* Governments, each made War or Peace with the *Indians* for itself: They were not united in these great Affairs, as Subjects of the same King ought to be, and so were much weaker.—Our wise King has now ordered Things better, and put all *Indian* Affairs under one general Direction.—I shall send a full Account of all that has passed between this Government and the *Indians,* on this present Occasion, to Sir *William Johnson,* to whom His Majesty has been pleased to commit the general Management of *Indian* Affairs, for his Approbation and Ratification; and as this Gentleman, in Quality of being the King's general Agent in this Part of *America,* has, in Conjunction with your Uncles the *Six Nations,* and all the Allies, kindled a general Council-Fire at his House, on the *Mohocks River,* I must insist upon it, that *Teedyuscung,* and a Deputation of your Chief Men, shall go to this Council-Fire, and there communicate every Thing to obtain Confirmation, and take Advice as to your future Conduct, that there may be a perfect *Union* both of Council and Measures, as well on the Part of all the *Indians,* as others his Majesty's Subjects, without which this great Work of Peace will never be brought to its just Perfection.

*A Belt.*

*Brother,* The good People of this Province, affected with the Distresses which their Brethren the *Indians* must needs suffer in this severe Season, for want of

Clothes and other Necessaries, have furnished me with a Quantity of Goods, to the Value of *Four Hundred Pounds,* to supply their Wants; a large Part of them is given by the People called *Quakers,* who are the Descendants of those who came over with *William Penn,* as a particular Testimony of their Regard and Affection for the *Indians,* and their earnest Desire to promote this good Work of Peace.

GOODS given at the Expence of the Province.

3 *Pieces of Blankets,*
1 *Piece of Matchcoat,*
1 *Piece of plain white Halfthicks,*
1 *Piece of napt Ditto,*
1 *Piece of purple Ditto,*
1 *Piece of Stroud,*
1 *Piece of Calicoe,*
1 *Gross of Scarlet Garters,*
3 *Pieces of Ribbons,*
3 *Dozen of Taylors Shears,*
6 *Dozen of Cuttoe Knives,*
6 *lb. of white and black Beads,*
1 *Gross of Womens Thimbles,*
1 *Gross of Mens Ditto,*
1000 *Fish-hooks,*
100 *Large Ditto,*
100 *Large Fish-hooks;*
6 *Dozen of Tobacco Tongs,*
6 *Gross of Morris Bells,*
5 *lb. of Vermillion,*
18 *Tin Kettles,*
20 *Shirts,*
6 *Hats,*
6 *Coats,*
2 *Gross of Awl-blades,*
100 *lb. of Powder,*
200 *lb. of Lead,*
1 *Piece of black Stroud,*
2 *Pieces of Bandanoe Handkerchiefs.*
1 *Piece of blue Stroud, was also given among the five* Mohocks *and two* Shawanese, *and one Shirt to each.*

GOODS given at the Expence of the People called *Quakers.*

2 *Pieces of striped Blankets,*
5 *Pieces of Matchcoat,*
2 *Pieces of Strouds,*
1 *Piece of purple Halfthicks,*
2 *Pieces of printed Calicoe,*
1 *Piece of striped Calimancoe,*
4 *Pieces of flowered Silk Handkerchiefs,*
2 *Dozen of Worsted Caps,*
40 *Pairs of Yarn Mittens,*
1 *Gross of Thimbles,*
5 *Parcels, about 6 1b. of Thread.*
3000 *Needles,*
2 *Pieces of Ribbon,*
24 *Small Brass Kettles,*
8 *Tin Kettles,*
20 *White Shirts,*
10 *Green Frize Coats,*
10 *Hats,*
2 *Gross of Bed-lacing,*
1 *Gross of Gartering,*
200 *lb. of Tobacco,*
3 *Gross of Pipes,*
48 *Weeding-hoes, for* Indian-Corn,
6 *lb. of small Beads,*
6 *lb. of Barley-corn Ditto,*
3 *Dozen of small Looking-glasses,*
12 *Silver Medals of King GEORGE,*
6000 *Black and White Wampum.*
*A Horse, Bridle and Saddle.*

*At a* CONFERENCE *held at* Easton, November 16, 1756.
PRESENT, The Honourable *WILLIAM DENNY,* Esq; Lieutenant-Governor.
William Logan, Richard Peters, Esquires.
The same Commissioners, Officers, Gentlemen, *Indians,* as before.

*The Governor acquainted* Teedyuscung *that he was ready to hear him.*

*Then* Teedyuscung, *taking a String of Wampum, spoke in these Words.*

*Brother,* I DESIRE you will hear me a few Words with Patience. You may remember I often desired you to endeavor to apprehend me aright, when I am speaking of Matters of Importance.

*Brother,* Hear me with Patience; I am going to use a Comparison, in order to represent to you the better what we ought to do.

When you chuse a Spot of Ground for Planting, you first prepare the Ground, then you put the Seed into the Earth; but if you don't take Pains afterwards, you will not obtain Fruit.—To Instance, in the *Indian Corn,* which is mine (meaning a native Plant of this Country) I, as is customary, put seven Grains in one Hill, yet, without further Care, it will come to nothing, tho' the Ground be good; tho' at the Beginning I take prudent Steps, yet if I neglect it afterwards, tho' it may grow up to Stalks and Leaves, and there may be the Appearance of Ears, there will only be Leaves and Cobs.—In like Manner, in the present Business, tho' we have begun well, yet if we hereafter use not prudent Means, we shall not have Success answerable to our Expectations.—God, that is above, hath furnished us both with Powers and Abilities.—As for my own Part, I must confess, to my Shame, I have not made such Improvements of the Power given me as I ought; but as I look on you to be more highly favoured from above than I am, I would desire you, that we would join our Endeavours to promote the good Work; and that the Cause of our Uneasiness, begun in the Times of our Forefathers, may be removed; and if you look into your Hearts, and act according to the Abilities given you, you will know the Grounds of our Uneasiness in some Measure from what I said before, in the Comparison of the Fire, that tho' I was but a Boy, yet I would according to my Abilities bring a few Chips; so with Regard to the Corn, I can do but little, you may a great deal; therefore let all of us, Men, Women and Children, assist in pulling up the Weeds, that nothing may hinder the Corn from growing to Perfection. When this is done, tho' we may not live to enjoy the Fruit ourselves, yet we should remember, our Children may live and enjoy the Blessings of this good Fruit, and it is our Duty to act for their Good.

*A String.*

*Brother,* I desire you will attend to these few Words, and I will, with all Diligence, endeavour to tell you the Truth; the great Log you mentioned, when kindled, will make a great Flame, but it will not kindle of itself, nor continue flaming, unless there be Air and Leaves, as well as Coals to make it kindle. I desire we may use our utmost Endeavours to make it kindle, though what I have told you may relate to Matters disagreeable to you, yet if we exert ourselves, and act according to the Abilities given from above, the Event will be agreeable, and pleasing to ourselves, and of Service to our Children.

*Brother,* Take Pains therefore, and though you are a Governor, do not put off these Things, from Time to Time, as our Forefathers did.

The Interpreter was desired to tell, in other Words, what was the Meaning of what was said in the two last Articles; and having requested Leave of *Teedyuscung,* he said, he alluded to the Beginning of the War; the Quarrels between the King of *France,* and the King of *England,* and their People on both Sides, and that their young Men were deluded by the *French;* this was the first and principal Cause, tho' other Things helped to make the Blow fall quicker and heavier.

*A String.*

*Brother,* I will now in a few Words, according to my Abilities, give you an Answer. You desired me to acquaint you what the Grounds of my Uneasiness were, and I complied, tho' it was not the main Thing which I came about. But when you put me in mind, I was pleased, for before, I thought it not proper to mention it in these difficult Times; it was not the Cause of the Stroke, tho' it was the Foundation of our Uneasiness. Now, Brother, in Answer to your Question: What will satisfy us? It is not usual, nor reasonable, nor can I tell you what the Damage is, and adjust, as in a Ballance, the true Value at that Time and these Times; formerly it might be lighter, but being delayed, it is now the heavier; the Interest is to be added. Besides, there are many more concerned in this Matter, not now present; and tho' many who have suffered are now in the Grave, yet their Descendants feel the Weight, and the more now for the Time they have waited.

Also, Brother, I require you would throw down the Fence that confines some of my Brethren and Relations in the *Jerseys,* that they may, if they see Cause, come and see their Relations. I do not want to compel any of them to come, or to stay against their Will. If they are inclined to stay and live among the *English,* I am quite willing they should come back again; but I want they should come and see me, that thereby I may convince their Relations, and the other Nations afar off, that I am now treating with, that they are not Servants, but a free People.

I do not request that all Men, Women and Children should come; but some, or as many as may be sufficient to convince other Nations that they are not confined, but have Liberty as well as we: In particular, one called *Philip,* he has a Wife, and Relations among us; to my Grief I heard he was carried to Goal, and there confined with some others, and put to Death; but I understand the Account of his Death was false. I desire he may have Liberty to come and see his Relations. I also request that you would apply to the Governor on the other Side the River (*viz.* of the *Jerseys*) and to use your utmost Endeavours with him, that he would give them Leave to come, and that they may come under your Protection, be they more or less, in the great Road to us opened by this Province.

But though you should not do this, yet I will use my utmost Endeavours to bring you down your Prisoners, there are only two in my Power. You may hear otherwise, but

I declare I have no more than two in my Power: There are more in the Possession of others, and these, with your Assistance, I may be able to bring down; and I will endeavour to gather and scoop in as many as I can, but I shall want your Help to do it.

*Brother,* I have to request you, that you would give Liberty to all Persons and Friends to search into these Matters; as we are all Children of the Most High, we should endeavour to assist and make use of one another, and not only so, but from what I have heard, I believe there is a future State besides this Flesh; now I endeavour to act on both these Principles, and will, according to what I have promised, if the Great Spirit spare my Life, come next Spring, with as great a Force of *Indians* as I can get, to your Satisfaction.

*A String.*

*Brother,* By this String now delivered, and lying before you, I assure you I have spoken on all Matters the best I could, according to my mean Capacity and Abilities. I shall depend on my Interpreter, who I believe is an honest Man, but I think it prudent, in order to prevent Misunderstandings, that I should be furnished with a Copy of what is done, as well in the Conferences held here last Summer as at this Time; for though I am not able to read, yet others may; it will be a great Satisfaction to have it in my Power to shew to others what has passed between this Government and me: What is committed to Writing will not easily be lost, and will be of great Use to all, and better regarded; and I would have the Names and Seals of all that have been concerned in transacting this Business put to it: I do not desire a Copy now, but that it may be ready for me when I come again.[14]—The Interpreter, *Pumpshire,* informed the Governor, that what *Teedyuscung* was going to say was not material, or of much Importance, as it related to himself; adding, though he might be considered as a simple Man, yet throughout all this Affair he had acted uprightly and honestly.

*Brother,* I will speak in Favour of the Interpreter; he acted as such in Governor *Morris*'s Time as well as yours; and I am pleased with his Conduct on both Occasions.—If we should have any further Business to transact, I desire he may be employed.—You know he lives in another Province, and is on that Account at some Expence; reward him well for his Services; and do it well for my Sake; but I shall leave it to you.

*Brother,* I have something, though of no great Consequence, yet to mention. I am in low Circumstances, and have not Things suitable; I wish I had——however, I have fifteen Deer Skins, which, as I see you love to have your Hands covered, I present you, to make Gloves of, or for any other Use you shall think proper. Eighty fine large Ones were brought at first, but on our Journey from *Diahogo* to *Wioming,* some of the *Indians* with me were so discouraged by Alarms, that they returned home, and took with them all but the Fifteen, which, I desire your Acceptance of.

The Governor returned him Thanks, and told him, he accepted of them as a Mark of his Affection, without regard to the Value of the Skins.—He then reminded *Teedyuscung,* that it was intended the Goods should have been delivered Yesterday, but as it grew late, and the Room in which they sat at Dinner was so small, it was agreed they should be brought here, and delivered, which was done, the Lists read, and the *Indians* left to divide the Goods.[15]

*At a* COUNCIL *held at* Easton, November 17, 1756.
PRESENT, The Honourable *WILLIAM DENNY,* Esq;
Lieutenant-Governor.
William Logan, Richard Peters, Esquires.

THE Commissioners advising the Governor to fix at this Meeting the Sum to be given in full Satisfaction of all Injuries done to the *Indians,* and to offer it to them now, Mr. *Weiser* was sent to consult with *Teedyuscung,* if this would be agreeable; and Mr. *Weiser* having done so, reported, That the King declared against it, saying, he had no Power to take any Sum, tho' the Governor should offer him never so much, the People to whom the Land belonged being absent; but he would endeavour to bring as many of them down as he could find to the next Meeting, when it might be further considered.[16]

Several Matters remaining to be mentioned to the *Indians,* the Governor sent for *Teedyuscung,* the four *Six Nation Indians,* the two *Shawanese,* and one or two *Delawares,* and in the Presence of the Commissioners, and some other Gentlemen, he spoke as follows.

*Brother,* Only one Thing of what was said Yesterday requires an Answer, which I am now going to give you.

By this String, you desired me to make Application to the Governor of *Jersey,* that the Fence might be broke down which confined the *Indians,* and that they, or some of them, might have Liberty to go into the *Indian* Country, and correspond with their Relations and Friends as formerly, and particularly to obtain this Liberty for one *Philip.*

The Province of *Jersey,* you know, is a different Government from this; I will use my best Endeavours with the Governor to grant your Request, but I apprehend I shall meet with this Difficulty, that as you have some of their People Prisoners with you, before they grant your Request, they will expect these shall be returned, which I think would be adviseable for you to do; particularly you have with you a Boy, whose Name is *Hunt,* taken near *Paulin's* Kiln, in that Province, whose Mother is now here, and requests he may be sent down among the first.

*A String.*

*Brother,* I consider you as the Counsellor and Agent of this Province, and as such obliged to assist us all you can. By this String, I confirm your Appointment.

*A String.*

*Brother,* As our Prisoners may suffer for Want of Clothes and other Necessaries in this severe Season, we would wish to have them as soon possible, and to that

End propose to send with you two Messengers who may collect them together, and bring them down; and I desire you will give them your Assistance, which will be a further Proof of your Sincerity.

*A String.*

*N. B. Two of the* Six Nations Indians *were employed in this Service.*

*Brother,* If any of our *Indians* shall incline to come into the Province, and live among their Brethren, the *English,* I do now assure you, that they shall be kindly received and supported, and live together in one Place, the most convenient that can be got for the Purpose.

Or as there is now a strong Fort at *Shamokin,* built at the Request of your Uncles, the *Six Nations,* for the Protection of the Friendly *Indians,* I propose to have a Store of Goods in it, the Direction and Management of which will be given to an honest Man, who shall not be suffered to impose upon the *Indians;* and I shall be glad all our Friendly *Indians,* who are scattered and distressed in these troublesome Times, will come and live near it; there they will be protected from the *French;* there they will have a large uninhabited Country to hunt in; and there they may be furnished with Clothes, and all other Necessaries of Life, at the easiest Rates.

*A String.*

*Brother,* You know that at the last Treaty the Road was opened for us to go to each other; I now give you this Belt to preserve the Communication free and clear of all Obstructions, let there be nothing in it that can hurt the Feet, or wound the Body of either.

*A Belt.*

*Brother,* Since I set out, I have heard of the Death of several of our *Indian* Friends by the Smallpox at *Philadelphia,* and particularly Captain *Newcastle* is dead, who was very instrumental, and joined with you as Agent, in carrying on this good Work of Peace. I wipe away your Tears; I take the Grief from your Hearts; I cover the Graves; eternal Rest be with their Spirits.

*A String of Wampum, eleven black Strouds, with some Handkerchiefs.*

*Brother,* Peace is now settled between us by the Assistance of the Most High; but the *Indians* in the *French* Interest still commit Murders on our Frontiers, and our Soldiers are in Pursuit of them. I desire you will order your young Men not to straggle about, but keep in the straight Path to your Towns, so that they may not be mistaken by our Soldiers for *French Indians.*

*Teedyuscung* thanked the Governor for his kind Speeches, and said, he was very glad that the Governor had thought of sending two Messengers with him for the Prisoners, and promised to assist them.

After the Condolance made on Captain *Newcastle*'s Death, the King made an Address as is usual to the other *Indians* on this mournful Occasion: They continued silent for some Time, and then one of the oldest of them spoke an Exhortation, in the Nature of a Funeral Oration; after which *Teedyuscung* expressed to the Governor, the great Satisfaction given to him at his condoling the Death of Captain *Newcastle,* who, he said, was a good Man, and had promoted the good Work of Peace with great Care; his Death would put him in Mind of his Duty, as it should all of us.

He then spoke in a warm and pathetick Manner in Favour of the Peace now settled, and implored the Assistance of the Most High to bring it to Perfection.

The Governor understanding that several of the *Indians* inclined to stay, desired *Teedyuscung* to give him the Names of such as would live with their Brethren the *English.—Teedyuscung,* mistaking the Governor, as if he had said, they must stay, answered, smiling, he did not understand any *Indians* were to be forced to stay, but left to their Liberty. If the Governor wanted any to stay, and desired it, he would stay himself, and his Wife and Family with him. The Governor set the Matter Right, thanked him, and wished him well; took his Leave of him, saying, they had met and parted Friends, and he hoped they would meet again as good Friends as now.

*Teedyuscung* shewed great Pleasure in his Countenance, and took a kind Leave of the Governor and all present.

*By his Honour's Command,*
RICHARD PETERS, Secretary.

*EXTRACT from the Minutes of the House of* REPRESENTATIVES *of the Province of* Pennsylvania, January 29, 1757.

"The four Provincial Commissioners, Members of this House, who were appointed to attend the Governor at the late Conference with the *Indians* at *Easton,* presented a Paper to the House, which was read, and is as follows," *viz.*

WE the Committee appointed to attend the Governor at the Conferences with the *Indians* at *Easton,* in *November* last, have perused the Copy of those Conferences, drawn up and signed by the Secretary, and laid before the House;

And as we apprehend it of Importance to the Province, that the Complaints made by the *Indians,* whether justly founded or not, should be fully represented, and their Sense of them understood, we think it necessary to observe to the House, that we conceive the Warmth and Earnestness with which they insisted on the Wrongs that had been done them in the Purchases of Land, are much too faintly expressed in this Account of the Conference. That we were not present at the palliating Hearsay Accounts of the Walking Purchase, said to be to given the Governor by Mr. *Weiser* and Mr. *Peters,* on the Fourteenth of *November;* tho', by the concluding Paragraphs under that Date, it may seem as if we were: But we well remember, that the Transaction of that Walk was at *Easton* universally given up as unfair, and not to be defended, even from the Accounts of some of our own People who were present at the Walking; even the Secretary, tho' he did say, that he *believed* Satisfaction was afterwards made the

*Indians,* and that this was the only Instance in which any Foundation of Complaint had ever been given them, yet this he allowed was (in his own Words) *unworthy of any Government.* We would farther observe, that when *Teedyuscung* claimed the Lands, even those on which the Conferences were held, no Objection was made, that neither he, nor any with him, had any Right to them; nor did we ever understand his Reason for not accepting Satisfaction to be as represented in the second Paragraph under *November* 17, for that "*the People* to whom the Land belonged were absent;"—but for that many of them were absent, and those who were absent had not impowered him to act for them in that Matter; but he would endeavour to bring them in the Spring.

The Offer of the Commissioners to furnish the Means of making the *Indians* immediate Satisfaction, not being fully related, we think it necessary to add, That the Reasons we gave the Governor for that Offer, were, 1. The Absence and great Distance of the Proprietaries, who being the sole Purchasers of Land from the *Indians* in this Province, ought, if the *Indians* were injured in such Purchases, alone to make the Satisfaction; but their Agents here had not the necessary Powers. 2. For that Promises [such being proposed] of enquiring into *Indian* Complaints, and doing them Right hereafter, had been so often made in other Governments, and so little observed, we imagined they could be of no Weight, and would rather be looked upon as a Denial of Justice; and therefore, we thought it better, as their Demands are seldom very high, to make them immediate Reparation for the Injuries they supposed they had received, and we would furnish the Goods, and risque the Proprietaries repaying their Value to the Province. The Secretary then told us, that he thought our Proposal very considerate and well-judged; that he was sure the Proprietaries would think themselves obliged to us, and repay the Money with Thanks: The Offer was accordingly made, but not accepted for the Reasons abovementioned. We then waited upon the Governor in a Body, and acquainted his Honour, That as we had made the Offer in Behalf of the Province, not from an Opinion that the Province ought to be at such Expence, but from the apparent immediate Necessity of the Thing, and on Account of the Proprietaries Absence as aforesaid; so now since the final Settlement of the *Indians* Claims was postponed to the Spring, and there would be sufficient Time to write to the Proprietaries and obtain their Orders to their Agents for the Payment of such Sums as should be found necessary, we looked on ourselves and the Province as totally disengaged from that Offer, and expected that the Proprietaries would be wrote to accordingly.[17]

*January* 29, 1757. Benjamin Franklin, Joseph Fox,
William Masters, John Hughes.

*A true Extract from the Minutes,*
William Franklin, *Clerk of Assembly.*

1. In April 1756, Pennsylvania had declared war on the Lenapes, put a price on scalps of Lenape men (130 dollars) and women (fifty dollars), issued bounties for their capture, and sent

a war belt to the League to ally with them against the Lenapes (Boyd, *Indian Treaties,* lxxii, lxxiv; Miller, *Philadelphia Printing,* 357). Franklin printed only the bounties, but in January had issued orders to one of Pennsylvania's companies that guaranteed forty dollars for the scalps of Indian enemies. At the time, he favored military rather than political responses to the Lenapes' attacks (Labaree, *Papers of Benjamin Franklin,* 6:354; Jennings, *Benjamin Franklin,* 143). On June 3, 1756, Governor Morris issued a proclamation calling for a cessation of hostilities against the Lenapes (Miller, *Philadelphia Printing,* 357). The latter proclamation came at the pressure of William Johnson and New York, who were furious not only that Pennsylvania had acted at cross purposes to their endeavors for peace but that the Quakers had sent the Six Nations a peace belt (and therefore not only meddled in business Johnson considered his prerogative but conveyed a mixed message regarding Pennsylvania's stance and leadership) (Wallace, *Conrad Weiser,* 437; Boyd, "Indian Affairs," lxxii–lxxiv). The leadership of the Assembly had passed into Anglican hands in 1756 as a result of anti-Quaker propaganda, both secretly and openly supported by Thomas Penn, which forced several Quaker Assemblymen to resign (Jennings, *Ambiguous Iroquois Empire,* 390; Jennings, *Benjamin Franklin,* 136–42). Their continued involvement in Indian affairs constituted a successful effort to maintain political influence in a climate hostile to their principles.

In the first wave of attacks that had hit the settlers outside of Pennsylvania's rightful borders in October 1755, some of the victims were "Paxton People above Hunters Mill" (Wallace, *Conrad Weiser,* 400). The war probably set the stage for the Paxton Boys incidents of the 1760s. As a result of the attacks, settlement in present-day Northampton, Berks, and Cumberland Counties receded toward the Pennsylvania border, and at least two settlements were completely wiped out (Boyd, *Indian Treaties,* lxx).

2. The succession of treaties from 1756 until 1762 will show how much at odds were the fundamental philosophies of British and Native Americans regarding prisoners. In most Indian nations, prisoners who were not killed were adopted into the nation as members and served to fill the place of relatives who had died. Often British subjects who underwent such adoption found that they preferred citizenship in their new nation to subjecthood in the British empire, particularly if they had been indentured servants or very young at the time of adoption.

3. When the term *king* is used to describe any Native American including Teedyuscung, it is inaccurate. The term *king* really refers to chiefs or sachems, who might come to office through heredity but who probably never held an office solely because of descent from a "royal" father. It appears, however, that the assertion of the title of king may be an attempt to emphasize to the British the principle of the equality of nations and the commensurability of their leaders in terms of authority to govern their nation.

4. The fact that Teedyuscung gives an immediate answer to Pennsylvania's overtures, here and elsewhere, may indicate a difference in Lenape philosophies and political practices regarding consensus, deliberation, and council protocol. It may, however, illustrate his inexperience.

Some contemporary observers believed that Weiser altered Teedyuscung's words to give the impression that he had claimed to be speaking for the League without authorization. Though this appears to be the case in later treaties, Teedyuscung's explanation that he had been in council with the Six Nations, who had deputed him to come to Easton at the time that Pennsylvania made contact with them regarding peace efforts, is detailed enough to be plausible. It is most likely that Weiser built his deceptions on the basis of factual circumstances.

This treaty is the first where Teedyuscung's rhetoric regarding the inadequacy of the Lenape's ancestors and their diplomacy appears. It seems a radical switch from the first several treaties, during which the Iroquois proudly display their skills at oral recall and their savvy in diplomatic matters. The "ancestors" to whom Teedyuscung refers are not the Lenapes themselves but the Iroquois, or those factions of the League that allied themselves with Pennsylvania in the 1730s to assert ascendancy over the Lenapes. It will become clear that certain other League factions agree with Teedyuscung in his critique, though they will deflect the blame away from themselves and toward Pennsylvania.

5. This passage is one of many that encouraged the linguistic hypothesis among Europeans that native languages could express much in few words.

6. Denny went to Easton under military guard because Teedyuscung refused to come to Philadelphia to meet him (Boyd, "Indian Affairs," lxxx). The act may have raised eyebrows in the Lenape delegation. The Lenapes placed a high value upon freedom of speech. The attempt to negotiate with others in the presence of arms was antithetical to that freedom (John Heckewelder, *History, Manners, and Customs of the Indian Nations who once Inhabited Pennsylvania and the Neighbouring States* (1819) (Philadelphia: Historical Society of Pennsylvania, 1876: 185–86). Iroquoian law proscribed the protection of peace delegations from other nations against attack during travel to and from negotiations (Mann, "Are You Delusional?," 39).

7. Franklin wrote the paragraph that was added to the answer. The Lenapes responded "jubilantly" when Denny asked the question. Israel "Pemberton saw such joy in their faces as he could not express. They "hurried across the Benches to offer the Governor their hands. One of them cry'd out, Oh! He is a good Man, there is no Evil in his Heart'" (Jennings, *Empire of Fortune*, 279). Pemberton was the leading Quaker in the Friendly Association for Regaining and Preserving Peace with the Indians by Pacific Measures. He is to be largely credited with bringing about the eventual peace, despite working in the background and through men like Franklin who were at first skeptical of the "pacific measures" he advocated.

8. If the pacing of this condolence and others seems too rapid for a kind of funeral ceremony, it is because a written text cannot capture the physical gestures, the pauses, and the spatial arrangement of the participants. The text abbreviates what was possibly a lengthy ceremony spaced by significant silences.

9. Broadhead had indeed been entrusted with a message from the governor, but it was not the message that Teedyuscung received. He was supposed to have gone to Wyoming to invite the Eastern Lenapes to a meeting in Pennsylvania, but before he left, his plantation had been attacked. It appears he blamed the attack on them.

10. Although Teedyuscung's speech is translated and recorded using the first person singular pronoun "I," it is likely that he speaks for the Eastern Lenapes or the Lenapes as a whole. Speakers of Algonquin and Iroquoian languages frequently use a grammatical form that conveys both the "I" and the "we" of the English language. Otherwise, he would be contradicting his denial to Broadhead in the previous paragraph, an unlikely possibility.

11. This speech is considered one of the most dramatic of this series of treaties, and is often quoted.

12. Clearly, the man who died was William Penn, and the children who forged the deed his sons. The "Kings" appear to be Nutimus and Mechkilikishu. Denny will later interpret them as the League and the Lenapes, possibly after the intervention by Weiser.

13. Note the absence of the commissioners. This would become the bone of the dispute over the accuracy of these minutes, mentioned in the final paragraphs.

14. Teedyuscung is likely not conceding to the British that writing preserves events with more accuracy than oral tradition. Rather, experience, the Indian grapevine, or the Quakers have probably tipped Teedyuscung off to the fact that the written documents do not cor-

respond accurately to the mutual agreements made between Pennsylvania and the Indian nations.

15. Though Pennsylvanians saw themselves as *giving* to the Indians without true reciprocity, Native Americans probably saw both parties as engaged in *gifting*. In noncapitalist societies, it is not unusual for the wealthier person to be expected to display greater largess, but the exchange is still seen as an act of reciprocity.

16. Note that the commissioners are apparently absent, though they are reported in the minutes as being present. Had they entered this council midway through the proceedings? See the note to November 14, 1756, above.

17. This extract is the second of two extraordinary addenda to the set of fourteen treaties that Franklin printed. It bears the mark of his personal intervention. The Assembly ordered this extract printed with the minutes when they sent it to Franklin's press, but as Franklin was an active member of that Assembly at the time, the order should not be seen as the result of an impersonal process (Labaree, *Papers of Benjamin Franklin,* 7:112). See also the last endnote to the 1753 treaty.

✠

# MINUTES OF CONFERENCES,

## HELD WITH THE *INDIANS*,

## At HARRIS'S FERRY, and at LANCASTER,

### In *March*, *April*, and *May*, 1757

*PHILADELPHIA:*
Printed and Sold by B. FRANKLIN, and D. HALL,
at the *New-Printing-Office*, near the Market. MDCCLVII.

## MINUTES OF CONFERENCES, &c.

*From* George Croghan, *Esq; to the Honourable Sir* WILLIAM JOHNSON, *Baronet, His MAJESTY's sole Agent, and Superintendent of the Affairs of the* Six Nations, *their Allies* and *Dependents.*[1]

*May it please your Honour,* IN Pursuance of your Instructions, as soon as I was informed of the *Indians* being come to *John Harris*'s, I set off from *Philadelphia* to meet them, and arrived at *John Harris*'s the 29th of *March*, 1757, where I met about One Hundred and Sixty *Indians*, Men, Women and Children, Part of eight Tribes.

The Thirtieth, I examined *Joseph Peepy*, and *Lewis Montour*, in regard to the Messages I had sent by them to the *Sasquehannah Indians.*[2]

They informed me, that *Teedyuscung* was gone to the *Seneca* Country, to get a Number of the *Senecas* to come down with him; and they delivered me a Belt of Wampum sent me by *Teedyuscung*, in Return of mine sent him by them; by which Belt he informs me that he will be down as soon as possible, with Two Hundred *Indians*, but could not tell, whether he would come in at *Easton* or at *John Harris*'s.

The remaining Part of this Day I spent in getting what Intelligence I could of the Strength of the *French* on *Ohio*, and the Disposition of the *Delawares* and *Shawanese;* and by the best Accounts I can get, I find the *French* have not had above Three Hundred Men in Garrison at *Ohio* this Winter, and that the *Delawares* and

*Shawanese* on *Ohio* were divided amongst themselves, one Half of each Tribe going down *Ohio* to where the Lower *Shawanese* are settled, and the other Half were determined to go off to the *Six Nations.*

I am informed, that all the *Sasquehanna Indians* are disposed for Peace, except the *Munseys,* or *Minisink Indians;* yet I understand that a Number of them will be down with *Teedyuscung.*

I am informed, by a *Six Nation Indian,* one of Reputation amongst them, that resided at *Diahogo,* that as soon as *Joseph Peepy* and *Lewis Montour* had delivered their Message there, the Council, that Night, dispatched two Men to the *Ohio,* to inform the *Delawares* and *Shawanese,* living there, of this Meeting, desiring some of them to come to it; but if none of them should chuse to come, these Messengers were then to insist that none of the *Delawares* and *Shawanese,* living on the *Ohio,* should come to War against the *English* till this Meeting was over, and they have Time, after returning Home, to let them know how it ended.

*At a MEETING of the* Six Nations *and their Allies, and* George Croghan, *Esq; Deputy Agent to the Honourable* Sir William Johnson, *Baronet, His Majesty's sole Agent and Superintendent of the Affairs of the* Six Nations, *their Allies and Dependents, and by his special Order, at* John Harris's *the First Day of* April, 1757.

PRESENT, The Reverend Mr. *John Elder,* Captain *Thomas McKee,*
Mr. *James Armstrong,* Mr. *Hugh Crawford,* Mr. *John Harris.*
*William Prentup,* Interpreter.

Mohawks.[3] *Tiahansorea, Cannadagaughia, Sogehoanna, Peter,* With 31 others, Men, Women and Children.

Oneidoes. *Thomas King, Scarroyady, Tawnaquanagis,* With Thirteen others, Men, Women and Children.

Tuscaroras. *Rut King,* With Twenty-six others, Men, Women and Children.

Onondagoes. *Ossaratonqua,* and his two Brothers, with Eighteen others, Men, Women and Children.

Cayugas. *Ogaratawrea, Orarroquare, Jenkasarone,* With 20 others, Men, Women and Children.

Senecas. *George,* With Eight more, Men, Women and Children.

Nanticokes. *Robert White, Joshua,* With Eleven more, Men, Women and Children.

Delawares. *Samuel, Joseph Peepy, Thomas Evans, Jonathan,* with 20 more, Men, Women and Children.

Connestogoes. *Sahays,* Captain *John,* With Twenty-nine more, Men, Women and Children.

*Brethren,* I AM sent here by the Honourable Sir WILLIAM JOHNSON, to represent him at this Meeting; and I desire you all to give Attention to what I am going to say to you in Behalf of your Brother *Onas* and the wise Men of this Government, who are truly sensible of your Afflictions, occasioned by the Death of many of your Counsellors and Warriors, since they had the Pleasure of seeing you in this Government; and as they have ever looked upon your Misfortunes as their own, they mix their Tears with yours, and have desired me to condole with you, agreeable to the antient Custom of our Forefathers.

*Gave a Belt.*

*Brethren,* With this Belt of Wampum I wipe the Blood off the Seats round your Council Fire, that your old Men at this critical Juncture, when convened in Council, may sit with Comfort, and direct their Warriors with Wisdom.

*Gave a Belt.*

*Brethren,* As I have wiped the Blood off the Seats round your Council Fire, I, with these Strouds, wrap up the Bodies of your deceased Friends, and bury them decently, covering their Graves with these Blankets and Halfthicks.

*Gave the Goods.*

*Brethren,* As the Blood is wiped off the Seats of your Counsellors, the Dead decently buried, and their Graves covered, I, with this Belt of Wampum, wipe the Tears from your Eyes, and desire you may mourn no more.

*Gave a Belt.*

*Brethren,* As you are now out of Mourning, I with this Belt of Wampum disperse the dark Clouds which are gathered over your Heads, that you may see the Sun clear, and shake Hands with your Brethren when you meet in Council.

*Gave a Belt.*

*Brethren,* As we have now gone through the antient Customs used by our Forefathers upon their Meeting, I with this Belt of Wampum heal your Hearts, and free your Minds from Trouble, that we may meet each other in Council, and brighten the Chain of Friendship.

*Gave a Belt.*

*Brethren,* I now wipe the Sweat off your Bodies after your long Journey, and bid you a hearty Welcome to this Government in the Name of your Brother *Onas.*

*Gave a String.*

*Sachems and Warriors of the* Six United Nations, *our Friends and Brethren,* I embrace this Opportunity of acquainting you, that last Year your Brother *Onas* held two Conferences at *Easton* with your Nephews the *Delawares,* and your Brethren the *Shawanese,* that live on *Sasquehannah,* in order to settle the Differences subsisting between them and us; but as that good Work could not be accomplished at that Time, they agreed to have a Meeting this Spring to finally settle all Differences subsisting between them and us their Brethren: And that this Meeting might be the more general, I dispatched Messengers up *Sasquehannah,* and to *Ohio,* and I wrote to your Brother, Sir *William Johnson,* desiring him to request a Number of you our Brethren, the *Six United Nations,* to be present at this Meeting, who I am heartily glad to see here; and when your Nephews and Brothers arrive, I am in great Hopes, by your Assistance, to be able to accommodate Matters to the mutual Satisfaction of both them and us their Brethren the *English* in the several Governments.

And by this Belt of Wampum, I request you to make use of all your Interest with your Nephews the *Delawares,* and Brothers the *Shawanese,* to bring about an Accommodation between them and us, that the Sun may once more shine upon us in Peace, and that the Peace may last as long as the Sun, the Moon and the Stars give Light.

*Gave a Belt.*

*At a* MEETING *with the* Indians, *at* John Harris's, April 2, *1757.*
PRESENT, The Reverend Mr. *Elder,* Captain *Thomas McKee,*
Mr. *James Armstrong,* Mr. *Hugh Crawford,* Mr. *John Harris.*
The Deputies of the *Six United Nations,* The *Delawares,* and *Nanticokes.*
*Scarroyady,* Speaker for the *Indians. William Prentup,* Interpreter.

*Brother,* YOU and our Brother *Onas* wisely considered the antient Custom of our Forefathers, in condoling with us, and mixing your Grief with ours: And as we make no Doubt but some of your wise Counsellors are dead since we were here, and many of our Brethren have been killed by the evil Spirit, we wipe the Blood off your Council Seats, and put them in Order with this Belt of Wampum.

*Gave a Belt.*

*Brother,* After wiping the Blood off your Council-Seats, we, with these few Skins, wrap up the Bones of our Brethren that died or were killed by the evil Spirit, and cover their Graves.

*Gave a small Bundle of Skins.*

*Brother,* We, by this Belt of Wampum, wipe the Tears from your Eyes, and desire you may mourn no more.

*Gave a Belt.*

*Brother,* We, with this Belt of Wampum, disperse the dark Clouds, that the Sun may always shine upon us in Friendship; we heal your Heart, and free your Mind from Trouble, that we may meet each other in Council, and brighten the Chain of Friendship made by our Forefathers; and that the Council Fire may burn clear, we throw a few Chips on it.

*Gave a Belt.*

This Evening I had a Meeting of the Sachems, and proposed the Going to *Philadelphia,* to hold the Treaty; but I could prevail on none of them, except the *Mohawks,* to go there; the rest were afraid of Sickness.

When I found they were not to be prevailed on to go there, I called a Council, and, with a Belt of Wampum, I removed the Council Fire to *Lancaster;* to which Place they all agreed to go, and wait the Arrival of *Teedyuscung,* with the *Senecas, Delawares,* and *Shawanese.*

*Gave a Belt, to remove the Council Fire to* Lancaster.

*April* the 7th, I arrived at *Lancaster* from *John Harris*'s; from whence Mr. *Shippen,* Mr. *Thompson,* Mr. *Boude,* and Captain *Cane,* with a Number of other Gentlemen, Inhabitants of that Borough, went out with me to meet the *Indians* (who I had left a few Miles behind) to bid them welcome to *Lancaster.*

As soon as the *Indians* were settled at the Place taken for them by *James Wright,* Esq; I then kindled a small Fire for them to sit by till they should hear from their Brother *Onas* of the Arrival of *Teedyuscung.*

*April* the 10th, I received a Letter from his Honour the Governor, acquainting me of the Arrival of Fifty *Delawares* and *Shawanese* at *Fort-Allen,* and that they were ordered to wait there the Arrival of *Teedyuscung,* with the rest of the *Indians* who were coming with him.

I immediately ordered a Meeting of the *Indians,* and acquainted them with what the Governor had wrote me about the Arrival of the *Delawares* and *Shawanese* at *Fort-Allen,* which was very agreeable to them.

I then acquainted them, by a Belt of Wampum, that their Brother *Onas* had prepared a very convenient Place for them within a Mile of *Philadelphia,* and that he proposed to hold the Conference at *Philadelphia,* as *Teedyuscung* had, at the last Treaty at *Easton,* given his Honour the Governor a Promise to come to *Philadelphia* this Spring.

*The* Indians, *after considering what had been said to them,*
*returned the following Answer.*

*Brother,* We have considered what you said to us from our Brother *Onas;* when you proposed to us, at *John Harris*'s, to go to *Philadelphia,* we refused for the Reasons we then gave you. By the Message you sent us by *Joseph Peepy* and *Lewis Montour,* we understood that the *Delawares* and *Shawanese* were to fix the Place of Meeting where they thought proper.

*Brother,* We tell you we will sit where we are till they arrive and fix the Place of Meeting with our Brother *Onas.*

*Returned the Belt of Wampum.*

*April* the 11th, I delivered the Goods purchased by *James Wright,* Esq; for the *Indians,* in the Presence of Mr. *James Webb,* which was well received by them.

After the Goods were divided, the Chiefs of the several Tribes came in a Body, and returned Thanks to the Government for the Cloathing they had received.

The 13th, the several Chiefs came to me, and told me, they observed that I gave no Cloathing to our Brothers the *Connestogoes,* and desired that I would give them some, else they should be obliged to give them Part of what had been given them.

*Gave a String.*

The 17th, I called a Meeting of all the *Indians,* and returned them Thanks for condoling with me at *John Harris*'s for the Loss we their Brethren the *English* had sustained by Death and the evil Spirit.

*Brethren,* I return you Thanks for mixing your Grief with ours, and wiping the Blood off our Council Seats.

*Gave a Belt.*

*Brethren,* I give you Thanks for wrapping up the Bones of our deceased Brothers, and covering the Graves, and wiping the Tears from our Eyes.

*Gave a Belt.*

*Brethren,* I return you Thanks for dispersing the dark Clouds from over our Heads, for healing our Hearts, and freeing our Minds from Trouble; and for brightening the Chain of Friendship made by our Forefathers.

*Gave a Belt.*

*April* the 20th, I received a Letter from his Honour Governor *Denny,* inclosing two Messages from *Teedyuscung* to the Governor, which were delivered to Major *Parsons* in *Easton* and forwarded by him.

As soon as I received his Honour's Letter, I called a Meeting of the *Indians,* and repeated over to them the Messages, and let them know, that *Teedyuscung*'s being so long detained on the Way was the Scarcity of Provisions; and then acquainted them, that his Honour the Governor had ordered a Supply to be sent to meet them, for which the *Indians* returned his Honour the Governor their hearty Thanks, and said, their Brother *Onas*'s sending Provisions to meet their Cousins on the Road, was giving them the strongest Assurances of his Regard and Esteem for them.

*Gave a String of Wampum.*

*April* the 23d, Six *Onondago* Warriors applied to me for Liberty to go to *Fort Cumberland,* to join the Southward *Indians,* who they understood were going to

War against His Majesty's Enemies at *Ohio;* I granted their Request, and fitted them out for their Journey.

*April* the 26th, *Scarroyady,* with a Party of *Mohawk* Warriors, came and told me that they were apprehensive the *French* would make some Attempt against *Fort-Augusta,* and desired I would fit them out to go there; to which I agreed, giving them Orders to reconnoitre the adjacent Woods, for a few Days, then to proceed towards the *Ohio,* and to reconnoitre the Country well as they went, and if they discovered any Body of *French,* or Parties of *Indians,* coming towards *Fort-Augusta,* or any Part of this or the neighbouring Governments, they were immediately to return and give Notice to the Commanding Officer at *Fort-Augusta,* or to the Commanding Officer of the Fort nighest to that Part of the Country where they should come into.

The 26th of *April, P. M.* the Chiefs of the several Tribes called a Meeting, and sent for me, and desired to know what Time they might expect their Brother *Onas* up, and their Nephews the *Delawares,* and Brothers the *Shawanese,* to hold the Conference.

To which I answered, I had not yet received any certain Account of the Arrival of the *Delawares* and *Shawanese;* and until the Governor had fixed the Place and Time of Meeting with *Teedyuscung,* I could not give them a full Answer.

To which *Little Abraham,* a *Mohawk* Sachem, spoke as follows, in Behalf of the Whole.

*Brother,* We have been here a great while, and the Spring is coming on fast: It is Time for us to think of going Home to plant. We have heard what you have said to us from our Brother *Onas,* both at *John Harris*'s and here, that our Brother *Onas* proposed to hold the Treaty at *Philadelphia.* Every Time you spoke to us upon that Head, we gave you our Objections against going so far down, which we expected would have been considered before now; but as our Brother *Onas* has not yet agreed to come here, we have determined in our own Minds to treat with our Brother *Onas* here, and go no further down the Country.

*Brother,* We have appointed three Men to go to *Philadelphia* to speak with our Brother *Onas,* and request of him to come up, and we desire you will find Horses for them to ride down, and a Man to go with them to the Governor.

And we have appointed three more to go and meet our Nephews the *Delawares,* and Brothers the *Shawanese* and bring them here, and we desire you will find them Horses, and a Man to go and take Care of them, and provide Necessaries for them on the Road.

*Gave a String.*

*May* the 5th, *P. M.* Captain *Trent* returned from *Bethlehem,* with the Deputies that went from here to meet the *Delawares* and *Shawanese,* and brought with them four *Delaware* Men, and one Woman.

About two Hours afterwards, Captain McKee returned from *Philadelphia,* with the Deputies who were sent down to the Governor to invite him here to hold the Conference.

*May* the 6th, I called a Meeting of the Chiefs of the several Tribes, when *William Logan,* Esq; a Member of his Honour the Governor's Council, returned the Governor's Answer to the Message sent him by *Thomas King,* and *Rut King.*

*Brethren, the Deputies of the* Six United Nations, *and your Cousins and Brethren the* Delawares, I am sent to you by your Brother *Onas,* from *Philadelphia,* as a Member of his Council, and your very good Friend, and I desire you will attend to what I am now going to say to you, and consider my Words as if they were spoken by *Onas* himself.

*Gave a String.*

*Brethren,* A few Days since, *Thomas King,* and *Rut King,* accompanied by *Thomas McKee,* as their Guide, came to me in *Philadelphia,* and informed me, by this Belt of Wampum, that you held a Council Fire at *Lancaster,* and had sent for our Friend *George Croghan* to it, and had made a Speech to him; in which you acquainted him, that on his Invitation you came to *John Harris*'s, understanding the Council Fire was to be kindled there; that after you had staid there some Time, you were desired to accompany him to *Lancaster,* and that I would meet you there; that therefore you had appointed these two *Indians* to wait on me, and to take me by the Hand, and invite me to your Council; that you had determined among yourselves to come no further, and would be glad to see me, and that my coming would rejoice your Hearts.

*Brethren,* You must be very sensible that in the transacting Publick Affairs, in these troublesome Times, many Difficulties and unforeseen Accidents happen which require my particular Attendance in *Philadelphia;* this is my present Case. And as *Teedyuscung,* the Chief of the *Delawares,* our Countryman, and your Cousin, with some other Chiefs and Head Men, of that Nation, has sent me lately a Message, acquainting me, that he was on his Way, with a great Number of *Indians,* coming to meet me, in order to finish the Treaty of Peace begun last Year by our late Governor and myself with the said Chiefs, and desired me to be ready with my Counsellors to assist in finishing the said Treaty which was so happily begun, and that I would be so kind as to send for *Moses Tatamy,* and *John Pumpshire* (two *Delaware Indian* Interpreters) from the *Jerseys,* to be present; and that as there was so great a Number of *Indians* who were coming with him, they would want Provisions on their Way, and desired I would send some to *Wyoming* for them, which I immediately complied with. These, Brethren, have been the Reason for my delaying my Journey to meet you at *Lancaster,* and for my desiring *George Croghan* would endeavour to prevail on you our Brethren to come to the Council Fire at *Philadelphia,* where the old wise People, who are your hearty Friends, would have been exceeding glad to see you; and as I have heard nothing from *Teedyuscung* very lately, I am uneasy lest some

Accident has happened to him. I thank you very kindly for your affectionate Invitation: I accept of it, and will, with great Pleasure, come and consult with you at your Council Fire at *Lancaster.*

*Gave a Belt of eight Rows.*

*May* the 9th, three of the Messengers I sent to the *Ohio* returned, and make the following Report.

That on their Arrival at *Venango* (an old *Indian* Town) on *Ohio,* they found several of the *Delawares* there, one, named *Castalago,* their Chief. They immediately called a Meeting, and delivered the Speeches sent by them, which were very well received by the *Delawares;* who told them, in Answer, That they would accept of the Invitation, and come down with them; but that they must first go and consult their Uncles the *Senecas,* who lived further up the River. The next Day they set off to a little Town further up the River *Ohio,* where they summoned a Number of the *Delawares* and *Senecas* together. After repeating the Messages over, one of the *Senecas,* named *Garistagee,* one of the Chiefs, said to the *Delawares;* Nephews, You must not accept of that Call, for the Belts which are sent you are not proper Belts on this Occasion. I know *George Croghan* very well, and would be very glad to see him; and if he will send a proper Belt, with Men wrought in it, for the several Tribes he wants to meet with (himself taking us by the Hand) made of old Council wampum, which is the Custom of the *Six Nations* on these Occasions, I will go down with you and see him: To which the *Delawares* agreed, and then returned the Belts.

They say that one of the Messengers proceeded further, to where the *Delawares,* that lived formerly at *Kittanning,* were now settled, on *Beaver-Creek,* with a View of finding out the Dispositions of them; and they expect he will be soon down, if not killed. These Messengers say, that there were but fifteen *Frenchmen* at *Venango,* and that the Fort there is very weak; and that the *Indians* in them Parts are very much distressed for Provisions.

They say that the *Ohio Indians* are much afraid of the Southern *Indians,* having been struck three Times by them this Spring, twice near *Fort Du Quesne,* and once at the *Logs-Town;* and that the *Indians* are moving fast up the *Ohio* towards the *Senecas.*[4]

They heard from the *Indians* there, that the *French* were defeated at *Fort William-Henry,* and that there was another Party defeated by Sir *William Johnson,* at the *German-Flats;* and the *French* were determined yet to make another Trial against the *English,* but that they could not tell where they intended to strike next.

They say the two Men killed at Fort *Augusta,* were killed by the *Delawares* and *French,* which was the only Party of *Delawares* or *Shawanese* that has come against us this Spring; that the other Parties that have been on the Frontiers of this and the neighbouring Provinces, were *Indians* from over the Lakes; that the *Delawares* made great Game of the Lake *Indians,* and told those Messengers, that one Party of them, who had been down, had, on their Return, killed and eat three of the *English* Prisoners, for want of Food; that there was an Account came there whilst they were at *Venango,* that the *French Conewagas* had differed with the *French,* because the *French* would not supply them with Provisions; the Difference rose so high at last, that they came to Blows; that Sixty of the *Conewagas* were killed, and a great Number of the *French.*

I quere the Truth of this News, as the *French* undoubtedly know their Interest too well to differ with the *Conewagas* at this Time.

These Messengers, on their Return, touched at *Diahogo,* where they met with *Teedyuscung,* who enquired of them what they had been doing at *Ohio;* they repeated over to him the Messages that had been sent by them from this Government, and the Answer they had received from the *Ohio Indians;* on which *Teedyuscung* sent the following Message by them to their Brother *Onas* and me.

*Brothers,* YOU have been at a great deal of Trouble in sending Messages to us, your Brothers the *Delawares* and *Shawanese;* but the Persons you employed are young Warriors, and not Counsellors, therefore unfit for such Business; likewise the Belts you have sent, in Comparison, are no more than Strings; but if you will send to call us together, and send proper Belts, and wise Men to take us by the Hand, we will come down with them, and give you a Meeting. In which Meeting I hope we shall settle all Differences subsisting between us; and I assure you, by this Belt of Wampum, that our Minds are well disposed, and that our Hearts are warm and true towards you our Brothers the *English;* and we desire that you, as Messengers from our Brothers, may take this Belt to Capt. *Thomas McKee,* and let him deliver it in our Name to our Brother *Onas* and *George Croghan.*

*Gave the Belt.*

*Brothers,* There is one Thing that gives us a great deal of Concern, which is, our Flesh and Blood that lives among you at *Bethlehem,* and in the *Jerseys,* being kept as if they were Prisoners. We formerly applied to the Minister at *Bethlehem,* to let our People come back at Times and hunt, which is the chief Industry we follow to maintain our Families; but that Minister has not listened to what we have said to him, and it is very hard that our People have not the Liberty of coming back to the Woods, where Game is plenty, and to see their Friends.

They have complained to us, that they cannot hunt where they are; and if they go into the Woods, and cut down a Tree, they are abused for it, notwithstanding that very Land we look upon to be our own; and we hope, Brothers, that you will consider this Matter, and let our People come into the Woods, and visit their Friends, and pass and repass, as Brothers ought to do.

*Gave a String.*

*Lancaster, Monday, May* the 9th, This Evening the Honourable WILLIAM DENNY, Esq; Governor of this Province, attended by a Number of his Council, a

Number of the House of Representatives, the Commissioners for the Province, with a great Number of other Gentlemen, arrived here.

*May* the 10th, The Sachems of the several Tribes, with a Number of their chief Warriors waited on the Governor at Mr. *George Gibson*'s, in *Lancaster;* when the Governor, with the Gentlemen that attended him, took them by the Hands, bid them welcome, and his Honour made them the following Speech.

*Brethren,* I give you a very hearty Welcome, agreeable to my Message by Mr. *Logan.* I have waited all this Time at *Philadelphia,* expecting the Arrival of *Teedyuscung,* as the principal Business to be transacted at this Meeting is between this Government and your Cousins the *Delawares* and *Shawanese;* but receiving your kind Invitation, I have hastened here, and am glad to see you.

*At a* MEETING *in the Court-House, in the Town of* Lancaster,
*on* Thursday, *the* 12*th of* May, 1757, P. M.
PRESENT, The Honourable *WILLIAM DENNY,* Esq; Lieutenant-
Governor of the Province of Pennsylvania, and Counties of *New-Castle,*
*Kent* and *Sussex,* on *Delaware.*
*James Hamilton, William Logan, Richard Peters, Lyn-Ford Lardner,*
*John Mifflin, Benjamin Chew,* Esquires, Members of
the Governor's Council.
*Isaac Norris, William Masters, Joseph Galloway, John Baynton,*
*George Ashbridge, William West,* Esquires, the Speaker,
and Committee of the House of Representatives.
The Magistrates of the Borough,
with a great Number of other Gentlemen.
The Deputies of the *Mohawks, Oneidoes, Tuscaroras, Onondagoes,*
*Cayugas,* with some *Senecas, Nanticokes,* and *Delawares.*
*William Prentup,* Interpreter for the Crown.
*Conrad Weiser,* Esq; Interpreter for the Province.

On opening the Meeting, his Honour the Governor asked me, as I represented the Honourable Sir William Johnson at this Treaty, if I was provided with a Secretary: Upon answering I was provided with one, his Honour then gave Orders that no Person else should take any Notes.

*Then the Governor made the following Speech.*

*Brethren of the* United Nations, YOU are sensible of the unhappy Differences that have subsisted for some Time past between us, the People of *Pennsylvania,* the *English* in the several Colonies, and our Brethren and Countrymen, the *Delawares* and *Shawanese,* your Nephews and Brothers.

By the Mediation of Sir *William Johnson,* His Majesty's sole Agent and Superintendent of *Indian* Affairs for the Northern District of *America,* a Cessation of

Arms was agreed upon; and they, at a Conference held in *Otsaningo,* promised to lay down their Hatchet; which Agreement they since ratified and confirmed in another Conference with that Gentleman in your Presence; at which Time Sir *William* desired to know what was the Cause of their committing Hostilities on their Brethren the *English,* which Question they did not then give a full Answer to. But at a subsequent Treaty with me at *Easton,* in *November* last, the same Question being put to *Teedyuscung,* he frankly acknowledged that their foolish young Men, being deluded by our Enemy, the false hearted *French* King, were perswaded to take up the Hatchet against us. This, he said, was the first and principal Cause; but that one Reason why the Blow fell the heavier on us was, that their Brother *Onas* had fraudulently possessed himself of some of their Lands, without having first purchased, or given any Consideration for them.

*Gave a Belt of nine Rows.*

Being very desirous that all Causes of Discontent should be removed, I proposed that the Matter should then be finally accommodated; but *Teedyuscung* declaring, that he was not sufficiently impowered to finish that Business, declined it, and desired another Meeting this Spring, when he engaged to bring with him those *Indians* to whom the said Lands belonged, at which Time this Complaint might be fully heard, and amicably adjusted.

*Gave a Belt of nine Rows.*

Having the greatest Confidence in the Friendship and Justice of our Brethren the *Six Nations,* I immediately acquainted Sir *William Johnson* with these Proceedings, and requested that he would be pleased to send some of the wise Men of those Nations to be present and assist at the proposed Meeting. I expected *Teedyuscung* would have been here before this Time, and am greatly concerned at his Stay.

It would afford me great Satisfaction, if it had suited your Conveniency to wait his Arrival; but as you have informed me your Business will not admit of being longer absent from your Country, if you can now think of any Measure that may be likely to promote the good Work in which we are engaged, and establish a firm and lasting Friendship between us and your Nephews, you shall find me sincerely disposed to join with you in doing every Thing in my Power conducive to so desirable an End. In Confirmation whereof, I give you this Belt of thirteen Rows.

*Gave the Belt.*

*At a* MEETING *in the Court-House,* Friday, May 13, 1757, P. M.
PRESENT, The Honourable *WILLIAM DENNY,* Esq;
Lieutenant-Governor.
The Council. The Committee of the Assembly. The Magistrates of the Borough, and a great Number of other Gentlemen. The same *Indians.*

*Thomas King,* an *Oneido* Sachem, *Little Abraham,* a *Mohawk* Sachem, Speakers for the *Indians.*
*William Prentup,* Interpreter for the Crown.
*Conrad Weiser,* Esq; Interpreter for the Province.

Little Abraham *opened the Meeting, addressing himself to the Governor as follows.*

*Brother,* AFTER you had done speaking to us Yesterday, you left the Appointing the Time for the next Meeting to us. We are now met in Council, and I desire you to listen to what we are going to say.

*Thomas King* then got up, and repeated over the two first Speeches made to them by the Governor Yesterday, and returned his Honour Thanks, for acquainting them with the particular Circumstances that happened during the Course of the Conference at *Easton* last Fall, between his Honour and the *Delawares* and *Shawanese;* and expressed the great Satisfaction it gave them to hear that their Brother *Onas* was so fortunate as to find out the true Causes from whence the Difference arose between their Brethren the *English,* and their Nephews the *Delawares,* and their Brothers the *Shawanese,* for that they had taken a great Deal of Pains to find it out without Success.

*Gave a Belt.*

*Thomas* then addressed himself to the Governor, and said, he hoped, that if they should make any Blunders, or have forgot any Part of the Speech, he would excuse them, as they could not write; therefore were obliged to keep every Thing in their Memory.[5]

*Gave a Belt.*

*Little Abraham* then desired the Governor to give Attention, as they were going to return an Answer to his Honour's last Speech; and after he had repeated over the last Speech delivered them by the Governor Yesterday, he spoke as follows.

*Brother,* You desired our Advice in Regard to the Differences that arose between you and our Nephews the *Delawares,* and Brothers the *Shawanese;* and you desired us to give you our Opinion which would be the best Method now to pursue to bring about an Accommodation: We have considered what you required of us. Brothers, We are disappointed, by the Heads of our Relations not coming to this Meeting; it was on their Account that we met our Brothers at this Time.—If they had come here at this Time, we should have sat still, and heard the Complaints on each Side, then we should have been the better able to judge who was in the Fault, and would have given our Opinion freely: However, as Things now stand, we must inform you, our Brothers, That in the Time of our Great-Grand-Fathers, and when the *Six Nations* first united, it was agreed that the *Seneca* Country should be the Door to the *Six Nations,* into which all Messengers should pass in Time of War, and there deliver their Messages, and the *Senecas,* our Brothers, were to forward the Messages to all the *United Nations.*

But in the Differences subsisting at present between you and our Nephews and Brothers, we have heard nothing from that Quarter, though we are sensible that Messengers arrived there upon this Affair. And as we, the *Mohawks,* are a Door to the Eastward of the *Six Nation* Country, established at the same time with that to the Westward, finding that they neglected their Offices, we took the Affair in Hand, and sent Messengers to *Otsaningo,* and there a Council was held, and the Deputies we sent charged them to get sober, as we looked upon their Actions as the Actions of drunken Men: This was the Substance of the Speeches sent to them.—They returned for answer, That they looked upon themselves as Men, and would acknowledge no Superiority that any other Nation had over them.—We are Men, and are determined not to be ruled any longer by you as Women; and we are determined to cut off all the *English,* except those that may make their Escape from us in Ships; so say no more to us on that Head, lest we cut off your private Parts, and make Women of you, as you have done of us. In the mean time, though they did not any longer acknowledge the *Six Nations* as their Uncles, yet they would listen to what *Anugh Kary Tany Tionen Hokorowy* should say to them.—Him only they acknowledged for their Uncle.—Notwithstanding this rash Speech, they afterwards, at the Instance of Sir *William Johnson,* agreed to a Cessation of Arms, to come to an Interview with him and their Brother *Onas.*

Now, Brother, our Advice is to you, that you send proper Messengers immediately to the *Senecas,* to invite them, with our Nephews the *Delawares,* and Brothers the *Shawanese,* to a Meeting with you here; and when they come, be very careful in your Proceedings with them, and do not be rash, and it will be in your Power to settle all the Differences subsisting betwen you and them: And we assure you, Brethren, by this Belt of Wampum, that we will continue our good Offices till this Affair is brought to a happy Conclusion.

*Gave a Belt, marked* G. R.

*At a* MEETING *at the Court-House,* Monday, May 16, 1757, A. M.
PRESENT, The Honourable *WILLIAM DENNY,* Esq;
Lieutenant-Governor.
The Honourable Colonel John Stanwix.
The Council. The Committee of Assembly. The Magistrates of the Borough, with a great Number of other Gentlemen.
The same *Indians.*
*William Prentup,* Interpreter for the Crown.
*Conrad Weiser,* Esq; Interpreter for the Province.
*Little Abraham,* a *Mohawk* Sachem, *Thomas King,* an *Oneido* Sachem,
Speakers for the *Indians.*

*The Governor spoke as follows.*

*Brethren of the* United Nations, I HAVE duly considered what you were so kind to say to me the other Day, in Answer to my Speech to you; and I return you my hearty Thanks for your Information and Advice as to what you judge proper to be done for the Restoration of Peace between us, your Cousins the *Delawares,* and Brethren the *Shawanese.*

We look upon your informing us of that close Connection, at present subsisting, between your Cousins and the *Seneca* Nations, of which we were till now ignorant, as the greatest Mark of your Regard and Esteem for us.——Brothers, Your Advice is good and wholesome, and I shall in Pursuance of it, send an Invitation to *Teedyuscung* to come down, and leave it entirely to his Choice to bring with him such and so many of his Uncles, and others his Friends, as he thinks proper, and will then cautiously and carefully pursue your Advice in treating with them.

In the mean time, if, on your Return, you should meet with *Teedyuscung,* I desire you will let him know what has been done between us at this Meeting, and advise him of the Continuance of the good Disposition of the People of this Province toward him and his People; and that we are ready to fulfil the Engagements we entered into with him at *Easton,* and shall be glad to see him and his Friends, as soon as they can conveniently come.

*Gave a Belt.*

*Little Abraham* then stood up, with the Belt delivered them by the *Governor* in his Hand, and repeated over the Speech made them on it; then addressing himself to the Governor, he spoke as follows.

*Brother* Onas, We return you Thanks for accepting of our Advice; and we make no Doubt, if you pursue the Measures we have recommended, but that your Endeavours will be crowned with Success.——We have come a great Journey, in order to see the Differences subsisting between you and our Cousins amicably settled, and could wish they had met here at this Time. On our Return, we assure you we will recommend it to our Nephews and Brothers, in the strongest Manner we can, to come down and meet you, in order to have all Differences subsisting between you settled in an amicable Manner.

*Gave a Belt.*

*At the Court-House* in Lancaster, Tuesday, May 17, 1757.
PRESENT, The Honourable *WILLIAM DENNY,* Esq;
Lieutenant-Governor.
The Honourable Colonel John Stanwix.
The Council. The Committee of the Assembly. The Magistrates of the Borough, with a great Number of other Gentlemen.
The same *Indians.*
*William Prentup,* Interpreter for the Crown.
*Conrad Weiser,* Esq; Interpreter for the Province.
*Little Abraham,* a *Mohawk* Sachem, *Thomas King,* an *Oneido* Sachem,
Speakers for the *Indians.*

*After the Minutes of the Treaty were read, and the* Indians *acquainted by the Interpreter with what had been doing, the Governor spoke as follows.*

*Brethren of the* Six United Nations, I DESIRE to be informed if you have any Complaints against this Province, with Regard to Purchases of Land, or for any other Cause whatsoever: In Expectation that you would freely open your Hearts to me on these Heads, I give you this Belt.

*Gave a Belt.*

I then acquainted the *Indians* by the Interpreter, that I was going to speak to them in Behalf of the Honourable Sir *William Johnson,* Baronet, His Majesty's sole Agent and Superintendent of the Affairs of the *Six Nations,* and their Allies and Dependents, and desired them to consider my Words as if spoken by himself.

*Sachems and Warriors of the* Six United Nations, *our Friends and Brethren,* When *Teedyuscung,* at the Treaty held at *Easton,* complained that the *Indians* had been defrauded of some of their Lands, this Government agreed to meet him upon his own Appointment this Spring; to which Meeting you were invited, that you might see and hear every Thing to be then transacted with your Nephews the *Delawares,* and Brothers the *Shawanese.* You are now here on that Invitation, and are Witnesses how ready this Government is to redress any Injuries or Injustice done to the *Indians* whenever they can make that appear, and that they, your Brethren of *Pennsylvania,* are now attending for that Purpose, and you must be convinced, from their Conduct towards you, that they are not come empty handed.

*Gave a Belt.*

*Brethren,* His Majesty's Subjects that have settled this and the neighbouring Provinces by Law, are not allowed to buy any of your Lands, and accordingly they have never done it; and if those who only have a Right from the Crown to purchase your Lands have done you any Injustice, or injured the *Indians* on this Account, the Governor of this Province, with a Number of the chief Men of this Government, are here, and appear hearty and willing to make Satisfaction; but if they, or the People of these Provinces, should refuse doing you Justice, when you make it appear that you are injured, I will then carefully represent your Case to the King of *England,* my Master, and your Father, in order to procure you ample and immediate Satisfaction.

*Gave a Belt.*

*Brethren,* As Deputies from most of the Tribes of the *Six Nations* are now here, who may not be present when *Teedyuscung* comes down, and as I am ordered and required by the Honourable Sir *William Johnson,* Baronet, His Majesty's chief Agent and Superintendent of the Affairs of the *Six Nations,* their Allies and Dependents, to enquire into and hear the Complaints made by the *Indians,* and, if justly grounded, to use my utmost Endeavours to get them redressed, I do insist upon it, that you open your Hearts to me without Reserve, and inform me of every Thing you know concerning Frauds complained of by *Teedyuscung,* or any other Injuries or Injustice done to you, or any of the Tribes of the *Six Nations,* or other *Indians* in Alliance with His Majesty King GEORGE, in this or the neighbouring Colonies, that I may be thereby enabled to represent the true State of your Grievances to His Majesty.—Brethren, after this candid Conduct towards you, and my thus pressing you to open your Minds to me, I do expect that you will hide nothing from me, but speak from the Bottom of your Hearts: And I expect that you will recommend it to your Nephews the *Delawares,* and Brothers the *Shawanese,* to come down and give your Brother *Onas* a Meeting, to make their Complaints appear, and have them adjusted, else I shall take it for granted that they have no just Cause of Complaint: To inforce what I have said, I give you this Belt of Wampum.

*Gave a Belt.*

*Brethren of the* United Nations, You remember that your Nephews the *Delawares,* and Brothers the *Shawanese,* in a Council with you at *Otsaningo,* promised to lay down their Hatchet, and in a subsequent Meeting with Sir *William Johnson,* at his House, in *July* last, ratified and confirmed it in the most solemn Manner in your Presence; then promising to deliver up all the *English* Prisoners that were by any Means brought to their Country, or in their Possession; and I desire that on your Return to your Country, you will remind your Nephews and Brothers of their Promises to Sir *William Johnson,* and recommend it strongly to them to bring down what *English* Prisoners they have amongst them, and deliver them up, as that is the only Proof they can give us of their Sincerity and good Disposition towards us.

*Gave a Belt.*

*Sachems and Warriors of the* United Nations, In that Meeting with your Brother *Warraigheyagey,*[6] your Nephews the *Delawares,* and Brothers the *Shawanese,* renewed and brightened the Chain of Friendship between them and us, and promised to fix their Eyes on you their Uncles, and regulate their Conduct by yours; and at the same time declared, in a publick Manner, by dancing, and singing the War Song, that they would turn the Edge of their Hatchet, in Conjunction with you their Uncles the *Six Nations,* against the *French,* the treacherous and faithless Invaders of the Property of Mankind. And I must now desire that you will insist upon their being ready, when called upon, to join His Majesty's Troops, in Conjunction with you our Friends and Allies, against our common Enemy.—That this Speech may have its full Force upon your Minds, I present you with this Belt of Wampum.

*Gave a War Belt.*

Little Abraham *then spoke as follows.*

*Brothers,* The Speeches you have just made are of great Consequence both to you and us.———We shall duly consider them, and, as soon as possibly we can, we will return you an Answer.

*May* 18, 1757. This Day four Persons that were killed on the Frontiers, in the Settlement of *Swetara,* by the Enemy *Indians,* were brought to this Town.—In the Afternoon the chief *Sachems,* with a Number of their Warriors, called a Meeting in the *Indian* Camp, and spoke to us as follows.

*Brethren,* We have called this Meeting with Tears in our Eyes, on Account of seeing so many of our Brethren killed by the evil Spirit; and we take this Opportunity, as we have a good deal of Business yet to do, to wipe the Tears from your Eyes, so that To-morrow, when we meet in Council, we may see each other with the same Good-will we have hitherto done.

*Gave a String.*

*Brethren,* Now we have wiped the Tears from your Eyes, agreeable to the antient Customs of our Forefathers, we clean the Blood off your Council Seats, that you may sit with Comfort, and hear what we have to say to you. No Doubt but the *French* King, who takes delight in Mischief, has taken this Opportunity to send his Children down to commit these Murders, with Expectation of breeding a Difference between you our Brethren and us; but we desire you will hold fast by the Chain of Friendship subsisting between us; and disappoint him in his Designs.

*Gave a Belt.*

*At a* MEETING *in the Court-House in* Lancaster,
Thursday, May 19, 1757, P. M.
PRESENT, The Honourable *WILLIAM DENNY,* Esq;
Lieutenant-Governor.
The Honourable Colonel John Stanwix.
The Council. The Committee of the Assembly. The Magistrates of the Borough, with a great Number of other Gentlemen.
The same *Indians.*
*William Prentup,* Interpreter for the Crown.
*Conrad Weiser,* Esq; Interpreter for the Province.
*Little Abraham,* a *Mohawk* Sachem, *Thomas King,* an *Oneido* Sachem,
Speakers for the *Indians.*

After reading over the Condolance Speeches made Yesterday by the *Indians,* on Account of our People that were killed by the Enemy, *Little Abraham,* addressing himself to the Honourable Sir *William Johnson,* Baronet, and the Governor, spoke as follows.

*Brethren,* EACH of you made us a Speech Yesterday on the same Subject; both which Speeches I now propose to answer at once, and then spoke as follows.

*Brothers,* Some Years ago, in the *Jerseys,* one of the Head Men of the *Delawares* had been out a Hunting.—On his Return, he called to see a Gentleman, a great Friend of his, one of your People, who he found in his Field: When the Gentleman saw him he came to meet him. It was rainy Weather, and the *Delaware* Chief had his Gun under his Arm.—They met at a Fence, and as they reached out their Hands to each other, the *Delaware*'s Gun went off by Accident, and shot him dead. He was very much grieved at the Accident, and went to the House, and told the Gentleman's Wife what had happened, and said he was willing to die, and did not choose to live after his Friend. She immediately sent for a Number of the Inhabitants.—When they were gathered, some said it was an Accident, and could not be helped; but the greatest Number were for hanging him, and he was taken by the Sheriff, and carried to *Amboy,* where he was tried, and hanged.—There was another Misfortune that happened.—A Party of *Shawanese,* who were going to War against their Enemies, in their Way through *Carolina,* called at a House, not suspecting any Harm, as they were amongst their Friends, a Number of the Inhabitants rose and took them Prisoners, on Account of some Mischief that was done there about that Time, suspecting them to be the People that had done the Mischief, and carried them to *Charles-Town,* and put them in Prison, where the chief Man, called *The Pride,* died.—The Relations of these People were much exasperated against you our Brethren, the *English,* on Account of the ill Treatment you gave their Friends, and have been continually spiriting up their Nations to take Revenge.——Brothers you desired us to open our Hearts, and inform you of every Thing we knew that might give Rise to the Quarrel between you and our Nephews and Brothers.—We must now inform you, that in former Times our Forefathers conquered the *Delawares,* and put Petticoats on them.—A long Time after that they lived among you our Brothers, but upon some Difference between you and them, we thought proper to remove them, giving them Lands to plant and hunt on at *Wyoming* and *Juniata,* on *Sasquehannah.*———But you, covetous of Land, made Plantations there, and spoiled their hunting Grounds; they then complained to us, and we looked over those Lands, and found their Complaints to be true. At this Time they carried on a Correspondence with the *French,* by which Means the *French* became acquainted with all the Causes of Complaint they had against you; and as your People were daily encreasing their Settlements, by this Means you drove them back into the Arms of the *French,* and they took the Advantage of spiriting them up against you, by telling them; "Children, you see, and we have often told you, how the *English,* your Brethren, would serve you; they plant all the Country, and drive you back; so that in a little Time you will have no Land: It is not so with us; though we build Trading-Houses on your Land, we do not plant it; we have our Provisions from over the great Water."—We have opened our Hearts, and told you what Complaints we have heard that they had against you; and our Advice to you is, that you send for the *Senecas* and them; treat them kindly, and rather give them some Part of their Fields back again than differ with them.—It is in your Power to settle all the Differences with them if you please.

*Gave two Belts, one for Sir* William Johnson, *and one for the Governor.*

Little Abraham *spoke again as follows.*

*Brothers,* As to what passed between you and *Teedyuscung* last Fall, respecting the Purchase of Lands, we know nothing of;—they are not here, and if we enquire, we can only hear what you say on that Head.—We should have been glad our Nephews the *Delawares,* and Brothers the *Shawanese* had been here at this Time, that we might have heard the Complaints on both Sides; then we should have been able to judge who was in the Fault, and we are determined to see Justice done to the Party aggrieved.—As they are not here, we can say nothing about it; but you yourselves, between whom the Business was transacted, must be the best Judges.

*Gave a String.*

*Brothers,* You acquaint us there are certain Persons empowered by the King to purchase Lands here from the *Indians:*—We are unacquainted with that; neither do we know how our Father, the King of *England,* has divided his Provinces.—You say, if you have done the *Indians* any Injustice, you are willing to make them Satisfaction. We are glad to hear it; and as you have Writings to refresh your Memories about every Transaction that has happened between you and our Nephews and Brothers, the *Delawares* and *Shawanese,* we recommend it heartily to you to do Justice.[7]—We are much concerned to see how you are used by them and the *French,* every Day having your People killed, and you sitting with your Heads between your Legs, and receiving the Blow, without resenting it, as if you could not, or would not, fight to defend yourselves.

*Brother* Onas, We desire that you may not think of great Expeditions far off.—Use your best Endeavours to defend your Frontiers, and protect the Lives of your People.—It is better for you to give up some Points to them, than to contend, provided they should be in the Wrong, and settle all Differences subsisting between you as soon as possible.

*Gave a Belt.*

He added, Brother *Onas,* take Pattern by Sir *William Johnson;* he always keeps large Parties patrolling across the Frontiers where he lives, and you do not hear of any Murders being committed there.—That is the Way to defend yourselves.—The Enemy is afraid to enter the Settlement there; and if you pursue the same Measures, they will be afraid to come into your Settlements.

Thomas King *then spoke as follows.*

*Brethren,* We have considered what you said to us, about our requesting the *Delawares* and *Shawanese* to bring down and deliver up all the *English* Prisoners they have, agreeable to their Promises to Sir *William Johnson.*—We will do every Thing in our Power that may induce them to do it, but perhaps it will not be in our Power to prevail on them to give them up.—Once more we desire that you would send for the *Senecas* and them, and endeavour to settle all those Differences.—It is in your Power to do it. When it is done, you will certainly see some of your own Flesh and Blood again.

*Gave a Belt.*

*Brethren,* It is true, we were present when the *Delawares* and *Shawanese* brightened the Chain of Friendship with Sir *William Johnson,* and promised to turn the Edge of their Hatchet against the *French.*—But you must know that last Fall, tho' they went out to War with us, they always turned back, and did not perform what they had promised; so that we cannot account for what they will do now.—But for our Parts, the *Six Nations,* we have been engaged in the War with you, and are always ready, when we see an *English* Flag, to join our Brothers, and to go with them, and share the same Fate.

*Gave a Belt.*

*At a* MEETING *in the Court-House, at* Lancaster,
Friday, May 20, 1757, P. M.
PRESENT, The Honourable *WILLIAM DENNY,* Esq;
Lieutenant-Governor.
The Honourable Colonel John Stanwix.
The Council. The Committee of the Assembly.
The Magistrates of the Borough, with a great Number of
other Gentlemen. The same *Indians.*
*William Prentup,* Interpreter for the Crown.
*Conrad Weiser,* Esq; Interpreter for the Province.
*Little Abraham,* a *Mohawk* Sachem, *Thomas King,* an *Oneido* Sachem,
Speakers for the *Indians.*

*After reading over the Speeches made the Day before, and the Interpreter acquainting the* Indians *with what had been doing, the Governor spoke as follows.*

*Brethren of the* Six United Nations, I RETURN you my hearty Thanks for the kind and open Manner in which you have informed us of the Causes from whence the Dissatisfaction of our Brethren the *Delawares* and *Shawanese* first arose; but, as you have observed, they are not present, it must be deferred until we have the Pleasure of seeing them.——I shall only assure you that I think your Advice good, and shall, with great Satisfaction, conform to it, by sending for the People you have so earnestly recommended to be sent for.—I think with you, that our Frontiers should be carefully and strongly guarded; and it shall be my particular Care to endeavour to have this done, in which I shall take kind any Assistance you will give me.

*Gave a Belt.*

*Brethren,* Soon after the present Troubles first broke out between us and the *French,* some of the *Six Nation Indians* requested of this Government to build a strong House at *Shamokin,* and a Store-house, with *Indian* Goods, and to give an Invitation to *Indians,* as well of the *United Nations* as *Delawares,* to come and live there; I must now inform you, that in Compliance with their Request this Government has built a strong House, where Goods will soon be sent, and sold as cheap as any where on this Continent.—To this Place I have appointed Mr. *Thomas McKee* to conduct as many of you as shall chuse to return that Way, and shall leave it to you to settle as many Families as shall incline to live there; promising you, that Care shall be taken by this Government, that as many as stay shall be furnished with such Necessaries as they may want till they can support themselves.

*Gave a Belt.*

*Brethren,* I shall immediately report the whole that has passed at these Conferences to Sir *William Johnson,* who is glad of all Occasions to shew his Attachment to our Friends the *Indians,* and promote His Majesty's Service.—It is that Gentleman's peculiar Province to treat and finish all Treaties with the *Indians.*———Let me add, my Brethren of the *United Nations,* that you shall find no Deceit in me, and I shall be happy if my Conduct deserves your Esteem and Approbation.

*Gave a Belt.*

*Brethren,* I have ordered the Presents provided by the good People of this Province to be carried to the *Indian* Camp early in the Morning; and inform you, that a Part of these Presents is given by those who are the Descendents of the Inhabitants that first came over to this Country with your old Friend *William Penn,* as a particular Testimony of their Regard and Affection for the *Indians.*

*I then spoke in Behalf of Sir* William Johnson.

*Sachems and Warriors of the* United Nations, You see how the *French,* the Enemies of Mankind, set on their Children to murder, in a barbarous Manner, your Brethren that are settled on the Frontiers of this and the neighbouring Provinces.—Brethren, I must now desire you, in the Name of the Great King of *England,* your Father, and my Master, that on your Return to your own Country, you will be active, and not suffer any of the *French,* or their Children, to pass over your Lands to murder your Brethren; and that you will let *Teedyuscung* and his People know, I expect he will do the same.—Tell them it is not, nor will not be, their Interest to carry on the War against their Brethren the *English.*—Their Father, the *French* King, makes Fools of them, and will, in the End, make Slaves of them: But you, Brethren, are convinced, that the *English* have always treated you as their Brethren, and I expect a due Regard and Performance to this Request on your Side.

*Gave a Belt.*

Little Abraham *made the following Answer to the Governor.*

*Brother* Onas, We return you our hearty Thanks for accepting of our Advice in sending for the *Delawares, Shawanese* and *Senecas,* and we hope, when you meet them, you will be able to settle all Differences to your Satisfaction.

*Brother* Onas, We likewise return you our hearty Thanks for your kind Invitation to us to settle at *Genossa,* and your Promise to supply those that will stay, or come and settle there, with Provisions and Goods.—We accept of the Invitation, and will take it into Consideration as we go Home, how many of us will stay there, or come back from our Towns to settle there; and we return you Thanks for appointing our Brother *Thomas McKee* to take Care of us, as he is a Person very agreeable to us.

*He spoke again as follows.*

*Brother* Warraighiyagey, We have all given Attention to what you have said to us by *Anaquarunda;*[8] and you may depend upon our being on the Active, and doing every Thing in our Power to prevent the *French* or their Children coming to murder our Brethren; and we will recommend it strongly to *Teedyuscung,* and his People, to do the same.—Brother, we must desire you will assist our Brother *Onas* in settling the Differences between him and our Nephews and Brothers, the *Delawares* and *Shawanese,* which will be the only Method to prevent these cruel Murders daily committed on our Brethren.

*May* the 21st. The Presents were delivered to the *Indians* in their own Camp; after which I condoled with them on account of some of their People who died of the Smallpox since they came here, and gave them a Piece of Stroud to cover the Graves of the Deceased, agreeable to the antient Custom of the *Six Nations.*

The several Chiefs returned their hearty Thanks for our condoling with them, and covering the Graves of their deceased Friends, agreeable to the antient Custom used by their Forefathers, and expressed great Satisfaction with the Treatment they met with in this Government, and returned Thanks for the Presents they had received.

*May* 22. I called a Meeting of the Chiefs of the several Tribes, and I repeated over to them the Messages going to be sent to *Teedyuscung* by this Government, agreeable to their Request; and at the same time I acquainted them, that there was a small Present provided by this Government for their Brethren the *Cherokees,* who had come into this Government, and was now waiting in Expectation of its being sent them, agreeable to their Request.——I then desired them to give their Opinion about the Message to be sent to *Teedyuscung,* and whether it was agreeable to them.

*To which they made me the following Answer.*

*Brother,* We have considered every Part of your Message to *Teedyuscung,* and we approve much of it, and think it will be acceptable to our Nephews and Brothers; and we likewise approve of our Brother *Onas*'s sending a Present to our Brothers the *Cherokees.*—You, our Brothers the *English,* took some Pains to bring about a

Peace between them and us, and we embrace this Opportunity of brightening the Chain of Friendship between us in your Presence.——We have appointed three Men to go with you to see them, and hope you will provide for them on the Road.

*Gave a String.*

*The Speech sent by the Governor to* Teedyuscung.

*Brother* Teedyuscung, AT the Treaty held at *Easton* last Fall, you complained unto me that the *Indians* had been defrauded of their Lands.——This you told me was one of the Causes that had alienated the Minds of our Brethren, the *Delawares* and *Shawanese,* from us your Brethren; upon which I told you, if you could make it appear that you had received any Injustice or Injuries from this Province, I was ready to hear it, and promised to make you Satisfaction.

*Brother,* You then informed me, that the People who claimed those Lands, as they did not expect that Affair would come under Consideration at that Treaty, were not present, and had not impowered you to transact that Business for them, and therefore you could not finish it at that Time, but that you would come down again in the Spring, and would bring with you as many of those *Indians* as could be got together, in order to a full Settlement of all Differences between us, that a firm and lasting Peace might be established for ever.

*Brother,* As you had thus promised to be down in the Spring, we were pleased to find a considerable Number of your Uncles, the *Six Nations,* were come amongst us, to be present and hear all your Complaints.——They staid a considerable Time for that Purpose, in Expectation of seeing you here; but as some Accident may have prevented your coming, your Uncles grew very uneasy at being detained here so long, and desired me to meet them at *Lancaster,* whither I went, and opened my Heart to them, giving them a full Account of all that passed between us at *Easton,* promising your Uncles, that I would take Care to see you redressed, either on account of your Lands, or any other Injuries you may have received from your Brethren of this Province.

*Brother,* Your Uncles, the *Six Nations,* at this Treaty, shewed a great deal of Kindness for you, and would have been extremely pleased to have seen you here, being resolved to see Justice done to you; but as you were not come in, they advised us to treat you very tenderly, and to advise you to bring with you some of your Uncles, the *Senecas,* that we might open our Hearts to one another freely, by which Means all Causes of Jealousies, or Misunderstandings between us, might be settled and taken away for ever, and that they would join their best Endeavours to bring about a firm and lasting Peace between you and your Brethren.

*Brother,* I gave your Uncles my hearty Thanks for their good Advice; and told them, that as I highly approved it, as good and sound Advice, I would act as they had so earnestly desired me to do, being sincerely disposed to hear all your Complaints, and to do you Justice, as I had formerly promised you at *Easton.*

*Brother,* As I have now informed you of the earnest Request of your Uncles, the *Six Nations,* and of my own Opinion, which is the same with theirs, I do by this Belt of Wampum invite you to come down as soon as it will suit your Convenience, and leave it to you to bring with you your Uncles, the *Senecas,* or such of them as will be most agreeable to you, to open your Hearts to us your Brethren; and if it shall appear that you have been defrauded of your Lands, or received any other Injuries from this Province, I do promise you shall receive Satisfaction.

*Brother,* By some late Letters received from your Brother *Onas,* in *England,* in Answer to my Representation of the late Conferences, and your Complaints at *Easton,* he acquaints me he is willing to have the Injuries complained of fully heard and settled as soon as possible.—If you rather chuse Sir *William Johnson* should determine these unhappy Differences, I most warmly recommend it to you to apply to that Gentleman, as he has the Honour to be appointed sole Agent and Superintendent of *Indian* Affairs in the Northern District.

*Gave a Belt.*

After this Speech was delivered to the Messengers, the Sachems of the several Tribes made the following Speech.

*Brother,* As we have finished the Business for this Time, and we design to part To-morrow, you must be sensible that we have a long Journey, and a hilly Country to pass over, and several of our old Men very weak, we hope that you will not send us from your Frontiers without a Walking-stick.*——In answer, I acquainted them, that the good People of this Province had provided some Cags for them on the Frontiers, which would be given them by the Persons employed to conduct them through the Settlements.

*A true Copy, taken by*

Charles Moore, Clerk of Assembly.

*The REPORT of* CONRAD WEISER, *the* Indian *Interpreter, of his Journey to* Shamokin *on the Affairs of* Virginia *and* Maryland; *his Mediation for accommodating the Differences between the* Indians *of the* Six Nations *and the said Province, delivered to the Governor in Council the* 21st *Day of* April, 1743.[9]

THE Ninth of *April,* 1743, I arrived at *Shamokin,* by Order of the Governor of *Pennsylvania,* to acquaint the neighbouring *Indians,* and those on *Wyoming,* that the Governor of *Virginia* was well pleased with his Mediation, and was willing to come to an Agreement with the *Six Nations* about the Land his People were settled upon, if it was that they contended for, and to make up the Matter of the late unhappy Skirmish in an amicable Way. The same Day *Shickallemo,* his Son, and *Suchsedowa,*

* Meaning a Cag of Rum.

who were sent to the *Six Nations,* returned from *Onondago;* and the next Day they, in open Council, delivered the following Message, directing their Speech, in Behalf of the *Six Nations,* to the Governor of *Pennsylvania,* according to what was agreed upon by the Council of the said *Indians* in *Onondago.*

*Brother* Onas, At this critical Time we received a kind Message from you, the Result of the good Friendship subsisting between you and us. For such Purposes a Road was cleared from our Country to yours, in which, at any Time, *Conrad Weiser* and *Shickallemo* may travel; we open our Doors with Chearfulness to your Messengers, and are glad to hear from you.

*He laid down two Strings of Wampum.*

*Brother* Onas, We thank you for the Concern you shew for the Misfortune that befel our Warriors in *Virginia.* We take it as a particular Mark of Friendship. We assure you, that notwithstanding the unjust Treatment our Warriors met with in *Virginia,* we did not allow our Heads to be giddy, nor to resent it as it deserved, which might have occasioned a Violation of Treaties, and the Destruction of many.

*He laid down four Strings of Wampum.*

*Brother* Onas, We thank you very kindly for the early Steps you made in calling your old and wise Men together to consult with them. It was a very prudent and good Advice they gave you to become Mediator betwixt us your Brethren, and the *Virginians* your Neighbours. We thank them for such good Advice: And we assure you, we will accordingly come to an amicable Accommodation with the Governor of *Virginia,* if he will come to reasonable Terms. And if a War should break out betwixt us and him, you will be convinced of his being the Author of it: For when in former Times we received a deadly Blow, we never returned it, if it was ever so dangerous; we always judged it to be given by disorderly People, and we used always peaceable Means to make it up; but when we received the second Blow, we judged that War was intended against us, and then we rose and knocked down our Enemies with one Blow, and we are still able to do the same, but we leave now our Case to you. We have ordered our Warriors, with the strongest Words, to sit down, and not revenge themselves: Therefore, Brother *Onas,* go on with Courage in your Mediation; we assure you we will not violate or do any Thing contrary to your Mediation. We desire you, and the old and wise Men of *Pennsylvania,* not to believe any Thing to the contrary, let it come from whom it will, till you receive Messages from us: We will do the same on our Side. In Confirmation of what we say, we lay down this Belt of Wampum before you.

*Then the Speech was directed to the Governor of* Maryland.

*Brother, the Governor of* Maryland, You have invited us to come to your Town; and you offered to treat with us concerning the Messages we sent to you by our Brother the Governor of *Pennsylvania,* and to establish good Friendship with us: We are very glad you did so; and we thank you for your kind Invitation.

*Brother,* We have a great deal of Business and Things of Moment under our Deliberation, and it will take us the best of the Day*, before we can finish them: We therefore desire you will set your Heart at Ease, and think on nothing but what is good. We will come and treat with you at *Canataquanny,* on *Sasquehannah,* To-morrow Morning,† since you live so near the Sea, and at such a great Distance from us. We accept kindly of your Invitation; our Brother, the Governor of *Pennsylvania,* recommended your Message to us, which he would not have done, if he had not been satisfied your Intention was good: We therefore promise you, by these Strings of Wampum, to come and treat with you at the aforesaid Place.

*The Speaker laid down four Strings of Wampum.*

*Then the Speaker directed his Speech to the Governor of* Pennsylvania *again, and said;*

*Brother* Onas, The *Dutchman* on *Scohooniady (Juniata)* claims a Right to the Land, merely because he gave a Little Victuals to our Warriors, who stand very often in Need of it. This String of Wampum serves (the Speaker then took two Strings of Wampum in his Hands) to take the *Dutchman* by the Arm, and throw him over the big Mountains within your Borders. WE HAVE GIVEN THE RIVER SCOHOONIADY (JUNIATA) FOR A HUNTING-PLACE TO OUR COUSINS THE DELAWARE INDIANS, AND OUR BRETHREN THE SHAWANESE; and we ourselves hunt there sometimes. We therefore desire you will immediately, by Force, remove all those that live on the said River of *Scohooniady.*

*Here he laid down two Strings of Wampum.*

*Brother, the Governor of* Pennsylvania, I live upon this River of *Ohio* harmless like a little Child: I can do nothing; I am but weak; and I do not so much as intend Mischief. I have nothing to say, and do therefore send these Strings of Wampum to *Catchcawatsiky,* the Chief Man, again; he will answer your Message, as he is the older, and greater, Man.

*Then* Sachsidora *took up the four Strings of Wampum, and spoke in Behalf of* Catchcawatsiky, *as follows.*

*Brother, the Governor of* Pennsylvania, The Place where I live, and the neighbouring Country, has been overshadowed of late by a very dark Cloud. I looked with a pitiful Eye upon the poor Women and Children, and then looked upon the Ground all along for Sorrow, in a miserable Condition, because of the poor Women and Children. In all that dark Time, a Message from you found the Way to *Shamokin;* and when it was delivered to us, the dark Cloud was dispersed, and the Sun immediately began to shine; and I could see at a great Distance, and saw your Good-will and kind Love to the *Indians* and the white People: I thank you, therefore, Brother *Onas,* for your kind Message; I am now able to comfort the poor Women and Children.

*Here the Speaker laid down four Strings of Wampum.*

* That is, this Summer.

† That is, next Spring

*Then the Speaker took up two Strings of Wampum, and directed his Discourse to the* Delaware Indians, *the* Shawanese, *and to* Onas.

*Cousins the Delawares,* We are informed that you can talk a little *English,* by which you have heard many Things amongst the white People; and you frequently bring Lies amongst the *Indians;* and you have very little Knowledge and Regard for Treaties of Friendship; you give your Tongue too much Liberty. This String of Wampum serves to tie your Tongue, and to forewarn you from Lies.

*Brethren, the* Shawanese, You believe too many Lies, and are too forward in Action. You shall not pretend to revenge our People that have been killed in *Virginia:* We are the Chief of all the *Indians;* let your Ears and Eyes be open towards us; and order your Warriors to stay at Home as we did ours.

*Brother* Onas, Your Back Inhabitants are People given to Lies, and raising of false Stories; stop up their Mouths; you can do it with one Word; let no false Stories be told; it is dangerous to the Chain of Friendship.

*The Strings of Wampum were delivered to the* Delawares.

After the Speaker had finished, an handsome *Indian* Dinner was given to all that were present by *Shickallemo*'s People.

After Dinner I delivered my Message to them, and presented the Company with two Rolls of Tobacco, about three Pound each Roll, to smoak whilst they were in Company together, to talk about the good News they had heard that Day, according to the Custom of the *Indians.*

*Shickallemo* told me, by Way of Discourse, that they (the Council of *Onondago)* had sent Strings of Wampum by him to all the *Indians* upon the River *Sasquehannah,* to tell them to use their Endeavours to stop all their Warriors, and not permit them to go to fight with the People of *Virginia;* and to acquaint them of what was agreed upon in *Onondago,* which was accepted of in every Town.——I enquired what Business of Moment the *Six Nations* had under Deliberation that prevented their coming down to treat with the Governor of *Maryland. Shickallemo* asked whether I could not guess at it. I told him no. Then he said, How should they come down with a Hatchet struck in their Head? The Governor of *Virginia* must wash off the Blood first, and take the Hatchet out of their Head, and dress the Wound (according to Custom, he that struck first must do it) and the Council of the *Six Nations* will speak to him, and be reconciled to him, and bury that Affair in the Ground, that it never may be seen nor heard of any more so long as the World stands.——But if the *Virginians* would not come to do that, he *(Shickallemo)* believed there would be a War; but I might assure the Governor of *Pennsylvania,* the Warriors would not come then within the inhabited Part of *Pennsylvania,* but direct their Course directly to *Virginia,* over the *Big Island,* in the North-West Branch of *Sasquehannah.*

1. Many in Pennsylvania were surprised when Johnson appointed Croghan to be his deputy (Wallace, *Conrad Weiser,* 467–68). The two had had contact in April 1755 when General

Braddock commissioned Johnson to be colonel in charge of the Iroquois. Johnson had ordered Croghan to join Braddock at Fort Cumberland with the Ohio warriors who had taken refuge on the trader's plantation near Carlisle. Braddock had treated the reinforcements contemptuously and was rewarded for sending them away by his defeat at Monongahela (Jennings, *Empire of Fortune,* 151–60). So while Croghan was in debt and discredited among many Pennsylvanians, Johnson may have had his reasons for appointing him. These very drawbacks might have made him easier to control.

2. The messages invited the Lenapes and Iroquois to a treaty, with Croghan in charge. Croghan promised Teedyuscung that he would do him justice (Jennings, *Empire of Fortune,* 335). Had Teedyuscung arrived at Lancaster in time for this treaty, with the Lenapes affected by the Walking Purchase, as he did several months later, they might possibly have received satisfaction (Jennings, *Empire of Fortune,* 328, 336). By July, Croghan had been definitely alienated from the Lenape cause.

3. Note that these are League Iroquois rather than Ohio Iroquois.

4. According to a letter written to Franklin by Charles Thomson (Thompson in the treaty records) in May 1758, General Forbes had recently attempted to "set the Cherokees upon the six Nations," acting in concert with public opinion (Labaree, *Papers of Benjamin Franklin,* 8:74). Whether this earlier fear that the Ohio Indians express resulted from older disputes between the southern and northern Indians west of British borders, from colonial instigation as part of the war effort, or both, is unknown. By summer of 1758, the Cherokees were seeking peace with the Lenapes and the League (Jennings, *Empire of Fortune,* 385).

5. This comment by the Oneida Thomas King is puzzling. His denigration of Iroquois memory may derive from contact with missionaries rather than a sudden loss of faith by the Iroquois at large in the adequacy of their ability to record historical events using wampum and oral recall.

6. William Johnson.

7. Note that the League does not itself raise any causes of complaint around land at this time. Instead, two paragraphs earlier, they refer to the disputes about the 1749 and 1754 sales when speaking of Wyoming and Juniata, and they characterize them as Lenape complaints rather than Iroquois ones.

8. George Croghan.

9. It is unclear why this report was being printed fourteen years after the fact. Because the war had started in part because of the 1744 "release" of all of Virginia's chartered lands by the League, it might have had some bearing on that question as debated in 1757.

✠

# MINUTES OF CONFERENCES,

## HELD WITH THE *INDIANS,* AT EASTON,

### In the Months of *July,* and *August,* 1757.

---

*PHILADELPHIA:*
Printed and Sold by B. FRANKLIN, and D. HALL,
at the *New-Printing-Office,* near the Market. MDCCLVII.

---

*Minutes of Conferences,* &c.

*At a MEETING with* TEEDYUSCUNG, *King of the* Delawares, *living on* Sasquehannah, *who is impowered by the ten following Nations,* viz. Lenopi, Wename, Munsey, Mawhickon, Tiawco, *or* Nanticokes, *and the* Senecas, Onondagoes, Cayugas, Oneidoes, *and* Mohawks *to settle all Differences subsisting between them and their Brethren the* English; *and* GEORGE CROGHAN, *Esq; Deputy Agent to the Honourable Sir* WILLIAM JOHNSON, *Baronet, His MAJESTY's sole Agent and Superintendent of the Affairs of the* Six Nations, *their Allies and Dependents, and Colonel of the same, at* Easton, *the Twenty-fifth Day of* July, 1757.

PRESENT,

*The Honourable* WILLIAM DENNY, *Esq; Lieutenant Governor, and Commander in Chief of the Province of* Pennsylvania, *and the Counties of* New-Castle, Kent *and* Sussex, *on* Delaware.

James Hamilton, William Logan, Richard Peters, Lyn-Ford Lardner,
Benjamin Chew, John Mifflin, *Esquires, Members of the Governor's Council.*
Isaac Norris, *Esq; Speaker of the House of Assembly.*
Daniel Roberdeau, *Esq; Member of the Assembly.*
William Masters, John Hughes, Joseph Fox, Joseph Galloway,
*Esquires, Provincial Commissioners.*

*A Number of Gentlemen of the City of* Philadelphia, *and others, Inhabitants of this Province.*
*Captain* Thomas McKee, *Interpreter for the Crown.*
Conrad Weiser, *Esq; Interpreter for the Province.*
*Mr.* John Pumpshire, *Interpreter for* Teedyuscung.
TEEDYUSCUNG, *King of the* Delawares, *attended by several Chiefs and Deputies of the Ten Nations he represents.*
*[The Number of the* Indians *here, at present, is about Three Hundred Men, Women and Children.]*

Teedyuscung *sent his Interpreter to call Mr.* Charles Thompson *to the Table, whom he had appointed his Clerk, to take down the Minutes of this Treaty.*[1]

*The Governor opened the Conference, directing his Discourse to* Teedyuscung, *and spoke as follows.*

*Brother,* I AM very glad to meet you once more with your People, and some of your Uncles the *Six Nations,* according to your Agreement with me at this Place, in *November* last. The Number of *Indians* you have brought down with you on this Occasion, and the Pains you have taken to carry the News of our good Dispositions for Peace to so great a Distance, confirms the good Opinion we have always had of you, and shews the Sincerity of the Professions you have made of your earnest Desire to restore the Friendship and Brotherly Love that always subsisted between us and the *Indians,* till your foolish Young Men were seduced by the evil Spirit, and turned against us.

*Brother* Teedyuscung, *and Brethren of the* Ten-united-Nations, We are now met together to finish, by the Assistance of the Almighty, the Great Work of Peace, and to make a new Chain of Friendship so bright, that it shall never rust, and so strong, that it shall never be in the Power of wicked Spirits to break it, that we may always hereafter be as one Man, with but one Heart and one Head. I invite you to join heartily and sincerely with me herein by this Belt.

*Gave a Belt.*

*Brother,* You may remember, that when we were here last Fall, I asked you what was the Cause of the Breach between our Brethren the *Delawares* and us; whether we, the People of *Pennsylvania,* had done you any Injury; and desired you would open your Hearts, and tell me your Mind freely. In answer to this you told me, that your foolish and ignorant young Men, when they saw the Proceedings of our Enemy, the *French* King, and believed the Things that were told them, were persuaded by this false hearted King to strike your Brethren the *English;* and that the Cause why the Blow came the harder on us was, that the Proprietaries had defrauded you of some of your Lands, and that you had been treated in the same Manner in the *Jerseys;* but that this was not the principal Cause of your striking us. I was willing to enquire into the Truth of this Charge at that Time, but you declined it, because few of the *Indians* then present originally owned those Lands; but said, that you would endeavour to bring as many of them down as you could find to the next Meeting.

*Brother,* According to the Promise I made you at our last Treaty, I laid all our Proceedings before Sir *William Johnson,* who, you have been often told, is appointed by our Great King his sole Agent for *Indian* Affairs in this District, to take Care of them as a Father, that no one may wrong them. Sir *William Johnson* has since deputed your and our Friend, Mr. *George Croghan,* who is well acquainted with your Affairs and Language, to act in his Behalf, to attend this Treaty, and enquire into every Grievance you may have suffered, either from your Brethren of *Pennsylvania,* or the neighbouring Provinces.

*Gave a String.*

*Brother,* I took Care, also to send Copies of our several Treaties with you to *England,* where they were laid before the King's Ministers, who, being desirous that Justice should be done you, ordered that Sir *William Johnson* should enquire into the Foundation of your Charge against this Province, in order that you may receive Satisfaction, in case any Injury has been done you.

*Brother,* I have freely opened my Heart to you, and am ready, with Mr. *Croghan,* His Majesty's Deputy Agent, whenever you think proper, to hear any Thing you may have to say to us about the Grievances you may think you labour under from this Province.

*Gave a String.*

*When the Governor had ended his Speech, I spoke as follows.*

*Brother* Teedyuscung, *and you my Brethren the Sachems and Warriors of the Ten Nations you represent at this Meeting,*

You have been informed by your Brother *Onas,* that the King of *Great-Britain,* your Father, has appointed Sir *William Johnson,* Baronet, to be His Majesty's chief Agent and Superintendent of the Affairs of the *Six Nations,* their Allies and Dependents in this District of *America,* and he has appointed me his Deputy, and ordered me to attend this Meeting, and hear any Complaints you have to make against your Brother *Onas,* in respect to his defrauding you of the lands mentioned in the Conference you held with this Government last Fall in this Town; or any other Injuries you have received from any of His Majesty's Subjects in this District. I am now ready to hear, what you have to say; and I assure you, in the Name of Sir *William Johnson,* I will do every Thing in my Power to have all Differences amicably adjusted to your Satisfaction, agreeable to his Orders and Instructions to me.

*Gave a Belt.*

When I had delivered my Speech, the Governor told *Teedyuscung* that we had done for the present; and that whenever he was ready to give an Answer, we should be ready to hear him. Then *Teedyuscung* replied, That he had something to say now; and, addressing himself to the Governor and me, spoke as follows.

*Brethren,* I will let you know in a few Words what my Desire is. I kindly receive your Words this Day: They are true, and make my Heart glad. By this Belt (holding up a Belt) I let you know I will speak To-morrow. I think it proper to speak my Mind with Openness. I think it my Duty to remember the Conduct of my foolish young Men. I see a great deal of Mischief done. I will first begin with cleaning up the Blood that has been shed, and removing the dead Bodies out of the Way: After that, I will make known my Grievances. I remember what Sir *William Johnson* said to me by the Messengers he sent to me: I sent back to him, by the same Messengers, and desired him, as he was a wiser Man than I, and of greater Abilities, that he would be strong, and lend his Assistance to cure this Wound.

*Gave a Belt.*

When *Teedyuscung* had ended his Speech, he told the Governor he thought he should be ready to speak To-morrow Morning at Eight o' Clock;—and that Time was accordingly appointed for the next Meeting.[2]

*At a* MEETING *in* Easton, Tuesday, July 26, 1757, A. M.
PRESENT, *The Honourable* WILLIAM DENNY, *Esq;*
*Lieutenant Governor,* &c.
*The Council. The same Members of the Assembly.*
*The Provincial Commissioners.*
*A Number of Gentlemen from the City of* Philadelphia,
*and others of the Inhabitants of this Province.*
*The same* Indians.
*Captain* Thomas McKee, *Interpreter for the Crown.*
Conrad Weiser, *Esq; Interpreter for the Province.*
*Mr.* John Pumpshire, *Interpreter for* Teedyuscung.

*I desired the Favour of Mr.* Jacob Duché *to assist Mr.* Trent *in taking down the Minutes.*

Teedyuscung *spoke to the Governor and myself, desiring us to give Attention; then directing his Speech to the King of* Great-Britain, *and all His Subjects, spoke as follows.*

*Brother,* YOU remember that you sent to me to come down to you, and invited me to bring down with me as many of the *Ten Nations* as I could, by Reason of the Difficulty of the Times. You then said to me, Brother, you are weak, I am strong: If you come down, I will put away all the Difference and Uneasiness that has happened, and will make a lasting Peace. Now, as I have brought some from each of the *Ten Nations* with me, I would have you remember your Promise, and exert your Power. Also, remember our Women and Children, that it may be well hereafter. Also, as you must remember the Blood that has been shed, and the dead Bodies that lie scattered up and down, I would have you join with me to remove these out of the Way, that we may see one another Face to Face, and after this we will proceed to other Business.

*Brother,* As you are a great deal stronger than I, you must exert your Power. When Differences arise between two Brothers, when one comes and makes Proposals of Peace, if the other does not accept them, nothing can be done. Now, as much Blood is spilt, I desire you will join with me to clear this away; and when that is done, we will proceed to other Business.

*Gave a Belt of eight Rows.*

*Brother,* According to the Promise I made you, that I would invite as many of the *Ten Nations* as I could, I have now brought with me as many as I could, who are here present, to witness what shall be transacted; but, in order to make a lasting and durable Peace, we must all exert our Abilities. When any Persons are engaged to lift a great Weight out of the Way, if all do not exert their Strength, they cannot remove it; but if all join, they will easily remove it. We, on our Parts, gather up the Leaves that have been sprinkled with Blood; we gather up the Blood, the Bodies and Bones; but when we look round, we see no Place where to put them; but when we look up, we see the Great Spirit above. It is our Duty therefore to join in Prayer, that he would hide these Things, that they may never be seen by our Posterity, and that the Great Spirit would bless our Children, that they may hereafter live in Love together; that it may never be in the Power of the evil Spirit, or any evil minded Persons to cause any Breach between our Posterity.

*Gave a Belt of seventeen Rows.*

*Brother,* As you remember you invited me to bring down some of the *Ten Nations,* so now some from each of them are here present, particularly some from my Uncles the *Five Nations.*[3] When we had endeavoured, as much as in our Power, to remove the dead Bodies, and the Mischief past, you also invited me to come, and take hold of your Hand. We accordingly now come, and take hold of one of your Hands, and the *Five Nations* also come and take of hold of the other Hand, that we may all stand together as one Man with one Heart. This now being done, when we look up, and see the clear Light, we shall enjoy it; we shall also enjoy, in Peace and Quietness, what the Land produces; and we shall enjoy the Comforts of the Day, and the Comforts of the Night; we shall lie down in Peace, and rise in Peace.

*Gave a Belt of twelve Rows, strung on Cords.*

*Brother,* The Reason of this great Cloud of Mischief that has been past is, that our old Standers, or Forefathers, never took regular Methods to have a lasting Peace: They never looked forward for their Children: They only had a View of this that decays, and what lies round about upon the Earth. When they came into Council, they only talked about the Things on the Earth, that are soon gone. They ought to have looked forward, and to have made such Agreements on both Sides, that their Children after might never disagree. And as we see their Mismanagement, let us do better, that we, as long as we live, may be faithful, and that by this our Meeting together our Children hereafter may enjoy a lasting Peace.[4]

*Gave a Belt of eleven Rows.*

*Brother,* You remember, according to your Orders, that Messengers have been sent to carry your Messages to distant Parts among us, in order to promote this good, this important Work of Peace, on which our Lives depend. One of these Messengers is now in a dangerous Condition, being shot by one of your young Men. Do not be too much grieved; but as I desire to be used with Justice, according to your Laws, I insist, if this young Man die, that the Man who shot him may be tried by your Laws, and die also, in the Presence of some of our People, who may witness it to all the Nations, that their Brethren the *English* have done them Justice. And if any Thing of the like Kind should happen on our Parts, we will do you the same Justice; that is, if any of our People shall murder any of yours, we will deliver up the Murderer, to be tried by your Laws. And as the Relations of the young Man must be grieved, I desire, as you have it in your Power, that you would remove the Grief and Sorrow from their Hearts.

*A String.*

The Governor then acquainted *Teedyuscung,* that we would take into Consideration what he had now said; and when we were ready to give an Answer, we would let him know.

As we were rising the King, by his Interpreter, told me, that what he had now said was of great Importance; he desired therefore we would take Time to consider it well; that he would wait with Patience till we were ready to give him an Answer.

*At a* MEETING *in* Easton, Wednesday, July 27, 1757, A. M.
PRESENT, *The Honourable* WILLIAM DENNY, *Esq; Governor*, &c.
*The Council. The same Members of the Assembly.*
*The Provincial Commissioners.*
*A Number of Gentlemen of the City of* Philadelphia,
*and others of the Inhabitants of the Province.*
*The same* Indians.
*Captain* Thomas McKee, *Interpreter for the Crown.*
Conrad Weiser, *Esq; Interpreter for the Province.*
*Mr.* John Pumpshire, *Interpreter for* Teedyuscung.

*The Governor opened the Conference by asking* Teedyuscung *if he was ready, and letting him know that Mr.* Croghan, *the King's Agent, joined him in the Speeches he was going to make, and then spoke as follows.*

*Brother,* YOUR Memory serves you faithfully, with Respect to what was promised by each of us in the last Conferences.

Our warmest Acknowledgments are due to you for your just Performance of your Engagements. You have made known our good Dispositions far and wide. You have brought down your Uncles, and some of each of the other Nations with whom you are joined. We are pleased to observe they have hearkened to you, and are come so well disposed to conclude and establish a firm and durable Peace. We return you very hearty Thanks in Behalf of His Majesty King *GEORGE,* the People of this Province, and all His other Subjects.

*Gave a Belt.*

*Brother,* We are sensible with you, that unless we both exert the utmost of our Strength, we shall not be able to accomplish the great Work we are mutually engaged in.

Whilst we see the dead Bodies of our People lying uncovered, and exposed to ravenous Birds, it is against Nature, and all the Principles of Religion and Humanity, to proceed to the Confirmation of Peace.[5]

We therefore, in Conjunction with you, diligently search for, and collect together, not only their dead Bodies and scattered Bones, but the very Leaves, Grass, and every Thing else that their Blood has touched; and join with you in looking up to Heaven, from whence the God of Peace beholds with Delight our Advances to Reconciliation, Concord and Unity. We pray he may cast a Veil over all that has happened in these unhappy Times, that it may be no longer remembered. We supplicate his Almighty Goodness to pardon all that is past. We pray him to dispose all the People of this, and the succeeding Generations, to the latest Posterity, to live in Love together. We entreat he will never permit the evil Spirit to enter so far into our Hearts, or evil minded Men so far into our Councils, as to interrupt the Course of Friendship, or blast the smallest Leaf in the Tree of Peace.

*Gave a Belt.*

*Brother,* Having now collected the dead Bodies, we agree with you to stand together, *English* and *Indians,* as one Man, with one Heart; we lay hold with you, your Uncles, and the *Ten Nations,* of the Belt of Friendship; we hold it fast with all our Strength. We bring with us all the Sincerity and Warmth of honest and upright Hearts. We rejoice to behold again the Light of the Sun shining in a clear Sky. We promise ourselves that, with the Blessing of the good Spirit, your Endeavours, united with ours, will be able to secure to us, and to our Children, and Childrens Children, durable Peace and Happiness, so that we may quietly enjoy the various Comforts of Life with which this fruitful Country abounds, and may sleep in Peace.

*Gave a Belt.*

*Brother,* Though our Forefathers and yours might make some Mistakes, and might not see far enough into the Consequences of some of their Measures, yet in general we can truly say, they were ever kindly disposed to one another; they were open and upright in their Intentions; they lived together in perfect Peace, and the mutual Exchange of good Offices.

It is very commendable in you to remind us that they have not been altogether regular, but confined their Views to the then present Times, and to the Interest of their own Generation, not so much consulting as they should have done the Good of future Generations. We shall be glad to join with you in promoting one general Interest, that may extend to the latest Posterity. We will lay aside all narrow partial Regards, and put Matters on a lasting Foundation, and endeavour to exceed our Ancestors, not only in the Goodness of our Measures, but in a more careful and exact Manner of doing Business.

*Gave a Belt.*

*Brother,* We have observed what you say, with respect to one of your Messengers. The Accident grieves us. In such Times, *Indians* should not go single, or into inhabited Parts, without proper Passports and Escorts.—We have careless and unthinking Men amongst us; we have bad Men too, who have mischievous Hearts. The Man who is supposed to have committed this Act is in Goal, and (in case the Messenger dies) shall be tried by our Laws, which require Blood for Blood, in the Presence of such *Indians* as you shall appoint to attend the Trial, of which you shall have due Notice. It is a Matter, firmly settled, by repeated Treaties, between us and the *Indians,* that whenever an *Englishman* kills an *Indian,* or an *Indian* kills an *Englishman,* the Murderer, or Person offending, shall be tried by our Laws, in the Presence of both Nations.

*Gave a String.*

*Brother* Moses Tetamy, You are the Father of the young Man who has been unfortunately wounded. It gives us great Concern that any Thing of this Kind should happen. We have employed the most skilful Doctor we have amongst us to take Care of him, and we pray that the Almighty would bless the Medicines that are administered for his Cure. We by this String of Wampum remove the Grief, from your Heart, and desire no Uneasiness may remain there. We have assured our Brother *Teedyuscung,* that strict Justice shall be done on the Trial, and we choose that you yourself should be a Witness of it.[6]

*Gave a String.*

*At a* MEETING *in* Easton, Thursday, July 28, 1757, P. M.
PRESENT, *The Honourable* WILLIAM DENNY, *Esq; Governor,* &c.
*The Council. The same Member of the Assembly.*
*The Provincial Commissioners.*
*A Number of Gentlemen of the City of* Philadelphia,
*and others of the Inhabitants of this Province.*

*Captain* Thomas McKee, *Interpreter for the Crown.*
Conrad Weiser, *Esq; Interpreter for the Province.*
*Mr.* John Pumpshire, *Interpreter for* Teedyuscung.
TEEDYUSCUNG, *King of the* Delawares,
*attended by several Chiefs and Deputies of the* Ten Nations *he represents.*

Teedyuscung *addressing himself to the Governor, spoke as follows.*

*Brother,* I DESIRE in a few Words to recollect what you told me the other Day, that the Great King, beyond the Water, had appointed a Man to oversee the Affairs of the *Indians,* viz. Sir *William Johnson,* who has nominated Mr. *Croghan* his Deputy. I am glad to hear this News, and to see the Man that is appointed. I hope, Brother, that it will be well accepted by both of us. It is our Duty to respect the Person that the King has appointed, and with Sincerity of Heart to join together, that as the present Business is well begun, it may end so. I hope he will execute his Commission with Justice. According to your Desire, what you mentioned in the last Treaty, and what you have said now, I will answer in a few Words; and we hope Mr. *Croghan* will be faithful to see Justice done on both Sides in the Name of the King.

*Gave a String.*

*Brother,* After I have opened the Passage from your Heart and Mind, that you may see and understand, by this Belt I desire you may fully understand what I now say. It is plain the Proceedings of our Ancestors were shorter than they ought to have been, in Respect and Behalf of their Children; and also their own everlasting Peace in the World to come. You may easily see the Reason, of the gloomy and dark Days; they have proceeded from the Earth. Our Misunderstanding or Mismanagement has proceeded from the Earth, as well as our Differences and Grievances that have passed and repassed. Though it was not the principal Cause that made us strike our Brethren the *English,* yet it has caused the Stroke to come harder than it otherwise would have come. Now it lies much in your Power to look strictly into your Hearts, as we always prefer and acknowledge you above us in Abilities, Strength and Knowledge. And as it lies a great deal in your Power to know whether what I have said, be true or not, it depends much on you, Brother, that it may be openly and publickly declared and published to the Province or Provinces under the Government of the Great King, both to his Satisfaction, and to the Satisfaction of those appointed to manage this Affair.—Brother, now as we have met together Face to Face to speak with great Sincerity, I will endeavour to lay every Thing plain before you, not to cover one Part, but to lay every Thing before you, that you may see plainly, in order that we may have true Satisfaction from one another, and that what may be proved to be our Right and Due, may be established for ever in a durable and lasting Peace.

*Gave a Belt.*

*Brother,* I would desire also that you would look with all Diligence, and see from whence our Differences have sprung. You may easily see they have sprung from the

Land or Earth, which was mentioned before, though it was not the principal Thing. If regular Methods had been formerly taken for an Habitation or Residence for the poor *Indians* in this Land, this would not have come to pass. Now as it lies much in your Power to search particularly into what was mentioned before, with respect to the Land, which was the Cause of our Differences, if I now can prevail with you, as I hope I shall, honestly to do what may be consistent with Justice, then I will, with a loud Voice, speak, and the Nations shall hear me. Then, it depends on you, Brother, as I shall speak with a loud Voice, and as you are of greater Abilities than I, to assist me, that what I speak to the Nations may be true, and that when I have made Proclamation with a loud Voice, by your Assistance, the Nations may hear and receive it with great Joy.

*Gave a Belt.*

Mr. *John Pumpshire,* being asked to explain what was meant by the first Part of this Speech, he said, the Meaning was this: The Land is the Cause of our Differences; that is, our being unhappily turned out of the Land, is the Cause: And though the first Settlers might purchase the Land fairly, yet they did not act well, nor do the *Indians* Justice; for they ought to have reserved some Place for the *Indians.* Had that been done, these Differences would not have happened.

*Brother,* I have now in a few Words to let you know what my Inclination and Desire is, agreeable to what have said. I now put it into your Power to make a lasting Peace, and that I may have my reasonable Enjoyment from this Land; as we are sensible that this Land was made by that Almighty Power that has made all Things, and has given this Land to us. I was the first to whom he gave it; and as it pleased him to convey you to us, and unite us in Friendship in the Manner already mentioned, which was well known by our Ancestors, it is now in your Power, and depends entirely on your Care and faithful Diligence, that it may not be broken as it has been; and if it be broken, it will be owing to you. I think it is my Duty to mention to you in publick, that I will comply with all Submission. This I ask, that I may have some Place for a Settlement, and for other good Purposes, in which we may both agree; but as I am a free Agent as well as you, I must not be bound up, but have Liberty to settle where I please.

*Gave a Belt of nine Rows.*

*Teedyuscung* informed the Governor, that he had done for this Time, and left it to the Governor's Pleasure to appoint a Time to answer him.

As the Governor had by Letter informed me, that *Teedyuscung*'s Speech appeared to him dark and confused, and desired me to call a Meeting in private with the *Indians,* and know what they meant; I accordingly, on the 30th of *July* at Five a Clock in the Morning, sent for the King, and some of his Counsellors, and desired them to call a Council, and consider well the Speeches the King had made, and afterwards to explain them to me. At Half after Nine o' Clock, King *Teedyuscung*, with *Jepiscauhunh, Epoweyowallund, Penawaghwottind, Lepaghpetund, Kuhtanamaku, Jangepapawey, Weneywalika,* his Counsellors, and *John Pumpshire,* Interpreter, met at my House, and explained his Speeches as follows.

The Complaints I made last Fall, I yet continue. I think some Lands have been bought by the Proprietary, or his Agents, from *Indians* who had not a Right to sell, and to whom the Lands did not belong. I think also, when some Lands have been sold to the Proprietary by *Indians* who had a Right to sell to a certain Place, whether that Purchase was to be measured by Miles or Hours Walk, that the Proprietaries have, contrary to Agreement or Bargain, taken in more Lands than they ought to have done, and Lands that belonged to others. I therefore now desire that you will produce the Writings and Deeds by which you hold the Land, and let them be read in publick, and examined, that it may be fully known from what *Indians* you have bought the Lands you hold, and how far your Purchases extend, that Copies of the Whole may be laid before King *GEORGE,* and published to all the Provinces under his Government. What is fairly bought and paid for, I make no further Demands about: But if any Lands have been bought of *Indians* to whom these Lands did not belong, and who had no Right to sell them, I expect a Satisfaction for these Lands. And if the Proprietaries have taken in more Lands than they bought of true Owners, I expect likewise to be paid for that. But as the Persons to whom the Proprietaries may have sold these Lands, which of Right belonged to me, have made some Settlements, I do not want to disturb them, or to force them to leave them, but I expect a full Satisfaction shall be made to the true Owners for these Lands, though the Proprietaries, as I said before, might have bought them from Persons that had no Right to sell them.

With respect to our Settlement, we intend to settle at *Wyoming,* and we want to have certain Boundaries fixed between you and us; and a certain Tract of Land fixed, which it shall not be lawful for us or our Children ever to sell, nor for you, or any of your Children, ever to buy. We would have the Boundaries fixed all round, agreeable to the Draught we give you, that we may not be pressed on any Side, but have a certain Country fixed for our own Use, and the Use of our Children for ever.

And as we intend to make a Settlement at *Wyoming* and to build different Houses from what we have done heretofore, such as may last not only for a little Time, but for our Children after us; we desire you will assist us in making our Settlements, and send us Persons to instruct us in building Houses, and in making such Necessaries as shall be needful; and that Persons be sent to instruct us in the Christian Religion, which may be for our future Welfare, and to instruct our Children in Reading and Writing; and that a fair Trade be established between us, and such Persons appointed to conduct and manage these Affairs as shall be agreeable to us.

I then asked him, as Fort *Augusta* was within the Lands he desired to be assigned to them, whether he would acknowledge that Fortress to belong to the King of *Great-Britain,* for the Use of His Subjects in *Pennsylvania,* and all His other Subjects;

and whether he would not be willing it should continue as a Trading-House, not only for the Good of us the *English,* and the Nations he represents, but of all the Nations that now are, or may be hereafter, in Alliance with us; and whether he will not engage, in Conjunction with the *English,* to defend it against any of His Majesty's Enemies that may come against it?

To which the King, in Behalf of the Nations he represents, replied, That he agrees that that Fort shall belong to the *English;* that it shall continue as a Trading-House; and he and his People, in Conjunction with their Brethren the *English,* engage to defend it against any of His *Britannick* Majesty's Enemies that shall come to attack it.

*At a* MEETING *in* Easton, Sunday, July 31, 1757, P. M.
PRESENT, *The Honourable* WILLIAM DENNY, *Esq; Governor,* &c.
*The Council. The same Members of the Assembly.*
*The Provincial Commissioners.*
*A Number of Gentlemen of the City of* Philadelphia, *and others, the Inhabitants of the Province.*
*Captain* Thomas McKee, *Interpreter for the Crown.*
Conrad Weiser, *Esq; Interpreter for the Province.*
*Mr.* John Pumpshire, *Interpreter for* Teedyuscung.
TEEDYUSCUNG, *King of the* Delawares,
*attended by several Chiefs and Deputies of the* Ten Nations *he represents, and a great Number of others.*

*King* Teedyuscung *desired that (before the Governor spoke) what passed between him and me in a private Conference Yesterday should be read in publick, which was accordingly done, and interpreted to the* Six Nations.

*Then the Governor made the following Speech.*

*Brother* Teedyuscung, *and Brethren Sachems and Warriors of the* Ten Nations, IT gives me Pleasure to hear you declare your Satisfaction at the Appointment our Great King has been pleased to make of Sir *William Johnson,* to be the Superintendent of the Affairs of the *Indians,* and that Sir *William* had appointed Mr. *Croghan* to be his Deputy; and further, to hear you so fully and openly acknowledge it to be the Duty of both of us to respect the Person whom the King has thought fit to entrust with so important a Commission. I thank you for these dutiful Expressions, and do not in the least doubt but they come from the Bottom of your Hearts.—I assure you, Brethren, I shall heartily join my Endeavours to yours, that the good Work of Peace, so well begun, may be happily finished to our mutual Satisfaction.

*Gave a String.*

*Brother,* You say that the Proceedings of our Ancestors were shorter than they ought to have been, in Respect and Behalf of their Children; and also of their own everlasting Peace. Brother, our Ancestors of this Province have been always esteemed a good, honest and wise People, and have always been distinguished for their brotherly Love and kind Treatment of the *Indians,* and their upright Dealing with them in their Publick Transactions. You say that the Cause of our Differences proceeded from the Land, and advise us to look strictly into our Hearts for the Truth of this. Brother, we have, according to your Desire, looked into our Hearts, and are not sensible that any of our Transactions with the *Indians,* either with Respect to Land, or otherwise, could have given Reason for the unhappy Breach betwen us. You have been so honest as to declare on all Occasions, that the Land was not the principal Cause why you struck us, but was only a Reason why the Stroke came the harder on us. As, then, it was not the Cause of our first Differences, it ought not to be any Obstacle to an immediate Conclusion of the Peace, which we are now met together with such good Intentions to establish. However we may differ in Opinion about Matters of Property, these are trifling Considerations, compared to the important Affair of uniting together in the firm Bands of Friendship. Let us therefore for the present suspend them, and all Matters of less Moment, and apply ourselves in the first Place heartily to the Great Work of Peace, so much wished for by both of us, and put Things on such a Footing, that the Great King over the Waters, and His Subjects, and all the *Indians,* shall be pleased with it.

*Gave a Belt.*

*Brother,* You say, that if you can prevail with us to do you Justice in your Complaint about Land, you will then with a loud Voice speak, and the Nations shall hear you. Brother, I must now inform you, that immediately after our last Treaty, I sent to the Proprietaries a Copy of the Complaints you then made of their defrauding you of your Lands, and received their Answer to it some Days before I set out to meet you here, wherein they express the greatest Concern that you, who they conceive have been so well treated both by their Father, *William Penn,* and themselves, should charge them with Crimes of so heinous a Nature as Fraud and Forgery, by which their Reputation (which to them and every honest Man is dearer than Life itself) is so deeply wounded. Your Complaint has likewise been laid before the King's Ministers, who, looking upon it as a Matter of great Importance, determined that it should be carefully enquired into, and examined, before some Person no ways concerned in Interest, on whose Honesty and Judgment they could depend; and therefore appointed Sir *William Johnson* to hear the Particulars of your Charge, and the Proprietary's Defence, and lay the whole Matter before His Majesty for his Royal Determination, in order that he may do you Justice himself, if you are injured.[7] Our great King looks on you as His Children; and therefore His Ministers have directed the same Method to be taken in hearing the Merits of your Complaint, as is used among His own Subjects, with this Difference only, that their Disputes are finally settled by Judges appointed for that Purpose; whereas, in your Case, His Majesty will determine it himself.

Before I received the Orders of His Majesty's Ministers, that your Complaints should be heard before Sir *William Johnson,* I fully intended, at this Meeting, to call on the Proprietaries Agents to answer the Charge you made against them, and to have the Matter strictly enquired into; but as I am the King's Servant, and bound by Duty as well as Inclination to obey His Orders, and His Majesty's Deputy Agent, Mr. *Croghan,* who is now present, informs me he has no Power to suffer any Altercations on this Complaint, and that he does not think it would be for the Good of His Majesty's Service, I must refer you on this Occasion to Sir *William Johnson,* to whom I shall send proper Persons to represent the Proprietaries, with Records, Deeds and Evidences, to shew the Justice of their Title at any Time he shall appoint, of which he will give Notice to you, and all Persons concerned. As that Gentleman is known to be a good Friend to the *Indians,* and a Man of Honour and Integrity, it gives me great Pleasure to find he is well approved of by you, and I do not doubt but you will most chearfully agree to leave the Examination of your Claims to him, and concur in the Method His Majesty has directed for settling our Differences, in which you will be certain of having strict Justice done you.

*Gave a Belt.*

*Brother,* I could give you many Instances of the great Affection and Regard the Proprietaries have for you, and all the *Indians;* and that they set a far greater Value on your Friendship, than on any private Interest or Advantage to themselves; they have lately given to you and the World a most convincing Proof of this. You no Doubt have heard, that the Proprietaries, about three Years ago, at a general Meeting of the *Six Nations,* held at *Albany,* fairly and openly purchased of them a great Country, lying on the West Side of the River *Sasquehannah;* but upon its being represented, that some of the *Indian* Tribes were dissatisfied with the Extent of that Grant beyond the *Allegheny* Hills, the Proprietaries chearfully agreed to surrender, and give up again to the *Indians,* the Lands Westward of those Hills, and have given their Agents Orders to release it to them at the proposed Meeting before Sir *William Johnson,* and to settle Boundaries with them.

*Gave a Belt.*

*Brother,* I have considered what you said about a Settlement for yourselves and your Posterity, and am informed by Mr. *Croghan,* that *Wyoming* is the Place you would chuse to settle at.

*Brother,* The Proprietaries have never granted away any Lands, though within the Limits of this Province, without first purchasing them of the *Indians;* and having never bought of them, the Lands between *Shamokin* and *Wyoming,* they have therefore never laid Claim to them under any *Indian* Purchase, and expresly desire this may be told to the *Indians,* lest evil-disposed Persons should have suggested any Thing to the contrary; and, in the Name of the Proprietaries, I now disclaim all such Right, of which I would have you take Notice. I am pleased you have made Choice that Place; it is perfectly agreeable to me, and I assure you I will heartily concur with you in using all the Means in my Power to have these Lands settled upon you and your Posterity, agreeable to your Request. As to the other Purposes for which you desire this Settlement of Lands, they are so reasonable, that I make no Doubt but, on my Recommendation of them to the Assembly, they will chearfully enable me to comply with them.

*Gave a Belt.*

*Brother,* I have now answered the Speeches you made me the other Day, and, I hope, to your Satisfaction, as I agree with you to submit the Differences about Lands to the Great King, which is your own Desire. I now assure you that I am heartily disposed and ready, with the King's Deputy Agent, to confirm the Peace which you and I have been for some Time taking Pains to establish.

*At a* MEETING *with the* Indians *in* Easton,
on Monday, August 1, 1757, P. M.
PRESENT, *The Honourable* WILLIAM DENNY, *Esq;* &c.
*The Council. The same Members of the Assembly.*
*The Provincial Commissioners.*
*A Number of Gentlemen of the City of* Philadelphia, *and others, the Inhabitants of the Province.*
*Captain* Thomas McKee, *Interpreter for the Crown.*
Conrad Weiser, *Esq; Interpreter for the Province.*
*Mr.* John Pumpshire, *Interpreter for* Teedyuscung.
TEEDYUSCUNG, *King of the* Delawares,
*attended by several Chiefs and Deputies of the* Ten Nations *he represents, and a great Number of others.*

Teedyuscung *addressing himself to the Governor, spoke as follows.*

*Brother, the Governor,* BY this Belt (holding up a Belt) I remember what you said Yesterday in the Evening. All was well accepted, and very good, only one Word, or one material Thing. When the several different Nations of us, that call ourselves the *Ten Nations,* that are present, I mean the Counsellors, had considered what you said, we approved all except one Thing. Also this Morning early, when we came to sit down by ourselves, and our Secretary with us, when we had done, and had fully understood one another, and agreed on every Word, we then ordered our Secretary to write it down.—[*John Pumpshire* said, I will just mention this in Addition; we ordered him to read it over three or four Times, and approved it.]—Having done that, we have the Words already written down, and if it please the Governor to hear it read; this that is written down is what was concluded on.

The Governor, in Answer, told him, Brother, you know that this is quite a new Method, and was never practiced before.

Brother, it is true, replied *Teedyuscung,* you are right; this was not formerly practised; it never used to be so. Don't you see that I aim, by having a Clerk of my own, to exceed my Ancestors, by having every Thing for the best. I endeavour, according to my Ideas, to look to those that have the Authority; as for Instance, if they take up a Handful of Corn or Pebbles, if they drop any, even one Grain, I will take Notice, and will speak of it, that they may take it up.

The Governor then applied to Mr. *Croghan,* to know whether this had ever been practiced in any Treaty; Mr. *Croghan* said it never was, and turning to the King, said, Brother, this is quite a new Method, and what was never before practised. I well know the *Indians* have good Memories, and can remember what was transacted twenty Years ago, as if Yesterday. I should therefore be glad the King would repeat himself what he has to say, as we are only treating with him.[8] Then *Teedyuscung* replied, Well, Brother the Governor, what we have consulted and concluded on this Morning is this; I remember you told me last Night, that what was transacted last Fall, was laid before the King's Ministers; and we took particular Notice that you told us, that some Time before you came from *Philadelphia,* you fully intended to make all Satisfaction to me at this Treaty about Lands and Deeds; but that you received a Letter, or Letters, from the King or Proprietaries, I am not certain which, you know best; in Consequence of which, you told us that you could not act in this Affair, but that Sir *William Johnson* was appointed to transact *Indian* Affairs, and Mr. *George Croghan* was appointed to act in his Name. We remember very well, when we had a private Conference with you at your Dwelling, that you and Mr. *Croghan* rose up, shook Hands with me, and you told us, this was the very Man that was appointed to act between the *English* and *Indians.* Now, in Consideration of these Things, why should we be obliged to go to Sir *William Johnson* to have the Proof of Lands and Deeds examined by him, when there is nothing in the Way, the Land Affair not being to be compared with the great Work of Peace, and should not be any Hindrance to our making a League of Friendship.

Now I will give you my Reasons for not going.

In the first Place, I do not know Sir *William Johnson;* he may be an honest and sincere Man. We do understand he treats his *Indians* very well; but we are sensible that some of the Nations are there that have been instrumental to this Misunderstanding, in selling Lands in this Province, having in former Years usurped that Authority, and called us Women, and threatened to take us by the Foretop, and throw us aside as Women. But, after a long Space, I believe it is evident, nay, there are Witnesses present, who can prove that it is otherwise. Also, when I have considered these several Particulars, as you told us there was nothing in the Way to hinder us from confirming a durable and lasting Peace, I at present desire nothing at all of my Brethren the *English* for my Lands, I only want, for the Satisfaction of the *Indians* of the *Ten Nations* present, and also of all other *Indians,* that the Deeds may be produced, and well looked into; and as you have told me that Mr. *George Croghan* was the Man that would settle Affairs for our Peace, here he is; I want nothing but to see the Deeds fairly looked into, and true Copies of them taken and put with these Minutes now taken. And, after they have been fairly taken down, if you agree to this, then I shall, by two Belts tied together, take you by the Hand, and, with my Uncles, confirm a lasting Peace with you; and if it please the Governor, and Mr. *Croghan,* let the Copy of the Deeds be sent to Sir *William Johnson,* and to the King, and let him judge. I want nothing of the Land till the King hath sent Letters back; then if any of the Lands be found to belong to me, I expect to be paid for it, and not before. Brother, another Reason for not going is, if we cannot agree to settle this Affair here, I am afraid the Nations that are watching and looking into what is done here, will have Reason to think we have not acted an honest Part, as they expect a real, true and lasting Peace will be settled here. I am also concerned on Account of our Women and Children back, and of our Brethren the *English* on the Frontiers. For these now present, who it was expected would go Home with great Joy, will go Home with their Finger in their Mouth, as every Body expected this would be the Time of confirming a real and lasting Peace. I told you I would proclaim with a loud Voice, and those present are Witnesses to what I said, and will not be easy if this is not done. I think nothing hinders us at all.

As you told us you had Letters from the King, or Proprietaries, I desire they may be produced and read, and put down with the Minutes. Now this is the Conclusion, and in Confirmation of what I have said, I give you this Belt.

*Gave a Belt.*

The King further said, I desire also that a Copy of what passed in private between you and me, may be given to be entered with these Minutes, and that it may be read in publick at our next Meeting.

As soon as the Meeting was over, I told the Governor, the Good of His Majesty's Service required, that *Teedyuscung*'s Request of having the Deeds and private Conferences read, and Copies of them given him, with a Copy of so much of the Proprietaries Letters as relates to having the Enquiry made by Sir *William Johnson,* should be granted.

*Easton, August* 2, 1757.

TEEDYUSCUNG, *with three* Nanticokes, *who arrived Yesterday, and three of his Council, came to me at my Lodgings, and desired I would hear what those* Nanticokes *had to say. Upon which the* Nanticoke *Chief made the following Speeches.*

*Brother,* THE chief Man of the *Nanticokes* has sent me here, to see the Governor and you; and desired me in his Name to wipe the Tears from your Eyes, which those troublesome Times may have occasioned; and I do it with this String of Wampum.

*A String.*

*Brothers,* You may have swallowed, since these Troubles arose, something bitter, which has given your Heart some Uneasiness: I, with this String of Wampum, remove all Grief from your Hearts, that your Minds may be as easy as they were in Times of Peace.

*A String.*

*Brothers,* I see a great deal of Blood spilt; I, with this String, clean the Blood from off your Beds, that you may sleep easy, and from off your Council Seats, that you may sit with Pleasure in Council with your Brethren; and with this Feather I open your Ears, which the great high Winds may have stopped, that you may hear what your Brothers may say to you.

*Brothers,* We must consider, and think it was not the good Spirit that has occasioned this Disturbance; no, it was the evil Spirit that surely occasioned all this Mischief, and I hope God will direct us to do every Thing in our Power to assist in the Good Work of Peace, that we may be once more united together, and live in Friendship, as the good Spirit has ordered us.

*Brothers,* I am come here to this Council Fire with our Cousins the *Delawares* and you, to give all the Assistance I can to the good Work of Peace, and to join my Cousin *Teedyuscung,* and the *Six Nations,* to gather up the dead Bodies and scattered Bones together, and will join in Prayer to the good Spirit to hide them; and when the Peace is confirmed, I will put both my Hands into the Chain of Friendship with you, and our Cousins the *Delawares* and the *Six Nations;* to confirm my Words, I give this String of Wampum.

*Gave a String.*

*At a* MEETING *with the* Indians *in* Easton,
*on* Wednesday, August 3, 1757, A. M.
PRESENT, *The Honourable* WILLIAM DENNY, *Esq; Governor,* &c.
*The Council. The same Members of Assembly.*
*The Provincial Commissioners.*
*A Number of Gentlemen from the City of* Philadelphia, *and others, the Inhabitants of this Province.*
*Captain* Thomas McKee, *Interpreter for the Crown.*
Conrad Weiser, *Esq; Interpreter for the Province.*
*Mr.* John Pumpshire, *Interpreter for* Teedyuscung.
TEEDYUSCUNG, *King of the* Delawares,
*attended by several Chiefs and Deputies of the Ten Nations he represents, and a great Number of others.*

*The Governor told* Teedyuscung, *that Five o' Clock Yesterday was appointed for the Time of Meeting; but understanding that the King was then particularly engaged with some Friends lately come in, he had deferred meeting them till this Morning.*

*The Governor spoke as follows.*

*Brother,* I HAVE well weighed and considered what you said to me at our last Meeting, and am sorry you do not incline to go to Sir *William Johnson* to have your Complaints strictly enquired into, and examined by him. It is true Sir *William* has, for some Time past, had a general Commission from the King to superintend *Indian* Affairs, and that he has given Mr. *Croghan* a Power to Act as his Deputy, under which he might have been justified in going into an Examination as well of your Complaints as the Proprietaries Defence, had not the King's Ministers lately been pleased to direct the Hearing to be before Sir *William Johnson* himself. Though you may think yourselves at Liberty, and may refuse to comply with these Directions, yet, as I told you before, I am the King's Servant, and obliged to obey, and cannot take upon me to go into a Defence of the Proprietaries Title at this Time. But as you so earnestly desire to see the Deeds for the Lands mentioned in your last Treaty, that you may be satisfied whether they are genuine, or whether the *Indians* who signed them had a Right to sell those Lands, I have brought them with me, and am willing to shew them to you now, or at any other Time you will appoint, and give you Copies of them, agreeable to your Request.

*Here the Deeds were laid down on the Table.*

And now let all further Debates and Altercations concerning Lands rest here, till they shall be fully examined and looked into by Sir *William Johnson,* in order to be transmitted to the King for His Royal Determination.

*Brother,* After having now gratified you in every reasonable Request, and being sincerely desirous to re-establish that Friendship and brotherly Love which so happily subsisted between your Ancestors and ours, I am ready, with the King's Deputy Agent, to take hold of the two Belts you mentioned with both my Hands, and confirm a lasting Peace, and exchange them with one prepared for that Purpose, in the Name of the King of *England,* and all His Subjects, as soon as we can agree upon the Terms.

*Brother,* The Orders of His Majesty's Ministers, on this Occasion, have been signified to me by the Proprietaries, which is the proper Channel through which they should come. That you may the better understand this, it will be necessary to inform you, that the Proprietaries are Governors in Chief over this Province, and I am appointed their Deputy, with the Approbation of the Crown. When, therefore, the last Treaty was laid before the King's Ministers, they gave the Proprietaries Notice of their Resolution, that the Matter should be heard before Sir *William Johnson* only, to whom they would send special Directions for that Purpose. The Proprietaries, for whom I act in this Case, have made me acquainted with the Ministers Orders, and desired me to regulate my Conduct by them. It would have been irregular and improper to have sent the Order itself to me, but I do not doubt the King's Ministers have transmitted it to Sir *William Johnson,* as an Authority for him to hear and examine our Differences, and that he has received it before this Time. As I could not suspect that you would have required a Copy of such of the Proprietaries Letters as relate to this Matter, I did not bring them with me here; wherefore, it is not in my Power to comply with your Request, to furnish you with Copies of them; and to confirm the Truth of this, I give you this Belt of Wampum.

When the Governor had ended his Speech, he asked the King whether he would have the Deeds read now, and Copies taken. Before the King returned an Answer, he took up the Belt which the Governor had just delivered, and rising up, spoke first to the *Delawares,* and then to the *Five Nations;* then turning to the Governor, said,

*Brother,* I understand the Words, you have said here; but they are not agreeable to your Knowledge, nor a full Answer to what I said. There are two Things not agreeable.

The Governor said, Will the King please to tell what these two Things are. No, replied the King, let the Governor find them out. The Governor said, he did not know what the King meant; he wished he knew what Answer to make.

*Teedyuscung* then said, If it please the Governor, in a few Words, what has been spoken on that Belt is as a Rumbling over the Earth, or Confusion about Lands. I did not want you to make Mention of them; when I expected an Answer in a loving Manner, I wanted you should come to the main Point, without having so many Words with it.

As the *Indians* seemed very much at a Loss about the Governor's Speech, I spoke to the King, and told him, that the first Part of the Governor's Speech was only to inform the King that the Deeds are now produced, and Copies will be given to him, agreeable to his own Request, that they may be sent to Sir *William Johnson,* to be by him transmitted to the King for his Determination. This done, we in the next Place now offer to take hold of the two Belts you mentioned at the last Meeting: That what was said about agreeing upon Terms, only referred to the Exchange of Prisoners, and other Things usual on making Peace; which *Teedyuscung* said he would do after the Peace was confirmed: That in the Conclusion of his Speech, the Governor only told the King, that the Proprietaries Letters, for a Copy of which the King asked, were at *Philadelphia,* for which Reason, the Governor could not comply with what the King requested, but that an Extract of as much of them as referred to this Affair, will be delivered to me some Time hence: In Confirmation of which the Governor gave the Belt.

As soon as the King heard this, he rose up; and taking up the two Belts tied together, he spoke as follows.

I desire you would with Attention hear me. By these two Belts I will let you know what was the ancient regular Method of confirming a lasting Peace. This you ought to have considered, and to have done; but I will put you in Mind. You may remember, when you took hold of my Hand, and led me down, and invited my Uncles, several of whom are present, with some from each of the *Ten Nations,* when we had agreed we came down to take hold of one of your Hands, and my Uncles came to take hold of the other Hand. Now, as this Day and this Time is appointed to meet and confirm a lasting Peace, we, that is, I and my Uncles, as we stand, and you, as you stand in the Name of the Great King, three of us standing, we will all look up, and by continuing to observe the Agreements, by which we shall oblige ourselves one to another, we shall see the clear Light, and Friendship shall last to us, and our Posterity after us, for ever. Now, as I have two Belts, and Witnesses are present who will speak the same, by these Belts, Brothers, in the Presence of the *Ten Nations,* who are Witnesses, I lay hold of your Hand (taking the Governor by the Hand) and brighten the Chain of Friendship that shall be lasting; and whatever Conditions shall be proper for us to agree to, may be mentioned afterwards: This is the Time to declare our mutual Friendship. Now, Brother the Governor, to confirm what I have said, I have given you my Hand, which you were pleased to rise and take hold of; I leave it with you. When you please, I am ready. Brother, if you have any Thing to say as a Token of confirming the Peace, I shall be ready to hear; and as you arose, I will rise up, and lay hold of your Hand. To confirm what I have said, I give you these Belts.

*Gave two Belts tied together.*

The Governor said, that he and I would be ready to give an Answer presently.

Then the King taking out another Belt, said, If the Governor please, I have a Word or two more to say to you. In remembering the old ancient Rules of making Friendship, I remember I was formerly represented as a Woman by my Uncles, the *Six* or *Five Nations;* but they gave me a Pipe, and good Tobacco; those present know it to be true; and what I say is in Behalf of all those present, and those afar off. That Pipe and good Tobacco of Friendship, I now deliver to you. Brother, when you shall smoke that good Tobacco, it will give you such a Relish, that you shall feel it as long as the Sun shines. That very good Tobacco and Pipe that I shall deliver into your Hand, represents among us a perpetual Friendship. Now I deliver you an equal Part of it, and I desire it may be a lasting Comfort in this World, and the World to come.

*Gave a Belt.*

After *Teedyuscung* had confirmed the Peace in Behalf of the *Ten Nations* he represents, his Honour the Governor, and myself, confirmed it in Behalf of the King, and all His Subjects, and exchanged the Belts in the following Manner.

*Brother* Teedyuscung, *and all our Brethren of the* Ten Nations, We your Brethren, all His Majesty's Subjects now present, have heard with Satisfaction, what you have said, and with great Pleasure receive the two Belts you have given us, which will confirm a lasting Peace to us and our Posterity, and we embrace this Meeting to exchange with you a Belt of Friendship, and take hold of you with one Hand, and of the *Five Nations* with the other, and confirm, in the Name of the King of *Great-*

*Britain,* and all His Subjects, a lasting Peace, that may continue as long as the Sun and Moon give Light; and we hope this Day may be always held in Remembrance by our Posterity; and we will be ready to consult with you at any Time about settling other Matters, as you yourself have said. We now rise and take you into our Arms, and embrace you with the greatest Pleasure as our Friends and Brethren, and heartily desire we may ever hereafter look on one another as Brethren, and Children of the same Parents: As a Confirmation of this we give you this Belt.

*Gave a very large white Belt, with the Figures of three Men in it, representing His Majesty King* GEORGE, *taking hold of the* Five Nation *King with one Hand, and* Teedyuscung, *the* Delaware *King, with the other, and marked with the following Letters and Figure,* G. R. 5 N. D. K. *for King* GEORGE, Five Nations, Delaware *King.*

This done, the King again asked the Governor for a Copy of the Conferences that had been held in private, that they might be read in Publick, and entered with the Minutes. The Governor said it was ready, and should be delivered immediately, and one was sent for it. The Governor then asked the King when it would be agreeable to him to have the Deeds read. The King said, To-morrow Morning, between Seven and Eight a Clock; which Time was accordingly agreed on; and the Reading of the Private Conferences was deferred till that Time.

I think it necessary to insert here the following Speech of *Laboughpeton,* a *Delaware* Chief, made to *Teedyuscung* at the Time he seemed at a Loss about the Governor's Speech to him, which is as follows.

"What, has not our Brother desired you to bring us down by the Hand to make Peace? why don't you do it? We have been here these twenty Days, and have heard nothing but scolding and disputing about Lands: Settle the Peace, and let all these Disputes stand till after."[9]

As soon as the Meeting was over, I let the Governor know I could not help taking Notice, that there was one Deed relative to those Lands wanting, which is mentioned in a Treaty held by this Government with the *Indians* in 1728, said there to be dated in 1718, and that I expected to see that Deed, and have a Copy of it; and likewise, Extracts of so much of the Proprietaries Letter to him as relates to the Desire of His Majesty's Ministers, signifying to them, that they ordered the Differences subsisting between them and the *Indians* to be examined by Sir *William Johnson.* And that as *Teedyuscung,* in Answer to a Message his Honour had sent by Mr. *Weiser* to him Yesterday Morning (which will appear as follows) said, that he would be contented, so he see all the Deeds relative to these Back Lands now in Dispute, and have Copies of them, and of the Proprietaries Letter; and further said, as soon as that was done, he would not say one Word more about the Disputes about Lands; I then let his Honour know, as *Teedyuscung* had now confirmed the Peace, I expected his Honour would now furnish me with a Copy of that Deed, and the Proprietaries Letter to him.

*Easton, August* 2, 1757.

THIS Morning, *Teedyuscung* sent *Samuel Evans* for me to come to him at Colonel *Weiser*'s Lodging: I went there, and found him with five of his Counsellors, and Mr. *Weiser.* Upon my coming in, Mr. *Weiser* told *Teedyuscung* that he wanted to have some Conversation with him. *Teedyuscung* asked him if it was by Order of the Governor. Mr. *Weiser* replied, it was by Consent of the Governor and Council.

Mr. *Weiser* then asked *Teedyuscung,* whether he wanted to see all the Deeds of the Province from the first Purchases, or only those relating to the Back Lands where we are. Mr. *Weiser* said, the Reason for his asking was, that he believed the whole of the Deeds were not brought up, but such only as were thought necessary, and relating to his Complaint, and the late Purchases.

*Teedyuscung* answered, I should be well pleased to have seen all the Deeds, as the Country, to the Sea Shore was first ours; but if there be the Deeds for these Back Lands, which is the main Point, I will be contented, so that I see them, and have Copies of them, and of the Letters, from the King's Ministers or Proprietaries; as soon as that is done, I will not say one Word more about the Differences or Lands, but confirm the Peace as soon as that is done.

This Evening the Governor wrote me, that his Letter from the Proprietaries was in *Philadelphia,* Extracts of which he would give me as soon as I went to Town. And he assured me, that he would give me a Copy of the Deed mentioned in the Treaty of 1728.

*At a* MEETING *with the* Indians *in* Easton, Thursday, August 4, 1757.
PRESENT, *The Honourable* WILLIAM DENNY, *Esq; Governor,* &c.
*The Council. The same Members of Assembly.*
*The Provincial Commissioners.*
*A Number of Gentlemen from the City of* Philadelphia, *and others, the Inhabitants of the Province.*
*Captain* Thomas McKee, *Interpreter for the Crown.*
Conrad Weiser, *Esq; Interpreter for the Province.*
*Mr.* John Pumpshire, *Interpreter for* Teedyuscung.
TEEDYUSCUNG, *King of the* Delawares,
*attended by several Chiefs and Deputies of the* Ten Nations *he represents, and a great Number of others.*

THE Conferences held in Council between the Governor and King *Teedyuscung* were produced, and read; and to them was added, by Order of the King, and approved by the Governor, a Paragraph relating to the King's insisting a second Time on having a Secretary, and the Governor's Answer.

The Deeds shewn Yesterday were again produced, and *Teedyuscung* was told, that Mr. *Charles Thompson,* his Secretary, had got Copies of them, and compared them with the Originals; and was asked if he chose to see the Originals. The King said, I am satisfied, as my Secretary has seen the Copies compared. If he is satisfied that they are true Copies, I am satisfied that they should be sent to the King for His Determination; then asked Mr. *Thompson* if he had seen them compared. Mr. *Thompson* said, he had seen and compared all the Deeds that were delivered Yesterday. The King then desired an Account of what Deeds were produced, which was accordingly taken, and is as follows. 1. A Paper Copy of the last *Indian* Purchase, 28th of *Sixth Month,* 1686. 2. A Release from the *Delaware Indians, August* 25, 1737. 3. A Release of the *Indians* of the *Five Nations* of the Lands on *Sasquehannah* River, *October* 11, 1736. 4. A Release from the *Six Nations* of Lands Eastward to *Delaware* River, dated *October* 25, 1736, with another indorsed on it, dated the 9th of *July,* 1754. 5. A Deed of Release for *Indian* Purchase, dated the 22d of *August,* 1749.

Note, *The above Deeds were shewn in open Council, and Copies of them delivered to* Teedyuscung, *which his Secretary acknowledged he had compared with the Originals, and that they were true Copies.*

When this was done, the Governor spoke to *Teedyuscung* as follows.

*Brother* Teedyuscung, *and all our Brethren of the* Ten Nations, As you and all His Majesty's Subjects are now united again in the firm Bands of Peace, it is our Duty to do every Thing in our Power to make each other happy; and it was stipulated at the Conferences held at this Place last Summer, that all Prisoners you had taken should be delivered up.

The Relations of those who yet remain Prisoners amongst you, have their Eyes fixed on me, expecting at my Return to see their Friends restored to them; but as few of them are brought down, and this will be a Bar to our Happiness, it is necessary for you to do every Thing in your Power to restore to us, as soon as possible, all our People that remain Prisoners amongst any of your Nations; and to procure those who are among any other Tribes in Amity with you, to be sent to us.

*Brother,* It is a Rule among Nations, upon confirming a Peace, to deliver up all Prisoners on both Sides. It is the only Method we can take to convince each other of our Sincerity; and we do insist on this being done. You will be so good, immediately on your Return, to convey them down by some of your young Men, who shall be well rewarded for their Trouble.

*Gave a Belt.*

When the Governor had delivered his Speech, and gave the Belt, *Teedyuscung* said, I will take no other Belt but the very same I have. Why have you done this now? Why did you not do it before? After we had finished, why do you make any Words about such Things? This was your Duty; you ought to have done it before. If you really believed I would be faithful and honest, you might be sure I would do it without your delivering a Belt. Now, as you have mentioned these Things, I also will mention, that you must deliver me my just Due about Lands. As you mention that your People look to you, expecting to see their Relations sent back at this Treaty, so the Nations that lay Claim to these Lands look to me for them.

*Returned the Belt.*

The Governor told *Teedyuscung,* that he did not do this, as if he had distrusted his Honour, the King having already given it full Proof of that, by delivering up some Prisoners, for which he thanked him; that he only meant to put the King in Mind of his Promise.

I then told *Teedyuscung,* that before the Peace was concluded, when I was explaining to him the Governor's Speech, that Part of it where the Governor says, "as soon as we can agree upon the Terms," related intirely to the Exchange of Prisoners, and *Teedyuscung* said, that should be settled afterwards.

*Teedyuscung* then applied to his Secretary, to know if any such Thing had been mentioned; and being informed by his Secretary, that it was entered in the Minutes, he *(Teedyuscung)* then rose up, and, having first consulted with his own People, and the *Five Nations* spoke as follows.

*Brother, the Governor,* Please to hear me in few Words. What you told me I have told to my Uncles the *Six Nations* present, and also to all the *Ten Nations.* We have consulted on these Words that you have now spoken: We now think they were very proper, and are very agreeable: We look on it as our Duty: Why should we keep your Flesh and Blood, or any of your People, when we have agreed as one, and look on one another as one, and treat one another as Brethren? After we have all considered, and all present have heard, we beg your Pardon, that we forgot to give you an Answer immediately. As it was written down by our Clerk in the Minutes Yesterday, it must be so; and as we are now sensible this Matter was mentioned Yesterday, we accept your Words, and look on it as our Duty to answer you, and to perform; whatever shall be in our Power, we shall endeavour to do. In Confirmation of which I give you my Hand.

*Gave the Governor his Hand.*

After this Speech the Governor again delivered back the Belt to the King, who readily accepted it.

The Governor then told the *Indians,* that a Present was prepared, and would be delivered to them To-morrow, as a Token of Friendship.

I told *Teedyuscung,* that as the Business was now nearly finished with *Onas,* I had something to say to him, in the Name of the King of *Great-Britain,* and that I would let him know when I was to speak to him.

After the Council broke up, the Governor sent for *Teedyuscung,* and some of his Counsellors, to his Lodgings, from whence we went to Mr. *Vernon*'s, where an handsome Entertainment was provided, at which were present, the Governor, his Council, the Speaker, and Members of Assembly, the Commissioners and Gentlemen in Town; the *Delaware* King, his Counsellors, Warriors, and all the *Indians,* Men, Women and Children, in Number about Three Hundred. After Dinner Peace was proclaimed in Form, and the Proclamation interpreted to the *Delawares* and *Six Nations;* at the Close of which, the Governor, by his Secretary, expressed his Satisfaction at being one of the happy Instruments of bringing about this Peace. His Honour recommended it to all Ranks and Professions of Men, to cultivate, to the utmost of their Power, a good Understanding with the *Indians,* and to treat them kindly, that they may daily see the Advantage of preserving our Friendship.

Having given this in Charge to the Freeholders present, he desired *Teedyuscung* to do the same to his People, that we might on both Sides forget what was past, and live affectionately together for the Time to come. A Detachment of the *Pennsylvania* Troops was drawn up in the Front of the Company, and fired three Vollies.

The Governor afterwards continued his Entertainment, at which there was a great Chearfulness. At Night was a large Bonfire, and a Variety of *Indian* Dances.

*At a* MEETING *with the* Indians *in* Easton, Friday, August 5, 1757.
PRESENT, *The Honourable* WILLIAM DENNY, *Esq; Governor,* &c.
*The Council.* Daniel Roberdeau, *Esq; Member of the Assembly.*
*The Provincial Commissioners.*
*A Number of Gentlemen from the City of* Philadelphia, *and others, the Inhabitants of the Province.*
*Captain* Thomas McKee, *Interpreter for the Crown.*
Conrad Weiser, *Esq; Interpreter for the Province.*
*Mr.* John Pumpshire, *Interpreter for* Teedyuscung.
TEEDYUSCUNG, *King of the* Delawares, *and the same* Indians *as before.*

THIS Morning another Sheet of Council Conferences was produced, which the Governor said was omitted to be delivered Yesterday; for which Reason they were delivered, and publickly read To-day, and ordered to be annexed to the Conferences in Council, delivered and read Yesterday.

After this was read, *Teedyuscung* arose and said, Brother, I am obliged to you; I hope, as it lies in your Power, you will act for our mutual Good. I take you as a Brother. When any Thing is omitted, I hope you will mention it to me; and I likewise will mention any Thing that I find you may have forgotten. I hope we both speak with an honest Heart. I trust much to my Interpreter. I thank you for making that Addition, and, in Token of Friendship, I give you my Hand.[10]

*The Governor then addressed the* Indians *as follows.*

*Brethren,* The Peace, so happily concluded, gives an universal Joy. I shall proclaim it far and wide, that all may hear and know it. The People of this Province are disposed to observe it faithfully, and will do the *Indians* every good Office in their Power.

Altho' we have now so solemnly entered into this Peace with each other, yet you are sensible there are still many Enemy *Indians,* who are daily doing Mischief on our Frontiers. Yesterday I received an Account of one Woman's being killed, and four Persons taken Prisoners, between *Tolhao* and *Monaidy.* As it will therefore be very difficult to distinguish between our Friends and our Enemies, I should be glad you would favour me with your Advice how to act in such a Manner, as not to hurt our Friends, or suffer our Enemies to escape.

*Gave a String.*

*Brethren,* The Governor, and People of this Province, observe, with a brotherly Compassion, the many Difficulties to which the *Indians* are exposed in these troublesome Times, and have therefore provided a Quantity of Goods to supply them in their Distress. You will, on your Return Home, proclaim the Peace, Union and Friendship, which is now established between us, and let every one know, as you have Opportunity, how well disposed you have found us. Accept these Presents, as a Testimony of the sincere Affection of us your Brethren towards you.

*To this* Teedyuscung *replied,*

*Brother,* I am obliged to you for putting me in Remembrance of these Things. I will take them into Consideration, and To-morrow, when I am ready to give you an Answer, I will let you know. He further added,

*Brother,* There is something which we intended to say before, but forgot, as we have not the Use of Writing. But better late than never; we will therefore mention it now. The Copy of the Deeds, and the Transactions of this Treaty, we entrust to our Clerk. We believe him to be an honest Man. Every Thing is done to Perfection. We hope you will not be against his making out a Copy, and giving it to Mr. *Isaac Norris,* whom we also appoint for us, to transmit to the King a Copy of the Deeds and Minutes of the Treaty, that, if one should miscarry, the other may go safe.

On which I acquainted *Teedyuscung,* that the Governor and myself had no Objection to Mr. *Norris*'s having true Copies of the Minutes of these Conferences and Deeds, to send to the King, as he requested.

Then, by Order of the Governor, Proclamation was made, that no One should cheat, defraud or purchase any of the Goods now ready to be given to the *Indians,* upon the Pain and Penalties that may fall thereon.

Then *Teedyuscung* said, he had yet one Thing more to mention.

*Brother,* I have some Complaints to make about Lands in the *Jerseys,* in Behalf of myself, *John Pumpshire, Moses Tetamy,* and others; which Complaints are contained in these two Papers: And as you represent Sir *William Johnson,* the King's Agent here, I desire you may take them under your Consideration, and see that Justice is done us on that Account, as it is the *King*'s Orders to you, to see Justice done to all the *Indians* in these Parts.

*Teedyuscung* then ordered Mr. *Thompson* to read the Papers, and give me true Copies of them, which he did immediately in publick Council.

The Papers delivered me are, a Copy of an old *Indian* Deed, and a Letter of Complaint about Lands in the *Jerseys,* signed by *John Pumpshire;* I then acquainted him, that I would take the Papers under my Consideration, and give him an Answer.

*Easton, August* 6, 1757.

THIS Morning I expected to have had a Meeting with the *Indians,* but as the friendly Association of *Quakers* had called the *Indians* together, to deliver them a Present, the *Indians* thought proper to put off the Meeting for this Time.

After this the three *Nanticoke* Messengers came to me, and congratulated the Governor and myself on the Conclusion of the Peace, and said, they had put both their Hands into the Chain of Friendship, as they were ordered by their Chief before they left Home, and, by a String of Wampum, desired that the Governor might send some Person with them to *Lancaster,* to take Care of them, and supply them with Necessaries on the Road, as they were come to take the Bones of their Friends which died at *Lancaster,* to their own Town, to be buried with their Relations.

*Gave a String.*

This Afternoon *Packsinosa,* the *Shawanese* Chief, with *Abraham,* a *Mohickon* Chief, and about Fifty or Sixty of their People, came to Town. Soon after Mr. *Peters,* and *Conrad Weiser,* went to them, and, with a String of Wampum, bid them Welcome, agreeable to the ancient Custom of our Forefathers. *Teedyuscung,* and the *Six Nation* Chief, did the same.

*At a* MEETING *with the* Indians *in* Easton, *on* Sunday, August 7, 1757,
*at Seven o' Clock in the Morning.*
PRESENT, Joseph Galloway, William Masters, Joseph Fox, John Hughes,
*Esquires, Provincial Commissioners.*
*Some Gentlemen from the City of* Philadelphia, *and others,*
*the Inhabitants of the Province.*
*Captain* Thomas McKee, *Interpreter for the Crown.*
Conrad Weiser, *Esq; Interpreter for the Province.*
*Mr.* John Pumpshire, *Interpreter for* Teedyuscung.
TEEDYUSCUNG, *King of the* Delawares, *and his Chiefs.*
Packsinosa, *Chief of the* Shawanese. *The* Nanticoke *Messengers.*
Abraham, *Chief of the* Mohiccons.
Anaquateeka, *Chief of the* Six Nations.

Teedyuscung, *taking out the Peace Belt that had been delivered to him by the Governor and myself, repeated over what had been said on it, informing* Packsinosa *and* Abraham *of the Peace concluded by him between the* English *and the* Ten *several* Nations *he represents, repeating over the Names of the* Ten Nations.

*After which I spoke to them, in the Name of Sir* William Johnson, *as follows.*

*Brother* Teedyuscung, *and all the Chiefs and Warriors of the* Ten Nations, *our Friends and Brethren,* As we are now become one People, we must look on the Enemies of the one as the Enemies of the other.

And I now, in the Name of the King of *Great-Britain,* your Father, and my Master, desire you will turn the Edge of your Hatchet against your and our common Enemies, in Conjunction with your Uncles the *Six Nations* and us; and that you will not suffer any of His Majesty's Enemies to pass through your Country to war against any of His Subject in this or the neighbouring Colonies: And if a Body of the Enemy, so large that you are not able to repel, should attempt to pass across your Country, I expect you will give the earliest Notice you can of it to your Brethren the *English,* either by Way of *Fort Augusta,* or any other Way you shall judge most convenient.

*Gave a Belt.*

*Brother,* You said, as soon as the Peace should be confirmed, that you would speak with a loud Voice, and the Nations around should hear you. As that good Work is now happily accomplished, I desire you may proclaim it aloud, that all the Nations may hear it.

*Brother,* You must be sensible that your Brethren, the *English,* are the most wealthy and powerful People on this Continent, and not only so, but the best inclined to help and assist their Brethren the *Indians* with the Necessaries of Life; all this you should let the Nations know that you speak to; and I assure you, in the Name of the King of *Great-Britain,* and of Sir *William Johnson,* His Majesty's sole Agent, and Superintendent of the Affairs of the *Six Nations,* their Allies and Dependents, in the Northern District, that they are ready to receive with open Arms all the Nations you shall speak to, that desire to take hold of the Chain of Friendship, and be united with the *Six Nations,* you, and us, your Brethren the *English.*

*Gave a Belt.*

*Brother,* The Papers you delivered me Yesterday, containing your, *John Pumpshire, Tundy,* alias *(Moses) Tetamy,* and others, Complaints of Lands you say you have been defrauded of in the *Jerseys;* I assure you I will do every Thing in my Power to have a strict Enquiry made about them, and when I can get the fair State of the Case, I will lay it before Sir *William Johnson,* for him to send to the King for His Royal Determination, unless the Difference can be settled here to your Satisfaction.

*Gave a String.*

*To this* Teedyuscung *answered,*

*Brother,* I will, in Answer to what you tell me, let you know what I intend to do. I shall, Brother, as I promised to speak with a loud Voice to the Nations, perform my Promise, and speak to the different Nations. I will faithfully let them know what you have promised, and, as we are Witnesses that you are wealthy and powerful, and well disposed to assist such as shall come in as Brothers, I will let them know it. And also, as I think it is very proper that I should do so, and as I think it my Duty, whatever Nation I see coming against the *English,* whenever I see them, I will make ready, and do every Thing in my power to vindicate the Cause of myself, and of my Brethren. If I am able, I will let them go no farther than where I tell them to stop. If they will not, by reasonable Terms, turn about, and join with me, I will then either make an End of them, or they of me. And if there is a great Number, so that I may not be able to withstand them, I will take all prudent Steps to let my Brethren the *English* know. And also, if I perceive that there is so great a Number, that it is not safe for my Women and Children, I will acquaint my Brethren the *English,* that they may assist me in defending my Women and Children, and I will leave my Country, and bring them down to you.

Now, you may remember I was stiled by my Uncles, the *Six Nations,* a Woman in former Years, and had no Hatchet in my Hand, but a Pestle or Hominy Pounder; but now, Brethren, here are some of my Uncles, who are present, to witness the Truth of this; as I had no Tomahawk, and my Uncles were always stiled Men, and had Tomahawks in their Hands, they gave me a Tomahawk. And as my Uncles have given me the Tomahawk, and I appointed and authorized me to make Peace with a Tomahawk in my Hand, I take that Tomahawk, and turn the Edge of it against your Enemies the *French.* In Confirmation of what I now say, I give you this String.

*Gave a String.*

*Brother,* I have just a Word or two more. I remember what you have spoken, in order that we may prevent any Mischief, by having a Signal: I should be glad that the *French* may not deceive us, that not one but several Signs and Methods may be fixed on by you. And whatever you shall think proper, I will agree to.

*Gave a Belt.*

I then returned *Teedyuscung* Thanks for his kind Speech, and let him know that I would consult with the Governor about settling the Signals, and would give him an Answer.

*Teedyuscung* then taking up four Belts, and a String, spoke to his Uncles, the *Six Nations,* telling them, that as they had empowered him, he had, in the Presence of these Witnesses they had sent, made a firm Peace with their Brethren the *English;* he, therefore, by these Belts desired, that they would perform their Part; and as they said they would take hold of the *English* by one Hand, and he by the other, he had now done it. And as the Chain of Friendship was now brightened, he desired they would be strong, and if they see any Enemies coming against us, they would look on it, that whoever strikes any one of us strikes all. These Belts he gave to *Anaqua-teeka,* and desired he would carry them to the *Six Nations.*

*Teedyuscung* then acquainted me that he had done; whereupon *Packsinosa* spoke to me as follows.

*Brother,* I heartily thank you for being so kind as to wipe the Sweat from our Faces, picking out the Briars, and taking away all bad Thoughts from our Minds, and cleaning the Passage from the Heart to the Throat, that we may see our Brethren, and be well from all our Wounds. By these Strings we return you Thanks.

*Gave a String.*

The same he said by another String to the *Six Nations* and *Delawares.*

Then the young Warrior, *Anaquateeka,* arose, and, directing his Speech to the *English,* and his Cousins, said,

*Brethren,* My Cousins have entrusted me with all that was here transacted, respecting the great Work of Peace here confirmed, to lay it before the *Six Nations.* I assure you I will execute the Trust reposed in me with Faithfulness, and lay it before the *Six Nations,* particularly before the *Senecas,* to whom I belong. I do not pretend to be a Counsellor: I am a young Warrior; yet the Affairs of War and Peace belong to us Warriors: And as I am entrusted, I assure you I will take Care that all the *Six Nations* may know what is here done.

Then his Honour the Governor, Mr. *Logan,* and Mr. *Peters,* came into Council. I acquainted the Governor, that I thought it was proper what had been transacted this Morning should be read, and it was accordingly done; after which the Governor addressed *Packsinosa* as follows.

*Brother* Packsinosa, You have been frequently invited by this Government to come and give us the Pleasure of a Visit. I am glad to see you, I take you by the Hand, and bid you heartily welcome, and thank you for bringing along with you *Abraham,* the *Mohiccon* Chief; he is likewise extremely welcome.

*Gave a String.*

*Brother,* We have often enquired after you, and always heard you continued to be our hearty Friend, and a Lover of Peace. Sir *William Johnson* was kind enough to send me an Account of the Conferences he lately held with you at *Fort Johnson,* and they gave me great Satisfaction.

*Brother,* With Pleasure I acquaint you, that Peace is now concluded, and it will add much to the Joy all feel on this successful Issue of our Conferences; and I am glad to see you and *Abraham* here to take hold of the Peace Belt.[11]

*Gave a Belt.*

*Brother,* We were in Hopes to have seen you with *Teedyuscung* when he came here. We heard you was not come, but would follow: I have staid some Time, in Expectation of your Arrival. I should have been glad to have spent more Time with you, but the Business of the Government obliges me to return to *Philadelphia* this Afternoon, so that you will please to use Dispatch in letting me know any Thing you may have to say to us.

Having finished this Speech, the Governor told *Packsinosa,* that some Presents were reserved for him and his Friends, which should be delivered presently.

Teedyuscung *then addressing himself to the Governor, spoke as follows.*

*Brother,* I have a Word or two more to say. You know when you employ your Soldiers, they are paid for their Services. As I am joined with you, you being rich, and I poor, as I am going against your Enemies, and carrying my Flesh against them, I think it would be proper, for the Encouragement of my young Men, to appoint some Reward for Scalps, and Prisoners, and that some Place may be fixed, where the Scalps and Prisoners may be brought in, and the Reward received, that my Men may return quickly from thence.

Then the Governor said, he would take into Consideration what he, *Teedyuscung,* had said, and in Half an Hour would return an Answer.

*Teedyuscung* further added; You may remember, when I mentioned *Isaac Norris,* the Speaker, I mentioned him alone; but I did not intend to mention him alone, but that he, with the Assembly, should look into it, and send Copies Home.—I then told *Teedyuscung,* that I had no Objection to Mr. *Norris,* with the Assembly, sending authentick Copies of the Minutes of this Treaty, and Deeds, Home.

*Sunday, August* 7, 1757.

PRESENT, *The Honourable the* Governor.

William Logan, Richard Peters, *Esquires, Members of the Council.*

Conrad Weiser, *Esq, Mr.* John Pumpshire, *Interpreter.*

Teedyuscung. *Seneca* Chief.

*Packsinosa, Shawanese* Chief. *Daniel.*

*Abraham, Mohickon* Chief. A *Nanticocke,* and 4 other *Delaware Indians.*

Teedyuscung *addressed the Governor as follows.*

*Brother,* WE have now finished. The Treaty is over. Peace is confirmed. I told you I thought of going to *Philadelphia,* but upon considering the Matter with more Attention, I think it will be more for the publick Service if I proceed immediately to *Diahogo:* Many Nations will be uneasy to know what has been done at this Council-Fire, and will take their Measures accordingly; I shall therefore make the best of my Way to *Diahogo,* and proclaim there, and to Nations still more distant, the Confirmation of the Peace with our Brethren the *English.* This will take up three or four Months; after which I may perhaps come and see you at *Philadelphia.* I wish the Governor a good Journey, and that we may both live to enjoy the Fruits of this happy Peace, which gives my People great Joy.

*To which the Governor returned the following Answer.*

*Brother* Teedyuscung, It gives me great Pleasure that we have brought the important Business we met about to so happy an Issue. You have very agreeably prevented my mentioning to you the Necessity of your returning Home, in order to publish to the *Indians* what has been transacted here. I thank you for the Change of your Purpose: It is a further Sign of your Zeal for Peace, and I make no Doubt but you will use your utmost Dispatch.

In Answer to what you requested this Morning, I assure you that your Warriors will always find this Government ready to reward them for any Services they shall do against the Enemy. I cannot at present give you a more particular Answer, but shall lay your Proposals before the Assembly, who meet To-morrow, and consult with them thereupon.

Teedyuscung *replied.*

*Brother, the Governor,* You have not so much as given us a rusty Iron to defend ourselves. If we meet an Enemy on the Road, what are we to do? We cannot defend ourselves against him. We have nothing to do it with. Our young Warriors think as much of themselves, and their Lives are as dear to them as white People's. But you have not given them any Encouragement to go against the Enemy. Can this be right? You know you have not. Consider this well Brother.

Further, Brother, I think it proper to tell you, if *English* and *Indians* shall go to War together, my young Men will not be subject to an *English* Captain; and if any of your People will go to War with me, I expect they will be subject to my Directions: We understand our own Way of Fighting better than you.

The Governor then said he had given Directions to Colonel *Weiser* to agree with him on proper Signals for the *Indians,* when they were coming towards the inhabited Parts of this Province, as this was a Matter that ought not to be spoke of in Publick.

They then took a kind Leave of each other, and the Governor set out for *Philadelphia.*

*Compared with the Original, by*
Jacob Duche, *Assistant Clerk to* Mr. Croghan.

1. Three versions of these treaty minutes survive, but they do not match. Franklin published Croghan's version, which Jacob Duché and William Trent recorded. Duché was a protégé of the leading anti-Quaker propagandist, William Smith, while Trent would later provide blankets to Colonel Henry Bouquet to carry out General Jeffrey Amherst's order that he spread smallpox among those Lenapes at odds with the British in 1763 (Jennings, *Empire of Fortune,* 447). (The incident at Fort Pitt is one of the most infamous of the smallpox blanket atrocities, but the Lenapes had suspected such intentional germ warfare and genocide as early as 1661 [Weslager, *Delaware Indians,* 134, 152]). Richard Peters and Charles Thomson also recorded versions of this treaty, for the Penns and the Lenapes respectively. Croghan's version is shorter than Peters's, which was apparently created to "counteract Thomson's version" (Jennings, *Empire of Fortune,* 342). These discrepancies write a cautionary tale for anyone who would use these Franklin printings as a dependable rendition of actual historical events.

Duché and Richard Peters's brother William accused Pemberton and Anglican Assemblyman Joseph Galloway of suggesting to Teedyuscung that he obtain his own clerk. Moses Tatamy claimed that the idea was his own and that the Lenape council at Wyoming had agreed upon it before departing for Easton (Jennings, *Empire of Fortune*, 344).

2. Until the Lancaster Treaty of 1757, Croghan had cooperated with Pemberton's Friendly Association and had acknowledged the legitimacy of the Lenapes' claims. At Easton 1757, Thomas Penn's placemen managed to manipulate him over to their side by threatening him with debtor's prison (Jennings, *Empire of Fortune*, 341–42). Thomson discovered that Croghan and Weiser were deliberately making and keeping Teedyuscung drunk so that he would be unfit to transact business. The deceptions afoot apparently brought several Lenapes in the delegation to the brink of reopening hostilities right in Easton around August 2, the day before peace was finally concluded (Wallace, *Conrad Weiser*, 481–82). Peters and Duché reported that when Indians met them in the streets, they would always ask whether they were Quakers. If they answered no, the Indians would frown and call them bad men and Governor's men. If they answered yes, they were "caressed" and called brothers and good men (Boyd, *Indian Treaties*, lxxxiv). This report casts doubt on scholars' conclusions that Teedyuscung was really only a mouthpiece for the Quaker genius that tried to outmaneuver Croghan. The Lenapes took help from those who offered it, but they argued their own case.

3. Of the approximately three hundred Indians at this treaty, 159 were eastern Lenapes, and the 119 Iroquois were mostly Senecas (Jennings, *Empire of Fortune*, 342). Given that the League Iroquois had waited in vain at Lancaster through April and most of May, it is unlikely that there was significant or official representation of the rest of the League nations at this treaty, particularly because no chiefs are named in these minutes. The record creates an appearance of consensus that the singular voice of Teedyuscung denies. The League almost never participated significantly in a treaty without speaking at least once. It appears from Anaquateeka's brief talk that the Onondaga Council had put responsibility for eastern Lenape affairs in the Senecas' hands.

4. See note 4 to the 1756 treaties. Teedyuscung may also be referring obliquely here to the British.

5. Though the meaning here is figurative, the bones and skulls from Braddock's defeat at Monongahela were still lying exposed on the field of battle in 1762 (Weslager, *Delaware Indians*, 223).

6. Moses Tatamy's son eventually died of the wound he received in this incident (Jennings, *Empire of Fortune*, 344n55).

7. The idea that William Johnson was in no way "concerned in interest" in this affair is laughable. By lobbing the problem into Johnson's court, Pennsylvania and the king of England effectively lobbed the Lenapes into the very coliseum of those who had ordered them out of the Tohiccon lands in the first place: the Anglo-Iroquois alliance. Johnson was not about to betray the reputation or confidence of the League.

8. Given that the British generally felt so secure in the superiority of writing over orality, Denny and Croghan are oddly nervous at the prospect of the Lenapes adopting their practices. This turnabout alone should tip the reader off to the bad-faith negotiations. It is particularly noteworthy that it is the reading of a written speech rather than the writing down of orally remembered and delivered speeches that threatens them. That it was the idea of Quaker interference that got them to admit publicly that "the *Indians* have good Memories, and can remember, what was transacted twenty Years ago, as if Yesterday" is remarkable.

9. In earlier treaties, the League nations refused to make peace until land disputes were settled. These exchanges between Lenapes and Pennsylvanians therefore seem irregular, be-

cause they seem to insist upon settling a peace before resolving land disputes. The difference seems to lie in the causes of the hostilities. In earlier cases, skirmishes and fighting had directly resulted from disagreements over land and rights of way; here, Teedyuscung has proclaimed the land issues to be of secondary consideration. While land rights, especially in the Ohio Valley, are clearly at the center of Lenape disaffection with the British, they may have fronted the French as the primary cause in this case because they recognized that no resolution could possibly be reached at this level. (Blaming the French was also an oblique way of blaming the English: for abandoning them when they asked for arms and for trying to invade the Ohio Valley.) The Walking Purchase, the 1749 purchase, and the 1754 purchases did not involve French claimants. Resolutions to them could wait until a peace was sealed.

If Teedyuscung was criticized internally by other Lenapes for delaying the peace as he argued about land, it may have resulted from the observation of Croghan's and Weiser's schemes and a wish to secure a peace before they managed to bribe him, as they had seen so many others succumb to bribery.

10. This short speech is a neat reversal of the one Canasatego had received in 1744 from Governor Thomas, which had implied that the written record and its procedures were superior to the oral one.

11. The peace that was concluded reached only as far as the eastern Lenapes, the League, and the dependent nations of the League. As subsequent treaties will show, the British had still to make peace with the western Lenapes and other Ohio Indian nations for whom Teedyuscung could not speak.

On September 6, 1757, Teedyuscung complained to Governor Denny that the treaty had not yet been printed and that the fact spoke to bad faith on the part of Pennsylvania. Franklin announced the printing of this treaty on October 13, 1757 (Miller, *Philadelphia Printing*, 372).

✠

# MINUTES OF CONFERENCES,

## HELD AT *EASTON*, In *OCTOBER*, 1758,

With the Chief SACHEMS and WARRIORS of the *Mohawks, Oneidoes, Onondagoes, Cayugas, Senecas, Tuscaroras, Tuteloes, Skaniadaradigronos,* consisting of the *Nanticokes* and *Conoys,* who now make one Nation; *Chugnuts, Delawares, Unamies, Mahickanders,* or *Mohickons; Minisinks,* and *Wapingers,* or *Pumptons.*

---

*PHILADELPHIA:*
Printed and Sold by B. FRANKLIN, and D. HALL,
at the *New-Printing-Office,* near the Market. MDCCLVIII.

---

## *Minutes of Conferences,* &c.[1]

*At a* MEETING *held at* Easton, *on the Seventh of* October, 1758.
PRESENT, The *Honourable* WILLIAM DENNY, *Esq;*
*Lieutenant-Governor of the Province of* Pennsylvania,
Lawrence Growdon, Richard Peters, Lyn-Ford Lardner,
Benjamin Chew, John Mifflin, *Esquires.*

THE Governor and Council coming to Town this Afternoon, *Teedyuscung,* accompanied with *Moses Tittamy, Daniel, Teepyuscung,* and *Isaac Stille,* waited on his Honour, and made the usual Salutations.

*Brother,* I am very glad to see you here again; you may remember that we have already made Peace, and you desired me to halloo loud, and give Notice of it to all the *Indians* round about.

I have spoke loud, and raised my Voice, and all the *Indians* have heard me as far as the *Twightwees,* and have regarded it, and are now come to this Place.[2]

I bid you welcome, and join with me in calling up our Eyes to Heaven, and praying the Blessing of the Supream Being on our Endeavours.

According to our usual Custom, I, with this String, wipe the Dust and Sweat off your Face, and clear your Eyes, and pick the Briars out of your Legs, and desire you will pull the Briars out of the Legs of the *Indians* that are come here, and anoint one of them with your healing Oil, and I will anoint the other.

*A String.*

The Governor returned him Thanks for the Visit and his good Advice, which he promised to comply with, and appointed a Meeting in the Morning for that Purpose.

*At a* CONFERENCE *held in the Town of* Easton,
*on the* 8*th of* October, 1758.
PRESENT, The *Honourable* WILLIAM DENNY, *Esq;*
*Lieutenant-Governor,*
Lawrence Growdon, William Logan, Richard Peters,
Lyn-Ford Lardner, Benjamin Chew, John Mifflin, *Esquires,*
*Members of the Governor's Council.*
Isaac Norris, Joseph Fox, Joseph Galloway, John Hughes,
Daniel Roberdeau, Amos Strickland, *Esquires,*
*Committee of the House of Representatives.*
Charles Read, Jacob Spicer, *Esquires,*
*Commissioners for* Indian *Affairs in the Province of* New-Jersey.
*A Number of Magistrates and Freeholders,*
*of this and the neighbouring Province,*
*and of the Citizens of the City of* Philadelphia,
*chiefly of the People called* Quakers.
George Croghan, *Esq; Deputy Agent for* Indian *Affairs, under*
*Sir* WILLIAM JOHNSON.

*INDIANS of several Nations,* viz.

MOHAWKS. Nichas, *or* Karaghtadie, *with one Woman and two Boys,* 4
ONEIDOES. Thomas King, Anagaraghiry, Assanyquou, *with* 3 *Warrior Captains,* 6 *Warriors, and* 33 *Women and Children* 45
ONONDAGOES. Assaradonguas, *with* 9 *Men, and* 9 *Women and Children,* 19
CAYUGAS. Tokaaion, *with* 8 *Men, and* 11 *Women and Children,* 20
SENECAS. Takeaghsado, Tagashata, *or* Segachsadon, *chief Man, with* 7 *other Chiefs,* 37 *other Men,* 28 *Women, and several Children, in all,* 83
TUSCARORAS. Unata, *alias* Jonathan, *with* 5 *Men,* 12 *Women, and* 2 *Children,* 20
NANTICOKES *and* CONOYS, *now one Nation.* Robert White, *alias* Wolahocumy Pashaamokas, *alias* Charles, *with* 16 *Men,* 20 *Women, and* 18 *Children,* 56
Kandt, *alias* Last Night, *with* 9 *Men,* 10 *Women, and* 1 *Child,* 21

| | |
|---|---|
| TUTELOES. Cakanonekoanos, *alias* Big Arm, Asswagarat, *with* 6 *Men, and* 3 *Women,* | 11 |
| CHUGNUTS. 10 *Men, and* 20 *Women and Children,* | 30 |
| CHEHOHOCKES, *alias* Delawares and Unamies. Teedyuscung, *with sundry Men, Women and Children,* | 60 |
| MUNSIES, *or* MINISINKS. Egohohowen, *with sundry Men, Women and Children,* | 35 |
| MOHICKONS. Abraham, *or* Mammatuckan, *with several Men, Women and Children,* | 56 |
| WAPINGS, *or* PUMPTONS. Nimham, Aquaywochtu, *with sundry Men, Women and Children, in all,* | 47 |
| | In all, 507 |

Conrad Weiser, *Esq; Provincial Interpreter.*
*Captain* Henry Montour,
*Interpreter in the* Six Nation *and* Delaware *Languages.*
Stephen Calvin, Isaac Stille, Moses Tittamy, Delaware Indians,
*Interpreters in the* Delaware *Language.*

*The Governor opened the Conferences with the following Ceremonies, addressing himself to all the* Indians *present, of every Nation.*

*Brethren,* IT gives me great Pleasure to see so many of you, and of so many different Nations, at this Council Fire. I bid you heartily Welcome.

*Brethren,* With this String I wipe the Sweat and Dust out of your Eyes, that you may see your Brethrens Faces, and look chearful. With this String I take all Bitterness out of your Breast, as well as every Thing disagreeable that may have gathered there, in order that you may speak perfectly free and open to us. With this String I gather the Blood, and take it away from the Council Seats, that your Clothes may not be stained, nor your Minds any Ways disturbed.

*Three Strings.*

Mr. *Weiser* interpreted the Substance of this Speech, and saying his Memory did not serve him to remember the several Ceremonies in Use on this Occasion, he desired *Nichas,* a *Mohawk* Chief, to do it for him, which he did, and it was afterwards interpreted by Captain *Henry Montour,* in the *Delaware* Language, to *Teedyuscung,* and the *Delawares.*

After a short Pause, *Tagashata,* the *Seneca* Chief, rose up, and repeating, as usual, each Paragraph distinctly as spoke by the Governor, he returned Thanks, and went through the same Ceremonies to the Governor, Council, and People of the Province, adding on the last String, that their Great Grandfathers had told them, that they had made a Road for them to travel to their Brethren the *English,* and that whenever it should be stopped, they would become a poor People. They were very glad to find the Road open to their Brethren, and should take Care to preserve it so on their Side.

*Three Strings.*

After Mr. *Weiser* had delivered this in *English,* and it was interpreted in the *Delaware* Language by *Moses Tittamy, Takeaghsado,* or *Tagashata,* proceeded;

*Brother* Onas, By this Belt you sent an Invitation to us to come to *Pennsylvania,* which reached our Towns about the Time that the Leaves put out last Spring, but we were then so much alarmed by the *French;* who were near us, that we could not then leave our Country. Some little Time ago we received another Belt from Sir *William Johnson,* which he informed us was sent to him by you, to be forwarded to us, to enquire into the Reasons why we did not come to you, according to your first Invitation, and Sir *William Johnson* desired us to come here to meet you in Council; upon which we immediately arose, and came as soon as we could to your Council Fire, and now we are here, as you see.

*Two Belts.*

*Brother,* Here is another Belt, by which we were invited lately to come to a Council Fire, that was kindled in an Island near the Sea: This surprized us, as we never heard of a Council Fire in an Island.* We know of no Council Fires, but the old Council Fire at *Philadelphia,* and the great Council Fire in *Albany.*

*Here he laid the Belt on the Table.*

Then taking four other Strings of Wampum, he said, These were sent to us by *Nichas,* the *Mohawk* Chief, with a Message, that he was arrived in this Province, and desired we would comply with the Invitation, and come down.

*Here he laid the four Strings on the Table.*

*Nichas* having acknowledged the Message, and taken up the Strings, *Tagashata* concluded, saying, These are your Belts, by which we were invited to this Council Fire; and as we are now come, we return them, and desire to see the Belts that were sent by us, particularly one, on which were several Images of Men holding each other by the Hand.

The Governor replied, that he would enquire for the Belts sent by them, and they should be returned.

The Substance of these last Speeches of *Tagashata* was interpreted to *Teedyuscung,* and the *Delawares.*

---

* Meaning *Burlington.*

*October* 9, 1758.

THIS Morning his Excellency Governor *Bernard* arrived at *Easton,* and desired a Meeting of the *Indians,* in order to make them the usual Compliments; but was acquainted by Mr. *Weiser,* that they were then in Council, deliberating on Matters necessary to be adjusted before the Meeting.

*October* 10, 1758.

THE *Indian* Chiefs continued in Council the greatest Part of this Day, and desired the Governors would not be impatient.

*October* 11, 1758.

THIS Morning the *Indian* Chiefs communicated to the Governors, by Mr. *Weiser,* the Business they had been consulting upon, and said they had concluded to speak to us this Forenoon. The Governors waited till One o'Clock, expecting the *Indians* to meet them, being told that they were gathering together for that Purpose; but they not coming, after several Messages sent to hasten them, it was agreed to meet punctually at Four o'Clock.

*At a* CONFERENCE *held at* Easton *with the* Indians,
October 11, 1758. P. M.
PRESENT,
*Governor* DENNY, *with his Council,*
*and the several* Pennsylvania *Gentlemen, as before.*
*Governor* BERNARD.
Andrew Johnson, Charles Read, John Stevens, Jacob Spicer,
William Foster, *Esquires,* Indian *Commissioners for* Jersey.

*TAGASHATA,* the *Seneca* Chief, intending to speak first, on Behalf of the *Indians,* had laid some Belts and Strings in Order on the Table.

As soon as the Company sat down, *Teedyuscung,* holding out a String, said he had something to deliver, and desired he might be heard first of all. Mr. *Croghan* requested to know, if what he was going to say was the Result of the *Delaware* Council, and if it was their Desire it should be spoke first; but no Answer was given him as to this.

Governor *Bernard* signifying his Desire to bid the *Indians* welcome, and just mention to them the Business he came upon, it was agreed he should speak first, which he did as follows.

*Brethren,* I am glad to see so many of you met together, to cultivate Peace with your Brethren and old Friends the *English.* I heartily bid you welcome; and wish that the good Work for which you are now assembled, may prosper in your Hands, and have that Success, which your wise Men, and all that wish you well, must desire, as a Thing much to your Advantage.

The Situation of the Province over which I preside, and the Disposition of its People, have hitherto afforded very little Occasion for Treaties with the neighbouring *Indians;* but having, some Months ago, sent a Message to the *Minisinks,* I received a Message from our Brethren the *Senecas,* and *Cayugas,* wherein they take upon them to answer my Message to the *Minisinks,* and desire that I would meet them at the Council Fire burning at this Place.

It is not usual for the King's Governors to go out of their Provinces to attend Treaties; but I am glad to have an Opportunity of shewing my good Disposition to establish Peace and Friendship with my Neighbours; and therefore I have waved all Forms, and am come here, according to the Invitation I received at *Burlington.*

To you therefore, our Brethren the *Senecas* and *Cayugas,* and your Nephews the *Minisinks,* I now speak, and desire that you would take into your most serious Consideration, my Message to the *Minisinks,* your Message to me, and my Answer thereto, and let me know what we are to expect from you.

What is past, we are willing to forget; but I must remind you, that if you are disposed to be our Friends for the future, you should give us that Proof of your Sincerity which I have desired in my Answer to your Message, and return us the Captives that have been taken out of our Province, and are now within your Power; this should be one of the first Steps, and will be the best that can be taken, towards restoring and confirming that Brotherly Love and Friendship between us, which I am convinced will be for the mutual Benefit of all Parties.

This was interpreted in the *Six Nation* Language by Mr. *Weiser,* and in the *Delaware* by Mr. *Stephen Calvin,* the *Indian* Schoolmaster in *West-Jersey.*

*Then* Teedyuscung *spoke.*

*Brethren,* I desire all of you who are present, will give Ear to me. As you, my Brethren, desired me to call all the Nations who live back, I have done so; I have given the Halloo, and such as have heard me are present. Now, if you have any Thing to say to them, or they to you, you must sit and talk together.

*Brethren,* I sit by, only to hear and see what you say to one another; for I have said what I have to say to the Governor of *Pennsylvania,* who sits here; he knows what has passed between us. I have made known to him the Reason why I struck him. Now I and the Governor have made up these Differences between him and me, and I think we have done it, as far as we can, for our future Peace.

*A String.*

The above Speech was interpreted in the *Six Nation* Language.

Tagashata *then rose up and spoke,*

*Brethren the Governors, and your Councils,* It has pleased the most High that we meet together here with chearful Countenances, and a good deal of Satisfaction; and as publick Business requires great Consideration, and the Day is almost spent, I chuse to speak early To-morrow Morning.

The Governors answered, that they should be glad to give all the Dispatch possible to this good Work they were engaged in; and desired the Chiefs would fix the Time of Meeting; but they declined it, saying, they were unacquainted with Hours, but would give Notice when they were ready.

*At a* CONFERENCE *held at* Easton *with the* Indians, *on the* 12*th of* October, 1758.
PRESENT, *The* GOVERNORS,
*The Gentlemen of their Councils, And others, as before.*

*TAGASHATA*, the *Seneca* Chief, taking the Strings and Belt of Wampum which Governor *Bernard* gave Yesterday, repeated, according to the *Indian* Custom, the Particulars of his Speech, and then added,

*Brethren,* We approve of every Article mentioned to us Yesterday by the Governor of *Jersey,* all that he said is very good; we look upon his Message to us as a Commission and Request from him, that we should bring Matters to a good Conclusion with our Cousins the *Minisinks.* They themselves sent for us to do the same Thing, on their Behalf, and, at their Request, we came here, have taken it in Hand, and will use our utmost Endeavours to bring about the good Work which Governor *Bernard* desires, and do not doubt but it will be done to his entire Satisfaction.

*Brethren,* I now speak at the Request of *Teedyuscung,* and our Nephews the *Delawares,* living at *Wyomink,* and on the Waters of the River *Sasquehannah.*

*Brethren,* We now remove the Hatchet out of your Heads that was struck into them by our Cousins the *Delawares;* it was a *French* Hatchet that they unfortunately made use of, by the Instigation of the *French;* we take it out of your Heads, and bury it under Ground, where it shall always rest, and never be taken up again. Our Cousins the *Delawares* have assured us they will never think of War against their Brethren, the *English,* any more, but employ their Thoughts about Peace, and cultivating Friendship with them, and never suffer Enmity against them to enter into their Minds again.

The *Delawares* desired us to say this for them by this Belt.

*A Belt.*

*Brethren,* Our Nephews, the *Minisink Indians,* and three other different Tribes of that Nation, have, at last, listened to us, and taken our Advice, and laid down the Hatchet they had taken up against their Brethren the *English.* They told us they had received it from the *French,* but had already laid it down, and would return it to them again.

They assured us, they would never use it any more against you, but would follow our Advice, and entreated us to use our utmost Endeavours to reconcile them to you their Brethren, declaring they were sorry for what they had done, and desired it might be forgotten, and they would for ever cultivate a good Friendship with you. These Declarations were made by the principal Warriors of Four Tribes of the *Minisink Indians* at giving us this Belt.

*A Belt.*

Then, taking eight Strings of Black Wampum, he proceeded.
*Brethren,* We let you know that we have not only brought about this Union with our Nephews on the Waters of the River *Sasquehannah,* but also have sent Messages to our Nephews the *Delawares* and *Minisinks,* and to those likewise of our own Nations, who are on the *Ohio,* under the Influence of the *French.* We have told all these that they must lay down the *French* Hatchet, and be reconciled to their Brethren the *English,* and never more employ it against them, and we hope they will take our Advice. We the *Mohawks, Senecas,* and *Onondagas,* deliver this String of Wampum to remove the Hatchet out of your Heads, that has been struck into them by the *Ohio Indians,* in order to lay a Foundation for Peace.

*Eight Strings of Black Wampum.*

*Tagashata* sat down, and then the *Cayuga* Chief, *Tokaaio,* arose and said,
*Brethren,* I speak in Behalf of the younger Nations, Part of, and confederated with, the *Six Nations. viz.* The *Cayugas, Oneidoes, Tuscaroras, Tuteloes, Nanticokes,* and *Conoys.*

A Road has been made from our Country to this Council Fire, that we might treat about Friendship; and as we came down the Road, we saw that (by some Misfortune or other) Blood has lately been spilt on it. By these Strings we make the Road wider and clearer;—we take the Blood away out of it, and likewise out of the Council Chamber, which may have been stained; we wash it all away, and desire it may not be seen any more, and we take the Hatchet out of your Heads.

*Gave three Strings.*

*Brethren, the Governors, and all the* English, I now confine myself to the *Cayugas,* my own Nation.

I will hide nothing from you, because we have promised to speak to each other from the Bottom of our Hearts.

The *French,* like a Thief in the Night, have stolen away some of our young Men, and misled them, and they have been concerned in doing Mischief against our Brethren the *English.*

We did not know it when it happened, but we discovered it since. The Chiefs of our Nation held their young Men fast, and would not suffer them to go out of their Sight, but the *French* came and stole them away from us, and corrupted them to do Mischief. We are sorry for it; we ask Pardon for them, and hope you will forgive them; we promise they shall do so no more, and now, by this Belt, we take out of your Heads the Hatchet with which they struck you.

*A Belt of ten Rows.*

He added, he had found out that some of their young People had been concerned in striking us four Times.[3]

*At a* CONFERENCE *with the* Indians, *held at* Easton, October 13, 1758.
PRESENT, *Governor* DENNY, *Governor* BERNARD,
*The same Gentlemen,* Indians, *Interpreters. &c. as before.*

AS soon as the *Indians* had taken their Seats, Governor *Denny* made the following Speech.

*Brethren, Chiefs and Warriors of the* United Nations, *and others your Brethren and Nephews, now met here,* Agreeable to your Request, at our first Meeting, I now return you the Belt, which the young *Seneca Indian* brought me, with your Answer to the Invitation I gave you to come down to this Council Fire.

*Here his Honour returned the Belt.*

*Brethren,* I invited you to come down to the Council Fire kindled at this Place by me and your Nephew *Teedyuscung,* with a Design to lay before you Matters of the greatest Consequence to you and us; I am now about to communicate them to you, and to answer all that has been said by you to me, since our meeting together; I therefore, by this String, open your Ears, that you may hear clearly, and carefully attend to what I shall say to you.

*A String.*

*Brethren,* I must first put you in Mind, that perfect Peace and Friendship subsisted between you and your Brethren, the *English,* in this Province, from our first Settlement among you, and that whatever little Disputes happened between your People and ours, they were amicably settled and adjusted by our wise Men at our Council Fires, according to an Agreement made by our first Proprietary WILLIAM PENN, and your Fathers. Had this wise Agreement been carefully observed, as it always ought to have been, our late unhappy Differences had never arose. But what is passed cannot be recalled, and shall be forgotten. Let us both resolve never to be guilty of the like Error for the future.

*A String.*

*Brethren,* You gave us Yesterday these two Belts, in Behalf of your Nephews the *Delawares* and *Minisinks,* and joined with them in taking out of our Heads the Hatchets with which we had been struck, acquainting us, "that these Hatchets were given to your Nephews by the *French,* and that they would not use them any more against us; but were heartily disposed to cultivate a firm Friendship with us for the future."

*Brethren,* We accept your Belts; we thank you for the Pains you have taken in enquiring of your Nephews into the true Cause why they struck us.

Now that the Hatchets are taken out of our Heads, and we are reconciled, we desire that your Nephews the *Delawares* and *Minisinks* will conceal nothing from you and us, that ever did, or now does, lie heavy on their Minds, that the End of this Meeting may be answered, which was, with your Assistance, to put Matters that have at any Time disturbed their Minds on such a just and reasonable Footing, that the Peace between us may never be interrupted, but continue firm to the remotest Ages.

*Two Belts.*

*Brethren,* By these eight Strings of black Wampum, you the *Mohawks, Senecas,* and *Onondagoes,* told us, that you had not only brought about an Union with the *Delawares* and *Minisinks,* on the Waters of the River *Sasquehannah,* but had also sent Messages to the *Indians* now on the *Ohio,* as well those of these two Nations, as those of the *Six Nations,* under the *French* Influence, desiring them to lay down the Hatchet, and enter again into Friendship with their Brethren the *English;* and, on their Behalf, you have taken the Hatchets out of our Heads, so far as to lay a Foundation for a future Peace.

*Brethren, the* Mohawks, Senecas, *and* Onondagoes, This was a very friendly Part, and we flatter ourselves they will hearken to you, as there are now Deputies here from those *Indians* on the *Ohio,* with Messages to us, which will be delivered in Publick.

We accept your Strings, and approve your taking the Hatchet, on the Behalf of the *Ohio Indians,* out of our Heads, so far as to make it the Foundation of a future Peace.

*Nine Strings.*

*Brethren, the* Cayugas, Oneidoes, Tuscaroras, Tuteloes, Nanticokes, *or* Conoys, *the younger Nations, who are Parts of, and united with, the* Six Nations, By these Strings you say, "That, as you came down the Road which has been opened from your Country to this Council Fire, you saw Blood lately spilt upon it, and have washed it away, not only out of the Road, but out of the Council Chamber, lest that should have been stained."

*Brethren,* We join, by these Strings, with you, in removing the Blood. We bury it deep in the Earth.

*Three Strings.*

*Brothers the* Cayugas, With this Belt "you justly lament the Folly of your young Men, who have suffered themselves to be stolen away from you by the *French,* and then, at their Instigation, to strike us. You take the Hatchet out of our Heads, you ask Pardon for them, and desire we will forgive the Mischief they have done us, and both you and they promise never to hurt us more."

*Brethren,* We accept the Belt in their Behalf, and give you this Belt in Token of our Friendship and Reconciliation.

*A Belt.*

*Brethren,* You may remember, that the Day before Yesterday, your Nephew *Teedyuscung* told me by this String, "that he had already said to me, at our former Meetings, every Thing he had to say, and had made me acquainted with the Cause why he had struck us, and that I knew what had passed between us.—That we had made up all Differences, and had done it, as far as we could, for our future Peace."

"That at my Request he had given the Halloo, and brought down to this Place you who heard him, and are now present; and that he would sit by, and hear what we said together."

*Brethren,* As there are a great many of you here, who were not present at our former Meetings, I think it proper, for your Information, to give you a short Account of what has passed between your Nephews the *Delawares* and us.

About three Years ago your Brethren the *English,* living on the Borders of this Province, were struck on a sudden, at a Time when they were in profound Peace with you, and following their Business, suspecting no Danger. Many were killed, and others carried away Captives.

We were surprised, and did not know who struck us, but sent Messengers up the *Sasquehannah,* as far as the *Six Nation* Country, to enquire whence the Blow came, and for what Reason.

On the Return of these Messengers, we were informed that the Hatchet had been struck into our Heads by our Countrymen the *Delawares* and *Shawanese.*

Some Time after this Discovery was made, a Cessation of Hostilities was brought about by the *Six Nations,* at our Request, made to them for that Purpose by Sir *William Johnson;* and, upon our Invitation, our Brother *Teedyuscung* came down, with a Number of *Delawares* and other *Indians,* to a Council Fire, kindled at this Place, where we have since had several Meetings.

At one of these Meetings *Teedyuscung* told us, that the Cause of the War was, their foolish young Men had been persuaded by the false-hearted *French* King to strike their Brethren the *English;* and one Reason why the Blow came harder was, that the Proprietaries of this Province had taken from them by Fraud the Ground we now stand on, and all the Lands lying between *Tohiccon-Creek* and *Wyomink,* on the River *Sasquehannah.*

At last all Blood was wiped away, and buried under Ground, and Peace Belts were exchanged between us and our Brother *Teedyuscung,* who then told us he acted in Behalf of Ten Nations, and promised to bring in and restore to us all our Fellow-Subjects that had been carried off Prisoners by them.[4]

For the Truth of this short Relation I refer you to our Brother *Teedyuscung,* who will confirm it to you more particularly.

*A Belt.*

*Brethren.* To continue our Friendship, it is absolutely necessary to preserve Faith, and keep the Promises we make with each other.

I will speak plainly to you, and from the Bottom of my Heart, as one Friend ought to another, that nothing may lie heavy on my Mind to disturb me hereafter; and I expect the same Openness and Freedom on your Parts.

I desire therefore to know the true Reason, why our Flesh and Blood, who are in Captivity, and in your Power, have not been delivered to us, according to the Promise made us by our Brother *Teedyuscung,* in Behalf of all the *Indians* he represented; and what is become of those Belts we gave him to confirm the Peace, and that Promise; for till that Promise is complied with, we can never sleep in Quiet, or rest satisfied in the Friendship of those who detain our Children and Relations from us.

*A Belt.*

After the Governor had done speaking, the *United Nations* gave the usual Shouts of Approbation, with great Solemnity, each according to Rank.

Then Governor *Bernard* delivered the Belts requested by the *Senecas, Cayugas,* and *Minisinks,* and spoke as follows.

*Brethren,* The Governor of *Pennsylvania* has given a particular Answer to what has been said to us both. So far as his Answer relates to the Province over which I preside, I confirm what has been said by this Belt.

*A Belt.*

Previous to what follows, it is necessary to observe, that *Pisquitomen,* and another *Ohio Indian,* having come to *Philadelphia* last Summer, acquainted the Governor, that the *Indians* in those Parts had not received any Account of the late Transactions with this Government, nor any Message from it; and that they might be persuaded to lay down the Hatchet, the Governor therefore took that Opportunity to send a friendly Message to those *Indians* by *Pisquitomen,* and appointed Mr. *Frederick Post,* a *German,* who understood the *Delaware* Language, to attend him, and acquaint the *Indians* at *Ohio* of the Peace made by the *Sasquehannah Delawares,* and other *Indians,* and the Disposition of this Government to forgive what was past, if they would return to their antient Alliance. This Message was accordingly delivered, and an Answer returned by *Frederick Post, Pisquetomen,* and *Thomas Hickman,* an *Ohio Indian,* who having come down together as far as *Harris*'s Ferry, *Frederick Post* went to wait on General *Forbes,* and left the two *Indians* to proceed with the Message, who being now arrived at *Easton, Pisquetomen,* who had the particular Charge of it, introduced it as follows.[5]

*Brethren,* When I was at *Allegheny,* the chief Men sat together as we do here now. I was employed by the Governor, *Teedyuscung,* and *Israel Pemberton,* these three Men, pointing to them; and the chief Men told me, that when I should come among the *English* Inhabitants, I must shake Hands for them with the Governor, *Teedyuscung,* and *Israel Pemberton* (here he shook Hands with them) and that what they had to say, was written down in a Paper, which he then produced, and said they desired it might be read in Publick. Now you, Gentlemen, who are Head Men, sent *Frederick Post* with me, desiring me to take and carry him in my Bosom there, and when I came there, to introduce him to the publick Council; I did this, and have brought him back safe again.

Then taking a Belt, and three Strings of Wampum, which were delivered with the Paper, he said he would interpret them; but as all that was said was truly set down in the Writing, it was not necessary. Let it be read.

Then *Pisquitomen* delivered the Paper, with the Belt, and three Strings of Wampum, who, on being asked afterwards to whom they were sent, answered, one was sent to the Governor, another to *Teedyuscung*, and another to *Israel Pemberton*. The Message was read in these Words.

*The* Indians *speak now. Brethren, hear what I have to say.*

*Brethren,* IT is a good many Days since we have seen and heard of you from all Sorts of Nations.

*Brethren,* This is the first Message which we have seen and heard of you; we have not yet rightly heard you.

*Brethren,* You have talked of that Peace and Friendship which we had formerly with you.

*Brethren,* We tell you to be strong, and always remember that Friendship which we had formerly.

*Brethren,* We desire you would be strong, and let us once more hear of our good Friendship and Peace we had formerly.

*Brethren,* We desire you to make Haste, and let us soon hear of you again.

*Gave a String.*

*Brethren,* Hear what I have to say; look Brethren, since we have seen and heard of you of all Sorts of Nations, we see that you are sorry that we have not that Friendship we formerly had.

Look Brethren, we at *Allegheny* are likewise sorry that we have not that Friendship with you we formerly had.

*Brethren,* We long for that Peace and Friendship we had formerly.

*Brethren,* It is good that you have held that Friendship which we had formerly amongst our Fathers and Grandfathers.

*Brethren,* We must tell you we will not let that Friendship quite drop, which was formerly between us. Now, Brethren, it is three Years since we dropped that Peace and Friendship which we formerly had with you. Now, Brethren, that Friendship is dropped, and lies buried in the Ground where you and I stand, in the Middle between us both. Now. Brethren, since I see you have digged up and revived that Friendship, which was buried in the Ground, now you have it, hold it fast. Do, be strong, Brethren, and exert yourselves, that that Friendship may be well established and finished between us.

*Brethren,* If you will be strong, it is in your Power to finish that Peace and Friendship well.

Now, Brethren, we desire you to be strong, and establish and make known to all the *English* of this Peace and Friendship, that it, over all, may be well established, as you are of one Nation, and one Colour, in all the *English* Governments.

*Brethren,* When you have made this Peace, which you have begun, known every where amongst your Brethren, and have finished and agreed every where together on this Peace and Friendship, then you will be pleased to send it to me at *Allegheny.*

*Brethren,* When you have settled the Peace and Friendship, and finished it well, and you send it to me. I will send it to all the Nations of my Colour; when I receive of you the Answer, and I have looked that every Thing is well done, so that I can send it to the Nations of my Colour, they all will join to it, and we all will hold it fast.

*Brethren,* When all the Nations join to this Friendship, then the Day will begin to shine clear over us. When we once hear more of you, and we join together, then the Day will be still; and no Wind or Storm will come over us to disturb us.

Now, Brethren, you know our Hearts, and what we have to say, be strong; if you do so, every Thing will be well; and what we have told you in this, all the Nations agree to join.

Now, Brethren, let the King of *England* know what our Minds are, as soon as possible you can.

*Gives a Belt of eight Rows.*

Received the above Speech from the under-written, who are all Captains and Counsellors, *viz.*

| | | |
|---|---|---|
| *Beaver King,* | *Owahanomin,* | *Macomal,* |
| *Shingas,* | *Cockquacaukeheton,* | *Popauco,* |
| *Delaware George,* | *Cuhshawmehwy,* | *Washascautaut,* |
| *Pisquitom,* | *Kekeknapalin,* | *John Hickoman,* |
| *Tassacomin,* | *Captain Peter,* | *Kill Buck.* |

The above Names is of Captains and Counsellors.

After this was interpreted in the *Six Nation* Language, and in the *Delaware,* the Three Strings were delivered to the Governor, *Teedyuscung,* and *Israel Pemberton.*

As the Governor was going to close the Conference, *Nichas,* the *Mohawk* Chief, spoke for some Time, with great Vehemence, pointing frequently to *Teedyuscung,* and Mr. *Weiser* was ordered to interpret it; but he desired to be excused, as it was about Matters purely relating to the *Indians* themselves, and desired Mr. *Montour* might interpret it; after some Pause, he said, perhaps it might be better if it was interpreted to the Governors, Councils, and Commissioners, in a private Conference. Mr. *Weiser* was desired to mention this to the *Indians,* and know of them what they would chuse should be done, whether it should be interpreted now, or at a private Conference, and they answered now; but soon after they said, that, at the Request of Mr. *Weiser,* they consented that it should be interpreted in the Morning, at a private Conference.

*October* 14, 1758. The *Indians* declined meeting To-day.

*At a private* CONFERENCE *with the* Indians *on the* 15*th of* October, 1758.
PRESENT, *Governor* DENNY, His Council,
and the Committee of Assembly.
*Governor* BERNARD, *and the* Jersey *Commissioners.*
*Chiefs of the* Mohawks, Senecas, *and* Onondagoes.
*Chiefs of the* Oneidoes, Cayugas, Tuscaroras, Nanticokes,
*or* Conoys, *and* Tuteloes.

Nichas, *the* Mohawk *Chief stood up, and, directing his Discourse to both Governors, said,*

*Brothers,* WE thought proper to meet you here, to have some private Discourse about our Nephew *Teedyuscung.*

You all know that he gives out, he is the great Man, and Chief of Ten Nations; this is his constant Discourse. Now I, on Behalf of the *Mohawks,* say, we do not know he is such a great Man. If he is such a great Man, we desire to know who has made him so. Perhaps you have, and if this be the Case, tell us so. It may be the *French* have made him so. We want to enquire and know whence his Greatness arose.

Tagashata, *on the Behalf of the* Senecas, *spoke next.*

*Brethren,* I, for my Nation, say the same that *Nichas* has said; I need not repeat it. I say we do not know who has made *Teedyuscung* this great Man over Ten Nations; and I want to know who made him so.

Assarandonguas *spoke next, on Behalf of the* Onondagoes.

*Brethren,* I am here to represent the *Onondagoes,* and I say, for them, that I never heard, before now, that *Teedyuscung* was such a great Man, and much less can I tell who made him so. No such Thing was ever said in our Towns, as that *Teedyuscung* was such a great Man.

Thomas King *spoke.*

*Brethren the Governors, and all present,* Take Notice that I speak in Behalf of Five Nations, who have their Deputies here present, *viz.* The *Oneidoes, Cayugas, Tuscaroras, Nanticokes,* and *Conoys,* who have joined together, and now make one Nation, and *Tuteloes.* We Five are all connected together, and if any Thing is said to one of us, it is communicated to all the rest.

On their Behalf I now tell you, we none of us know who has made *Teedyuscung* such a great Man; perhaps the *French* have, or perhaps you have, or some among you, as you have different Governments, and are different People. We, for our Parts, entirely disown that he has any Authority over us, and desire to know from whence he derives his Authority

*A Belt.*

Tokaaio, *the* Cayuga *Chief spoke.*

*Brethren,* I speak now to you, on Behalf of the Nations just now mentioned to you. You may remember, that you said the other Day, you could not be easy without your Prisoners were returned. We have considered this, and I now assure you that they shall be returned.

We speak from the Bottom of our Hearts; we will look carefully into all our Towns for them. You shall have them all. We will keep none. If there be any of them that have gone down our Throats, we will throw them up again. You told us, a tender Father, Husband, Wife, Brother, or Sister could not sleep sound, when they reflected that their Relations were Prisoners. We know it is so with us, and we will therefore use our Endeavours to make your Hearts easy, and we give you this Belt as a Promise, that we will perform our Words.

*A Belt.*

Nichas *spoke next, in Behalf of the* Mohawks, Senecas, *and* Onondagoes.

*Brethren,* I speak now on Behalf of my own Nation, and my two other Brethren, Deputies of the *Senecas* and *Onondagoes.* We remember you desired us to leave nothing in our Hearts, but speak open on every Matter, and you said you would do the same to us.

You told us, that you could not sleep sound whilst your Prisoners were detained from you, nor could you have any Confidence in the Friendship of those who did detain them.

We of these three Nations promise, that we will use our best Endeavours to make you easy. When we return, we will enquire of every Town for the Prisoners. We will call our Councils, and lay what you have said before them, and make diligent Enquiry for them through all our Towns, and all that we can find you shall see.

If any of them are gone down our Throats, we will heave them up again.

*A String of seven Rows.*

*At a* CONFERENCE *with the* Indians, *on the* 16*th of* October, 1758.
PRESENT, *The* GOVERNORS, *and the Gentlemen of their Councils,* &c.

THE Minutes of the preceding Conferences were read, and approved.

Those of Yesterday's private Conference were read at the particular Desire of the Chiefs of the *Eight Nations,* and interpreted to *Teedyuscung,* and the *Delawares,* in the *Delaware* Language, by Mr. *Stephen Calvin.*

The Governors then spoke separately; Governor *Denny* beginning as follows.

*Brethren, the* Mohawks, Onondagoes, Senecas, Oneidoes, Cayugas, Tuscaroras, Nanticokes *and* Tuteloes. In a Conference held with you Yesterday, you told me, that we know your Nephew *Teedyuscung* gives out, that he is the great Man, and Chief of ten Nations, and that this was his constant Discourse; by this Belt therefore you denied him to be so great a Man, and desired to know of me who made him so, or gave him any Authority over you.

*Brethren,* I will answer you truly, and tell you, in a few Words, all that I know of the Matter; I have already informed you, that after the *Delawares* had struck us, you, our good Friends the *United Nations,* advised them to sit still, and do us no more Mischief; and that soon after this, we invited the *Delawares* to meet us at a Council Fire kindled at this Place.

We received an Answer to our Message from *Teedyuscung* as a Chief among the *Delawares.* At the Time appointed he came, and told us, that he represented ten Nations, amongst which the *United Nations* were included, that he acted as a chief Man for the *Delawares,* but only as a Messenger for the *United Nations,* who were his Uncles and Superiors; to whom he would faithfully carry every Thing that should be transacted between us, that they might do as they saw Cause.

We believed what your Nephew told us, and therefore made him a Counsellor and Agent for us, and desired him to publish to all Nations of *Indians* what we did at our Council Fires, and to let them know we were sincerely disposed to be at Peace with them.

*Brethren,* I can only speak for myself, and do assure you, that I never made *Teedyuscung* this great Man, nor ever pretended to give him any Authority over you; and I must do him the Justice to declare to you, that, at our former publick Treaties, *Teedyuscung* never assumed any such Power, but, on many Occasions, when he spoke of you, called you his Uncles and Superiors.

I never shall attempt to nominate or impose a Chief on any *Indian* Tribe or Nation, but, on all Occasions, will pay due Regard to those who are chosen by their Countrymen.

If any others have made *Teedyuscung* so great a Man, as to set himself above you, I am sorry for it. It is more than I know, and they who have done it must answer for themselves.

I should be greatly concerned, that any Uneasiness should arise among you; and hope you will guard against it, and preserve that Harmony which ought to subsist between Friends and Relations.

*Brethren,* By this Belt and String, you promised me to make diligent Search in your Towns for our Flesh and Blood, who are Prisoners among you, and return them to us.

*Brethren,* We have always found you honest, and punctual in the Performance of your Promises; your Words therefore give me great Comfort, and fill all our Hearts with Pleasure.

We rely upon you that no Time may be lost in fulfilling an Engagement, on which our Peace and Quiet so greatly depend.

*A Belt and String.*

*Then Governor* Bernard *spoke.*

*Brethren of all the Confederated Nations,* As you proposed your Question, concerning *Teedyuscung,* separately, I think it proper to give you a separate Answer thereto.

I know not who made *Teedyuscung* so great a Man; nor do I know that he is any greater than a Chief of the *Delaware Indians,* settled at *Wyomink.* The Title of King could not be given him by any *English* Governor; for we know very well, that there is no such Person among *Indians,* as what we call a King. And if we call him so, we mean no more than a Sachem or Chief. I observe, in his Treaties, which he has held with the Governors of *Pennsylvania* (which I have perused since our last Meeting) he says he was a Woman till you made him a Man, by putting a Tomahawk in his Hand; and through all of those Treaties, especially in the last, held at this Town, he calls you his Uncles, and professes that he is dependent on you; and I know not that any Thing has since happened to alter his Relation to you. I therefore consider him to be still your Nephew.

*Brethren,* I heartily thank you for your kind Promises to return the Captives which have been taken from us. I hope you will not only do so, but will also engage such of your Allies and Nephews, who have taken Captives from us, to do the same. That you may be mindful of this, I give you this Belt.

*A Belt.*

After the Governors had done speaking, and their Answers were interpreted in the *Six Nation* and *Delaware* Languages, the *Indian* Chiefs were asked if they had any Thing more to say; on which *Tagashata* arose, and made a Speech to his Cousins the *Delawares* and *Minisink Indians,* directing his Discourse to *Teedyuscung.*

*Nephews,* You may remember all that passed at this Council-Fire. The Governors who sit there have put you in Mind of what was agreed upon last Year. You both promised to return the Prisoners. We, your Uncles, put you in Mind of this Promise, and desire you will perform it. You have promised it, and you must perform it. We, your Uncles, have promised to return all the *English* Prisoners among us, and therefore we expect that you, our Cousins and Nephews, will do the same. As soon as you come home, we desire that you will search carefully into your Towns for all the Prisoners among you, that have been taken out of every Province, and cause them to be delivered up to your Brethren. You know that this is an Article of the Peace that was made between you and your Brethren, in Confirmation of which you received a large Peace Belt; of which Belt we desire you will give an Account, and let us know what is become of it, and how far you have proceeded in it.

*A Belt.*

After this was interpreted in the *Delaware* Language, it was observed, that there were no *Minisink Indians* present; the Governors therefore desired Mr. *Read* and

Mr. *Peters* would procure a Meeting of the Chiefs of the *United Nations,* with the *Delawares* and *Minisinks,* and cause the Speech of *Tagashata* to be interpreted to the *Minisinks,* in the Presence of their Uncles.

*Robert White,* the *Nanticoke* Chief, arose, and said he was going to speak in the Behalf of seven Nations, and, directing his Discourse to the Governors, he delivered himself in the *English* Language, as follows.

*Brethren,* It is now more than two Years past, since we heard of our Cousins the *Delawares* taking up the Hatchet against the *English.* At the first, Sir *William Johnson* sent a Message to the Head Nations, and when they received it, they sent one to us at *Otsaningo,* telling us, that, as we lived close by our Cousins, they desired we would invite them to meet at our Town, and accordingly we invited them, and they came to a great Meeting at our Town of *Otsaningo.* We then gave our Cousins a Belt of a Fathom long, and Twenty-five Rows in Breadth, and desired them to lay down the Hatchet that they had taken up against the *English,* and to be easy with them; and if they would follow this Advice, we told them, that they would live in Peace, until their Heads were white with Age, otherwise it might not be so with them.

Not hearing from our Cousins of some Time, what they did in Consequence of this Belt, we sent to them two other Belts, one of Sixteen, and the other of Twelve Rows, desiring them once more to be easy with their Brethren the *English,* and not to strike them any more; but still we heard nothing from them: Indeed, some Time afterwards we understood the *Delawares* should say, that the *Indians* at *Otsaningo* had grey Eyes, and were like the *English,* and should be served as *Englishmen;* and we thought we should have had the Hatchet struck into our Heads. We now want to know what is become of these Belts; may be they may be under Ground, or they have swallowed them down their Throats.

*Brethren,* As our Cousins have been loath to give any Answer to these Belts, we now desire they may let us know, in a publick Conference, what they have done with them.

*A String.*

*October* 17, 1758.

THE *Indians* were in Council all Day; and acquainted the Governors, that they could not be ready to meet before Morning.

*At a* CONFERENCE *held at* Easton, *on the* 18*th* of October, 1758.

PRESENT,

*The* GOVERNORS, *Council, Gentlemen, and* Indians,
*with the Interpreters as before.*

MR. *Read,* and Mr. *Peters,* acquainted the Governors, that, at a Meeting of the Chiefs of the Older and Younger Nations, with the several Tribes of the *Delaware* and *Minisink Indians* on *Monday* Night, the Speech of *Tagashata,* delivered that Morning in the Publick Conference, respecting the giving up the Prisoners, was interpreted in the *Delaware* Language by *Stephen Calvin;* and another Belt, on the Part of the Governors, being joined to *Tagashata*'s Belt, they were both delivered to the *Delaware* and *Minisink* Chiefs, to enforce the Matter. When this was done *Tagashata* spoke to the *Minisink* Chief, *Egohohowen,* saying, we were told by you that you had delivered up the *English* Prisoners, and we believed you: But our Brethren have told us that they were not delivered up; and therefore we earnestly desire that they may be made easy on this Article. You know, Cousins, that their Hearts will always be in Grief till they see again their Flesh and Blood. It is natural that they should be so. It would be so with us, if it was our Case. We desire you will be extremely careful to perform this Matter fully, and soon. Let there be perfect Peace over all the *English* Country. And let it now be published, that we may all live in Peace, and with Satisfaction, now, and for ever. I told you, *Egohohowen,* when you was in my Town, to bring with you the *English* Prisoners, and that our Brethren would expect it. I wish you had done it. But however do it now with all Speed, and it will be well.

*Egohohowen* answered, it is true, I was at my Uncle's Fire, and I believe he desired me to bring the Prisoners down; but I suppose it was not interpreted to me, for I did not understand it clearly, but I now understand it.

The *Minisink* and *Delaware Indians* were desired to collect all their Warriors together, and give them these Belts, and receive from them their Answer, it being necessary they should concur heartily in whatever should be concluded.

*Nichas,* the *Mohawk* Chief, acquainted the Governors, that, as Counsellors, they had finished, having nothing to propose at this present Meeting. The Warriors were to speak now, and *Thomas King* was appointed to deliver their Words, who thereupon arose, and began with an Exhortation, as well to all concerned in publick Affairs, Governors and their Councils, and *Indian* Chiefs and their Councils, as to Warriors of all Nations, White People and *Indians,* desiring all present to attend carefully to what was going to be related, as Matters of great Consequence, which would serve to regulate the Conduct of *English* and *Indians* to each other. He added, that the Relation going to be made, had taken a great deal of Trouble to put it into Order, and it was made on Information given by the several *Indians* now present, who were acquainted with the Facts. Brethren, we the Warriors have waited some Time, in Hopes our Counsellors would have taken this Matter in hand, but as they have not done it, we have, at their Desire, undertaken it, and they have approved of every Thing. I say, the Counsellors of the Five Younger Nations, as well as the Three Older Nations, have approved of what the Warriors are going to relate; and take Notice, that the Speech is not only the Speech of all the Warriors of the Elder and Younger Nations, but of our Cousins the *Delawares* and *Minisinks.*

This was interpreted in the *Delaware* Language; and *Thomas King* then proceeded, directing his Speech to the Governors, and all the *English* upon the Continent.

*Brethren,* You have been inquisitive to know the Cause of this War; you have often enquired among us, but perhaps you did not find out the true Cause of the Bitterness of our Hearts, and may charge us wrong, and think that you were struck without a Cause by some of our own Warriors, and by our Cousins. But if you look a little about you, you will find that you gave the first Offence. For in Time of profound Peace, some of the *Shawanese,* passing through *South-Carolina,* to go to War with their Enemies, were taken up, and put in Prison. The *English* knew they were going to War, and that they used to do it every Year; and yet, after they had persuaded them in a friendly Way into their Houses, they were taken up, and put into Prison, and one, who was an Head Man of that Nation, lost his Life, and the others were severely used. This first raised Ill-will in the Minds of the *Shawanese,* and as the *French* came a little after this happened to settle on the *Ohio,* the *Shawanese* complained of it to them, and they made an artful Use of it, set them against the *English,* and gave them the Hatchet. Being resolved on Revenge, they accepted it, and likewise spoke to their Grandfathers the *Delawares,* saying, Grandfathers, Are not your Hearts sore at our being used so ill, and at the Loss of one of our Chiefs? Will not you join us in revenging his Death? So by Degrees our young Men were brought over to act against you. On searching Matters to the Bottom, you will find that you, in this Manner, gave the first Offence. This we thought proper to let you know. It may be of Service for the future. You may be induced by this to take better Care in conducting your Council Business, so as to guard against these Breaches of Friendship; or, as soon as they happen, in corresponding immediately with one another, and with the *Indian* Nations, who are in any wise concerned, on such Occasions.[6]

*Eight Strings of black Wampum.*

*Brethren,* This was the Case of the *Shawanese,* that I have just now related. Another of the like Nature has since happened to the *Senecas,* who have suffered in the same Manner.

About three Years ago, eight *Seneca* Warriors were returning from War, through *Virginia* having seven Prisoners and Scalps with them; at a Place called *Green Briar,* they met with a Party of Soldiers, not less than One Hundred and Fifty, who kindly invited them to come to a certain Store, and said, they would supply them with Provisions; and accordingly they travelled two Days with them in a friendly Manner, and when they came to the House, they took their Arms from the *Senecas:* The head Men cried out, here is Death; defend yourselves as well as you can, which they did, and two of them were killed on the Spot, and one, a young Boy, was taken Prisoner. This gave great Offence, and the more so, as it was upon the Warriors Road, and we were in perfect Peace with our Brethren. It provoked us to such a Degree, that we could not get over it.

*Brethren,* You have justly demanded your Prisoners; it is right, and we have given you an Answer. And therefore, as we think this young Boy is alive, and somewhere among you, we desire you will enquire for him. If he be alive, return him; if you have swallowed him down your Throats, which perhaps may be the Case, let us know it, and we will be content. His Name is *Squissatego.*

*Six Strings of white Wampum.*

*Brethren,* We have one Word more to mention of the same Nature, and which was the very Cause why the *Indians* at *Ohio* left you.

*Brethren,* When we first heard of the *French* coming to the *Ohio,* we immediately sent Word to the Governors of *Virginia* and *Pennsylvania;* we desired them to come, and likewise to supply us with such Things as were proper for War, intending to defend our Lands, and hinder the *French* from taking the Possession of them. But these Governors did not attend to our Message; perhaps they thought there was no Foundation for our Intelligence. The *French,* however, came, and became our Neighbours, and you neither coming yourselves, nor assisting us with warlike Stores, our People, of Necessity, were obliged to trade with them for what we wanted, as your Traders had left the Country. The Governor of *Virginia* took Care to settle on our Lands for his own Benefit; but when we wanted his Assistance against the *French,* he disregarded us.

*A Belt.*

*Brethren,* At this Treaty you justly demanded to see your Flesh and Blood. We have pressed this on our Cousins the *Minisinks,* and they, by this String, desired us to assure you, the Governors, that they would make strict Search in their Towns, and sincerely comply with your Request, and return all the Prisoners in their Power.

*Two Strings of black and white Wampum.*

Then directing his Discourse to the Governor of the *Jersey,* he proceeded.

*Brother, the Governor of* Jersey, Our Cousins the *Minisinks* tell us, they were wronged out of a great deal of Land, and the *English* settling so fast, they were pushed back, and could not tell what Lands belonged to them. If we have been drunk, tell us so. We may have forgot what we sold, but we trust to you the Governor of *Jersey* to take our Cause in Hand, and see that we have Justice done us. We say that we have here and there Tracts of Land, that have never been sold. You deal hardly with us; you claim all the wild Creatures, and will not let us come on your Land to hunt after them. You will not so much as let us peel a single Tree; this is hard, and has given us great Offence. The Cattle you raise are your own; but those which are wild, are still ours, and should be common to both; for our Nephews, when they sold the Land, did not propose to deprive themselves of hunting the wild Deer, or using a Stick of Wood, when they should have Occasion. We desire the Governor take this Matter into his Care, and see Justice done in it.[7]

*Two Strings of white Wampum.*

*Brethren,* All that has been said has been of one Nature, that is, of Matters that are Subjects of Dispute; this that I am now going to speak upon is of another Nature.

Then, directing himself to the Governor of *Pennsylvania,* he said,

We must put you in Mind, that four Years ago, you bought at *Albany* a large Tract of Land over *Sasquehannah,* extending from the Mouth of *John Penn*'s Creek to the *Ohio.* The Proprietaries Agents then paid *One Thousand Pieces of Eight* for the Part which was settled by your People, that have been since driven off and killed. We acknowledge to have received Payment for those Parts that were settled, but for the other Part that we have not received Payment for, that we reclaim. Our Warriors, or Hunters, when they heard that we had sold such a large Tract, disapproved our Conduct in Council; so now we acquaint you, that we are determined not to confirm any more, than such of the Lands as the Consideration was paid for, and were settled; tho' included in the Deed, they are our hunting Grounds, and we desire the Request may be granted, and Notice taken, that it was made in open Conference.[8]

*Three white Strings.*

Then *Thomas King* sat down.

The *Six Nation* Chiefs being asked if they had any Thing to say, answered, that they had done; and having eased their Minds of all that lay heavy upon them, they would return home.

The Governors promised attentively to consider what was said, and give them an Answer.

Teedyuscung *then arose, and spoke.*

*Brethren,* I should have said something at the Time our Uncles laid before you their Grievances, or Causes of Complaint, in Behalf of my Countrymen who lived near *Goshen.* About three Years ago nine of their People were killed at *Goshen,* when they were in Peace. I will not take upon me to say that the Land had never been sold, but there was no Dispute about this at that Time. I verily believe that they killed those nine *Indians,* for no other Reason than because they were hunting on that Land. I speak to all the *English* when I mention this, as what was very wrong.

*Three white Strings.*

*Brethren,* One of the *Waping* Tribes, or *Goshen Indians,* tells me, that, as soon as those nine Men were killed, he went with three Belts, and Tears in his Eyes, to *George Freeland*'s, in order to have the Matter made up; but he never received an Answer to this Day, tho' he told him that he would send the Belts to the Governor, and as soon as he should receive his Answer, he would send for him, and let him know it; but he has never yet received any Answer.

*Brethren,* I give you this String, to enquire what became of the three Belts, and what Answer was made to them.

*Three Strings of white Wampum.*

*Brethren,* You may remember we made Peace last Year, and a Peace Belt was made, a Fathom long, and of Fifteen Rows. Mr. *Croghan* was present, so were some of my Uncles, and the *Minisinks.* They all saw it. You have asked me what is become of that Belt, and how far it went. I will tell you; I sent it up the *Sasquehannah* to *Diahoga;* from thence it went to *Assintzin;* thence to *Secaughkung.* The chief Men there got together to consider what was best to be done with it. They all concluded that it should be sent to our Uncle. He is a Man, and often told us he ought to see Things first, and consider what is to be done. The *Senecas* had the Belt the first, and then all the *United Nations* afterwards; they had it almost a Year. Now it is come back, and in *Lapachpeton's* Hands, who is one of the *Delawares,* and lives at *Secaughkung.* How far the Peace Belt went, I don't know; but I suppose it went thro' all my Uncles, and I assure you I will do as my Uncle does. He has promised you he will deliver up all your Captives, and I assure you I will do so, wheresoever I find them, in all my Towns. Four Tribes, now present, have agreed to this, *viz. Delawares, Unamies, Mohiccons,* and *Wapings,* who are settled as far as *Secaughkung.* This Belt confirms my Words.

*A Belt.*

*Brethren,* I did let you know formerly what my Grievance was. I told you, that from *Tohiccon* as far as the *Delawares* owned, the Proprietaries had wronged me. Then you and I agreed that it should be laid before the King of *England;* and likewise you told me you would let me know, as soon as ever he saw it. You would lay the Matter before the King, for you said he was our Father, that he might see what were our Differences; for as you and I could not decide it, let him do it. Now let us not alter what you and I have agreed. Now let me know if King GEORGE has decided the Matter between you and me. I don't pretend to mention any of my Uncles Lands, I only mention what we the *Delawares* own, as far as the Heads of *Delaware.* All the Lands lying on the Waters that fall into the *Sasquehannah,* belong to our Uncles.

*A Belt.*

*Teedyuscung* then took up another Belt, designing to speak to his Uncles the *United Nations;* but whilst he was delivering the above, their Chiefs had one after another left the Council, seemingly much displeased, he therefore declined speaking it.[9]

*October* 19, 1758.

THE Governors, having prepared their Answers, desired the *Indians* to meet, but they continued holding private Councils among themselves all that Day, till late in the Afternoon; and as the Governors were going to the Place of Conference, the *Indians* sent Mr. *Weiser* out of Council, to desire they would defer meeting till the next Morning, their own private Business not being finished.

*At a private* CONFERENCE *with the* Indians, *held at* Easton,
October 19, 1758. P. M.

PRESENT,

*His Excellency Governor* BERNARD, *The Commissioners of* New-Jersey,
*The Chiefs of the* United Nations, *and of the* Minisinks *and* Wapings,
George Croghan, *Deputy to Sir* WILLIAM JOHNSON,
Andrew Montour, *His Majesty's Interpreter,*
Stephen Calvin, *Interpreter of the* Minisink *and* Waping *Language.*

HIS Excellency reciting the Request of the *United Nations* to him, to do Justice to their Nephews the *Minisinks,* concerning their Claims to Lands in *New-Jersey,* said, he would make diligent Enquiry what Lands were remaining unsold by them; but as that would be a Work of Time and Expence, he wished that some Means could be found to give them Satisfaction at this Meeting. The People of *New-Jersey* said, that they had bought all, or the greatest Part of the *Minisink* Lands; and the *Minisinks* said they had a great Deal of Land unsold.

He could not tell who was in the right; but would suppose there were some Lands unsold, and upon that Supposition would give them some Money, by Way of Consideration, for them, if they would propose a reasonable Sum; and desired they would advise about it, and give an Answer.

The *United Nations* said it was a very kind Proposal, and recommended it to the Consideration of the *Minisinks.*

The same Day *Teedyuscung* waited on Governor *Denny,* at his House, bringing with him *Isaac Stille,* for his Interpreter, and his Grandson; and, in the Presence of Governor *Bernard,* Mr. *Andrew Johnson,* and Mr. *Peters,* acquainted the Governor, that the *Delawares* did not claim Lands high up on *Delaware* River; those belonged to their Uncles; and he thought proper to let the Governor know this, that there might be no Misunderstanding of what he had said in the publick Conference.

*At a* CONFERENCE *with the* Indians, *held at* Easton, October 20, 1758.
PRESENT, The GOVERNORS, *Council, Gentlemen and* Indians,
*with the Interpreters, as before.*

GOVERNOR *Denny* desired to know of *Teedyuscung,* if he proposed to speak, as the abrupt Departure of the *Six Nation* Chiefs from the Conference Yesterday, had prevented him from finishing what he had to say.

Then *Teedyuscung* arose, and, addressing himself to the *Six Nation Indians,* said,

*Uncles,* According to our old Custom, we used to speak to one another at home; but we are now met here on Business, I must speak to you in the Presence of the *English* Governors; and what I shall say, I desire both you the *English,* and my Uncles, who are here, will attend to.

*A Belt.*

*Uncles,* I take this Opportunity of speaking to you in the Presence of our Brethren the *English,* and two of their Governors; please to take Notice what I am going to say.

*Uncles,* You may remember that you have placed us at *Wyomink,* and *Shamokin,* Places where *Indians* have lived before. Now I hear since, that you have sold that Land to our Brethren the English; let the Matter now be cleared up, in the Presence of our Brethren the *English.*

I sit there as a Bird on a Bow; I look about, and do not know where to go; let me therefore come down upon the Ground, and make that my own by a good Deed, and I shall then have a Home for ever; for if you, my Uncles, or I die, our Brethren the *English* will say, they have bought it from you, and so wrong my Posterity out of it.

*A Belt*

*Governor* Denny *then requested the Attention of the* Indians, *and spoke.*

*Brethren, Chiefs and Warriors of the* Six United Nations, *and your Nephews, here assembled,* I am much obliged to you for the Account you gave me the Day before Yesterday, of the true Cause of the Bitterness of your Hearts towards us, and the Reasons which induced some of your young Men first to strike us, and others to side with the *French* on the *Ohio.*

The Advice you gave us, to take better Care and guard against any Breach of Friendship between us for the future, is very kind and wholsome; we will join with you, and endeavour to prevent the like Evils for the Time to come.

I promise you, that I will immediately send to the Governor of *Virginia,* to enquire after the *Seneca* Boy, *Squissatego,* who you say was left a Prisoner in his Country, and if he is alive, you may depend on his being returned to you.

*A Belt.*

*Brethren,* By these Strings you put me in Mind, that the Proprietaries, four years ago, bought of you at *Albany,* a large Tract of Land over *Sasquehannah,* from the Mouth of a Creek called *Kayarondinhagh,* or *John Penn*'s *Creek,* to the *Ohio,* and were paid by the Proprietaries Agents *One Thousand Pieces of Eight,* as the Consideration Money for such Parts as were settled by our People; but that, as your Warriors disapproved of your Conduct in Council for making that Sale, you now reclaimed such of the Lands contained in that Grant, as you have not received a Consideration for.

*Brethren,* The Proprietaries of this Province have, on all Occasions, manifested their particular Regard for you; they prefer your Friendship and the publick Good to their own private Interest. Their former Conduct gives you no Room to doubt the Truth of this; what I am about to tell you is a further Confirmation of it; therefore give me your Attention, and listen to what I shall say. You may remember, that, at a Treaty you held with your good Friend Sir *William Johnson,* three Years ago, some of your wise men told him, that there were some among them who were dissatisfied with the Sale of the above Lands, made by them at *Albany,* and were desirous that Part of it should be reserved for them; though the Proprietaries had purchased it fairly of them, and paid *One Thousand Pieces of Eight,* which was all they were to receive, till our People settled to the Westward of the *Allegheny,* or *Appalaccian Hills.* Sir *William Johnson* represented this Matter to the Proprietaries, in your Behalf, whereupon they cheerfully agreed to release to you all that Part of the Purchase you have reclaimed, and, by a Letter of Attorney, empowered *Richard Peters,* and *Conrad Weiser,* to execute a Deed to you for those Lands, on your confirming to them the Residue of that Purchase. On this Subject therefore you will please to confer with them, and settle the Boundaries between you, that they may release the Lands to you accordingly, before you leave this Place, and set your Minds at Ease.

*A String.*

*Brethren,* I thank you for the Pains you have taken with your Nephews, to prevail with them to return us such of our Brethren as are Prisoners among them, and we depend on the speedy Performance of their Promise.

*Brethren,* I have something to say to you which is of the utmost Importance to us all; it requires your particular Attention and Consideration. Providence has brought you and your Nephews together at this Meeting, Face to Face with us, that every Thing may be settled, and nothing remain, not so much as a Doubt, to create any Uneasiness in our Hearts hereafter. You know, Brethren, that there is an old Agreement between the Proprietaries and you, that you will not sell any of the Lands lying within this Province to any one but them, and they never take Possession of Lands till they have bought them of the *Indians.* You know also, that the *United Nations* have sold Lands to the Proprietaries, which your Nephews the *Delawares,* now claim as their Right. This is the Case with Regard to some Part of the Lands lying between *Tohiccon* Creek and the Head of *Delaware* River, which *Teedyuscung,* in your Hearing, the Day before Yesterday, said, the Proprietaries had defrauded him of. The Proprietaries are desirous to do strict Justice to all the *Indians,* but it cannot be supposed they can know in which of you the Right was vested. It is a Matter that must be settled among yourselves; till this is done, there will probably remain some Jealousy and Discontent among you, that may interrupt both your and our future Quiet, which we should guard against by all Means in our Power.

*A String.*

*Brethren,* I now acquaint you, that a Store of all Sorts of Goods for your Use is opened at *Shamokin* where the *Indians* may be supplied, at the most reasonable Rates, with any Goods they want, and the best Prices will be given to you for such Skins, Furs and Peltry, as you shall bring them. Another Store is intended to be opened at *Fort Allen,* and you may depend upon it that such Persons will be placed there, who shall use you with the strictest Justice in all their Dealings.

*A String.*

*Brother* Teedyuscung, As I understood at our last Meeting, that you were prevented at that Time, by the Absence of some of the *Six Nation* Chiefs, from finishing what you then had to say, I defer answering, for the present, such Parts of your Speech as relate to me. But I shall soon take an Opportunity of doing it.

This was interpreted to the *Delawares* by *Isaac Stille.*

After the Governor had done speaking, *Tagashata* and *Nichas* arose, and said, they did not rightly understand that Paragraph relating to the Lands, and requiring them to settle Matters among themselves; they said the Governor had left Matters in the Dark; they did not know what Lands he meant. If he meant the Lands on the other Side of the Mountain, he knew the Proprietaries had their Deeds for them, which ought to be produced and shewn to them. Their Deeds had their Marks, and when they should see them, they would know their Marks again.

And then *Conrad Weiser* being desired to bring the Deed, Governor *Bernard* informed the *Indians* he was going to speak to them; on which they acquainted him, that they chose to be spoke to by one Governor only at a Conference; for that when they both spoke, their Belts were mixed, and they were thereby confused in their Councils. Whereupon he deferred his Speech to another Time.

The Deed was then produced to the *Indians,* and *Nichas* said, this Deed we well remember; we know our Chiefs who signed it; some of them are present now; we sold the Land, and were honestly paid for it; the Land was ours, and we will justify it. They were desired to take it with them into their Council Room, and confer on it, and settle the Matter among themselves.[10]

*The Conference then broke up.*

*Teedyuscung* having Yesterday requested of the Governor, that two Belts, which he then presented to him, might be sent as their joint Belts to the *Ohio Indians:*

This Day the Chiefs of the *United Nations,* and *Teedyuscung,* had a Meeting with two Members of Governor *Denny*'s Council, at which the following intended Answer from Governor *Denny* to the *Ohio Indians,* being first interpreted to the *Indians,* was considered, settled, and approved by all present.

*Governor* DENNY*'s Answer to the Message of the* Ohio Indians, *brought by* Frederick Post, Pisquitomen, *and* Thomas Hickman.

BY this String, my *Indian* Brethren of the *United Nations* and *Delawares,* join with me in requiring of the *Indian* Councils, to which these following Messages shall be presented, to keep every Thing private from the Eyes and Ears of the *French.*

*A String.*

*Brethren,* We received your Message by *Pisquitomen* and *Frederick Post,* and thank you for the Care you have taken of our Messenger of Peace, and that you have put him in your Bosom, and protected him against our Enemy *Onontio* and his Children, and sent him safe back to our Council Fire, by the same Man that received him from us.

*A String.*

*Brethren,* I only sent *Post* to peep into your Cabbins, and to know the Sentiments of your old Men, and to look at your Faces, to see how you look. And I am glad to hear from him that you look friendly, and that there still remains some Sparks of Love towards us. It is what we believed before-hand, and therefore we never let slip the Chain of Friendship, but held it fast on our Side, and it has never dropped out of our Hands. By this Belt we desire you will dig up your End of the Chain of Friendship, that you suffered, by the Subtilty of the *French,* to be buried.

*A Belt.*

*Brethren,* It happened that the Governor of *Jersey* was with me, and a great many *Indian* Brethren, sitting in Council at *Easton,* when your Messengers arrived, and it gave Pleasure to every one that heard it; and it will afford the same Satisfaction to our neighbouring Governors, and their People, when they come to hear it. I shall send Messengers to them, and acquaint them with what you have said.

Your requesting us to let the King of *England* know your good Dispositions, we took to Heart, and shall let him know it, and we will speak in your Favour to His Majesty, who has, for some Time past, looked upon you as his lost Children. And we can assure you, that, as a tender Father over all his Children, he will forgive what is past, and receive you again into his Arms.

*A Belt.*

*Brethren,* If you are in Earnest to be reconciled to us, you will keep your young Men from attacking our Country, and killing and carrying Captive, our Back Inhabitants. And will likewise give Orders that your People may be kept at a Distance from *Fort Duquesne,* that they may not be hurt by our Warriors, who are sent by our King to chastise the *French,* and not to hurt you. Consider the commanding Officer of that Army treads heavy, and would be very sorry to hurt any of his *Indian* Brethren.

*A large Belt.*

*And Brethren,* The Chiefs of the *United Nations,* with their Cousins, our Brethren the *Delawares,* and others now here, jointly with me send this Belt, which has upon it two Figures that represent all the *English,* and all the *Indians* now present, taking Hands, and delivering it to *Pisquitomen,* and we desire it may be likewise sent to the *Indians,* who are named at the End of these Messages*; as they have all been formerly our very good Friends and Allies; and we desire they will all go from among the *French* to their own Towns, and no longer help the *French.*

*Brethren on the* Ohio, If you take the Belts we just now gave you, in which all here join, *English* and *Indians,* as we don't doubt you will; then, by this Belt, I make a Road for you, and invite you to come to *Philadelphia,* to your first old Council Fire,

* Sastaghretsy, Anigh Kalickon, Atowateany, Towigh Towighroano, Geghdageghroano, Oyaghtanont, Sisaghroano, Stiaggeghroano, Jonontadyhago.

which was kindled when we first saw one another; which Fire we will kindle up again, and remove all Disputes, and renew the old and first Treaties of Friendship. This is a clear and open Road for you; fear therefore nothing, and come to us with as many as can be, of the *Delawares, Shawanese,* or of the *Six Nation Indians.*[11] We will be glad to see you; we desire all Tribes and Nations of *Indians,* who are in Alliance with you, may come. As soon as we hear of your coming, of which you will give us timely Notice, we will lay up Provisions for you along the Road.

*A large white Belt, with the Figure of a Man at each End, and Streaks of black, representing the Road from the* Ohio *to* Philadelphia.

*Brethren,* The *Six Nation* and *Delaware* Chiefs join with me in those Belts, which are tied together, to signify our Union and Friendship for each other; with them we jointly take the Tomahawks out of your Heads, and bury them under Ground.

We speak loud, so as you may hear us; you see we all stand together, joined Hand in Hand.

*Two Belts tied together.*

The *Indian* Chiefs being asked, if it would not be proper to insert in the Message an Account of the Situation of our Army to the Westward, and to desire them to join General *Forbes,* against the *French;* they replied, that they would by no Means advise this Government so soon to press them to take up the Hatchet, because their Wounds were not yet healed, nor Peace made, which must first be done. They said further, that as the *French* had many *Indians* fighting for them, and they by Intermarriages were related to the *Indians* who sent the Messages, it could not be expected they would easily be persuaded to join the *English,* lest they should kill their own Flesh and Blood, adding, that the only proper Measure that could now be taken, was to advise them to sit still, and keep out of the Way, and this Advice they believed would be hearkened to.

They then desired, that at least two of our Inhabitants might accompany *Pisquitomen* and *Thomas Hickman,* the two Messengers, to the *Ohio.* The *Six Nation* Chiefs promised to send two of their own People with them; and *Teedyuscung* said he would send one, if not two *Delawares.*

*At a private* CONFERENCE *with the* Indians, *held at* Easton,
October 21, 1758.
PRESENT, *His Excellency Governor* BERNARD,
*and the* Jersey *Commissioners;*
Thomas King, *Chief of the* Oneidoes, Tagashata, *Chief of the* Senecas,
Tokaaio, *Chief of the* Cayugas, Egohohowen, *Chief of the* Minisinks,
Nimham, *Chief of the* Wapings,
*with other* Indians *of the several Nations;*
George Croghan, *Deputy to Sir* WILLIAM JOHNSON,

Andrew Montour, *His Majesty's Interpreter to the United Nations,*
Stephen Calvin, *Interpreter of the* Delaware *and* Minisink *Language.*

HIS Excellency informed them, that he met them to agree about the Price of the uncertain Claims of the *Minisinks, Wapings,* and other *Indians,* Claimants of Land in the Northern Parts of the Province of *New-Jersey,* and desired that it might be considered, that they knew not what they sold, and he knew not what he bought; therefore the Price ought not to be large.

That they might propose a Sum to him, or he would make an Offer to them; or it should be left to their Uncles to consider of a Price, as would please them best.

The *Mingoes,*[12] or *Six United Nations,* by *Thomas King,* said, that the *United Nations* had no Claim to the Lands of the *Minisinks,* or others their Nephews, on the East Side of *Delaware,* and should therefore leave the fixing a Price to them.

Then the *Minisinks* and *Wapings* withdrew to consult upon it; and being returned, *Egohohowen,* the *Minisink* Chief, said, they would chuse the Governor should make an Offer, as they might perhaps demand too much.

His Excellency, having consulted the Commissioners, offered them *Eight Hundred* Spanish *Dollars* for their Claim in *New-Jersey,* as an extraordinary Price.

The *Minisinks* said, they should be glad of the Opinion of their Uncles in the Matter.

The *Mingoes,* or *United Nations,* by *Thomas King,* said, that it was a fair and honourable Offer, and that if it were their own Case, they would chearfully accept of it; but as there were a great many Persons to share in the Purchase-money, they recommended it to his Excellency to add *Two Hundred Dollars* more; and if that was complied with, the Report of it would be carried to all the Nations, and would be a great Proof of the Affection and Generosity of their Brethren the *English* on this Occasion, and would be very agreeable to them.

His Excellency desired to know of the *Minisinks,* and other Claimants, if they approved of the Proposal of their Uncles, and they informed him that they did.

The Governor, after consulting the Commissioners, said, it was more than he had intended to give; but as the *United Nations* had given themselves the Trouble of being Mediators between them, he could not refuse their Recommendations, and was glad of the Opportunity he had of shewing his Regard to the *United Nations,* and his Benevolence to the *Minisink* and other *Indians,* who had resided in the Province where he presided, and therefore complied with their Request.

His Excellency then desired them to remember, that this Consideration Money was to be in full for the Claims of all the *Minisink* and *Waping Indians,* and all others who claim any Lands in a Map, which was laid before them at the same Time, which included all the Lands from the Line between the Provinces of *New-York* and *New-*

*Jersey,* and down *Hudson*'s River, to the Mouth of *Rariton,* up the same to *Laometang* Falls, on the North Branch of *Rariton* River; thence on a strait Line to *Pæqualin* Mountain, where it joins on *Delaware* River; and thence up the *Delaware* to *Cushyhink;* and recommended it to them to have respect to this in the Division of the Consideration Money.

Then *Tagashata,* the *Seneca* Chief, arose, and, addressing himself to the *Minisinks,* and other *Indian* Claimants, spoke as follows.

*My Nephews,* I desire you will now give over all Thoughts of your Land, and that we may hear no more Complaints about it.

Now you must remember the Friendship between you and your Brother, and transmit it to your Children; and make them acquainted with the Transactions of this Day. I recommend this to you, not from my Lips only, but from the Bottom of my Heart. I hope it will also make a deep Impression in your Hearts.

It seems as if your Grandfathers had not told you of the Treaties they used to have with their Brethren, but carried them with them to the Grave. But we hope you will not do so, but carefully inform your Children of your Agreements. We have given you this Advice, and hope you will follow it. We also expect you will take Care of your young Men, that they do no more Violence to their Brethren the *English.*

*Egohohowen* then addressed himself to the Governor, and desired to be heard.

*Brother,* We are now thoroughly satisfied, and we still retain a Friendship for our Brethren the *English,* and we desire, that if we should come into your Province to see our old Friends, and should have Occasion for the Bark of a Tree to cover a Cabbin, or a little Refreshment, that we should not be denied, but be treated as Brethren; and that your People may not look on the wild Beasts of the Forest, or Fish of the Waters, as their sole Property, but that we may be admitted to an equal Use of them.

The Governor answered, that, as soon as he got home, he should issue a Proclamation to notify to the People of his Province, that he had made a Peace with them; and to order, that, for the future, they should be treated as Brethren, which he hoped would be done; but desired that they would not go into those Parts where they had lately committed Hostilities, till the Peoples Passions were cooled; for he could not be answerable for his Peoples Behaviour, whilst their Losses were fresh upon their Minds.

On the 21st of *October* the Members of the *Pennsylvania* Council received a Message from Mr. *Weiser,* that the Chiefs of the *United Nations* were met in Council, with their Nephews the *Delawares,* at the House of *Nicholas Scull,* and that the *Delawares* had something to say to their Uncles, which they desired some of the Members of that Council, and Commissioners, should be Witnesses of, and hear.

Messieurs *Growdon, Chew,* and *Mifflin,* attended accordingly, with Messieurs *Galloway, Fox,* and *Hughes,* Commissioners, and *Israel Pemberton, Isaac Zane,* and some other *Quakers,* who were present at this particular Request of the *Delawares.*

PRESENT,

*All the* Six Nation Chiefs, Teedyuscung, Tapiscawen, *alias Samuel Davis,* Nowalekeeka, *or Four Steps,* Compass, Awehela, *alias James Davis,* Lappink, Neccochoon, *Munsey Chief,* Moses Tittamy, Conrad Weiser, Andrew Montour, Isaac Slille, *Interpreters.*

Teedyuscung, *on Behalf of the* Delawares, *arose, and spoke as follows.*

*Uncles,* I DESIRE you will hear me. We have gone so far at this Treaty as to talk of Lands; I therefore thought proper to meet you here, to let you know that I have consulted with all my Brethren, your Cousins, here present, about the Deed you, our Uncles, signed to the Proprietaries of *Pennsylvania,* shewn to us Yesterday, for the Lands beyond the *Kittochtinny* Hills.

We have seen the Deed, and know it well. *Nutimus,* one of our Chief Men, has signed it, and here sits one of our Men, named *Philip Compass,* who was present when the Sale was made; and remembers that *Nutimus,* our Chief, received *Forty-four Dollars,* as his Part or Share of the Consideration Money. We agree to it, and acknowledge that the Land was fairly sold. We give it up, and now confirm it. Let there be no Difference, nor any Thing more said about it. This is not the Land I have disputed with my Brethren the *English.* That Land lies between *Tohiccon* Creek and the *Kittochtinny* Hills.

*Gave a String.*

*Tokaaion,* the *Cayuga* Chief, stood up and spoke as follows, addressing himself to *Teedyuscung.*

*Cousin,* I thank you for your Openness and Honesty on this Occasion, freely to declare the Truth. We wish our Brethren the *English,* naming the Governors of *Pennsylvania, Virginia, Carolina* and *Jersey,* were so honest and precise.

They have called us down to this Council Fire, which was kindled for Council Affairs, to renew Treaties of Friendship, and brighten the Chain of Friendship. But here we must hear a Dispute about Land, and our Time is taken up, but they don't come to the chief Point.

The *English* first began to do Mischief; we told them so. They only thanked us for our Openness and Advice, and said they would take Care for the future, but healed no Wounds. In short, when they speak to us, they do it with a shorter Belt or String than that which we spoke to them with; tho' they can make Wampum, and we cannot.[13]

They ought not thus to treat with *Indians* on Council Affairs. Several of our strong Belts are lost in their Hands entirely. I fear they only speak from their Mouth, and not from their Heart.

On the same Day, *P. M. Pisquitomen* and *Thomas Hickman* came to take their Leave of the Governor, accompanied with Captain *Bull, William Hayes,* and *Isaac*

*Stille,* the Persons appointed to attend them to the *Ohio,* who were particularly recommended to their Care and Protection by a String of Wampum,

The Belts and Strings were numbered, as well in the written Paper containing the Messages, as on Labels tied to each of them, and delivered to *Pisquitomen,* and the written Message was delivered, with the Passports, to Captain *Bull.*[14]

The 22d of *October,* the *Six Nation* Chiefs held a private Council, and named two of their People to send to the *Ohio,* viz. *Tojenontawohy,* a *Cayuga* Chief, and the youngest *Shick Calamy,* who joined *Pisquitomen,* and set off this Afternoon. As they were setting out, Mr. *Frederick Post* arrived with News from General *Forbes,* that a large Body of *French* and *Indians,* having attacked his advanced Post at *Loyal Hanning,* were repulsed with great Loss on their Side; which News he communicated to the *Indians.*

At Noon the Governors, being prepared for a Conference, proposed a Meeting of the *Indians,* which they desired might be deferred till the Morning.

*October* 23, 1758.

This Morning one of the *Seneca* Chiefs died; Condolence Ceremonies, and Presents being made as usual, he was decently interred, a Number of the Inhabitants attending the Funeral. This took up the Forenoon.

*At a* CONFERENCE *with the* Indians, *the same Day,* P. M.
PRESENT, *The* GOVERNORS, *and*
*the Gentlemen of their Councils,* &c. *as before.*

THE Minutes were read, and approved, to the End of the publick Conference on *Friday* last; after which Governor *Denny* spoke.

*Brethren,* By this Belt, we heal your Wounds, we remove your Grief; we take the Hatchet out of your Heads; we make a deep Hole in the Earth, and bury the Hatchet so low, that no Body shall be able to dig it up again.

*A Belt.*

*Brethren,* Now we have healed your Wounds, we, by this Belt, renew all our Treaties; we brighten the Chain of Friendship; we return to our first Affection; we confirm our antient Union; we put fresh Earth to the Roots of the Tree of Peace, that it may bear up against every Storm that can blow, and live and flourish to the End of Time, whilst the Sun shines, and the Rivers run. And we desire you would publish it among your own, and all other *Indian,* Nations, who are your Friends and Allies; and engage them to join with you in a firm Peace with His Majesty, and all His Subjects; in whose Behalf I give you this Belt.

*A large Peace Belt.*

*Brethren,* We now open a Road to the old Council Fire, which was kindled by your and our Fathers in the City of *Philadelphia.*

Be assured, that you will always find this Road open, easy and pleasant to travel in, and, for the future, whenever Occasion calls, we shall be glad to see you there.

*A Belt.*

*Brethren of the* United Nations, *and all our other Brethren, your Cousins and Nephews,* We thank you for the Care and Diligence with which you have attended to the several Matters recommended to you in these Conferences, which has yielded us Abundance of Satisfaction.

This Treaty will convince all our Enemies, that we are now united in the firmest Band of Amity; and whilst we join our Strength together; it will not be in their Power to hurt either you or us.

*A Belt.*

*Brethren,* As a Token of the Love we your Brethren of this Province bear to you, I shall make a Present of a Quantity of Goods, which we have prepared for you; and desire your Acceptance of them; sensible of the approaching Season, and of the many Difficulties you live under, from the present War. We give it with an hearty Goodwill.

Here his Honour delivered a List of the Goods, and desired Mr. *Weiser,* and Mr. *Montour,* would interpret it to them at a proper Time.

*INVOICE of* Indian *GOODS brought to* Easton.

3 Groce of narrow starred Gartering.
4 Ditto of broad Star.
2 Ditto of middle Star.
4 Ditto of narrow *Scotch.*
2 Ditto of middle *Turkey.*
2 Ditto of broad *Turkey.*
4 Ditto of best *Scotch.*
5 Ditto of mixt figured.
2 Ditto of narrow Calimancoe.
2 Ditto of broad Calimancoe.
2 Ditto of spotted.
2 Ditto of Leaf.
1 Ditto of *London* lettered.
2 Ditto of plad.
3 Ditto of middle Scarlet.
4 Ditto of broad Scarlet.
3 Ditto of superfine.
2 Ditto of Boys, lettered.
2 Ditto of broad white lettered.
2 Ditto of coloured Pigeon.
1 Piece of brown Halfthicks.
2 Ditto of white Ditto.
1 Piece of blue Broadcloth.
5 Laced Coats.
8 Plain Ditto.
50 Pair of Shoes.
3 Dozen and one Pair of Womens Worsted Stockings.
1 Ditto of Yarn Ditto.
4 Pieces and 2 Bandanoe Handkerchiefs.
1 Ditto Lungee Romals.
1 Ditto of Cotton Romals.
4 Ditto of Nonsopretties.
8 lb. Coloured Thread.
3 Dozen and ten Worsted Caps.
2 Ditto of Knives.
1 Ditto of Tobacco-boxes.
1 Ditto of coarse Linen Handkerchiefs.

2 Ditto of Camblet.
33 Painted Looking-glasses.
8 Pieces of red Stroud.
4 Ditto.
14 Ditto of Mazarine Blue.
1 Ditto.
1 Ditto black
1 Ditto red, and one blue.
2 Pieces of 6–qr. blue Duffil.
2 Ditto of 7–8ths Ditto.
1 Ditto napped.
1 Piece of stamped Serge.
1 Piece of red Halfthicks.
4 Pieces of figured Gartering.
4 Ditto of blue and white flowered Handkerchiefs.
3 Dozen and ten plain Hats.
2 Dozen of Taylors Shears.
6 Gun-Locks.
1 Bunch of black Beads.
3 Groce and an Half of Sleeve Link Buttons.
4 Dozen of Ivory Combs.
1 Groce of Womens Thimbles.
100 Blankets.
160 Matchcoats.
246 Shirts, plain.
187 Ditto, ruffled.

*Brother* Teedyuscung, By this Belt you put me in Mind, that we formerly referred our Dispute about Lands to our Father King GEORGE, and you desired to know if he has decided it.

*Brother,* You should consider the Circumstances of the Affairs of your Father King GEORGE; His Majesty lives at a very great Distance from us, is now engaged in a War with the *French,* and the Business of War takes up a great deal of Time and Attention; besides, in Time of War, we have but few Opportunities of hearing from him.

As yet I have had no Answer relative to your Affairs. You may depend upon it, as soon as I receive one, it shall be communicated to you. And I can assure you, the Proprietaries have pressed Dispatch, and will do every Thing they can to bring it to a speedy Determination.

*A Belt.*

Then Governor *Bernard,* requesting the Attention of the *Indians,* addressed them as follows.

*Brethren of the* United Nations, By this String you spoke on Behalf of our Brethren the *Minisinks,* and said that they were wronged in their Lands; that the *English* settled so fast, that they were continually pushing them back; and when they asked for their Lands, they were told that they had sold their Lands, and had got drunk, and forgot it. If they had swallowed their Lands, they must be content, but they did not believe that they had swallowed all, but that some was left. They desired that I would enquire after their Lands that were left, and do them Justice.

*Brethren,* I am glad I have an Opportunity, in the Presence of so many Nations, to express the Desire I have of doing Justice to every one. The Throne of the Great King is founded on Justice, and I should not be a faithful Servant to him, if I neglected to give Redress to all Persons that have received Injuries from the People over whom the Great King has placed me.

I have therefore had a Conference with the *Minisinks,* in the Presence of some of their Uncles, and have come to a full Agreement with them; the Proceedings of which are now ready to be read to you.

*Brethren,* I have another Proof to give you of the Uprightness and Justice of our Province. We have come to an Agreement with the *Delaware Indians,* and other *Indians,* for the uncertain Claims they had on the Southern Parts of our Province; I hereby produce the Deeds that have been executed on this Occasion, that the Subject of them may be explained to you, and be had in perpetual Remembrance by all the Nations present; and I desire that you may all remember, that, by these two Agreements, the Province of *New-Jersey* is entirely freed and discharged from all *Indian* Claims. In Confirmation of which I give you this Belt.

*A Belt.*

*Brother* Teedyuscung, By this String you tell me, that, after the killing the nine *Indians* near *Esopus,* you carried three Belts to *George Freeland* who undertook to give them to the Governor, and you ask what is become of those Belts.

*Brother,* I can only say, that I never heard of those Belts before; nor do I know what Governor *George Freeland* undertook to carry those Belts to. The proper Governor was the Governor of *New-York;* for in his Province was this Mischief committed. And probably the Governor of *New-York* had these Belts; for I have heard that he issued a Proclamation for apprehending the Perpretrators of this Fact. This Fact has been blamed by all good and wise Men; and I am glad it was not done by the People of my Province. I will acquaint the Governor of *New-York* with what you have said upon this Occasion, and I will enquire after those Belts, and give you in Answer.

*A String.*

Governor *Denny,* being obliged to return to *Philadelphia,* on urgent Business, took his Leave of the *Indians.*

*Brethren,* It gives me great Pleasure that the Business of this Treaty has been carried on with so much Satisfaction.

I am sorry I am now to inform you, that I am obliged to leave you, having received last Night an Express from General *Forbes,* who is now near the *Ohio.* My Business calls me to Town; I shall therefore leave Mr. *Logan* and Mr. *Peters* to transact the Remainder of the Business, and doubt not but they will act to your Satisfaction.

I assure you of my Affection for you, and wish you all Manner of Happiness.

*Teedyuscung* arose, and desired to be heard on Behalf of the *Wapings,* or *Wapinger Indians,* called the *River Indians,* living near *Esopus,* and produced a short broad Belt of white Wampum, having in the Center two Hearts, of a reddish Colour, and in Figures 1745, wrote after the following Manner, 17♥♥45. The Belt had a round

Circle Pendant, representing the Sun; he then produced two Certificates, one from Governor *Clinton,* and the other from Governor *Hardy,* both which were much in Favour of the *Wapinger* Tribe of *Indians.* He said the Belt was given them by the Government of *New-York,* and represented their Union, which was to last as long as the Sun should continue in the Firmament.

*Teedyuscung* addressed Governor *Bernard,* desiring, by a String of Wampum, that he would extend his Protection to the Tribe of the *Wapings;* and as their Chief was old and infirm, he requested the Favour of a Horse to carry him home, which was readily granted.

*Takeaghsado,* or *Tagashata,* made the same Request to Governor *Denny,* which was likewise granted.

The *Six Nation* Chiefs consulted together, and, in a little Time, *Nichas,* in their Behalf, returned an Answer to the Speeches of the Governors, laying the Belts and Strings upon the Table in the Order they were delivered, and repeating distinctly what was said on each of them. At the End of every Article he returned Thanks, and expressed the highest Satisfaction, particularly on the ratifying the Peace, and the large Belt given thereupon, which he said should be sent to all the distant Nations of *Indians,* to whom it would be very agreeable; he likewise promised, that every Thing transacted in these Conferences, which, he again said, had afforded him great Pleasure, should be laid before the great Council at *Onondago,* whose Answer should be carefully transmitted. He thanked Governor *Bernard* for making up all the Differences between the Government and the *Minisink Indians,* so much to their Satisfaction. He made an Apology for the Want of Wampum, and the Exchange of other Belts, to give in Confirmation of their Performance of the several Things mentioned in the Governor's Speeches, agreeable to *Indian* Customs. Then wished Governor *Denny* a good Journey.

*October* 24, 1758.
Mr. *Peters,* and Mr. *Weiser,* the Proprietary Agents,
held a private Conference with the Chiefs of the *United Nations,*
at the House of *Adam Johe,* in *Easton;* at which were present,
William Logan, *Esq; of the Council.*
George Croghan, *Esq; Deputy Agent to Sir* William Johnson,
Charles Swaine, *Esq; Prothonotary, of* Northampton *County,*
*Mr.* Henry Montour, *Interpreter, and*
*Mr.* John Watson, *Surveyor, in the County of* Bucks.
*And there were likewise present the following* Indians.

*Kuriahtaaty,* Chief of the *Mohawks*
*Seguchsonyont,* Chief of the *Oneidoes,*
*Assaradungua,* Chief of the *Onondagoes,*
*Tagashata,* Chief of the *Senecas,*
*Tokaaio,* Chief of the *Cayugas,*
*Nichaquantaquoah,* Chief of the *Tuscaroras,*
*Conniach,* Chief of the *Conoys,*
*Robert White,* Chief of the *Nanticokes,*
and Several other *Indians.*

MR. *Peters*, and Mr. *Weiser*, in Virtue of a Power of Attorney from the Proprietaries of *Pennsylvania* to them, under the Great Seal of the said Province, having previously settled with the *Indian* Chiefs the Limits of the Lands to be released by the said Proprietaries, and of the Lands to be confirmed by the *United Nations*, the Proprietary Release, and the *Indians* Deed of Confirmation were read and interpreted, and the *Indians* expressing their Satisfaction at every Part thereof, and particularly with the Limits, as described in the Draught annexed to their Confirmation Deed, they were both executed in the Presence of *William Logan, George Croghan, Henry Montour, Charles Swaine*, and *John Watson*, who subscribed their Names, as Witnesses thereto. A Belt was given to the *Indians* at the Delivery of the Release; and it was agreed, that both Deeds should be produced at the next publick Conference, in order to be acknowledged.

On the 25th of *October* the *Indians* were employed all Day in dividing the Presents among their several Tribes.

*At a* CONFERENCE *held at* Easton, *with the* Indians, October 26, 1758.
PRESENT, *His Excellency Governor* BERNARD,
William Logan, Richard Peters, Andrew Johnson, Charles Read,
John Stephens, *Esquires.*
George Croghan, Conrad Weiser, Charles Swaine, *Esquires.*
*Major* Orndt, *The Sheriff and his Officers, Mr.* John Watson,
*The Chiefs of the* United Nations,
*and of the other Nations of* Indians, Moses Tittamy, *and*
James Davis, *and several other* Delawares.

THE Secretary having observed to the *Six Nation* Chiefs, that the Governors were charged, by *Tokaaio*, with having omitted some Things in their Answers, and desired to know what they were; *Thomas King* said they were afterwards supplied, and recommended some Things to be more particularly mentioned than they had been; and agreeably to this Advice the following Speech was spoke by the Members of the *Pennsylvania* Council.

*Brethren*, As we have now settled all Differences, and confirmed the antient Leagues of Amity, and brightened the Chain of Friendship; we now clean the Blood off your Council Seats, and put them in Order, that when you hold Councils at Home, you may sit as you formerly used to do in your Seats, with the same Peace and Tranquility.

*A String, consisting of One Thousand Grains of Wampum.*

*Brethren*, With this String of Wampum, we condole with you for the Loss of your wise Men, and for the Warriors that have been killed these troublesome Times, and likewise for your Women and Children; and we cover their Graves decently, agreeable to the Custom of your Forefathers.

*A String of One Thousand Grains of Wampum.*

*Brethren,* We disperse the dark Clouds that have hung over our Heads during these Troubles, that we may see the Sun clear, and look on each other with the Chearfulness our Forefathers did.

*A String of One Thousand Grains of Wampum.*

Mr. *Peters* and Mr. *Weiser* produced the Confirmation Deed, executed by the Chiefs of the *United Nations,* as before set forth, which the *Indian* Chiefs acknowledged to have been their voluntary Act and Deed, and that they clearly understood the Contents thereof, together with the Limits described in the Draught annexed to it; and the same being handed from *Indian* to *Indian,* it was re-delivered to the Proprietaries Agents.

After which the *Indian* Chiefs produced the Proprietary Deed of Release, executed by Mr. *Peters,* and Mr. *Weiser,* the Proprietary Agents, who acknowledged it to be their Act and Deed, in Behalf of their Constituents, and re-delivered it to the *Indians,* together with the Belt.

His Excellency Governor *Bernard* produced the following Deeds; one executed by five *Indian* Attorneys, appointed by a Council of the *Delaware* Nation, for all the Lands lying in *New-Jersey,* South of a Line from *Paoqualin* Mountain, at *Delaware* River, to the Falls of *Laometung,* on the North Branch of *Rariton* River, and down that River to *Sandy-Hook;* dated the 12th of *September* last, with Endorsements thereon, made by *Teedyuscung, Anawalleckon,* and *Tepascouon,* signifying their Agreement thereto, and Acknowledgment of their having received Satisfaction thereon, witnessed by three Chiefs of the *United Nations,* who, in Behalf of the *United Nations,* approved the Sale; and also by several *English* Witnesses.

Another Deed, dated the 23d of *October* Instant, at *Easton,* from the Chiefs of the *Munseys,* and *Wapings,* or *Pumptons,* Sixteen in Number, and included all the remaining Lands in *New-Jersey,* beginning at *Cushetung,* and down the Division Line between *New-Jersey* and *New-York,* to the Mouth of *Tappon-Creek,* at the *North* or *Hudson's River,* and down the same to *Sandy-Hook;* then to the Mouth of *Rariton;* then up that River to *Laometung Falls;* then on a strait Line to *Paoqualin,* where it joins on *Delaware* River; and up *Delaware* to *Cushetung;* endorsed by *Nimham,* a Chief of the *Pumptons,* or *Wapings,* who was sick at the Execution thereof, and approved by the *United Nations,* which was testified by three of their Chiefs, signing as Witnesses. And Governor *Bernard* desired all present might take Notice of the same, the *Indian* Title to all the Lands in the Province of *New-Jersey* being conveyed thereby; which being interpreted in the *Six Nation* and *Delaware* Languages, his Excellency addressed the *Indians,* as follows.

*Brethren,* I am very glad this good Work has been so happily finished. I came among you, wholly unacquainted with your Forms, and therefore if I have omitted any Ceremonial, you will readily excuse me. But in whatever I have been deficient, I am sure I have not wanted a good Heart towards you.

The Circumstances of our Province have hitherto rendered us unable to give you any great Proofs of our Regard for you; but I shall endeavour to persuade my People to do you good Service for the future, by opening a Communication with you, which, if rightly managed, will be much to the Advantage of both People. And, for my own Part, I shall be always ready to do you Justice, and desire that whenever you have Cause of Complaint against my People, you will take Care to signify it to me.

*A String.*

The *Five Nation* Chiefs having laid all the Belts and Strings on the Table, that were delivered at this and the last Conference, the *Cayuga* Chief, *Tokaaio,* desired the Governors, and all present, would hearken to what *Thomas King* was going to say on Behalf of the *United Nations* (now Eight in Number) on which *Thomas King* arose, and taking up the first Belt, which was given by *Teedyuscung,* when he requested a Deed for the *Wyomink* Lands, he addressed the *Delawares, Teedyuscung* not being present, as follows.

*Cousins,* By this Belt *Teedyuscung* desired us to make you the Owners of the Lands at *Wyomink, Shamokin,* and other Places on the *Sasquehannah* River; in Answer to which, we who are present say, that we have no Power to convey Lands to any one; but we will take your Request to the great Council Fire, for their Sentiments, as we never convey or sell any Lands, before it be agreed in the great Council of the *United Nations.* In the mean Time you may make use of those Lands, in Conjunction with our People, and all the rest of our Relations, the *Indians* of the different Nations in our Alliance, which being interpreted in *Delaware,* the String of Wampum was given to *Moses Tittamy,* and *James Davis,* to be delivered to *Teedyuscung,* as he was not present.

Then taking up each Belt and String, in the Order it was delivered in this and the last Conference, he proceeded to repeat distinctly what had been said under each Article, returning Thanks for all those good Speeches, which he said were extremely agreeable: He made particular Mention of the large Peace Belt, saying, the Nations were vastly pleased, that all the antient Treaties made here, at *Albany,* and elsewhere, were renewed, as well as that the old Council Fire at *Philadelphia* was kindled again, and a good Road made to it, that might be travelled without any Danger; these in particular, as well as every other Matter transacted at these Conferences, we will make known to our own Nations, and to every other in Friendship and Alliance with us; and we are sure they will be very well received.

Then, addressing Governor *Bernard,* they thanked him for his Farewel Speech, saying, it was a very kind one, and that they were very glad at his having been present and given his Assistance at this Treaty, which had given them an Opportunity of gaining an Acquaintance with him, which they would ever remember with Pleasure. After a Pause, he desired to be excused in mentioning something that had been omitted by the Governors and their Councils. You have forgot to bring with you Ammunition, of which we always used to receive a sufficient Quantity, not only to serve us in our Journey, but support us in our hunting Season, that we might be enabled to make Provision for our Families. You have given us Gun-Locks without Guns, which are of no Manner of Use to us; and therefore this must surely have been forgot, as it is impossible for *Indians* to subsist without Guns, Powder and Lead, of which we have received none.

*Brethren,* As many of us are old and infirm, we desire our Brethren will be so good as to furnish us with a Number of Waggons to carry such of us as are not able to walk with the Goods you have been pleased to give us, as far as *Wyomink,* where we have left our Canoes, and then we will discharge the Waggons. We further desire a Supply of Provisions may be put into the Waggons, enough to serve us till we get to our respective Habitations.

He then took up the Proprietary Release, and returned Thanks for it. He said that, when the *United Nations* first made the Request to Sir *William Johnson,* to be transmitted to *Onas,* they had no Doubt but *Onas* would comply with it, having always found him ready to grant all their Requests; with him we have never had any Difference, he has always settled our Affairs without giving us any Trouble, and to our Satisfaction. We heartily thank *Onas.* This Act confirms us in the good Opinion we have always had of him.

Then, addressing himself to the *Delawares,* with a String of Wampum, he spoke as follows.

This serves to put *Teedyuscung* in Mind of his Promises, to return the Prisoners. Remember Cousin, you have made this Promise in our Presence; you did it indeed before, and you ought to have performed it; it is a Shame for one who calls himself a great Man to tell Lies; let us, as Counsellors, perform our Engagements and Promises; Cousin, you must not now fail to perform your Word; we are all one People, and we must all of us be punctual in the Performance of our Engagements. This was interpreted in the *Delaware* Language, and the String was given to *Moses Tittamy* for *Teedyuscung.* He then said the *United Nations* had finished what they had to say.

Looking round the Room, he espied Mr. *Vernon,* the Person who had the Care of furnishing the *Indians* with Provisions, and he desired, that, now Council Business was over, he might be ordered to take the Lock off the Rum, and let it run freely; that, as they were going away, their Hearts might me made glad, and we could very well spare it, as it was of no Use to us.

Some Wine and Punch was then ordered in, and the Conferences were concluded with great Joy and mutual Satisfaction.

*The END*

1. Between the Treaty at Easton in August 1757 and this treaty of the following year, Governor Denny had issued two proclamations forbidding the sale of liquor to Indians, in preparation for Teedyuscung's party's arrival. They were printed on July 5, 1758, and September 22, 1758 (Miller, *Philadelphia Printing,* 380).

2. On June 15, 1758, Isaac Norris wrote to Franklin in London, saying, "except a very few skulking Parties now and then in Small Numbers, we have not had much Damage on the frontiers, but it is probable, we may hear of more, during the harvest, unless the large Bodies of Soldiers now dispersd Thro' the back Counties should deter the Enemy from the attempt, which is not probable" (Labaree, *Papers of Benjamin Franklin,* 8:105). The western Lenapes had never received the peace belts that had been sent to them. Two Ohio Lenape chiefs, Pisquetomen and Keekyuscung, told Peters that the belts intended for them had been "detained somewhere." This comment and Pennsylvania's decision to begin communicating and treating directly with the Ohio Lenapes rather than through Teedyuscung make it unlikely that "the *Indians* have heard me as far as the *Twightwees,*" especially because Peters also learned that there were Miamis supporting the French at Fort Duquesne (Jennings, *Empire of Fortune,* 386, 401–2). These western Lenapes for their part had no interest in treating through Teedyuscung either. Not only were the eastern Lenapes clearly junior members of the League from which the westerners were carefully maintaining their independence, but the two Lenape nations were by no means inherently related to one another as political entities (Jennings, *Empire of Fortune,* 394). Most of the Ohio leaders descended from Tulpehocken Lenapes, while Teedyuscung's Wyoming group was mainly from the Forks.

3. This is the first reference in this series of treaty councils to the fact that Iroquois warriors had been involved in the attacks. It is unclear whether these warriors resided in Cayuga proper or in the Ohio Valley, though it appears from later discussions regarding prisoners that they resided in Iroquoia, not Ohio.

4. This paragraph is an example of how Weiser and Peters falsified the record to make it look like Teedyuscung was claiming to act on the behalf of the League itself.

5. Pisquetomen and Keekyuscung came to Philadelphia in the early summer of 1758 when rumors of a peace reached them despite the fact that the belts had not. The Ohio Indians were interested in peace and unhappy with the French (Jennings, *Empire of Fortune,* 385–86).

6. This paragraph tends to reinforce the mythic association of Indians with revenge. It is to be hoped that this series of treaties dispels these concepts: that Native Americans always sought immediate revenge when wronged and that they conceived of the world in terms of retaliation rather than justice. Both the Iroquois and the Lenapes consistently act with utmost patience and measured forethought in response to the most egregious violations of their human and political rights by British subjects and British governments.

7. Many contemporary Indian nations still retain hunting and fishing rights through treaty agreements with the United States government, though the fact is not well known, nor is the principle of their special relationship with the United States, as compared to other "minority" groups widely recognized (Pevar, *Rights of Indians and Tribes,* 189–208).

8. See also Wallace, *Conrad Weiser,* 360.

9. Though we know that the League's earlier displeasure with Teedyuscung was carefully manufactured and set in motion by Weiser and Peters, it is unclear whether this unprecedented public snubbing was a continuation of it. At least three aspects of Teedyuscung's speech could have provoked the reaction. First, it is possible that they were displeased at his speaking at all, rather than raising his points in their councils ahead of time to be included or excluded from Thomas King's speech by consensus. Second, the Goshen incident alone might have been considered more proper to be included in King's detailing of the grievances that led to war. The Six Nations may have resented that he held it back and thereby elevated himself to a position of commensurability with King. Finally, his mention of his uncle's lands in the final paragraph might easily have been misinterpreted to them, and raised again the false spectre

that he was claiming to speak for the League as well as his own nation (See Jennings, *Empire of Fortune,* 399). The context of both this instance and the earlier one involving Weiser and Peters was a pattern of European powers propping up leaders of their own choice to represent Indian nations in order to bypass the legitimate leaders of those nations and of their towns and clans.

10. The exact lands referred to in the deed produced here are conveniently left out of the treaty record. As Teedyuscung will point out on October 21, it is not the Walking Purchase that the deed refers to at all. It may be a deed for a minor sale of land in the same vicinity of William Logan's iron mine near Durham Creek, made in 1726, although this treaty locates the deed "beyond the Kittochtinny Hills" (Jennings, *Ambiguous Iroquois Empire,* 309, 331).

11. That is, the Six Nations Indians of Ohio.

12. This word usually refers to Ohio Iroquois, and is normally considered a slur (Mann, "Are You Delusional?" 37). Why it appears here to describe League Iroquois is a mystery.

13. After this figurative pronouncement by Tokaaion, the British literally begin to count the grains of wampum and the lengths of their belts! It is one of the more ridiculous outcomes of the dialogue toward peace. Tokaaion is not actually concerned with the length of the strings and belts they receive, even though there is a relationship between the size of wampum and the importance of the message sent. Rather, he wants sincerity, honesty, directness, and good faith. The League is in essence here acknowledging that the eastern Lenapes are getting the runaround from Penn's henchmen (Weiser, Peters, and Croghan) and ultimately from Denny, despite his apparent forthrightness in continuing to raise the land issue while these three are attempting to bury it.

14. Apparently the Ohio Lenapes, like Teedyuscung, had also caught on to the mismatch between their records and Pennsylvania's written records.

✠

# MINUTES OF CONFERENCES,

HELD AT *EASTON*, In *AUGUST*, 1761.

With the Chief SASCHEMS and WARRIORS

of the *ONONDAGOES, CAYUGAS,*

*ONEIDAS, NANTICOKES, MOHICKONS,*

*DELAWARES, TUTELOES, CONOYS.*

---

*PHILADELPHIA:*
Printed and Sold by B. FRANKLIN, and D. HALL,
at the *New-Printing-Office*, near the Market. MDCCLXI.

---

*Minutes of Conferences*, &c.

*At a* CONFERENCE *with the* Indians *at* Easton,
*on* Monday *the Third of* August, 1761.[1]
PRESENT, *The Honourable* JAMES HAMILTON, *Esq;*
Lieutenant-Governor;
Richard Peters, *and* Benjamin Chew, *Esquires,*
*of the Council of the Province;*
Joseph Fox, *Esq; one of the Provincial Commissioners, and several other Gentlemen from* Philadelphia *and other Parts of the Province;*
The Deputies of the Onondagoes, Cayugas, Oneidas, Mohickons,
Nanticokes, Delawares, Tuteloes, Conoys;
*Men, Women and Children, about Four Hundred in Number,*
*which encreased afterwards to near Five Hundred.*
Seneca George. *Speaker.* Samuel Weiser, James Sherlock, Joseph Pepy,
*Interpreters.*

THE Governor opened the Conference with the usual Ceremonies of giving them a String, to bid them heartily welcome, and another to wipe the Sweat from their Bodies, to take the Thorns and Briars out of their Legs and Feet, to clear their Throats, and to open their Hearts; after which he acquainted them, that he then was, or would at any Time be ready, upon their giving him Notice, to attend to any Thing they had to say to him.

Then *Seneca George* stood up, and spoke as follows, *viz.*
Brother Onas, I am very glad to meet you here at this Time, and to find that the Sky is clear, and that the Road is open and safe to travel in: I speak this in Behalf of Seven Nations, and all their Cousins, Captains and Warriors, and thank the Almighty that he has once more brought us all together, to shake Hands.

*A String.*

*Brother* Onas, We suppose, that during the late Troubles, you may have lost many of your People, either by Sickness or War, since we were last together; by this String, therefore, we wipe away the Tears from your Eyes, clear your Throats, wash away the Blood from your Bodies, sweep the Council Chamber, and throw the Dirt out of Doors, that you may see and speak to us clearly at the present Conference.

*A String.*

*Brother* Onas, We the Seven Nations,[2] and all our Cousins, are sorry, from the Bottom of our Hearts, for the Death of your Men, Women and Children; and by this Belt we collect all their Bones together, bury them in one Grave, and cover them up.

*A black Belt of eight Rows, streaked with White.*

*Brother* Onas, We the Seven Nations, and our Cousins, are at a great Loss, and sit in Darkness, as well as you, by the Death of *Conrad Weiser,* as since his Death we cannot so well understand one another: By this Belt we cover his Body with Bark.

*A white Belt of seven Rows, with four black Streaks.*

*Brother* Onas, By the last Belt I mentioned to you that we both sat in Darkness, now by this Belt I remove the Clouds from before the Sun, that we may see it rise and set, and that your Hearts may be eased from Sorrow, on Account of what I mentioned before.

*A white Belt of five Rows, with three black Bars.*

After the Delivery of the Belt, he added (having forgot it before) We pray the Great God above, who can enlighten our Hearts, that we may live in Love and Peace until Death.

*Brother* Onas, Having taken Notice of the Death of *Conrad Weiser,* and the Darkness it has occasioned amongst us, I now, by this Belt (taking Hold of the Belt in the Middle) raise up another Interpreter, by whose Assistance we may understand one another clearly.

*Brother* Onas, (Speaking with the other Part of the Belt) You know that in former Times, when great Men grew old and died, we used to put others in their Places; now as *Conrad Weiser* (who was a great Man, and one Half a Seven Nation *Indian,* and one Half an *Englishman)* is dead, we recommend it to the Governor to appoint his Son (pointing to *Samuel Weiser,* then present) to succeed him as an Interpreter, and to take Care of the Seven Nations and their Cousins. We take Hold of this Belt, and clasp our Hands together in Friendship, and desire you will not neglect our Request.

*A black and white Belt of eight Rows.*

*Brother* Onas, *Jenochiaada,* the Chief of the *Onondagoes,* sends this String, by *Ashenoch,* to his Brother the Governor, saying,

*Brother,* When I receive a Letter from you, I cannot understand it, which I think very hard, and we ought to have some body living among us, who can understand and interpret your Messages, and the Letters you send to us; wherefore I take my Child, *James Sherlock,* by the Hand, and present him to you, that with your Leave he may live amongst us, and serve us as an Interpreter on all Occasions.

*Three Strings.*

*Brother* Onas, Having by the last String recommended *James Sherlock* to you, as an Interpreter, we have no more to say to you at present, but to inform you that we have sufficiently rested ourselves, after the Fatigue of our Journey, eased our Hearts of all Sorrow, and are ready to hear any Thing you have to say to us.

*Three Strings.*

The Governor then informed them, that he thanked them for what they had said, and would return them an Answer at another Time, and in a more convenient Place, of which he would give them timely Notice.

*At a* CONFERENCE *with the* Indians,
*on* Wednesday *the* 5th *of* August, 1761.
PRESENT, *The Honourable* JAMES HAMILTON, *Esq;*
*Lieutenant-Governor;*
Richard Peters, Benjamin Chew, *Esquires, of the Council of the Province,*
&c. &c. &c. *as before;*
Samuel Weiser, Isaac Stille, David Seisberger, *Interpreters.*

Tokahaio, *the* Cayuga *Chief stood up and spoke.*

*Brother* Onas, BY this Belt, three Years ago, at a Treaty held here at *Easton,* the Governor invited us to come down in greater Numbers, as we were not all then present; and now that we do all appear, we return you the Belt, that had been given us at the making the Peace, and are glad to see you here Face to Face.

*A very large white Belt of eighteen Rows.*

*Brother* Onas, You told us by this Belt, three Years ago, that you removed this, which is but a little Fire, to *Philadelphia,* where our Ancestors formerly kindled their great Fire, and made all their Alliances and Treaties.

*Brother* Onas, By this other Belt, you at the same Time cleared the Road to the Great Council Fire, at *Philadelphia,* and removed all Obstructions out of it, that it might be open for us to pass in Safety.

*Two Belts joined together.*

*Brother* Onas, By this Belt, you at the same Time told us, that you cleared our Ears; that all the Nations might hear what you had to say to us.

*A white Belt of seven Rows, striped.*

*Brother* Onas, At the same Time you told us, that our Eyes were bad, and that by this String you cleared them, that we might be able to see a great Ways, and every Thing that passed.

*Six white Strings.*

*Brother* Onas, You also gave us this String, and told us we seemed a little shy; but desired we would lay aside all such Thoughts; for you had no ill Intentions against us.

*Three white Strings.*

*Brother* Onas, This String was sent to us, the *Six Nations,* by Seven Nations of *Indians* over the Lakes; who have formerly been in the *French* Interest, but have lately entered into an Alliance with us, desiring that they might lay Hold, with us, of one End of the Chain of Friendship, that subsists between us and the *English;* and we desire the Governor, that they may be accepted as Friends.

The Names of the Seven Nations, abovementioned, are as follow, *viz.*

| | | | |
|---|---|---|---|
| *Warontas,* | *Schesova,* | *Cochnawagechrona,* | *Neoquechta.* |
| *Scheiquoucchrona,* | *Connechsatagechrona,* | *Chesochechrona,* | |

*Ten white Strings.*

*Brother* Onas, When we came as far as *Fort-Allen,* you sent us this String by Mr. *Horsefield,* inviting us to come down to *Easton;* and now that we are come, we return it you again.

*Four white Strings.*

*Brother* Onas, By this String you told us, on *Monday* last, that you were very glad to see us all well here; we are likewise glad to see you; and return it you again.

*Three white Strings.*

*Brother* Onas, By this String you wiped the Sweat from our Bodies, took the Thorns from our Legs and Feet, cleared our Throats, and opened our Hearts; we thank you, and return it you again.

*Four Strings, chequered.*

*Brother* Onas, These three Belts were brought to us, the *Onondagoes,* by the *Oneidas,* but they brought no Speeches with them; we therefore return them to you again, for, as they are your own Belts, you may know their Meaning;———we do not.

*One Belt of eleven, one of eight, and one of seven Rows, black and white.*

Being asked whether they were brought all together, or at different Times, they answered, that they were all brought by one Messenger, about a Year ago, which Messenger was an *Oneida,* but that they do not know his Name.——Being asked how the *Oneida* came by them, and what he said, they answered, that he said no more, but that they were about the Governor's Business.

*Papounan,* by one of his *Indians,* called *Tougachena,* living at *Wighalousin,* then spoke to the Governor as follows.

Agreeable to your Request, when I was at *Philadelphia* last Summer, I carried your Message to *Achoan,* the Chief of the *Minisinks,* respecting his sending the *English* Prisoners, and I now deliver to you *Achoan*'s Answer.

*Brother* Onas, "You desired me last Year that I should clear myself, as your Brothers that live at *Wighalousin* did, by which you would have a Proof of my Friendship. After I received your Message, I took it away to my Uncles, the *Senecas,* and delivered to them what you had said to me, upon which they advised me to deliver up all the Captives: Now, Brother, I would have you not be impatient, and I will come as soon as possible. I will hunt up all the Captives that are amongst us, and will not leave one, but will bring them all;——but I have not yet found them all. I expect to come when the Corn is ripe; but if I should fail then, I will certainly come by the Spring."

*Three white Strings.*

*At a* CONFERENCE *with the* Indians, *the same Day, in the Afternoon.*
PRESENT, *as before.*

Teedyuscung, *the Chief of the* Delawares, *stood up and spoke.*

*Brother, and all the rest of my Brethren and Uncles, attend.* I INTEND to take no other Method, than what I have already agreed with the Governor. Brother, now I take the soft Feather to clear your Ears, which our Grandfathers used for the same Purpose, that you may hear distinctly whatever I may say.

*Four chequered Strings.*

*Brother,* I desire you would now hear me; I beg you would frame that good Heart God has given you in a right Way, that you may sensibly feel, and have a right Understanding, of what I am going to say to you.

*Four chequered Strings.*

*Brother,* I am come here to this Place, where we met about three Years ago. I then told you, I would take that Medicine which our Maker has ordered for us, to apply to any Wounds we may have. I likewise told you, that I do not apply it any where but where the Wound is——I have now come to see whether the Wound is healed, or no.

*A Belt of eight Rows.*

*Brother,* You then told me, when you looked on the Road our Grandfathers laid out, that you observed many Bushes and much Grass grown there, so that you could not see me. You then took me by the Hand.

*Brother,* All my young Men, as far as the *Tweteeway* Nations, have let me know, that they intend firmly to join in and stand to whatever you and I have agreed on; and also those young Men I have with me, *Mohickons, Opies* and *Delawares,* say they will not take Notice of what few Drops of Blood have stained our Road, but will look steady to our Agreement.

*A black Belt of seven Rows, and five chequered Strings.*

*Brother,* Observe what I am going to say, and I will let you know we have cleared ourselves, as far as *Makahelousink, Papounan*'s House. I will assure you, that I want to make a Peace between us as lasting as the World. I call the Almighty to witness, that I have no Captives in my Possession, as far as *Makahelousink.*

*Seven chequered Strings.*

*Brother,* I have one Thing more to say: I would not have you look to me any more for any Thing, for I believe nothing will ever make us differ again, except it is your Fault, for I am sure nothing on my Part shall cause it; therefore, if any Thing should fall out, examine your own Hearts, for it must spring from you, because all our young Men have put it into the Care of their Chiefs to manage Affairs.[3]

*Three chequered Strings.*

*Brother,* Our Grandfathers used to hold great Treaties of Peace and good Friendship, now we that succeed them will do the same; they used to agree that we should have one Ear and one Eye, now you sit at *Philadelphia,* and I am away in the

Country, and whatever one hears or sees, the other should hear it and see it also, because we are Brothers.

*Thirteen chequered Strings.*

*Brother,* As I told you just now that we have one Ear, I desire you would hear me: My Uncles, the *Seven Nations,* that sit here now, desire me to leave *Wyoming,* for Fear; I answered, I will not leave it so suddenly; but, if I should see any Danger, I will endeavour to jump out of the Way of that Danger.

*A black and white Belt of six Rows.*

*Brother,* My Uncles have now put some Tobacco in my Pouch; they tell me, I must steadily look towards the Mountains, and "if you see *English* Brethren coming over the Mountains, you must light your Pipe, and come to us (the *Mingoes)* and we will receive you."

*A white Belt of six Rows, striped.*

*Brother,* It is about three Years ago that I desired my Uncles would give me a Deed for the Lands at *Wyoming,* but as they have not done it, I believe I shall get up and leave it; for you know, according to your Custom, you hold all Lands by Deeds, and if our Uncles had given us a Deed, our Children would enjoy them after us: If they had given me a Deed, my Children and Grandchildren would live there as long as the World lasts; but as that is not done, I believe I shall leave it.[4]

*A white Belt of twelve Rows.*

*At a* CONFERENCE *with the* Indians *at* Easton,
*on* Friday *the Seventh of* August, 1761,
PRESENT, *The Honourable* JAMES HAMILTON, *Esq;*
*Lieutenant-Governor of the Province of* Pennsylvania;
Richard Peters, *and* Benjamin Chew, *Esquires,*
*of the Council of the Province;*
Joseph Fox, *Esq; one of the Provincial Commissioners,*
*and several other Gentlemen from* Philadelphia
*and other Parts of the Province;*
*The Deputies of the* Onondagoes, Cayugas, Oneidas, Nanticokes,
Mohickons, Delawares, Tuteloes, Conoys;
*Men, Women and Children, about Four Hundred in Number.*

The Governor, addressing himself to the *Indians* present, spoke as follows, *viz.*

*Brethren of the* Six Nations, *and of all the other* Indian *Nations now present.* HEARKEN to me, while I return an Answer to your Speeches of *Monday* and *Wednesday* last.

*Brethren,* It gives me Pleasure to hear that you have found the Sky clear, and the

Road to this Council Fire open and safe, and I join with you in returning Thanks to the Almighty; that he has once more brought us all together, to speak to one another, as Brethren and Friends, Face to Face.

*A String.*

*Brethren,* We thank you for remembering those whom we have lost, during the late Troubles, either by Sickness or War, and for wiping away the Tears from our Eyes, clearing our Throats, washing away the Blood from our Bodies, and sweeping clean the Council Chamber; in return, we most heartily condole with you, the *Seven Nations,* and all your Cousins and Warriors, for the Death of all our *Indian* Brethren, who have died or been killed since we last met in Council, and with this String we wipe away the Tears from your Eyes, clean your Throats, wash away the Blood from your Bodies, sweep the Council Chamber, and throw the Dirt out of Doors, that there may be nothing to interrupt our present friendly Conference.

*A String.*

*Brethren,* With this Belt we collect together the Bones of all your Men, Women and Children, and most affectionately bury them in one Grave, that they may rest in Peace for ever.

*A Belt.*

*Brethren,* We are very sensible, with you, that both of us have sustained a very heavy Loss, by the Death of our old and good Friend *Conrad Weiser,* who was an able, experienced and faithful Interpreter, and one of the Council of the *Seven Nations;* and that since his Death we, as well as you, have sat in Darkness, and are at a great Loss for Want of well understanding what we say to one another: We mourn, with you, for his Death, and heartily join in covering his Body with Bark.

*A Belt.*

*Brethren,* By this Belt we dispel the dark Clouds, which you have justly observed the Death of our good Friend has occasioned, and make the Sky perfectly clear again, that we may behold the Light all the Day long: We ease your Hearts from the Grief you were under, on this mournful Account, and we pray God that we may for ever live together in Peace and Love.

*A Belt.*

*Brethren,* Having thus paid our Regards to our deceased Friend, we cannot but observe, with you, that there is a Necessity of appointing some other Person to succeed him, by whose Assistance we may be enabled to find the true Sense and Meaning of what there may be Occasion to say to one another, either in Council, or by Letters, or Messages.

*Brethren,* In Conformity to the ancient Custom of taking from among the Relations of any great Man who dies, some fit Person to supply his Place (as Mr. *Weiser* was by Adoption one of the *Six Nations,* though by Birth one of us) we think you did well to cast your Eyes upon one of his Children; and, inasmuch as *Samuel Weiser* is the only one amongst them who has any Knowledge of the *Indian* Language, and has lived among you, we shall be glad to make Trial of him for the present, and if we find him capable of serving in the Office of an Interpreter, and in the Management of *Indian* Affairs (in both which Capacities his Father so well acquitted himself) we shall appoint him to that Service. We look upon this Choice of yours as a Mark of your grateful Affection for *Conrad Weiser,* who was always your sincere Friend; and we join this Belt to yours, in Token of our Concurrence, so far as to make Trial of him.

*Their Belt, and another.*

*Brethren,* I have now answered every Thing that you, of the *Seven United Nations,* said to me at our last Meeting, I now address myself to *Jenochryada,* the *Onondagoe* Chief, to answer the Message he sent to me by *Ashenoch.*

*Brother* Jenochryada, You tell me that *James Sherlock* has for some Time past lived with you: I am glad to hear he has behaved in such a Manner as to obtain your good Opinion of him, and I hope he will continue to prove himself worthy of your Confidence: I have no Objection to his living among you, or to your employing him in any Business you may have to transact with us, which you think him capable of executing; but as he is a young Man, and quite a Stranger to me, I cannot consent to employ him as an Interpreter for this Government, until I have as full an Experience of his Abilities and good Disposition as you have had. In the mean Time, if I should have any Occasion of sending Messages or Letters to your Nation, I shall commit the Care of them to Messengers of my own; and desire you will observe the same Method, as the likeliest Means to our right understanding of one another, and preventing Mistakes, which might otherwise happen.

*A String.*

*Brethren of the* Seven United Nations, You told me, that three Years ago, at a Treaty held here, I invited you, by this Belt, to come down in greater Numbers, as you were not then all present; and that, as you all were now here, you returned me this Belt, and were glad to see us here Face to Face.

*Brethren,* My Counsellors well remember, that this Belt was given you by the late Governor of this Province, at the last Treaty, but you seem to have mistaken the End and Purpose for which it was given; I must therefore inform you, that it was given to you as a Peace Belt, by which we then renewed our old Treaties, brightened the Chain of Friendship, confirmed our former Union, and put fresh Earth to the Roots of the Tree of Peace, that it might bear up against every Storm, and live and flourish to the End of Time, whilst the Sun should shine, and the Rivers run; and we then further desired you would publish this good News among your own and all other *Indian* Nations, who were your Friends and Allies, and engage them to join with you in a firm Peace with our great King, and all his People. All this appears by the Minutes of that Treaty, taken down in Writing at that Time; you ought therefore to preserve this Belt, as a Bond or Earnest of the Engagements we then made to one another, and keep it safe in your Bosoms, and I now return it you for that Purpose.

*The Peace Belt returned.*

*Brethren,* You informed us, that this String was sent from Seven Nations of *Indians* over the Lakes, who have formerly been in the *French* Interest, but have lately entered into your Alliance, desiring they might lay Hold, with you, of one End of the Chain of Friendship, that subsists between you and the *English.*

*Brethren,* It gives me great Pleasure to hear that you have strengthened your Interest, by entering into an Alliance with these Seven Nations of *Indians,* who have been formerly in the Interest of the *French.* You and I are one Flesh and Blood, and I shall love and esteem all *Indians* whatsoever, who are in your Friendship. I will take this String, and send it to the King's Commander in Chief, and Sir *William Johnson,* and let them know the Desire those *Indians* have of entering into Friendship and Alliance with the *English,* and I make no Doubt but they will receive them with open Arms. To confirm my Words, I give you this String.

*A String.*

*Brethren,* I am very much surprised to hear from you, that these three Belts were brought to the *Onondagoe* Council, by an *Oneida Indian,* about a Year ago, without any Speeches or Messages to attend them. I can assure you, I did not send these Belts to the *Onondagoe* Council, and therefore I am at a Loss to know the Meaning of them, or from whom they came. I have frequently sent Messages into the *Indian* Country, to put them in Mind of their Promise to return to us our Flesh and Blood, who are Prisoners among them, and to press them to fulfil that Promise; and it is possible, that the Belt sent with the Messengers for that Purpose, may have been forwarded to the *Six Nation* Council by Mistake; I therefore now return you the Belts, that you may make further Enquiry of the *Oneidas* about them.

*The Belts returned.*

*Brethren,* You acquainted me, by these three Belts, first, that you were coming to see me, and were got as far as *Wyoming;* by the second, you desired me to meet you at *Easton;* by the third, you desired me to stop strong Drink, and send you Waggons, Provisions and Paint. As I have complied with these several Requests, I now return you the Belts.

*The three Belts returned.*

The several other Belts and Strings which you received from us at the last Treaty, and were returned by you to me the Day before Yesterday, I have accepted, and put into the Council Bag.

*Brethren,* Whatever may be the Occasion of your coming down at this Time, I can truly say, I am glad to see my old Friends and Brethren once more, and take them by the Hand, and will make you as welcome and easy, while you stay among us, as I possibly can. I have only further to say to you at present, that as we are now Face to Face, we should open our Hearts to one another, and let nothing remain upon our Minds; if you, on your Part, have, any Thing to offer or communicate to me, that relates to the private Interest or Concerns of this Province, or that can tend to promote and confirm our Friendship, and prevent all future Causes of Jealousy and Discontent, I shall be glad to hear it

*A Belt.*

*At a* CONFERENCE *with the* Indians,
*on* Saturday *the Eighth of* August, 1761.
PRESENT, *The Honourable* JAMES HAMILTON, *Esq;* &c. *as before.*

Joseph Pepy *stood up, and spoke as follows,* viz.

*Brother* Onas, I AM to speak a few Words to you. We had a great Council Fire at *Albany,* when a Friendship was first made with our Grandfathers; after which, about seven Years ago, our Brother General *Johnson* moved the Council Fire from *Albany* to his own House, where he said to us, "I am one Half *Indian,* and one Half *English:* What I say to my dear Brethren, the *Seven Nations,* shall be true."——The *Seven Nations* were accordingly all assembled to the Place where he had kindled the Fire, at which Time he took up a Tomahawk gave it them, and told them, he was going to War against the *French,* and desired them to join with him, and promised them, that after the *French* were all conquered and removed, Trade should be made open and free to them, and all Kinds of Goods should become more cheap, and that their Furs and Skins should bear a good Price.———

Last Year General *Johnson* appointed his Brethren, the *Seven Nations,* to meet him at *Oswego,* upon which they did assemble there; at which Time General *Johnson* observing that their Chiefs and Warriors were not all come, he sent a second Message, desiring them all to attend him there, and when they did come he said,

*Brethren,* "I am very glad to see you here. I see many of your Chiefs are dead. I am now going against the *French,* and out of the Prisoners that I shall take from them, I will put as many in their Room."——Now, Brother *Onas,* as General *Johnson* has not performed his Promise to us, we see Death coming upon us, and the God above knows he has wronged us.

*Brother* Onas, We give no Belt or String upon this Occasion, and only relate it as Matter of Information to you.

*Brother* Onas, Listen to what your Brethren of the *Seven Nations* say, in Answer to what you told us Yesterday.

You desired us to open our Hearts, that nothing unknown might lay hid there, but that every Thing may come out: We desire, by this Belt, that you may do the same.

*A white Belt of eight Rows, with three black Bars.*

*Brother* Onas, We see, Brethren, on each Side of us: On the one Side, the Governor of *Virginia,* who does not speak or do right to us; on the other Side, General *Johnson,* who does the same. We have often heard you speak, and you always do and speak right and justly to us; every Time you speak it does our Hearts good. When we look towards you, General *Johnson,* and the Governor of *Virginia,* we esteem you all as One; how comes it then that you do not all speak alike.[5] We, your Brethren of the *Seven Nations,* are penned up like Hogs. There are Forts all around us, and therefore we are apprehensive that Death is coming upon us. We want nothing but Friendship with you, so long as the Sun shall shine, and the Waters run.

*A white Belt of nine Rows, and four black Bars.*

*Brother* Onas, Hearken to what your Brethren, the *Seven Nations,* are going to say to you. When our Grandfathers first made a Friendship together, God saw it: Now we, and all the Nations, would stand to the Agreement they made, and when any Nations smile upon us, we will join with them. Now, dear Brother, may God Almighty give us Strength and Knowledge to continue our Friendship. We look at no other, but to you, to hold fast the Chain of Friendship. We are crushed on all Sides, so that we cannot stir ourselves, nor look any Way but to you.——Now, dear Brother, that we see you Face to Face, we desire that you would not slack your Friendship, but hold it fast.

*A black and white Belt of seven Rows.*

*Brother* Onas, I would only let you know, in a few Words, how our Brother General *Johnson* served us.——When we come to him for Ammunition, and bring our Skins, he does not give us the Worth of our Skins, but only a Handful of Powder; and for that Reason we think there is certain Death coming upon us.——

He shuts up his Powder from us, and will not give us more than will serve us two or three Days. We only mention this to you, but if you will continue to smile on us, we will look to you.

*A white Belt of six Rows, and three black Bars.*

*Brother* Onas, We are now sensible, that we were under a Mistake with Respect to the Meaning of this Belt (holding up the large Peace Belt) We should not have brought it back to you again, if we had known what it meant: We are very glad that you have explained it to us: We look upon it as the Belt of Peace, and will shew it to all the Nations over the Lake, and will lodge it in the *Onondagoe* Council, where the only General Council Fire is kept, and where it ought to remain.

*Brother* Onas, This is all your Brethren of the *Seven Nations* have to say.

*At a* CONFERENCE *with the* Indians,
on Monday *the Tenth of* August, 1761.
PRESENT, *The Honourable* JAMES HAMILTON, *Esq;* &c. &c. *as before.*

Tokahaio *stood up and spoke as follows,* viz.

*Brother* Onas, YOU will please to hear what the *Six Nations,* are going to say to you. Some of the *English* have settled upon our Lands, but we don't know from whence they came. We hope, that as you are strong, you will assist us in preventing them from settling upon our Lands, that we may not be wronged out of them.

*A Belt of seven Rows, with six Diamonds and a Bar.*

*Brother* Onas, We have heard that this Land has been sold, but we do not know for certain by whom. The *Six Nations* have not sold it, and never intended it as yet. Whoever has sold the Land, stole it from us, and only did it to fill their Pockets with Money, but we have heard that two *Tuscaroras,* one *Oneida,* and one *Mohawk,* have sold it, unknown to the *Six Nations.*

*A String of four Rows.*

*Brother* Onas, Hear what we are going to say to you.———You know there is a Line made between you and us, and we desire that none of the *English* would settle on the other Side of that Line. [Being asked what they meant by that Line, they answered, the Line of the Purchase last made by this Province from the *Six Nations.*] Some People have already settled over that Line, which People we do not like, and hope you will be strong, and assist us in having them removed.

*A Belt of seven Rows, with three black Diamonds.*

*Brother* Onas, We are very poorly off, as we have no Trade stirring among us, and as we have mentioned to you that the Things we buy from General *Johnson* are very dear, we hope you will have Pity on us, and erect a Trading-house at *Diahoga,* that we may be able to buy our Goods cheaper. We are in great Want of all Kinds of Goods, but especially of Powder and Lead, and hope you will supply us plentifully with them. We desire you would not allow any strong Liquor to be sent among us, as we shall fetch that ourselves, whenever we shall want it. As soon as we see your People come with Goods, we will acquaint all our young Men with it, both far and near, and if your Goods are sold reasonable, we suppose that General *Johnson* will also sell his Goods cheaper than he now does.——We desire that you would send a good and honest Man to trade with us.

*A Belt of seven Rows and four black Bars.*

*Brother* Onas, You have frequently sent us Messages by straggling *Indians, Delawares,* and others, upon whom there is no Dependance: They sometimes lose the Belts and Messages, and sometime drink them away; but if they do happen to reach us, they are nothing but Nonsense. We desire you, therefore, that whenever you have Messages to send, you will send them by trusty Persons to our Great Council Fire at *Onondago,* that we may be able to understand them rightly; and as we have chosen *Samuel Weiser* for that Purpose, you can always send your Messages by him.

*A chequered String of four Rows.*

*Brother* Onas, You have often made Mention of your Flesh and Blood, who are Prisoners among us. "Tis true, Brother, there was some of your Blood among us; there were Ten among the *Cayugas,* but our Brother General *Johnson* also often spoke of them to us, and we have delivered them all up to him; there is none amongst us at present—You must now look for them amongst the *Delawares,* our Cousins.

*A Belt of five Rows, with three black Bars.*

*Brother* Onas, We have nothing further to say, and as we have been here a great While, we desire the Governor to make Haste to dismiss us.

(*James Sherlock* reports, that he had a Belt from the *Onondagoes* to the *Delawares,* at *Chugnot,* above *Diahoga,* demanding the *English* Prisoners they had; that he received one Woman from them, and was coming off with her in a Canoe, but that *Mechtochkaway,* the *Delaware* King, followed him, and took her from him, telling him that the *Delawares* would not deliver up their Prisoners, till they heard what their Brothers, the *English,* should say.)

*At a* CONFERENCE *with the* Indians,
*on* Tuesday *the Eleventh of* August.
PRESENT, *The Honourable* JAMES HAMILTON, *Esq;* &c. *as before.*

The Governor, addressing himself to the *Seven United Nations,* spoke as follows, *viz.*
*Brethren of the* Seven United Nations, *and all our* Indian *Brethren now present,* YOU desire me to open my Heart, and conceal nothing from you. I give you this String, to assure you that I will always communicate to you every Thing that comes to my Knowledge, or that rises up in my Mind, which concerns our common Interest, and keep nothing secret, but will agree that you and I shall have but one Eye, one Ear, and one Heart.

*A String.*

*Brethren,* I am very sorry to hear that you apprehend General *Johnson* has been unkind to you. I am afraid the Evil Spirit is again endeavouring to blind your Eyes, and mislead you. You well know that General *Johnson* has, for a great Number of Years past, manifested his Love and Friendship for the *Indians,* on many Occasions, and you have as often given Proofs of your Esteem and good Opinion of him. You should not therefore suffer the Confidence and Trust you have reposed in him, to be interrupted by any Jealousies or Suspicions; but you should open your Hearts to him, and tell him your Minds freely. I am persuaded he is a very worthy Gentleman, and your good Friend, and if you will lay your Grievances before him, I am sure he will do you Justice, if you have been injured, and remove all your Uneasiness.

*A Belt.*

*Brethren,* You say that you are afraid Death is coming upon you, and seem to apprehend yourselves to be in great Danger; I am much surprized to hear this, nor can I find out what has given Rise to your Fears, as there is now a perfect Peace and Friendship betwixt you and all your Brethren the *English;* you must not therefore make yourselves uneasy without any just Grounds or Foundation. I speak to you from the Bottom of my Heart, and do assure you that I never heard, nor do I believe that there are any ill Designs forming against you.

*A Belt.*

*Brethren,* I thank you for the particular Affection you express for the People of this Province. We have always made it a Rule to speak to you plainly, and from the Bottom of our Hearts, and to treat you not only justly, but with Brotherly Love, and Kindness. And it now gives us great Satisfaction to hear that you think so well of us. I assure you we desire nothing more, than to live in perfect Peace and Friendship with you, as long as the Sun and Moon endures. We will always hold the Chain of Friendship in our Hands, and keep it Bright and Free from Rust, and in all our future Conduct to, and Dealings with you, continue to use you well, and give you every Proof of our Affection and Regard for you.

*A Belt.*

*Brethren,* I have carefully considered that Part of the Speech you made Yesterday, wherein you say that some Lands have been stole from you, and sold by some *Indians,* who have no Right to them, to the *English,* who have settled upon them. I know of no Lands lying within this Province, which have not been purchased of you, that have been settled by the *English,* except a Tract lying on or near the River *Delaware,* about Fifty Miles above the *Blue Mountains.* Brethren, I am glad to have this Opportunity of speaking to you on this Head: It is a Matter of great Consequence, and has given me much Concern; listen attentively, therefore, to what I shall say to you about this Matter.—You know that an Agreement was made, a great While ago, between your Ancestors and your Brother *Onas* (which has been often renewed and confirmed by many of your Chiefs now living) that your Brother *Onas* would never settle any Lands in this Province, till he had fairly purchased them of the *Indians,* who engaged that they would never sell any Lands in this Province to any other

Person than their Brother *Onas.* That you may refresh your Memories, and call to Mind this Agreement, I give you this Belt.

*A Belt.*

*Brethren,* A great Number of People who lived in *Connecticut* Government, came about a Year ago, and settled near this River, beyond the Line of the Lands purchased of you, at a Place called *Cushetunk,* and claimed all the Lands from thence quite up to *Wyoming.* As soon as I heard of it I sent Messengers to them, informing them these Lands had never been purchased of the *Indians,* and desiring them to remove away. They sent me back, for Answer, that they had purchased all those Lands of you, and under that Pretence had a Right to them, and would hold them. Now, Brethren, as you have told me you will hide nothing from me, I desire you will tell me truly, whether you have sold these Lands to these Strangers, who have settled them, against my Will and Consent?—(To which Question the *Six Nations* made Answer, That those were the Lands which they mentioned Yesterday to have been sold by four straggling *Indians,* without the Knowledge or Consent of their General Council, and that they understood *Thomas King.* an *Oneida Indian,* was one of those who had sold those Lands.)

Upon which Answer the Governor said,

*Brethren,* You know all such private Sales are of no Force. I therefore join this String to the Belt, and desire you will send for those *Indians* into the Great Council at *Onondagoe,* and reprove them for their Conduct, and cancel their Deeds.

*A Belt and a large String.*

*Brethren.* I have already, by the Consent of my Wise Men, set up two great Stores, or Trading-houses, to furnish the *Indians* with all Sorts of Goods, at a cheap Rate, one at *Pittsburgh,* and the other at *Shamokin;* at the last of which Places you may easily supply yourselves with whatever you want. The Expences, Losses, and many Difficulties which attend our sending Goods to these two Places, are so great, that I cannot set up another Store-house at so great a Distance as *Diahoga,* according to your Desire.——I am sorry to refuse you any Thing; but if I should agree with you, to do more than I can perform, you would have just Reason to charge me with deceiving you. You must not therefore take it amiss, that I always speak plainly to you, and tell you my Mind.

*A Belt.*

*Brethren.* I told you before, that if I should have Occasion to send you any Messages, I would commit the Care of them to Messengers of my own; and as *Samuel Weiser* is a Person recommended by you for that Purpose, I will use him for the future.

*A String.*

*Brethren,* I am pleased to hear you sent to General *Johnson* our Flesh and Blood, who were Prisoners among the *Cayugas.* We esteem it as the strongest Proof of your Friendship that you can possibly give us.——You all agreed, at the Treaty held here three Years ago, that you would search all the Towns and Places in the *Indian* Countries for them, and deliver them up to us, without leaving one behind; and that if they had gone down your Throats, you would heave them up again. I am sorry that but very few have yet been brought back, though I know there are a great many scattered up and down among the *Indians.* We cannot help thinking that you speak only from your Lips, and not from your Hearts, whatever Professions of Regard you make for us, till this Promise is performed, and we see our Fathers, Mothers and Children, who have been carried into Captivity, restored to us, this Promise was the Condition on which the Peace Belt was exchanged between us.——Some among you have been faithful, and sent back all the Prisoners they had; I do not therefore address this Part of my Speech to them, but take them to my Heart; it is intended only for such of the *Indians* as have deceived us, and still detain our Flesh and Blood. I sincerely wish to be Friends with you all, and therefore once more put you in Mind of your Engagements, and insist on your immediately complying with them, by restoring the Prisoners, that nothing may remain to make any Difference between us to the End of Time.

*A Belt.*

The Governor, addressing himself to *Teedyuscung,* spoke as follows, *viz.*
Brother, Agreeable to your Request, I have taken into serious Consideration what you said to me on *Wednesday* last, and shall answer you with the same good Will and Sincerity that true Friends always use to one another.

*A String.*

*Brother,* I readily acknowledge that you have been a great Instrument in bringing about the great Work of Peace; and, according to the Promises you made us at this Place three Years ago, the Peace Belt has been sent to several Nations of *Indians,* who have since joined their Hands to it; so that, by the Blessing of the Most High, the Wound, by the Means of the Medicine you have applied, is intirely healed. And it shall be my Endeavour, as you say it shall be yours, to keep the Wound from ever opening again.

*A Belt.*

*Brother,* You tell me that all your young Men as far as the *Twightwees,* and those now with you, *Mohickons, Opies* and *Delawares,* intend to join in, and stand to, whatever you and I have agreed to; and that they will not take Notice of whatever Drops of Blood may have stained the Road, but will look steadily to our Agreements.

*Brother,* I very much commend this Resolution;—it is a Mark of Prudence and real Love for Peace; considering how many wicked Men there are in the World, it must be expected that private Mischiefs, and even Murders, will now and then be committed: When this happens, we shall do well to let one another know of it, and join in taking all proper Measures to detect and punish the evil Doers. This being done, the public Peace can never be affected or hurt.—By this Belt I assure you that this is my Disposition and Resolution, as well as it is yours.

*A Belt and String.*

*Brother,* I take special Notice of your declaring that you have cleared yourself as far as *Wighalousin, Papounan*'s Town, as far as that Place, you say you have no Prisoners, but they are all delivered up, and you want to make a Peace as lasting as the World; Brother, I take this public Declaration of yours very kindly; I believe you say true; if all like you would do the same Thing,—and they are engaged, and have often promised, to do it,—the Peace would last for ever. On the Part of this Government all Engagements shall be punctually observed; this String confirms my Words.

*A String.*

*Brother,* You say you would not have me look to you for any Thing further, for nothing will ever make a Difference betwixt you and me, and therefore if any Thing happens, it must spring from me, as your young Men have put all their Affairs into the Hands of their Chiefs. Brother, assure yourself that my Heart is good towards you, and that I shall take all the Pains in my Power to prevent any Breach of the Peace; keep but your young Men sober, and in Order, and let them do no Mischief to the Inhabitants, and I am well assured we shall always remain on good Terms, and enjoy all the Benefits of Peace.

*A String.*

*Brother,* I agree with you that friendly Conferences between us are of great Use, as they give us an Opportunity of settling Matters that may arise from time to time, which might otherwise breed Misunderstandings between us.—I shall be your Ear, and inform you constantly of any Thing that may concern you.

*A String.*

*Brother,* I thank you for your Information respecting what you told me was said to you by the *Seven Nations.* You are now all together; speak your Minds to one another freely and affectionately, as Friends and Relations should do, and agree now on all Points. If you really mean to continue at *Wyoming,* let your Uncles know it, and they will, I doubt not, consent to it. They seem to apprehend that Danger is nigh to you as well as themselves; but I hope what I have said to them of the good Disposition of General *Johnson,* will quiet both their and your Fears. By this Belt I assure you that I will give you the earliest Notice in my Power if any Harm should ever be intended against you. At present I know of none; I am assured that there is none.

*A Belt.*

*Brother,* I shall be very sorry if you remove from *Wyoming;* this Province has chearfully, and at a considerable Expence, assisted you to build Houses, and make your Settlements there commodious to you as long as you live; there you will always find us disposed to assist you, if you go away, it will not be so much in our Power. Consider this well; your Uncles, who now hear me speak to you, will not, I hope, after placing you there, and after the Expence that has been laid out by us in building Houses for you, desire you to go to live at another Place, without your giving them some Cause of Complaint; and that I hope you never will do. In Confirmation of the Truth of what I now say to you, I give you this Belt.

*A Belt.*

The Governor then addressing himself to the *Papounan,* spoke as follows. *Brother* Papounan, I thank you for your Care in sending my Message to *Achoan,* and for delivering his Answer. I shall give you no more Trouble in this Matter, nor send him any more Messages; but expect his Uncles, the *Seven Nations,* will acquaint him with what I have so strongly urged upon them, during these Conferences, with Respect to the Delivery of the Prisoners.

*At a* Conference *with the* Indians, *the same Day, in the Afternoon.*
PRESENT, *as before.*

IN Consequence of the Governor's pressing Demand, for the *Indians* to deliver up all the *English* Prisoners they had now with them, they produced one Girl, and delivered her up to the Governor in Form.

The Governor then spoke to the *Indians.*

Brethren, I am now to inform you, that since our last Meeting at this Place, three Years ago, the Road has been stained with a few Drops of Blood. The first Thing of this Kind happened over *Sasquehanna,* where one *Indian* Man, his Wife, and two Children, were found dead, having been either murdered or drowned in the River *Coneduganníct.* It no sooner came to my Knowledge, but I issued a Proclamation, offering *Two Hundred and Sixty-six Dollars,* as a Reward for detecting and apprehending all such as should be concerned in this Murder; but, notwithstanding all my Endeavours, nothing certain has yet been discovered.

About two Months ago, our very good Friend *Thomas Hickman* was found shot in the *Tuscarora Path Valley.* One Person is now in Goal, on Suspicion; two others were put into Prison, but set at Liberty again, at the Instance of the *Indians,* it appearing to them that they were innocent. All possible Endeavours are now using to find out who did this wicked Act; a Reward has been offered, by public Proclamation, for their Apprehension, and I hope we shall find them.

There may have been some few more of such Instances, which I may not have been particularly informed of; but these are all that have reached my Ears.

*Brethren,* These are Accidents, which ought not to affect the Peace made between us: It is as grievous to me as to you to hear of these wicked Acts, and let them be who they will that have been guilty of these Murders, they shall die themselves, as soon as convicted thereof, by a lawful Trial. With this Belt I collect their Bones, and put them all into one Grave.

*A Belt.*

I fill up their Graves, and cover their Bodies with these Strouds.

*Strouds.*

With these Handkerchiefs I wash off the Blood from your Bodies, and wipe away the Tears from your Eyes.

*Handkerchiefs.*

With this Belt I take all Sorrow out of your Hearts, I clear your Throats, Eyes and Ears; and desire you will no more mourn for them.

*A Belt.*

*Teedyuscung* then informed the Governor, that he desired to speak a few Words to him, and to his Uncles the *Six Nation;* whereupon the Governor desired him to begin, and he spoke as follows.

*Uncle,* I beg you will hearken to what I am going to say. You may remember, some Years ago, at our Council Fire, you took me by the Hairs of my Head, and shook me, and told me to go and live at *Wyoming,* for you gave me the Land there, where I might raise my Bread, and get my Living; now again you desire me to move off from thence, and would place me somewhere else. The Reason why I complied with your first Request was, because I thought you would give me the Lands at *Wyoming,* in the Room of some of our Lands you had sold the *English;* I assure you now, that if I move from thence, some *English* will come and settle there, in the Midst of our Road, so that we cannot pass from thence to this Province; and we shall lose the Land, so that neither you nor me will have any Benefit from it.

Addressing himself to the Governor, he said,

*Brother,* I am really very glad to hear you say the Wound is healed up; we are all pleased at it; since this is the Case we expect you will pay us for the Lands we have been complaining about. It was left to King GEORGE. You told me as soon as ever you heard from the King, you would let me know of it; but I have not heard you say any thing about it since: Now, Brother, as there are some here present, who have never been paid for some of their Lands, we desire you would pay them now; but as for the *Munsies,* and some others at *Allegheny* who also claim Lands near this Place, they will agree with you when they see you.

The Governor replied, that he would take into Consideration what he had said, and would answer him in the Morning.

Being asked what Lands he desired to be paid for; he answered, that the Lands are where we now stand, betwixt the Mountains and *Tohickon Creek;* but acknowledged that some Lands about *Durham,* four Miles square, were paid for.

Tokahaio *then stood up and spoke.*

*Brother* Onas, We the *Seven Nations,* especially the *Nanticokes* and *Conoys,* speak to you.——About seven Years ago we went down to *Maryland,* with a Belt of Wampum, to fetch our Flesh and Blood, which we shewed to some *Englishmen* there, who told us they did not understand Belts, but if we had brought any Order in Writing from the Governor of *Pennsylvania,* they would let our Flesh and Blood then come away with us; but as this was not done, they would not let them come:——Now we desire you would give us an Order for that Purpose.

*A white String of five Rows.*

*Brother* Onas, We would have you make some Satisfaction to our Cousins here, the *Delawares,* for their Lands, as we suppose they desire it.—Some of them are now present, who claim some Lands here, and are often thinking of it, particularly one (pointing to *Joseph Pepy.*)[6]

*At a private* CONFERENCE,
*on* Wednesday *the Twelfth of* August, 1761.
PRESENT,
*The Honourable* JAMES HAMILTON, *Esq; Lieutenant-Governor,* &c. &c.
Richard Peters, Lewis Gordon, *Esquires;*
*The Chief of the* Onondagoes, Ashenoch, *Speaker;*
James Sherlock, *Interpreter.*

*Brother* Onas, IT is a long Time since we last met together, and we are now glad to see you. Brother, we request it of you that you would give us a Duplicate of this Deed (shewing a Deed of Release from *Richard Peters,* and *Conrad Weiser,* Esquires, Proprietary Attornies to them at the last Treaty) because it is the Desire of *Jenochryada,* and in Order that the *Mohawks* may have the Original, and we keep the Copy.

*A chequered String of three Rows.*

To which Request the Governor assented, and desired *Lewis Gordon,* Esq; to prepare an exemplified Copy of the above-mentioned Release for them.

Jeoquanta *then Spoke to the Governor.*

*Brother* Onas, My old Mother and Children, who are here at present, are not able to walk, I desire therefore that my Brother would help me to a Horse, as I have a great Way to go Home, and cannot make a Canoe at this Time of the Year.

*A black Belt of seven Rows.*

*Brother* Onas, I have come a great Way, and have brought with me a Pack of Beaver. Our Brother General *Johnson,* and those who live near him sell their Goods very dear, and give us nothing for our Skins, but as I heard our Brothers of this Province gave better Prices for our Skins, I have brought them here, and hope my Brother will see Justice done me in the Sale of them. And if my Brother thinks I can get a better Price for them by carrying them to *Philadelphia,* I should be obliged to him for his Information.

*A chequered String of three Rows.*

*At a public* CONFERENCE *on the same Day.*
PRESENT,
*The Honourable* JAMES HAMILTON, *Esq;* &c. &c. *as at the former public Conferences.*

*The Governor, addressing himself to* Teedyuscung, *spoke as follows.*

*Brother,* AS to the Lands lying between the *Kittochtinny Hills* and *Touhickon Creek,* which you say you have never been paid for, you know the Proprietaries of this Province have always insisted that they were fairly purchased of the *Delawares,* before you were born, who received the Consideration Money for them; you know also that the Dispute between you and the Proprietaries about these Lands was, by your own particular Desire, referred to our Great King over the Water, who, from his Love of Justice, and Regard to you, has taken upon himself to settle it, and has ordered General *Johnson* to hear your Complaint, and enquire into the Truth of it, and make Report to him, that he may direct what is right to be done; of this General *Johnson* gave you Notice, by a Letter, above a Year and an Half ago, and desired you to appoint a proper Time and Place to meet him on this Occasion, that the Affair might be speedily settled. I have waited ever since in Expectation that you would comply with General *Johnson*'s Request; and I now inform you that I am, and at all Times shall be, ready, on my Part, to send the Proprietary Commissioners to support their Claim, whenever you shall appoint the Time and Place of Meeting; it is therefore your own Fault if the Matter is delayed any longer.

Addressing himself to the *Seven Nations,* he said.

*Brethren of the* Seven United Nations, I have considered what you said to me on Behalf of the *Conoys* and the *Nanticokes,* who have some of their Brethren still remaining in the Province of *Maryland:* As I am not Governor of that Province, I have no Power to order the People there to suffer their Relations to come away; I will, however, afford them all the Assistance I can, and will not only give the Messenger they send to *Maryland* a Passport, or safe Conduct, but will write to the Governor, and request him to permit their Brethren to come away, without Interruption.

*Brethren,* You desire me to make Satisfaction to your Cousins the *Delawares* for these Lands which they claim, as they often think of it; had you known, as well as I do, how groundless and unjust this Claim of theirs was, I am sure you would not have taken any Notice of it. Your old Men must remember, that at a full Council held with the *Six Nations,* at *Philadelphia,* in the Year 1742, the Claim the *Delawares* now make for these very Lands was laid before them, and the Deeds from them to the Proprietaries perused and considered by the *Six Nations;* who, upon a full Hearing of the Matter, then were convinced that the Proprietaries had fairly purchased them of the *Delawares,* and paid for them. Whereupon the *Six Nations* ordered the *Delawares* to remove off from them, and go to *Wyoming,* which they accordingly did. *Teedyuscung,* some Time ago, referred his Complaint about these Lands to our Great King, who has ordered General *Johnson* to enquire into the whole Matter, and let him know how it is circumstanced, that Justice may be done as well to the *Delawares* as to us; and I am ready to send my Commissioners to General *Johnson,* to lay before him the Proprietaries Deeds for, and Right to, these Lands, whenever *Teedyuscung* will appoint a Time and Place for this Purpose.

*Tokahaio* addressed the Governor, in Behalf of the *Tuteloes,* as follows.
*Brother* Onas, We desire our Brother will be so good as to furnish us with three Waggons, to carry home our Sick, who are not able to walk, as we intend to go home as soon as we can;——which Request the Governor granted, and left the Number of Waggons to be provided for them, to the Direction of *Joseph Fox,* Esq;

Tokahaio *then added,*

*Brother* Onas, We have been here at this Council Fire, and heard what good Words you have spoke to us. We have no more to say at present, and we see likewise that you have nothing more to say to us; we are therefore going to part. When we return home, we will acquaint all our People with what we have heard. We heartily thank you for the good Usage we have received from you.

The Governor informed them, that he had brought up with him a Present from the Government to them, which Mr. *Fox* would distribute amongst them To-morrow; and then concluded the Treaty, by shaking Hands with the Chiefs of the *Indians.*

In the Afternoon the Governor and his Company set out for *Philadelphia.*

*THE END.*

1. On February 21, 1760, Governor James Hamilton had issued a proclamation offering a reward for persons who had murdered a party of Indians in Cumberland County. On Febru-

ary 20, 1761, he issued another proclamation that forbad people from settling on Indian Lands. These events may indicate the extent to which a peace had been achieved. Franklin and Hall's press printed another such proclamation on June 2, 1763 (Miller, *Philadelphia Printing,* 401, 408, 422).

2. This reference to the Seven Nations is confusing, as there is no modern record of the League having become seven nations after the admission of the Tuscaroras into full membership early in the eighteenth century (Johansen and Mann, *Encyclopedia,* 7–10). Jennings conjectures that the seventh nation is the Nanticoke-Conoy nation (Jennings, "Descriptive Treaty Calendar," 193). Possibly, though, Seneca George was merely referring to the seven nations then present (Onondaga, Cayuga, Oneida, Mahican, Nanticoke-Conoy, Delaware (Lenape), and Tutelo). A translator or scribe could easily turn the reference mistakenly or intentionally into a political designation that was never meant. The later reference to the seven nations over the Lakes only makes matters worse!

3. This indicates a shift back to peacetime government from war governance.

4. Teedyuscung would never leave Wyoming. In April 1763, he was assassinated by being burned to death in his cabin. He had been encouraged to stay by all the rivals to Connecticut's claim to the Wyoming—the eastern Lenapes, the League, and Thomas Penn—as well as William Johnson. His presence and that of the eastern Lenapes was meant to "hold off intruders to preserve the rights of the Iroquois and the Penns." The same squatters from Connecticut's Susquehannah Company who torched his house drove his people out of the region (Jennings, *Empire of Fortune,* 434–36). That night, twenty other Lenape houses were set ablaze (Wallace, *King of the Delawares,* 258). The incident marks the end of Lenape nations presence in eastern Pennsylvania. Those Lenape who remained were not organized around indigenous polities with identifiably ancient roots. They were mainly Christian converts and others who had chosen to intermarry with British subjects and become incorporated into Euramerican society. Six months later, Teedyuscung's son led an expedition of a Lenape war party that killed the Connecticut settlers responsible for his father's death (Wallace, *King of the Delawares,* 260).

5. This complaint renews and recalls Canasatego's urgings that the British colonies speak with one voice as the League did.

6. Though minimalized in this treaty, this statement is an extraordinary shift in Iroquois policy regarding the Walking Purchase. Since 1742, when Canasatego had effectively neutralized Lenape resistance to that land grab, the League had been virtually silent. As recently as 1758, they had seemed to tip toward the British on the matter of deeds to these lands. Here, Tokahaio (Tokaaion) stands on the side of the Lenapes in their complaint. His silence when Pennsylvania replies to his request is extraordinary.

✠

# MINUTES OF CONFERENCES,

## HELD AT *LANCASTER,* In *AUGUST* 1762.

### With the Sachems and Warriors of several Tribes of *Northern* and *Western* INDIANS.

---

*PHILADELPHIA:*
Printed and Sold by B. FRANKLIN, and D. HALL,
at the *New-Printing-Office,* near the Market. MDCCLXIII.

---

## *Minutes of Conferences,* &c.

*At a* COUNCIL *held at* Lancaster,
*on* Wednesday *the Eleventh of* August, 1762.
PRESENT, *The Honourable* JAMES HAMILTON, *Esq;*
Lieutenant-Governor;
William Logan, Richard Peters, *and* Benjamin Chew, *Esquires.*

THE Governor having been informed last Week, at *Philadelphia,* that in Consequence of several Invitations sent by this Government, at sundry Times, to the *Indians* living on and near the *Ohio,* the *Delaware* Chief *Beaver,* and the Deputies of other Tribes of Western *Indians,* would be at *Lancaster* on the Eighth Instant; sat out from *Philadelphia,* attended by several Gentlemen, and came here on the Ninth Instant, and found that the *Indians* had arrived the Evening before.

On the Tenth the Governor, attended by the Gentlemen abovementioned, with several of the Inhabitants of this Town, paid a Visit to *Beaver,* and the other *Indians,* at their Encampment, about a Mile from the Town, where he took them by the Hand, and bid them heartily welcome; and having seen that they were well accommodated, took his Leave, and came back to Town.

The Governor Yesterday Afternoon received a Message from *Beaver,* that having been a long Time from Home, they would take it very kindly if he would be pleased to open the Conferences with them To-morrow Morning, without waiting any longer for the *Six Nations,* as he and those *Indians* with him were the first invited, and were only made acquainted with the coming of the *Six Nations* since they left their Homes.

The Governor returned them for Answer, that the Interpreter was not come; but as soon as he should arrive, he would immediately proceed to Business with them, and give them Notice when to attend.

This Afternoon arrived Six *Tuscarora Indians,* who waited on the Governor, and acquainted him, that they were sent to him by those of their Nation, living at *Onohoquage,* on the Upper Waters of the *Sasquehannah,* with a Letter; which, after the Ceremony of opening his Eyes and Heart, by a String of Wampum, they delivered to him, and it follows in these Words.———

*Lower Tuscarora, Onohoquage, July* 8, 1762.

*Great Brother,*

"I the Bearer, *Augus,* Chief of the Nation, am, and ever have been, a Friend and Brother to the *English,* and to the Interest of *Great Britain,* now wait upon your Excellency, by Agreement, to transact Affairs of Importance; and heartily rejoice that the *Five Nations* have agreed to, and (as I hear) have actually returned the *English* Prisoners, to enjoy the Liberties of their own Nation.——And I the said *Augus,* Chief, with my whole Tribe, have ever been for Peace with the *English* Colonies in *America,* and have minded the Things of Religion, and of a private Life. And as true Friends to the Protestant Cause, we congratulate your Excellency, our Brother, and all the *British* Nation, on the various Conquests obtained against the common Enemy, and especially on the total Reduction of *Canada,* with its Dependences, being greatly delighted with the happy Prospect that now arises, without Clouds. As we rejoice to hear that the Prisoner are resigned, so we hope a Peace will be established between us, the *Five Nations,* and the *English* Colonies on the Continent; a Peace that shall be lasting and undisturbed, while the Waters run, and the Grass grows.——We should be glad to be informed of the State and Behaviour of our Brethren in *Tuscarora Valley,* and to have some Directions about the Way, as we propose to make them a Visit; and also should be glad of a Pass, or Recommendation in Writing, that we may be friendly received on the Way, and at the Valley.

*I am your Brother, AUGUS, Chief.*"

The above was taken from the Mouth of the said *Augus, Tuscarora* Chief, by the Help of an Interpreter, by me

*ELI FORBES, Missionary at* Onohoquage.

After the Governor had read the Letter, they delivered him a Belt of Wampum, to confirm the Sincerity of their Professions contained in the said Letter.

They then delivered the Governor another Belt from the *Nanticokes* and *Conoys,* as a Testimony of their joining with the *Tuscaroras* in the same sincere Professions.

The Governor acquainted them that he would take the Letter into Consideration, and at a proper Time return them an Answer.

*At a* CONFERENCE *with the* Indians *held at* Lancaster,
*on* Thursday *the Twelfth of* August, 1762.
PRESENT, *The Honourable* JAMES HAMILTON, *Esquire,*
Lieutenant-Governor, *&c.*
William Logan, Richard Peters, Benjamin Chew, *Esquires,*
*of the Council of the Province;*
Joseph Fox, George Ashbridge, James Wright, Samuel Rhoads,
James Webb, *Esquires, of the Assembly, and several Magistrates,*
*and a Number of Gentlemen from* Philadelphia,
*and other Parts of the Province;*

Tomago, *or* Beaver, Wendocalla, Tissacoma, *Chiefs of the* Ohio Delawares, *and Twenty-two others, most of them Warriors;*

Akis, Lenaskocana, Enasquana, *Chiefs of the* Tuscaroras;

Miskepalathy, *or* Red Hawk, Wapemashehawy, *or* White Elk, Magalacutway, *Chiefs of the* Shawanese, *and Ten other Warriors;*

Cakakey, Micathie, *Chiefs of the* Kickapoe *Nation;*

Teacott, Wiougha, Weatona, *Chiefs of the* Wawachtanies;

Paoughawe, Cottalinnea, Nenaouseca, Sawnaughakey, *Chiefs of the* Twightwee *Nation;*

Isaac Stille, *and* Frederick Post, *Interpreters.*

AFTER the *Indians* had taken their Seats, the Governor opened the Conferences with the following Speech.

*Brethren* the *Delawares, Shawanese, Twightwees. Wawachtanies, Tuscaroras,* and *Kickapoes,* With this String I clean your Bodies from the Dust and Sweat, and open your Eyes and Ears, that you may see your Brethren with Chearfulness, and hear distinctly what I have to say to you at this Conference.

*A String* (480)

*Brethren,* With this String I open the Passage to your Hearts, that you may speak freely, and without Reserve, as Brethren ought to do when they meet together.

*A String* (260)

*Brethren,* It is now a great while since we have had the Pleasure of meeting one another in Council, wherefore I take this Opportunity of condoling with you for the Losses you may have sustained by the Death of any of your People, and with this

String I gather up the Bones of our deceased Brethren, and bury them decently, according to the Custom of our Forefathers.

*A String* (460)

*Brethren,* With this String I disperse the dark Clouds, which for many Years have hung over our Heads, and prevented our seeing each other, that we may for the future meet and confer together, as our Fathers used to do, and brighten and renew the Covenant Chain of Friendship, for our mutual Benefit and Advantage.

*A String* (300)

*Brethren,* As the Council-Chamber hath contracted much Dust, for Want of Use for some Years past, and hath also been stained with Blood, I, with this String, sweep it quite clean, and wipe all Blood from off the Seats, that we may sit down and confer together, without seeing any Thing to interrupt us, or make us uneasy.

*A String* (280)

*Brethren,* Having now wiped your Eyes, opened the Way to your Hearts, and cleansed the Council Seats, I, by this Belt, take you by the Hand, and bid you heartily welcome, and assure you, that I am ready to do every Thing in my Power to strengthen and preserve that Brotherly Love and Friendship, which so long subsisted between your Ancestors and His Majesty's Subjects of this Government.

*A Belt.*

The Governor then told them he had finished what he had to say to them at present, and that if they were prepared to speak to him at this Time, he was ready to hear them; if not, he would appoint another Time for that Purpose.

Beaver, *the Chief of the* Delawares, *then spoke to the Governor as follows.*
*Brother,* We all rejoice to hear what you have said to us, and are glad that you have cleansed us, and have spoke to us in the Manner which our Forefathers used to do to one another. As we speak different Languages, we shall be glad of an Opportunity of consulting among ourselves, and shall deliver what we have to say to you To-morrow Morning.

*At a* CONFERENCE *with the* Indians, *held at* Lancaster,
*on* Friday *the Thirteenth of* August, 1762.
PRESENT, *The Honourable* JAMES HAMILTON, *Esquire,*
Lieutenant-Governor, *&c.*
William Logan, Richard Peters, Benjamin Chew, *Esquires,*
*Members of the Council.*
Joseph Fox, Samuel Rhoads, James Wright, John Morton, *Esquires,*
*of the Assembly.*
*The Chiefs and Deputies of the several Nations of* Indians *as before.*

The Governor having told the *Indians* that he was ready to hear them,

Beaver, *the* Delaware *Chief, spoke as follows.*

*Brother,* I HAVE heard what you said to me Yesterday, and am well pleased with it. You have cleansed me, opened my Eyes, and cleaned my Ears in the same Manner as our Forefathers used to do. You will now listen to me attentively; with this String I also open your Eyes, and clean your Ears, that you may see me, and hear what I have to say to you.

*A String.*

*Brother,* When our Grandfathers used to meet together, they wiped the Tears from one anothers Eyes, and with this String I now wipe the Tears from your Eyes, that you may see clearly your Brothers now before you.

*A String.*

*Brother,* When our Grandfather used to meet our Brethren, they cleansed each others Hearts, and took away all Grief and Sorrow out of them:—By this String I do likewise clean your Hearts, and remove all Sorrow and Grief from them, and strengthen your Breath, that you may speak more freely to your Brothers here before you.

*A String.*

*Brother,* It is a great While since we saw one another; we here present are really very glad to see you and all our Brethren well.—It is about four Years ago since we first received any Messages from you, and ever since we have been employed in carrying good News to all the Nations round, who were rejoiced to hear it from you. And we have been likewise ever since endeavouring to bring in your Flesh and Blood, as you required it of us. Mr. *Croghan,* and the Commander at *Fort-Pitt,* know that we have delivered many of them, and now we bring a few more of them to you. There are some behind yet, and they meet with good Usage, and live as we do, and chuse to stay with us; but I hope they will come to you after some Time, because you live better than we do.

*A Belt.*

*Brother,* I heard you Yesterday, and was much rejoiced to hear you, as were all your Brethren here present. You told me you had removed all the dark Clouds that hung over us. I am rejoiced that the dark Clouds are dispersed, so that we can see one another clearly.

By this Belt I do, on my Part, disperse the Clouds. Now, Brother, let us join heartily, and put our Hands together, to put away the Clouds.

If we should see the Clouds rise again, let us join to remove them, and keep Peace together, so that our Children and Grandchildren, when they meet, may rejoice to see one another, and live to great Ages in Peace.

*A Belt.*

*Brother,* We are rejoiced to see one another; all the dark Clouds are now scattered, and the Sun shines clear upon us, and all the Nations who are our Friends. We see plainly that good Road which our Grandfathers used, when they travelled to your Council Fire, to consult about our Affairs, when we lived in Friendship.

*Brother,* We will join with you to keep that Road open and good; I assure you it was never yet quite stopt up; we find our old Council Fire, which our Grandfathers made, is still burning; now by this Belt I collect dry Wood to put to the Fire, and make it bigger, so that the Smoke may rise to the Skies; when other Nations see it, they will know by the Light that I have been in Council with my Brethren.

*A Belt.*

Beaver *then got up, and holding a Belt in his Hand, said,*

This Belt we received last Fall from Sir *William Johnson,* at *Fort-Detroit,* who then informed us, that he had heard of the good Work of Peace in which we had been engaged with our Brethren the *English;* which Belt represents us, the *Delawares,* in the Middle, and the Western Nations of *Indians* at one End, and the *English* at the other, Hand in Hand, together holding fast the Chain of Friendship; and assured us, that if we held this Chain of Friendship fast, our Children and Grandchildren should grow up, and live to great Ages.—We were so pleased with this, that we put it into our Hearts, and have always kept it there till now.

And now, Brother, you have heard from me what passed between Sir *William Johnson* and me.—I assure you I will actually do what was desired of me, and hold fast this Chain of Friendship. I assure you I will always do my Part in keeping this Friendship firm, and the Nations to the Westward will do the same. I desire all you, my Brethren, will be strong, and join heartily in keeping this Friendship alive; which if you do, you and your Grandchildren shall arrive at a great Age.

*A Belt.*

*Brother,* I desire you will take Pity on those of our Brothers that live or come amongst you, and be kind to them. Our Brethren live among you, because they love you. When any of our Brothers the *English* come amongst us, we always take Pity on them, and give them Victuals, to make their Bodies strong; and we desire that you will do the same to such of us as come amongst you, or live with you.

*A Belt.*

*Brother,* I have no more to say at present; I shall wait to hear what you have to say to us at another Time. You desired me to bring other Nations of *Indians* with me, and I have brought them a great Way, who also wait to hear what you have to say.

The Governor then acquainted *Beaver,* that he was well pleased to hear what they had said to him; and that he received it into his Heart, and should take a proper Opportunity to give them an Answer.

The Governor rose and went to the Place where the *English* Prisoners sat, and received them one by one, from the Hands of King *Beaver,* and here follow their Names.

| | | | |
|---|---|---|---|
| *Thomas Moore,* | taken from | *Potowmack,* | *Maryland.* |
| *Philip Studebecker,* | | *Conegocheague,* | Ditto. |
| *Ann Dougherty,* | | | *Pennsylvania.* |
| *Peter Condon,* | | | Ditto. |
| *Mary Stroudman,* | | *Conegocheague,* | Ditto. |
| *William Jackson,* | | *Tulpehocken,* | Ditto. |
| *Elizabeth M<sup>c</sup>Adam,* | | *Little Cove,* | Ditto. |
| *John Lloyd,* | | Ditto, | Ditto. |
| *Eleanor Lancestoctes,* | | | Ditto. |
| *Dorothy Shobrin,* | | *Big Cove,* | Ditto. |
| *Richard Rogers,* | | | *Virginia.* |
| *Esther Rogers,* | | | Ditto. |
| *Jacob Rogers,* | | *South Branch,* | Ditto. |
| *Archibald Woods,* | | | Ditto. |
| *Christopher Holtomen,* | | Ditto. | |
| *Rebecca Walter,* | | | Ditto. |
| *Hans Boyer,* a Boy, | | not known from whence. | |

Friday, August 13, 1762. This Afternoon *Tokahaion,* and a Number of the *Six Nation Indians* coming to Town, about Fifteen of them waited on the Governor, at his Lodgings, and *Tokahaion* spoke to the Governor as follows.

*Brother,* We were some Time ago invited by you, and our Brethren the *Quakers* of this Province, to come to this Treaty at *Lancaster,* with our Cousins the *Delawares.* Agreeable to this Invitation, we came down as far as *Harris*'s Ferry, where we heard that you intended to return Home To-morrow, which induced us to make all the Haste we could to this Place, that we might have the Pleasure of seeing you. On our Way one of our Brethren died, but our Hurry was so great that we threw his Body aside, and did not so much as stay to bury him. We are just come to Town, and pay you this Visit to take you by the Hand, and let you know we are glad to see you. We must request of you to order your People to lock up all Rum, and not let our *Indians* have any, till the End of our Conferences.——He added, that they had seen the Cabbins which had been built to accommodate them, but that they were at so great a Distance from the Place where their Cousins the *Delawares* were lodged, that they could not conveniently discourse with them; wherefore he desired that others might be provided near to them To-morrow.

The Governor took them by the Hand, and after bidding them welcome, told them that they were misinformed respecting his designing to return Home To-morrow; that as he heard they were on their Way, he had waited some Days, in Expectation of their coming, and was now glad to see them; that he would do every Thing in his Power, during their Stay here, to render their Situation easy and agreeable to them, and would give strict Orders that no Rum should be sold to them; that the Field where the *Delawares* were encamped, being too small to accommodate them, he had pitched on a Place which he judged most convenient, where Cabbins had been built, by his Order, for their Reception, at a considerable Expence of Time and Money, which he hoped they would be well pleased with; but if, on Trial, they should still be dissatisfied with that Situation, he would remove them where they thought most proper; and that when they had rested themselves, after the Fatigues of the long Journey they had come, he would speak to them, and give them sufficient Notice of the Time, that they might be prepared to meet him in Council.——They were refreshed with a Draught of Beer, and then took their Leaves, and departed.

*At a* CONFERENCE *with the* Indians, *held at* Lancaster,
*on* Saturday *the Fourteenth of* August, 1762.
PRESENT, *The Honourable* JAMES HAMILTON, *Esquire,*
Lieutenant-Governor, *&c.*
William Logan, Richard Peters, *and* Benjamin Chew, *Esquires,*
*of the Council.*
Joseph Fox, James Wright, Samuel Rhoads, John Morton,
George Ashbridge, Joseph Gibbons, David McConaughy, *Esquires,*
*of the Assembly,* &c.
*The Western INDIANS, as before;*
Hinderuntie, *or the* Garr, Hogastees, Hajentora, *Speaker,* &c., *Senecas;*
Tokahaion, Totinyentunya, Onechsogaret, Gachradodo, Soghiowa,
Dochneghdoris, *or* John Shacalamy, *Cayugas;*
Diohaguaande, Hoghsetagegle, Cagentorongua, *Onandagoes;*
Thomas King, Conogoragheri, *or* Hans George, Tiokoraghta, *Oneidas;*
Ganigal, Tionaskocto, *Tuskaroras;*
Teedyuscung, Tapeskohonk, *or* Samuel, Wehololahund, *or* Joseph Peepy,
Memenowal, *or* Augustus, Kakolopomet, *or* Compass, Naywolaken,
Penowotis, *or* John Philip, *Delawares;*
Ullauckquam, *or* Robert White, Olaykenawightamen,
*or* Jemmy, Canahatch, *or* Last Night, Tuchsat, *or* Sam,
Packsowamuchquis, *or* Charles, Packetellam, *or* Sam Adams,
*and several others, Nanticokes* and *Conoys.*
*A List of the Northern* Indians, *including Men, Women, and Children,*
*at the Treaty at* Lancaster, August 1762.[1]
Oneidas, Onondagoes, Tuscaroras, Nanticokes, Conoys, 156.
Senecas, 97.
Cayugas, *and* Saponys, *and a Mixture of* Shawanese *and* Munseys, 128.
Teedyuscung, *and the* Delawares *with him,* 176. *In all,* 557.

THE Governor sent a Message to the *Six Nations,* and those that came along with them, to acquaint them, that he was going into Conference with the Western Nations, at which they might be present, if they pleased; and on their coming in, and taking their Seats, the Governor spoke to the Western *Indians* as follows.

*Brethren* the *Delawares, Shawanese, Twightwees, Wawachtanies, Tuscaroras,* and *Kickapoes,* I return you Thanks for your Speeches of Yesterday, which were very agreeable to me; and I shall now give you an Answer to such Parts thereof as require one,

*Brethren,* Before I take Notice of what you said Yesterday, let me remind you of the strict Friendship which was established with your Forefathers, by our old Proprietor *William Penn,* on his first Arrival in this Country, and how happily it subsisted between them and their Children, till the Troubles which unfortunately broke out some few Years ago, and stopt up the Road between us. The many Messages which we have since, from Time to Time, sent you, by *Frederick Post* and *Teedyuscung,* and the great Pains we have taken to drive away the Evil Spirit, plainly shew how sincerely we have been disposed to renew that Friendship.

*Brethren,* You acquainted me, that after receiving our first Message about Peace, which was about four Years ago, you made it known to all the *Indian* Nations on this Side, and over the Lakes, who were glad to hear the good News; and as we desired you to deliver up our Flesh and Blood, you say that you have, from Time to Time, delivered up many at *Fort-Pitt,* to the Commanding Officer, and to Mr. *Croghan,* and that you now have brought in a few, which you delivered to me Yesterday. You likewise say, you have yet others in your Possession, and that some of them chuse to live with you; but you made no Doubt of their coming to us some Time hence, as we live better than the *Indians.*

*Brethren,* For the Prisoners that you have delivered at *Fort-Pitt,* as well as for those you have now brought along with you, and delivered to me, I return you my hearty Thanks; but you must remember, that on re-establishing and renewing the antient Chain of Friendship with us, you repeatedly engaged to deliver us all our Flesh and Blood, which you have taken from us, by the Instigation of the Evil Spirit. On these Assurances and Engagements we have relied, and as we cannot enjoy the Blessings we expected from that Peace, till the Parents and Relations of those Prisoners have them restored to them, I must insist on your taking every Measure in your Power to deliver them up, agreeable to your Engagements, which will be the only Means of strengthening and establishing a lasting Peace, to us and our Children, yet unborn.

*A large Belt of Thirteen Rows.*

*Brethren,* You Yesterday, by this Belt, said you would join with me in dispersing the dark Clouds, which have for some Time hung over our Heads; and desired I would join with you, in hearty Endeavours to prevent any more Clouds from rising, or if they should chance to rise, from coming to an Head.

*Brethren,* GOD, who made all Things, has given us Eyes to see, and Tongues to speak to each other, freely and openly; and I assure you, if I should see any little Clouds arise, at never so great a Distance, I will take every Measure in my Power to prevent their encreasing, and communicate it to you forthwith; and if you do the same to me, at all Times, it will prevent any Clouds from gathering to an Head, so as to disturb the public Peace and Tranquility, which have been lately so happily established between us.

*A Belt of Seven Rows.*

*Brethren,* It gave me great Satisfaction Yesterday, to hear you declare your Intentions to keep open the Council Road between your Nation and us. As a small Interruption on that Communication may be attended with dangerous Consequences to us both, I heartily join with you in keeping the Road open, and perfectly clear from Obstructions, for our mutual Use and Advantage.

I likewise take it kind in you to heap up dry Wood on our Council Fire, and I, on my Part, shall still add more Wood to it, that the Smoke thereof may be seen by the most distant Nations of *Indians,* to the Sun-setting, that are in Friendship with His Majesty's Subjects.

*A Belt of Nine Rows.*

*Brethren,* Yesterday you shewed me a Belt, with the Figures of three Men in it, which you say you received from Sir *William Johnson* last Fall, at the Conference he held with all the Western Nations of *Indians,* at *Fort-Detroit,* repeating what he said to you on it; all which Transactions there I am acquainted with, by Sir *William Johnson,* who, as His Majesty's Superintendant of *Indian* Affairs, did then renew the antient Covenant Chain of Friendship, in Behalf of all his Majesty's Subjects, with all those Western Nations of *Indians.* You say further, that since you received that Covenant Belt, you laid it close to your Heart; and, by this Belt, you assure me that you, and all the Western Nations, are determined to adhere strictly to that Treaty and Renewal of Friendship; and desire me to be strong, and hold it fast.

*Brethren,* You must remember, that you then not only promised Sir *William Johnson* to deliver up all our Flesh and Blood, who were Prisoners in your several Towns and Countries, but that this Promise was an express Condition of that Treaty, made between him and you. This Matter lies so near to my Heart, that I should not act as your true and sincere Friend, if I did not speak with the greatest Freedom and Plainness to you about it, and tell you again, that it is impossible we can look upon you as our Brethren, if you detain from us our Flesh and Blood; we cannot sleep quietly in our Beds, till we see them all; our very Dreams are disturbed on their Account; we demand of you nothing more than the Right which God and Nature has given us.

If we had among us ever so few of your Children, would you think that any Professions of Friendship we could make to you were sincere, if we withheld them from you but for one Day? Your Brother *Teedyuscung* may remember, that at our first confering with him, at *Easton,* we had then one of your People in Prison, and he thought it so grievous a Thing, that he told us he could not speak freely to us, and should look upon what we said as coming not from our Hearts, but from our Mouths only, until the said Prisoner was restored to him; which was immediately done. Can you then delay doing us that Justice, which you yourselves expected and received from us! We do not well understand your Meaning, when you say, some of the Prisoners chuse to live with you.[2] If you intend it as a Reason for not delivering them up, till they consent to come, we must inform you, that we cannot admit of it. They were born Subjects of our Great King, and as such, he has a Right to demand them. You have, it is true, by the Delivery of some of the Prisoners, performed your Agreement in Part; but as we know, and you acknowledge, there are a great many yet behind, we now insist positively, that you do not fail, immediately on your Return, to collect every one that remains among you, and deliver them up to us. Relying therefore on your Honesty, and that you will faithfully comply with an Engagement you have so solemnly made with us, I do, by this Belt, in Behalf of all His Majesty's Subjects of this Province, lay Hold of that Covenant Belt, and will keep it fast, that we, our Children, and Grandchildren, may long enjoy the Blessings of Peace, and live together as Brethren, till they are old Men.

*A Belt of Fifteen Rows.*

*Brethren,* I thank you for the kind Entertainment which you always give to any of our People who live with you, or come among you. I am persuaded, that such of you who have either lived or come amongst us occasionally, have always found that we received and treated them with the same Kindness that we used to do. We are Brethren, and while we live and love like Brethren, we shall be sure to give one another a Share of what we have.

*A Belt.*

*At a* CONFERENCE *with the* Six Nation Indians,
*held at* Lancaster, *on* Monday *the Sixteenth* of August, 1762.
PRESENT,
*The Honourable* JAMES HAMILTON, *Esquire,*
Lieutenant-Governor, *&c. &c. as before.*

THE Governor, addressing himself to the *Indians* present, spoke as follows.
*Brethren of the* Six Nations, *and all other our Brethren now present,* We are glad to see you, and with this String we bid you heartily welcome.

*A String.*

*Brethren,* So long a Journey as you have now taken must have been very fatiguing, and made your Bodies very dirty; with this String therefore I clean your Bodies, and wipe off all the Sweat and Dirt from them.

*A String.*

*Brethren,* As you came along, you must have hurt your Feet with the Stones, and torn your Legs with the Bushes and Briars; I therefore apply some healing Oil to them, and make them well.

*A String.*

*Brethren,* With this String I open your Eyes, and clean your Ears, that you may see your Brethren clearly, and hear distinctly what they shall have to say to you.

*A String.*

*Brethren,* With this String I clear your Throats, and open the Passage to your Hearts, that we may confer together freely and affectionately, as our Forefathers used to do.

*A String.*

*Brethren,* Having now cleansed your Bodies, opened your Eyes and Ears, cleared your Throats, and made a Passage to your Hearts, I am now ready and disposed to hear every Thing that you have to say to me.

*Then* Thomas King *stood up, and spoke as follows,* viz,

*Brother,* We are well pleased to hear what you have said to us, and as we are of different Nations, and speak different Languages, we shall take Time to consider and explain what you have said; and To-morrow, after Breakfast, I shall give you Notice when we shall be ready to speak to you.

*A String.*

*Brother,* I take this Opportunity to acquaint you, that all our Guns, Hatchets, and other Things, are out of Repair, and we beg you will give Orders that they may be forthwith mended.

*A String.*

The Governor granted them their Request, and told them their Guns, *&c.* should be mended, and desired that they might be brought to the Council House, for that Purpose.

*At a* CONFERENCE *with the Western* Indians,
*held at* Lancaster, *on* Monday, *the Sixteenth of* August, 1762.
PRESENT,
*The Honourable* JAMES HAMILTON, *Esquire,*
Lieutenant-Governor, *&c. &c. as before.*

THE Governor having acquainted the *Indians* that he was ready to hear what they had to say,

Beaver, *a* Delaware *Chief spoke as follows.*

*Brother,* I do not chuse to speak now myself, as I do not speak clearly and distinctly, and therefore shall appoint this *Indian,* named *Cleghiccon* (in *English, Simon)* to speak for me.

*Then* Cleghiccon *spoke.*

*Brother,* The Day before Yesterday you spoke to me, and I have heard you, and we your Brethren, the Western *Indians,* have all been consulting about it.

*Brother,* I now inform you, in Behalf of my Grandchildren, the *Tawwas,* they have none of your Flesh and Blood left in their Towns, for they have delivered them all up to you: Likewise in Behalf of my Grandchildren, the *Twightwees,* they have delivered them all up also, and have none left: Also on Behalf of the *Wawaghtanies,* they have none of your Prisoners, for they have also delivered them all up: And lastly, on Behalf of another Nation, called the *Kickapoes,* they say they never had any Prisoners.

*Brother,* The Day before Yesterday I heard what you said, and I assure you I am very well pleased with it. From what you have said, I suppose this Matter of the Prisoners to be the principal Business for which you invited us here.

*Brother,* I have told you I left some of your Flesh and Blood where I came from, and I assure you I look upon them as my own Flesh and Blood and I assure you again, you shall see them some Time hence.

*Brother,* I am very well pleased that you have demanded them now, and assure you, you shall have every one of them that remain with us.

*Brother,* You may remember that you told me, we should deliver all the Prisoners at *Pittsburgh,* and I shall be glad you would now shew to me the Persons here whom you shall appoint to receive those our Friends, and we shall be glad of it.

*A Belt of Seven Rows.*

*Then* Beaver *stood up, and spoke.*

*Brother,* This is all I have to say to you. We, the Western *Indians,* have nothing further to say to you. You know that we spoke three Days ago to you, about the Friendship between us.

*Brother,* The next Nation that have a Mind to speak to you are our Grandchildren, the *Shawanese,* and they are now about to speak.

*Then* Miskapalathy, *a* Shawanese, *rose up and spoke.*

*Brother,* I have heard what you and the Chief Men have been confering about, and now I desire you will hear your younger Brothers, the *Shawanese.* Our Chief Men are not here, but we are sent by the Chief Men, to speak for them, and what we say comes from their Hearts. There are several of our Nation here, though but two of us are deputed by our Chiefs.

*Brother,* I am very well pleased to hear you have cleansed our Council House. Now, though we who are left are like Boys, I assure you we will assist you to cleanse our Council Chamber, and we will do it always from our Hearts.

*A Belt of Eight Rows.*

*Brother,* You have heard what I had to say last Fall: *George Croghan* knows it, and I suppose you know it. I told him then, that I would cut all the Prisoners loose, and set them at Liberty.

*Brother,* I have heard what you said to my Grandfathers, the *Delawares,* respecting the Demand of your Flesh and Blood, and I am very well pleased with your Demand; and I now assure you I am in a Hurry to get Home, for they, your Flesh and Blood, yet remain there.

*Brother,* I have heard what you said. Now I shall depart very soon. I expect to meet my People, and all the Prisoners, at *Pittsburgh,* where I shall deliver them up, and you shall then hear what I shall have further to say to you.

*A String.*

*Brother,* Now you have heard what I have said to you, and it is all I intend to say to you.

*Brother,* I now want to mention something to you about our Trade with you.

*Brother,* We of the *Shawanese, Twightwees, Ottaways, Wawaghtanies,* and *Kickapoes,* desire you will take Pity on us. Our Chief Men at Home have their Eyes on us Boys, who came with our Grandfathers, the *Delawares,* to talk with you about Friendship. We have now concluded our Friendship with you. I now desire you will open a Trade with us, and that you will not be too hard in it. If you open a Trade among the back Nations, we desire to know at what Prices you can afford your Goods.

*A Belt of Seven Rows.*

The Governor asking the Names of the two *Shawanese* Chiefs, or Deputies, was informed they were called *Miskapalathy,* or the *Red Hawke,* and *Wapemashaway,* or the *White Horse.* The Governor told them he had heard what they had said, and it was very agreeable to him, and that he would give them Notice when he should return them an Answer.

*At a* CONFERENCE *with the Western* Indians,
*held at* Lancaster, *on* Wednesday, *the Eighteenth of* August, 1762.
PRESENT,
*The Honourable* JAMES HAMILTON, *Esq;*
Lieutenant-Governor, *&c, &c. as before.*

THE Governor, addressing himself to *Beaver,* and the *Delawares* from the *Ohio,* spoke as follows, *viz.*

*Brethren,* Listen to me, while I give you an Answer to the Speeches that you made to me on *Monday.*

You spoke to me in Behalf of your Grandchildren, the *Tawwas, Twightwees, Wawaghtanies,* and *Kickapoes,* acquainting me that they had respectively delivered up all our People, who were Prisoners in their Towns during the War.

*Brethren,* Let them know, that we esteem this as the greatest Mark they could have given us of the Sincerity of their Friendship, and by this Belt we return them our hearty Thanks.

*Brethren,* You told us that our demanding the Prisoners at this Time, and in the Manner we have done it, was very agreeable to you; and you supposed it was the principal Business for which we invited you here.

*Brethren,* You judge right, in thinking that the Affair of our Prisoners was a principal Reason of our inviting you here; it really was so, for we had it very much at Heart.

Another Reason of our desiring to see you was, that we might renew our antient Friendship, and brighten and strengthen the Covenant Chain, which so long and happily subsisted between our Ancestors. This last has now been done to our mutual Satisfaction, and it has given me, and all the good People present, the highest Pleasure to hear from your own Mouths that, agreeable to our Demand, you are determined to deliver up all the Prisoners that remain in your Towns, to such Persons as I shall appoint to receive them, at *Pittsburgh.*

*Brethren,* I have not yet concluded upon the Persons to be sent to *Pittsburgh,* for that Purpose, but you may be assured I shall very soon; who, when they come, will bring with them a Message and full Credentials from me, by which you will know, that they are deputed by me to receive the Prisoners from you. I propose they shall be at *Pittsburgh* the Second Day of *October* next, by which Time I expect you will have collected all of them, and brought them to that Place.

*A String.*

*Brethren,* We shall now return an Answer to your Grandchildren the *Shawanese.*

*Brethren the* Shawanese, You told me, at your last Meeting, that you were pleased to hear what had passed between us and your Grandfathers, and with our having cleaned the Council Chamber, which you said you would always assist in keeping clean. You told us also, that your Chief Men are not here, but have deputed you to speak for them, and that what you shall say comes from their Hearts.

*Brethren,* As we have been very sincere and open in every Thing we have said to your Grandfathers, we should have been glad that more of your Chiefs had been here, to have heard it; but as they are not, we desire you will acquaint them, and all your Nation, that we are extreamly well disposed towards them, and are determined to hold fast the Chain of Friendship that has been so happily renewed between us, and are glad to hear you will always readily assist us to keep the Council Chamber clean.

*A Belt.*

*Brethren,* You told me that you had sent me Word last Fall, by Mr. *Croghan,* that you would cut all the Bands of the Prisoners loose, and set them at Liberty; that you were pleased to hear the Demand I made of your Grandfathers, that they might all be delivered up; that you expect to meet your People, and all the Prisoners, at *Pittsburgh,* where you will deliver them; and that you are in a Hurry to go Home, for that Purpose.

*Brethren,* Mr. *Croghan* delivered me your Message last Fall, and I was very well pleased to hear you had concluded to set our People at Liberty; and I am the more so, to hear that you expect your People may be on the Way to *Pittsburgh,* with the Prisoners, and that you will deliver them up immediately; and your desiring to return Home forthwith, for that Purpose, convinces me you are in earnest, and I much approve of it.

*Brethren,* You desired we would open a Trade with you, and the other Western Nations, and not be too hard in our dealing with them. I must address my Answer not only to you, but to the *Delawares,* and all present, who I desire may listen attentively to it.

*Brethren,* Trade is a Business of Importance, and what I intended to mention to you all at this Meeting. You know that, for some Years past, this Government hath kept a great Store at *Pittsburgh,* in order to supply you with Goods, in Exchange for your Skins and Furs, near your own Homes. Good Men have been appointed to regulate the Prices of our Goods, and your Skins, and great Care has been taken that you should not be cheated, or imposed upon, by those who have, from Time to Time, kept the Provincial Store; but I am sorry to inform you, that the Charges of carrying our Goods, and bringing back your Skins, so many Hundred Miles, on Horseback, are so high, that it is a great Discouragement to that Trade, and we lose a great Deal of Money by it every Year, insomuch that I fear it will drop, unless your Uncles, the *Six Nations,* will consent to let us go, with our Canoes, up the West Branch of *Sasquehannah,* as far as we can, and build a few Store-houses on the Banks of that River, to secure our Goods in, as we pass and re-pass. This will cut off a long Land Carriage, and may be a Means of encouraging the Continuance of the Trade with you, and enabling our People to sell their Goods to you at a reasonable Rate.— We intend to speak to your Uncles on this Subject.

*Brethren,* I have now finished my Answers to your several Speeches, but I have still something particularly to say to *Beaver,* and our Brethren of the *Delaware* Nation, living at *Allegheny,* and desire you will attend to me.

*Brethren the* Delawares, I take this Opportunity to inform you, that about Six Years ago your Brother *Teedyuscung* made a Complaint against the Proprietaries, wherein he charged them with defrauding the *Delawares* of a Tract of Land, lying on the River *Delaware,* between *Tohiccon-Creek* and the *Kittatinny Hills.* He alledged, that this Complaint was not made by him, on his own Account but on Behalf of the Owners of the Land, many of whom, he said, lived at *Allegheny.* This Dispute, Brethren, was, by mutual Consent, refered to our Great King GEORGE, who ordered Sir *William Johnson* to enquire fully into the Matter, and make his Report to Him, that Justice might be done you, if you had been wronged. Accordingly Sir *William,* about two Months ago, came to *Easton,* where, on the Proprietaries Commissioners producing and reading sundry Writings and Papers, *Teedyuscung* was convinced of his

Error, and acknowledged that he had been mistaken with Regard to the Charge of Forgery made against the Proprietaries, having been misinformed by his Ancestors, and desired that all further Disputes about Land should be buried under Ground, and never heard of more; offering that such of the *Indians* as were then present should sign a Release for the Land in Question, and that he would endeavour to persuade the rest of his Brethren who were concerned to do the same at this Treaty at *Lancaster.* Now, Brethren of *Allegheny,* as we are Face to Face, be plain, and tell whether you are satisfied with, and approve of, what was done at the last Treaty at *Easton,* and whether you lay any Claim to those Lands, that there may be no Room left for any future Dispute about it among our Children.

*A small Belt.*

*To which* Beaver *said,*

*Brother,* As to my own Part, I know nothing about the Lands upon the River *Delaware;* but since you request it, I will first speak to my own People about it.

Then *Beaver* consulting with his Counsellors, returned the following Answer.

*Brother,* I must acknowledge I know nothing about the Lands upon the *Delaware,* and I have no Concern with Lands upon that River. We know nothing of the *Delawares* Claim to them. I have no Claim myself, nor any of my People. I suppose there may be some Spots or Pieces of Land, in some Parts of the Province, that the *Delawares* claim; but neither I nor any of my People know any Thing of them. As to what you and our Brother *Teedyuscung* have done, if you are both pleased, I am pleased with it. As to my Part, I want to say nothing about Land Affairs; what I have at Heart, and what I came down about, is to confirm our Friendship, and make a lasting Peace, so as our Children and Grandchildren may live together in everlasting Peace, after we are dead.

*Teedyuscung* and his *Delawares* being present, something passed between them, which was not interpreted.

*The Governor, addressing himself to* Beaver, *said,*

I am very much pleased with what you have said; you speak like an honest Man, and I hope that the Friendship that has been made between us and our Brethren, the *Delawares,* will remain firm, as long as the Sun shines, and the Rivers run.

Teedyuscung *then stood up, and addressing himself to the Governor, said,*

*Brother,* Before all these *Allegheny Indians* here present, I do now assure you, that I am ready and willing to sign a Release to all the Lands we have been disputing about, as I told you I would at *Easton,* and desire no more may be ever said or heard of them hereafter.

On which the Governor told *Teedyuscung,* that he was pleased with what he had said, and that on that Occasion he had acted like an honest Man.

*The Governor then concluded.*

*Brethren,* Your Brothers, the Proprietaries, about three Years ago, directed me, as soon as *Teedyuscung*'s Complaint against them was determined, and Justice done to their Characters, to make their old Friends, the *Delawares,* a Present, in their Name, to supply your Wants, and as a Mark of their Affection and Regard for you, and to convince you that they had no ill Will in their Hearts against you, but looked upon you as formerly to be their good Friends and Brothers. Now as that Dispute is happily at an End, I am at Liberty to follow their Direction, and shall accordingly order a Present of Goods to be delivered to you from the Proprietaries.

*At a* CONFERENCE *with the Northern* Indians, *held at* Lancaster, *on* Thursday, *the Nineteenth of* August, 1762.
PRESENT, *The Honourable* JAMES HAMILTON, *Esquire, &c, &c. as before.*

THOMAS KING, a Chief of the *Oneidas* stood up, and spoke as follows, *viz.*
*Brother,* Hearken to what I am going to say, in Answer to your Speech to me the Day before Yesterday. I return you my Thanks; it gives me Pleasure that we see one another, in the same Manner as our Forefathers used to do.——Then taking up the Strings delivered by the Governor in their Order, he repeated what had been said upon them.

We are all very glad to see you, and your Brethren that are with you, in Health. All the *Six Nations,* and our Nephews, have had interpreted to them all that you said, and they are pleased with it, and very glad to see you, and that it has pleased the Great GOD, who has all Power in his Hands, to suffer us to come together, to speak to one another freely.

*A String.*

Then taking another String, he repeated the Governor's Words spoke upon it; and, in the Name of all the *Indians* present, returned him Thanks for his taking the Briars out of their Legs, and healing the Bruises that were made in their Feet by the Stones.

*A String.*

*Brother,* The other Day you cleared my Ears, and my Cousins here, for which I return you Thanks; and now, by this String, I clear your Ears in the same Manner, that you may hear what I have to say to you.

*A String.*

*Brother,* You told me the other Day, that as we were come from afar, and the Roads were very dusty, you cleansed our Throats from the Dust, and opened a Passage to our Hearts; we all return you Thanks that you have cleansed us so far, and we do in the same Manner clean your Throats and Hearts.

*A String.*

*Brother,* You likewise told me you wiped the Tears from my Eyes, for the Loss of my Friends, that we may see one another clearly, for which we all return you our Thanks.

*A String.*

*Brother,* It is now three Years since you first demanded of us your Flesh and Blood. Now hear me, as to what I and all our Nations and our Allies, that live as far as the Sun-setting, have done.

*Brother,* I assure you, in Behalf of all of us present, and the Western *Indians,* of whom you have been demanding your Flesh and Blood, that I have them here, and that it is not my Fault, neither can I say our Maker has been the Cause, but the *French* have been the Cause why you have not had them sooner.

Then directing his Discourse to his Brothers and Cousins, the *Delawares,* he proceeded, and said,

I never had Occasion to go to War with the *English* Nation; the People I had Occasion to go to War with live to the Southward; it has been so from all Ages, and we have always gone to War against the Southern *Indians;* I never had Cause to go to War with the *English,* this was owing to the Evil Spirit, the Devil. When I used to go to War with the Southern *Indians,* and brought Prisoners Home, I thought they were mine, and that no Body had any Right to meddle with them. Now since I joined with you, I went to War again, and I brought *French* People Home with me, as Prisoners, and you took them from me; this makes me think it was owing to the Evil Spirit.

*Brother,* I desire you to be strong. I have heard you often say, you would be very glad if I would bring you the Captives, and you would make me Satisfaction, because you know I am not as you are; I am of a quite different Nature from you; sometimes I think you are not in Earnest with me, in telling me you will make me Satisfaction.

*Brother,* We have heard you, and so have all my Brothers and Cousins to the Westward heard what you have said about giving us Satisfaction; your Words seem to be very sweet to us. You told us if we did so and so, you would do so with us.

*Brother,* You know we are different Nations, and have different Ways. We could not immediately perform what you required of us, in returning your Flesh and Blood, because every one of these Nations have different Ways; that is the Reason why we could not so soon perform it.

*Brother,* I am sorry it is so difficult for us to understand each other: If we could understand one another, we would put one another in Mind of the Friendship that subsisted between us and our Forefathers; but as we do not easily understand one another, we are obliged to deliver you the Substance in short of what we have to say, which makes it tedious.——(Meaning that they are obliged to interpret in two or three Languages, before it is told to us.)

*Brother,* You have often told me, if I would bring your Flesh and Blood you would be very glad, and would give such Prisoners Liberty to return with them, if they did not incline to stay with you, and to go where they pleased.

*A Belt of Eight Rows.*

*Thomas King* being asked, who it was that promised the Prisoners should be left to their Choice, to return with them, or to go where they pleased? He answered, the Governor promised it at *Easton,* and there were two Governors there at that Time.——(Meaning Governor *Denny,* and Governor *Bernard,* of *New-Jersey.*)

*Brother* Onas, You have been requiring your Flesh and Blood these three Years; I promise you I will give you them, and now I will deliver all I have brought.

*A Belt of Eight Rows.*

*Brother* Onas, I am sorry we cannot speak to one another any faster, because we cannot understand one another without so many Interpreters, and this takes up much Time, so that we must be slow in telling our Business.

*Brother* Onas, You have told us, of the *Six Nations,* that we must assist you to see your Flesh and Blood. If we assist you, you say you shall see your Flesh and Blood.

*Brother,* We have done what we can, and that is the Reason why you see so many of your Flesh and Blood; some *Indians* part with them with Reluctance, and want to keep them longer; they are unwilling to part with them; this brings a great deal of Trouble on us, the *Six Nations.*

*Brother* Onas, You have often told us, the *Six Nations,* that we should assist in getting your Flesh and Blood. I have done my Endeavour, and taken great Pains: I have got a great many of them, though at first with great Difficulty: When I brought them by the *English* Forts, they took them away from me; all along from *Oswego* to the Carrying-Place, and so to *Niagara,* till I got to *Shamokin,* they got them all from me, and I believe they have made Servants of them: This is the Reason why I brought so few of them: No Wonder they are so loath to come, when you make Servants of them: You know that you have told me that I should assist you, you cannot deny it: By and by you will say, I never told you to assist me, and that I tell Lies when I say so.

*Brother* Onas, You told me you would be very glad if I would bring you your Flesh and Blood, and that you were able to make me Satisfaction for them: You said you had Rooms full of Goods, and that we should never want any Thing while you have Goods: You told me, we shall have a Recompence for our Trouble in bringing them down. I assure you, I have brought all your Flesh and Blood that I could get at this Time; there are some behind yet, but they belong to such People as are gone to War against the *Cherokees,* and we could not take them without their Leave, and when they return from War, we will certainly bring them.

*Brother* Onas, I have brought Fourteen of your Flesh and Blood, that is all I could get this Time; for as I told you, your People in the Forts have got them all away from me, they have stole them, or persuaded them to run away from me, and have hid them in the Bushes. As I told you, there are few left that belong to those *Indians* that are gone to War against the *Cherokees,* with whom we have been at War from all Ages, and they are at War with you; I assure you when they return, we will bring them all to you. You used to tell me, I always came unawares upon you, when I did come; you certainly knew that I was coming ever since last Spring, and you might have got every Thing ready for me. There is one Captive at the Camp that says he will not come; he says the Governor has seen him, and talked with him at the Camp; all the rest are here.

*A Belt.*

*Brother* Onas, It may be there are two Governors of you; your Messages and your Words do not agree together; when I repeat what you have said to me, it seems disagreeable to you.

Here the Governor asked what he meant by two Governors, and desired him to explain himself, for he could not understand him.

*He answered,*

*Brother,* You want to know what my Meaning is, by saying there are two Governors. In every Country there is always one Head Governor, but here are two Governors. It will not do for me to point out People, for you must certainly know there is more than one Governor. I hear one say such a Thing, and another say such a Thing; but I will not point out any Body, lest you should differ. You will hear of it hereafter. I heard that both Governors came from *Philadelphia,* but perhaps I may be misinformed.

The Governor desired to know, whether any Messages had been delivered to them in their own Country, and by whom, and what the Messages were. He insisted on their giving him a plain Answer.

They answered, that the *Cayugas,* who were at *Philadelphia* in the Spring, brought the Messages to them; but do not pretend that they were delivered in the Governor's Name, but they might have brought what passed only in private Conversation.

*Brother* Onas, As I have now brought your Flesh and Blood, I would have you to take Care of them, and keep them fast. I brought a Girl to *Easton,* and she run away: When I came Home, I found her there. Bless me! says I, there is my Wife. I was sorry that I had delivered her, but to my Surprize I found her at Home. You know it is hard to part with a Wife.

*Brother,* I have brought an *English* Prisoner, who I love as my own Wife: I have a young Child by her. You know it is very hard for a Man to part with his Wife. I have delivered her, therefore take Care of her, and keep her safe, that she dont make her Escape.

*Brother* Onas, Our Grandfathers used to tell us, we should keep fast Hold of the Chain of Friendship, and always advised us to observe it; but now, in latter Days, as soon as I came across the Hatchet, I got Hold of it, and really I did not know what I was about, and stuck it into your Heads. By this Belt, I take the Hatchet out of your Head; it belongs to you and the *French;* you are both of one Colour. It has been the Fault of the *French* that we struck you, and therefore we take the Hatchet out of your Head.

*A Belt of Eight Rows.*

*Brother* Onas, Now that I have taken the Hatchet out of your Head, I gather your Bones, which lie scattered in so many Places, that I cannot name them particularly.

*Brother,* There is a large Pine Tree in the *Oneida* Country, which I take and pull up by the Roots, and then it makes a great Hole; when I look down the Hole, I see a great River, running very strong at the Bottom. By this Belt I gather all your Bones, wherever I can find them, and bury them in that Hole, and the Hatchet with them; when I put them down the Hole, they fall into that strong Stream, and float down it, I know not where. I stick that Pine Tree down again in the same Hole, and then no Body can discover that there has been a Hole; so that neither you nor I, nor our nor your Grandchildren, shall ever be able to know where your Bones are laid. This is the Custom of our Forefathers, that when any Difference arose between them and their Brethren, they buried it in this Manner.

*A Belt.*

*Brother,* I own you are my eldest Brother. The eldest Brother should always teach the youngest Brother, when they misbehave; I therefore desire when you see us misbehave, that you would tell us of it, and teach us better.

*A Belt of Seven Rows.*

*Brother* Onas, Our late Differences have been the Cause why the Clouds have hung over our Heads, and made it dark. Now by this Belt I take away all the Clouds, that we may see the Sky clear, and the Sun rise and set. We Fourteen Nations, now present, tell you this.

*A Belt of Six Rows.*

*Brother* Onas, I don't doubt but there is some Foulness come into your Heart, through your Throat. My Grandfathers used to tell me, that whenever we found our Brother's Heart and Throat to be foul, that they had left me the best Medicines, and desired me to put it to your Mouth, to drink as a Physic, and that it would cleanse their Throat and Heart, and pass quite through their Body down to the Ground; and, Brethren, by this String I bury it in the Ground, so that your Heart and Throat may be for ever clean. We Fourteen Nations tell you so.

*A String.*

*Brother* Onas, I have removed all the Filthiness from your Body, and since I have cleansed it out and in, I shall go about that good Work of Peace.

*Brother* Onas, It was we of the *Mohocks, Oneidas, Senecas, Onondagoes, Cayugas,* and *Tuscaroras,* that first brought about the good Work of Peace.—He added, that the *Mohocks* and *Oneidas* were the eldest of the *Six Nations,* and both of a Height.

*Brother* Onas, I will acquaint you further, that I have more Brothers to the Westward, and that we are all Brothers down as far as to the Sun-set; my Friends are so many, that I cannot tell how many they are.

*Brother* Onas, I will let you know, that though the *Mohocks* are the eldest, yet they are the furthest off to the Eastward: When they hear any Thing, they pass through the *Oneidas* to the *Onondagoes,* where the Council Fire burns: Likewise, when the *Senecas* hear any Thing, they come to the *Cayugas,* because they are next to the *Onondagoe* Council; so that whenever they hear any Thing to the East or West, it is carried to the *Onondagoe* Council. (Meaning, that when you shall send any Messages to the *Onondagoe* Council, they must be sent either to the *Senecas* or *Mohocks.*

*Brother* Onas, I will mention our old Friendship; I will make it new again; I will brighten up our old Chain of Friendship. Our Grandfathers used to tell one another they had one Heart, and here it is; they both had Hold of it: They used to tell one another they had one Head, here it is. I tell you the same; you and we have one Head, and one Heart. We Fourteen Nations tell you so.

*They delivered a Belt of Nine Rows, representing the Figure of two Men in the Middle, with a Heart between them, and Six Diamonds on each Side; one of the Men represents the* Indians, *the other the* English.

*Brother* Onas, Now we have renewed our old Friendship, I am a little afraid your Fire is almost out, it is not good; now I will take all that bad Fire away, and kindle it again, and make a good Fire of it; I will take good dry Wood, and kindle up the Fire afresh that our Grandfathers have made, and so make the Smoke rise up so very high, that all distant Nations shall see it, and thereby know that there is a Council Fire here. There was a good Fire at *Easton;* that was really a good Fire, for when I came to that good *Easton* Fire, I could have my Belly full of Victuals, and Plenty of Drink; but now I come here, I have little to eat; I am sure I have no other Drink than dirty Water, which almost choaks me.

*A Belt of Six Rows.*

*Brother* Onas, What we have hitherto said, concerning Peace, has been concluded upon by our old Counsellors. We also desired our chief Warriors to be strong, and assist the old Counsellors; and desired, if any Thing should be wanting in the old Counsellors, they would assist them in it, in order that our Friendship may be lasting; for the Counsellors can do nothing, unless the Warriors should give their Consent to it. We Fourteen Nations tell you so.

*A Belt with Seven Rows, with Two Diamonds in it, representing the Counsellors and Warriors, united in Council together.*

*Brother* Onas, Our Friendship seems to go on very kindly. I will tell you one Thing, you are always longing after my Land, from the East to the West; you seem to be longing after it. Now I desire you will not covet it any more; you will serve me as you have done our Cousins, the *Delawares;* you have got all their Land from them; all the Land hereabouts belonged to them once, and you have got it all.

*Brother* Onas, I desire you to go no further than *Nixhisaqua* (or *Mohonoy)* I desire you will settle no higher up, for if you keep pressing on me, you will push me out, for I shall have no Place to live on, nor hunt in, neither for me nor my Grandchildren; so I desire you will press no further. I desire another Thing, that you will not take it from me by Force: If you take this Land by Force, it will never go well with either of us. You may remember that GOD gave us this Land, and you some other; yet I have parted with some of it to you.

*A Belt of Six Rows.*

*Brother* Onas, You have desired me to assist you, in order to bring in your Flesh and Blood, which now you see I have done. You used to tell me, if I would bring in your Flesh and Blood, or assist you therein, you would satisfy those who brought them in; these are mighty pleasing Words to me, and I hope you will do so. Some of our Warriors who are here have no Guns, and if you will bestow any on them, I desire they may be good. You are daily making Rifles; I do not know what you do with them. When you gave me any Guns, you gave me yellow-stocked ones, that are worth nothing. I have asked you now four Times. At *Easton* you gave me only Gun-Locks: What think you could I do with them, without Stocks and Barrels? I make no Guns. After I got the Gun-Locks, I joined myself with General *Forbes,* and went to War with him, as you ordered me, against the *French;* and as soon as I had done it, you still gave me only Gun-locks.

*A Bunch of Ten Strings, mostly black.*

*Brother* Onas, Having finished what I had to say to you, I am now going to speak to my Cousins. Please to hearken to what I shall say to them.

*Then directing his Discourse to the* Delawares, *he spoke as follows.*

*My Cousins,* I could hardly get along. I heard such frightful News, that indeed I could not get along, if I had not had good Courage. *Teedyuscung,* before I sat off from Home, I heard you should say, you would poison us all, so that we should not hold this Treaty. Thinks I to myself, I will come nevertheless; if I die, it will be well; I can die but once; so then I came along as far as *Wyoming.*

*My Cousins,* As soon as I came there, *Teedyuscung* began to make his Complaints that he had no Fire; so says I, Cousin, there is certainly some Fire, for I made one here for the *Shawanese, (Cacawasheca)* and I made another Fire at *Shamokin,* for *Alammapis;* another Fire I made at *Wighalousin;* another Fire I made at *Diahoga.* All those Fires are there yet.[3] The Fire at *Wighalousin* is a good Fire, for I heard no bad Stories there; that Fire at *Shamokin* is not yet out; if any Body stirs it, it will soon blaze. I made the Fire at *Wyoming* for the *Shawanese;* perhaps they will still return to that Place. Then I came along as far as *Harris*'s Ferry; there I heard another Piece of bad News from *Teedyuscung,* who said he had got a Sort of Poison that will give the *Indians* the Bloody Flux, and as soon as they come, he would give it to them, that they might get the Flux, and die along the Road as they go. But, notwithstanding these Discouragements, I came along, and got here. I now suspect there is a Bag of Poison somewhere about this Camp, that will give us the Flux as we go Home; and I think it will be great Shame, if it should be so, because our *English* Brethren sent for us; and if any of us should die, it will appear to them as if they had lost so many of their own People, because it was they that sent for us.[4]

Now, *Teedyuscung,* I must teach you better; I will correct you; you must not talk of such a Thing, for if any of us die, it will be said *Teedyuscung* was the Cause of it; so you should not say such Things. By this Belt I make a Fire for *Teedyuscung,* at *Wyoming;* I tell him to sit there by the Fire Side, and watch that Fire; but I dont give it to him, for our *English* Brethren cast an Eye upon that Land; therefore I say to *Teedyuscung,* watch that Fire, and if any White People come there, tell them to go away, for that Land belongs to your Uncles, the *Six Nations.* The *Six Nations* want to keep up that Fire, that they may hear from their Brethren the *English,* and others.

*The Belt was given to* Tipiscohan.

*Then turning to the Governor, he said,*

*Brother,* This is all I have to say at present, but I have more in my Heart, which I cannot speak now, having staid so long that I am quite fatigued.

The Governor then acquainted *Thomas King,* that he had been attentive to all he said, and that he thanked him for it, and when he had considered of it, would at a proper Time return him an Answer; but told him, that he had not yet delivered him the Prisoners, and as this was in improper Place, he desired a few *Indians* would take them to the Court-House, where he would receive them.

The Conference then broke up, and the Governor, his Council, and the Commissioners, went with some *Indian* Chiefs to the Court-House, to receive the Prisoners; where being come, the Governor acquainted *Thomas King,* that he was now ready to receive the Prisoners from him, and that they need not be under any Apprehensions of being used ill, for that he would be kind to them, and treat them like Children, and restore them to their Parents and Relations.

*Then they delivered to the Governor the Prisoners, as follow.*

*Elizabeth Williams,* a young Woman, delivered by *Mussause,* a *Munsey Indian; Henry Williams,* about Eighteen Years of Age, Brother to *Elizabeth Williams,* delivered by *Conoyhocheratoquin,* a *Munsey; Peggy Dougherty,* delivered by *Eckgohson,* a *Munsey; Mary Tidd,* and her Child, taken near *Samuel Depui*'s, by *Eckgohson; Abigail Evan,* and her Child, taken at *Stony-Creek,* in *Virginia,* by *Cowachsora,* a *Seneca.*

A Boy, by *Meightong,* a *Munsey;* a little Girl, by *Eckgohson,* a *Munsey;* a little Boy, by *Pessewauck,* a *Munsey;* a Boy, of about Fourteen Years, by *Eckgohson,* a *Munsey;* a Boy, of Twelve Years, by *Cowockslaira,* a *Seneca;* a little Boy, of Seven Years, by *Corocksaara,* a *Seneca;* a little Girl, of Six Years, by *Contaronque,* a *Seneca.* These Childrens Names unknown, as they cannot speak *English,* or give any Account from whence they were taken.

*John Brightwell,* of *Lower Marlborough,* near *Patuxent,* in *Maryland,* a Deserter from the First Battalion of *Royal Americans.*

Lancaster, August 22, 1762.

*At a* CONFERENCE *at* John Hambright*'s*
*(where the Governor delivered to the* Delaware Indians
*the Presents made to them, by himself and the Province)*
PRESENT, *The Honourable* JAMES HAMILTON, *Esquire,*
Lieutenant-Governor, *&c.*
William Logan, *Esq; Member of the Council;*
Joseph Fox, James Webb, *Esquires, Members of the Assembly;*
Israel Pemberton, Jeremiah Warder, Isaac Greenleafe, Benjamin Hooton;
Beaver *and* Teedyuscung, *Chiefs of the* Delaware *Nation at*
Allegheny *and* Wyoming;
Joseph Compass, *alias* Catepackeaman, Joseph Peepy, Tayshiccomen,
Taqualaw, *Counsellors to the Chiefs.*

THE Governor opened the Conference, and spoke to the *Indians* as follows, *viz.*

*Brother* Beaver, I told you, a few Days since, of the Disputes that had happened between your Brothers, the Proprietaries, and *Teedyuscung,* about Land; and that I had their Orders, as soon as that Dispute should be ended, and the Proprietaries Characters cleared, to make the *Delaware Indians* a Present of considerable Value, as a Mark of their Affection to their old Friends. To which Present from the Proprietaries, the good People of this Province have been pleased to make an Addition, of equal Value.

*Brothers,* Teedyuscung *and* Beaver, As that Dispute is now happily settled, I do (in Consequence of the Proprietaries Orders, and upon what was agreed upon at *Easton,* upon that Subject, between me and your Friends, the People of this Province) make you a Present of the Goods and Money now lying before you, to be equally divided between you, as a Proof of the Regard, both of the Proprietaries, and People, for their old Friends, the *Delaware* Nation.

*Brother* Beaver, As this is the first Time we have seen you, and our Friends from the Westward, since the late Disturbances; and as some of them have been at Expence in collecting and bringing down our Flesh and Blood, which they have now delivered to us, I, and your Friends of this Province, have thought fit to make you this further Present, to testify the Pleasure we have in seeing you, after so long all Absence, and our Thankfulness for your having restored the Prisoners.—As you know better than we, in what Manner to divide the Present now made you, we desire you will do it amongst those who come with you, in the most just and equitable Manner, paying a particular Regard to those who have now, or at any other Time, been at Trouble and Expence in collecting and restoring our Flesh and Blood.

*Brother* Teedyuscung, We have had frequent Opportunities of shaking you by the Hand, since the War, and you, upon many Occasions, received the strongest Proofs of our Reconciliation and Friendship for you. Nevertheless, as we observe that a greater Number than common of your Friends are come down with you, in order to enable you to shew your Kindness to them, we think fit to make you this additional Present.

And now, Brothers, I heartily wish the Peace and Friendship, which have been renewed betwixt us at this Treaty, may continue and grow stronger, as long as the Sun shall shine, or the Rivers run; to which you may be assured we, on our Parts, shall contribute to the utmost of our Power, as we doubt not you will also on yours.

After the Governor had finished his Speeches to *Beaver* and *Teedyuscung,* the latter rose up, and addressing himself to *Beaver,* desired him to take Notice, that he now delivered up all his Right and Claim to the Lands on the River *Delaware,* that have been in Dispute between him and the Proprietaries of *Pennsylvania;* and that he now, as he (*Beaver*) saw, received this Money and Goods from his Brethren the *English.* He further desired *Beaver* to acquaint all the *Indians* at *Allegheny,* that the *Delaware* Nation have now no Right or Claim to any of the Lands on the Waters of the River *Delaware,* that have been in Dispute.

*Then turning to the Governor, said to him,*

Now Brother Governor, our Children and Grandchildren shall never be able to say hereafter, that they have any Right or Claim to the Lands that have been in Dispute upon that River.

The Governor, directing his Discourse to *Beaver* and *Teedyuscung,* told them, that as they had now received a considerable Sum of Money, he cautioned them against giving too much of it to their young Men, who, instead of laying it out in Things necessary and useful, might be tempted to debauch themselves with strong Liquors, which might occasion them to quarrel, and do Mischief, not only to one another, but also to their Brethren, the *English;* which might endanger the Chain of Friendship betwixt them and us, and would be a very ungrateful Return for all the Kindness we had shewn them.

*To which they both answered,*

That they were obliged to the Governor for his Advice, in which they thought he had their Good at Heart, and promised to follow it, and heartily thanked him for it.

The Governor then delivered to *Beaver* and *Teedyuscung* respectively, *Two Hundred Pounds,* in milled Dollars, and the Value of *Four Hundred Pounds* in Goods, to be equally divided between them. He further presented to *Beaver,* and those who came with him from the *Ohio,* the Value of *Four Hundred Pounds* in Goods; and the Value of *Two Hundred Pounds* in Goods to *Teedyuscung,* and his Friends and People. And after taking them both by the Hand he departed, and the Conference ended.

*At a* CONFERENCE *with the Northern* Indians, *held at* Lancaster, *on* Monday, *the Twenty-third of* August, 1762.
PRESENT, *The Honourable* JAMES HAMILTON, *Esquire, &c. &c. as before.*

THOMAS KING stood up, and addressing himself to the Governor, spoke as follows, *viz.*

*Brother* Onas, It is about three Years ago that you asked me, whether I was willing you should build a Fort at *Shamokin;* you said you wanted to build a Fort there, to stand against the *French,* and to defend the Inhabitants; that our Great King had commanded you to build Forts. You said you would keep a Fort there as long as the War continued, but that you did not want any of our Land there.

*Brother* Onas, You likewise asked me to let you build a Fort there, to defend my Land, and to defend yourself; you told me, that you did not desire any greater Quantity of my Land than what the Fort took up. I granted you Liberty to build a Fort, because you told me it was the Great King GEORGE desired you might build one on my Land; and I endeavoured to assist you. You also told me, as soon as ever the Peace was concluded you would go away; or that at any Time when I should tell you to go away, you would go away, and that I might do what I would with the Fort.

*Brother* Onas, Now all the different Tribes of us present, desire that you will call your Soldiers away from *Shamokin;* for we have concluded a Peace, and are as one Brother, having one Head and one Heart.

If you take away your Soldiers, we desire you would keep your Trading House there, and have some honest Man in it, because our Cousins follow their Hunting there, and will want a Trade. This is the Way for us to live peaceably together.

*Brother* Onas, I must tell you again, these Soldiers must go away from *Shamokin* Fort; I desire it, and let there be only Traders live there; you know who are the honest People; we desire that only honest People may live there, and that you will not be too hard with us, when they may buy our Skins and Furs, and such Things as we may have to sell. This will be the Way for us to live peaceably together; but for you to keep Soldiers there, is not the Way to live peaceable. Your Soldiers are very often unruly, and our Warriors are unruly, and when such get together they do not agree. For as you have now made Peace with all our Nations, there is no Occasion for Soldiers to live there any longer.

*Brother* Onas, We, the *Six Nations,* have all consulted, and concluded on this Matter of your removing the Soldiers from *Shamokin;* for you know we go to War with the Southern *Indians,* the *Cherokees;* we have been at War with them ever since we were created, and the Place where the *Shamokin* Fort stands is right in our Warriors Path, and you know that Warriors are always an unruly People. For this Reason we desire you to take away your Soldiers, and place some honest Man there, that he may supply our Warriors with Ammunition, and any other Necessaries that they may want, when they go to War against the *Cherokees.* We must press you to take away your Soldiers from *Shamokin,* as our Warriors are unruly. You have planted Corn there, and if our Warriors come there, they may cut some of your Cornstalks, and then you will be angry. The Fort you have there does not now do any Good, for you have many other Forts all around you; this one therefore can be of no Use to you; it stands as it were at your own Doors.

*A Belt of Twelve Rows.*

*Note.* He said he had forgot a Word in this Belt, which was to tell the Governor, that he might chuse and appoint such Men as pleased to trade; and also a Blacksmith and Gun-smith, to mend their Guns and Hatchets, or do any Thing they may want.

*He then added,*

We desire that the present Store-keepers at *Shamokin* may be removed, and honest Men placed there in their Room; for our Hunters, who have been down there, complain that when *Indians* come there, and want Provisions and Goods, they find the Store sometimes shut up, and they cannot be supplied with what they want.

*Brother* Onas, For my Part, I think *John Harris* is the most suitable Man to keep Store; for he lives right in the Road where our Warriors pass, and he is very well known by all of us in our Nation, as his Father was before him; we all know him. If you chuse *John Harris,* we desire you will order him to keep Provisions and Cloaths, to give to our People, who sometimes come there naked; and likewise Ammunition for our Warriors, for that is their Path. We desire you may have no Trading Houses higher up the *Sasquehannah* than *Shamokin;* let the *Indians* come there, or to *John Harris*'s; if they want to trade, let them come down to these Trading Houses. We also desire you will send your Messages to *John Harris*'s, so that we may hear from one another, because where he lives the Road seems to divide, and spread, and it goes to many Places. And we further desire you will give him a Commission for these Things, in Writing.

*Thomas King* being asked, if they meant that *John Harris* was to be furnished with Goods to sell or to give to the *Indians?* He answered, that they desired there might be a Trading House there, and that this was what they requested; and desiring to be excused, if they forgot any Part of their Speeches, as they were very long.

*He proceeded.*

*Brother* Onas, I have now mentioned two Places for you to keep Store Houses at, *Shamokin* and *John Harris*'s; but perhaps they will sell at different Prices, and if we have a Mind to have Goods cheapest, we may go to *John Harris*'s. We therefore desire you will let us know, what Prices you set upon your Goods.

*A Belt of Ten Rows.*

*Brother* Onas, I will also acquaint you of another proper Trading Place, and who we think will be a suitable Man to keep that Store House, and that is *George Croghan,* who is very well known by all our Nations, and several others. We desire you will appoint him to keep Store at *Bedford,* because that is also in our Warriors Path. We desire likewise, that there may be a Black-smith and Gun-smith, because my Cousins will be there a hunting, and will want their Things mended. This will be known every where, throughout all our Nations; for as the Peace is made, our young Men will set themselves to hunt, and bring Skins there, and will have nothing else to do but hunt.

*A Belt of Eight Rows.*

*Brother* Onas, I will also acquaint you of another Trading Place, which is the Place they call *Patowmack,* in *Maryland.* One *Daniel Cressap* has sent me Word, by many Warriors, this Spring, and he tells me, that if the Governor would order him to keep a Store there, he would provide every Thing for the Warriors; for his Father used to maintain all the *Indian* Warriors that passed and re-passed that Way. He likewise tells me, if the Governor would let him know what he should do, and if he should be allowed to do this, he would provide for the Warriors. We now desire, that he may be the Person appointed to receive Messages, and that you would acquaint the Governor of *Maryland* with this, that the Warriors may pass and re-pass that Way, without any Molestation.

*A Belt of Seven Rows.*

*Brother* Onas, We desire you to acquaint the Governor of *Virginia,* that we may pass and re-pass through his Province, when we go to War with the *Cherokees;* for our Warriors Road is stopped up in many Places; *English* People have settled on it. And now we desire that a Road may be opened, that we may pass safely. We desire nothing but Love and Friendship with our Brethren, the *English,* as we pass through. We desire you will send a Letter, with this Belt, to the Governor of *Virginia,* as from us, as soon as possible; for I do not know how soon my People may go that Way; our Warriors have already the Hatchet in their Hands, and perhaps they may go there before your Letter gets there; for which Reason I desire you will make Haste in this Business.

*A Belt of Five Rows.*

*Brother* Onas, We now desire you to be strong, and that you will give us Powder; I do not think that you will refuse to let me have Powder, for you are able. Our Brother, General *Johnson,* though but a single Man, supplies all our People with

Powder; when we go to see him, he fills all our Powder-horns with it. I see a great many of you here, and I think you are more able than he. Our own People at Home will have their Eye upon us, and expect that we shall bring them some Powder, and Presents; we therefore hope you will consider us in this, and make them larger than common as we do not come to see you often.

*A Belt of Nine Rows.*

*Brother* Onas, I now speak in Behalf of our Warriors. When we heard your Words come to our Countries, they were very pleasing to us, that you would make Presents to your Brethren, when they come to see you, and would give them any Thing they might want. Now we desire you will give us some Vermilion, for you know that the eldest Brother has always Pity and Compassion on the youngest Brother; we know you are able, as you make all these Things in yourselves. We have all concluded Peace now, but we have given our young Men Liberty to go to War with the Southern *Indians;* this is the Reason of our wanting the red Paint; you see the Warriors always paint themselves, when they go to War.

*A String.*

*Brother* Onas, I shall now speak a few Words, without any Belt or String. Whenever the *French* were asked for Paint, or any Thing else, they always gave it to the *Indians* readily; and it is no Wonder that so many *Indians* liked the *French,* since they were so kind to them.

You see several of our *Indians* here dressed in *French* Cloaths; and we desire the Governor will be strong, and supply us with every Thing.

*Brother* Onas, I have not left any Thing in my Heart; I have said every Thing material I had to say; and now I desire you will help me as far as *Shamokin,* and supply me with Provisions; for perhaps some of our People, if they are hungry, may hurt some of the Inhabitants Corn or Fruit, and cause Differences to arise. When I came from *Easton* last, I had no Provisions given me to eat, so that when I got Home I was almost starved, and a mere Skeleton.

*A String.*

*Brother* Onas, We want a little Lad that lives among you; he is *Keisheta*'s Son; the old Man ordered that he should live at *Philadelphia,* in order to learn *English,* to be an Interpreter; we think by this Time he has learned it, and we now think it Time for him to come Home; his Relations, that are present, desire that he may go Home now with them.[5]

*A String.*

*Brother* Onas, You may remember, three Years ago, that this Man (pointing to *Samuel Curtiss)* mentioned something to you about his Daughter, that was stolen from him in *Dorset* County, in *Maryland,* about Fourteen Years ago. I spoke to you once before about it, and I have heard nothing from you concerning her.

*A black and white String.*

*Brother* Onas, I am now going to speak to you in Behalf of *Tokahaion's* two Daughters. They desire the Governor will give them a Horse; they hear the Governor is very kind, and gives many People Horses; they have two Plantations, at which they plant Corn, and want Horses to carry their Corn, to ease their Backs, because when at Home, their Corn Fields are at a considerable Distance from them.

*A String.*

*Then* Seneca George *rose up, and spoke as follows,* viz.

*Brother* Onas, *and all our Brethren with you,* We all desire you to remember our Son, *Robert White,* who carries all our Messages; he is old, and we desire you will give him a Horse; you did give him a Mare before, but she is dead; she was with Foal, and died.

*A Belt of Eight Rows.*

Thomas King *then spoke as follows,* viz.

*Brother* Onas; This is all I have to say; I have nothing more in my Mind; I beg you will consider of all that I have said, and take Time to do it; it looks as if you were in Haste to go Home, but I desire you will be patient, and stay; I came a great Way, and will contentedly stay as long as may be convenient.

*TUESDAY, the Twenty-fourth of* August.

*THOMAS KING,* in Behalf of the Chiefs of the *Six Nations,* waited on the Governor, and acquainted him, that as their Speeches to him of Yesterday were long, he suspected he might have forgot something; and desired he would give him the Opportunity of bearing every Thing he had said repeated to them.

On which the Governor appointed a Meeting at the old *Lutheran* Church, at which were

PRESENT,

*The Honourable* JAMES HAMILTON, *Esquire,* Governor, *&c.*

William Logan, Richard Peters, *Esquires, of the Council;*

Joseph Fox, James Wright, Samuel Rhoads, *Esquires, of the Assembly;*

Thomas King, Tokahaion, Kinderuntie,

*and several other Chiefs of the* Six Nations;

Andrew Montour, *and* Isaac Stille, *Interpreters.*

WHEN the *Indians* were seated, the Governor, laying the several Belts and Strings in their Order, as delivered him Yesterday, directed the Secretary to read the

Minutes, which were distinctly interpreted to them, Paragraph by Paragraph, and declared by the *Indians* to be right.

*After which* Thomas King *arose, and spoke as follows.*

*Brother* Onas, I mistook when I told you Yesterday, that I would have you keep a Store at *Bedford;* I meant that Sir *William Johnson* should have a Store there, and that you should have the Care of the Stores at *Shamokin,* and *John Harris*'s. As *George Croghan* is under Sir *William Johnson,* I wanted that he should appoint Mr. *Croghan* to keep the Store at *Bedford.*

*Then* Tokahaion, *a* Cayuga *Chief, spoke to the Governor as follows.*

*Brother* Onas, My Cousins, that live at *Wighalousin,* tell me, they went to the *Easton* Treaty to hear something about the Land Affair, between the Governor and *Teedyuscung;* these, my Cousins, went to the Governor, to enquire about their own Lands. The Governor made Answer to them, and told them, that he had bought their Land from their Uncles.—What they wanted to know about their Land is this, that if they found it was not sold by the *Six Nations,* they think they ought to be paid for it. And since my Cousins made this Complaint to the Governor, at *Easton,* they have asked me, whether I had sold the Land, or not. And I told them, that I did not know that I had sold any Lands belonging to my Cousins; but (speaking to the Governor) said, you know it, because you have Writings.

*He further added,*

You can tell whether you have bought the Land, or not; if it is not sold to you by the *Six Nations,* it still belongs to them; but I do not want to sell Land, that you have already bought.

The *Indians* having finished what they had to say, the Governor acquainted them, that *Thomas* King had promised him, the other Day, that they would deliver up all the Prisoners that were in their Camp, and that he understood some were there yet, and desired to know the Reason of their not being delivered up.

Thomas King *answered,*

*Brother,* I acknowledge to have said, I would deliver up all the Prisoners, and I thought it had been done, and that all were delivered up that remained in the Camp; but we have gone too far, in engaging to deliver up all the Prisoners in the *Indian* Country, that belong to the absent Warriors. However, we suppose they will be delivered up, and we will do our Endeavours that it shall be so, and will consult with those that have the Prisoners.

*Then* Kinderuntie, *the* Seneca *Warrior, spoke.*

*Brother,* There are yet two White Men in the Camp; one of them, though he came with us, yet it was not by our Consent; he would follow us; he belongs to a Warrior, that is gone to War against the *Cherokees,* and we had no Right to bring him, without the Warrior's Consent; you see him every Day; he is at Liberty. The other is a Deserter; he came among us of his own Accord; we informed Sir *William Johnson* of it, and Sir *William* said, that perhaps he might have misbehaved, and that we might keep him; perhaps he might learn the Language, and be of Service as an Interpreter, and that he might stay with us, if he would; he did not come to us as a Prisoner, and as he has his Liberty, you may talk with him, if you please.

*The Governor made Answer,*

That as to the Captive, he expected they would deliver him up; and desired that they would bring the Deserter to him To-morrow Morning, that he might speak with him.

*To which* Kinderuntie *replied,*

*Brother,* I cannot deliver up the Captive to you; he does not belong to me; he belongs, as I told you, to those that are gone to War; he came here of his own Accord; he followed me down, and if I should deliver him now, the Warriors would say that I had sold him, and that will make me ashamed; I therefore desire my Brother will not force me to deliver him at this Time, to make me ashamed. As to the Deserter, I will bring him to you at any Time.

The Governor concluded, by saying to them, that he would have them consider of this Matter in their Council again, and reflect seriously upon it, as he should have no Dependance on all they had already said, about restoring the Prisoners, unless they now delivered up this one to him.

The *Indians* then broke up, and went to their Camp.

*At a* CONFERENCE *with the Northern* Indians,
*held at* Lancaster, *on* Thursday, *the Twenty-sixth of* August, 1762.
PRESENT, *The Honourable* JAMES HAMILTON,
*Esquire, &c. &c. as before.*

THE Governor, first addressing himself to the *Minisink* Nation, spoke to them as follows.

*Brethren of the* Minisink *Nation,* You have, since I saw you, lost a great Man. With this String I condole with you, and share your Grief on that Occasion; and with this Stroud I cover his Grave, and desire you may mourn for him no longer.

*A String and Stroud.*

*Brethren,* By this String I desire you may consult among yourselves, and appoint a Man to sit in Council in his Place, which will be agreeable to me.

*A String.*

The Governor then, addressing himself to the *Six Nations,* returned the following Answer to the several Speeches made by *Thomas King,* the *Oneida* Chief.

*Brethren,* You have, according to the antient Custom of your Ancestors, upon my bidding you welcome, and cleaning you, performed the usual Ceremonies on like Occasions; with which I am well pleased, and return you Thanks.

*A large String.*

*Brethren,* (*Holding up the Belts and Strings that they gave*) By these Belts you have made me several Speeches, respecting my requesting you to use your Influence with your Nephews, and all other *Indian* Nations, to restore to us all our Flesh and Blood. I make no Doubt you have met with some Difficulties on that Head, as I am very well acquainted with the Manner in which you carry on War against one another, and that what Prisoners you take, you claim an absolute Property in, by adopting them into your own Nation, as soon as they bring them Home.

But, Brethren, the Case is quite different between you and us. We do not look upon you to have the same Sort of Right over our Flesh and Blood, as over your own. As we are of a different Colour from you, so we have different Customs. It is a constant Rule with us White People, that upon making of a Peace with those with whom we have been at War, the Prisoners on both Sides are faithfully delivered up. Besides, you may remember it was a positive Engagement between us, upon re-establishing the antient Chain of Friendship, that those Nations who had taken any of our People Prisoners, should deliver them all up; and this, Brethren, I must insist upon, as the only Means of burying every Thing that has passed between us. I thank you for the Influence you have used, and the Trouble you have taken, upon this Occasion; but we are informed, by such as have lately passed through the *Indian* Countries, that there yet remain a great many of our People, as Prisoners, in some of your Towns, particularly among our Brothers, the *Senecas.* It is, I suppose, as you say, that some of them may belong to the Warriors, who are gone to War against the Southern *Indians,* with whom you are always at War; but whether they belong to them, or any other People, we expect that you will acquaint them with your repeated Engagements, that they shall all be delivered up, and therefore that they will no longer continue unwilling to part with them.

*Brethren,* As to what you say about our Promises of paying you for our Flesh and Blood, you must have been mistaken; for I never either told you so, or sent you any such Message. If you have received any Messages to that Effect, they must have come from some other People. But I must be plain with you on this Subject, and tell you, that it is never our Custom to purchase our Flesh and Blood of any Nation whatsoever. But, Brethren, what I have told you, and what I now again tell you, is this, that for any Services you may have done, with any of the Nations, on that Account, or for any Trouble or Expence they may be at, in bringing them down to me, I will make you and them a suitable Satisfaction.

*Here gives three Belts, and a Bunch of Wampum.*

*Brethren,* As to what you say about making Servants of our Prisoners, we are entirely ignorant of it; we do no such Thing, but as soon as we receive them from your Hands, we deliver them up to their Parents and Relations, if they happen to be present, and if not, we cloath them, and take Care of them, till we can get an Opportunity of sending them to their Friends. They are our own Flesh and Blood, and we use them as tenderly as is in our Power; if any have been treated otherwise, it is owing to your not delivering them to me. We have, indeed, at the Instance of some of your own People, put the Prisoners into the Court-House, till we could take their Names, and be informed of the Places of their Abode; and as soon as we were told this, they were all cloathed, and forthwith sent along, with some good Persons to take Care of them, to their Habitations; therefore do not entertain any Notion that we make Servants or Slaves of them, and when you return Home, let all your Nations know that this is truly the Case, and that the Prisoners are at Liberty to go to their Relations, as soon as they are delivered up to us; or, if they have no Relations, they go into such Places where they can best get Employment, in order to maintain themselves.

*Brethren,* I think it my Duty to tell you, that such of our White Men who want to stay with you, are either Deserters from the Army, or have behaved ill amongst us, and were they to stay with you, they would be very apt to be very mischievous, and make ill Blood between us; we desire therefore you will not encourage them, but deliver all such up as you have amongst you; and if you place any Dependance upon them, either in Peace or War, they will certainly deceive you, as they have done us.

*A String.*

*Brethren,* It grieves me that any Occasion should have been administered to you, to observe to me, in so public a Manner, that there are others besides myself who concern themselves in Affairs of Government. If it be as you say, I must tell you, Brethren, that it is a great Presumption, and an high Infringement of the Rights of Government, for any Person whatsoever, within this Province, except by my special Order or Commission, to send or deliver Messages to you, or to any other Nations of *Indians,* or to treat with you, or them, on any public Matters.[6] I am the only Person intrusted by His Majesty, and the Proprietaries, with the Administration of public Affairs within this Province; and I desire you to take Notice, that in order to prevent any Thing of this Kind for the future, all Messengers I shall send to you shall be furnished with proper Credentials, and my Speeches in Writing, under the usual Seal; and if any Persons, *Indians* or others, should take upon them to deliver to you any Messages in my Name, unless they bring with them such Credentials as above mentioned, I desire you will pay no Regard to them, and acquaint me therewith.

*A Belt.*

*Brethren,* You acquaint me, that your Grandfathers advised you never to have any Difference with your Brethren, the *English.* It had been well you had constantly taken their Advice, but as you say the Evil Spirit got the better of your Understandings, and compelled you to strike us, you, the other Day, by this Belt of

Wampum, took the Hatchet out of my Head. It is possible, Brethren, that as you struck us, and obliged us to strike you, that you also have been hurt by us; I therefore, by this Belt, take the Hatchet out of your Heads.

*A Belt.*

*Brethren,* By this Belt I join with you in collecting all our and your Bones, wheresoever scattered, and in burying them, with the Hatchet, and do heap up Earth about the Roots of the great Tree in the *Oneida* Country, where they and the Hatchet are buried; so that the Smell thereof may never offend us hereafter.

*A Belt.*

*Brethren,* By this Belt you tell me that I am your elder Brother, and whenever you misbehave, you desire me to give you Advice. Brethren, my real Regard to your Welfare, as we are Brethren, will always induce me to take Notice of any Thing wrong that I shall observe in your Conduct; and by this Belt I stop your Ears against hearkening to any but myself.

*A Belt.*

*Brethren,* I join with you in dispersing the dark Clouds that have gathered together, during our Differences, and hid the Light from us, that we may see the Sky clearly, from Sun-rising to Sun-setting.

*A Belt.*

*Brethren,* By this String of Wampum you tell me, that some Foulness may have got into my Heart, through my Throat, and that with a Medicine, left you by your Fathers, you make it pass quite through my Body to the Ground, and bury it there. As you may have contracted the like Foulness, by this String of Wampum I thoroughly purge your Body, and remove every Defilement.

*A String.*

*Brethren,* You tell me, by this Belt, that there are only two Doors, the *Mohawks* and *Senecas,* to the *Onondagoe* Council, one to the Westward, the other to the Eastward, through one of which all the Messages to that Council should properly come.

As I understand, by this Information, that you expect that this Method should always be observed by me, I shall very readily conform to it, and think it a very prudent Establishment of yours, for the Dispatch and regular Transaction of Business.

*A Belt.*

*Brethren,* By this Belt you take Notice, that our old Council Fire is almost out, and not good, and that you now put to it the same good dry Wood, such as your Ancestors used, and make it burn as bright as ever. You add further, that your Entertainment has not been as good here as at *Easton.*

*Brethren,* I take it kind and friendly in you, that you have kindled up the old Fire; and by this Belt I heap up some good dry Wood, and join with you in putting it on the Council Fire, that it may burn as bright as ever. I am very sorry there should be any Cause of Complaint given you here, with Respect to your Accommodations; I took all the Pains in my Power that there should be none, and I hope now every Thing is made agreeable to you, with Respect to your good Accommodation.

*A Belt.*

*Brethren,* By this Belt you acquaint me, that your Warriors have assisted the Counsellors in making firm the good Work of Peace, and that without their Concurrence and Assistance the Counsellors can do nothing effectually.

*Brethren,* It gives me Pleasure to hear that your Warriors are united with you in Council, and are become unanimous in establishing the Peace, which has been so happily brought about. I am sensible of their Importance, and hope that the Harmony which now subsists may long continue; and I shall be ready to serve them, as well as you, as long as their future Conduct shall merit it.

*A Belt.*

*Brethren,* By this Belt you tell me, that the *English* have a longing Eye after your Land, and desire that we may not covet any more of your Land; and say further, that we have got all the Land belonging to the *Delawares,* and shall serve you as we have done them.

*Brethren,* It is true the *Delawares* had a large Tract of Land in this Province, bordering on the River *Delaware,* which the Proprietaries of this Province have from Time to Time, fairly purchased of them, and have honestly paid them for it, which they have acknowledged, in your Presence.

*Brethren,* By the same Belt you desire we will not think of making any more Purchase of Land, or settling your Lands by Force; for if we do, we shall push you back, and leave you no Land to live or hunt upon; and desire we would confine ourselves to *Nixhisaqua,* or *Mohonoy,* and settle no higher up.

*Brethren,* The Proprietaries of *Pennsylvania* have never forced a Purchase of Lands from any of their Brethren, the *Indians,* since they have owned this Province. It is very well known, that the Native *Indians* very readily sold their Lands to the Proprietaries, as soon as he arrived here in their Country, about Eighty Years ago. And about Thirty Years ago the *Six Nations,* observing greater Numbers of White People than those old Purchases could accommodate, voluntarily sold to the present Proprietaries some Lands, lying further West. And their Number still increasing, at *Albany,* in the Year 1754, they sold them more Lands, as far as the Limits of the Province to the West, to be bounded by a Line agreed upon to the Northward.

And let me remind you of their Kindness to you, in this Respect; for no sooner were they informed that you repented of this last Sale, than they immediately gave Orders to their Agents here, to execute a Release to you for all the Lands over the *Al-*

*legheny Hills,* which was accordingly done at *Easton,* in the Year 1758, in public Council; when a Draught of the Part of the Country, which the Proprietaries held, by the *Six Nations* Deed, on this Side the *Allegheny Hills,* was shewn to, and approved by, the *Six Nations,* some of whom are now present; and the Draught, and Copy of the Proprietary Release, were delivered in open Council to them, who returned their hearty Thanks to the Proprietaries for their Goodness. I hear those Chiefs put the Release and Draught into Sir *William Johnson*'s Hands, and desired him to keep it for them, together with many other Deeds and Papers, at the same Time. Now, Brethren, as no Time has been fixed for the running of the North Line, or Boundary of this last Purchase, I desire you to apply to Sir *William Johnson,* and whenever you and he shall think it necessary to run that Line, I shall always be ready to join with you; and until this be done, agreeable to your Deed, I shall not suffer any of my People to settle beyond it. By your Speech it appears to me, that you think the Line is fixed at *Mohonoy;* but by the Deed, which I have not brought with me, and so cannot now produce it, to the best of my Remembrance, the Line begins at a certain Mountain, by the River Side, about a Mile above the Mouth of *Mohony.* I must therefore desire, that none of your People be permitted to disturb any Persons within the Limits of that Purchase, till that Line be settled.

*A Belt.*

*Brethren,* By this String you desire me to give some Guns, telling me that you had already made this Request four Times.

*Brethren,* At the Conclusion of this Treaty I propose to make you a Present, Part of which will consist of some good Guns, which I hope will please you.

*Brethren,* I have heard attentively what you said to your Cousins, and to *Teedyuscung* in particular. Among other Things you say, you formerly kindled a Fire at *Shamokin,* for *Allumapes;* another at *Wyoming,* for the *Shawanese;* and others at *Wighalousin* and *Diahoga.* You say to *Teedyuscung,* that the *English* cast an evil Eye on the Lands at *Wyoming,* and that he is to watch that Fire, and if any White People come there, to tell them to go away; for that Land belongs to the *Six Nations.*

*Brethren,* Some of you may remember, that at the Treaty held last Year, at *Easton,* the *Six Nations* complained to me, that some *English* had settled upon their Lands, and desired me to assist them in preventing that Settlement, that they might not be wronged out of their Lands. They told me further, that they heard the Land had been sold; that the *Six Nations* never sold it, and that those who sold it stole it from them; that it was two *Tuscaroras,* one *Oneida,* and one *Mohawk,* who sold it, unknown to the *Six Nations.* To this Request I answered, that a Number of People, from *Connecticut* Government, had settled at a Place on the River *Delaware,* called *Cushietunck,* about Fifty Miles North of the *Blue Hills,* being the Settlement complained of, and claimed all the Lands from thence quite up to *Wyoming;* that I had sent Messengers to them, to inform them that those Lands belonged to the *Six Nations,* and ordered them to remove away; but they refused to do it, assuring me, by the Messengers, that they had purchased all those Lands of the *Six Nations,* and under that Pretence had a Right to hold them.

As there are now many more of the *Six Nations* present than were at *Easton* last Year, I again request you to tell me plainly, whether these Strangers are settled there by your Consent or not, and why no Measures have been taken, if, as some of you told me at *Easton,* the Lands were not sold by you, to oblige those private *Indians,* who stole the Land from you, to procure a Surrender of their unjust Deed, from the People to whom they have made it, that it might be brought into the *Onondagoe* Council, and there cancelled or destroyed.

*Upon which* Thomas King, *without consulting any of the other Chiefs, rose up and spoke.*

*Brother,* It is very well known that the Land was sold by the *Six Nations;* some are here now that sold that Land; it was sold for *Two Thousand Dollars,* but it was not sold by our Consent in public Council; it was as it were stolen from us. Some People said that my Name was to it, on which I went down immediately to *Connecticut,* to see whether it was or not, and found it was not. I brought a Paper back from *Connecticut,* which I shall shew to the Governor. Had I not gone down to *Connecticut,* the Lands would have been all settled up to *Wyoming,* as far as *Awicka,* Twelve Miles on this Side *Chenango.*

*Thomas King* being then asked, whether those Lands at *Cushietunck* were a Part of those Lands that were stolen from them? He answered, they had nothing to do with them; they belonged to the *Delawares.*

Then the Governor asked, whether the Lands above the Hills, and at *Cushietunck* in particular, belonged to the *Six Nations,* or to the *Delawares?* this was asked of all the *Six Nations* present, and the Governor desired they would all give an Answer to it, *Thomas King* having already said that those Lands belonged to the *Delawares.* They answered, that they would take it into Council, and give him an Answer in Writing.

Whereupon the Conference broke up for the present.

*At a* CONFERENCE *with the* Indians, *held at* Lancaster,
*on* Friday, *the Twenty-seventh of* August, 1762.
PRESENT, *The Honourable* JAMES HAMILTON,
*Esquire, &c. &c. as before.*

THE Governor continuing his Speeches to the *Six Nations,* spoke as follows.
*Brethren,* By this String I inform you, that a few Days since your Cousins, the Western *Indians,* applied to me about our Trade with them, and told me that we sold our Goods very dear, and desired we would sell them cheaper; on which I informed them that I had, for their Benefit, opened a large Store of Goods at *Pittsburgh,* and had appointed honest Men there to deal justly with them, and made no Doubt but they had done so; but that our Land Carriage was so long, and made the Expences so very

high, that we lost Money by the Trade every Year; and that I knew of no other Method, by which we could supply them cheaper, than by your suffering us to go up the Western Branch of the *Sasquehannah* River, with Boats or Canoes, and to build some small Store Houses, to put our Goods and Skins in, as we went up and came down that River. This Liberty I told them I would apply to you for, and I now desire you will be free, and tell me whether you will consent that we should build such Store Houses there, being unwilling to do any Thing of that Kind, without having first obtained your Appprobation, or to give you the least Reason to think we intend to settle any of the Lands there.

If you approve of this Proposal, I will send proper Persons to view that River, and to see how far Boats or Canoes can go up it; and I desire the People I shall send upon that Service may be under your Protection, and treated as your Friends, by any of your People they may happen to meet with in their Journey.

*A String.*

*Then* Kinderuntie, *the head Warrior of the* Seneca *Nation, suddenly rose up, and spoke as follows.*

*Brother* Onas, You have laid out two Roads already; one you told me was a good one, the other leads from *Potowmack,* and now you want another Road to go by Water; we cannot grant it to you, because our chief old Men are not here; we are chiefly Warriors here; I am almost as chief a Man as any among them, but we cannot grant it to you, because our chief Men are not present, and the Matter has not been consulted in Council. I give you this Answer now, because I have the Care of those Lands; but if it is agreed upon in our Council, that will be another Thing; but at present we deny you entirely.

*Brother,* You may remember you told me, when you was going to *Pittsburgh,* you would build a Fort against the *French;* and you told me that you wanted none of our Lands; our Cousins know this, and that you promised to go away as soon as you drove the *French* away, and yet you stay there, and build Houses, and make it stronger and stronger every Day; for this Reason we entirely deny your Request; you shall not have a Road this Way.

*A Belt.*

*To which the Governor answered,*

*Brethren,* This Request did not arise from me; I only mentioned it, in order to oblige your Cousins, the *Delawares,* who desired a Trade with us, and I did it that they might have their Goods cheaper; but this is an indifferent Matter to me; it particularly concerns your Cousins, the *Delawares,* and the Western *Indians;* and since the *Six Nations* disapprove of our going up and down the West Branch, and building Store Houses there, I shall say nothing further upon this Subject.

*To which the* Seneca *Chief made Answer,*

*Brother,* I am glad to hear you, as you say it did not come from you, but that it came from our Cousins; I thought it had been your own Proposal. I really quite wonder at my Cousins, that they did not tell me this; but since they have swallowed up all their own Land, and live to the Westward, I believe they are growing proud. The Lands do belong to me where they live; I conquered it with my Sword; but they are grown proud, and will, I suppose, not own us for their Uncles.[7]

The Governor answered, that if he expressed himself in such a Manner to them, as if the Application did come from himself, he was mistaken; for that he meant to express himself that he did it in Consequence of the *Delawares* desiring a Trade with us, and that our Goods might come cheaper to them, and that he knew of no other Method of rendering them so, but by Means of a Water Carriage; and therefore he told the *Delawares* that he would apply to their Uncles, the *Six Nations,* for Liberty to carry our Goods up the West Branch of *Sasquehannah;* and he desired that they should not think the *Delawares* in Fault, on this Account, as they did not propose this Method to him; and that no Blame should be imputed to them at all in this Affair; and that as he found it disagreeable to the *Six Nations,* he would say nothing further about it.

*The Governor then proceeded to speak to the* Six Nations *as follows.*

*Brethren,* By this Belt you desired, that as there was no War now between you and us, and the Fort at *Shamokin* stood upon your Warriors Path, the Soldiers might be removed from that Garrison; but that the Trading House might still continue, that your Hunters and Warriors might be supplied with Goods; and further desired to know what Prices we set upon our Goods.

*Brethren,* You must be sensible, that though an End be happily put to the War between the *Indians* and us, yet it still continues as warm as ever between us and the *French;* and therefore without His Majesty's express Orders, at whose Instance you acknowledge it was built, by your own Consent, I cannot remove the Soldiers from that Garrison. I shall give particular Directions to the Commanding Officer, that the Soldiers behave very well, both to your Warriors and Hunters, when they come there; and if the Warriors behave well on their Parts and keep sober, there can be no Differences between them.

*Brethren,* You further desire, by this Belt, that the Person who has the Care of the Provincial Store may be removed, and an honest Man put in his Place.

*Brethren,* The Agent at *Shamokin* has, so far as I know, supported the Character of an honest Man; but as it seems he is not agreeable to you, I will consult with the Gentlemen who are joined with me in the Direction of that Store House, when I return to *Philadelphia,* and give you an Answer at a proper Time.

As to the Trading House, it shall continue, for your Convenience and Accommodation; but it is not in my Power to fix any certain Price upon our Goods. You know we don't make the Goods ourselves; they are made in *England,* and the transporting them over the Seas is dangerous in War Time, and very expensive, so that they must come much dearer now than in Time of Peace, and their Prices change, as the Risque and Demand for them is greater or less; but I am told, that they are sold to you as cheap as they can be afforded, and cheaper than they can be purchased from private Traders, and Care will be taken that they be good in their Quality.

*A Belt.*

*Brother,* By this Belt you give it as your Opinion, that *John Harris*'s House, standing on your Warriors Path, would be a good Place for a Trading House, for the Accommodation of your Warriors and Hunters, and desire one may be erected there, and recommend *John Harris* to be Store-keeper.

*Brethren,* By the Relation you gave me at *Easton,* in 1758, when you was relating the Causes of the War, it appears that you were of Opinion, one of the principal Reasons which made you join the *French* against us, was owing in a great Measure to the ill Treatment your Warriors met with in *Virginia,* in those Places where your War Path passes through the settled Part of that Colony; and you have now desired me to write to the Governor of *Virginia,* that as there are Settlers on your War Path, whereby it is stopped, he would cause it to be opened.

Now, Brethren, I must acquaint you, that all the Way from *Harris*'s Ferry to *Potowmack,* the White People are settled very thick, so that should your Warriors now use that Path, frequent Differences between them and the Inhabitants might probably arise, by means whereof, the Peace so lately established between us may be endangered. And I must desire you, for this Reason, to use your best Interest with your Warriors, in case they are determined to go to War, that they would pursue the old War Path from *Shamokin,* which lies along the Foot of the *Allegheny Hills,* and which is the nearest Way they can go to their Enemies Country.

*A Belt.*

*Brethren,* As you tell me you intend to apply immediately to Sir *William Johnson,* to give Orders that the Warriors be supplied with Necessaries, through Mr. *Croghan,* at *Rays-Town,* I must refer you to him, that the same may be done in other of the King's Garrisons, along the War Path.

*Brethren,* As *John Harris*'s House is a great Deal out of the Way, if more Trading Houses shall hereafter be thought necessary than there are at present, which we shall consider of, we shall take Care to fix them at the most convenient Places, for the Accommodation of our *Indian* Brethren, and appoint honest Men to take the Direction of the Trade, who will deal justly and kindly with all the *Indians.*

*A Belt.*

*Brethren,* By this Belt you desire a Trading House may be erected on *Potowmack,* at *Daniel Cressip*'s House, and that he may have the Care of it, for the Supply of your Warriors, and that I will send your Request to the Governor of *Maryland.*

*Brethren,* Your Belt, and all you have said upon it, shall be carefully sent to Governor *Sharpe.*

*Brethren,* I shall also, agreeable to your Request, transmit your Belt, and what you have said upon it, to the Governor of *Virginia;* and I shall lose no Time in doing it, as your Warriors, you tell me, are now ready to set out.

*A String.*

*Brethren,* Some red Paint, or Vermilion, is provided for you, and it shall be delivered to you.

*Brethren,* Agreeable to your Request, the Persons whom I shall appoint to attend you, on your Return Home, will have Orders to furnish you with Provisions, as far as *Shamokin.* I have received several Complaints of great Mischief being done by the *Indians,* in their coming here, and therefore must insist upon it that you restrain your young Men from committing any further Violence, or from taking any Thing from the Inhabitants in their Return; for this must have a natural Tendency to raise ill Blood in the Minds of the People.

*A String.*

*Brethren,* The little Boy, *Kisheta's* Son, is, I hope, on his Way here, having sent for him to *Philadelphia.*

*Brethren,* Since you spoke to me, I am told *Samuel Curtis* is informed where his Daughter is, and if he pleases to go and see her, and desires my Passports, he shall be furnished with them.

*A String.*

*Brethren,* A Horse shall be delivered to *Tokahaion,* for the Use of his two Daughters.

*Brethren,* A Horse will likewise be given to *Robert White,* in Lieu of the one that died.

*Brethren,* As to the Application made by your Friends at *Wighalousin,* with respect to Lands they lay Claim to beyond the Mountains, I am surprized this should be mentioned to me by *Tokahaion,* after what passed at *Easton,* in the Year 1758, between me and the *Six Nations,* respecting those Lands. Their Deed to the Proprietaries for those Lands was then produced, and was acknowledged to have been executed by the *Six Nations,* some of whom were then present. They further added, that they had sold the Land in Question, and were honestly paid for it, and that the Land was theirs, and they would justify it; these were their Expressions. This being the Case, and we being unacquainted with any Rights they have, must refer them to you, and desire you will settle this Matter among yourselves.

*A String.*

*Brethren,* By this Belt you tell me, that your Grandfathers advised you to keep fast Hold of the Chain of Friendship, and that you, the *Mohawks, Oneidas, Senecas, Onondagoes, Cayugas,* and *Tuscaroras,* have brought about the Peace; that you have more Brothers, Friends and Allies to the Westward, as far as the Sun sets, so many that you cannot tell their Numbers; and in Behalf of them and yourselves, who now make up fourteen Nations; you make our old Friendship new again, and brighten the Covenant Chain.

*Brethren,* You know that when the Peace was concluded first between us, at *Easton,* as well as in several friendly Conferences held afterwards, we both of us took great Pains to send the Peace Belt among all your Nations, and among your Friends and Allies, to the most distant Parts; and we have heard you say with Pleasure, and we have ourselves likewise received Messages from several *Indian* Nations, that they were glad to hear we had made Peace together, and joined heartily in it.

*Brethren,* We thank you for renewing your old Friendship; we very heartily join with you in it, and in brightening the Covenant Chain, and confirm our Words with this Belt. When you return Home, we desire you will shew this Belt to your own People, and to all the Nations in your Alliance, and let them know how friendly your Brothers have received you; advise them not to hearken to any Stories that bad People may tell them, to our Prejudice; desire them to stop their Ears to all such Stories, and assure them that we shall, on all Occasions, preserve our Friendship with our *Indian* Brethren, and their Allies. And we hope, that both you and we shall be so careful as not to give the least Occasion of Difference, so long as the World lasts.

*A very large Peace Belt.*

*Brethren,* As I have now finished all my Business with you, I inform you, that as the good people of this Province think you may want some Cloathing, and other Necessaries, they have, from the Regard they have for you, put into my Hands a considerable Present of Goods, which I shall deliver to such Persons as you shall appoint to receive and divide them; and I desire, that in the dividing them you will pay particular Regard, and give an handsome Present to such *Indians* who have been at any Expence and Trouble in bringing down the Prisoners.

*Thomas King* desired that the Governor would stay a little longer, for that they had something further to say to him.

*Then the* Onondagoe *Chief,* Deogwanda, *rose up, and addressing himself to the Governor, said,*

*Brother* Onas, I mentioned to you, the other Day, my Desire that there should be a Store House kept at *John Harris*'s, and that he might have the Care of the Store for the Warriors. I desired, at the same Time, that the Road might be opened for the Warriors, to pass through the back Settlements to the Southern *Indians;* you know we are, and always have been at War with them, and I shall now begin to strike them. You told me, in Answer, that you thought it best that that Road should be stopt up, lest any Differences should arise between your People and our Warriors; and desired, if any Warriors did go to War, they would take the old Road that led to the Southward, under the Mountains; and I now tell you, that as you desired that Road should be stopt, it shall be so, and I will take the old Road. We don't now desire a Store

House should be kept at *John Harris*'s for the Warriors, but that he may be supplied with Provisions, and other Necessaries, for our Chiefs and old Men, as they pass to and fro about the good Work of Peace. We know *John Harris,* and he is known among all the *Indian* Nations, and we desire he may be the Man appointed for the Care of this Matter.

*A String.*

*At a* CONFERENCE *at Mr.* Slough*'s House, after the public Conferences.*
August 27, 1762.
PRESENT, *The Honourable* JAMES HAMILTON, *Esquire,*
Lieutenant-Governor, *&c.*
William Logan, Richard Peters, *Esquires.*

*KINDERUNTIE,* in Company with some other *Six Nation Indians,* having, agreeable to the Governor's Desire, brought *Peter Weese,* one of the Captives, mentioned to him in the old *Lutheran* Church; the Governor took *Peter* into a private Room from the *Indians,* to confer with him respecting his Inclination to stay among the *Indians,* lest he should be under any Fear of speaking his Mind freely in their Presence; when, after a free Conference, *Peter* desired he might not now be detained among the White People, but left to his Liberty to return with the *Indians,* and that on his Way he would call on his Brother, who lived near *Pittsburgh,* and speak with him, and return to the Governor in the Spring, and gave several Reasons for his staying with them this Winter. On which the Governor consented to his Request, and went with him to the *Indians;* and then acquainted the *Six Nation* Chiefs present, that as he had now consented that the Prisoner, *Peter Weese,* should stay among them, agreeable to his Inclination, and their Desire, he hoped they would be as honourable, on their Part, in delivering up the other Prisoner, who was a Deserter from the Army, and now in their Camp; and that they would do every Thing in their Power, on their Return to their own Country, to collect every Prisoner among them, and deliver them up faithfully, agreeable to their Promises.

Kinderuntie *answered.*

That he was well pleased with what the Governor had done; that he would now deliver up the Deserter to him, and that he should make it his particular Business, when he returned Home, to make a thorough Search every where in their Towns for all the Prisoners that are among them that the Governor might rely upon these Endeavours, and that as soon as he had done this he would faithfully deliver them all up, and use his Interest with all others to do the same.

The Deserter was brought soon after to the Governor, who assured him of his receiving him with Kindness, and he would grant him his Protection, if he would consent to come among the *English.* He answered, that as he confided in the Governor's Assurances, he was very willing to return among the *English* again, and if he would grant him a Pass, he would go down into *Maryland* to his Parents and Relations there.

Kinderuntie *then said,*

*Brother,* As both you and we are in a great Hurry to have the Business of the Treaty finished, that we may all return Home, I shall not detain you; and shall only at this Time request you to grant to *Totiniontonah* a Rifle Gun, of your own Make, and a Saddle for my Friend, this young Man here.

*A String.*

The Governor said, he would consider of what they said, and return them an Answer To-morrow Morning; and should be glad at that Time to see all the chief Men of the *Six Nations,* that he might deliver them the Presents, and take his Leave of them, as it is now growing late.

*SATURDAY, the Twenty-eighth of* August, 1762.

EARLY in the Morning *Deogwanda* and *Kinderuntie* waited on the Governor, at his Lodgings, and told him, that they had agreed in Council not to say any Thing further about Lands; but would take what the Governor had said to them on *Thursday,* respecting the Lands above the Hills, and at *Cushietunck,* and also what he said the next Day, respecting the Lands claimed by the *Minisink Indians,* at *Wighalousin,* to the *Onondagoe* Council, to be there considered.

On the same Day, in the Afternoon, the following *Indians* waited on the Governor, at his Lodgings, *viz.*

PRESENT, *Kinderuntie,* the *Seneca* Chief, *Totiniontonah,* a *Cayuga,*
*John Shakalamy,* and two *Seneca* Warriors;
William Logan, Richard Peters, Esquires.

Who complain against *Nathaniel Holland,* at *Fort-Augusta,* as a Man who always treats the *Indians* who come there with ill Usage, and bad Language, insomuch that they are very often so provoked as to do him Violence; and as the public Business is now over, they intreat the Governor to remove him, and put a more quiet Man in his Place. They further say, that as the Governor has acquainted them that the War has occasioned a Rise in the Price of Goods, they hope the Governor will give Orders that they may be paid a higher Price for their Skins and Furs in Proportion.

The Governor made Answer, that he would take this Matter into Consideration, and do in it whatever was thought reasonable; and further acquainted them, that the small Presents they had requested of him the Day before should be granted them.

*AUGUST the Twenty-ninth.* Sunday *Morning.*

THE Governor having ordered all the Goods intended as a Present to the *Six Nation Indians* to be taken to Mr. *Hambright's* Malt-House, and appointed this Morning for those *Indians* to meet him there, to receive them; they accordingly came, when being seated, and the Goods divided into four different Parcels, in Proportion to the Numbers of the different Tribes, the Governor, in the Presence of *William Logan,* Esq; Member of the Council, *Joseph Fox, Samuel Rhoads,* Esquires, of the Assembly, and some Gentlemen from *Philadelphia,* acquainted them that, agreeable to what he told them on *Friday* last, he had now provided a handsome Present of Goods, and desired they would accept of them, as a Mark of the Affection and Regard of the good People of this Province for them; and having laid aside a Parcel of the same, to a considerable Value, by themselves, he told the *Indians,* that that particular Parcel was to be divided among such *Indians* as had been at any Expence or Trouble in bringing down the Captives.

The Governor then delivered the Goods, amounting to about *Eight Hundred Pounds,* and taking his Leave of the *Indians,* left them to divide them among themselves, as they should think proper.

*The END*[8]

1. This list makes clear that the northern Indians referred to in the treaty's title are the League and their allies or adoptees, and that the western Indians are the Ohio Lenapes and their allies.

2. This contradiction proves the preceding analogy somewhat false. The British "prisoners" were not considered prisoners in the Indian nations where they resided, but adoptees. They were not confined in jails or otherwise limited indefinitely in their freedom of mobility, though this may have been the case upon their initial capture.

3. In this context, a fire means a place to live rather than a council fire, or place of negotiation between two or more nations.

4. Given that Thomas King had been accused in the previous treaty of 1761 of being one of the men who illegally sold land to the Connecticut individuals settling in the Wyoming region, one might infer that King had correctly learned of a plan by the eastern Lenapes to assassinate him. However, there appears to be no independent evidence to clarify this accusation regarding the poison. King will later deny the charge of selling the land.

5. Comparing this paragraph to the 1744 offer by Virginia to educate Iroquois boys, it seems that Keisheta made this decision on his own, whereas the offer extended by Virginia and rejected by the League would have been a decision of confederacy policy with further reaching implications.

6. It appears that the Governor suspects the Quakers in this matter.

7. It is unclear why the Lenapes are sometimes referred to as nephews by the League spokespersons and sometimes as cousins. This practice can be seen in these treaties as early as 1742.

8. Franklin and David Hall dissolved their partnership in 1766. Pennsylvania was involved in at least three more treaties with the League: one at Fort Pitt in April–May 1768 and two at Fort Stanwix in October–November 1768 and October 1784.

## GLOSSARY OF PERSONS AND GROUPS MENTIONED IN THE TREATIES

*(listed in order of appearance)*

### First Mentioned in the 1736 Treaty

Conrad Weiser: The main interpreter and ambassador between Pennsylvania and the Iroquois League nations between 1731 and 1760. Weiser and his parents were Palatine Germans who first settled in the Schoharie Valley near Mohawk country in New York colony on a tract that four Mohawk ambassadors to England had given to Queen Anne in 1710. He had learned Mohawk as a youth before relocating to the Tulpehocken Valley in Pennsylvania.

Thomas Penn: One of the second Proprietors of Pennsylvania. Thomas was the second son of William Penn (*Brother Onas*), the first Proprietor of Pennsylvania, by his second wife, Hannah Callowhill. William Penn's sons John, Thomas, and Richard inherited his estate because their father disinherited William Penn Jr., his oldest son by his first wife, Gulielma Springett. Thomas Penn took an active role in Pennsylvania affairs despite being an absentee landlord for much of his tenure. Richard Peters kept him informed through their correspondence. At first patronized by Thomas Penn, Franklin acquired a great contempt for him during his diplomatic mission to England to unravel the Walking Purchase deceit. The Indians addressed Penn and the Penn sons as *Brother Onas. Onas* means *feather;* it is a translation of the last name, which sounds like pen.

James Logan: Secretary to William Penn from 1699 until his death in 1718, Logan continued as Pennsylvania Secretary until Thomas Penn removed him in 1732 for embezzling from William Penn and buying land directly from Lenapes, who were obliged by treaty to sell only to the proprietors. Logan was thickly involved in the Indian trade and in speculation of lands that he controlled for the Penns by proxy.

Shikellamy: Also known as Onkiswathetami, Swatana, Ungquaterughiathe. Shikellamy was a French national who had been captured and adopted into the Oneida nation.

He served as a liaison between the League and the Shawnees and as the latter's nominal "supervisor," though how much authority this position entailed is debatable. He may have acted more as a protector or speaker in international affairs. He helped Logan and Weiser craft the alliance between the League and Pennsylvania.

William Penn: Also referred to as *Brother Onas.* The Proprietor of Pennsylvania from 1681 until 1718. A Quaker, he was renowned for his honesty and fairness in dealing with the Indian nations who occupied the land that fell within the chartered borders of Pennsylvania. He established Pennsylvania as a colony where freedom of religion was guaranteed (though, ironically, after his death, Quakers became one object of religious persecution) and where the people had the right to representation in an elected assembly.

Great Council at Onondaga: The Iroquois Confederacy met in the middle nation of the confederacy. The location of this council fire was near present-day Syracuse, New York.

Civility: A Conestoga chief in 1721 who appears to have had a vexed, and possibly antagonistic, relationship with the League. He informed William Logan that the Senecas were unhappy with Pennsylvania's squatters on the Susquehanna.

## First Mentioned in the 1742 Treaty

George Thomas: Lieutenant Governor of Pennsylvania from 1738 to 1747. Thomas was instrumental in enforcing Iroquois prerogative over the Lenapes during and after the first Walking Purchase controversy.

Canasatego: A speaker for the Iroquois League at the treaties of 1742, 1744, and 1745. Canasatego may have been a hereditary chief of the League, a chief of the Onondaga nation, or simply a speaker for the chiefs of the League, the nation, or both. He had enormous influence during the period from 1742 until 1750, when he was apparently assassinated for political reasons.

Olumapies: Also known as Sassoonan. A chief of the Tulpehocken Lenapes. Politically manipulated by James Logan, he was a key signatory to a series of land deals that dispossessed these Lenapes of their lands. In 1741, he attempted to appoint the less cooperative Pisquetomen as his successor, after having killed a young man whom Logan was trying to groom for the same position.

Pishquiton: Possibly a variant spelling of Pisquetomen. Also recorded as Pisquitom. Also spelled Pisquitomen. Brother of Shingas, Beaver, and Nenatchehan. Originally a Tulpehocken Lenape who was his uncle Olumapies's chosen successor, he relocated to the Ohio from Shamokin after that line of succession was frustrated by Logan, Weiser, and Shickellamy's refusal to acknowledge him. One of the signatories to the release of the Lebanon Valley in September 1732, but also a leader of the Lenape resistance to English and French encroachment in the Ohio. In the summer of 1758, he and Keekyuscung arrived in Teedyscung's town at Wyoming to make overtures to a peace that they had been hearing about by rumor. He and Frederick Post went back to the Ohio to arrange the Easton conference of October 1758. His name means "he that keeps on though it is getting dark." Also, a translator for Nutimus at some treaties.

Nutimus: A chief of the Forks Lenapes and one of those whose land was stolen as a result of the Walking Purchase. Nutimus helped stage a resistance to that land fraud until the League-Pennsylvania alliance of 1742 quelled it.

## First Mentioned in the 1744 Treaty

Thomas Lee: A commissioner for Virginia, Lee was the manager of Virginia's Fairfax estate and architect of the plan to gain the Ohio Valley for Virginia by "release" from the League. Lee corresponded with Weiser about the government, religion, and social mores of the League and wished to unite all the English colonies and the League in a common alliance.

Edmund Jennings: A commissioner for Maryland with whom Weiser also corresponded, along with Thomas Lee, regarding the League's structure and culture.

Tachanoontia: Also spelled Tagunhuntee, Tocanuntie, Tachanuntie, Takanuntie. Also known as the Black Prince. An Onondaga whom Wallace reports was a chief of major influence without whom the French would not treat. Apparently, Tachanoontia was about sixty years old in 1744. He was a great warrior and had tattooed multiple designs on his chest with gunpowder, perhaps a record of those war deeds or of visions.

Conoy-uch-such-roona: Probably the Conoys. The other tribal names—Coch-now-was-roonan, Tohoa-irough-roonan, Connutskin-ough-roona, and Sachdagugh-roonaw—remain somewhat obscure to the modern scholar. *Roona-* is an Iroquoian suffix designating a people. In Mohawk, the word for men is *rononkwe.*

Tuscarroraws: The Tuscaroras, or Sixth Nation of the Iroquois League. They became incorporated into the League by the 1730s after having become refugees of the colonial trade wars of the Carolinas, where they were residing upon contact.

John Armstrong: A trader among the Lenapes who, along with traders Woodward Arnold and James Smith, was killed by a Lenape man named Mushemeelin on the Juniata River. Armstrong stole the horse of Mushemeelin's wife after holding it as collateral for a trading debt that he represented fraudulently upon Mushemeelin's attempt to repay him.

Catawbas: A tribal nation residing in what is now the borderland between North and South Carolina near Charlotte. In 1751, there were seven towns and upwards of two thousand people. The Iroquois League was engaged in ongoing conflicts with them throughout the century, interrupted only occasionally by peace efforts. They were allies of the English in the Tuscarora War. The Catawbas are speakers of a Siouan language (distantly related to Iroquoian languages).

Thomas Cressap: A Virginia trader and a partner in the Ohio Company of Virginia. He and Hugh Parker ran a storehouse for the company at Wills Creek (today's Cumberland, Maryland).

Gachradodow: A Cayuga speaker and possibly a chief of the League, of whom little else is known outside the Iroquois oral tradition. He assisted Weiser in the 1754 Albany Purchase and was paid one hundred pieces of eight, or forty pounds.

Conoys: A tribal nation of Algonquin language family speakers who lived between the Potomac River and Chesapeake Bay at the time of contact with the English. Sometimes referred to as the Piscataways. They were adopted into the League as a result of pressures from the Susquehannock-Maryland alliance and conflict.

Praying Indians of Canada: This designation could refer to many different groups residing near or among the French. Its use in these treaties is confined to the groups at Caughnawaga, Akwesasne, and possibly Oka/Kanesatake (all in modern-day Quebec, Ontario, and far northern New York), several of whom were Mohawks or others of the Six Nations.

## First Mentioned in the 1745 Treaty

Roger Wolcot(t): Lieutenant Governor of Connecticut in 1741 and Governor in 1754 when Connecticut purchased land from the League in a deal that they subsequently disavowed.

William Shirley: Governor of Massachusetts. In March 1755, Franklin responded to Shirley's request to Pennsylvania for military support for Massachusetts by getting the Assembly to go around the governor (Morris). Shirley was a rival of William Johnson's. He became commander in chief of the British land forces in North America in late 1755. He used John Henry Lydius, the man who purchased lands from the Iroquois in 1754 under Pennsylvania's nose, as one of his agents. He was replaced in 1756 by his rival, Thomas Pownall, an ally of William Pitt's.

Peter Chartier: A crossblood Shawnee trader who led some Ohio Shawnees on an attack against the British traders in the Ohio in 1745. His Euramerican father, Martin Chartier, had been a trader for James Logan. Logan alienated Peter after his father's death in 1718 by making him responsible for the latter's debts, seizing his property, and evicting him from his home. Peter Chartier subsequently had established a trading post at Paxtang.

## First Mentioned in the 1747 Treaty

Benjamin Shoemaker: A Quaker member of the Pennsylvania Council during the time when Teedyuscung's complaints arose, and who was deliberately excluded from Council decisions on the matter.

Joseph Turner: William Allen's business partner and a trustee of Pennsylvania's German schools with Allen, Peters, Franklin, and Weiser. Allen was one of the indirect beneficiaries of the Walking Purchase and a patron of Franklin's.

William Logan: A Quaker member of the Pennsylvania Council during the time when Teedyuscung's complaints arose, and who was absent from Council decisions on the matter. Son to James Logan. Cousin to Israel Pemberton, but severe tension developed between them over the Walking Purchase matter and Logan's perceived complicity with the Penns' placemen. William Logan had represented his incapacitated father and the Penns in a meeting with Nutimus in October 1734.

John Harris: The man for whom Harris' Ferry, now Harrisburg, was named, and an intelligence informant for Weiser during the Lenape war.

George Croghan: A trader of Irish origin who established a trading site at Cuyahoga (Cleveland) in 1744. He became influential with many Ohio Indians despite his debts and poor reputation among many Pennsylvanians. French raids destroyed his trading business in 1753. He was appointed as William Johnson's deputy in 1756 and continued in that position until the early 1770s.

## First Mentioned in the 1748 Treaty

Andrew Montour: Also known as Sattelihu, Eghuisera, and possibly as Henry Montour. A crossblood (French-Iroquois) interpreter for the Iroquois, Lenapes, Shawnees, and Miamis at several treaties and meetings. The multilingual Montour also knew both French and English. Virginia bribed him at the 1752 Logstown treaty to work in their interest while nominally Pennsylvania's interpreter. In 1753, he and Croghan diverted presents intended for the Ohio Indians into their own private stores. Some believe he was a member of the Onondaga Council of the Confederacy. Others have him as a member of the Onondaga Council *for the Ohio Indians.* The Montour family was well known in Pennsylvania, though not always favorably.

Scarouady: Also spelled Scarrowyady, Scarroyady. Also known as Monacotoocha. An Oneida who shared with Tanaghrisson responsibility for some of Shikellamy's duties after his death in 1748, particularly "supervision" of the Ohio Shawnees.

Neucheconno: Also spelled Newcheconner. Chief of the Shawnees. Though it appears that he turned against the British in the 1740s, he was responsible for informing them of how the Shawnees had turned away the 1726 invitation of the League to join in a war upon them.

Kekewatcheky: Also spelled Cackewatcheka, Catchcawatsiky. Chief of the Shawnees whose people had lived at the Forks and the Minisink before moving to Wyoming and then Ohio. Maintained friendship with Weiser and with Pennsylvania in general.

## First Mentioned in the 1753 Treaty

James Hamilton: Lieutenant Governor of Pennsylvania from 1748 to 1754 and 1759 to 1763. An advocate of intercolonial union and joint reconciliation of the colonies with the Indians. Defended Pennsylvania against Connecticut's incursions. A supporter of the Penns.

Richard Peters: Pennsylvania Secretary and one of Thomas Penn's most faithful informants and allies. An Anglican minister. The minutes that Peters wrote for the 1756, 1757, and 1758 treaties are cautionary examples of how these treaties cannot be relied upon as accurate renditions of history. Though Peters often sowed the seeds of suspicion over Franklin's power with Penn, he also described Franklin's virtue and honesty as uncorrupted.

Isaac Norris Jr.: The Speaker of the Pennsylvania Assembly who appointed Franklin and Israel Pemberton to the Indian Affairs committee that uncovered the imbalance in monetary support for Indian expenses between the Penns and the people of Pennsylvania. A frequent correspondent of Franklin's during his antiproprietary lobbying in England and leader of the Quaker party.

Half King (Tanaghrisson): A Catawba by birth who had been adopted into the Seneca nation at a young age. He represented the Onondaga council to the Ohio Indians of several nations. In 1752, he nominally "appointed" Shingas as chief of the Lenapes by authorization from the Six Nations, but Shingas had already been selected by the Lenapes as their chief without permission from the League.

Guest: Christopher Gist. An agent for Virginia and for the Ohio Company of Virginia.

William Trent: A captain in the British forces. One of those responsible, in 1763, for deliberately presenting to Shingas, Beaver, and other Ohio Lenape chiefs blankets that they knew were contaminated with smallpox. Shingas and Pisquetomen are believed to have died as a result of the germ warfare, which effectively crippled resistance to the illicit takeover of the Ohio by the British.

Michael Taaf(e) and Robert Callender: Two traders among the Indians who were associates of George Croghan.

Cayanguileguoa: Also spelled Cayenquiragoa. Also known as Jonathan Cayenquiloquoa. A Mohawk orator and Weiser's adoptive brother.

William Fairfax: A commissioner for Virginia at the 1753 Winchester conference that preceded the 1753 Carlisle conference.

Outawas: The Ottawa Indians. Allied with the French through much of the eighteenth century until the end of the Seven Years' War. They are Algonquin language family speakers who lived north of Lake Ontario upon contact. Trade wars with the League in the seventeenth century pushed them into Michigan, Wisconsin, and northern Illinois, though they may have partially reoccupied the northern territory, with Ojibwa help, after 1675. The Ottawas were part of the Covenant Chain with Great Britain in 1710 and again in 1760 and traded with the League during this century, indicating their independence from France despite their military alliances between these dates.

Cheepaways: Usually spelled Chippewa. The Ojibwa Indians, who were allied with the French through much of the eighteenth century until the end of the Seven Years' War. They are Algonquin language family speakers who lived north of Lake Huron and north, south, and west of Lake Superior upon contact. Though not directly involved in the Great Lakes trade wars of the early seventeenth century, they helped the Ottawas and other nations allied with the French to push the Five Nations back below Lake Ontario and to the margins of Lake Erie.

Caghnawagas: The Caughnawagas. See Praying Indians of Canada, above.

Adirondacks: An unidentified nation apparently living in the Adirondack mountains and allied to the League.

Governor Dunwiddie: Robert Dinwiddie, Lieutenant Governor of Virginia and a partner in the Ohio Company of Virginia, who likely gained his post through the influence of the company and who consistently maintained their interest in his official capacity. He commissioned George Washington in 1753 to warn the French out of Ohio.

## First Mentioned in the July 1756 Treaty

Newcastle: Sometimes Captain Newcastle. Also known as Kanuksusy, Cassiowea. Son of a woman known as Queen Allaquippa (possibly a clan matron, possibly the Jigonsase of the Senecas). A war chief of the Senecas and one of the few Indians who assisted Braddock at the battle of the Monongahela. He was appointed by the Six Nations to transact any business at the 1756 meeting that did not concern the Lenapes. He made it clear that Teedyuscung was empowered to act on behalf of his own group of Lenapes, though the two appear to have been in dispute over this point. He withdrew that authorization before the November 1756 conference.

Newcastle acted as an "agent" for Pennsylvania along with Teedyuscung. He died from smallpox in late 1756. Also, a Quaker and favorably disposed toward the Quaker peace contingent.

Jagrea: Also known as Satacaroyies. A Mohawk, who was Scarouady's son-in-law, he acted as a messenger for Pennsylvania during the peace negotiations. He was murdered by a Conestoga man named Bill Sock in 1758, possibly for refusing to attack the English.

William Locquies: A Lenape who acted as a messenger for Pennsylvania during the peace negotiations.

Sir William Johnson: A merchant and plantation owner of Irish origin who came to New York colony in 1738. He was very influential among the Mohawks. He served as New York's agent for Indian affairs until 1751. In 1755, General William Braddock commissioned him to be royal superintendent of Indian affairs. He was one of the most powerful men in the colonies throughout the middle of the eighteenth century.

Paxinosa: A Shawnee who was chief man at Wyoming. In 1754, he and Teedyuscung helped carry a message from the Six Nations to the Indians at the Moravian mission of Gnadenhutten demanding that they move to Wyoming. He and the families of thirty warriors (Shawnee and Lenape) remained neutral during the Lenape war with Pennsylvania.

Aroas: Also known as Silver Heels. A Seneca warrior and one of the few Indians who assisted Braddock at the battle of the Monongahela.

Mr. Spangenberg: Bishop Augustus Gottlieb Spangenberg. A German-born Moravian who came to Pennsylvania in 1735 and stayed until 1762. A friend and correspondent of Franklin's who admired his common sense and leadership. Also a friend of Weiser's.

Teedyuscung: Leader of the eastern Lenapes during the 1750s and 1760s. Died by political assassination on the part of Connecticut settlers in 1763.

Robert Hunter Morris: Lieutenant Governor of Pennsylvania who was in league with Thomas Penn and lied to General Braddock about the Assembly's willingness to grant moneys in support of the army. He turned down a Lenape request for arms in the summer of 1755 without asking the Assembly for support. In April 1756, he declared war on the Lenapes at the advice of the Assembly's commissioners, angering New York, which was working toward a peace conference. Quaker protest forced him to rescind his scalp bounties. In June 1755, Franklin described him as "the rashest and most indiscreet Governor that I have known."

Joseph Fox: A Quaker member of the Pennsylvania Assembly who with Pemberton,

Hughes, Franklin, and Galloway was very involved in exposing the Penns' duplicity with the Lenapes over the Walking Purchase. He was disowned by the Quakers during the Lenape war for advocating military defense.

John Hughes: A Quaker member of the Pennsylvania Assembly who with Pemberton, Fox, Franklin, and Galloway was very involved in exposing the Penns' duplicity with the Lenapes over the Walking Purchase.

William Edmonds: A Moravian who acted as intermediary between Governor Denny and Teedyuscung in 1757. A "constant companion" of Franklin's "during the troubles in Northampton" County.

## First Mentioned in the November 1756 Treaty

William Denny: Lieutenant Governor of Pennsylvania succeeding Morris, who stepped down after the scalp bounty controversy. A protégé of the Duke of Cumberland, Thomas Penn appointed him upon the duke's advice.

William Masters: A colleague of Franklin's and an Anglican member of the Assembly. A trustee of the Academy of Philadelphia.

Major (William) Parsons: An old friend of Franklin's and a partner in his Junto, as well as a neighbor of Weiser's, whom he helped fight against Connecticut's purchase of the Wyoming lands. Member of the Pennsylvania Assembly and advocate for the proprietary party.

Moses Tattamy: A Presbyterian Forks Lenape interpreter who bought back from the Penns the lands they had purchased from his family. His testimony regarding the Walking Purchase and Quaker-Lenape interactions during its public airing has helped twentieth-century historians piece together the actual events as against proprietary propaganda.

## First Mentioned in the Lancaster 1757 Treaty

Reverend John Elder: A Presbyterian minister in Paxton.

Captain Thomas McKee: A trader and interpreter from near Big Island (seventy miles above Shamokin), from Paxton, and from Hunter's Fort. He signed an affidavit with Weiser in early August 1757 that denied that Teedyuscung represented the eastern Lenapes faithfully. McKee had been shot in the hand during the October 1755 violence. In 1744, he had been involved in the search for John Armstrong's body and earlier had informed Pennsylvania about the skirmish between Six Nations Indians and Virginians.

James Armstrong: A justice from Paxton, possibly related to John Armstrong.

William Prentup: A smith and interpreter who lived among the Onondaga-Tuscarora community at Ganasaraga, and who tended to be pro-English and anti-French.

Tiahansorea: This may be Teiorenhsere or Little Abraham. See Little Abraham entry below.

Cannadagaughia: Possibly Canadagaye, a Mohawk leader questioned in 1745 about rumors being spread among his people and refusing to answer in private forum.

Thomas King: Also known as Sagughsuniunt and probably the variant Seguchsonyont (1758). An Oneida whom the Onondaga Council used as a speaker and also as a messenger in the attempt to remove Connecticut settlers from the Wyoming.

Thomas Evans: Teedyuscung's half-brother.

Mr. Shippen: Probably Edward Shippen, a trading partner of the late James Logan, who had one of the biggest fur trade businesses in the province. He was father-in-law of James Burd, the commander at Fort Augusta, after Weiser stepped down in 1758.

Mr. Thompson: This is probably Charles Thomson. See below.

Little Abraham: A speaker for the League from the Mohawk nation who resisted land encroachments. Also a warrior during the Seven Years' War. Nephew of Hendrick through his father.

Joseph Galloway: The son of a Maryland landowner who had moved to Philadelphia as a youth. He was related to both the Shippens and the Pembertons. He was married to the daughter of a former speaker of the Assembly, Lawrence Growdon. He was a strong ally and frequent correspondent of Franklin's, especially after Franklin went to England for his anti-proprietary activities. He was speaker of the Assembly from 1766 to 1775. He presented a plan of union to the First Continental Congress that was modeled upon Franklin's Albany Plan of Union from 1754. His plan, which was not a plan for independence from England, was rejected, and Galloway eventually fled to England as a Loyalist.

Anugh Kary Tany Tionen Hokorowy: By process of elimination using a reference in Wallace to the Onondaga's "absent Brother Oughcarrydawy dionen Horarrawe," I determined tentatively that this name refers to the Senecas. During a 1743 meeting with the Council of the United Nations, Weiser heard this phrase. At the time, representatives of all the nations of the confederacy had arrived, except for the Senecas. Because they are the westernmost nation and most involved in Ohio affairs, this acknowledgment of them as the Lenape's uncles makes sense. Wallace further specifies in his index that Ounghcarrydawy signifies the Doorkeepers of the Snipe Clan, while Dyionenhogaron signifies the Doorkeepers of the Wolf Clan, and that the names together name the Seneca nation when in council. The

Senecas were designated the keepers of the western door of the longhouse when the League was created. Diplomatic messages were supposed to travel through them or through the Mohawks toward Onondaga.

Colonel John Stanwix: A British army officer with whom Israel Pemberton exerted his influence in order to move peace proceedings along.

## First Mentioned in the Easton 1757 Treaty

Wename: Wename is a variant spelling for Unami. It appears that by naming the Lenopi, Wename, and Munsey as nations, these treaty minutes mean to show that all three of the near contemporary groupings of Lenapes were represented in some way: the Unalimi, or people up the river (probably the Forks Lenape), referred to as Lenopi; the Unami, or people down the river (probably the Tulpehocken Lenape), referred to as Wename; and the Munsee Lenape, or people of the stony country. The Unalachtigo, or people near the ocean, had already been incorporated into other groupings.

Tiawco/Nanticokes: A tribal nation of Algonquin language family speakers who lived south of the Lenapes on the shores of Chesapeake Bay and the Atlantic Ocean at the time of contact. They relocated to the Susquehanna starting around 1722 and while being incorporated into the League between around 1747 and 1756, living first along the Juniata, then at Wyoming, and finally at Otseningo.

Daniel Roberdeau: An Anglican (or possibly Huguenot) member of the Pennsylvania Assembly who replaced one of the outgoing pacifist Quakers and whose character was falsely attacked by anti-Quaker and anti-Catholic propagandist William Smith.

Charles Thomson: Teedyuscung's clerk, one of the official writers of treaty minutes for the province, and the author of *An Enquiry into the Causes of the Alienation of the Delawares and Shawanese Indians* (1759). This pamphlet exposed the Penns' dealings in the Walking Purchase and the other controversial land sales of the mid-1700s. He was a Presbyterian teacher at the Friends' school. Also, Secretary of Congress during the American Revolution and a long-term friend of Franklin's.

Jacob Duché: A scribe working with Peters to keep the Walking Purchase facts from the public.

Laboughpeton/Lepaghpetund: Probably Lappachpitton, Lappapitton, whom Weiser used to try to prove that Teedyuscung was dwelling on land matters to the dissatisfaction of the other members of his delegation. In 1732, he, Olumapies, Pisquetomen, and others had signed away the Lebanon Valley to the Penns. In 1747, Weiser had tried unsuccessfully to appoint the man chief, to succeed Olumapies, over the Tulpehocken Lenapes, against their will.

Samuel Evans: Teedyuscung's half-brother.

Abraham: Also known as Shebosh, Mammatuckan. The chief of the Mahicans who with Teedyuscung in 1754 had relocated sixty-five to seventy Lenapes from Gnadenhutten to Wyoming.

## First Mentioned in the 1758 Treaty

Tuteloes: The Tutelos lived in the mountain regions of present-day Virginia near nations such as the Saponi, Manahoac, and Monacan. They are Siouan language family speakers of Catawban ancestry who were adopted into the League through the Cayugas around 1753. It is conceivable that this nation is one of those unidentified nations named during the 1744 treaty.

Chugnuts: These are probably Nanticoke-Conoy who were residing at a place called Chugnut (now Vestal) in southern New York near Owego and Chenango on the eastern branch of the Susquehanna River.

Wapingers, or Pumptons: A tribal nation of Algonquin language family speakers related to the Mahicans. They lived around present-day New York City and northward (near the Munsee Lenape) at the time of contact.

Lawrence Growdon: Father-in-law to Joseph Galloway and first a member of the Council in 1747, he had also been a speaker of the Assembly.

Charles Read: A New Jersey commissioner described by Peters as a "tool of I.P." or Israel Pemberton. He helped Pemberton pressure Denny through Governor Bernard. He was Pemberton's cousin.

Nichas, or Karaghtadie: Also spelled Karaghialalie, Karochyaktatty. A Mohawk chief, father-in-law to George Croghan, who was instrumental in the attempt to undermine Teedyuscung's authority in international relations. Nichas and Tagashata were leaders of "two mutually distrustful factions" within the League.

Tokaaion: Also spelled Tokaaio, Tokahaio, Tokahaion. A Cayuga chief who reportedly helped inform Weiser that Tagashata had participated in the Pennsylvania hostilities with the Lenapes, but who appears to have maintained his independence from the proprietary faction quite openly.

Tagashata, or Segachsadon: A Seneca chief who had previously inquired of Teedyuscung why the Lenapes attacked the Pennsylvania English. At that meeting, *according to proprietary sources,* Teedyuscung had abruptly declared to Tagashata the Lenapes' independence from the League. It seems more likely, given Tokaaion's support of the Lenapes and suspicion of the English, that the decision was mutual or part of an elevation of the Lenapes *within* the League. However, Teedyuscung may have said some indiscreet things under the influence of the proprietary faction's liquor. Tagashata was also one of the signatories to the controversial 1754 deed to Pennsylvania.

Captain Henry Montour: Possibly an alternate name for Andrew Montour.

Stephen Calvin: A Lenape interpreter, who in 1777 appears to have forged signatures on a petition to New Jersey that asked the state to release the trust lands of the Brotherton Indians so that they could sell the land and remove to the Ohio. Calvin acted as a proxy for Killbuck, but it is unclear whether he acted with Killbuck's approval.

Governor Bernard: Francis Bernard, Governor of New Jersey from 1758 to 1760 and Governor of Massachusetts from 1760 to 1769.

Mr. Frederick Post (Christian Frederick Post): A Moravian missionary to the Lenapes, originally from Germany. At first a messenger with Charles Thomson to Teedyuscung from Pemberton and Denny, Post became one of the emissaries who went back with Pisquitomen to the Ohio to begin arrangements for the formal peace between the western Lenapes and Pennsylvania. He also carried intelligence about French position and strength to General John Forbes. His journals make it clear that the Lenapes wanted the English out of their Ohio territory.

Thomas Hickman: Also known as Iecasso. Part of Pisquitomen's delegation from Ohio in the quest for peace. A warrior in the resistance to British encroachment in the Ohio that continued after the end of the Seven Years' War.

General Forbes: A brigadier general in the British army originally from Scotland chosen by William Pitt, who was leader of the British ministry after December 1756 and a political enemy of the Duke of Cumberland and Lord Loudon. Pitt had made the capture of Quebec the policy of the British government during the Seven Years' War and insisted for the first time in years on cooperation with the colonial assemblies in military matters. Forbes created an unlikely alliance with pacifist Israel Pemberton in the effort to achieve peace with the Lenapes. On November 25, 1758, he seized Fort Duquesne from the French and renamed it Fort Pitt.

Israel Pemberton: A leading Quaker, a wealthy merchant, and a member of the Pennsylvania Assembly from 1750 to 1756 who formed alliances with Teedyuscung, Franklin, Forbes, and several others to investigate what actions by Pennsylvania and the proprietors had caused the Lenapes to turn against them in 1755. After helping to achieve the peace, Pemberton engaged in trade from Fort Pitt amounting to at least 4,400 pounds worth of goods. Pennsylvania's post-independence government created a loyalty oath that disenfranchised Pemberton and his fellow Quakers, many of whom, including him, were exiled/deported to West Virginia in 1777.

Beaver King: Better known as Beaver or Tamaqua. A leader of the Ohio Lenapes and possibly their peace chief, with brother Shingas acting as their war chief, though these roles are not clear in the records. It appears that he refused the French in 1755 when they offered to back a Lenape attack against the British, succeeding with Shingas in this offer. With Shingas and his other brothers, Pisquetomen and Nenatchehan, he had been one of Scarouady's party at the 1753 Winchester and Carlisle treaties. On November 28, 1758, he urged Forbes through Post to leave Fort Pitt and the region to the Lenapes and other Ohio Indians. He participated in Pontiac's War and the peace negotiations that followed it, having survived the 1763 germ warfare of the British. His town was located south of present-day Canton, Ohio, in present-day Tuscarawas County, near where the Moravians later founded the second Gnadenhutten.

Shingas: Chief of the Ohio Lenapes after 1752 and champion of their independence from the British, the French, and the Iroquois. When George Washington went to his town in 1753 with the charge from the Ohio Company of Virginia that they planned to build a fort there, Shingas gave Washington the run-around. In 1755, he helped the British smuggle information about Fort Duquesne out of that fort, but after General Braddock made it clear to him and others in his delegation that the Lenapes would be disinherited once the British won the Ohio, he and his nation refused to fight with Braddock. This withdrawal of Lenape support led to Braddock's ignominious defeat. Shingas joined the French in the attack on Pennsylvania in 1755 after the British refused to arm the Lenapes against them, negotiated for peace in 1758, and was killed by germ warfare in 1763.

Delaware George: Also known as Nenatcheehunt or Nenatchehan. One of the Winchester-Carlisle delegation of 1753. With Shingas, he helped the British smuggle out information about Fort Duquesne. An Ohio Lenape warrior.

Captain Peter: Probably John Peter, one of the Ohio Lenapes who with Shingas led war parties into the disputed Pennsylvania Lenape territories in 1755.

Kill Buck: Also spelled Killbuck. One of the Ohio Lenapes who with Shingas led war parties into the disputed Pennsylvania Lenape territories in 1755. Kill Buck lived until at least 1776 and was a traditionalist who opposed Christian missionaries and allowing Christian Lenapes to remain as members of the Lenape nation.

Sastaghretsy: Along with Anigh Kalickon, Atowateany, Towigh Towighroano, Geghdageghroano, Oyaghtanont, Sisaghroano, Stiaggeghroano, and Jonontadyhago, it appears to be the Iroquoian name for a western Indian nation. The Atowateany is recognizably a possibility for the Ottawa. The Towigh Towighroano are probably the Miamis (Twightwees or Towick Towicks). All appear to be former Covenant Chain allies. In 1744, when Weiser wrote to Thomas Lee regarding the Iroquois, he listed Iroquois allies, some of whom correspond to some of these names: the Unich-Kalliagon, who lived from west of Lake Erie to the strait of Lake Huron and numbered 3,000 warriors; the Towwichtowich-Roonu on the Thunackgi River, numbering 300 warriors; the Gechdagech-Roonu on the Mississippi, numbering 500 warriors; Oyjachdanich-Roonu on the Black River, numbering 1,000 warriors; and the Zisagech-Roonu, who had three large cities east of Lake Huron and 2,400 warriors. Some of these may be Iroquoian names for wholes or parts of the following peoples: Attiwandaronks, Eries, Hurons, Kah-Kwahs, Neutrals, Ojibwas, Squawhihaws, Wenros, or Wyandots.

Nicholas Scull: The surveyor who accompanied the persons hired by the Penns to "walk" out the boundaries of the Walking Purchase. It appears that by 1758, he was keeping a tavern in Easton, though this may be a different man.

Isaac Zane: A Quaker and member of the Friendly Association for Regaining and Preserving Peace with the Indians by Pacific Measures, headed by Pemberton.

Tapiscawen: Also known as Samuel Davis. Probably the same as Tepascouon and Tipiscohan. A counselor to Teedyuscung.

Captain Bull: Teedyuscung's son, who was captured in 1764 by an Iroquois war party allied with the British. His capture came after having attacked Connecticut settlers (some probably responsible for his father's murder) in the Wyoming Valley in the fall of 1763 as part of Pontiac's War, in what is sometimes called the first Wyoming massacre. He also attacked settlers in Northampton County, an area of the Walking Purchase.

Governor Clinton: George Clinton, Governor of New York from 1741 to 1753 and a patron of William Johnson's.

Governor Hardy: Sir Charles Hardy, Governor of New York from 1755 to 1757.

Major Orndt: Jacob Arndt, formerly a captain. An officer at Fort Norris and later Fort Allen (present-day Allentown). During Ardnt's escort of Lenapes from Fort Allen to the Easton treaty in 1757, Moses Tattamy's son William wandered off from the party and was shot by a fifteen-year-old boy near Bethlehem. A member of the Supreme Executive Council during the Revolution.

## First Mentioned in the 1761 Treaty

Samuel Weiser: Conrad Weiser's son and an interpreter for Pennsylvania.

David Seisberger: David Zeisberger. A Moravian missionary and expert in the Lenape language who was assisted by John Heckewelder, the missionary whose writings were the source of James Fenimore Cooper's Indian materials. Author of *History of the Northern American Indians*, *Zeisberger's Indian Dictionary* (which contained cross-references among German, English, Onondaga, and Lenape), and *Grammar of the Language of the Lenni Lenape or Delaware Indians,* which Peter Stephen Du Ponceau, the second president of the American Philosophical Society after Franklin, translated into English and that contributed to Wilhelm von Humboldt's development of theories of linguistic diversity and hierarchy.

Papounan: A traditionalist chief at Machachlosing, where in 1760 Teedyuscung and Christian Frederick Post found a cultural renaissance in progress.

## First Mentioned in the 1762 Treaty

Samuel Rhoads: A friend of Charles Thomson and the carpenter who built Franklin's house in 1764. He served as mayor of Philadelphia in 1774 and was a member of the Assembly from 1761 to 1763 and again later. He became a delegate to the First Continental Congress. He was involved in Franklin's Library Company and the Pennsylvania Hospital.

Joseph Gibbons: An Assembly representative from Chester County and a Quaker who tended to support Franklin and his allies in their votes.

David McConaughy: An Assembly representative from York County from 1753 to 1765. He appears to have voted in the interests of the proprietary party and he opposed Franklin's appointment as agent in England in 1764.

Dochneghdoris, or John Shacalamy: Also spelled Tachnechdorus. One of Shikellamy's four sons, Tachnechdorus took over his duties for the Six Nations at Shamokin after his death in 1748. He protested to the Pennsylvania government the arrival of settlers from Connecticut and advised the Lenapes, Shawnees, and Mahicans living in Wyoming to protest to the League. However, he also helped Weiser with Pennsylvania's controversial 1754 purchase.

Memenowal, or Augustus: Husband of the sister of Teedyuscung's wife and a peace emissary at the start of the 1755 Lenape-Pennsylvania war.

Tawwas: A tribal nation living south of Lake Erie. Possibly part of or related to the Ottawas.

Mary Tidd: Possibly the wife of a man named John Tidd, who was killed, scalped, and mutilated in the summer of 1757 in the Delaware Water Gap region above Easton.

Governor Sharpe: Horatio Sharpe, who was governor of Maryland from 1753 to 1769. He was something of a political rival of Franklin's because Franklin anonymously attacked the proprietary government of Maryland (Lord Baltimore proprietor) in an attempt to weaken proprietary governments in the colonies in general. Sharpe issued a rebuttal to Franklin's argument.

Nathaniel Holland: The storekeeper at Fort Augusta, he was assaulted and almost killed by an Indian trading at the fort in 1760, probably because of his treatment of those Indians with whom he traded.

In all cases, I have used information from the sources in my notes to create this glossary. For the sake of simplicity and ease of reading, I have generally chosen not to cite each individual source and page number used for each entry. Main sources are Francis Jennings, *The Ambiguous Iroquois Empire;* Francis Jennings, ed., *The History and Culture of Iroquois Diplomacy;* Paul A. W. Wallace, *Conrad Weiser* and *The White Roots of Peace;* Leonard W. Labaree, ed., *The Papers of Benjamin Franklin;* C. A. Weslager, *The Delaware Indians* and *The Delaware Indian Westward Migration;* Daniel K. Richter and James H. Merrell, eds., *Beyond the Covenant Chain;* Bruce Johansen and Barbara Mann, eds., *Encyclopedia of the Haudenosaunee;* Dean Snow, *The Iroquois;* and Anthony F. C. Wallace, *King of the Delawares.* See also http://www.hiddenhistory.com/PAGE3/swsts/marylnd1.HTM; http://www.rootsweb.com/~nybroome/seward/sunion.htm; and http://www.dickshovel.com/wap.html.

# INDEX


Abraham (Mahican chief), 418; at 1757 Easton conferences, 282, 285–86; at 1758 conferences, 292, 294, 296, 298, 305, 308, 313–14, 323. *See also* Little Abraham
Achoan (Munsee Lenape chief), 338, 352
Adirondack (nation), 169, 173, 413
adoption: of individuals, 122n11, 342, 392, 405n2, 407, 412–13; of nations, 140n4, 410; Native American philosophies of, 7, 223n2
Akwesasne, 410. *See also* praying Indians
Alammapis. *See* Olumapies
Alaska, 23. *See also* land releases: Myth of Iroquois Empire "release" (1744)
Albany (town of), 33, 50, 60n2, 68, 92, 95, 98–99, 103–4, 106, 142–43, 147n1, 293, 330; Congress, 33, 43n64; Plan of Union, 26–27, 33, 416; relocation in 1754 of council fire at, 344; as site of 1745 treaty, 29, 31, 123–24, 134, 136, 140n1, 140n6; as site of 1754 land sale, 268, 312, 315–16, 395; trade monopoly with the Mohawk nation, 15, 17
alcohol, 343, 346–47, 384; coercion to accept trade in, 170; enforcement against use at treaty conferences of, 365; problems caused by, 56–57, 59–60, 62n10, 174; regulation of, 57, 59, 62n10, 177n1, 331n1; requests to regulate, 170, 343, 346; requests to restrict use at treaty conferences of, 364; sale of, 177n1; trade use of, 57, 59–60, 170, 174, 177; use at treaty conferences of, 18, 44n88, 60, 61n5, 66–67, 81–83, 87, 108, 111, 115, 119, 139, 171, 174, 250, 288n2, 331, 365, 418–19
alcoholism, colonizing production of, 170, 177
Algonquin (nations north of St. Lawrence), 10, 84n9
Algonquin languages, 224n10, 410, 413, 417–18
Algonquin peoples, 2
Allegheny Hills, 162, 169, 268, 316, 395–96, 400
Allegheny Indians. *See* Ohio Valley, Indian nations of the
Allegheny River, 18, 30, 33, 56–57, 59, 65, 100, 153, 163–64, 176, 301–3, 354, 373–74, 383–84
Allen, William, 17, 411
Allentown, 421. *See also* Fort Allen
Allumapes. *See* Olumapies
Amboy, 244
American Revolution, 27, 38, 417, 421; Supreme Executive Council of, 421
Amherst, General Jeffrey, 287n1
Anaquarunda, 248. *See also* Croghan, George
Anaquateeka (a war chief of the Iroquois Confederacy), 282, 284–85, 288n3; speeches of, 285
Anawalleckon (Lenape leader), 329
Andaste. *See* Susquehannock
Andros, Edmund, 11–12. *See also* New York: Governors of
Anglicans, 222n1, 287n1, 412, 415, 417
Anglo-Iroquois alliance. *See* Chain of Friendship, Pennsylvania's; Silver Covenant Chain
Anglo-Saxons, 28. *See also* Franklin, Benjamin: "Observations concerning the Increase of Mankind, Peopling of Countries, &c"; race
Annapolis, 119, 128. *Also in text as* Annapolis-Royal

Anoyiuts. *See* Oneida
anti-Catholicism, 417. *See also* Smith, William
antlers: in Iroquois peacetime chief installation ceremony, 176, 179n12
Anugh Kary Tany Tionen Hokorowy, 239, 416. *See also* Seneca
Apess, William, 41n39. *See also* land: speculation
Appalachia Mountains, 23, 98–99, 103–4, 174, 252, 316
approbation, reported expressions of, 147, 301
Aquila, Richard, 15, 38nn1–2, 41n34, 41n38, 44n74
armaments, requests for, 143, 163–64, 288n9, 311
Armstrong, James, 227, 229, 415
Armstrong, John (member of the Pennsylvania Assembly), 165
Armstrong, John (trader), 100, 108–9, 409, 415
Arndt, Jacob, 328, 421
Arnold, Woodward, 409
Aroas (Seneca warrior), 183, 414. *See also* Silver Heels
Articles of Confederation, 26–27
Aschicanhcook (nation), 132
Ashbridge, George: at 1757 Lancaster conferences, 236–37, 239–40, 243, 246; at 1762 conferences, 360, 365, 368–69, 371, 375
Ashenoch (speaker for Jenochiaada), 336, 342, 354; speech delivered by, 354
Asheton, Ralph: at 1736 conferences, 49, 52, 54, 56; at 1742 conferences, 63, 68, 74–75. *Also in text as* Assheton
Asopus, 75
Assaragoa, 87, 90, 97–99, 103, 106–7, 111, 114, 116–18, 162. *See also* Virginia, Governors of
Assarandonguas (Onondaga chief), 291, 294, 296, 298, 304–5, 308, 313–14, 323; speeches of, 304
Assintzin, 313
Atlantic Ocean, 103, 106, 162, 355, 417
Atotarho (twelfth-century Onondaga chief), 4–6, 20, 38n4; as Flint, 4
Atsaningo. *See* Otseningo
Attiwandaronks, 421
Attowawie, 131
Augus (Tuscarora chief), 359
Augustus. *See* Memenowal
authority over Indian affairs, as residing at the federal level, 140n6
Awehela (Lenape chief), 322, 328, 330
Awicka, 397

Bacon's Rebellion, 11
Bad Medicine Woman. *See* Sky Woman
Bagley, Carol L., 41n52, 42n60, 44n76. *See also* Canasatego: assassination of
Baird, Patrick, 84
Baltimore, Lord, 105, 107–8, 422
Bartram, John, 43n66
Bartram, William, 43n66
Baynton, John, 236–37, 239–40, 243, 246
beaver: blankets, as gift and mnemonic, 168, 173–74; coats, as gift and mnemonic, 53; skins, 152, 168; trade, in 103, 355
Beaver, or Beaver King. *See* Tamaqua
Beaver Creek, 32, 162, 234
Bedford, 387, 390
beer. *See* alcohol
Belt, The (Iroquois warrior), 179n9
Ben (interpreter for the Lenapes), 187, 189–90, 194, 196, 199
Berks County, Pennsylvania, 222n1. *See also* Lenape-Pennsylvania war
Bernard, Francis, 294–96, 298, 301, 304, 315, 317, 319–20, 325–30, 377–78, 418–19; speeches of, 294–95, 301, 307, 321, 325–26, 329–30. *See also* New Jersey: Governors of
Berner, Robert L., 25, 42n59
Berwick, Pennsylvania, 14. *See also* Nutimy's Town
Bethlehem, Pennsylvania, 37, 183, 196, 232, 235, 421
Beverly, Colonel William, 86–91, 93, 96–97, 100–102, 105, 107–13, 119–20
Bierhorst, John, 5, 8, 38n3, 39nn12–14
Big Cove, Pennsylvania, 364
Big House Ceremony, 8. *See also* Lenape (nations): oral traditions
Black River, 421
blanket, as diplomatic symbol, 76
Blue Mountains, 19, 177n1, 210, 348, 396–97, 404
Blue Ridge chain of Appalachia Mountains, 23
boarding schools, in Native American history, 122n14
boiled heads metaphor, 143, 147n3
border conflicts, 12, 88, 250
borderlands, 177n1
Boston, 132
bounties. *See* prisoner bounties; scalp bounties

Bouquet, Colonel Henry, 287n1
Boyd, Julian, ix, xi, 121nn7–8, 140n1, 177n1, 178n7, 222n1, 224n6, 288n2
Braddock, General Edward, 179n9, 253n1, 288n5, 413–14, 420
brethren: meaning of articulated, 155
bribery, 32, 36, 38, 61n5, 288n9; possible uses at treaties of, 18, 20, 31
British, xi–xiii, 9–16, 18, 20–22, 24–31, 33–34, 36, 409–12, 414, 416, 418–21; in 1736 minutes, 60nn1–2, 61n7, 62n8, 62n11; in 1742 minutes, 67, 84nn1–5, 84n8, 84n9; in 1744 minutes, 89, 91–92, 94–96, 112, 116, 119, 120n2, 121n4, 121n10, 122nn11–12; in 1745 minutes, 125–29, 131, 133–38, 140nn5–6; in 1747 minutes, 142–47; in 1748 minutes, 151–57, 159n3; in 1753 minutes, 162, 164, 167–73, 175, 177, 178nn5–7, 179n9, 179n11; in July 1756 minutes, 181–82, 184, 189–90, 192–93, 195, 197; in November 1756 minutes, 200, 203, 207, 212–14, 217, 220–21, 223nn2–3, 224n14; in 1757 Lancaster minutes, 227, 229, 231, 234–39, 241–42, 244–48, 253, 254n4; in 1757 Easton minutes, 255–56, 258, 260–63, 266–67, 270, 273, 275–76, 278, 282–87, 287n1, 288n4, 288nn7–9, 289n11; in 1758 minutes, 292–94, 296–300, 303, 307–12, 314–15, 318–23, 325, 329, 332n6, 333n6, 333n13; in 1761 minutes, 336–38, 340, 343–44, 346–48, 352–54, 357n4; in 1762 minutes, 359, 363, 376–80, 382, 384, 387, 393, 395–96, 399, 403, 405n2; and Iron Act, 28
British colonials, 147n3, 148n4
British colonies, xiii, 9, 11–12, 14–16, 20–21, 24, 26–29, 31, 33, 36–37, 42n55, 409, 422; in 1736 minutes, 53, 58; in 1742 minutes, 64, 67, 74, 77; in 1744 minutes, 88, 91, 120n1; in 1745 minutes, 126, 128, 130, 138, 140n6; in 1748 minutes, 151, 154–56; in November 1756 minutes, 207, 211–14, 222; in 1757 Lancaster minutes, 229, 232, 234, 236, 241, 245; in 1757 Easton minutes, 257, 263, 265, 283; in 1758 minutes, 295, 304, 307, 309; in 1761 minutes, 345, 357n5; in 1762 minutes, 359; coast-inland split 177n1; Governors of the, 151, 154, 295, 307, 314, 318 (*see also governors listed under the specific colonies*); historical expertise regarding the, 24; independence of, 26. *See also specific colonies*
British empire, xi, 18–19, 26, 122n11, 179n9, 179nn11–12, 223n2
British laws, 75
British traders, 32, 33, 178nn5–6, 179n9, 179n11. *See also* traders
Broadhead, Charles, 207, 210, 212, 224nn9–10
brother (metaphor of elder-younger), 379–80
Brotherston, Gordon, 61n3
Brotherton Indians, 419. *See also* reservations
Brown, Joseph Epes, 158n1
Buchanan, William, 164
Bucks County, Pennsylvania, 13, 327
Buffalo, New York, 37
Bull, Captain, 322–23, 421. *See also* Teedyuscung: sons of
Burd, James, 416
Burlington, New Jersey, 293, 295

Cacawasheca, or Cackewatcheka, or Cackewatcheky. *See* Kekewatcheky
Caghnawaga. *See* Caughnawaga
Caiyouquos. *See* Cayuga
Callender, Robert, 164, 175, 412
Callowhill, Hannah, 407
calumet pipe, 152, 155–56, 158n1, 171–72, 174; ceremony, 158n1
Calvin, Stephen, 292, 294–96, 298, 305, 309, 314, 320, 323, 419
Canada, 10, 23, 37, 38, 54, 67, 70, 103, 127–28, 132–33, 135–38, 143–44, 146, 151, 153, 359, 410, 413; Governors of, 67, 89, 116, 127, 135, 137–38, 143–44, 151, 169
Canadagaye (Mohawk leader), 416
Canada-Indians. *See* France: Indian allies of
Canajoherie, 131
Canasatego (Onondaga leader), 19–20, 23–24, 26–27, 29, 31, 42n55, 44n76, 177n1, 289n10, 357nn5–6, 408; at 1742 conferences, 63, 66–68, 71, 75, 78–80, 83, 84n2, 84nn9–10; at 1744 conferences, 87, 90, 92–93, 96, 105, 108, 111, 114–16, 119–20, 121n3, 122n13; at 1745 conferences, 132, 136, 138–39, 140n6; assassination of, 31, 177n1, 408; compared unfavorably to William Blackstone, 84n9; gift of union speech, 24, 26, 29, 118–19, 140n6, 357n5; gift of union speech given back to Ohio Indians, 167; gifts to, 120. *Also in text as* Canassateego; Canassatego
Canasatego, speeches of: at 1742 conferences, 64–67, 71–73, 79–82; at 1744 conferences, 93–96, 105, 108–9, 114–19; at 1745 conferences, 132–34, 136–39, 140n6
Canataquanny, 252
Canawa River, 169
Canay. *See* Conoy

Canayiahaga River, Indians living at the, 145–47
Cane, Captain, 230
Canestogo. *See* Conestoga (town)
Cannadagaughia. *See* Canadagaye
cannibalism, 1, 4–7, 147n3, 158n1, 178n5, 234; as metaphor for adoption or execution, 305, 350
Canoyias. *See* Conoy; Nanticoke
Canso, 128, 137
Canton, Ohio, 420
Canyingoes. *See* Mohawk (nation)
Cape Breton, 128
Cape Henlopen, 10
captives, 300–301, 310–11, 315, 407. *See also* prisoners
Carlisle, Pennsylvania, 32–33, 153n1, 160, 164–65, 167, 178n3
Carolina. *See* North Carolina; South Carolina
Carson, John, 164
Castalago (Ohio Lenape chief), 234
Catawba (nation), 16, 104, 106, 113–14, 117, 122n11, 135–36, 138–39, 409–10, 412, 418. *Also in text as* Catawbaws
Catchcawatsiky. *See* Kekewatcheky
Catepackeaman. *See* Compass, Joseph
Caughnawaga (nation), 169, 173, 235, 410, 413
Caxhayn (Onondaga diplomat), 50, 68, 83–84. *Also in text as* Caxhayion
Cayanguileguoa (Mohawk orator), 165, 413
Cayuga (nation), 6, 15, 17, 23, 410, 418; at 1736 conferences, 50; at 1742 conferences, 68; at 1744 conferences, 87, 107; at 1757 Lancaster conferences, 227, 236–37, 239–40, 243, 246; at 1757 Easton conferences, 255; at 1758 conferences, 290–91, 294–99, 301, 304–6, 308–9, 313–14, 319, 322–23, 330, 332n3; at 1761 conferences, 334–36, 338, 340–42, 344–47, 350–52, 354–55, 357n2; at 1762 conferences, 365, 368, 375, 378, 380, 385, 390, 401, 404, 405n1. *Also in text as* Cayogoes; Cayooges
cease-fires, 88, 136, 158, 187, 190, 222n1, 236–37, 239, 300
*Century of Dishonor, A* (Jackson), 22
chain metaphor: origin of, 95
Chain of Friendship, Pennsylvania's, 14, 30, 33, 35; in 1736 minutes, 53–54, 56, 58–59; in 1742 minutes, 64, 67, 70–72, 78, 80; in 1744 minutes, 89–91, 94, 97, 101, 104–5, 107, 112–18, 120n2; in 1747 minutes, 143; in 1748 minutes, 151–52, 154–57; in 1753 minutes, 166–67, 169, 172; in July 1756 minutes, 184–85, 191–92, 198; in November 1756 minutes, 202, 204–5; in 1757 Lancaster minutes, 228–29, 231, 242–43, 246, 253; in 1757 Easton minutes, 256, 261, 267, 270, 272, 275, 282–84, 288n7; in 1758 minutes, 317–18, 322–23, 328; in 1761 minutes, 337, 342–43, 345, 348; in 1762 minutes, 361, 363, 366–67, 372, 378, 380, 384, 392, 401–2
Champlain, Samuel de, 10
Chanandoah. *See* Shenandoah River
Charles, Robert, 60
Charles-Town, South Carolina, 176, 244
Charlotte, North Carolina, 410
Chartier, Martin, 410
Chartier, Peter, 138, 154, 410
Cheepaways. *See* Ojibwa
Chehohockes. *See* Lenape (nations); Lenape (nations): Unami
Chenango, 397, 418
Cherokee (nation[s]), 16, 106, 118, 122n11, 138, 248, 254n4, 385–87, 390, 392, 400, 402. *Also in text as* Cherikee
Chesapeake Bay, 92, 410, 417. *Also in text as* Chessapeak
Chesapeake peninsula, 13
Chester County, Pennsylvania, 13, 422
Chew, Benjamin: at July 1756 conferences, 187, 190, 194–96, 198; at 1757 Lancaster conferences, 235–37, 240, 243, 246; at 1757 Easton conferences, 255, 258, 260, 262, 266, 272, 277, 280; at 1758 conferences, 290–92, 294–96, 298, 303–5, 308–9, 314, 321, 323; at 1761 conferences, 334, 336, 338, 340, 344, 346–47, 352, 355; at 1762 conferences, 358, 360–61, 365, 368–69, 371, 375
chief-making, by Europeans, 332n9
Chippewa. *See* Ojibwa
Choptank River, 92
Christianity: missionaries for, 254n5, 265, 420; voluntary adoption of, 265
Chugnut (nation), 290, 292, 294, 296, 298, 305–6, 308, 313–14, 323, 347, 418. *Also in text as* Chugnot
Civility (Conestoga leader), 17, 59, 408
Clark, Joshua V. H., 39n11. *See also* League, story cycle of the
Clapham, Colonel, 183
Cleghiccon (Simon), speaker for Tamaqua, 370
Clements, William, xivn5. *See also* oral traditions and discourses: mediation of

Cleveland, Ohio. *See* Cuyahoga
Clinton, George, 327, 421. *See also* New York: Governors of
Coch-now-was-roonan (nation), 98, 409
coercion: absence of, 155; in British diplomacy, 159n3; government by, 25; by squatters, 34; in treaty settings, 224n6
Cohongorooton, or Cohongoronta, or Cohongorontas, or Cohongoronto, or Cohongoruton. *See* Potomac River
Colden, Cadwallader, 27, 37, 44n91, 120n2, 122n5
Collinson, Peter, 28
Colville, Colonel Thomas, 86–91, 93, 96–7, 100–102, 105, 107–9, 111–15, 119, 120
communitism, xii–xiii
Compass, Joseph (Lenape delegate), 365, 368–69, 375, 383
Compass, Philip (Lenape delegate), 322
Condolence Ritual, xi, 5–6, 158n1, 161, 165–68, 178n3, 224n8, 229, 231, 243, 248, 292, 323, 359
Condolence Ritual, language of: at 1736 conferences, 50, 52–53, 56, 58–59, 61n4; at 1742 conferences, 64–66, 70–71, 76, 78; at 1744 conferences, 99–101, 108–9, 112–13, 115; at 1745 conferences, 126–27, 137; at 1748 conferences, 150–51, 155; at 1753 conferences, 165–68, 175; at July 1756 conferences, 183, 186–87, 190–91; at November 1756 conferences, 200–201, 206, 211–12, 220–21; at 1757 Lancaster conferences, 228–29, 231, 243, 253; at 1757 Easton conferences, 258–63, 271–72, 285; at 1758 conferences, 291–92, 297–300, 323, 328; at 1761 conferences, 335, 337–39, 341, 350, 352–53; at 1762 conferences, 360–62, 368–70, 372, 375–76, 379–80, 391–92, 394
Conedogwainet, 93
Coneduganniet River, 352
Conegocheague, 64, 364. *Also in text as* Conegocheegoe
Conestoga (nation), 12, 14, 16–17, 22–23, 37, 59, 64, 69, 96, 106, 227, 231, 408, 414. *Also in text as* Conestogo; Conestogoe. *See also* Susquehannock
Conestoga (town), 17, 69
Conewaga Falls, 17
Conewagas, French. *See* Caughnawaga
Confederated Nations. *See* Iroquois Confederacy
confederation, principle of, 26–27
conflict: prevention of, 174, 177; resolution of, 34
Connecticut, 12, 33–34, 410, 412, 416; at 1745 conferences, 123–26, 128, 131, 134, 140n6; Governors of, 128, 146, 410; Wyoming settlers from, 34, 349, 357n4, 396–97, 405n4, 414, 421–22
Connecticut River, 129
Connestogoes. *See* Conestoga (nation)
Connutskin-ough-roonaw (nation), 98, 409
Conoy (nation), 12, 14–17, 23, 53, 98, 109–10, 118–19, 409–10, 418; at 1742 conferences, 69; at 1758 conferences, 290–91, 294, 296–99, 304–6, 308–9, 313–14, 323; at 1761 conferences, 334–36, 338, 340–42, 344–47, 351–52, 354–55, 357n2; at 1762 conferences, 359, 365, 368, 375, 385, 391, 397, 405n1; reservations, 109–10. *Also in text as* Conoy-uch-such-roona
conquest, discourse of, 11, 20–23, 60, 72; at 1744 conference, 88, 96–98, 103, 106, 399; in Iroquois-Lenape relationship, 80–81, 84n9
consanguinity: discourse of international, 53–54, 56, 58, 61n7, 67, 70, 78, 89, 92, 94–95, 101, 116, 133, 147, 154–56, 167, 184, 192, 198, 256, 259, 261, 279, 283, 319, 331, 343, 380, 385
consensus, in Iroquois diplomacy, 21. *See also* Iroquois Confederacy: diplomacy of
consent, government by, 25
Constitution, U.S.: controversy over Iroquois contributions to, 23–27, 43n64, 118–19
Constitutional Convention, 42n57, 43n64
Continental Congress, 26–27, 416, 422
Cooper, James Fenimore, 421
Corlaer, 162. *See also* New York: Governors of
corn, 1, 4–5, 8–9, 389; as Mother Corn, 9; as time marker, 338
Council of the United Nations. *See* Iroquois Confederacy: Grand Council of the
Coursey, Colonel Henry, 103
Covenant Chain. *See* Silver Covenant Chain
Covenant Chain between Iroquois Confederacy and Lenapes, 192
Crawford, Hugh, 227, 229
Cressap, Daniel, 387, 400. *Also in text as* Cressip
Cressap, Thomas, 105, 387, 410
Croghan, George, 27, 32–33, 35–36, 44n88, 147, 156, 411–12, 418; at 1753 conferences, 160, 163, 169, 175–76, 177n1, 179n9, 179n11; at 1757 Lancaster conferences, 226–37, 239–43, 246–48, 253n1, 254n2, 254n8; at 1757 Easton conferences, 255, 257–58, 260, 263–66, 268–

77, 279–82, 284–87, 287n1, 288n2, 288nn8–9; at 1758 conferences, 291, 294, 296, 298, 305, 308, 313–14, 319, 323, 327–28, 333n13; mentioned at 1762 conferences, 362, 366, 371–73, 387, 390, 400; secretary of, 236; speeches of, 227–29, 231, 241–42, 257, 275–76, 283
Crown. *See* Great Britain, King of
crying, diplomatic use of, 164, 178n7, 312
Cumberland, Duke of, 415, 419
Cumberland, Maryland, 410
Cumberland County, Pennsylvania, 160–61, 165, 167, 171, 173, 222n1, 356n1
Cumberland River, 7–8
Curtis, Samuel, and daughter, 388, 401. *Also in text as* Curtiss
Cushetung, 321, 329, 349, 396–97, 404. *Also in text as* Cushetunk; Cushietunck; Cushyhink
Cusick, David, 147n3
Cuyahoga, 411

dances, Native American, 280. *See also* warrior dance
Daniel (Lenape Indian), 286, 290
David (Iroquois Confederacy Indian), 183
Davis, James. *See* Awehela
Davis, Samuel. *See* Tapiscawen
death penalty, 75, 100. *See also* jurisdiction, matters of legal; killing, accidental
debate, differing cultural styles of, 25
decentralization of power, 26
deer, 5, 73, 81, 95, 110, 118
Deganawida (twelfth-century co-founder of Iroquois Confederacy), 3–7; as Sapling, 3–4
Delaware (colony/state), 10, 13
Delaware (nations). *See* Lenape (nations)
Delaware Bay, 10–12
Delaware George. *See* Nenatchehan
Delaware River, 7–8, 10, 12–13, 16, 19, 31, 79–80, 86, 123, 160, 208, 217, 236, 255, 278, 313–14, 316, 320–21, 329, 348–49, 373–74, 384, 395–96; Forks region of the, 13, 16, 19–20, 36, 75–77, 79–80, 186, 412
Delaware Valley, 17–19
Delaware Water Gap, 13, 422
deliberation, 38; as a diplomatic principle, 121n3; in Iroquois diplomacy, 21, 121n3
DeMallie, Raymond, xivn11, 42n60
democracy, concepts of, 25–26, 29, 43n64
Dennis, Matthew, 6, 38n4, 39nn15–16, 42n55, 61n7
Denny, William, 35, 120n2, 415, 418–19; at November 1756 conferences, 199, 201–5, 210–11, 216, 219, 224n6, 224n7, 224n12; at 1757 Lancaster conferences, 230–33, 235–41, 243, 245–46, 248–49; at 1757 Easton conferences, 255–58, 260, 262–64, 266, 269–82, 284–87, 288n8, 289n11; at 1758 conferences, 290–97, 301–5, 307–9, 311–15, 317, 322–23, 326–28, 330, 331n1, 333n13; at 1762 conferences, mentioned, 377–78. *See also* Pennsylvania, Governors of
Denny, William, speeches of, 35; at November 1756 conferences, 201, 204–5, 211–15, 219–20; at 1757 Lancaster conferences, 233–34, 236–37, 239–40, 241–42, 243–44, 246–47, 249–50; at 1757 Easton conferences, 256–57, 261–62, 266–69, 273–74, 275–76, 278, 280–81, 285–87; at 1758 conferences, 292, 298–301, 305–6, 315–19, 323–25, 326
Deogwanda (Onondaga chief), 402, 404; speeches of, 402–3
Devil. *See* evil spirit, references to
Diahoga, or Diahogo. *See* Tioga
Dinwiddie, Robert, 176, 413. *See also* Virginia, Governors of
diplomacy: dangers for Indian messengers in, 260, 262; intercontinental, 140n5; Native North American, 20, 25, 140n5, 158n1, 163, 178n3, 178n4, 178n7, 235, 267, 274–79, 288n9; U.S. toward Indian nations, 27. *See also* Iroquois Confederacy: diplomacy of; Lenape (nations): diplomacy
disease, 9, 12, 51, 61n5, 121n10, 124, 126, 220, 230, 248, 287n1, 335, 341, 356, 414
Dochneghdoris. *See* Shikellamy, John
domestic, dependent nation, 84n1
Dongan, Thomas, 17. *See also* New York: Governors of
Dorset County, Maryland, 389
Duché, Jacob, 258, 287, 287n1, 288n2, 417
Dudensing-Reichel, Beatrix, 122n14
Dunaway, Wilma, 38n1, 43n63
Dunwiddie, Governor. *See* Dinwiddie, Robert
Du Ponceau, Peter Stephen, 422
Durham, Pennsylvania, 354
Durham Creek, as site of William Logan's iron mine, 333n10
Dutch, 9–11, 94–95, 252

eastern Indians, 125, 128
Easton, Pennsylvania, 33, 44n88, 179n12, 318, 373, 378, 380–81, 383, 390, 394, 402, 421–22;

as site of July 1756 conferences, 181, 187, 190, 194–96, 198–99, 278, 367; as site of November 1756 conferences, 202–3, 210, 216, 219, 221, 223n4, 224n6, 257; in 1757 Lancaster minutes, 226, 228, 230–31, 237–38, 240–41, 249–50; as site of 1757 Easton conferences, 255, 260, 262, 266, 269, 271–72, 277, 280, 282, 287n1, 288n2, 307, 331n1, 421; as site of 1758 conferences, 290–91, 294–96, 298, 301, 306, 308, 313–14, 319, 324, 327–29, 331n1, 336, 339, 377, 396, 401, 409; as site of 1761 conferences, 334, 336, 339–40, 343, 374, 388, 396–97
economics, relationship to speech and ideology, 62n11
Edmonds, William, 187, 190, 194, 196, 415
education: of Indian children, 122n14; offer to Iroquois from Virginia, 114, 117, 122n14, 405n5; requests for western-style, 265
Egohohowen (Munsee Lenape chief), 292, 294, 296, 298, 305, 309, 313–14, 319–21, 323; speeches of, 309, 321
"Eight Nations" (1758). *See* Conoy; Iroquois Confederacy; Nanticoke; Tutelo
"eight tribes": mentioned in 1757 Lancaster conferences, 226. *See also* Cayuga; Conestoga (nation); Lenape; Mohawk (nation); Nanticoke; Oneida; Onondaga (nation); Seneca; Tuscarora
Elder, John, 227, 229, 415
electoral-hereditary leadership, 25
Elizabeth Town Point, 140
Endless Mountains, 18, 63, 69. *See also* Kittochtinny Hills
England. *See* Great Britain
English. *See* British
English language, 2, 383, 388, 411, 422
*Enquiry into the Causes of the Alienation of the Delaware and Shawanese Indians from the British Interest, An* (Thomson), 36, 417. *See also* Thomson, Charles
environmental discourse, modern, 178n7
equality, political and economic concepts of, 25
Erie (nation), 7, 421
Erie, Pennsylvania. *See* Presque Isle
escorts, during wartime, 262
Esopus (nation), 36
Esopus (town), 326
Evans, Samuel (Lenape delegate), 277, 418
Evans, Thomas (Lenape delegate), 227, 416
evil spirit, references to, 130, 186, 191, 202, 213, 229, 231, 243, 256, 259, 261, 272, 347, 366, 376, 393

Fairfax (estate), 409
Fairfax, Colonel William, 165, 413
famine, 66–67, 69, 84n2
far nations of Indians. *See* western Indians, or western Indian nations
federalism, 26
Fenton, William N., x, xi, xivn1, xivn4, 39n7, 39n11, 39n14, 41n50, 42n53, 61n3, 120n2, 121n4
Finger Lakes, 4
fire metaphor, 408; in 1736 minutes, 51–53, 56, 58–59; in 1742 minutes, 68, 70–71, 78; in 1744 minutes, 89, 92–93, 96, 112, 120n2; in 1745 minutes, 136, 138; in 1747 minutes, 143, 145; in 1748 minutes, 151; in 1753 minutes, 162–63, 166; in July 1756 minutes, 184, 186–89, 191; in November 1756 minutes, 202, 204–5, 208, 212–14; in 1757 Lancaster minutes, 228–30, 233–34; in 1757 Easton minutes, 272, 286; in 1758 minutes, 292–93, 295, 297–98, 300, 306–7, 309, 317–19, 322–23, 330; in 1761 minutes, 337, 341, 344–45, 347, 353, 356; in 1762 minutes, 363, 367, 380–82, 394–96, 405n3
Five Nations. *See* Iroquois Confederacy
"five nations" (1753). *See* Iroquois Confederacy; Lenape (nations); Miami; Shawnee; Wyandot
"Five Nations" (1758). *See* Cayuga; Conoy; Nanticoke; Oneida; Tuscarora; Tutelo
Flint, 2–4. *See also* Sky Cycle
Forbes, Eli, 359
Forbes, General John, 254n4, 301, 319, 323, 326, 381, 419–20
Forks region. *See* Delaware River: Forks region of the
forts, 345; British, 129, 232, 377, 400; forts, building of, 32–33, 162, 169, 177n1, 420; French, 162
Fort Allen, 199, 203, 208–9, 230, 316, 337, 421
Fort Augusta, 187, 220, 232, 234, 247, 265, 283, 385–86, 399, 404, 416, 423
Fort Cumberland, 231, 253n1
Fort Detroit, 363, 367
Fort Duquesne, 33, 234, 318, 332n2, 419–20. *See also* Fort Pitt
Fort Johnson, 181, 190, 285
Fort Necessity, 33
Fort Norris, 421

Fort Pitt, 287n1, 362, 366, 398, 405n8, 419. *See also* Fort Duquesne
Fort Stanwix, 405n8
Fort Venango, 234
Fort William Henry. 234
Forty Years War, 37, 181–82, 212, 217, 222n1, 234, 246, 409. *See also* Lenape-Pennsylvania war; Seven Years' War
Foster, Michael K., 6, 39n14, 41n50, 61n3
Foster, William, 294, 296, 298, 304–5, 308, 314, 319, 320, 323
Four Steps. *See* Nowalekeeka
"Fourteen Nations": mentioned in 1762 conferences, 379–80, 402. *See also* Cayuga; Conoy; Kickapoo; Lenape (nations); Miami; Lenape (nations): Munsee; Nanticoke; Oneida; Onondaga (nation); Saponi; Seneca; Shawnee; Tuscarora; Wawachtanies
Fox, Joseph, 414–15; at July 1756 conferences, 187, 190, 194, 199; at November 1756 conferences, 201, 203–5, 211, 216, 219, 221–22, 224n13, 224n16; at 1757 Easton conferences, 255, 258, 260, 262, 266, 269, 272, 277, 280, 282; at 1758 conferences, 291, 294, 296, 298, 303–5, 314, 321, 323; at 1761 conferences, 334, 336, 338, 340, 344, 346–47, 352, 355–56; at 1762 conferences, 360–61, 365, 368–69, 371, 375, 383, 385, 389, 391, 397
France, 1, 14–15, 19, 29–34, 36–37, 60n1, 122n12, 128, 140n2, 147n3, 413; Indian allies of, 1, 29–30, 64, 113, 116, 119, 127–30, 133–34, 137–38, 147n3, 155, 161, 193, 195, 203, 220, 232, 234–35, 243, 247–48, 281, 317, 323, 413; King of, 70, 112, 115, 128, 131, 136–37, 158, 162, 207, 217, 237, 243, 247, 256, 300. *See also* French
Franklin, Benjamin, ix–xi, xiii, 1, 11, 14–15, 17–19, 21, 26–37, 43n66, 62n10, 120nn1–2, 147n3, 222n1, 254n4, 287n1, 289n11, 332n2, 356n1, 405n8, 407, 410–12, 414–17, 419, 422; as commissioner, 27, 32–33, 35, 62n10, 161, 163–65, 167–68, 171, 173, 175–77, 177n1, 178n3, 179n9, 179n12, 199, 201, 203–5, 211, 216, 219, 221–22, 224n7, 224n13, 225n16; diplomatic mission to Great Britain, 407, 412, 416, 422; influence of Native American discourse on, 120n2, 179n12; interventions in treaties and treaty politics, 15, 179n13, 225n17; Junto of, 415; Library Company of, 422; "Narrative of the Late Massacres, A," 37; "Observations concerning the Increase of Mankind, Peopling of Countries, &c," 28; partnership with David Hall, 405n8; political ambitions of, 19; as president of the American Philosophical Society, 422; press of, 177n1, 225n17, 356n1; on printing announcements of treaties, 49, 63, 86, 123, 142, 149, 160, 181, 226, 255, 290, 334, 358; propaganda use of treaties, 15, 27, 35; speeches written by, 35, 120n2; view of Walking Purchase, 221–22; volunteer militia organized by, 30, 147n3
Franklin, William (son of Benjamin), 30, 37, 222
freedom of religion, 25, 408
freedom of speech, 25, 224n6
Freeland, George, 312, 326
French, 9–11, 14–15, 29–32, 37, 44n76, 60n1, 84n2, 140n2, 147n3, 159n2, 177n1, 178n4, 178n5, 178n7, 179n9, 179n12, 288n9, 332n2, 332n5, 407, 409–11, 413, 416, 419–20; in 1736 minutes, 54, 57; in 1742 minutes, 66–67, 70; in 1744 minutes, 88–89, 95, 103, 110, 112–16, 119; in 1745 minutes, 127–38; in 1747 minutes, 143–46; in 1748 minutes, 151, 153–55, 157–58; in 1753 minutes, 161–64, 168–72, 177; in July 1756 minutes, 185, 193, 195, 197; in November 1756 minutes, 202, 212, 217, 220; in 1757 Lancaster minutes, 226, 232, 234–35, 237, 242–48; in 1757 Easton minutes, 256, 266, 283–84, 286–87; in 1758 minutes, 293, 296–300, 304, 310–11, 315, 317–19, 323–25; in 1761 minutes, 337, 343–44; in 1762 minutes, 376, 379, 381, 385, 388, 398–400; as enemies to God, 130. *See also* France
French and Indian War. *See* Seven Years' War
French Canadians, 179n12
French empire, 23
French Indians. *See* France: Indian allies of
French language, 411
Friendly Association for Regaining and Preserving Peace with the Indians by Pacific Measures, 224n7, 282, 288, 421
frontier: as opposed to borderlands models of history, 24, 34 (*see also* borderlands); Iroquoia as, 88 (*see also* Iroquoia)

Gachradodow (Cayuga speaker), 23, 105, 107, 120, 365, 368, 375, 385, 391, 397, 410; gifts to, 120; speeches of, 105–7. *Also in text as* Gachradodo
Gáiwoh. *See* Iroquois: concept of righteousness

Galloway, Joseph, 415–16, 418; at 1757 Lancaster conferences, 236–37, 239–40, 243, 246; at 1757 Easton conferences, 255, 258, 260, 262, 266, 269, 272, 277, 280, 282, 287n1; at 1758 conferences, 291, 294, 296, 298, 303–5, 308, 314, 321, 323
Gamwing. *See* Big House Ceremony
Ganasaraga, 416
Garistagee (Seneca chief), 234
Garr, The. *See* Kinderuntie
Gashasdénshaa. *See* Iroquois: concept of power
gender: and emotion, 178n7; political discourses of, 23, 42n55, 80, 84n9, 106, 192, 196–97, 239, 244, 270, 275, 284, 307; and reciprocity, 8
genocide, 287n1
Genossa. *See* Shamokin
German-Flats, 234
German language, 422
Germans, 301, 414, 419; Palatine, 14, 60n1, 407
German schools of Pennsylvania, 411
germ warfare, 287n1, 412, 420
Gibbons, Joseph, 365, 368–69, 371, 375, 422
Gideon. *See* Teedyuscung
gifts, 178n3, 178n6; from British colony to Indian nation, 32–33, 88, 90, 106–7, 111, 113–14, 118–19, 135; from Indian nation to Pennsylvania, 54, 171, 174; from Pennsylvania to Indian nations, 54–55, 57–60, 68–70, 72–74, 76, 78–79, 139, 145, 147, 156, 161, 164, 166–68, 175, 187, 189, 192, 194, 203, 211, 214–15, 218, 228, 231, 247–48, 279, 281, 286, 323–25, 328, 331, 356, 375, 377, 383–85, 388, 396, 402, 404–5, 411; to Pennsylvania governor, 66; private, 176, 196, 198 (*see also* bribery: possible uses at treaties of); and reciprocity, 54, 225n15; from Teedyuscung to Denny, 218
Gist, Christopher, 32, 163, 412
Gnadenhutten, 414, 418, 420
Gooch, Governor William, 121n8. *See also* Virginia, Governors of
goods. *See* gifts
Gordon, Lewis, 354
Goshen, 312, 332n9
*Grammar of the Language of the Lenni Lenape or Delaware Indians* (Zeisberger), 422
Grandmother. *See* Sky Woman
Great Britain, 1–2, 11, 14–15, 18, 30–31, 35, 70, 92, 95, 112, 128, 146, 250, 257, 286, 332n6, 359, 376, 407, 412–13, 416; armed forces of, 410, 412, 417, 419; cooperation with colonial assemblies in military matters, 419; government of, 121n7; Parliament, 25, 28; Prince of, 130
Great Britain, King of, 22–23, 31, 33–36, 58–60, 66–67, 69–70, 74, 77, 84n4, 88–89, 92–93, 97–98, 103–4, 106, 108, 111–12, 114–15, 117, 119, 123, 126–31, 136, 149–51, 154–56, 162, 187, 207, 213–15, 217, 226–27, 232, 236, 238–43, 245–47, 255–58, 260–61, 263, 265–83, 288n7, 295, 303, 313–14, 318, 320, 323, 325–26, 343, 353, 355–56, 361, 367, 373, 385, 393, 399–400; ministers of the, 257, 267–68, 270, 273, 277; Privy Council of the, 36
Great Fire. *See* Iroquois Confederacy: Grand Council of the
Great Lakes, 10, 68, 137, 143–45, 158n1, 234, 366, 413; Indian nations of the, 10, 143–46
Great Meadow Fort, 134
Great Mountain. *See* Blue Mountains
Great Peace, 4–7. *See also* League, story cycle of the
Green Briar, Virginia, 310
Green Corn Ceremony, 8–9. *See also* Lenape (nations): oral traditions
Greenleafe, Isaac, 383
grief, 50, 65–66, 109, 126, 137, 167, 323, 335, 341, 353, 362, 391; and mourning in Iroquois oral tradition, 2–6
Griffitts, Thomas, 49, 52, 54–56
Grinde, Donald A., Jr., 25, 29, 42n57, 42nn59–61, 43nn63–65, 62n11, 148n4
Growdon, Lawrence, 290–92, 294–96, 298, 303–5, 308–9, 314, 321, 323, 416, 418
Guest, Christopher. *See* Gist, Christopher

Half King. *See* Tanaghrisson
Hall, David, 30, 160, 181, 226, 255, 290, 334, 356n1, 358, 405n8
Hambright, John, 383, 405
Hamell, George R., 25, 42n59
Hamilton, James, 160, 177n1, 412; at 1757 Lancaster conferences, 235–37, 239–40, 243, 246; at 1757 Easton conferences, 255, 258, 260, 262, 266, 269, 272, 280; at 1761 conferences, as governor, 334, 336, 338, 340, 344, 346–47, 349–50, 352–56, 356n1; at 1762 conferences, as governor, 358–66, 368–69, 371, 374–75, 378, 382–91, 397–99, 402–5; speeches of, 340–44, 347–53, 355–56, 360–61, 366–69, 371–75, 383–84, 391–98, 399–402
handkerchiefs, as gift and mnemonic, 175, 220, 353

hand shakes, as diplomatic symbol, 279–80, 301, 335, 336, 356, 358, 361, 364, 384–85
Hardy, Sir Charles, 181–82, 327, 421. *See also* New York: Governors of
Harris, John, 146, 226–27, 229–33, 386, 411
Harris, John, Jr., 386, 390, 400, 402–3
Harrisburg, Pennsylvania, 14, 17, 411; as Harris's Ferry, 226, 301, 364, 382, 400, 411
Hassell, Samuel, 55–56, 63, 71, 74–75, 77–78, 83, 142, 144–45
hatchet, 127, 129–30, 133, 137, 143–46, 162–63, 181–82, 184, 187, 190, 193, 213, 237, 242, 246, 253, 283–84, 296–301, 308, 310, 319, 323, 379, 387, 394; metaphor of burying the, 163, 296, 319, 323, 344, 379, 394
Hatchet River, 157
Haudenosaunee, x, xiv, 1, 3. *See also* Iroquois Confederacy
Hayes, William, 322
Heckewelder, John, 20, 40n19, 41n51, 224n6, 421
He-holds-the-earth, 39n16. *See also* Sky Cycle
Hendrick (Mohawk leader), 43n64, 416
hereditary leadership, 25, 223n3
Hewitt, J. N. B., 5, 38n4, 39n16
Hiawatha (twelfth-century co-founder of Iroquois Confederacy), 4–6, 38n4, 39n11
Hickman, Thomas, 301, 317, 319, 322, 352, 419
hieroglyphs, 8
higher power, references to, 81, 106, 129–30, 163, 166, 174, 183, 189, 216, 218, 220, 206, 259, 261–62, 264, 272, 291, 295, 335
Hinderuntie. *See* Kinderuntie
history: preservation of history, 21; research methodologies in the field of, 23–26, 38, 42n57, 412
*History of the Five Indian Nations* (Colden), 28
*History of the North American Indians* (Zeisberger), 421
Hockbruck, Wolfgang, 122n14
Hohio. *See* Ohio River; Ohio Valley
Holder of the Heavens, 7, 39n16
Holland, Nathaniel, 404, 423
Holler, Lieutenant, 203
Hooton, Benjamin, 383
Hopkinson, Thomas, 144–45, 149–50, 152–54, 157–58, 158n1
horn, ceremonial. *See* antlers
Horsfield, Mr., 199–200, 337. *Also in text as* Horsefield
Horsmanden, Daniel, 124
hospitality, cultural differences over, 59–60, 62n11
Howard, Lord, 103. *See also* Virginia, Governors of
Hudson, Henry, 10
Hudson Bay, 10
Hudson River, 10, 140n4, 321, 329. *Also in text as* Hudson's River
Hughes, John, 415; at July 1756 conferences, 187, 190, 194, 199; at November 1756 conferences, 201, 203–5, 211, 216, 219, 221–22, 224n13, 225n16; at 1757 Easton conferences, 255, 258, 260, 262, 266, 269, 272, 277, 280, 282; at 1758 conferences, 291, 294, 296, 298, 303–5, 308, 314, 321, 323
Humboldt, Wilhelm von, 28, 422
Hunter's Mill & Fort, 222n1, 415
hunting economy, 121n10
Huron confederacy, 1, 10, 30, 421
Hutchinson, Thomas, 124–26, 131

*ignorant,* connotation of, 28, 43n69
Illinois River, 8
immortality, 218
*Importance of Gaining and Preserving the Friendship of the Indians to the British Interest, The* (Kennedy), 27–28
Indian as romanticized figure, xii, 178n7
Indian attorneys, 329
Indian "Kings" as Pretenders, 188, 213, 223n3, 224n12
Indian nations, political relations among, 20–21
Indians, figured as children, 178n7
individual rights, concept of, 25
intelligence, mutual military, 71–72, 88, 112, 155, 208, 212, 283–84, 339–40, 347, 351
intermarriage, 357n4
international nature of British-Indian and Indian-Indian relations, xii–xiii, 84n1, 84n5
Irish, 177n1, 411, 414
iron goods, mending at treaties of, 92–93, 158, 174, 331, 369, 386–87
Iroquoia, 1, 4, 12, 15–16, 19, 30, 37–38, 94, 137, 140n2, 143, 177n1, 210, 219, 237–39, 293, 297, 300, 313, 332n3, 332n9, 343, 350, 378, 381–82, 388–90, 401, 403; as frontier or neutral zone, 88, 113, 115–16, 135, 137–38, 283; boundary line between Pennsylvania and, 346, 349, 395–96; boundary line between Virginia and, 103–4, 121n10; water route to Ohio through, 373
Iroquoian languages, 39n7, 224n10, 409–10, 420. *See also* Iroquois: languages

Iroquoian peoples, 2, 4, 7

Iroquois, xi–xiii, 2–8, 10–12, 14–27, 29–31, 33, 35, 39n7, 43n64, 60n1, 61n3, 61n7, 62n8, 62nn10–11, 84n4, 84n9, 121nn3–4, 147nn1–3, 158n1, 177n1, 179n8, 181–82, 184–99, 253n1, 254n2, 254n5, 254n7, 288n3, 288n7, 332n3, 332n6, 405n5, 411; agriculture in history of the, 4–5, 232; concept of health, 7; concept of justice, 7; concept of madness, 7; concept of righteousness, 7; concept of power, 7; culture, 6, 409; fishing and hunting in history of, 4–5; gender relations among, 4; influence on British discourse, 120n2, 121n7; influence on U.S. government, 148n4; languages, 292, 295, 303, 307, 342; metaphors, 120n2, 148n4 (*see also* boiled heads metaphor; brethren; brother; cannibalism; chain metaphor; Condolence Ritual, language of; consanguinity; fire metaphor; hatchet; kettle metaphor; kinship relations; nephew metaphor; road metaphor; woman); of Ohio, 15, 27, 29–32, 142–46, 147nn1–2, 149–54, 156–58, 158n1, 160–62, 164–65, 167–68, 170–73, 175–77, 179n9, 254n3, 297, 299, 333nn11–12; oral tradition of, 410 (*see also* League, story cycle of the; Sky Cycle); philosophy of land rights, 381; possible origin story of the, 94; reservations and reserves, 37–38; theology, 106; thought, 24–26. *See also* Iroquois Confederacy

Iroquois Confederacy, x–xiii, 1–8, 10–12, 14–37, 43n64, 407–18, 420–22; at the 1736 conferences, 49, 52–56, 58–60, 60nn1–2, 61n3, 61n5, 61n7, 62nn8–11; at the 1742 conferences, 63–71, 74–77, 79–83, 84nn1–4, 84n6, 84n9, 85n10; at the 1744 conferences, 86–120, 121nn3–4, 121nn6–12, 122n14; at the 1745 conferences, 123–28, 130–39, 140nn1–2, 140n4, 140n6; at the 1747 conferences, 142–43, 145–46, 147nn1–3, 148n4; at the 1748 conferences, 149–58, 158n1; at the 1753 conferences, 160–62, 164–65, 167–68, 170–73, 175–77, 177n1, 178n4, 179nn8–9, 179n12; in the 1756 minutes, 181–82, 199–202, 206–7, 210–11, 214–15, 219–20, 222n1, 223n4, 224n12; at the 1757 Lancaster conferences, 226–29, 233–34, 236–42, 246–53, 253n1, 254nn2–5, 254n7, 254n9; at the 1757 Easton conferences, 255–59, 261, 263, 266, 268–72, 274–80, 282–85, 288n3, 288n7, 288n9, 289n11; at the 1758 conferences, 297, 299–301, 305–8, 312–31, 332n3, 332n6; at the 1761 conferences, 337–38, 340, 342–43, 346, 349, 351–53, 356, 357n2, 357nn4–6; at the 1762 conferences, 358–59, 365, 368, 373, 375, 377, 380, 382, 385–91, 395–99, 401, 403–5, 405n1, 405n5, 405nn7–8; adopted nations of the, 23, 84n9, 140n4, 405n1; allies of the, 53–54, 60n1, 62n8, 68, 103, 108, 151, 405n1; chiefs, hereditary of the, 6, 20, 84n9, 121n3, 147n2, 223n3, 276, 380, 395, 398, 408 (*see also* antlers); clan mothers of the, 20–21, 32, 413; complaints to British of poor treatment, 404; consent requested for water right-of-way to Ohio, 397–98; Constitution of the, 43n64; customs regarding prisoners of war, 376–78, 390–93, 405n2; diplomacy of, 5–6, 14, 21, 61n6, 76, 121n3, 223n4, 238–39, 253, 398, 405n5, 416–17 (*see also* diplomacy, Native North American); diplomatic doorkeepers of the figurative Longhouse of the, 238–39, 394, 416–17; factions within the, 44n76, 418; governance during war versus peace, 143, 145, 147n2, 357n3; Grand Council of the, 20, 31–32, 34, 36, 51–52, 56, 65, 68, 82, 84n1, 90, 97–98, 127, 143, 147n2, 151, 171, 173–74, 179n8, 179n12, 186–87, 190, 197, 251, 253, 288n3, 312, 315, 327, 330, 341, 343, 345, 347, 349, 380, 394, 397–98, 404, 408, 411–12, 416; importance to British of peace with the, 88–89; invitation in 1726 to other nations, 60n1, 412; law of the, 224n6; longhouse as symbol of the, 416–17; neutrality of the, 67, 84n2, 88, 119, 125, 127, 135, 137–38, 143, 146; political structures of the, 27, 147n2, 409; practice of adoption of nations, 23; protection of peace delegates, 224n6; resistance to assimilation, 376; response to British confiscation of French prisoners of, 376; role of women in the, 4, 42n55; Tree of Peace, 323, 342; use of economic leverage by, 404; war chiefs of the, 147n2, 380, 395, 398; warning to British against asking for more lands, 381, 385–86, 395, 398; war roads of the, 99–100, 103–4, 106, 110, 310, 386–87, 399–400, 402–3; wars with the Cherokees & Catawbas, 376–78, 387–88, 390, 392, 402 (*see also* Catawba; Cherokee). *See also* Iroquois

Iroquois empire, myth of, 18, 20–23, 30

Iroquois League. *See* Iroquois Confederacy; League, story cycle of the

Jackson, Helen Hunt, 22, 42n54
*Jago*, 189
Jagrea (Mohawk diplomat), 181, 183, 185, 414
Jeffry, Ensign, 199, 201, 204–5, 211, 216
Jennings, Edmund, 86–91, 93, 96–97, 100–102, 105, 107–9, 111–15, 119–20, 409
Jennings, Francis, xivn1, 15, 19, 25–26, 28, 38n1, 39nn14–15, 39n17, 40nn18–19, 40nn22–29, 40nn31–50, 42nn55–56, 42nn58–59, 43n63, 43n66, 43n68, 43nn70–74, 44nn76–87, 44n89, 60nn1–2, 61nn5–6, 62n13, 84n9, 120n2, 121n10, 122n12, 140n2, 140n4, 147n3, 177n1, 178n5, 179n9, 179n12, 222n1, 224n7, 253n1, 254n2, 254n4, 287n1, 288nn2–3, 288n6, 332n2, 332n4, 332n9, 333nn12–13, 357n2, 357n4, 423
Jenochiaada (Onondaga chief), 336, 342; speeches of, 336. *Also in text as* Jenochryada
Jenontowanos. *See* Seneca
Jeoquanta, 355; speeches of, 355
Jigonsaseh (founding clan mother of the Iroquois Confederacy), 4, 413; as Lynx, 4. *Also in text as* Jigonsase
Johansen, Bruce, 25, 29, 41n50, 42n55, 42n57, 42nn59–61, 43nn63–65, 62n11, 148n4, 357n2, 423
John Penn's Creek, 312, 315
Johnson, Andrew, 294, 296, 298, 304–5, 308, 314, 319–20, 323, 328
Johnson, William, 27, 33, 35–37, 181–82, 187, 207, 210, 214, 222n1, 357n4, 410–11, 414, 421; in 1757 Lancaster minutes, 226–27, 229, 234, 236–37, 239, 241–43, 245–48, 250, 253n1, 254n6; in 1757 Easton minutes, 255, 257–58, 263, 266–68, 270–71, 273–74, 276, 281, 283, 285, 288n7; in 1758 minutes, 291, 293, 300, 308, 314–16, 319, 327, 331; in 1761 minutes, 343–47, 350–51, 355–56; in 1762 minutes, 363, 367, 373, 387, 390–91, 396, 400
Juniata (region), 110, 169, 254n7
Juniata River, 31, 33, 72–73, 121n9, 177n1, 244, 252, 409, 417
jurisdiction, matters of legal, 56–57, 65–66, 75–76, 84n8, 99–101, 109–10, 121n9, 260, 262, 353
justice: differing national and cultural theories of, 106; discourse of doing oneself, 73–75, 82, 91, 93–94; as opposed to revenge, 332n6

Kah-Kwahs, 421
Kakwatcheky. *See* Kekewatcheky
Kandiaronk (Wyandot leader), 42n55
Kanickhungo (Seneca speaker), 50, 52; speeches of, 50–51, 52–54, 58–59
Kanienke. *See* Mohawk (nation)
Karaghtadie. *See* Nichas
Kayarondinhagh Creek. *See* John Penn's Creek
Kayukwa. *See* Cayuga
Keekyuscung (Ohio Lenape chief), 332n2, 332n5, 409
Keisheta and his son, 388, 401, 405n5
Keith, William, 14. *See also* Pennsylvania, Governors of
Kekachtaninius Hills. *See* Kittochtinny Hills
Kekewatcheky (Shawnee chief), 153–54, 156, 252, 381, 412; speech of, 252–53
Kennedy, Archibald, 27–29
Kent County, Pennsylvania (now Delaware), 86, 123, 160, 236, 255
kettle metaphor, 76, 143–44, 147n3
Kickapoo (nation), 37, 360–61, 365, 369–71. *Also in text as* Kickapoe
Killbuck (Ohio Lenape war chief), 303, 419–20
killing, accidental, 244
Kinderuntie (Seneca leader), 365, 368, 375, 385, 389–91, 397–98, 403–4; speeches of, 390–91, 398–99, 403–4
King, Colonel Robert, 86–91, 93, 96, 97, 100–102, 105, 107–9, 111–12, 119–20
King, Rut (Tuscarora chief), 227, 233
King, Thomas (Oneida chief), 349, 416; at 1757 Lancaster conferences, 227, 233, 238–40, 243, 245–46, 254n5; at 1758 conferences, 291, 293, 296, 298, 304–5, 308–9, 312–14, 319–20, 323, 328, 330, 332n9; at 1762 conferences, 365, 368–69, 375, 377, 382, 385–86, 389, 391, 397, 402, 405n4; plot to assassinate, 405n4; speeches of, 238, 245–46, 304, 309–12, 330–31, 369, 375–82, 385–89, 390, 397
King George's War, 14, 29, 66–68, 70, 112–16, 127–29, 131–34, 136–37, 143–44, 146, 147n3, 154, 158, 389
King Philip's War, 12, 140n4
Kinsey, John, 74, 76, 83, 140
kinship relations: as metaphor for political relationship, 122n12, 140n4
Kirkland, Samuel, 27
Kisheta's son. *See* Keisheta and his son
Kittanning, 30, 234. *See also* Logstown
Kittatinny Mountains, 13, 19, 373. *Also in text as* Kittatinny Hills

Kittochtinny Hills, 18, 55, 63, 72, 322, 333n10, 354–55. *See also* Endless Mountains

Labaree, Leonard W., 41n46, 43nn63–69, 43n73, 44nn85–91, 120n2, 177n1, 222n1, 225n17, 254n4, 332n2
Laboughpeton (Lenape counselor), 265, 276, 313, 417
Lafitau, Joseph François, 3, 39n7
Lake Erie, 7–8, 15, 146, 157, 161, 413, 421–22
Lake Huron, 413, 421
Lake Michigan, 158n1
Lake Ontario, 3, 10–11, 140n2, 161, 413
Lake Superior, 413
Lakota (nations), xivn11, 158n1
Lancaster, 37, 282; as site of 1744 conferences, 36, 86–87, 90, 93, 96–97, 100–102, 105, 107–8, 110–11, 115, 135, 138, 140n6; as site of 1748 conferences, 149–50, 153–54, 157–58; as site of Spring 1757 conferences, 226, 230, 233, 235–37, 239–40, 243, 246, 249, 254n2, 288n3; as site of 1762 conferences, 358, 360–61, 364–65, 368–69, 371, 374–75, 383, 385, 391, 397
Lancaster County, Pennsylvania, 150, 154, 158
land: claims, 23, 32, 35, 58–60, 74, 76–77, 79–80, 87–89, 91–101, 103–5, 108–9, 209–11, 221–22, 268, 281–83, 288n2, 314, 320–22, 325–26, 353–56, 373–74, 401, 404, 417; as compensation for service to Penns, 85n10, 177n1; disputes, 18, 58–60, 72–77, 79–81, 90–96, 103–4, 116–17, 121n8, 121n10, 203, 208–11, 213–14, 241, 244–45, 249–50, 254n7, 267–68, 273, 276–77, 288n9, 325–26, 355, 373–75, 383; early negotiations with Lenapes for, 7, 10, 12–14; fraud alleged, 17, 19, 31, 33–34, 208–10, 221–22, 237, 241–42, 249–50, 256–57, 263–65, 267–68, 270–71, 273, 276–79, 283, 300, 311, 313, 316, 325–26, 333n13, 373–74, 409; grants, 31, 33, 69, 100, 104, 268; greed for, 24, 38, 84n5, 244, 416; justice in dealings over, 203, 207, 311, 325, 408; lottery, 17; power to buy and sell, 59, 63–65, 80–81, 84n1, 84n9, 96, 213, 222, 241, 245, 265, 270, 273, 316, 330, 348–49, 407, 419; quitrents paid for, 29, 177n1; rights-of-way through, 398–99; speculation, 15, 41n39, 84n6, 209, 407; surveyors, 74; title, 17, 24, 101, 108, 111, 329 (*see also* land claims); value of, 72–73, 84n6, 106, 178n6, 217; of the Walking Purchase, 16–20
land deeds, 265, 268, 270–71, 273–74, 276–78, 317, 322, 330, 333n10, 340, 356, 357n6, 396–97, 401; related to Walking Purchase (1686), 278; deed of, 1718 requested by Croghan, 276; from the Iroquois Confederacy to Maryland (1744), 108; deed of release (1749), 278; New Jersey deeds (1758), 329; "deed" to Virginia from the Iroquois Confederacy (1744), 33, 44n76, 111; Walking Purchase deed (1737), 278, 333n10. *See also* land purchases and sales; land releases
land pressures, coercive, 38, 381, 395–96
land purchases and sales (cessions), 9–10, 12–17, 19, 21–22, 23, 31–34, 55, 59, 64–66, 69, 72–73, 76–77, 79–81, 84n1, 97, 99, 101–2, 105–8, 111, 114, 177n1, 208–11, 213–14, 221–22, 241, 244–45, 249–50, 264–65, 268, 277, 316–17, 322, 329, 333n10, 410–11, 415, 417; coercive tactics in, 15–17; Iroquois Confederacy to Pennsylvania (1749), 31, 177n1, 254n7, 278, 288n9; Iroquois Confederacy to Connecticut (1754), 33–35, 254n7, 288n9, 346, 349, 405n4; Iroquois Confederacy to Pennsylvania (1754), 33–35, 254n7, 268, 278, 288n9, 312, 315–16, 328–29, 354, 395–97, 410, 419, 422; Ohio Iroquois to Virginia (1752), 32
land releases: by Iroquois Confederacy of Delaware lands (1736), 17–19, 265, 278; by Iroquois Confederacy of Susquehanna lands (1736), 18, 55, 58, 63, 69–70, 72, 278; by Iroquois Confederacy of the Lebanon Valley (1732), 408; by Iroquois Confederacy to Maryland (1744), 101, 105, 108; by Lenapes of the Walking Purchase lands (1737), 278; by Lenapes of the Walking Purchase lands (1762), 373–74, 383–85; Myth of Iroquois Empire "release" (1744), 23, 32–33, 36, 44n76, 111, 254n9
land rights, 10, 12, 20, 23, 30, 88, 94, 98, 101, 103–5, 222, 252, 356, 357n4 (*see also* land claims; land title); theories of, 94, 106
land use: agreements about, 10, 99, 209, 235; disputes over, 73, 81, 95, 103, 106, 110, 118, 209, 235, 311, 312, 321; myths regarding, 121n10; rights, 332n7
Langhorne, Mr., 77
Langlade, Charles, 178n5
Laometang Falls, 321, 329
Lapachpeton. *See* Laboughpeton
Lardner, Lyn-Ford: at 1757 Lancaster conferences, 235–37, 239–40, 243, 246; at 1757 Easton conferences, 255, 258, 260, 262, 266, 269, 272, 277, 280; at 1758 conferences, 290–92, 294–96, 298, 303–5, 308–9, 314, 323

Lawrence, Thomas, 52, 54–55, 63, 71, 74–79, 83, 140, 142, 144–45
leader as servant, concept of, 25
League. *See* Iroquois Confederacy
League, story cycle of the, 2–7, 38n4; madness in, 5–6; relationship to Sky Cycle, 2–5
League of the Haudenosaunee. *See* Iroquois Confederacy; League, story cycle of
Lebanon Valley, 408, 417
Lee, Thomas, 86–91, 93, 96–97, 100–102, 105, 107–13, 119–20, 121n8, 409, 420
legislative structures, 26
Lehigh River, 13, 16, 19, 209
Lehigh Valley, 19
Lenape (language), xi, 8, 292–93, 295, 301, 303, 305, 307, 309, 320, 329–31, 421–22; Munsee dialect, 8, 314, 320; Unami dialect, 8; use of first person in, 224n10
Lenape (nations), xii–xiii, 6–20, 23, 29–38, 53, 60n1, 61n3, 161–62, 407–9, 411–22; at the 1742 conferences, 69, 72, 76–77, 79, 82, 84n9; in the 1744 minutes, 100, 108–10; at the 1748 conferences, 150–51, 153–54, 156–58; at the 1753 conferences, 161–62, 164–68, 170–75, 177, 179n9; at the 1756 conferences, 181–85, 187, 189–90, 193–214, 216–22, 222n1, 223n4, 224n6, 224nn9–10, 224n14; at the 1757 Lancaster conferences, 226–50, 252–53, 254n2, 254n4, 254n7; at the 1757 Easton conferences, 255–87, 287n1, 288n2, 288nn8–9; at the 1758 conferences, 290, 292–300, 305–10, 313–23, 326, 328–31, 332n6, 332n9; at the 1761 conferences, 334–36, 338–42, 344–47, 350–52, 354–56, 357n2, 357n4, 357n6; at the 1762 conferences, 358, 360–67, 369–71, 373–76, 381, 383–85, 392, 395–99, 405n7; agriculture, fishing, and hunting in history of, 8–10; Brandywine, 13–15, 30; chiefs of, 10, 14, 30, 199, 207, 211, 219, 221, 223n3, 307, 347; Christian, 357n4, 421 (*see also* Lenape [nations]: Moravian); concepts of responsibility and revelation, 8; diplomacy, 223n4 (*see also* diplomacy: Native North American); eastern (*see also* Lenape [nations]: Wyoming), 34, 36, 224nn9–10, 288n3, 289n11, 301, 357n4, 405n1, 405n4, 414–15, 420; Forks, 13–14, 16–20, 30–31, 34, 36, 69, 76–77, 79, 82, 84n9, 332n2, 409, 415, 417; funeral oration, 221; governance during war versus peace, 420; independence from Iroquois Confederacy, 418; Jersey, 13, 199; Moravian, 11, 37; Munsee, 8, 10, 13, 19, 84n9, 208, 212, 227, 255, 290, 292, 294–99, 301, 305–9, 311, 313–14, 319–23, 325–27, 329, 338, 354, 365, 382–83, 391, 404, 405n1, 417–18; northern, 10; Ohio, 15, 30–34, 36, 57, 60n1, 62n9, 150–51, 153–54, 156–58, 160–62, 164–68, 170–75, 177, 358, 360–67, 369–71, 373–74, 383–85, 405n1, 412, 420; Okehocking, 13; oral traditions, 8–9; political structures of, 8, 13; population loss among and causes of, 12; reservations and reserves, 38; southern, 7, 10; Tulpehocken, 13–15, 30, 60n1, 332n2, 408, 417; Unalachtigo, 12–13, 417; Unalimi, 13, 417; Unami, 8, 12–13, 255, 290, 292, 294, 296, 298, 305, 308, 313–14, 323, 417; western (*see also* Lenape [nations]: Ohio) 34, 36, 160, 289n11, 332n2, 333n14, 419; Wyoming, 34–36, 226, 332n2
Lenape-Pennsylvania war (1755), 33–36, 182, 190, 193, 203–4, 212, 217, 220, 222n1, 332n2, 366, 371, 383–84, 399, 411, 414–15, 418, 420, 422; causes of, 33–36, 186, 190, 205–10, 212, 216–17, 237–38, 244, 249, 256, 263–64, 267, 288n9, 295, 300–301, 310–12, 315, 332n9, 400; cease-fire of, 300; Iroquois involvement in, 332n3. *See also* Forty Years War; Seven Years' War
Lenopi. *See* Lenape (nations)
Lepaghpetund. *See* Laboughpeton
Le Tort, 65–66, 75
Lewes, Delaware, 10
liberty, concept of. *See* political freedom(s), concept of
linguistic theories, 422
literacy, western, 218
Little Abraham (Mohawk chief), 232, 238, 239–40, 242–43, 245–46, 248, 416; speeches of, 232, 238–39, 240, 242–43, 245, 248
Little Cove, Pennsylvania, 364
Locke, John, 24
Locquies, William (Lenape diplomatic messenger), 181–83, 414
Logan, James, 15–18, 60n1, 407–8, 410–11, 416; at the 1736 conferences, 49, 51–52, 54–58, 60, 61n5, 62n10; in the 1747 minutes, 144–45, 147; at the 1742 conferences, 63, 66, 68, 71, 74–79, 81, 83; correspondence of, 88, 96, 98; embezzlement of Penn's money by, 407; speeches of, 50, 56–58, 59–60. *See also* Pennsylvania, Presidents of
Logan, William, 408, 411; at the 1747 conferences, 142, 144–45; at the 1748 conferences, 149–50, 152–54, 157–58, 158n1; at the 1756

conferences, 187, 190, 194–96, 198–99, 201–5, 210–11, 216, 219; at the 1757 Lancaster conferences, 233, 235–37, 239–40, 243, 246; at the 1757 Easton conferences, 255, 258, 260, 262, 266, 269, 272, 277, 280, 285, 286; at the 1758 conferences, 291–92, 294, 296, 303–5, 308, 314, 323, 333n10; at the 1762 conferences, 358, 360–61, 365, 368–69, 371, 375, 383, 385, 389, 391, 397, 403–5; iron mine of, 333n10
Logstown, 30, 32, 145, 161–62, 164, 169, 178n5, 234; Council at, 145, 161–62, 168
London, 36, 332n2
Loudon, Lord, 419
Louisburgh, 128
Lower Marlborough, Maryland, 383
Loyal Hanning, 323
Lydius, John Henry, 410
Lynx, 2–4

Machachlosing, 339, 422
Magna Charta, 24
Mahaniay, 72–73
Mahican (nation), 8, 12, 36, 418, 422; at the 1745 conferences, 130–31, 140n4; in the 1756 minutes, 184–85, 199, 202; at the 1757 Easton conferences, 255–61, 263, 266, 269, 272, 274–75, 277–79, 282–83, 285–86; at the 1758 conferences, 290, 292, 294, 296, 298, 305–6, 308, 313–14, 323; at the 1761 conferences, 334–36, 338–42, 344–47, 350–52, 354–55, 357n2. *Also in text as* Mahickanders
Makahelousink. *See* Machachlosing
Mammatuckan. *See* Abraham
Manahoac (nation), 418
Manhattan Island, 10
Mann, Barbara A., 1–4, 38nn1–4, 39nn5–10, 41n50, 41n52, 42n55, 61n6, 62n12, 224n6, 333n12, 357n2, 423
Maquas. *See* Mohawk (nation)
Maryland, 11–12, 18, 20–23, 57–60, 72–75, 77, 354–56, 364, 383, 387, 389, 400, 404, 409–10, 416, 422; at the 1744 conferences, 86–94, 96–98, 100–102, 104–15, 117–20; citizens of, 355; in Weiser's 1743 report, 250–51, 253
Maryland, Governors of, 58–60, 74–75, 77, 87–94, 96, 98, 100, 104, 107, 114, 251, 253, 355–56, 387, 400, 422; speeches of, 91–92
Massachusetts (or Massachusetts-Bay), 12, 29, 123–26, 131–32, 134–35, 140n6, 410, 419; Assembly of, 124; Council of, 124; Governors of, 128–29, 146, 410, 419
Masters, William, 415; at November 1756 conferences, 199, 201, 203–5, 211, 216, 219, 221–22, 224n13, 225n16; at 1757 Lancaster conferences, 236–37, 239–40, 243, 246; at 1757 Easton conferences, 255, 258, 260, 262, 266, 269, 272, 277, 280, 282; as trustee of the Academy of Philadelphia, 415
Mawhickon. *See* Mahican
McAlpin, Lieutenant, 199, 201, 204–5, 211, 216
McConaughy, David, 365, 422
McConnoll, Michael N., 30, 41n35, 43nn71–73
McKee, Thomas, 415; at 1757 Lancaster conferences, 227–29, 232–33, 235, 247–48; at 1757 Easton conference, 256, 258, 260, 263, 266, 269, 272, 277, 280, 282
Mechkilikishi (Lenape chief), 16, 19, 224
Mechtochkaway (Lenape chief), 347
mediation. *See* oral traditions and discourses: mediation of
mediators. *See* peacemakers, diplomatic
Memenowal (Lenape leader), 365, 422
Memeskia (Miami chief), 178n5
memory, 53, 98, 104, 116, 197, 238, 245, 254n5, 261, 269–70, 280–81, 288n8, 292. *See also* speech
Memskies, 184–85. *See also* Lenape (nations): Munsee
Merrell, James H., 40n23, 122n11, 423
metempsychosis. *See* reincarnation
Miami (nation), 15, 30, 32, 37, 54, 62n8, 65, 76, 290, 332n2, 339, 350, 411, 420; at the 1748 conferences, 149–52, 154–58, 158n1, 159n2; at the 1753 conferences, 161, 163, 165–69, 171–75, 177; at the 1762 conferences, 360, 361, 365, 369–71; attacked by the French, 163, 178n5; ceremonial meaning of green for, 172–73; hereditary office, 172–73; chiefs of the, 168, 172
Mifflin, John: at July 1756 conferences, 185, 187, 190, 194–96, 198; at 1757 Lancaster conferences, 235–37, 239–40, 243, 246; at 1757 Easton conferences, 255, 260, 262, 266, 269, 272, 277, 280; at 1758 conferences, 290–92, 294, 296, 298, 303–5, 308–9, 314, 321, 323
Mihesuah, Devon, 44n93
military, political control over, 147n3
military leadership, negotiations over, 287
military support, requests by Indians for, 163–64, 179n9, 287, 410, 414, 420
Miller, C. William, 41n41, 41n46, 177n1, 222n1, 289n11, 331n1, 356n1
Miller, Jay, 8, 40nn19–21

Mingoes, 320. *See also* Iroquois Confederacy
Minisink (language). *See* Lenape (language): Munsee dialect
Minisink (nation). *See* Lenape (nations): Munsee
Minisinks (place), 193, 412
minutes, 218, 256, 269–71, 276, 279, 281, 286, 343; accuracy of, 221–22, 224nn13–14, 225n16, 287n1, 390, 412; addenda to, 177, 179n12, 221–22, 224n13, 225n17, 250–53; alterations of, 17, 20, 332n4, 333n14; reading of the, 389–90
Miskepalathy (Shawnee chief), 360, 370–71; speeches of, 370–71. *Also in text as* Miskapalathy
Mississippian cultural zone, 158n1
Mississippi River, 154, 157, 158n1, 421; French forts on the, 157
Mohawk (language), xi, 189, 409
Mohawk (nation), 1, 5, 10–12, 14–15, 17, 36, 43n64, 50, 60n2, 122n12, 125–27, 133, 165, 170, 215, 346, 354, 380, 394, 396, 401, 407, 410, 413–14, 416–18; at the 1757 Lancaster conferences, 227, 230, 232, 236–40, 243, 246; in the 1757 Easton minutes, 255; at the 1758 conferences, 290–94, 296–99, 303–5, 308–9, 313–14, 323
Mohawk River, 214
Mohegan (nation), 140n4
Mohiccons, or Mohickons, or Mohickon, or Mohiggans. *See* Mahican
Mohocks. *See* Mohawk (nation)
Mohongely River. *See* Monongahela River
Mohongialo Forks. *See* Monongahela River
Mohonoy, 381, 395–96
Monacan (nation), 418
Monaidy, 281
Monongahela (region), 32
Monongahela, battle of the, 179n9, 253n1, 288n5, 413–14, 420
Monongahela River, 32–33, 162, 169
monopoly (in land purchases), 84n1
Montour, Andrew (interpreter), 32, 411, 419; at 1748 conferences, 150, 152–54; at 1753 conferences, 160–61, 163–65, 171, 176, 177n1, 179n12; at 1758 conferences, 314, 320, 322–24; at 1762 conferences, 389; brother of, 164; family of, 411
Montour, Captain Henry, 292, 294, 296, 298, 303–5, 308, 327. *See also* Montour, Andrew
Montour, Lewis, 226–27, 230
Montreal, 127, 137
Montrose, Louis, 27, 42n58
Moore, Charles, 250
Moravian, 199, 414–15, 419–21. *See also* Lenape (nations): Moravian
Morris, Robert Hunter, 185, 187, 209, 218, 222n1, 410, 414–15; gifts to, 209; speeches of, 182–83, 185–88, 190–92, 194, 197–98
Morton, John, 361, 365, 368–69, 371, 375
mourning, role in relation to war, 122n11
Muhlenberg, Frederick, 27
Munsee, or Munsey, or Munsies. *See* Lenape (nations): Munsee
multiculturalism, 24
Murray, Joseph, 124
Mushemeelin (Lenape individual), 409
mutilation, 158n1

Nanticoke (nation), 16, 23, 417–18; at the 1742 conferences, 69; at the 1748 conferences, 150–51, 153–54, 157–58; at the 1757 Lancaster conferences, 227, 229, 236–37, 239–40, 243, 246; at the 1757 Easton conferences, 255–59, 261, 263, 266, 269, 271–72, 274–75, 277–79, 282–83, 286; at the 1758 conferences, 290–91, 294, 296–99, 304–6, 308–9, 313–14, 323; at the 1761 conferences, 334–36, 338, 340–42, 344–47, 351–52, 354–55, 357n2; at the 1762 conferences, 359, 365, 368, 375, 385, 391, 397, 405n1
"Narrative of the Late Massacres, A" (Franklin), 37
Native American speech genres, xii, xivn6, 2–6
Native American Studies, ix, xiii, xivn8
Native languages, European views of, 224n5
Neccochoon (Munsee Lenape chief), 322
Nena chy haut. *See* Nenatchehan
Nenatchehan (Ohio Lenape warrior), 32, 69, 303, 408, 420
nephew metaphor: in relation to cousin metaphor, 405n7
Neshaminy Creek, 16
Neucheconno (Shawnee chief), 153, 156, 411–12
Neutral (nation), 4, 421
Newcastle, Captain (Seneca war chief), 181, 183, 185–87, 190–92, 195–98, 413–14; as agent for Pennsylvania, 196–98, 414; death of, 220–21
Newcastle County, Pennsylvania (now Delaware), 86, 123, 160, 236, 255
New England, 12, 124, 129, 140n4, 146
New France, 14. *See also* France; French empire

New Hampshire, 128
New Historicism, 24–27
New Hope, Pennsylvania, 13
New Jersey, 13, 37, 57, 182, 187, 190, 194, 207–9, 217–19, 233, 235, 244, 256, 281–83, 418–19; at the 1758 conferences, 291, 294–96, 301, 304, 314, 318–21, 326–27, 329–30; citizens of, 295, 314, 321, 326; Council of, 296, 298, 304–5, 308, 314, 319, 323, 330; Governors of, 37, 217, 219, 294–97, 301, 304–5, 307–9, 311–13, 315, 318–23, 325–30, 377–78, 419
New Netherlands, 11. *See also* New York
New York, 11–17, 24, 29, 33, 35–38, 58, 60n1, 68, 89, 147n1, 181, 198, 222n1, 224n12, 320, 326–27, 329, 407, 410, 414, 418, 421; at the 1745 conferences, 123–26, 128, 133–35, 140nn1–2, 140n6; Assembly of, 134; Governor's Council of, 124–26, 134; Governors of, 17, 37, 68, 92, 95, 97–98, 103, 122n12, 123–28, 130–36, 138, 142–43, 146, 147n1, 162, 181, 326–27, 421; merchants of, 17
New York City, 135, 140, 418
Niagara, 4, 161, 194, 377
Nichas (Mohawk chief), 36, 291–93, 296, 298, 303–5, 309, 313–14, 317, 323, 327, 418; speeches of, 303–5, 327
Nimham (Wapinger chief), 292, 294, 296, 298, 305, 308, 313, 319, 323, 329
Nishamekatchton Creek, 203
Nixhisaqua, 381, 395–96
nonhereditary leadership, concept of, 25
Norris, Isaac, 33, 332n2, 412; at the 1753 conferences, 160–61, 163–65, 167–68, 171, 173, 175–77, 178n3, 179n12; at the 1757 Lancaster conferences, 236–37, 239–40, 246; at the 1757 Easton conferences, 255, 258, 260, 262, 266, 269, 272, 277, 280–81, 286; at the 1758 conferences, 291, 294, 296, 298, 303–5, 308, 314, 323
North America, 67, 68, 74
Northampton County, Pennsylvania, 203, 222n1, 327, 415, 421
North Carolina, 16, 23, 322, 409–10
northern and northwestern Indians (of Canada), 140n2
"Northern Indians" (1762). *See* Cayuga; Conoy; Lenape (nations): eastern; Lenape (nations): Munsee; Nanticoke; Oneida; Onondaga (nation); Saponi; Seneca; Shawnee; Tuscarora
North River. *See* Hudson River
North Wind, in Iroquois oral tradition, 2
Nowalekeeka (Lenape chief), 322
Nutimus (Lenape chief), 16–17, 19, 69, 76, 79, 224, 322, 409–11
Nutimy's Town, 14, 19

"Observations concerning the Increase of Mankind, Peopling of Countries, &c" (Franklin), 28
Ohio Company of Virginia, 31–32, 410, 412–13, 420
Ohio Indians. *See* Ohio Valley, Indian nations of the
Ohio Iroquois. *See* Iroquois: of Ohio
Ohio Lenape. *See* Lenape (nations): Ohio
Ohio River, 7–8, 18, 33, 57, 109–10, 120, 144–46, 149–54, 156–58, 158n1, 160–64, 168–70, 175–76, 179n9, 179n11, 210, 226–27, 229, 232, 234–35, 252, 310–12, 315, 318–19, 323, 326, 333n11, 408–9
Ohio settlers, attempted expulsion of, 169
Ohio Valley, 15, 23, 29–32, 34, 36, 44n76, 60n1, 140n6, 159n2, 177n1, 178n7, 179n9, 179nn11–12, 195, 288n9, 332n3, 409–10, 412–13, 416, 419–20; British claims to, 179n9, 398, 409; French claim to, 162–63, 169, 409; Indian requests for empires to vacate, 161–63, 169
Ohio Valley, Indian nations of the, 29–34, 36, 185, 195, 234–35, 253n1, 254n4, 289n11, 297, 299, 301, 311, 317, 327, 332n5, 405n1, 411–12, 420; at the 1747 conferences, 142–46, 147n1, 147n3; at the 1748 conferences, 149–58, 158n1; at the 1753 conferences, 160–77, 177n1, 178n3, 178n5, 179nn8–9, 179nn11–12; at the 1762 conferences, 374 (*see also* Kickapoo; Lenape [nations]: Ohio; Miami; Shawnee; Tuscarora; Wawachtanies); relationship with Iroquois Confederacy, 171, 173
Ojibwa (nations), 26, 168, 413, 421
Oka/Kanesatake, 410. *See also* praying Indians
Olumapies (Lenape chief), 14, 17, 69, 76, 79, 382, 396, 408, 417
Onandago, or Onandagoes. *See* Onondaga (nation)
Onantio. *See* Onontio
Onas, 407–8; in 1736 minutes, 52; in 1742 minutes, 64–65, 72, 80; in 1744 minutes, 87, 90, 92–93, 95, 98–100, 104, 107–9, 114–15, 118, 120; in 1745 minutes, 136, 138; in 1748 minutes, 151–52; in 1753 minutes, 162, 166, 168–73, 176; in July 1756 minutes, 183–84; in

1757 Lancaster minutes, 228–33, 235, 237–40, 242, 245, 248, 250–53; in 1757 Easton minutes, 257, 279; in 1758 minutes, 293, 331; in 1761 minutes, 335–38, 344–49, 354–56; in 1762 minutes, 377–81, 385–90, 398, 402. *See also* Penn, John; Penn, Thomas; Penn, William; Pennsylvania
Onayiuts. *See* Oneida
Oneida (nation), 6, 15, 50, 68, 87, 94, 136, 150, 161, 407, 411, 416; at the 1757 Lancaster conferences, 227, 229, 236, 238–40, 243, 246, 254n5; in the 1757 Easton minutes, 255; at the 1758 conferences, 290–91, 294, 296–99, 304–6, 308–9, 313–14, 319, 323; at the 1761 conferences, 334–36, 338, 340–47, 349, 351–52, 354–55, 357n2; at the 1762 conferences, 365, 368, 375, 379–80, 385, 389, 391, 394, 396–97, 401, 405n1; Pine Tree at, 379, 394. *Also in text as* Oneides; Oneido; Oneidoes; Onenniote
Onohoquage, 359
Onondaga (language), 422
Onondaga (nation), 4–5, 14–15, 20, 31–32, 39n16, 44n76, 50, 56, 63–68, 87, 90, 94, 97–98, 143, 147n2, 151, 408–9, 416–17; at the 1757 Lancaster conferences, 227, 231, 236–37, 239–40, 243, 246, 251; in the 1757 Easton minutes, 255; at the 1758 conferences, 290–91, 294, 296–99, 304–6, 308–9, 313–14, 323; at the 1761 conferences, 334–36, 338, 340–47, 349, 351–52, 354–55, 357n2; at the 1762 conferences, 365, 368, 375, 380, 385, 391, 397, 401–2, 405n1
Onondaga Council. *See* Iroquois Confederacy: Grand Council of the
Onondagoes, or Onontakes. *See* Onondaga (nation)
Onontio, 116, 151, 155, 162–63, 169, 317. *See also* Canada: Governors of
Onontio's children. *See* France: Indian allies of
Onontogoes. *See* Onondaga (nation)
Ontario, 410
Opies (nation), 339, 350
oral historiography, reliability of, 121n6, 223n4
oral traditions and discourses, xiii–xiv, 1–6, 21, 39n7, 53, 103, 106, 116, 121n4, 121n6, 224n14, 288n8, 289n10; mediation of, x, xiii, xivn5, 2–3, 20–21, 42n55
oratory, x, xii
orenda. *See* spiritual power
Orndt, Major Jacob. *See* Arndt, Jacob
Oswego, 127, 137, 140n2, 344, 377; trading house at, 127, 137
"other five nations, the," 188, 198
Otseningo, 181, 184, 190–91, 237, 239, 242, 308, 417. *Also in text as* Otsaningo
Otsitsa. *See* Sky Woman
Ottawa (nation), 31, 168, 371, 413, 420, 422. *Also in text as* Ottaways; Outawas
Ouabache River, 151, 157
Owego, 418
Owendaets. *See* Wyandot

Pacific Ocean, 22
pacifism, 34, 37, 147n3, 415, 417, 419
Packsinosa. *See* Paxinosa
Paeoqualin Mountains. 321, 329. *Also in text as* Paoqualin Mountains
Palatine Germans. *See* Germans, Palatine
palingenesis. *See* reincarnation
palisades, of League cycle tradition, 1
Palmer, Anthony, 52, 54, 142, 144–45, 147. *See also* Pennsylvania: President of
Papounan (Lenape chief), 338–39, 351–52, 422; speeches of, 338
Parsons, Major William, 199, 201, 204–5, 209, 211, 216, 231, 415
passports, 104, 262, 323, 356, 359, 404
Patowmack. *See* Potomac River
Patuxent River, 92, 383
Paulin's Kiln, 219
Paxinosa (Shawnee chief), 182–83, 282, 285–86, 414; speeches of, 183, 285
Paxtang, 14, 17, 410. *See also* Harrisburg, Pennsylvania
Paxton, Pennsylvania, 415
Paxton Boys, 11, 37, 222n1
peace, British efforts to enforce among Indian nations. *See* Catawba; Cherokee
Peace, Great. *See* Great Peace
peace, in Iroquois thought, 61nn6–7
peacemakers, diplomatic, 84n9
Peepy, Joseph (Lenape delegate): at July 1756 conferences, 187, 189–90, 194, 199; at 1757 Lancaster conferences, 226–27, 230; at 1761 conferences, 334, 338, 340, 344, 346–47, 352, 354–55; at 1762 conferences, 365, 368, 375, 383, 385, 391, 397; speeches of, 344–46
Pemberton, Israel, 27, 224n7, 287n1, 301–3, 321, 383, 411–12, 414–19, 421
Penn, John, 15–17, 19, 23, 27, 29, 34–38, 60n1, 123, 210, 407, 411–12, 415, 417, 421. *See also* Pennsylvania, Proprietor(s) of

Penn, Richard, 16, 112, 123, 407, 411–12, 415, 417, 421. *See also* Pennsylvania, Proprietor(s) of

Penn, Thomas, 15–19, 23, 27, 29, 32, 34–38, 49–52, 54–58, 60, 60n1, 64, 66, 70–73, 76–77, 79, 83, 123, 147n3, 177n1, 210, 222n1, 250, 288n2, 333n13, 357n4, 407, 411–12, 414–15, 417, 421; nephew of (John), 37. *See also* Pennsylvania, Proprietor(s) of

Penn, William, 13–17, 27, 50, 70–71, 78, 83, 112, 182, 184, 191, 193–94, 202, 205, 210, 215, 224n12, 247, 267, 298, 348, 366, 407–8; death of, 407–8; fairness in dealings with Lenapes, 13, 205, 267, 408; sons of, 84n6, 85n10, 177n1, 205, 209–11, 224n12, 250, 287n1, 407, 411–12, 415, 417, 421 (*see also* Penn, John; Penn, Richard; Penn, Thomas; Penn, William, Jr.); wives of, 407 (*see also* Callowhill, Hannah; Springett, Gulielma)

Penn, William, Jr., 407

Pennsylvania, x–xi, 1, 4, 7–9, 12–21, 24, 27, 29–37, 407–12, 414–22; in 1736 minutes, 52–55, 58–59, 60nn1–2, 62nn9–10, 62n13; in 1742 minutes, 63–65, 69, 72–74, 76–78, 80, 83–84, 84n1, 84n9; in 1744 minutes, 86–87, 89, 105, 107–8, 110–13, 115, 118–19, 121n3, 121n5, 121n9; in 1745 minutes, 123, 125–26, 134–36, 138–40, 140n1, 140n6; in 1747 minutes, 142–46, 147n1, 147n3; in 1748 minutes, 149, 151, 154–55, 157, 158n1, 159n2; in 1753 minutes, 160–67, 169, 174, 177n1, 179n9, 179n11; in 1756 minutes, 181–87, 190–94, 197–202, 204–5, 207, 209–10, 212–15, 217–22, 222n1, 223n4, 224n9, 224n14; in 1757 Lancaster minutes, 228–29, 231, 235–36, 238–43, 246–53, 253n1; in 1757 Easton minutes, 255–58, 260–63, 265–70, 272–73, 277, 280–83, 285, 287, 288n7, 288n9, 289n11; in 1758 minutes, 290–95, 298, 300, 301, 315, 319, 322, 324, 326–28, 332n2; in 1761 minutes, 334, 336, 340, 342, 344, 346, 348, 351–53, 355–56, 357n4, 357n6; in 1762 minutes, 358, 360–61, 364, 373–74, 383–84, 393, 395–96, 402, 405, 405n8; citizens of, 80, 121n5, 147n3, 166, 177n1, 183–85, 190–91, 193–94, 198, 225n15, 254n1, 288n9, 292, 348, 383, 408, 411–12; Commissioners of, 121n7, 334, 336, 338, 340, 344, 346–47, 352, 354–55; costs of Indian nations diplomacy to, 177n1, 412; diplomacy, 24; militia of, 29–30, 187, 190, 194, 199, 200, 222n1, 280; President of, 50–51, 88, 96, 142, 144–45, 149; proclamations of, 222n1 (*see also* Pennsylvania, Governors of: proclamations of the); proprietary party of, 415, 418–19, 422; Secretary of, 95, 144–45, 147, 153, 158, 195, 328, 407, 412; Treasurer of, 83

Pennsylvania, Council of, 37, 147n3, 411, 418; at the 1736 conferences, 49, 51–52, 54–56, 58, 60; at the 1742 conferences, 63, 71, 74–79, 81, 83, 112; at the 1747 conferences, 142, 144–45, 147; at the 1748 conferences, 149; at the July 1756 conferences, 187, 190, 194, 198; at the 1757 Lancaster conferences, 233, 235–37, 239–40, 243, 246, 250; at the 1757 Easton conferences, 255, 258, 260, 262, 266, 269, 272, 277, 280, 286; at the 1758 conferences, 290–92, 294–96, 303–4, 317, 321, 327–28, 330; at the 1761 conferences, 334, 336, 338, 340, 344, 346–47, 352, 354–55; at the 1762 conferences, 360–61, 365, 368–69, 371, 375, 383, 385, 389, 391, 397, 405; speeches of the, 328–29; *Also in text as* Governor's Council

Pennsylvania, Governors of, 10, 21, 31, 35, 37, 50, 177n1, 222n1, 224n9, 356n1, 408, 410, 412, 414–15; at the 1742 conferences, 63–71, 73–79, 81–83; at the 1744 conferences, 86–91, 93, 96–97, 100–102, 107–13, 115–16, 119–20; in the 1745 minutes, 123, 135–36, 138–40; in the 1747 minutes, 142; in the 1748 minutes, 151, 153–54, 156–57; in the 1753 minutes, 160–62, 164–69, 174–77; at the July 1756 conferences, 181–83, 185, 187, 189–90, 192–99; at the November 1756 conferences, 199–212, 216, 218–22, 224n7; at the 1757 Lancaster conferences, 230–33, 235–41, 243, 245–46, 248–53; at the 1757 Easton conferences, 255–58, 260, 262–64, 266, 269–82, 284–87, 288n2; at the 1758 conferences, 290–97, 301–5, 307–9, 311–15, 317, 322–23, 326–28, 330; at the 1761 conferences, 334, 336, 338, 340, 342, 344, 346–47, 349–50, 352–56; at the 1762 conferences, 358–66, 368–69, 371, 374–75, 377–78, 382–91, 397–99, 402–5, 405n6, 408, 410, 412, 414–15; proclamations of the, 177n1, 331n1, 352–53, 356n1; reports to the (*see* Weiser, Conrad); Secretary of the, 280; speeches (1742), 65–68, 69–71, 73–74, 78–79, 82–83; speeches (1744), 87–90, 100–101, 112–13, 119, 120; speeches (July 1756), 182–83, 185–88, 190–92, 194, 197–98; speeches (November 1756), 201, 204–5, 211–15, 219–20; speeches (1757 Lancaster), 233–34, 236, 237, 239–40, 241–42, 243–44, 246–47, 249–50; warnings against interference in public business by, 393

Pennsylvania, Proprietor(s) of, 13, 15–17, 29, 34–36, 407–8, 416, 418–19, 421; in the 1742 minutes, 64–66, 71–73, 76–77, 79, 83; in the 1744 minutes, 110; in the 1745 minutes, 123; in the 1748 minutes, 157; in the July 1756 minutes, 182; in the November 1756 minutes, 205, 209–11, 222; in the 1757 Easton minutes, 256, 265, 267–68, 270–71, 273–74, 276–77; in the 1758 minutes, 298, 300, 312–13, 315–17, 322, 325, 328; in the 1761 minutes, 355–56; in the 1762 minutes, 366, 373–75, 383–84, 393, 395–96, 401; agents of the, 14, 222, 265, 268, 288n2, 312, 315, 327–29, 354–55, 373, 411; propaganda of the, 415. *See also* Penn, Thomas; Penn, William

Pennsylvania Assembly, 29, 32, 34–35, 37, 74, 76, 78, 83, 112, 125, 135, 139, 147n3, 177n1, 179n9, 181, 221–22, 222n1, 225n17, 408, 410, 412, 414–15, 417–19, 422; at the 1753 conferences, 165; at the 1757 Lancaster conferences, 236–37, 239, 240, 243, 246, 250; at the 1757 Easton conferences, 255, 258, 260, 262, 266, 269, 272, 277, 280, 286–87, 287n1; at the 1758 conferences, 291, 294, 303–4; at the 1762 conferences, 360–61, 365, 368, 371, 375, 383, 385, 389, 391, 397, 405; Clerk of the, 222, 250; committees of the, 291, 294, 303–4, 321; Secretary of the, 221–22; Speaker of the, 74, 83, 236, 255, 280, 286, 412, 416, 418. *Also in text as* House of Representatives

*Pennsylvania Gazette,* 17

Pennsylvania Hospital, 422

Pepy, Joseph. *See* Peepy, Joseph

Perdue, Theda, 122n11

Peter, Captain John (Ohio Lenape leader), 303, 420

Peters, Richard, 31, 33, 35, 177n1, 407, 411–12, 417–18; at 1742 conferences, 75, 79, 83; at 1744 conferences, 120, 121n7; at 1747 conferences, 144–45, 147; at 1753 conferences, 160–61, 163–65, 167–68, 171, 173, 175–77, 178n3, 179n13; at 1756 conferences, 185, 187, 190, 194–96, 198–99, 201–5, 209–11, 216, 219, 221; at 1757 Lancaster conferences, 235–37, 239–40, 243, 246; at 1757 Easton conferences, 255, 258, 260, 262, 266, 269, 272, 277, 280, 282, 285–86, 287n1, 288n2; at 1758 conferences, 290–92, 294–96, 298, 303–5, 308–9, 314, 316, 323, 326–29, 332n2, 332n4, 332n9, 333n13; at 1761 conferences, 334, 336, 338, 340, 344, 346–47, 352, 354–55; at 1762 conferences, 358, 360–61, 365, 368–69, 371, 375, 385, 389, 391, 397, 403, 404

Peters, William, 287n1

Pevar, Stephen L., xivn7, 332n7

Philadelphia, 10, 12–13, 15, 17, 19, 29–31, 37, 179n9, 416; as site of the 1736 conferences, 49, 51–52, 54–57, 59; as site of the 1742 conferences, 63–64, 66, 68–69, 74, 76–78, 81; in the 1744 minutes, 86, 89, 97, 100, 110–11, 119–20; in the 1745 minutes, 123, 136, 138, 140; as site of the 1747 conferences, 142, 144–45; in the 1748 minutes, 149, 156; in the 1753 minutes, 160, 164–65, 174, 176; in the 1756 minutes, 181, 185, 187, 190, 194, 198–99, 206, 209, 211, 214, 220, 224n6; in the 1757 Lancaster minutes, 226, 230, 232–33, 236; in the 1757 Easton minutes, 255–56, 258, 260, 262, 266, 269–70, 272, 274, 277, 280, 282, 286–87; in the 1758 minutes, 290–91, 293, 301, 318–19, 323, 326, 330, 332n5; in the 1761 minutes, 334, 337–40, 355–56; in the 1762 minutes, 358, 360, 364, 378, 388, 399, 401, 405; Mayor of, 52, 422; Recorder of the city of, 52

Philip (Jersey Indian), 217, 219

Piankasha (nation), 172–73, 175

Pickawillany, 178n5

pictographs, 8

pipes, 158n1, 188, 194–95, 275

Piscatawa (nation), 11–12, 410. *Also in text as* Piscataways

Pisquetomen (Lenape leader), 32, 69, 79, 301–3, 317–19, 322–23, 332n2, 332n5, 408–9, 412, 417, 419, 422; speeches of, 301–3. *Also in text as* Pishquiton; Pisquitom; Pisquitomen

Pitt, William, 410, 419

Pittsburgh, 33, 349, 370–73, 397–98, 403

pity, discourse of, 184, 189, 191, 363, 371, 388

Plan of Union. *See* Albany: Plan of Union

Plumsted, Clement, 49, 52, 54–56, 63, 66, 68, 74–75, 77, 79, 83

poisoning, possible threat at 1762 conferences of, 405n4

political freedom(s), concept of, 25, 29

political philosophies: European, 24–25; Native North American, 23–26

Pontiac's War, 420–21

popular sovereignty, concept of, 25

Post, Frederick, 301–2, 317, 323, 360–61, 365–66, 368–69, 371, 409, 419–20, 422

Potomac River, 20, 64, 96, 98, 103, 105, 364,

387, 398, 400, 410. *Also in text as* Potomac; Potomack; Potowmack
poverty, discourse of, 73, 106, 118, 139, 184, 189, 195, 218, 286, 293
power, sacred or supernatural. *See* spiritual power
Pownall, Thomas, 410
prayer, 158n1
praying Indians, 116, 138, 143, 146, 410, 413
Prentup, William, 227, 229, 236, 238–40, 243, 246, 416
Presbyterian, 415, 417
Presque Isle, 32
Preston, Samuel, 49, 51–52, 55–56, 63, 68, 71, 74–78, 83
Pride, The (Shawnee chief), 244
prisoner bounties, 222n1, 286
prisoners, 223n2, 244, 405n2; feared coercion of, 403; (Indian) held by colonies, 244; opting to stay with Indian nations, 362, 366, 368, 377; proposed compensation for release of, 278, 377, 381, 392, 402, 405; releases of, 352, 363–64, 382–83; reluctance of Indian nations to release due to colonial treatment of, 377, 392–93; suspicions regarding keeping of free Indians as, 235; as wives of Indians, 378. *See also* Iroquois Confederacy: customs regarding prisoners of war
prisoners, negotiations over release of, 32, 34–35; at the July 1756 conferences, 182, 184, 186, 191–92; at the November 1756 conferences, 213–14, 217, 219–20; at the 1757 Lancaster conferences, 235, 242, 245; at the 1757 Easton conferences, 274, 278–79; at the 1758 conferences, 295, 300–301, 305–7, 309–11, 313, 316, 331, 332n3; at the 1761 conferences, 338–39, 343–44, 347, 350–52, 354, 356; at the 1762 conferences, 359, 362, 366–68, 370–73, 376–78, 381–84, 390–93, 402–3, 405
private property, discourse of, 82
promises: advocacy of adherence to, 177; discourse of Indians keeping, 129–30, 146, 242, 279, 300–301, 305–7, 316, 322, 331, 343–44, 350, 367, 377, 403; injunction for Pennsylvania to keep, 222
propaganda, religious, 417
proprietary form of governance, 422
Protestantism, 359
Pumpshire, John (Lenape interpreter), 233; at July 1756 conferences, 187, 189–90, 194, 199; at November 1756 conferences, 201, 204–5, 211, 216, 218; at 1757 Easton conferences, 256, 258, 260, 263–66, 269, 272, 277, 280–83, 286
Pumptons. *See* Wapinger

Quakers, 16–17, 29, 34–35, 37, 179n9, 408, 411–12, 414–15, 417, 419, 421–22; efforts toward peace, 181, 222n1, 224n7, 224n14, 288n2, 288n8, 364, 405n6; exile to West Virginia of, 419; impact of loyalty oath upon, 419; pacifism of, 37 (*see also* pacifism); propaganda against, 22n1, 287n1 (*see also* propaganda, religious); as sponsors of gifts, 215, 247, 282; as witnesses to treaty conferences, 187, 190, 194, 291, 294, 296, 298, 305, 308, 314, 319, 323
Quebec, 137–38, 410, 419
Queen Allaquippa, 413
Queen Anne, 407
Queen Anne's War, 14, 163; peace talks ending, 163

race, xii, 28, 106, 177n1, 303, 392
Rafert, Stewart, 158n1
Rariton River, 321, 329
rationality, discourse of superior, 91
Rays-Town, 400
Read, Charles, 52, 54–55, 291, 294, 296, 298, 303–5, 308, 314, 319, 323, 328, 418
Read, James, 124
rebirth. *See* reincarnation
Red Hawk. *See* Miskepalathy
regionalism, 177n1
reincarnation, 3–4
religious persecution, 408. *See also* propaganda, religious; Quakers: propaganda against
reparations, postponing of, 219, 222
reservations, 13–14, 110, 264–65, 269, 419. *See also* Conoy: reservations; Iroquois: reservations and reserves; Lenape (nations): reservations and reserves
revenge, myths surrounding, 332n6
Revolutionary War. *See* American Revolution
rewards, for criminal suspects, 353, 356n1
Reynolds, Captain, 199, 201, 204–5, 211, 216
Rhoads, Samuel, 360–61, 365, 368–69, 371, 375, 385, 389, 391, 397, 405
rights: human, 332n6; hunting and fishing, 332n7 (*see also* land use: rights); political, 332n6
right to representation, 408

River Indians. *See* Mahican; Wapinger
road metaphor, 52–53, 59, 61n6, 65–66, 70–71, 76, 78, 99–101, 108–9, 112–13, 115, 118, 138, 151, 154–55, 157, 163, 186–87, 191, 217, 220, 251, 292–93, 297, 299, 318–19, 323–24, 330, 335, 337, 339, 341, 350, 352–53, 363, 366–67, 375
Roberdeau, Daniel, 417; at 1757 Easton conferences, 255, 258, 260, 262, 266, 269, 272, 277, 280; at 1758 conferences, 291, 294, 296, 298, 303–5, 308, 314, 323
*-roona* suffix, 409
Royal American Regiment, 187, 190, 194, 199, 383
Ruckman, Jo Ann, 41n52, 42nn60–61, 42n76
rum. *See* alcohol
rumors, 78, 80, 125–27, 132, 200–201, 203, 217, 253, 332n5, 402, 409, 416

Sachdagughroonaw (nation), 98
Sachsidora (Shawnee speaker), 252
Samuel (Davis). *See* Tapiscawen
Sandy-Hook, 329
Sapling, in Iroquois oral tradition, 2–4
Saponi (nation), 365, 405n1, 418. *Also in text as* Saponys
Sarris, Greg, 84n9
Sasquahannah, or Sasquehannah, Indians. *See* Lenape (nations): eastern; Iroquois Confederacy; Shawnee: in the 1756 minutes and conferences; Shawnee: 1757 Lancaster minutes; Shawnee: 1757 Easton conferences; Susquehannock
Sasquahanna, or Sasquahannah, or Sasquehanna, or Sasquehannah. *See* Susquehanna River
Sasquehannah Delawares. *See* Lenape (nations): eastern
Sassoonan. *See* Olumapies
Satagarowyes. *See* Jagrea
savage, connotation of, 28–29, 43n69; images of, 34
savagist ideology, 28–29, 37, 177n1
Scaiohady. *See* Scarouady
scalp bounties, 222n1, 286, 414–15
scalps, 65, 76
scarcity, discourse of. *See* supply and demand, discourse of
Scarouady (Oneida official), 32, 34, 411, 414, 420; at the 1747 conferences, 144, 147; at the 1748 conferences, 150, 153–54; at the 1753 conferences, 161–68, 170, 173–76, 178n3, 179n9; in the July 1756 minutes, 181, 183, 187; at the 1757 Lancaster conferences, 227, 229, 232; speeches of, 166–67, 168–71, 229–30. *Also in text as* Scaroyady; Scarrooyady; Scarrowyady; Scarroyady
Schahkook, 131–32
Schickcalamy. *See* Shikellamy
Schlesinger, Arthur, Jr., 24–25, 42n57
Schoharie Valley, 407
Schohooniady. *See* Juniata
Schoolcraft, Henry Rowe, 39n11
Schuylkill River, 10, 13, 17, 31
Scottish, 419
Scull, Nicholas, 17, 79, 321, 421
Secaughkung, 313
Segachsadon. *See* Tagashata
Seisberger, David. *See* Zeisberger, David
Seneca (nation), 1, 6, 14–15, 31, 36, 50, 66–69, 84n2, 87, 124, 126, 226–27, 230, 234, 236–40, 243–44, 246, 248–50, 255, 285–86, 288n3, 290–92, 294–99, 301, 304–6, 308–10, 313–15, 319, 321, 323, 338, 365, 368, 375, 380, 383, 385, 389–92, 394, 397–98, 401, 404, 405n1, 408, 412–14, 416–18; Snipe Clan of the, 416; Wolf Clan of the, 416
Seneca George (Iroquois speaker), 334–36, 338, 340, 344, 346–47, 352, 355, 357n2, 389; speeches of, 335–36, 389
separation of powers, 26
Sequeheton (Shawnee chief), 153
"seven nations" (1758), 308
Seven Nations (1761), 335–36, 338, 340–42, 344–47, 351–52, 354–55, 357n2. *See also* Cayuga; Conoy; Lenape (nations); Mahican; Nanticoke; Oneida; Onondaga (nation); Tutelo
"seven nations of Indians over the lakes," 337, 343, 345, 357n2
Seven Years' War, 1, 15, 26, 34, 179n9, 182, 193, 203–4, 212, 217, 220, 222n1, 232, 234–35, 243, 246–48, 281, 287, 325, 335, 341, 344, 359, 371, 381, 385, 404, 413, 416, 419; deserters from the, 383, 391, 393, 403–4
Shacalamy, John. *See* Shikellamy, John
Shackamaxon (now Philadelphia), 12
Shakalamy, John. *See* Shikellamy, John
Shamokin, 14, 19, 49, 69, 80, 100, 109, 187, 220, 247–48, 250, 252, 268, 315–16, 330, 349, 377, 381–82, 385–86, 388, 390, 396, 399–401, 408, 415, 422; fort at (*see* Fort Augusta); request to remove fort and soldiers from, 385–86; right to build fort at, 385–86 (*see also* Fort Augusta)

Sharpe, Horatio, 400, 422. *See also* Maryland, Governors of
Shawnee (nation[s]), 6–8, 14–17, 23, 30, 32–37, 57, 60n1, 62n9, 120, 135, 408, 410–12, 414, 422; at the 1742 conferences, 63, 65–66, 69, 76; at the 1748 conferences, 150–51, 153–54, 156–58, 158n1, 159n3; at the 1753 conferences, 161–62, 164–68, 170–77, 179n9; in the 1756 minutes and conferences, 181–82, 184–85, 190, 199, 202, 215, 219; in the 1757 Lancaster minutes, 226–32, 234–36, 238–42, 244–46, 248–49, 252–53; at the 1757 Easton conferences, 282, 286; in the 1758 minutes, 300, 310, 319; at the 1762 conferences, 360–61, 365, 369–72, 381, 396, 405n1; chiefs of, 154; Ohio, 150–51, 153–54, 156–58, 410–12; prisoners in Carolina, 176, 310; *Also in text as* Shawanaes; Shawanese; Shawanoes; Shawnese; Shawonese; Shawunogi
Shekallamy. *See* Shikellamy
shell, in treaty ceremony, 172, 174
Shenandoah River, 20, 23, 58
Sherlock, James, 334, 336, 338, 340, 342, 344, 346–47, 352, 354–55
Shikellamy (Oneida "supervisor" of the Shawnees), 50, 55, 64, 68, 75, 78–79, 83, 100, 250–51, 253, 323, 407–8, 411, 422; *Also in text as* Shicalamy; Shickalamy; Shickallemo; Shick Calamy; Shickellamy; Shikalamy; Shikelimo
Shikellamy, John (second "supervisor" of the Shawnees), 365, 368, 375, 385, 391, 397, 404, 422
Shingas (Ohio Lenape chief), 30, 32, 303, 408, 412, 420
Shippen, Edward, 230, 416
Shirley, William, 128, 198, 410
Shoemaker, Benjamin, 142, 144–45, 149–50, 152–54, 157–58, 158n1, 185, 411
silencing, xi–xii
Silver Bowl, 163
Silver Covenant Chain, 12, 14–16, 89–90, 95, 103–5, 112, 115–16, 126–27, 130–32, 140n1, 148n4, 178n5, 242, 246, 288n7, 361, 367, 372, 402, 413, 420; wampum belt of the, 367
Silver Cup, 163
Silver Heels (Seneca warrior), 179n9. *See also* Aroas
sincerity, discourse of, 322, 350
Sineka. *See* Seneca
Siouan (languages), 410, 418
Six Nations, or Six United Nations. *See* Iroquois Confederacy
Skaniadaradigronos. *See* Conoy; Nanticoke
Skénon. *See* Iroquois: concept of health
skins, 53–55, 58–59, 66, 73–74, 76, 81, 83, 118, 132, 139, 158, 170–71, 229; beaver, 152; deer, 24, 55, 153, 209, 218; negotiations over price of, 158
Sky Cycle, 2–5, 38n4, 39n16. *See also* Iroquois: oral tradition of
Sky Woman, 2–4, 38n4, 39n16
smallpox-infested blankets, 412
Smith, James, 409
Smith, William, 287n1, 417
Snow, Dean, 21, 38n2, 38n4, 39n7, 39n8, 41n34, 423
sobriety, discourse of, 239
Sock, Bill, 414
Sonatziowanah (Shawnee chief), 153
Sonontowane. *See* Seneca
South Branch, Virginia, 364
South Carolina, 23, 32, 35, 176, 244, 310, 322, 409–10; Governors of, 176, 322
Southern Indians, 68, 103–4, 135, 231, 234, 254n4. *See also* Catawba; Cherokee
South Mountains, 19
sovereignty, xii, 84n1, 178n7
Spain, King of, 67
Spangenberg, Augustus Gottlieb, 183, 414
Spanish, 112, 114; America, 67; dollars, 320
speech: preservation of, 53, 121n4 (*see also* history: preservation of); reproduction of, 21
speeches, 121n4; delivery of, 122n13; mending of, 65, 116, 175, 208, 238; proposal among colonies for joint, 124–26; unity urged in, 345. *See also* individual speakers
Spicer, Jacob, 291, 294, 296, 298, 303–5, 308, 314, 319, 323
spiritual power, 8, 39n16, 61n3
Spotswood, Alexander, 103–4. *See also* Virginia, Governors of
Spring, Cornelius (interpreter for the Lenapes), 69, 79–80
Springett, Gulielma, 407
squatters, 12–15, 17, 19–21, 23–25, 31, 33–34, 38, 60n1, 77, 190, 222n1, 265, 312, 315, 346, 348–49, 357n4, 400, 408, 421–22; efforts to remove, 348, 356n1; north of the Kittochtinny Hills at Juniata; 72–74, 177n1; possibility of alliance between Indians and, 177n1; requests to remove, 72, 77, 100, 252, 346; re-

striction of, 177n1, 395–96; west of Maryland, 58, 72–74, 96, 400; warnings by Pennsylvania against disturbance of, 396; west of Virginia, 58, 72–73, 96, 99–100, 104, 400
squatting, 84nn5–6; efforts to prevent, 177n1, 348, 356n1, 396–97; requests to prevent, 346
Squawhihaw (nation), 421
Squissatego (Seneca prisoner in Virginia), 311, 315
Stanley, Colonel, 124, 126, 131
Stanwix, Colonel John, 239–40, 243, 246, 417
Starna, William, 25, 42n59
starvation, 12, 34, 84n5, 121n10, 388
Staten Island, 8
state's rights, 26
Stenton, 49, 51
Stevens, John, 294, 296, 298, 304–5, 308, 314, 319–20, 323, 328
Stille, Isaac: at the 1758 conferences, 290, 292, 294, 296, 298, 305, 308, 313–14, 322–23; at the 1761 conferences, 336, 338, 340, 344, 346–47, 352, 355; at the 1762 conferences, 360–61, 365, 368–69, 371
St. Lawrence River, 1, 10
Stoddart, John, 124–26, 131
Stony-Creek, 383
Strettell, Robert, 63, 68, 71, 74–79, 83, 142, 144–45
Strickland, Amos, 291, 294, 296, 298, 303–5, 308, 314, 323
strouds, as gifts and mnemonic, 64–65, 84, 175, 220, 353, 391
Stroudsburg, Pennsylvania, 8, 13
Suchraquery (Ohio Valley Indian), 158
Suchsedowa (Indian from Shamokin), 250, 252
Sunbury, Pennsylvania, 14
supply and demand, discourse of, 81
Susquehannah Company of Connecticut, 357n4
Susquehannah Indians. *See* Lenape (nations): Wyoming
Susquehanna River, 8, 10, 12, 14, 17–18, 31, 33, 37, 49, 53, 55, 57–60, 63, 69, 72–74, 98, 105, 177, 181, 183–85, 195, 208, 228–29, 244, 252–53, 255, 268, 278, 296–97, 299–300, 312–13, 315, 330, 352, 359, 373, 386, 398–99, 408, 417–18; Big Island in the, 253, 415
Susquehanna Valley, 4, 14, 17–18, 60n1, 63, 95
Susquehannock (nation), 7, 10–12, 14–16, 18, 22–23, 84n9, 92, 96, 410. *See also* Conestoga (nation)
Sussex County, Pennsylvania (now Delaware), 86, 123, 160, 236, 255
Swaine, Charles, 327–28
Swedish presence in seventeenth-century North America, 9–10
Swetara, 243
syllabaries, 8
Syracuse, New York, 37, 408

Taafe, Michael, 164, 175, 412
Tachanoontia (Onondaga chief), 22–23, 87, 97–98, 100, 409; speeches of, 97, 98–100
Tachnechdorus. *See* Shikellamy, John
Tagashata (Seneca chief), 291, 293–98, 304–5, 307–9, 313–14, 317, 319, 321, 323, 327, 418–19; speeches of, 292–93, 295, 296–97, 304, 307, 309, 321, 327. *Also in text as* Takeaghsado
Tamaqua (Ohio Lenape chief), 32, 36, 303, 358, 360–65, 369–71, 373–74, 383–85, 408, 412, 420; speeches of, 361, 362–64, 369–70, 374, 384
Taminy Buck (Shawnee chief), 157
Tanaghrisson (Seneca official), 32, 162–65, 176, 178n5, 178n7, 411–12
Tapeskohonk. *See* Tapiscawen
Tapiscawen (Lenape counselor), 322, 329, 365, 367, 369–71, 373, 376, 380, 382, 397–99, 401, 421. *Also in text as* Tapascawen
Tappon-Creek, 329
Taqualaw (Lenape advisor), 383
Tarachawagon, 117. *See also* Weiser, Conrad
Tattamy, Moses (Lenape interpreter), 415, 421; at the July 1756 conferences, 203–4; in the 1757 Lancaster minutes, 233; at the 1757 Easton conferences, 262, 281, 283, 287n1, 288n6; at the 1758 conferences, 290, 292–93, 296, 298, 305, 308, 313–14, 322–23, 328, 330–31; son of (*see* Tattamy, William). *Also in text as* Tatamy, Moses
Tattamy, William, 260, 262, 421
tattoos, 409
Taway (nation), 65. *See also* Miami
Tawwas, 370–71, 422. *Also in text as* Ottaways. *See also* Ottawa
Taylor, Abraham, 63, 68, 71, 74, 76–79, 83, 142, 144–45
Tayshiccomen (Lenape advisor), 383
Teaogon. *See* Tioga
Teedyuscung (Wyoming Lenape chief), 34–36, 44n88, 357n4, 409, 411, 413–19, 421–22; at the 1756 conferences, 183, 187–88, 190, 192–201, 203–5, 208–12, 214, 216–22,

223nn3–4, 224n6, 224nn9–10, 224n14; in the 1757 Lancaster minutes, 226–27, 230–33, 235–37, 240–42, 245, 247–49, 254n2; at the 1757 Easton conferences, 255–60, 262–66, 269–72, 274–87, 287n1, 288nn2–4, 288n9, 289n11; at the 1758 conferences, 290, 292–96, 298, 300–308, 312–14, 316–17, 319, 322–23, 325–31, 331n1, 332n2, 332n4, 332n9, 333n10, 333n14; at the 1761 conferences, 338, 350, 353, 355–56; at the 1762 conferences, 365–68, 373–75, 381–85, 390–91, 396–97; as agent for Pennsylvania, 192, 196–98, 219–20, 306, 414; assassination of, 357n4, 414, 421; complaints regarding Wyoming by, 381–82; grandsons of, 199, 314; references to two kings/chiefs, 188, 193; role to secure Wyoming against Connecticut for Iroquois Confederacy, 382, 396; rumor of his plan to poison participants at the 1762 treaty, 382; sons of, 193, 199, 357n4; wife and family of, 221

Teedyuscung, speeches of: at July 1756 conferences, 183–85, 188–90, 192–93, 194–95, 196, 197, 198; at November 1756 conferences, 200–202, 205–10, 216–19, 224nn10–11; at 1757 Easton conferences, 258–60, 263–64, 265–66, 269–71, 274–75, 278–79, 281, 283–84, 286, 287; at 1758 conferences, 290–91, 295, 312–13, 314–15, 322, 326–27; at 1761 conferences, 338–40, 353–54; at 1762 conferences, 374, 384

"ten nations" (1756, 1758), 188, 189, 193, 196, 202, 206, 300, 304, 306. *See also* "Ten Nations" (Easton 1757)

"Ten Nations" (Easton 1757), 255–61, 263, 266, 269, 272, 274–75, 277–80, 282–83. *See also* Cayuga; Lenopi; Mahican; Mohawk (nation); Munsey; Nanticoke; Oneida; Onondaga (nation); Seneca; Wename

Tepascououn. *See* Tapiscawen

termination, U.S. policy of, xii

terror, discourse of, 91, 93–94

Tetamy, Moses. *See* Tattamy, Moses

Thomas, George, 123, 250–53, 289n10; at 1742 conferences, 63–71, 73–79, 81–83; at 1744 conferences, 86–91, 93, 96–97, 100–102, 107–13, 115–16, 119–20; speeches of, 65–68, 69–71, 73–74, 78–79, 82–83, 87–90, 100–101, 112–13, 119, 120. *See also* Pennsylvania, Governors of

Thomas, Philip, 86–91, 93, 96–97, 100–102, 105, 107–9, 111–15, 119–20

Thomson, Charles, 27, 36, 44n88, 230, 254n4, 256, 269–70, 277–79, 281–82, 287n1, 288n2, 416–17, 419, 422. *Also in text as* Thompson, Charles

Thunackgi River, 421

Tiahansorea, 416. *See also* Little Abraham

Tiawco. *See* Nanticoke

Tidd, John and Mary, 422

Till, William, 142, 144–45

Tioga (town), 34, 183, 185–87, 189, 191, 196, 199, 201, 203–4, 218, 227, 235, 286, 313, 346–7, 349, 382, 396

Tipiscohan. *See* Tapiscawen

Tittamy, Moses. *See* Tattamy, Moses

tobacco, 87, 152, 194–95, 253, 275, 340; as part of pipe ceremony, 152, 158n1

Tocarry-hogan, 107, 111, 114, 117–18; *See also* Maryland, Governors of

Tohiccon Creek, 13, 16, 19, 36, 208, 210, 288n7, 300, 313, 316, 322, 354–55. *Also in text as* Tohickon Creek

Tohoa-irough-roonan (nation), 98

Tojenontawohy (Cayuga chief), 323

Tokaaion (Cayuga chief), 418; at 1758 conferences, 291, 293, 296–98, 305, 308, 314, 319, 322–23, 328, 330, 333n13; at 1761 conferences, 336, 346, 354, 356, 357n6; at 1762 conferences, 358, 364–65, 368, 375, 385, 389–91, 397; daughters of, 389, 401; speeches of, 297–98, 305, 322, 336–38, 346–47, 354, 356, 364, 390. *Also in text as* Tokaaio; Tokahaio; Tokahaion

Tolhao, 281

Tomago. *See* Tamaqua

tomahawk. *See* hatchet

Tooker, Elisabeth, 25, 40n26, 41n52, 42n59

Tougachena (Lenape speaker), 338

Touhickon Creek. *See* Tohiccon Creek

trade, 6–7, 9–12, 15, 17–18, 31, 38n1, 57–60, 60n2, 62n7, 62n10, 62n13, 81–83, 84n3, 95, 103, 106, 110, 122n11, 127, 137, 140n2, 158, 169–70, 173–74, 265–66, 311, 344–46, 349, 355, 371, 373, 385–87, 390, 397–400, 402–3, 407, 419; in arms and ammunition, 73, 170, 179n9, 321, 381, 386–87, 396; commissioners support requests to regulate, 173–74, 177; costs of Ohio, 373, 397–400, 404; debts, 409; deception in, 170; in flour, 170; honesty requested in, 385, 397, 399; regulating prices of goods in, 373; regulation of, 62n10; requests to regulate, 58–60, 169–70, 173–74; routes for, 398

traders, 30, 32–33, 38, 57–60, 62n10, 65, 81–83, 100, 105, 110, 118, 135, 138–39, 147, 154, 158, 163–64, 169–70, 173–74, 177, 311, 316, 399–400, 409–12, 415–16. *See also* British traders
trade war, Carolinas, 409. *See also* Tuscarora
trade wars, seventeenth century, 1, 7, 10–12, 15, 30–31, 54, 413
trading house, 140n2
translation, 122n14; delays at treaty conferences caused by, 376–77
transmigration of souls. *See* reincarnation
treaties: Dutch-Iroquois Treaty (1613), 94; English-Iroquois Treaty (1666), 95; Maryland-Susquehannock Treaty (1645), 92; Silver Covenant Chain Treaty (1677), 92, 103, 140n4; First Pennsylvania Treaty (1682), 395; Albany (1684), 92, 103; Walking Purchase deed as treaty (1686, unratified), 76–77; Albany (1722), 99, 103–4, 121n10; Philadelphia (1728), 276–77; Philadelphia (1732), 49, 51–57, 60n1, 70–71, 136, 395; Philadelphia (1736), 14, 49–62, 64, 69, 72, 74, 84n9, 91, 93, 96–98, 103, 136; Philadelphia (1742), 14, 19–20, 23, 31, 36, 63–85, 87, 91, 93–94, 97, 112, 211, 353, 357n6, 405n7, 408–9; Lancaster (1744), 14, 20–24, 26–27, 31–32, 86–122, 135, 138, 140n6, 177n1, 289n10, 405n5, 408; Albany (1745), 14, 29, 31, 123–41, 408; Philadelphia (1747), 14, 29–30, 142–48; Lancaster (1748), 14, 30, 149–59; Logstown (1752), 32, 411; Carlisle (1753), 15, 32–33, 62n10, 160–80, 225n17, 413, 420; Winchester (1753), 32, 160–61, 163, 413, 420; Albany (1754), 33–34, 268; Philadelphia (1755), 179n9; William Johnson's estate (1755), 315; Easton (July 1756), 15, 181–99, 213, 218, 220, 228, 233, 278, 288n4, 412; Easton (November 1756), 15, 33, 35, 62n10, 179n12, 199–225, 228, 230, 233, 237–38, 241, 249–50, 257, 267, 270, 273, 288n4; Lancaster (Spring 1757), 15, 35, 226–54, 288nn2–3, 412; Easton (Summer 1757), 15, 35–36, 44n88, 255–89, 330, 331n1, 421; Easton (1758), 15, 44n88, 290–333, 336–37, 339–40, 342–43, 350, 352, 354, 396, 400, 401, 409, 412; Easton (1761), 15, 334–57, 396–97, 405n4; Fort Detroit (1761), 367; Lancaster (1762), 15, 36, 358–406; Fort Pitt (1768), 405n8; Fort Stanwix (1768), 405n8; Philadelphia (1775) 43n64; Fort Stanwix (1784), 405n8; addenda to, 177, 179n12, 221–22, 224n13, 225n17, 250–53; as dramas, x–xi; as historical documents, ix, xi; language contexts of, xi, 3–6, 8, 20–21, 24–25, 53, 61n3, 61n4, 61n6, 62n12; as literature, x–xi, 120n2; sales in Great Britain of, 120n1
treaties, participants at, 50, 68, 153, 198–99, 227, 256, 265, 291–92, 303, 318, 322, 327, 360, 365, 383. *See also individual names of major participants*
treaty minutes. *See* minutes
Trent, William, 163, 232, 258, 287n1, 412
Trenton, New Jersey, 10, 13
tributary, connotation of, 84n3
Tsanandowans. *See* Seneca
Tulpehocken, 49, 69, 364. *Also in text as* Tulpehokin; Tulpyhoken
Tulpehocken Valley, 17, 60n1, 407. *Also in text as* Tulpehokin; Tulpyhoken
Tundy, Moses. *See* Tattamy, Moses
Turner, Joseph, 142, 144, 149–50, 152–54, 157–58, 158n1, 185, 411
Turtle Island, 2
Tuscarawas County, Ohio, 420
Tuscarora (nation), 23, 133, 346, 357n2, 409–10, 416; at the 1736 conferences, 50; at the 1742 conferences, 68; at the 1744 conferences, 87, 98, 118; at the 1757 Lancaster conferences, 227, 236–37, 239–40, 243, 246; at the 1758 conferences, 290–91, 294, 296–99, 304–6, 308–9, 313–14, 323; at the 1762 conferences, 358–61, 365, 368–69, 371, 375, 380, 385, 391, 396–97, 401, 405n1. *Also in text as* Tuscaroraes; Tuscarroraws; Tuscarroros; Tuskaroras; Tuskarores; Tuskaroroes
Tuscarora (Path) Valley, 352, 259
Tuscarora-British war, 409–10
Tutelo, 418; at the 1758 conferences, 290, 292, 294, 296–99, 304–5, 308–9, 313–14, 323; at the 1761 conferences, 334–36, 338, 340–42, 344–47, 351–52, 354–56, 357n2
Tweteeway, or Twightwee, or Twigtwees. *See* Miami
Twins. *See* Flint; Sapling

Unamies. *See* Lenape (nations): Unami
union: intercolonial, 412; political, 24, 26, 28–29, 43n64, 124–25, 130, 133–34, 140n3, 140n6, 155, 166–67, 198, 202, 214
United Nations. *See* Iroquois Confederacy
United States, ix–xiii, xivn8, 23–27, 37–38, 84n5, 178n7, 332n7; history of the, 25; intellectual heritage of the, 23–26; literature of the, 34; political philosophies of the, 23–

26; political structure of the, 23, 25–26; Secretary of the Congress of the, 417; Supreme Court of the, 84n1

Van Doren, Carl, xi
Van Etten, Captain, 193, 199, 201, 204–5, 211, 216
Venables, Robert W., 25, 42nn59–60
Venango, 32, 234
Vestal, New York, 418
Virginia, 10–12, 18, 20–23, 31–33, 36, 44n76, 56–60, 135, 138, 310–11, 315, 322, 364, 383, 387, 400–401, 405n5, 409–13, 415, 418, 420; at the 1744 conferences, 86–90, 93, 96–105, 107–16, 118–20, 121n8, 121n10, 122n14; and the 1753 Winchester treaty and Ohio Valley crisis, 160–63, 169, 171, 176, 177n1, 178n5; boundary line between Iroquoia and, 103–4, 121n10; Council of, 96–97, 121n8; Indian allies and tributaries of, 103; Raleigh's founding of, 97–98; and Weiser's 1743 report, 250–51, 253, 254n9
Virginia, Governors of, 59, 87–90, 96, 103–4, 113, 120, 121n8, 162, 169, 176, 250–51, 253, 311, 315, 322, 345, 387, 400–401, 413; speeches of, 103–5
Vizenor, Gerald, x, xivn3, 26–27, 38, 42n61, 44n92
Voloshinov, V. N., xivn6, 62n11

Wabash River, 7
Wah'kon-tah, 158–59n1
Wainwright, Nicholas B., 43n65
Walking Purchase, 16–20, 23, 34–36, 179n9, 407–9, 411, 415, 417, 421; actual walks of the, 16–17, 19, 221; Assembly rescinds offer to fund reparations for the, 222; Denny's initial denial of fraud in the, 213; fraud made public at November 1756 conferences, 203, 208–11, 213–14, 216–17, 219, 221–22; original Lenape owners of the, 210, 219, 222, 237, 249, 257, 265, 373; raised at 1757 Lancaster conferences, 237–38, 241–42, 249–50, 254n2; raised at 1757 Easton conferences, 256–57, 263–65, 267–68, 270–71, 273, 276–79, 288n9; raised at 1758 conferences, 300, 313, 316, 322, 333n10, 333n13; raised at 1761 conferences, 354–56, 357n6; raised at 1762 conferences, 373–74, 383–85, 390, 401; refereed in 1742 by Iroquois Confederacy, 76–77, 79–82, 84n7
Wallace, Anthony F. C., 41n48, 357n4, 423
Wallace, Paul A. W., 39n5, 39nn8–11, 39n13, 39n16, 40n33, 41n48, 43n65–66, 44n75, 44n82, 44n86, 44n88, 84n7, 84n9, 121n5, 121n8, 177n1, 178n7, 179n9, 222n1, 253n1, 288n2, 332n8, 409, 416, 423
Walum Olum, 8
wampum, 5–6, 8, 21, 50, 58, 61n3, 94–95, 99, 121n4, 121n10, 146, 152, 156, 167, 171, 195–98, 207, 234, 254n5, 297, 299, 310–12, 322, 326–29, 392; importance of correspondence between belt and action, 333n13; mislaying of strings of, 179n10; misunderstandings about, 333n13; peace belts of, 6, 196–97, 222n1, 282, 285, 300, 307, 313, 330, 332n2, 342–43, 345, 350, 402; relation to speech, 171, 317; separation of belts from speeches, 338, 343, 346–47; war belts of, 130, 137, 222n1, 242
wampum, belts of, 61n3, 332n2, 332n5; given at 1736 conferences, 52; given at 1742 conferences, 65, 70, 72–73, 80; given at 1744 conferences, 89–92, 94, 96–97, 99–101, 105–6, 112–18; given at 1745 conferences, 126–27, 129–36, 138–39; given at 1747 conferences, 143, 146; given at 1748 conferences, 155, 157; given at 1753 conferences, 161, 165–69, 172, 176; given at July 1756 conferences, 182, 184–88, 191–93, 195–98; given at November 1756 conferences, 200–202, 204–8, 212–14, 220; given at 1757 Lancaster conferences, 226, 228–31, 233–35, 237–43, 245–47, 250–51; given at 1757 Easton conferences, 256–64, 267–69, 271, 273–76, 278–79, 282–85; given at 1758 conferences, 293–94, 296–309, 311–15, 317–19, 322–27, 329–30, 333n13; given at 1761 conferences, 335–55; given at 1762 conferences, 359, 361–63, 366–68, 370–72, 374, 377–82, 386–89, 392–96, 398–402. *See also* wampum, peace belts of; wampum war belts of
wampum, strings of, 5, 61n3; given at 1736 conferences, 50; given at 1742 conferences, 66, 70–71, 73, 75, 77, 79–81; given at 1744 conferences, 91, 93, 96–99, 101, 108–9, 114–15, 117–18, 120; given at 1745 conferences, 125, 127, 131–32, 135–36; given at 1747 conferences, 144, 146–47; given at 1748 conferences, 151–56; given at 1753 conferences, 161, 165–66, 168–76, 179n10; given at July 1756 conferences, 183–90, 194–96, 198; given at November 1756 conferences, 200–201, 204–8, 212–13, 216–20; given at 1757 Lan-

caster conferences, 228, 231–33, 235, 243, 245, 249, 251–53; given at 1757 Easton conferences, 257, 260, 262–63, 266, 271–72, 281–85; given at 1758 conferences, 291–300, 302–3, 305–6, 308, 310–13, 315–17, 322–23, 325–31, 333n13; given at 1761 conferences, 335–44, 346–47, 349–51, 354–55; given at 1762 conferences, 359–62, 368–69, 371–72, 375–76, 379, 381, 388–89, 391–94, 396–98, 401, 403–4
Wapamashehawy (Shawnee chief), 360, 371. *Also in text as* Wapemashaway
Wapinger (nation), 290, 292, 294, 296, 298, 305, 308, 312–14, 319–20, 323, 326–27, 329, 418. *Also in text as* Waping
Wapinger language, 314
war: declarations of, 30, 145, 222n1, 414; discussions at treaties of, 66–68, 70; proposals of, 29–30, 67, 125–27, 129–30, 133, 143–46, 283–84
Warder, Jeremiah, 383
warfare in North America, decisiveness of Indian participation in, 179n9
Warraigheyagey, 242, 248. *Also in text as* Warraighiyagey
Warrior, Robert, xivn8
warrior dance, 137, 147, 242
Washington, D.C., 11, 43n64
Washington, George, 33, 179n9, 413, 420
Washington Crossing, Pennsylvania, 13
Watson, John, 327–28
Wawachtanies (nation), 360–61, 365, 369–71
Weatherholt, Captain, 199, 201, 204–5, 211, 216
Weaver, Jace, xii, xivn9
Webb, James, 231, 360, 383
Webb, William, 75, 84n7
Weese, Peter, 403. *See also* prisoners: opting to stay with Indian nations
Wehololahund. *See* Peepy, Joseph
Weiser, Conrad, 14, 18, 20, 27, 30–31, 33, 35, 44n88, 60n1, 84n9, 85n10, 121n8, 254n9, 407–18, 420–22; at the 1736 conferences, 49–50, 52, 55–57, 59; at the 1742 conferences, 63, 67, 69, 76–83; at the 1744 conferences, 87, 89–91, 93–94, 96–97, 100–102, 104–5, 107–8, 110–17, 119–20; at the 1745 conferences, 134–35, 137–39; at the 1747 conferences, 142, 144–46; at the 1748 conferences, 150, 153–54, 156; at the 1753 conferences, 161, 164–65, 170, 176, 177n1, 178n6, 179n9; at the 1756 conferences, 182, 185–87, 189–90, 194–96, 199–201, 203–5, 210–11, 216, 218–19, 221, 223n4, 224n12; at the 1757 Lancaster conferences, 236, 238–40, 243, 246, 250; at the 1757 Easton conferences, 256, 258, 260, 263, 266, 269, 272, 276–77, 280, 282, 286–87, 288n2, 288n9; at the 1758 conferences, 292–96, 298, 303, 305, 308, 313–14, 316–17, 321–24, 327–29, 332n4, 332n9, 333n13; in the 1761 minutes, 335–36, 341–42, 354; April 1743 report to Pennsylvania Governor, 250–53, 254n9; death of, 335–36, 341; son of (*see* Weiser, Samuel)
Weiser, Samuel, 334, 336, 338, 340, 342, 344, 346–47, 352, 355, 421
Wells, Samuel, 124–26, 131
Wename. *See* Lenape (nations): Unami
Wendal, Jacob, 124–26, 131
Weningo, 161–62
Wenro (nation), 421
Weslager, C.A., 39n17, 40n20, 40nn23–24, 40nn30–33, 41n37, 41n50, 44n92, 84n9, 287n1, 288n5, 423
West, William, 236–37, 239–40, 243, 246
"Western Indians" (1762), 358, 360–61, 363, 365, 367, 369–71, 373, 376, 380, 397–99, 401. *See also* Kickapoo; Lenape (nations): Ohio; Miami; Ohio Valley, Indian nations of the; Shawnee; Tuscarora; Wawachtanies
western Indians, or western Indian nations, 130, 133, 420
West-Jersey, 295
Weyser, Conrad. *See* Weiser, Conrad
*Whish-shicksy,* 189–90
whiskey. *See* alcohol
White Elk. *See* Wapamashehawy
White, Robert (Nanticoke-Conoy chief), 291, 294, 296, 298, 305, 308, 313–14, 323, 365, 368, 375, 385, 391, 397; speeches of, 308
Wighalousin, 338, 351, 382, 390, 396, 401, 404
Williamsburg, 119
Wills Creek, 410
Wilmington, Delaware, 10
Winchester, Virginia, 32, 160, 163, 165, 171, 176
Wioming. *See* Wyoming
Wolcott, Roger, 124, 126, 131, 410. *See also* Connecticut, Governors of
woman, diplomatic definition of, 23
women, participation in treaty conference by: at July 1756 conferences, 196–97; at November 1756 conferences, 199; at 1757 Lancaster conferences, 226–27, 229, 232, 236–37, 239–40, 243, 246; at 1757 Easton conferences, 256, 280; at 1758 conferences,

291–92; at 1761 conferences, 334, 336, 338, 340, 344, 346–47, 352, 355; at 1762 conferences, 365, 368, 375, 385, 391, 397. *See also* gender
writing, 53, 95, 104, 111, 121n6, 140, 155, 213, 218, 224n8, 224n14, 238, 245, 256, 265, 267–71, 276–78, 281–82, 286, 288n8, 289n10, 301–2, 343, 354, 386–87, 389–90, 393, 397; Native North American forms of, 8; precontact in the Americas, 61n3
Wright, James, 165, 230–31, 360–61, 365, 368–69, 371, 375, 385, 389, 391, 397
Wroth, Lawrence C., x, xivn2, 120n1, 121n5
Wyandot (nation), 30, 32, 42n55, 161, 165–68, 171, 173, 175, 177, 178n2, 179n9, 421
Wyoming Valley, 14, 19, 31, 34–36, 80, 181–84, 207–8, 210, 212, 218, 224n9, 233, 244, 250, 254n7, 265, 268, 287n1, 296, 300, 307, 315, 330–31, 340, 343, 349, 351–53, 356, 357n4, 381–83, 396–97, 405n4, 409, 412, 414–18, 421–22. *Also in text as* Wyomen; Wyomink
Wyser, Conrad. *See* Weiser, Conrad

yo-hah, 89–92, 94, 101, 107, 112–13, 115, 117–20, 121n5. *See also* approbation, reported expressions of
York County, Pennsylvania, 422
youth, discourse of, 202

Zaccheus, 203
Zane, Isaac, 321, 421
Zeisberger, David, 40n19, 336, 338, 340, 344, 346–47, 352, 355, 421–22
*Zeisberger's Indian Dictionary,* 421

SUSAN KALTER is an associate professor of American literature at Illinois State University. She specializes in the literature and culture of North America prior to 1920s, especially the United States and Native America. She has published numerous articles and is the coeditor (with the San Diego Bakhtin Circle) of *Bakhtin and the Nation.* She is currently working on a long-term project examining the literature of the Louisiana Territory and its multilingual, multinational history and culture.

The University of Illinois Press
is a founding member of the
Association of American University Presses.

---

Composed in 10/12.5 Adobe Minion
with Hoefler Fell Type display
by Type One, LLC
for the University of Illinois Press
Manufactured by Thomson-Shore, Inc.

University of Illinois Press
1325 South Oak Street
Champaign, IL 61820–6903
www.press.uillinois.edu